Transforming Public Administration Through AI-Driven Predictive Analytics

Pradeep Kumar
Infrastructure University Kuala Lumpur, Malaysia

Abu Bakar Abdul Hamid
Infrastructure University Kuala Lumpur, Malaysia

Parma Nand
Sharda University, India

Rajeev Kumar
Moradabad Institute of Technology, India

IGI Global
Scientific Publishing
Publishing Tomorrow's Research Today

Vice President of Editorial Melissa Wagner
Director of Acquisitions Mikaela Felty
Director of Book Development Jocelynn Hessler
Production Manager Mike Brehm
Cover Design Jose Rosado

Published in the United States of America by
IGI Global Scientific Publishing
701 East Chocolate Avenue
Hershey, PA, 17033, USA
Tel: 717-533-8845 | Fax: 717-533-7115
Website: https://www.igi-global.com E-mail: cust@igi-global.com

Library of Congress Cataloging-in-Publication Data

Names: Kumar, Pradeep, 1980- editor | Abdul Hamid, Abu Bakar, 1958- editor | Nand, Parma, 1967- editor | Kumar, Rajeev, 1985- editor
Title: Transforming public administration through AI-driven predictive analytics / Edited by Pradeep Kumar, Abu Bakar Abdul Hamid, Parma Nand, Rajeev Kumar.
Description: Hershey, PA : IGI Global Scientific Publishing, [2026] | Includes bibliographical references and index. | Summary: "This book aims to explore the transformative impact of artificial intelligence (AI) and predictive analytics on governance, policy implementation, and public service delivery"-- Provided by publisher.
Identifiers: LCCN 2025017544 (print) | LCCN 2025017545 (ebook) | ISBN 9798337337609 hardcover | ISBN 9798337337616 paperback | ISBN 9798337337623 ebook
Subjects: LCSH: Public administration--Technological innovations | Artificial intelligence--Data processing | Blockchains (Databases)
Classification: LCC JF1525.A8 .T725 2026 (print) | LCC JF1525.A8 (ebook)
LC record available at https://lccn.loc.gov/2025017544
LC ebook record available at https://lccn.loc.gov/2025017545

British Cataloguing in Publication Data
A Cataloguing in Publication record for this book is available from the British Library.

Editorial Advisory Board

S. Gayathri, *University of Madras, India*
Utpal Ghosh, *Sarojini Naidu College for Women, India*
J. Nandha Gopal, *Velammal Institute of Technology, India*
Himani Grewal, *Moradabad Institute of Technology, India*
Sachin Gupta, *MAIT, India*
V. Basil Hans, *Srinivas University, India*
Balqees Talal Hasan, *Ninevah University, Iraq*
Nazia Hasan, *Teerthanker Mahaveer University, India*
Akhtar Husain, *Mahatma Jyotiba Phule Rohilkhand University, India*
S. Mahaboob Hussain, *Vishnu Institute of Technology, India*
Grace Hannah J., *Women's Christian College, India*
Rajkumar Jagdale, *Vishwakarma University, India*
Sukrati Jain, *Teerthanker Mahaveer University, India*
Vijay S. Jariwala, *Sardar Patel University, India*
S. Jeyakumar, *Garden City University, India*
Rishabh Jha, *Lambton College, Canada*
Sudhanshu Kumar Jha, *University of Allahabad, India*
Gudditti Viswanath Jntua, *Sri Venkatesa Perumal College of Engineering and Technology, India*
Ankush Joshi, *COER University, India*
Sonia Juneja, *IMS Engineering College, India*
Sriprasadh K., *SRM Institute of Science and Technology, India*
K. Kalaiarasi, *Cauvery College for Women, India*
Vijay H. Kalmani, *Rajarambapu Institute of Technology, India*
Amol Kasture, *Ajeenkya DY Patil University, India*
C. Kathiravan, *Roever Engineering College, India*
Ihtiram Raza Khan, *Jamia Hamdard, India*
Mohd Vaseem Khan, *APJ Abdul Kalam Technical University, India*
Mudassir Khan, *King Khalid University, Saudi Arabia*
Wasim Khan, *KL University, India*
Ajay Khunteta, *Poornima University, India*
Sachin Kulkarni, *Lexicon Management Institute of Leadership and Excellence, India*
Ajay Kumar, *NIIT China (Shanghai) Ltd., China*
M. Vinoth Kumar, *Vel Tech Rangarajan Dr. Sagunthala R&D Institute of Science and Technology, India*
Prahlad Kumar, *University of Allahabad, India*
S. Venkata Siva Kumar, *Vardhaman College of Engineering India*
S. Vinoth Kumar, *Vel Tech Rangarajan Dr. Sagunthala R&D Institute of Science and Technology, India*

Sanjeev Kumar, *G. L. Bajaj Institute of Technology and Management, India*
Jomon Jose M., *Holy Grace Academy, India*
Mahesh K. M., *Jain Evening College, India*
Suman Madan, *ATLAS SkillTech University, India*
Rajiv Mahajan, *Lamrin Tech Skills University, India*
Vijaya Kittu Manda, *PBMEIT, India*
Oleksandra Mandych, *State Biotechnological University, Ukraine*
Nimish Mathure, *Loras College, USA*
Janelli M. Mendez, *LORMA Colleges, Philippines*
Manvi Mishra, *Dr. A. P. J. Abdul Kalam Technical University, India*
Nandita Mishra, *Chetana's Institute of Management and Research, India*
Saurabh Mishra, *Parul University, India*
Siddhartha Mishra, *Samsung Research, India*
Suyash Mishra, *Nice Actimize, India*
Pratik Mungekar, *Savitribai Phule Pune University, India*
Kolluru Venkata Nagendra, *JNTUA, India*
Vaibhav E. Narawade, *D. Y. Patil University, India*
Pranav Paranjpe, *Indore Institute of Science and Technology, India*
Jaykumar Shantilal Patel, *Chaudhari Technical Institute, India*
Tanuja Patgar, *Dr. Ambedkar Institute of Technology, India*
Basavaraj Patil, *Dayananda Sagar College of Engineering, India*
Pramoda Patro, *S. R. University, India*
A Noble Jebakumar Thanthai Periyar, *Bharathidasan University, India*
Vijay Pithadia, *Narmada D.M.C., India*
K. Prabhakar, *Central University of Jammu, India*
A. Renuka Prasad, *Sai Rajeswari Institute of Technology, India*
Manjunath B. R., *Tecnologico de Monterey, Mexico*
P. Radha, *JAIN University, India*
R. Raffik, *Kumaraguru College of Technology, India*
S. Mohan Raj, *Indo-American College, India*
D. Rajasekar, *AMET University, India*
D. Rajesh, *Vel Tech Rangarajan Dr. Sagunthala R&D Institute of Science and Technology, India*
Pranati Rakshit, *JIS College Of Engineering, India*
Ramarao, *Woxsen University, India*
H. Srinivas Rao, *Babu Jagjivan Ram Government Degree College, India*
Srinivasa Rao, *Kasisomayajula Koneru Lakshmaiah Education Foundation, India*
Divya Rastogi, *Sharda University, India*
Inderpreet Kaur Rayat, *Bahra University, India*
Anitha S., Rajeswari, *College of Engineering, India*

Table of Contents

Preface xvi

Acknowledgment xxi

Chapter 1
AI-Driven Predictive Approaches for Mitigating Cyber Attacks on Electric Vehicle Charging Networks in Public Infrastructure 1
Paritosh Biswas, Marwadi University, India
Sushil Kumar Singh, Marwadi University, India
Habib Khan, Gachon University, South Korea

Chapter 2
AI-Driven Predictive Analytics for Secure IoT-Enabled Smart Agriculture and Public Administration Perspectives 49
Harshita Singh, Marwadi University, India
Sudhriti Bari, Marwadi University, India
Sushil Kumar Singh, Marwadi University, India
Om Prakash Suthar, Marwadi University, India

Chapter 3
Business Intelligence in Public Administration Integrating Predictive Analytics and Organizational Adaptation 95
Mohammad Al Khaldy, University of Petra, Amman, Jordan
Amjad Aldweesh, College of Computing and Information Technology, Shaqra University, Saudi Arabia
Ahmad Al-Qerem, Computer Science Department, Faculty of Information Technology, Zarqa University, Jordan

Chapter 4
E-Governance Services Using AI: Effective or Wasteful? 115
Hanifa Maylasari, Diponegoro University, Indonesia
Nilam Adini Rakhma, Diponegoro University, Indonesia
Ali Roziqin, Universitas Muhammadiyah Malang, Indonesia

Chapter 5
Hybrid AI and Blockchain Systems for Digital Identity in Developing Countries: Predictive Governance for Public Inclusion and Efficiency............. 147
Sónia Calado, University of Aveiro, Portugal
Cláudia Miranda Veloso, University of Aveiro, Portugal

Chapter 6
Improving Cybersecurity and Risk Management Techniques in AI Blockchain Governance Systems 177
Puneet Chauhan, Swami Vivekanand Subharti University, India
Krishan Pal, Swami Vivekanand Subharti University, India
Almash Saifi, Swami Vivekanand Subharti University, India
Vikas Sharma, SRM Institute of Science and Technology, Delhi, India
Tarun Kumar Vashishth, IIMT University, Meerut, India
Kajal Choudhary, IIMT University, Meerut, India

Chapter 7
Proactive Governance: Leveraging Predictive Analytics for Citizen-Centric Public Service Delivery 209
Hina Hashmi, Moradabad Institute of Technology, India

Chapter 8
Transforming the Cyber World Through Blockchain-Driven Enlightenment .. 249
Abhay Bhatia, Roorkee Institute of Technology, India
Anil Kumar, Roorkee Institute of Technology, India
Pankhuri Bhatia, Kunwar Satyavira College of Engineering and Management, Bijnor, India

Chapter 9
Street-Level Bureaucracy in Health Services During COVID-19 Outbreak in Indonesia 275
Mohammad Jafar Loilatu, Universitas Muhammadiyah Malang, Indonesia
Tri Sulistyaningsih, Universitas Muhammadiyah Malang, Indonesia
Bambang Irawan, Mulawarman University, Indonesia
Saiman Saiman, Universitas Muhammadiyah Malang, Indonesia
Paisal Akbar, Mulawarman University, Indonesia
Muhammad Nurul Huda, Universitas Muhammadiyah Karanganyar, Indonesia
Inamyza Nurziana Putri, Universitas Muhammadiyah Malang, Indonesia

Chapter 10
The Ethical Integration of AI in Advancing Transparency Fairness and Employee Well-Being 297
Raed Atef, United Arab Emirates University, UAE

Chapter 11
The Evolution of Public Administration in the AI Era 327
Ankush Joshi, COER University, Roorkee, India

Chapter 12
AI-Driven Governance: Predictive Analytics and Blockchain for Smart Public Administration 343
R. N. Ravikumar, Marwadi University, India
S. Aarthi, Marwadi University, India

Compilation of References 373

About the Contributors 431

Index 441

Detailed Table of Contents

Preface..xvi

Acknowledgment...xxi

Chapter 1
AI-Driven Predictive Approaches for Mitigating Cyber Attacks on Electric Vehicle Charging Networks in Public Infrastructure 1
Paritosh Biswas, Marwadi University, India
Sushil Kumar Singh, Marwadi University, India
Habib Khan, Gachon University, South Korea

The rapid adoption of Electric Vehicles (EVs) is transforming sustainable mobility and creating new demands for secure public charging infrastructure. The digital integration of EV charging networks creates vulnerabilities exposed to various cyber threats, including denial-of-service, malware, ransomware, and man-in-the-middle attacks are significant concerns. These vulnerabilities can lead to service disruption, financial loss, and reduced public trust. This chapter provides a comprehensive review of cybersecurity risks within the EV infrastructure, emphasizing the role of AI-driven approaches in mitigating risks through the use of machine learning, anomaly detection, and adaptive defence strategies. Predictive analytics help identify and respond to emerging threats. The chapter also covers secure communication protocols and encryption mechanisms. Integration of predictive intelligence in the development of secure and resilient public EV infrastructure ensures operational continuity and trust in digital EV infrastructure.

Chapter 2
AI-Driven Predictive Analytics for Secure IoT-Enabled Smart Agriculture and Public Administration Perspectives 49
Harshita Singh, Marwadi University, India
Sudhriti Bari, Marwadi University, India
Sushil Kumar Singh, Marwadi University, India
Om Prakash Suthar, Marwadi University, India

This chapter explores how AI and predictive analytics, as well as advanced next-gen technologies, are transforming traditional agriculture into smart farming with IoT technologies in the Smart City Environment. Integration of IoT devices, AI, blockchain, drones, 6G networks, edge computing, and digital twins enables real-time monitoring of various agricultural activities. AI-backed predictive models help in forecasting irrigation needs, identifying early crop health monitoring, and optimizing resource usage. Blockchain and smart contracts help in ensuring data security and transparency. However, challenges include cybersecurity risks, limited rural connectivity, and the need for improved digital literacy is evident. The chapter discusses and highlights both advancements in technology and the role of policy, governance, and digital inclusion in achieving secure and efficient smart agriculture.

Chapter 3
Business Intelligence in Public Administration Integrating Predictive Analytics and Organizational Adaptation 95
Mohammad Al Khaldy, University of Petra, Amman, Jordan
Amjad Aldweesh, College of Computing and Information Technology, Shaqra University, Saudi Arabia
Ahmad Al-Qerem, Computer Science Department, Faculty of Information Technology, Zarqa University, Jordan

Business intelligence (BI) in public administration involves the synthesis of large data sets to support evidence-based decision-making. Researchers have identified organizational barriers, technical complexities, and governance gaps that hinder BI initiatives in the public sector. This chapter investigates how agencies can use predictive analytics to strengthen service outcomes, focusing on strategies for effective implementation. The analysis draws on examples of AI-assisted processes in diverse contexts, revealing that organizational structures and leadership practices determine the success or failure of predictive models. Findings indicate that robust data governance, staff training, and mechanisms for accountability foster sustainable BI use. This chapter contributes by offering a structured discussion of BI adoption and outlines future paths for integrating neural-network-driven insights in public administration.

Chapter 4
E-Governance Services Using AI: Effective or Wasteful? 115
Hanifa Maylasari, Diponegoro University, Indonesia
Nilam Adini Rakhma, Diponegoro University, Indonesia
Ali Roziqin, Universitas Muhammadiyah Malang, Indonesia

Rapid development of technology is marked by the emergence of Artificial Intelligence (AI) .This study is important, because public services using e-governance create social dynamics. The method used is document analysis by comparing public service systems in developing and developed countries that use AI technology from relevant scientific literature. This chapter finds that developing countries emphasize digital foundations and technology accessibility developed countries. Developing countries have not yet reached a more mature regulatory stage, minimal public involvement in the policy-making process, and need to examine more deeply the ethical standards of AI management. Developed countries are able to be a reference in determining public service regulations using AI, because they are able to use e-governance services in a more structured manner and involve the role of civil society. The existence of this study is expected that governance regulations in developing countries in implementing e-governance services using AI can run accountably and effectively to the entire community.

Chapter 5
Hybrid AI and Blockchain Systems for Digital Identity in Developing Countries: Predictive Governance for Public Inclusion and Efficiency 147
Sónia Calado, University of Aveiro, Portugal
Cláudia Miranda Veloso, University of Aveiro, Portugal

The digital transformation of public administration demands innovative solutions that balance operational efficiency with inclusive governance. This chapter proposes a hybrid framework using predictive AI and blockchain to address a key barrier in developing countries: the lack of formal digital identities. By applying AI-driven predictive analytics to biometric verification and leveraging blockchain for data integrity and decentralization,it is demonstrated that integrated systems can support secure, scalable identity infrastructures. These systems expand access to public services and generate real-time data that help governments forecast needs, reduce exclusion and allocate resources strategically. Drawing on empirical studies and case examples, the chapter explores opportunities, implementation challenges and policy implications, focusing on algorithmic transparency, ethical data governance, and institutional readiness, while showing how AI-powered predictive technologies can transform public administration through inclusive, data-informed and accountable digital identity systems.

Chapter 6
Improving Cybersecurity and Risk Management Techniques in AI Blockchain Governance Systems 177
Puneet Chauhan, Swami Vivekanand Subharti University, India
Krishan Pal, Swami Vivekanand Subharti University, India
Almash Saifi, Swami Vivekanand Subharti University, India
Vikas Sharma, SRM Institute of Science and Technology, Delhi, India
Tarun Kumar Vashishth, IIMT University, Meerut, India
Kajal Choudhary, IIMT University, Meerut, India

The combination of AI with Blockchain or AI-Blockchain integration disrupts existing governance structures. Cybersecurity however becomes an important area of concern in system fortitude, data trust, and public confidence. The focus of this chapter is the AI-Blockchain governance system's cybersecurity vulnerabilities such as smart contracts' flaws, AI model attacks, and other blockchain specific weaknesses like

51% and Sybil attacks. Addressing these concerns, some of the focus areas include Protecting AI model training, issuing decentralized identities, end-to-end encryption, and blockchain auditors to enhance security. More importantly, fostering proactive threat intelligence, robust governance policies and frameworks, and resilient design architectures for active defences against sophisticated cyber threats is paramount.

Chapter 7
Proactive Governance: Leveraging Predictive Analytics for Citizen-Centric Public Service Delivery 209
Hina Hashmi, Moradabad Institute of Technology, India

This chapter explores how predictive analytics is transforming public administration from reactive to proactive, citizen-centered governance. It examines how governments can use historical, real-time, and multi-source data—such as demographic, health, infrastructure, and social media information—to anticipate societal needs and intervene early. Drawing on welfare and public health examples, it demonstrates how predictive models support timely detection of service demands, risks, and policy gaps, enhancing operational efficiency and crisis management. The chapter also addresses ethical and regulatory challenges, including algorithmic accountability, data privacy, and transparency. By emphasizing AI, digital twins, and real-time analytics, it offers a data-driven framework for building inclusive, responsive, and future-ready governance systems.

Chapter 8
Transforming the Cyber World Through Blockchain-Driven Enlightenment .. 249
Abhay Bhatia, Roorkee Institute of Technology, India
Anil Kumar, Roorkee Institute of Technology, India
Pankhuri Bhatia, Kunwar Satyavira College of Engineering and Management, Bijnor, India

The cybersecurity landscape through blockchain technology in India involves leveraging the decentralized nature and consensus mechanisms of blockchain to enhance security measures. This approach aims to ensure transaction authenticity, prevent unauthorized alterations, and strengthen cybersecurity defences across various sectors, from critical infrastructure to government records. Despite the promising advantages of blockchain in cybersecurity, challenges such as scalability, interoperability, and regulatory frameworks need to be addressed for successful integration into India's cybersecurity framework. By exploring specific use cases, real-world examples, and case studies, this transformation can be more potential of blockchain technology in cybersecurity with artificial intelligence offers insights into fortifying India's digital security infrastructure and fostering a more secure and trusted digital ecosystem for better world.

Chapter 9
Street-Level Bureaucracy in Health Services During COVID-19 Outbreak in Indonesia 275
Mohammad Jafar Loilatu, Universitas Muhammadiyah Malang, Indonesia
Tri Sulistyaningsih, Universitas Muhammadiyah Malang, Indonesia
Bambang Irawan, Mulawarman University, Indonesia
Saiman Saiman, Universitas Muhammadiyah Malang, Indonesia
Paisal Akbar, Mulawarman University, Indonesia
Muhammad Nurul Huda, Universitas Muhammadiyah Karanganyar, Indonesia
Inamyza Nurziana Putri, Universitas Muhammadiyah Malang, Indonesia

This study seeks to elucidate the interaction between healthcare professionals and the government through health service indicators during the COVID-19 epidemic in South Sulawesi. This study used a qualitative methodology to perform a content analysis of online media coverage about health workers, the government, and health services during the COVID-19 epidemic in South Sulawesi. This study demonstrates a direct correlation between health professionals and the government with health indicators, including front-line services, stigma, duty, equipment assistance, protection, and engagements. These findings affirm that health professionals and the government are accountable for the efficacy of front-line bureaucracy, services, bureaucratic responsibilities, health facilities and infrastructure, health protection, and stakeholder engagement. The government has not succeeded in cultivating a favorable perception of health workers as the front-line of the bureaucracy delivering quality health services.

Chapter 10
The Ethical Integration of AI in Advancing Transparency Fairness and Employee Well-Being 297
Raed Atef, United Arab Emirates University, UAE

This chapter examines AI's role in fostering trustful work environments and enhancing employee well-being. AI-driven technologies improve transparency, fairness, and integrity by detecting corruption, reducing bias, and promoting ethical practices. They enhance fairness in recruitment and career progression while alleviating stress through automation and wellness monitoring. Despite these benefits, ethical concerns regarding data privacy and bias remain. Responsible AI implementation, with clear guidelines and employee involvement, is crucial to maximizing its potential. When applied ethically, AI can create more transparent, inclusive, and supportive workplaces.

Chapter 11
The Evolution of Public Administration in the AI Era 327
Ankush Joshi, COER University, Roorkee, India

This chapter explores the transformative impact of Artificial Intelligence (AI) and predictive analytics on public administration. It traces the evolution from traditional bureaucratic governance to AI-powered systems that enhance efficiency, transparency, and responsiveness. The chapter examines how AI automates administrative tasks, supports data-driven decision-making, and enables proactive policy formulation. It presents global case studies across sectors such as smart cities, healthcare, and law enforcement. Ethical concerns, including bias, transparency, and data privacy, are critically analyzed. The chapter concludes with future directions, emphasizing ethical frameworks, human-AI collaboration, and inclusive digital governance for the 21st century.

Chapter 12
AI-Driven Governance: Predictive Analytics and Blockchain for Smart Public Administration 343
R. N. Ravikumar, Marwadi University, India
S. Aarthi, Marwadi University, India

This chapter explores how Artificial Intelligence (AI) and blockchain technologies are transforming public administration into a transparent, efficient, and citizen-centric ecosystem. It examines the role of predictive analytics in enabling proactive decision-making and resource optimization, while blockchain ensures data integrity, trust, and decentralization. Through real-world case studies of Estonia and Singapore, the chapter highlights successful implementations of these technologies in digital identity systems, smart urban planning, and public service delivery. It also addresses ethical, legal, and governance challenges, proposing strategic frameworks for responsible adoption. The chapter offers a roadmap for future-ready, technology-driven governance that is inclusive, accountable, and resilient.

Compilation of References 373

About the Contributors 431

Index 441

Preface

INTRODUCTION

The 21st century has ushered in an era marked by rapid technological advancements, where data has emerged as a vital resource for both private enterprises and public institutions. In this context, the public sector, historically slower to adopt cutting-edge technologies, now faces a pivotal moment of transformation. One of the most promising avenues for this transformation lies in the integration of Artificial Intelligence (AI), particularly predictive analytics, into public administration.

This book, *Transforming Public Administration Through AI-Driven Predictive Analytics*, is a response to the growing need for innovative tools and frameworks that can enhance decision-making, increase efficiency, and ultimately deliver better outcomes for citizens. It emerges from both academic inquiry and practical engagement with the evolving landscape of governance, where AI is no longer a futuristic ideal but a present-day reality.

Predictive analytics, as a branch of AI, involves the use of historical data, statistical algorithms, and machine learning techniques to forecast future outcomes. Within the private sector, these tools have been leveraged for years to predict consumer behavior, manage supply chains, and optimize marketing strategies. However, their application in the public sector is only now gaining momentum.

Governments and public institutions possess vast amounts of data on health, education, crime, transportation, demographics, and more, collected over decades. Unfortunately, much of this data has remained underutilized. With the introduction of predictive analytics, public administrators now have the ability to transform raw data into actionable insights. For example, predictive models can anticipate spikes in hospital admissions, identify at-risk student populations before dropout occurs, or forecast infrastructure needs based on urban growth patterns.

Such applications are not just about efficiency; they are about fundamentally reshaping how public services are designed and delivered. AI-driven predictive analytics can help shift governance from reactive to proactive, enabling authorities to prevent problems before they arise rather than merely responding to crises after the fact.

The integration of AI into public administration represents a paradigm shift, from traditional, bureaucratic systems to more agile, adaptive, and evidence-based governance structures. This shift is not merely technological; it is organizational, cultural, and strategic.

At the heart of this transformation is the recognition that data and algorithms, when used responsibly, can augment human judgment and support more equitable, transparent, and accountable governance. By uncovering patterns and trends that may not be immediately visible to human decision-makers, AI systems can highlight areas of concern, prioritize resource allocation, and offer alternative scenarios for policy consideration.

Consider the potential of predictive analytics in social welfare: by analyzing data on unemployment, housing, and education, predictive models can help governments identify vulnerable communities before crises escalate, allowing for early intervention and more targeted support. Similarly, in law enforcement, predictive tools can aid in crime prevention by identifying high-risk areas and times, thereby improving patrol strategies while reducing unnecessary police interventions.

This book explores such transformative applications in detail, offering both theoretical grounding and practical case studies. It also critically examines the challenges and ethical considerations involved in implementing AI within public institutions.

While the benefits of AI-driven predictive analytics are substantial, their adoption in the public sector is not without challenges. One of the most pressing concerns is the ethical use of AI, particularly with regard to bias, transparency, accountability, and data privacy.

Predictive models are only as good as the data they are trained on. If historical data contains biases—racial, gender-based, or socio-economic—then those biases can be perpetuated or even amplified by AI systems. It is therefore crucial for public institutions to approach AI implementation with a clear understanding of algorithmic fairness, data ethics, and inclusive design.

Moreover, public trust is essential in democratic governance. The opacity of some AI algorithms, often referred to as "black boxes," can hinder transparency and accountability. Citizens have a right to understand how decisions affecting them are made, especially when those decisions involve access to services, benefits, or legal outcomes. This book emphasizes the need for explainable AI, participatory design, and robust governance frameworks to ensure that technology serves the public interest.

Another significant challenge lies in organizational readiness. Many public agencies lack the technical infrastructure, skilled personnel, and agile workflows necessary to leverage predictive analytics fully. As such, digital transformation must be accompanied by capacity-building efforts, cross-sector collaboration, and sustained investment in data infrastructure and workforce development.

This book takes a multidisciplinary approach to the subject, drawing insights from data science, public policy, management studies, ethics, and systems thinking. The aim is to create a bridge between technical innovation and administrative practice.

ORGANIZATION OF THE BOOK

Each chapter is designed to serve a distinct purpose: from laying out foundational concepts in AI and predictive analytics to exploring real-world applications across domains such as healthcare, education, public safety, urban planning, and environmental management. We also present frameworks for ethical governance, policy recommendations, and strategies for overcoming institutional resistance to change.

This volume opens with Chapter 1, which addresses the emerging cybersecurity threats posed by the rapid expansion of Electric Vehicle (EV) charging infrastructure. As public systems become increasingly digitalized, this chapter explores how AI-driven predictive analytics—through machine learning and adaptive defense strategies—can mitigate vulnerabilities such as ransomware and denial-of-service attacks. It emphasizes the need for secure communication protocols and resilient infrastructure to protect public trust and operational continuity.

In Chapter 2, the focus shifts to the agricultural sector within smart city environments, showcasing how IoT and AI integration is revolutionizing farming practices. The chapter presents predictive tools for irrigation and crop health monitoring, enhanced by blockchain, drones, and edge computing. It underscores the critical role of public administration in fostering digital inclusion, improving rural connectivity, and addressing cybersecurity and policy challenges inherent in deploying smart agriculture systems.

Chapter 3 delves into the integration of business intelligence (BI) and predictive analytics in public administration. Drawing from a variety of global case studies, the chapter analyzes how organizational structures, leadership, and data governance influence the successful adoption of BI tools. It provides a roadmap for enhancing evidence-based decision-making and adapting public institutions to leverage data-driven insights sustainably.

Chapter 4 presents a comparative study of e-governance initiatives in developed and developing countries, questioning whether AI-enabled public services enhance or hinder governance outcomes. The chapter highlights digital infrastructure disparities, regulatory maturity, and civil society involvement, emphasizing that effective AI adoption in e-governance requires not just technological investment but ethical oversight and inclusive policymaking.

In Chapter 5, a hybrid framework using AI and blockchain is proposed to address the persistent challenge of digital identity in developing countries. Through predictive analytics and decentralized technologies, this chapter demonstrates how inclusive digital identity systems can improve access to public services, strengthen governance, and reduce exclusion. Policy considerations around data ethics, algorithmic transparency, and institutional capacity are central to its analysis.

Chapter 6 examines the complex cybersecurity landscape emerging from the convergence of AI and blockchain technologies. With an emphasis on proactive threat detection and resilient system design, the chapter discusses vulnerabilities in smart contracts, AI models, and blockchain networks. It recommends robust governance frameworks and auditing mechanisms to bolster public confidence and data security in AI-blockchain systems.

In Chapter 7, the narrative turns to citizen-centric public service delivery, showing how predictive analytics enables governments to move from reactive problem-solving to proactive governance. Using diverse data sources, predictive tools help anticipate social needs, manage crises, and optimize resource distribution. The chapter also confronts the ethical implications of algorithmic decision-making, advocating for transparency and privacy safeguards.

Chapter 8 explores India's strategic adoption of blockchain to strengthen national cybersecurity across sectors. Focusing on decentralization and consensus mechanisms, the chapter highlights use cases where blockchain fortifies digital records and infrastructure security. It also discusses the hurdles of scalability and regulation, offering a vision of a secure digital future bolstered by AI and blockchain integration.

Chapter 9 provides a grounded, qualitative analysis of street-level bureaucracy during the COVID-19 outbreak in Indonesia. It reveals the essential, and often underappreciated, role of frontline health workers in shaping health outcomes and institutional trust. The study illustrates the need for supportive policy environments, adequate resources, and positive public narratives to empower bureaucrats and improve public service efficacy.

Chapter 10 investigates the ethical integration of AI in fostering transparency and employee well-being within public organizations. It highlights how AI can detect corruption, minimize workplace bias, and support mental health monitoring. The chapter calls for responsible AI deployment strategies that center human values, ensuring ethical standards are upheld while promoting inclusive and transparent work environments.

Chapter 11 offers a macro-level perspective on how AI and predictive analytics are transforming public administration. Tracing its evolution from traditional bureaucracy to intelligent systems, the chapter presents global examples from smart cities, healthcare, and law enforcement. It concludes with a forward-looking vision of collaborative, ethical, and digitally mature governance that can adapt to the demands of the 21st century.

Finally, Chapter 12 synthesizes the transformative potential of AI and blockchain in creating smart, citizen-centric public administration ecosystems. Through case studies from Estonia and Singapore, it illustrates how predictive analytics and distributed technologies enhance decision-making, trust, and accountability. The chapter proposes a strategic framework for responsible implementation, aiming to guide governments toward inclusive, resilient, and future-ready digital governance.

CONCLUSION

Importantly, the book does not advocate for technology as a panacea. Rather, it recognizes AI as a tool, one that must be wielded with care, guided by human values, and embedded within systems of democratic accountability. The future of public administration lies not in replacing human judgment with machines, but in creating symbiotic systems where data-driven insights enhance human wisdom.

Transforming Public Administration Through AI-Driven Predictive Analytics is intended for a diverse readership. Academics and researchers will find a wealth of references and theoretical frameworks to support further investigation. Policymakers and administrators will gain practical insights into implementation strategies and policy implications. Data scientists and technologists will benefit from understanding the unique challenges of applying AI within the public domain. Lastly, students and emerging professionals will find a comprehensive introduction to one of the most dynamic intersections of technology and governance.

The book contributes to an ongoing dialogue about the digital transformation of public institutions. By bringing together theory, practice, and ethics, it aims to inform and inspire a new generation of public leaders who are prepared to harness the power of AI not only for efficiency but for equity, resilience, and social progress.

The digital transformation of governance is not a destination but a journey, one that will evolve alongside technological advances, societal expectations, and global challenges. As climate change, pandemics, and economic disruptions reshape the global landscape, the need for agile, data-informed public administration has never been greater.

Acknowledgment

The journey of bringing together this edited volume, *Transforming Public Administration Through AI-Driven Predictive Analytics*, has been both intellectually enriching and collaborative in the truest sense. We extend our deepest gratitude to all the contributing authors whose scholarly insights, rigorous research, and diverse perspectives have shaped the core of this book. Their commitment to exploring the intersection of artificial intelligence, predictive analytics, and public governance has been invaluable.

We are especially thankful to the reviewers and subject matter experts who offered constructive feedback throughout the editorial process. Their critical evaluations helped enhance the quality, clarity, and impact of each chapter.

We extend our sincere appreciation to the academic and institutional partners who provided an enabling environment for this project. We are particularly grateful to Moradabad Institute of Technology, Moradabad, Uttar Pradesh, India, whose encouragement and support have been instrumental in realizing this endeavor.

We also acknowledge the efforts of the editorial and production team, whose professionalism ensured the smooth execution of this publication, from manuscript preparation to final printing.

Finally, we dedicate this work to researchers, practitioners, policymakers, and students who continue to push the boundaries of innovation in public administration. We hope that this volume will serve as a catalyst for meaningful discourse and data-driven decision-making in governance.

Chapter 1
AI-Driven Predictive Approaches for Mitigating Cyber Attacks on Electric Vehicle Charging Networks in Public Infrastructure

Paritosh Biswas
https://orcid.org/0009-0000-4506-9827
Marwadi University, India

Sushil Kumar Singh
https://orcid.org/0000-0003-0030-5691
Marwadi University, India

Habib Khan
Gachon University, South Korea

ABSTRACT

The rapid adoption of Electric Vehicles (EVs) is transforming sustainable mobility and creating new demands for secure public charging infrastructure. The digital integration of EV charging networks creates vulnerabilities exposed to various cyber threats, including denial-of-service, malware, ransomware, and man-in-the-middle attacks are significant concerns. These vulnerabilities can lead to service disruption, financial loss, and reduced public trust. This chapter provides a comprehensive review of cybersecurity risks within the EV infrastructure, emphasizing the role

DOI: 10.4018/979-8-3373-3760-9.ch001

of AI-driven approaches in mitigating risks through the use of machine learning, anomaly detection, and adaptive defence strategies. Predictive analytics help identify and respond to emerging threats. The chapter also covers secure communication protocols and encryption mechanisms. Integration of predictive intelligence in the development of secure and resilient public EV infrastructure ensures operational continuity and trust in digital EV infrastructure.

INTRODUCTION

Smart cities are founded on the application of digital technologies and public infrastructural connectivity to develop the level of urban life, energy, and rational level of emissions. Electric Vehicles form one of those ecosystems, as they are pushing business to be profitable in the transport sector on the one hand and are in contact with the city public infrastructure literally all the time, such as charging points, traffic control system, and bus and tram network. This amount of connectivity renders EV communications systems vulnerable to cybersecurity threats and an attacker can disrupt the traffic pattern, control of energy, or privacy of personal data. This may also involve man-in-the-middle attack which may arise when EVs are attached to the public chargers via mobile apps or through a city Wi-Fi, which should be highly encrypted and authenticated. The unification of the artificial intelligence and Internet of Things (IoT) technologies to help in controlling the EV traffic and supply it with a source of power adds even more to the attack surface. The modern base of all EV systems is IoT and connects them to the automobiles, charge-up, grid, and personal mobile applications using the various sensors to monitor the battery level, navigation preserves, and service warnings. However, vulnerability of these IoT devices due to their interdependence nature poses a dangerous cybersecurity threat as the poorly secured IoT devices may be remotely accessed resulting to erroneous invoice or the unavailability of a service. Many of the Internet of Things architecture protocols suffer poor authentication and encryption which results in vulnerability to spoofing and denial of service attacks. In order to ensure the security of these networks we have to consider, the integrity of firmware and secure boot processes, software patches in time, anomaly detection using machine learning in real time. Smart EV networks are networks that are fully incorporated with EVs, charging infrastructure, energy providers and cloud platforms that interact using intelligent platforms and means of maximizing the charging, route planning, energy usage and predictive maintenance. These networks in spite of the benefits brought about have a high chance of being attacked by cyber-attacks that include data manipulation, denial-of-service, firmware hacking, and the man in the middle attack, all these expose them to the risk of losing their service interruption, monetary looting, and safety. A layered protection will be required in good security involving an encrypted communication, anomaly detection, secure firmware management, and restricted access control.

Moreover, there is the need to protect privacy since user driving behaviour, location and financial data is sensitive information. With the spread of intelligent transport systems and self-driven vehicles, it is of paramount importance that the smart EV networks should be secured in order to have safe, reliable, and trustworthy transportation. Standardizing on this, the Internet of Electric Vehicle (IoEV) is the network public infrastructure that provides real-time communication between the electric vehicles, charging system, grid services, traffic management system and cloud computing. This model is a development of the Internet of Vehicles (IoV) technology, which provides vehicle monitoring, vehicle diagnostics, battery management solutions, automated billing, and traffic aware routing. The need of IoEVs to be connected to wireless and the cloud however presents the issue of cybersecurity challenges that include false injection of data, spoofing, denial-of-service attacks and unauthorized access to data. Imperilled modules emit data leaks, loss of monetary gain and backdoor control over the vehicle. Some of the Mitigation requires strong authentication, end-to-end encryption, blockchain-based identification, or intrusion detection in real-time. Edge computing may reduce cloud reliance because the critically sensitive data can be processed locally. The protection of IoEVs infrastructure is an important part of keeping established safety, privacy, and operational integrity given its convergence into smart cities and smart grids.

In the continuation of this work, the current study of the Electric Vehicle Charging Networks (EVCNs) attempts to study the vexational security issues that are associated with the interconnection of EVs, charging public infrastructure and the power grid. The importance of EVCNs to the adoption of EVs has made its cyber-physical relationships present many attack surfaces that are prone to complex cyberattacks. In this paper, the current vulnerabilities are reviewed based on the communication protocols, hardware, and software elements and the need to increase security, which should be dependent on the updated threat posed. Through an in-depth scoping of the various security concerns like man-in-the-middle attack, data breach, denial of service and firmware hijacking, the study shows the need to implement multi-layered defence systems like machine-learning based anomaly detections and secure authentication protocols as well as strong encryption standards. Proactive cybersecurity infrastructures are an important component of IoT and smart grid integration in EVCNs, where operational efficiency and resilience have to counteract the new and emerging cyberattacks. Such a study supports the necessity of creating scalable, agile, and privacy-preserving solutions to protect the integrity, confidentiality, and availability of EV charging network infrastructures in order to deliver reliable services and generate a trustworthy user base to achieve sustainable developments in electric mobility. Overview of EV charging station in IoEV within a smart city public infrastructure is shown in Figure 1.

Figure 1. Overview of EV charging station in IoEV within a smart city public infrastructure (Sabzi & Vaijta, 2023)

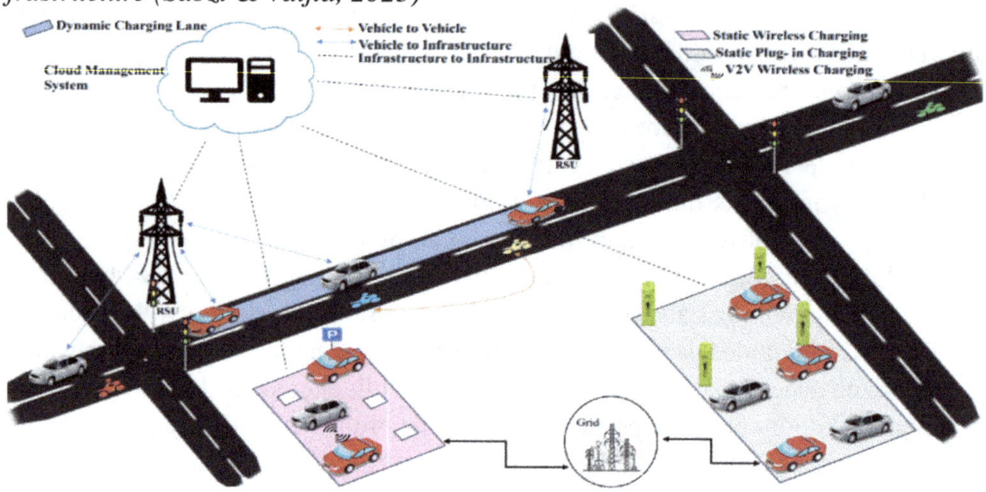

Research Contribution

In search of suitable sources, we included Google Scholar on one hand and the big-publisher databases (IEEE Xplore, Springer, ScienceDirect, etc.) on the other hand and used the following keywords: Cyber Security, Threat Detection, Electrical Vehicle Charging Networks, Internet of Electric Vehicles, Threat Detection on Electrical Vehicles under the 2020-2025 period. Consequently, we come across 120 research studies, and after examining these articles to make them relevant, we have finally incorporated 40 articles in this review.

The main contributions of our research are as follows:

- This research establishes the foundation for investigating Electric Vehicle Charging Networks (EVCNs) within the framework of cybersecurity and AI-driven predictive defence, serving as a guide for strengthening the resilience of public infrastructure.
- The chapter presents in detail the cybersecurity threats targeting EVCNs, highlighting vulnerabilities, attack vectors, and operational risks that undermine reliability and trust.

- A comprehensive tabular representation of cyberthreats, risks, and weaknesses in EVCNs is provided, offering a clear overview of potential vulnerabilities and their impacts.
- Future research directions are discussed, emphasizing the role of predictive analytics, machine learning, and adaptive defence models in securing EVCNs within public systems.
- The chapter examines security implications of cloud, fog, and edge computing in EV infrastructures, outlining associated risks, challenges, and mitigation strategies.
- Finally, it explores emerging AI-driven cybersecurity technologies that can proactively detect, predict, and prevent attacks, supporting secure and sustainable EV charging infrastructures.

Organization

Literature on the topic of cybersecurity in EV systems is greatly obsessed with finding vulnerabilities in the key elements of cybersecurity in EV systems, which comprises charging infrastructure, vehicle-to-grid (V2G) and onboard control units. The research articles only show the way in which we can adopt a more sophisticated approach to data like deep learning, ensemble learning and anomaly detection systems to find and eliminate various cyber threats like false data injection, spoofing, and denial-of-service (DoS) attacks. The paper looks at some of the platforms, which include smart grids, EV charging channels and real-time communication protocols. It addresses the issues of such fields as autonomous systems, power electronics, and connected mobility systems. Even though these initiatives are wonderful milestones, it has its setbacks. The current models are imprudent and cannot alter in real time and this is of essence in changing environments. Moreover, there still exist no standardised procedures that would hamper down the interoperability of the EV systems and platforms. The next potent limitation that can be also referred to is the use of such models in the actual application, which causes the fact that many solutions obtained are not widely applicable and can be viewed as hypothetical or experimental. The mentioned gaps highlight the need to have near and flexible cybersecurity models that are more standardized in offering an all-inclusive security regarding the electric vehicle ecosystem.

Figure 2. Few cyber attacks in electrical vehicle charging networks in public infrastructure

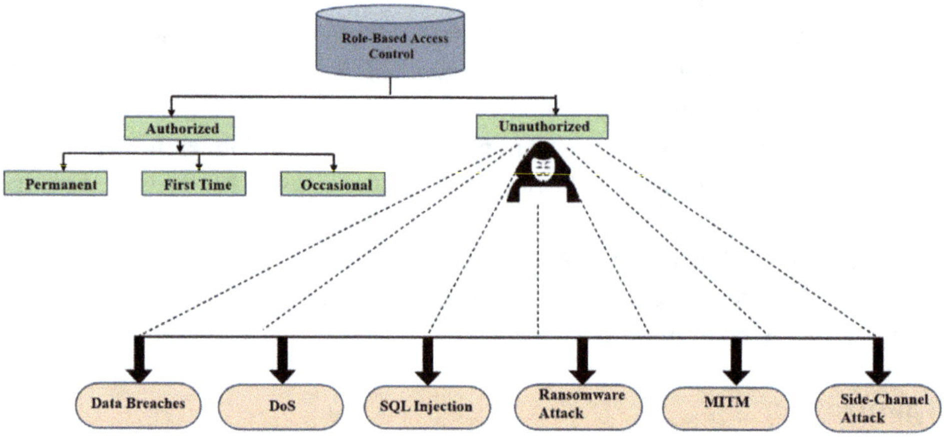

Man-in-the-Middle attacks are cases when evil actors can intercept the messages that two parties exchange with one another, including that between an electric vehicle and a charging station or between a charging station and central servers. Through such attacks, the hackers can overhear the traffic, alter the transmitted data, or send fake commands, and can also be deployed to affect billing data and charge mechanisms, eavesdrop on users, or steal their authentication information. Not surprisingly, the exposure to this type of attack is specifically on the increase in the EVCS domains where communication protocols such as OCPP are not secured. This much impacts on integrity, privacy and the capability of controlling EV charging operations. The vulnerabilities related to the protocols have been discussed by Sani, Hassan, and Chen (2022), which emphasized secure encryption and authentication is required to extend the exposure of the risks of MitM, and safeguard the EV charging ecosystem. The data breaches in EVCS are illustrated as the input of the sensitive data on the user or the system, e.g. payment data, user identity, vehicle data, and logs. This kind of information is usually stored or transmitted to cloud servers or grid operators that increase the attack surface as well. They may be related to access by insecure APIs, database misconfigurations and encounters with malware. Such breaches can result in possible identity theft, fraud, and data abuse, lower user trust, and punishment in laws, such as GDPR. Among the cybersecurity concerns of the EVCS infrastructural system, Hamdare et al. (2023) presents the situation on the information confidentiality problem and the need to implement powerful and effective security to minimize the risk of the threat to unauthorized access to the information and the fact of information exposure. A Few Cyber Attacks in Electrical Vehicle Charging Networks in public infrastructure are shown in Figure 2.

Denial of Service (DoS) and Distributed Denial of Service (DDoS) pour on the network or service structure of EVCS, such that it is unavailable to legitimate users. The attackers may overwhelm communication ports, APIs, or any cloud interface, and in many cases use compromised IoT devices as part of DDoS attacks to increase the effects. This interference will frustrate the EV charging system, disrupt grid communications, and disrupt the charging or reservation systems, thus causing massive operation and financial losses to the operators, especially public transportation and fleet operators. Morrison (2018) gives a thorough explanation of DDoS attacks against EVCS and the power grid, and the necessity of mitigation plans to ensure the security of the grid and the availability of its services. SQL injection-based attacks can be used to attack the database query interface in electric vehicle charging networks to gain unauthorized access to, modify, or even remove vital information, including user identities, billing accounts, and charging schedules. These are the attacks that destroy charging services, enable financial fraud, breach sensitive information and endanger operational integrity and negatively affect both network availability and trust afforded to the user.

Despite these 36-referenced papers mainly dealing with wider aspects of cybersecurity, including intrusion detection, security of firmware and vulnerabilities in protocols, none of the papers directly examine SQL injection in the EV charging system. This gap demonstrates one of the possible areas of future investigations that tend to contribute to the raising of database safety in EVCN systems. Side-channel attacks utilize indirect physical emissions, e.g., timing, electromagnetic signal, or power consumption of electric vehicle charging networks, to retrieve sensitive information, e.g., cryptographic keys or credentials, without directly accessing software or protocols. Such attacks compromise the privacy of the user, the integrity, and the safety of systems, which may lead to loss of service and wastage of money.

RELATED WORK

In this section, we discuss existing related work with some parameters such as limitations, merits, objectives, and all, preliminaries based on this chapter title.

Preliminaries

The provided section provides the body of knowledge based on which it will be possible to understand the issues regarding cybersecurity in the electric vehicle ecosystem. The EV infrastructure comprises an upstream and downstream network of systems, including electric vehicles, charging infrastructure (private- and publicly-owned) electric utility grid connection, which can also be controlled or managed via standard communication protocols, including OCPP and ISO 15118. The systems will form a part of the broader platform of the smart grid system whose operation is based on the bidirectional communicational capability to regulates energy management and vehicle-to-grid (V2G) services. The multiple embedded controllers found in the electric vehicles used are the Battery Management Systems (BMS), the Powertrain Control Modules (PCMs) and the Telematics Units (TCUs). Such embedded controllers introduce novel attack areas of cyber-physical aspects. Security is a challenge to majorly since implementation of V2G capability and the IoV capability nickel attacks surfaces and introduces real-time activities in control. Technologies that would alleviate such risks, i.e., use of edge computing, secure communication protocol, and intrusion detection system, constitute the technical foundation of the present work.

Electric Vehicle Infrastructure

Electric Vehicle infrastructure would comprise the simple infrastructure, which makes possible the implementation and integration of the electric vehicles. It is a combination of inter-connected components such as charging points, the vehicles themselves and interface with the utility grid. These charging points could be either own by a business or power business and have different power rangers, Level 1 which is low power charging point to Level 3 which are fast charging point. They will be equipped with special equipment like charging, transformers, power-supply units and communication modules as well as data exchange modules. In addition, EVs have charging ports making them plug to charging points. The communication between the vehicle-charging station is significant in ensuring the proper communication of energy and the standardized protocol e.g. OCPP and the ISO 15118 ensure that the systems will interoperate. The overall energy grid within which the electric vehicle infrastructure is probably to be the focus of the connection relies on the smart grid so that the electricity distribution could be performed in an arguably consistent manner. This kind of integration can solve smart charging, demand response, and Vehicle-to-Grid (V2G) capabilities too, which increases grid stability even further. An Overview of the ENCS Public Infrastructure is shown in Figure 3.

Figure 3. An overview of ENCS public infrastructure

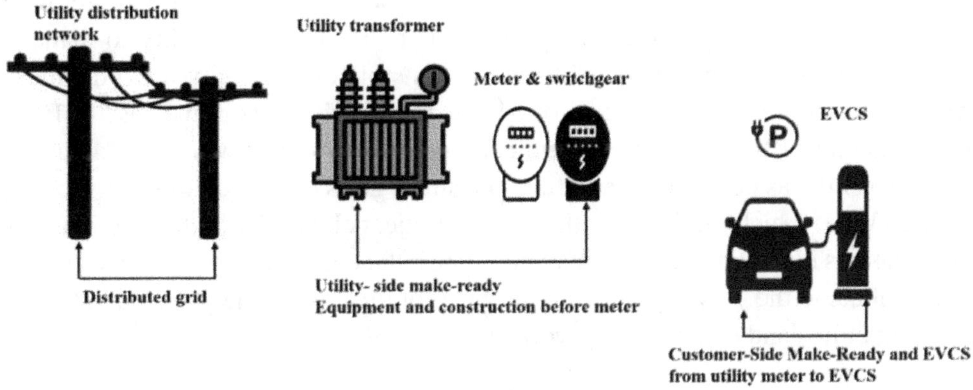

Communication Protocols (OCPP, ISO 15118)

The electric vehicle (EV) ecosystem relies and relies a lot on the communication protocols such as Open Charge Point Protocol (OCPP) and ISO 15118. OCPP is an open protocol standard that would enable a form of communication between charging stations and central management systems and consequently provide them with the capability of such processes as remote diagnostics, monitoring, and billing. It enables charging points of different producers to collaborate with each other, and, hence, is a compulsory battery of norms in the premises of the EV. In its turn, ISO 15118 is aimed at secure communication between the electric vehicle and the charging station. It helps to support such features as Plug-and-Charge, where an auto will be capable of authenticating itself without any introduction of such equipment as RFID cards. Exchange of secure data is also defined in ISO 15118 to ensure that the information on the user is not revealed and also ensuring the integrity of the charging process. The significance of the two protocols in the creation of an effective and stable EV charging system is that they enable a high-performance capacity system to address areas related to energy management and interoperability effects, as well as security issues of various charging systems.

Smart Grid Networks

Smart electrical grid system (smart grid) uses digital communication mode to respond, detect and protect any local change in usage by automatically reacting. It allows two-way communication between consumers and the energy suppliers where the monitoring of the energy use and distribution can be made in a real-time. In the electric vehicles (EVs) case scenario, the smart grids can be used to encourage renewable energy sources such as the solar and wind into the grid and facilitate effective flow of energy. One high point of a smart grid is its ability to manage demand response and make the grid adjust the supply of electricity when the maximum demands are about to create overloads in the grid. This in the case of EVs, means that the charging can be dynamically planned in such a way so as to burden the grid as little as possible. In addition, the smart grids can accommodate vehicle-to-grid (V2G) which implies that the EVs can inject electricity in the grid in times when there is high demand. This may facilitate balancing energy in general, as well as contribute to the growing trend of electric mobility where the powered vehicles, charging points and electricity network flows are best balanced.

Bidirectional Communication for Energy Management and V2G

To optimize energy management and realize the Vehicle-to-Grid (V2G) technology, Electric Vehicles (EVs) and energy grid require bi-directional communication. In the old regimes, charging is one way, with energy being transferred to EV, grid-to-EV. But in case of bidirectional communication, EVs are not only able to obtain power through the grid but also able to inject some energy into the grid when one requires it. It is especially helpful in ensuring the grid is stabilized in cases of high demand. V2G can offer a more efficient model of energy distribution given that EVs can be used as mobile energy storage batteries and offer their energy to the grid in case of energy surplus or shortage. Bidirectional nature necessitates utilization of advanced level of communication protocols, real-time monitoring system as well as smart grid technologies. Moreover, the Battery Management System (BMS) of the vehicle is instrumental in making sure that it does not overcharge – or under-charge the battery too much. It is also important to note that secure communication between EVs and charging stations is important in curtailing unauthorized access to the network as well as maintaining integrity in the data being exchanged.

Embedded Controllers (BMS, PCMs, TCUs)

Embedded controllers are essential to electric vehicles (EVs), which can be handy in the manipulation and coordination of its systems. Battery Management System (BMS), Powertrain Control Module (PCM) and Telematics Control Unit (TCU) are some of the major controllers. The BMS is assigned a responsibility of monitoring state of charge (SOC) of the battery, state of health (SOH), temperature and much more in order to make sure that battery operates securely and competently. The PCM also tracks the powertrain of EV and manages circulation of electricity flow through the battery into motors and further transfers electricity management to achieve optimal performance. TCU is concerned with data exchange between the automobile and external environment, it may be the charging station, fleet management or the cloud. The above control units form an inseparable part of the Automobiles and their significance in the EVs upgrading is turning out to be increasingly crucial in automobile safety, viability and vehicle connectivity. They are also possible source of weakness since the cyberattack of these controllers threatens the vehicle functions and safety.

Cyber-Physical Vulnerabilities

Cyber-physical vulnerabilities are pointers to the potential cyber-system security risk due to the interdependent relationship between cyber-systems and physical systems (such as electric vehicles (EVs)) and EV-infrastructure. These vulnerabilities are founded on the incorporation of embedded controllers, communications tasks and also cloud-based frameworks on EVs. The exploitation of these interconnected systems should also enable hackers to hijack any of the functions of the vehicle, extract valuable data, and make the charging and other energy managing systems fall offline as well. Any embedded devices such as Battery Management System (BMS) and Powertrain Control Modules (PCMs) present in EVs can be attacked and create dangerous scenarios like overheating the battery pack, failures in the operations of the vehicle, or misuse of the confidential data. Furthermore, the charging process of power control or other user-related details can be handled by attackers as the EV and charging networks are highly reliant on the communication protocols, e.g., OCPP and ISO 15118, and they can be easily manipulated. The extensiveness of V2G and IoV implementation, the bigger the cyber-physical attack surface, and therefore, cybersecurity is one of the key concerns in the future evolution of the framework and implementation of the electric vehicle infrastructure.

Vehicle-to-Grid (V2G) and Internet of Vehicles (IoV)

Smart or intelligent vehicle to grid (V2G) and Internet of Vehicles (IoV) are novel technologies that will facilitate adoption of electric vehicles (EVs) in any smart city. The technology involved to have the electric vehicles push back the extra power, which can be utilized to energize the grid in high energy demand, is known as V2G. This two-way communication and energy exchange is between EVs and smart grid systems which manage charging and post-charging duties of EVs in real-time. The connected vehicles network, whereby the cars communicate with one another and with the infrastructure like the traffic lights, road sensors, charging stations, is, however, known as IoV. It is based on this data exchange that improved traffic management, predictive maintenance and safety are possible.

Another relevant activity which can be improved by IoV is smart vehicle usage and autonomous driving: EVs being both a vehicle and a power resource. The two facilitating technologies, V2G, and IoV, play a critical role in guaranteeing a more sustainable energy-efficient transport environment.

Attack Surface Expansion and Real-Time Control

With the growth of the eco-system of the electric car, the area of attack grows. The fact that EVs are composed of a gourmet, the charging system, smart grid and the cloud system also entails that EVs are so easily hacked at the weakest point as hackers are very crafty. This form of management of energy in terms of real-time management would be very effective if it as well accommodates the cyber culprits to bring in manipulation of data or make business processes to a screeching halt. As an illustration, after gaining access to the control unit of the charging station, an attacker can vandalize a charging station and even end up dysregulating the charging schedules and/or cause power outage. Moreover, potential hacking of real-time data will result in inefficient use of the system of distribution of energy or theft of circulating grid resources without authorizations. To minimize the risks of the penetration of the security of the cyberspace such as intrusion detection systems, firewalls and encrypted channels, the security of the cyberspace should be mounted on different levels.

Edge Computing

The edge computing is the processing of data near the origin of data instead of being processed using a centralized cloud system. This is especially significant in the EV charging systems, where the issues of latency and real-time decision-making matter. As an example, regarding the V2G systems, that is, by using edge computing, rather than all the data being sent to the centralized cloud server, the energy transfer data is processed instantaneously between vehicles and the grid. This minimizes load on communication systems as well as increases response time and improves the stability of the grid and the performance of charging locations. Edge computing helps in maintaining data security and privacy as well since sensitive information is stored in the area devices instead of being shared on the web. But there are also new vulnerabilities, as in today, edge devices can be an object of attack indeed.

Secure Communication Protocols

To ensure secure communication within the electric vehicle ecosystem, several protocols are implemented to protect data exchanges between EVs, charging stations, and the grid. HTTPS, TLS/SSL, and ISO 15118 are some of the key protocols used to safeguard communications. These protocols ensure that data, including payment information, vehicle identification, and energy transfer details, is encrypted and protected from unauthorized access. The implementation of secure communication protocols is essential for maintaining operational integrity and safeguarding users' sensitive data from cyber threats such as man-in-the-middle attacks, eavesdropping, and data tampering. As more EVs and charging stations become interconnected, the importance of these protocols in ensuring overall security cannot be overstated.

Seminal Contribution

The interdependence of the electric vehicle, charging systems and power grid is an area of close examination into the flaws and threats to the EV cybersecurity. In addition to that, (ElKashlan et al., 2023) machine learning-based abnormality classifiers to IoT data to identify distributed denial-of-service (DDoS) attacks targeting EV charging systems to put into focus concerns related to the intrusion detection of networked systems. Finally, a greater advancement has been made by Hussain, Yadav, and Ravikumar (2024), who introduced a model of anomaly detection based on Bi-LSTM as successful on a Hardware-in-Loop testbed, which can demonstrate them to be efficient in cyber-physical security of the EV charging station, (Bielawski et al., 2020). A machine learning solution with the introduction of machine learning algorithms together with blockchain into the process of identifying false data injection attacks system with peer-to-peer energy exchange between connected EVs was introduced. Elkhail et al. (2021) has examined the dangers of over-the-air software upgrades to the ECUs in cars, and presented the case for the necessity of a mechanism that can secure the security in upgrading the software. In a systematic discussion survey designed and implemented by Dehrouyeh et al. (2024), it was confirmed that system categorization of malware and cyber-threats in intelligent vehicle networks and also in the EV charging ecosystems, can be systematically categorized, and important factors to consider are the detection and mitigation procedures involved. Observation of Our Study Relative to the Existing Survey is discussed in Table 1.

Table 1. Observation of our study relative to the existing survey

Related Research	Technology	Environment	Methodology/ Algorithm	Advantage	Limitation
ElKashlan et al. (2023)	Cybersecurity, ML, IoT	EV Charging Systems	Random Forest, Naive Bayes, SVM	High accuracy in DDoS detection	Focused mainly on DDoS attacks
Hussain, Yadav, & Ravikumar (2024)	Cybersecurity, DL	EVCS	Bi-Directional Long Short-Term Memory (Bi-LSTM)	Detects cyber anomalies in real-time	limited to binary classification scenarios
Said, Elloumi, M., & Khoukhi (2022)	Blockchain, ML	P2P Energy Trading Security	Support Vector Machine	Improved data integrity	Depends on data quality
Bielawski et al. (2020)	Cybersecurity	EVCS	Mitigation Mapping	Provides detailed framework	Focuses only on firmware
Dey & Khanra (2020)	ML	CAN Bus Intrusion Detection	CNN	Identify external & internal malicious ECUs	High sensitivity to voltage noise
Elkhail et al. (2021)	Malware detection techniques	Smart EVCS	CAN, LiDAR	Enables real-time protection	Signature methods fail on unknown threats
Dehrouyeh et al. (2024)	ML	EV Infrastructure	TinyML (on-device ML with ESP32)	Low power consumption	Hardware limitations
Saadat, Maingot, & Bahizad, 2020)	ANPR	EV charging station	ANPR with loop RFID	Improved security	Hardware cost
Nasr et al. (2022)	Reverse Engineering, Penetration Testing	EVCS	Reverse engineering	Uncovered zero-day vulnerabilities	Not real-time protection
Mitikiri, Srinivas, & Pal, 2025)	LSTM, FGSM	EV charging ports	LSTM-based autoencoder	High detection accuracy	Sensitive to model tuning
Singh et al. (2025)	AI	EV charging stations	AI-SGF	Real-time detection	Requires significant data
Rewini et al. (2020)	LiDAR, Radar	Vehicle Sensor	Three-tier Auto VSCC	Covers threats across multiple sensor	Lacks of real-time response
Scruggs et al. (2024)	Neural Network	AEVs	Feed-forward Neural Network	Handles replay, DoS, and integrity attacks	Requires training data

continued on following page

Table 1. Continued

Related Research	Technology	Environment	Methodology/ Algorithm	Advantage	Limitation
Benfarhat et al. (2025)	TCN	EVCS Protocol Security	TCN	Low computation cost	Focuses only on OCPP
Sardar et al. (2023)	ML	Electric Vehicles	RF, XGBoost	High accuracy	Limited to detection

The charging environment is resource-constrained, so it poses a challenge of cyberattacks, (Saadat, Maingot, & Bahizad, 2020); the optimization approaches, such as TinyML can eliminate the risks, (Saadat, Maingot, & Bahizad, 2020). Authentication enhancements suggested by Nasr et al. (2022), included the multi-level hardware checking strategies. In addition, Mitikiri, Srinivas, and Pal (2025) says that there exist grave zero-day vulnerabilities in EV charging station management systems, and so companies are advised to tighten their firmware to at greater extent. Such models of anomaly detection through machine learning are continuously evolving, such as the application of LSTM-based autoencoder to detect spoofing attacks on EV charging data (Singh et al., 2025) or the usage of intelligent frameworks based on AI to detect threats in real time with high accuracy in the smart grid, (El-Rewini et al., 2020). The other works refer to sensor-specific defence measures, (Scruggs et al., 2024). The autonomous EVs, on the other hand, have had approaches to autonomous EVs detection advanced in the automotive cybersecurity regime, and they are based on neural networks, (Benfarhat et al., 2025). The researchers have also reported increased application of AI techniques in the OCPP assault detection based on deep learning models, (Sardar et al., 2023). The methodology is an intrusion detection system that seeks unauthorized access and anomalies in the EVs using a few machine learning algorithms and explainable AI (XAI) tools, e.g., SHAP. The gaps, which are noticed by some of the studies, such as the unrealistic nature of the application and absence of experimental confirmation, and the impossibility of scaling and tailoring of detection models to various types of attacks, are outlined as well. Overall, all these works prove that there is a critical need to create a competent, strong, scalable, and flexible sub-system that camouflages the ever-expanding EV charging ecosystem and its integration in the smart grid infrastructure.

EMERGING TECHNOLOGY-BASED CYBER ATTACKS ON ELECTRICAL VEHICLE CHARGING PUBLIC NETWORKS

In this section, we discuss security challenges and solutions for Electric Vehicle Charging Public Networks and show how to use emerging technologies such as Blockchain, Artificial Intelligence, Machine Learning, and all for this network.

Security Challenges for EVCNs

Intrusion Detection System (IDS) bypass enables bad traffic to take place without detection within the network as the attackers will be able to simulate normal patterns of the traffic. This APT technique compromises the normal security mechanisms, this necessitates flexible IDS systems that can dynamically identify the changing threats, (Nasr et al., 2022). Replay Attacks imply that the malefactor uses a fault in the usage of this communication protocol, retransmitting a legitimate data packet, thus providing access or causing a duplicated service, (Niu et al., 2019). Taken together, these threats highlight the dire need to have strong authentication schemes and IDS development. Firmware Hijacking is the implementation of malicious code into an embedded application, which can control charging behaviour or even destroy infrastructure, (Hamdare et al., 2025). Such an attack cannot be detected using basic methods, and therefore, a secure, authenticated, and encrypted firmware update system is required. False Data Injection attacks also encompass the attack, where the incorrect data is passed, which may hinder the processes in the grid or fail to provide billing accuracy, (Nasr et al., 2022). The security of firmware is particularly effective to support the data-input integrity, a verification tier of such attacks, which attempts to exploit software and network vulnerabilities within EVCS that may lead to disabling critical functions or support stealing data. This threat will require effective physical and network security with back-ups in the form of anti-malware tools and integrity check-up tools. Protocol Spoofing may lead to service interruption and financial abuse, especially when it is applied to popular communication standards like OCPP, (Basnet & Ali, 2023). Any kind of strong authentication and encryption should be implemented in communication protocols as well as enhancing the protections put in place against malware threats.

On the other hand, the attack called Command Injection attacks are a source of danger and offer attackers an opportunity to execute dangerous scripts in the vulnerable input fields and, in some cases, terminate important systems or compromise them. To avoid such an attack, intense execution control and input validation are pertinent. The risks that are associated with the threats found in STRIDE have a broad range of risks, which is inclusive of spoofing, tampering and denial of service, and they exist through injection and protocol compromise. Approaching the issue of STRIDE on an aggregate level will ensure that these disparate defences are combined into a comprehensive security initiative. DDoS routed attacks hijack the EVCS capabilities and prevent charging capacity and may cause power grid instability, (Bozdal et al., 2020). This necessitates the implementation of network security parameters and traffic policing systems will facilitate the eradication of the same. In real-time, cyber anomaly detection using IDS and other monitoring tools identifies malicious actions and enables a system to withstand DDoS and its variants, (Acharya et al., 2024). Anomaly detection, hence, comes in handy as an addition to protection as defined by STRIDE and as defined by DDoS consequences. Data corruption happens when significant data has been modified without the user's permission, and this influences the billing and the operation of decisions. Cryptographic methods and secure communications required in successful anomaly detection systems support the integrity of data. All these dangers concern energy trading systems, due to firmware security and Vehicle-to-Grid (V2G) security weaknesses, producing the need to provide secure firmware upgrades and additional authentication protocols. A combination of all these layers provides reliability of the system, whether it is data forwarding or communication within the grid.

When there are some vulnerabilities in firmware, it is usually wise to observe that sticky patches and high-security updates are essential in hindering any illegal passage into the system and failure of the system. By taking advantage of Controller Area Network (CAN) bus intrusion, the attackers can see through the communications channels between the parts of the same vehicle that are not secured and conduct attacks against charging and control systems, (Moravec & Krumnikl, 2017). Vehicular networks adopt the applications of encryption and authentication to complement the firmware defences. The effect of indirect grid threats will be experienced when grid stability will be affected due to compromise of the EVCS and therefore require including grid security procedures in the procedures monitored by EVCS. The navigation and the obstacle detection inputs can be changed through sensor spoofing attacks and this can lead to unreliable vehicle decisions, (Singh & Patro, 2019). One must strive to preserve the integrity of the validity of sensor data and this can be done based on secured communication and firmware systems of the sensor. Authentication tokens cloning and unauthorized access can be realized because of the RFID vulnerability as well as billing fraud, (Gravenor & Adedoyin, 2023). Such vulnerabilities could also be diminished by superior encryption standards, and which also tie sensor protection to bigger security in communication.

The risk accompaniments emanating because of Mixed-Integer Linear Programming (MILP) based Attacks are associated with running of data in optimization algorithm that have a risk of overloading the grid or loss of money. It is possible to prevent such interruptions by verification of data injected into the processor and protection of algorithmic process which on its part interconnects the data integrity and the operating stability. The only glaring feature of the hardware is that it impedes the application of better security plan in the field on account of custom constriction of resources and the hardware must be updated and must operate on software that is optimized. Hardware capability is another of those factors that one should look into when it is going to employ all-out security measures. The compromise of ANPR and RFID creates a threat to the accuracy of the identification and billing, (Dayanikli et al., 2020). Safe authentication and encryption provide security of a system of identity management. That is, zero-day vulnerabilities are vulnerable (Yang et al., 2018) and they comprise unidentified vulnerabilities that, when exploited, can be acted on prior to patching. The practices also make it resistant to environmental changes in the attack environments. Fast gradient sign method (FGSM) is an example of other approaches that trick the machine learning models by adding insensible changes to its input. Such evasion is also easy to detect through adversarial training and AI designs that are strong. An AI model can be at risk of over-dependence on the information, contamination, and manipulation, and to ensure predictive success, it is recommended to use as many different sample sets of information as possible; validation tests should be repeated. Security of AI models and increase confidence in the system and detect inconsistencies.

The actuator and sensor attacks compromise the charging process as they damage the charging process or the peripheral physically, and this needs to be guarded during communication, and this needs a regular inspection of the device. The Multi-sensor Threats are based on the correlations of the sensors to create erroneous information or anomalies, which could be prevented by fusing sensors and cross-checking. Overcharge of batteries and Denial-of-Charge (DoC) attack threats exist, resulting in compromised battery health and safety, inducing a necessity of high regulation of charging and real-time monitoring. These physical security threats are integrated with the entire cybersecurity system. The taskonomy classification of sensor-related threats determines the existence of vulnerability, including spoof, jam, and data manipulation, and was used to develop the focus on the mitigation methods. The communication standard and protocols used in the communication have vulnerability that facilitates interception and tampering, so it is important to follow the best practices and update the communication standard and protocols. Cybersecurity threats on Digital Twin are attacks on replica virtual systems, which calls on the need to ensure secure information transfer and access regulations, (Giechaskiel & Rasmussen, 2019). These systematic activities enhance the surveillance and threat detection of the system and the security of the system in general. Those exploits are performed with the help of spatio-temporal correlation, which allows anticipating the actions of systems or designing attacks that can be avoided through data anonymization and access control. The weakness of Open Charge Point Protocol (OCPP) is based on the fact that it lacks the execution of sufficient protection, which allows an incursion to be made without substantive Authority, (Manso, Moura, & Serrão, 2019). Deployment and enhancement of secure protocols are quite crucial for successful trusted communication. The threats of routing and charging optimization are due to the possibility of the manipulated algorithm making the system inefficient, and weaknesses can be circumvented by input validation and secure implementation of the algorithm.

The explainability of AI decreases transparency and introduces a barrier to trust; this is the reason why explainable AI models ought to be implemented. Privacy and anomaly detection solutions integration experiences a trade-off between user data privacy and the ability to detect a threat that will be addressed via federated learning and differential privacy, (Kovacevic & Gligoric, 2024). Safe updating means are provided so that no malicious code is added to system software updates and system integrity is maintained. The problem with the threat generated by adversarial machine learning is that such models and their structures during training must be efficient enough so that systems perform reliably. Due to these complex cybercrimes within the networks of electric vehicle charging, the protection needs multiple layers of defence in the hardware, the code, the connectivity, and even the AI components. Among possible solutions to keep the EV structure secure, there should be solutions to eliminate the vulnerabilities in the intrusion detection, firmware, protocols, and AI models. The availability, integrity, confidentiality, and privacy statement offers durability and plausibility of the user and stability of the grid; thereby, assured and sustainable EV charging system. Cybersecurity Threats, Impacts, and Mitigation Strategies for Electric Vehicle Charging Networks are discussed in Table 2.

Table 2. Cybersecurity threats, impacts, and mitigation strategies for electric vehicle charging networks

Related Research	Security Threat	Description	Impact/ Consequences	Mitigation Measures/ Recommendations
Alqahtani (2024)	IDS Bypass	Attackers mimic normal traffic patterns to evade detection.	Malicious actions remain undetected for extended periods.	Adaptive IDS systems capable of detecting evolving threats dynamically.
Alqahtani (2024)	Replay Attacks	Retransmitting valid data packets to exploit communication protocol weaknesses.	Unauthorized access or duplicated services, disrusdxpting operations.	Implement strong authentication protocols and secure communication channels.
Falas, Konstantinou, & Michal (2021)	Firmware Hijacking	Malicious code injected into embedded software.	Manipulates charging behaviour or damages infrastructure.	Secure, authenticated, and encrypted firmware update mechanisms.

continued on following page

Table 2. Continued

Related Research	Security Threat	Description	Impact/ Consequences	Mitigation Measures/ Recommendations
Niu et al. (2019)	False Data Injection	Transmitting misleading data to disrupt system operations.	Compromises grid operations or billing accuracy.	Real-time data validation and secure input mechanisms.
Nasr et al. (2022)	Malware Injection	Malware targeting software and network vulnerabilities within EVCS.	Disables critical functions, facilitates data theft, or infrastructure damage.	Strong physical and network protections, anti-malware measures, integrity verification.
Hamdare et al. (2025)	Protocol Spoofing	Exploiting vulnerabilities in widely used communication protocols (e.g., OCPP).	Service disruption, financial fraud, and system corruption.	Strong encryption and authentication for communication protocols.
Nasr et al. (2022)	Command Injection	Unauthorized commands executed through insecure input interfaces.	Disables chargers, extracts sensitive data.	Rigorous input validation, execution controls.
Nagrare, Sindhwad, & Kazi, 2023)	STRIDE Threats	Spoofing, tampering, and denial-of-service risks.	Increased vulnerabilities through injection and protocol weaknesses.	Comprehensive security framework integrating STRIDE risk mitigation strategies.
Basnet & Ali (2023)	DDoS Attacks	Distributed Denial-of-Service attacks overwhelming EVCS with traffic.	Disrupts charging availability, destabilizes power grids.	Implement network security protocols, traffic monitoring, and anomaly detection.
Manso, Moura, & Serrão (2019)	Real-Time Cyber Anomaly Detection	IDS and monitoring tools to identify malicious activities.	Enhances resilience against DDoS and similar attacks.	Effective anomaly detection systems integrated with IDS.
Makhmudov et al. (2025)	Data Integrity Issues	Unauthorized modification of critical data.	Compromised billing and operational decisions.	Cryptographic methods, secure communications for data integrity.
Cao et al. (2019)	Firmware and V2G Security	Risks in Vehicle-to-Grid (V2G) and firmware vulnerabilities.	Compromises grid operations, exposes systems to attack.	Secure firmware updates and authentication mechanisms.
Bozdal et al. (2020)	CAN Bus Intrusion	Attack on in-vehicle communication channels.	Compromises charging control, data theft, and vehicle system integrity.	Encryption and authentication for CAN bus security.

continued on following page

Table 2. Continued

Related Research	Security Threat	Description	Impact/ Consequences	Mitigation Measures/ Recommendations
Acharya et al. (2024)	Indirect Grid Threats	Compromised EVCS affecting grid stability.	Risk of destabilizing power grids.	Integrate grid security protocols with EVCS monitoring systems.
Cao et al. (2019)	Sensor Spoofing	Manipulation of sensor inputs affecting navigation and detection systems.	Leads to erroneous vehicle decisions, endangering vehicle operation.	Secure communication and firmware systems for sensor integrity.
Moravec & Krumnikl (2017)	RFID Vulnerabilities	Cloning of RFID tokens for unauthorized access.	Billing fraud, unauthorized access.	Implement advanced encryption for RFID systems.
Bhattar & Pindoriya (2024)	MILP-Based Attack Risks	Data manipulation within optimization algorithms.	Leads to grid overloads, financial losses.	Validate input data, secure algorithmic processes.
Singh & Patro (2019)	Hardware Limitations	Inability to deploy advanced security measures due to resource constraints.	Compromises overall security implementation.	Upgrade hardware and optimize software for improved security.
Gravenor & Adedoyin (2023)	ANPR & RFID Exploits	Exploitation of Automatic Number Plate Recognition (ANPR) and RFID systems.	Unauthorized access, billing fraud, system exploitation.	Enhanced authentication and secure protocols for ANPR and RFID systems.
Zhou (2022)	Zero-Day Vulnerabilities	Unidentified flaws before patches are released.	Exploited vulnerabilities, potential system compromise.	Proactive security assessments and rapid patch deployment.
Zhao, Alwidian, & Mahmoud (2022)	Adversarial Attacks (FGSM)	Attacks that manipulate machine learning models using subtle input alterations.	Deceives machine learning models, evading threat detection.	Robust AI models with adversarial training and detection mechanisms.
Kure et al. (2025)	Data Poisoning in AI Models	Manipulation of AI training data to deceive models.	Loss of predictive accuracy, compromised anomaly detection.	Dataset diversity, rigorous validation, and privacy-preserving AI frameworks.
Dayanikli et al. (2020)	Physical Sensor & Actuator Attacks	Physical attacks on sensors and actuators.	Disrupts charging operations, damages equipment.	Secure communication protocols, regular hardware inspections.

continued on following page

Table 2. Continued

Related Research	Security Threat	Description	Impact/ Consequences	Mitigation Measures/ Recommendations
Yang et al. (2018)	Multi-Sensor Threats	Exploiting interdependencies among sensors.	Induces false data or inconsistencies, impacting system performance.	Sensor fusion, cross-verification methods for multi-sensor threat mitigation.
Hong et al. (2022)	Battery Overcharge & DoC Attacks	Overcharge or denial of charge attacks on batteries.	Risk to battery health, safety, and charging integrity.	Strict charging protocols, real-time monitoring, and safety measures.
Alabdulatif (2025)	Sensor Threat Taxonomy	Categorization of sensor vulnerabilities (e.g., spoofing, jamming).	Informed mitigation strategies for sensor-specific attacks.	Mitigate sensor spoofing, jamming, and manipulation risks.
Reda et al. (2021)	Communication Protocol Vulnerabilities	Weaknesses in IEC 61850, ISO 15118, and OCPP standards.	Vulnerable data transmission, potential for interception and tampering.	Regular protocol updates, secure communication channels.
Zhao, Foo, & Tian (2022)	Digital Twin Cyber Risks	Risks involving digital replicas of physical systems.	Security risks to virtual system models and data integrity.	Secure data transmission, access controls for digital twin systems.
Chen et al. (2015)	Spatio-Temporal Correlation Risks	Exploiting data patterns to predict system behaviours or attacks.	Risk of system manipulation or attack planning.	Data anonymization, access control for sensitive system information.
Alabdulatif (2025)	Privacy in Anomaly Detection	Balancing user privacy with effective threat detection.	Challenges in ensuring privacy while detecting anomalies.	Federated learning, differential privacy techniques for secure anomaly detection.

Existing Solutions for Cyber Threat Detection on EVCNs

In bypassing the Intrusion Detection System (IDS) bypass, where the attackers simply use the legitimate messages to avoid detection, resilient and dynamic frameworks are required. Ganesan, Patel, and Chokhalingam (2024) also designed an AI-powered Smart Grid Framework (AI-SGF) with the ability to monitor charging data in real-time intelligently, thanks to machine learning technology that has allowed the researchers to get high precision and recall in identifying cyber-physical attacks and thus enhanced the adaptability of IDS. In addition to this, Makhmudov et al. (2025) proposed an online IDS that uses Adaptive Random Forest, and ADWIN concept drift detection in order to dynamically adapt to changing threats, increasing the vulnerability to IDS evasion, (Said, Elloumi, & Khoukhi, 2022). Antoun et al. (2020) Also had an attempt at using the STRIDE threat model to determine the type of attacks and suggested using AI to detect anomalous behavior with network segmentation, hence curbing an all-round IDS evasion and replay attacks. Vulnerabilities associated with firmware and false data injection attacks endanger EV charging systems severely. Hamdare et al. (2023) examined the vulnerability of infrastructure and firmware and vulnerabilities of EVCS, paying special attention to the real-time validation of data in order to maintain the integrity of systems. Sabzi and Vajta (2023) and Saadat, Maingot, and Bahizad (2020) made an effort to check the data-integrity of bean-table information in the e-beam energy transactions in the EV environment by using neural networks like SVM and RF.

Malware injection, protocol spoofing, command injection and STRIDE threats violate the security token of ENCS. Hamdare et al. (2023) raised the issue of software and network vulnerability, which is used to realize such attacks, particularly affecting the OCPP standard, raising the requirement of robust authentication and encryption. Antoun et al. (2020) was able to identify the categories of risks using the STRIDE modelling and suggested an AI-based anomaly detection with network segmentation to prevent command injection attacks and other similar threats. Extensive message manipulation and message spoofing exploits, with the emphasis on message hardening and secure messaging. The EV security is affected both by firmware patching and CAN bus intrusion. Muhammad et al. (2023) identified constant update of firmware as an important defence measure against unauthorized access, and Muhammad et al. (2023) experimentally provided evidence of the possibility of CAN bus illicit intrusion and recommended encryption and authentication as a protection measure in vehicle communications. The threats of navigation sensor spoofing are discussed by Scruggs et al. (2024), who recommend the data-driven security that is specific to the sensor-vulnerabilities. selecting authentication tools, Nasr et al. (2022) suggested multi-layer authentication in which RFID and physical verification will be combined in order to reduce the chance of cloning and unauthorized action.

The risks in the security of EVCS are driven by the optimisation algorithm hazards and limitation in the hardware. This idea was proposed by Das et al. (2024), which used a Mixed-Integer Linear programming (MILP) model to prevent the spreading of the malware and managing to prevent the overloading of the grid, which could be caused by manipulated inputs of data. Hardware barrier for the deployment of the complex protocols might be an exception, however some solutions seem to have quite common grounds of discussion. In Nasr et al. (2022), the exploits in ANPR and RFID as well as enhanced authentication were covered. The results provided in works by Mitikiri, Srinivas, and Pal (2025) with the application of penetration testing methods pointed to zero-day vulnerabilities and rapid remediation and testing of the security statutes in advance. To identify and protect the Fast Gradient Sign Method (FGSM) of adversarial test in EV charging ports, the authors applied LSTM-based autoencoders in adversarial training. In Sani, Hassan, and Chen (2022), the risks of data poisoning on the AI models were outlined, and it was stated that the diversity and validation of the dataset to be used have to be included in privacy-preserving system. Sensor and actuator attacks based on physical have an impact on physical functionality of EVCS, (Scruggs et al., 2024). Automobile sensor exploits were mapped and recommended data-based cybersecurity approaches like sensor fusion and cross-verification in the framework of sensor-based threat mitigation delegation, (Mohammadi et al., n.d.). The overcharging of the battery and denial charging of charges was modelled and the significance of the strict charging protocols and its real-time monitoring on to the battery safety were indicated.

Muhammad et al. (2023) talked about a taxonomy of sensors, threats of spoofing and jamming, and suggested mitigation and strategy, (Rahman et al., 2024). Hamdare et al. (2023) reviewed the flaws of communication protocols, IEC 61850, ISO 15118 and OCPP and focused on encryption and regular update. Bielawski et al. (2020) was dedicated to the cyber risks of digital twins and advocated the concept of the data transfer security and access to virtual system replicas. Use of spatio-temporal correlation along with the weaknesses of protocol compromises the credibility of EVCS. The study mainly among Singh et al. (2021) built a graph convolutional model to forecast the charging demand of EV to predict the threat of a cyberattack and Hamdare et al. (2023) demonstrated the vulnerability of OCPP and highlighted the value of secure implementation of the protocol that would ensure trusted communication between EV chargers. The analysis done of the risks of the routing and charging optimization under the assumptions of the MILP models suggested that the check of the input and use of secure algorithms should be done to prevent the inefficiency of the system and grid stability. The explainability restrictions to AI-based threat detection lowers transparency and confidence, which may be addressed with the introduction of the deep learning explanation of a CNN and LSTM combination with the enhancement of transparency with SHAP, Singh et al. (2021). tried to combine privacy with anomaly detection via federated learning and differential privacy, which ensures safe threats detection and does not entail sacrifices to the data of its users. Choi et al. (2022) emphasizes the necessity to use some secure update protocols that could prevent a malicious code during software update of the automotive ECUs. The recommendation provided by Singh et al. (2025) is the adversarial trained LSTM autoencoders that can be applied in the approaches to EV charging cybersecurity to minimize the effect of the machine learning attacks and increase the stability of modelling. An overview of Cybersecurity Models for Electric Vehicle Networks is shown in Table 3.

Table 3. Overview of cybersecurity models for electric vehicle networks

Related Research	Technology	Environment	Methodology/ Algorithm	Advantage	Limitation
Ganesan et al. (2024)	EV Charging Systems	Charging Systems	STRIDE Threat Model, AI-based anomaly detection, Network segmentation	Secure charging and enhanced cybersecurity using AI	Protocol-related vulnerabilities, and costs associated with upgrades
Hamdare et al. (2023)	Cyber Security	EV Charging Network, EVs	Real-time charging session data analysis, Cybersecurity risk analysis	Identification of key vulnerabilities and protocol risks	Insufficient attention to the evolving attack patterns
Makhmudov et al. (2025)	IDS	EV Charging Systems, Grids	Adaptive Random Forest, (ARF), ADWIN	Real-time adaptability	Requires substantial computational resources for real-time updates
Gabriel Hurtado et al. (2025)	CAN Bus System	EV Charging Networks	CAN bus monitoring for malicious alterations, Cyberattack simulation	Detects cyberattacks like overcharging or undercharging	Limited to CAN bus-based attacks, other attack vectors might be missed
Sani et al. (2024)	ML, FL	Electric Vehicle Networks, IoT	Privacy-preserving	Ensures privacy while enhancing the security of EV networks	Privacy-preserving techniques add complexity, potential data silos
Rahman et al. (2024)	DL, Neural Networks	EV Charging Networks	CNN-LSTM hybrid model for anomaly detection	High accuracy in detecting malicious behaviour	Model complexity increases computational load and training time

Emerging Technology-Based Cyberattack Detection Solutions for EVCNs

AI-Powered IDS

Attacks are on the increase, and this has led to the application of AI and ML-based IDS which aid in improving the security of EVCNs. These systems detect real-time information and predictive analytics apply in detecting abnormal pattern that tells of possible attack by cybercriminals. Concept drift detection The technique of concept drift detection can be integrated into IDS as machine learning methodology (i.e., Adaptive Random Forest (ARF) and ADWIN (Adaptive Windowing)), allowing IDS to dynamically adapt to the emerging threats, (Nasr et al., 2022). This combination enhances the performance of the detection by enabling the systems to detect the new and unfamiliar attack vectors. As an illustration, the AI-powered Smart Grid Framework (AI-SGF) processes real-time information with high precision to identify cyber-physical attacks through machine learning algorithms. This model increases the flexibility of IDS and this enables it to detect the emerging threats which would otherwise not have been detected, (Nasr et al., 2022). Consequently, the IDS systems based on machine learning contribute to infrastructure security as they respond to malicious activities in a short period. Using machine learning, IDS is capable of constantly improving detection measures. This allows the system to be current of all threats and gives a proactive defence mechanism. The use of machine learning in security in EVCNs contributes to its security in the context of the vulnerability to the ever more designed cyberattack techniques.

Anomaly Detection Using Deep Learning Models

Running anomaly detection inside EVCNs with deep learning models, specifically Long Short-Term Memory (LSTM) based autoencoders is gaining momentum as well. Those models will work effectively when it comes to identifying abnormal behaviours in the EV charging system, such as inconsistent charging future or sensor readings, which may be the signatures of cyberattacks. Such models can then be trained to detect such advanced attacks, such as the Fast Gradient Sign Method (FGSM) that is designed to perturb the input data in an imperceptible way so as not to be detected when trained using adversarial training techniques. LSTM is used to implement autoencoders to examine sequential data and discover abnormalities so as to make sure that a system can learn anomalies that can lead to development of a malicious conduct. With such models, the EVCNs will be in position to detect new threats in favor of time and prevent potential attacks that could affect or disrupt the charging structure. This anomaly detection process helps it in identifying known and unknown attack vectors. The primary advantage of the LSTM based models is that they effectively store and learn the long-term time dependency and accordingly, they would be very appropriate to monitor continuous and dynamic data streams generated by the EV charging stations. This adds predictability to the models in ascertaining trends and tendencies over time when 24/7 systems prevail. Finally, all these advanced neural networks feed more security doctrines to EVCNs making the charging system more secure. They provide our infrastructure with very good opposition to unknown and also direct cyber threats and increase the network capacity and network and user trust.

Blockchain for Data Integrity

Blockchain technology is becoming a well-known idea to alleviate data integrity and assure communication in EVCNs. Through the application of immutable decentralized distributed ledgers, blockchain makes data tamper resistant. That explains why it will be hard to change transaction logs in the system or any communication that has taken place in the system thus making the entire data authentic and untampered. The main benefit of Blockchain lies in the preservation of data authenticity, which is essential in shielding against multiple cyber-risks, including the replay attack, malware injection, or firmware hijacking. Blockchain can be used to prevent replay attacks where an attacker retransmits the valid data to confuse the systems. Data use vulnerabilities, such as malware injections and firmware hijacking, can also be minimized, as such, any input of data, as well as firmware updates, must be verified securely. Besides, the blockchain facilitates the utilization of smart contracts and blockchain authentication systems, which delivers extra security levels. These systems endorse the integrity of data and firmware updates and prohibited any illegal interventions in that area, thus being certain that only confirmed, legitimate actions can be performed in the network. As such, blockchain transparency and security features have offered a good defensive tool against a cyberattack, ensuring both data and communication integrity in EVCNs. This will guarantee not only the infrastructure security but also its maintenance, which will lead to a trusty approach to the system and facilitate the increase in cybersecurity across the board, (Fala, Konstantinou, & Michael, 2021; Sani, Hassan, & Chen, 2022).

Federated Learning for Privacy-Preserving Anomaly Detection

Because of the current appeal of its application in recent times, block chain technology is proving to be one of the finest and most efficient mechanisms in the verification of data integrity as well as the safety of conveying data between various points within the EVCNs. Blockchain employs unchangeable distributed ledgers and seals and encrypts the information and makes it tamper-proof. This makes it difficult to exploit the mechanism of attackers to tamper with contents of the transaction logs and interpersonal communication within the system; hence, being assured that all the information held in the system is actual and not wry. The most critical benefit of blockchain is that, it ensures authenticity of the data being processed thus paramount in the fight against any form of cyber attack including the replay attack, insertion of malware and take-over of the firmware, (Ezzeddine et al., 2024). The feature of the blockchain clearness removes cases of replay attacks through sending of valid information multiple times to mislead the systems. Likewise, firmware Hijacking, and Malware injection can also be eliminated by providing a secure data- verification of inputs and firmware update, (Liu et al., 2021). In addition, by applying blockchain, it becomes possible to incorporate authentication (with blockchain) along with smart contracts, thereby providing some extra security layers. One can observe that such systems can provide integrity of the information and upgrades of the firmware to avoid the illegal manipulated exercise and ensure nothing, except various legal safe services can be provided within the network. In fact, the implementation of a blockchain, its transparency, and defence characteristics contribute to the establishment of an efficient defence system against cyberattacks that guarantees data and communication integrity in the EVCNs. This renders the infrastructure dynamic and secure, whose trust in the system increases and there is enhanced cybersecurity at large.

Machine Learning for Anomaly Detection in EVCNs:

The algorithm of such transformation is anomaly detection of EVCNs conducted by machine learning. They can read real time data, identify patterns, trends, and anomalies to anticipate possible cyberthreats and train their models using very large quantities of information. Machine learning in the form of supervised machine learning and unsupervised machine learning can be used to train EVCNs to recognize and identify known and unknown attack vectors and can thereby triage these types of attacks in the attacking vehicle or preferably in the cloud service that delivers the EVCN as a service to many vehicles to detect potential visible markers of more subtle indicators of an actively ongoing attack such as anomalous charging patterns and off centre sensor data. As the system is also evolving in its progress, therefore, in the long run a better level of detection can be achieved because, the system is learning about the new information being provided to it and hence can be permitted to act against newer threats. Besides, to allow the maximization of the overall effectiveness of the anomaly identification and, more so, to ensure that the privacy of the users remains intact, the machine learning models may be realised through the application of the privacy protecting methods called the differential privacy, (Aljumah & Ahanger, 2020). These are measures that will make certain that the sensitive data of the users used to develop the models is on the safe-side and cannot be accessible to the cloud centralized systems. Strategies of privacy in this direction can offer good security even of the new threats: cybersecurity to the charging infrastructure, as well as privacy of the user information in relationship with the machine learning models, and thus cybersecurity of the machine learning models disabled. The advantage of such conjunction of strong anomaly detection and data privacy protection results in a better security environment of EVCNs in general and provides real-time security assumption without facing an intermediate loss of privacy, (Kim, Hakak, & Ghorbani, 2024).

Digital Twin Technology for Cyber Risk Prediction

Digital twin technology can play a role in securing cybersecurity in EVCNs, which is becoming a convincing solution. It entails generation of simulated versions of physical systems resembling real life systems that allow the real-time digital reflection of the infrastructure. It is these virtual models through which potential loopholes or cyberattacks can be predicted before they reflect on the physical infrastructure. Having a constant observation of the digital twin, the flaws in the system become known within a short time and this means that proactive security measures could be developed. This helps curb the risks before they develop into real forces, thus the maintenance of the infrastructure is ensured. Cybersecurity using digital twins can offer a solution early in the process to detect issues such that corresponding interventions are made at the right time. Moreover, digital twins allow testing and checking new cybersecurity solutions in a simulated environment. This activity would help in first testing new strategies and technology to ensure efficiency in the implementation in the live system. It minimizes the chances of interruption through security arrangements that have not been tried. Digital twin can be used to improve cybersecurity by offering predictive risk analysis, as well as implementing cybernaut positioning before attacker's strike. By simulating and testing the different scenarios, more informed decisions can be made thus making the cybersecurity strategies powerful and efficacious in protecting the EVCNs, (Qureshi et al., 2023).

CLOUD, FOG, AND EDGE COMPUTING FOR DETECTING CYBER THREATS ON EVCN

The EVCNs will be critical in intelligent transportation systems of smart cities because they create and move tremendous quantities of data among electric vehicles, charging networks, the grid, and cloud applications. Such flow of data demands secure measures of data storage, processing, authorization, and evaluation in order to ensure a reliable and secure functionality of the interrelated systems. In the recent years, cloud, fog, and edge computing coupled with blockchain have built secure and efficient mechanisms in the management and analysis of data bits transmitted and stored by EVCNs. The Edge computing is located close to the data source and facilitates a low-latency process, which boosts real-time decision-making and the security of the location. The Fog computing acts as an intermediate plane, extending the computing source and data storage to the edge, making it less prone to delays and increasing the security even more. Cloud computing provides the ability to scale, the centralization of processes and massive information storage to handle the marine volumes of information generated. Along with the capacity to bear exogeneity and liabilities, blockchain makes data transactions persist to stay secure and reliable, where trusted and reliable sources guarantee reliability and impossibility of alterations, (Zhou, Guo, & Deng, 2019). The interacting technologies are all designed to provide security to the communications, privacy to communications, and also the integrity of the whole infrastructure that is controlled. The offer of reliable, secure, and efficient services by taking advantage of the advanced solutions provided by EVCNs in smart cities could facilitate the development of the sustainable and intelligent transportation systems. Combination of cloud and fog computing, edge, and blockchain not only provides superior security but also enhances performance and scalability, thus making these networks more robust against cyber-attacks and other operational difficulties.

Cloud Computing for Secure ENCNs

The possibility of cybersecurity threats that cloud computing brings are various and require proper deployment of defence strategies, (Alwakeel, 2021). One of the main threats, data breaches, implies that due to unauthorized access to sensitive user and operational data stored in clouds, violations of privacy rights, financial loss, and fines may occur. Since cloud services keep huge number of information belonging to users such as billing information, vehicle information and location information, securing this information is mandatory. Malware on cloud infrastructure (Ransomware) can sabotage the services, lock system-critical areas, and hold ransom the access to them, which interferes with charging station resilience and general network performance. One more major vulnerability is SQL injection that attacks cloud databases used to store user sessions and charging information. Such attacks might enable the attackers to manipulate, erase and steal sensitive data. The same applies to firmware hijacking through cloud updates, which poses a threat in the event of an unauthorized access to the over-the-air (OTA) updates, where a hacker can upload malware into cloud-controlled systems and take charge of the charging points or the working of EVs. The cloud level injection of malware may also be an issue as the attackers may infect the components of cloud services resulting in the disruption in a network and unauthorized job of data. An overview of Cloud Computing in EVCNs is shown in Figure 4.

Figure 4. Overview of cloud computing in EVCNs

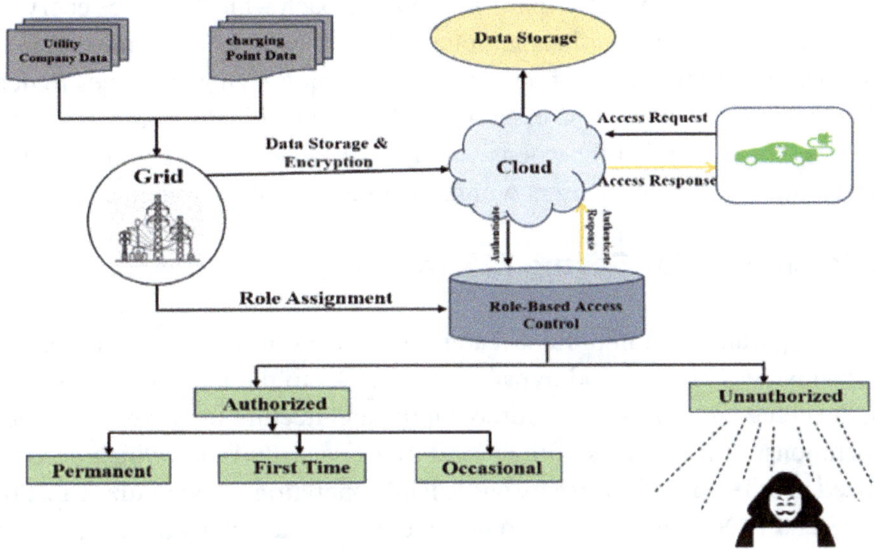

The process of the cloud services communicating to other levels in the network (edge and fog) is vulnerable to man-in-the-middle (MitM) attacks. These kinds of attacks may eavesdrop and tamper with information being transmitted, and this may jeopardize the integrity of sensitive transactions like that of charging and one that makes the bill. The prevalence of authentication and authorisation attacks poses a threat to the identity management systems of cloud-based infrastructure, as, in many cases, it is implemented through blockchain technologies that might be used to violate access control and access the system unauthorised. Also, since data kept on the cloud contains personal data, infringement of privacy is widespread, and personal data, including driving habits, billing details, and vehicle location, is kept and likely to be erupted in the clouds. To address these issues, secure updating procedures are required so that malicious update can be sabotaged to the cloud software and firmware systems, and hence safeguarding updates to the EVs and charging stations. In addition, the cloud-based machine learning models might be prone to vulnerabilities that can be exacerbated in terms of explainability gaps or adversarial machine learning risks wherein models can be tricked into behaving in a manner that would breach network security. The risk of data dependency and poisoning in cloud AI systems as well is quite high because the attackers can alter training data corruptions with the help of AI algorithms that are supposed to detect anomalies, optimize routes, and balance loads. Direct deployment of DDoS attacks on cloud services compounds this vulnerability by presenting cloud resources with an immense task and causing the halt in important services to create service downtimes, (Chang et al., 2022). Based on these challenges, the best way to secure cloud services in EVCNs is to involve multi-layered approach which involves encryption, anomaly detection, secure authentication methods as well as real-time threats mitigation methods. Exploration of adaptive, privacy-preserving strategies to deploy cloud-connected EV systems is essential to develop resilient infrastructure that is able to meet the demand of the extensive growth experienced in EV popularity and the safety and privacy of the users within the interconnected systems.

Fog Computing for Secure EVCNs

Fog computing is an important feature of EVCNs allowing computing within their locality, less latency, and transferring of tasks to the intermediate nodes between the cloud and the devices. Although the architecture improves efficiency of the operations, it also comes with several cyber security risks, which need to be addressed in order to achieve secure and reliable operations, (Tanyildiz et al., 2025). The DoS and DDoS attacks are also considered as one serious threat as it attacks fog network components and local aggregators. Such attacks flood fog nodes with requests monopolising real-time data processing which is essential in voice response, charging schedules and optimisation of energy. Preventing the vulnerability of these fog computing nodes towards those attacks is basic in ensuring the availability of EVCNs, (Sabella et al., 2024). These would be accompanied by the avoidance and circumvention of the IDS as another major issue. The attackers can use anomaly evasion mechanisms installed at the nodes in fog computing, causing the attackers to perform malicious operations without being detected, (Banik, Kothamali, & Dandyala, 2024). In order to address this, it is vital to conduct studies on adaptive IDS models capable of detecting the new attack patterns in fog so as to offer real-time protection. Security in fog computing of EVCNs is even complicated by data integrity challenges. Fog nodes are prone to attacks as the node concentrates and transports the information between various locations such as charging stations and electric vehicles. This has the potential to tamper with integrity of billing systems, user information, or grid management procedures. Data aggregation methodologies and strong abilities to create validation processes are essential to yield competent and reliable data. Moreover, there is a serious concern of security of optimization algorithms used in fog computing to accomplish operations like local charging schedule and course planning. As an example, the MILP-based optimisation malware may compromise the process and impact the efficient functioning of charging stations and energy management.

Thus, the study of the design of secured algorithms and breeding malware to make them specific to fog-level optimization is significant to deter the said attacks. A flaw in protocol and standards such as a crack in the Open charge point protocol

(OCPP) that is most used in interaction between charging stations and network is also a key point of weakness. With these vulnerabilities in place one can perhaps get unauthorized access or identify methods of hacking or controlling charging stations so as to prevent a service, as well as, creating a financial fraud. Improvement of the communication procedure and protocols like the secure and latest versions of OCPP and other standards fall in the area of significant research. Unauthorized ones like recharging, re-play or frauds can also be carried out because of the attacks like replay (Attackers have the right to intercept and retransmit genuine connectivity between fog nodes). They can avoid such attacks through the utilization of encrypted communications and validity verification of messages. The other form of attack on the fog computing is the spatio-temporal correlation attacks which are quite difficult to avert. Fog computing suffers an attack of spatio-temporal correlation in which the malicious users get to see the behaviour of the information present in the fog and subsequently use the information to predict the behaviour of the system which they will follow up with malicious operations. These trends can be reasons of service outage or alteration of data whereby the attacker leaps to the forecast of charging trends or consumptions of energy. This risk ought to be minimized by making the anomaly detecting systems recognize the interrelation between the temporal and spatial data in the continual surveillance of security.

Moreover, the next type of attack to fog nodes is firmware update attacks since the weaknesses in the process of updating the firmware can be extremely dangerous. The security update mechanisms like signed and verified firmware updates are also important to stop unauthorized firmware updates. A common framework of detecting possible attack vectors that target the fog infrastructure can be found in the STRIDE framework (Spoofing, Tampering, Repudiation, Information Disclosure, Denial of Service, and Elevation of Privilege). There is a need to research on each of these threats in a fog environment such as spoofing of charging stations or altering charging data in a bill. Besides, the AI in the fog layer, data poisoning and adversarial attacks on the AI model are essential issues. Transportable memory systems There is a risk of an AI-based system and a machine cantered form of anomaly detection reliant on fog being attacked by manipulating training data, impacting the precision of the threat detection, (Sheikh et al., 2025). It is thus necessary to investigate powerful AI models that can resist adversarial attacks to ensure the intelligence level of the fog computing experience. Attacks through false data injection into aggregated data at fog nodes may hamper the process of making decisions regarding the distribution of power and vehicle charging. Data validation protocols are necessary at every fog node so that attackers should not get a chance to feed false data into the system. Segmentation of networks and protocol spoofing are other issues on fog-layer communications. Fog nodes handle aggregation of information of different sources, and an attacker can use segmentation vulnerability to add malicious data or breach the network frontiers.

Such risks will be alleviated through research on the network segmentation methods and protocol hardening in fog computing environments. Finally, digital twin cyber risks pose a growing threat to fog computing. Predictive analysis can be carried out to the digital twins (which are virtual models of real-world systems, e.g. charging station, EV or energy grid), but digital twins can be attacked and manipulated to write inaccurate predictions, which may cause inefficiencies in the operation or blackout the service. A priority research area that can laser out these types of emerging risk is to ensure the security of digital twin systems and the integration of real-time monitoring tools. The effective mitigation of these cybersecurity issues, is highly beneficial to the safe and effective functioning of the EVCNs, thus continued growth and reliability in the EVCNs. An overview of Fog Computing in EVCNs is shown in Figure 5.

Figure 5. Overview of fog computing in EVCNs

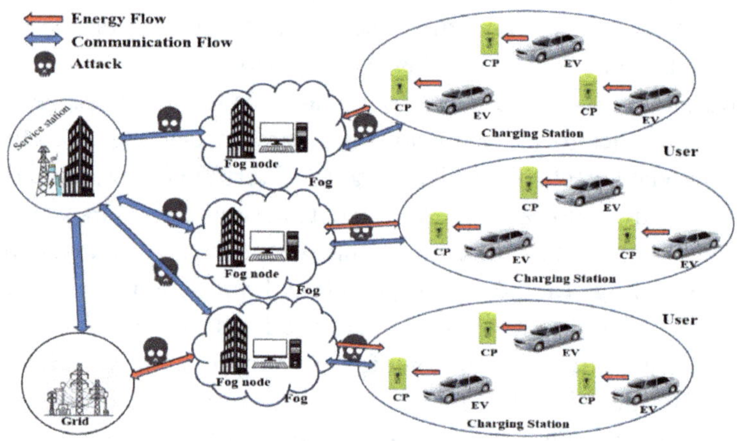

Edge Computing for Secure EVCNs

The application Edge computing on EVCNs is also significant since local processing and decision-making may be undertaken at the edge of the network, with smaller latencies, or contribute to offloading the computing procedures to the core cloud. This kind of decentralization is enhancing the accountability and effectiveness of the system in real-time charging and provision of energy. However, the smooth transition of edge computing to EVCNs is associated with gross cybersecurity challenges that must be addressed to ensure integrity, privacy and security of the system. Another important threat which may occur between the EV and charging station is the MitM attacks. In such attack, attackers intercept and modify the conversation leading to unauthorized charging, theft or modification of charging pattern. One should also ensure that the modes of communication e.g. an encrypted channel or powerful authentication procedure avoid such faults at the edge. Another risk is restraints due to hijacking and interference with their firmware. Insecure firmware update mechanism enables the attackers to load the system with malicious codes making the attacker be able to make the charging functions controllable, tamper data or even terminate service. Such attacks on the edge need to be addressed by investigations of secure firmware update processes as well as authenticated update mechanisms. The final risk can be an attack in the form of injecting malware into car control units or charging stations. Malicious codes can be introduced into the system to destroy or cripple the working capacity of a system. This could in case of EVCN result in service interruption, financial heist, or even ransacked of charging operations.

What matters most is the creation of anti-malware and edge-based capabilities of real-time monitoring which would serve to reduce this risk. Besides, data privacy and the integrity of the system are sensitive to the side-channel attacks originated based on the physical emissions (timing, electromagnetic, or power consumption) of charging gadgets or ev embedded systems. Such attacks can access confidential applications to include cryptographic keys without physically interacting with the software. Moreover, such threat can be countered to a larger extent by securing hardware; as well as by application of data masking. Replay attacks utilize communication protocols between the devices on the edge whereby an attacker seizes valid data packets and retransmits the data to deceive the systems to perform unauthorized operations. This can lead to false charging session or inappropriate charging. One effective means of preclusion against replay attack is the MACs (message authentication codes) and timestamping operations. The other type of attacks is the command injection that was a consequence of compromised input interface of the chargers. The attacker can inject malicious instructions in order to alter functionality of the charger, or rather, this may lead to hardware loss or a loss of charging processes. Verification of stringent inputs and provision of safe command execution processes at the edge is imperative in preventing such attacks. The edge is also a major element of concern with actuator attacks and sensor spoofing. The attackers can toy with navigation sensors or battery sensors and bring about negative alterations in the charging behaviour of the vehicle, energy expenditure, or route planning. Such risks can be reduced through sensor fusion, over checking of multiple sensors and implementation of anomaly detection algorithms. The next threat that can affect the functioning of both the vehicle and the charging system in case the attackers exploit the vulnerability of the internal communication network over the vehicle is CAN Bus intrusion. Besides this, all that are required to solidify the system against these weaknesses are to ensure that vehicle to grid (V2G) communication protocols are secured and finally ensure that the CAN Bus communication is encapsulated and authenticated too, which is one of the vital research areas. The other phenomenon is the RFID vulnerability in charging access control. The working RFID tags present in the form of tokens would be copied or disrupted to grant access to charging stations to wrong hands. Bypassing of these types of security breaches may be done by employing extremely sophisticated encryption technologies and a sealed RFID token in the edge.

Besides, the physical components of the EV as well as the charging system also can be attacked through overcharging of battery and through Denial-of-Charge (DoC) attacks, which may therefore either destroy the battery of the car or denies services altogether. These kinds of attacks are protectable, through strict charging procedures, real time monitoring and protection on the edge. Another threat is the IDS bypass at the border, where intruders can (in a bid to evade capture) replay a pattern exactly like the regular traffic or manipulate flow of information. It is necessary to understand adaptive IDS model that is dynamic and can adjust to the strategies that work of the attackers. False data injection attacks can also be the aim of the local data aggregation process at the edge nodes, leading to an unreliable charging decision or inappropriate charges. Data manipulation in sensitive layers of the system would be prevented when the system would consider installing important components like data validation and verification techniques at all edge nodes. Another threat is the protocol spoof, e.g. an OCPP (Open Charge Point Protocol), which entails unauthorized access to charging points or fraudulent charging point invoicing. The greatest step in mitigating this risk is the improvement of communication processes and tight verification. The methods that the threats in sensors could be undertaken through could be spoofing, jamming and manipulating the data that could mislead the system to give wrong decisions. The research on trusted sensor networks and sensor data integrity is important towards making sure that even at the edge, the attackers were not able to exploit this aspect. At the same note, ANPR and RFID exploits as other RFID vulnerabilities, pose a threat to local physical access control systems in charging stations. Such dangers can be mitigated in terms of strengthening authentication and the physical protection. A limited hardware resource of processing power and available memory could also constrain the possibility of programming their embedded devices (e.g., charging stations or vehicle onboard units) to develop an advanced security feature. One of the ways to do it may be the improvement of the security of all the operations at the edge by eliminating some of the hardware security problems and ensuring that the lightweight cryptography solutions are applied to the embedded systems. An Overview of Edge Computing in EVCNs is shown in Figure 6.

Figure 6. Overview of edge computing in EVCNs

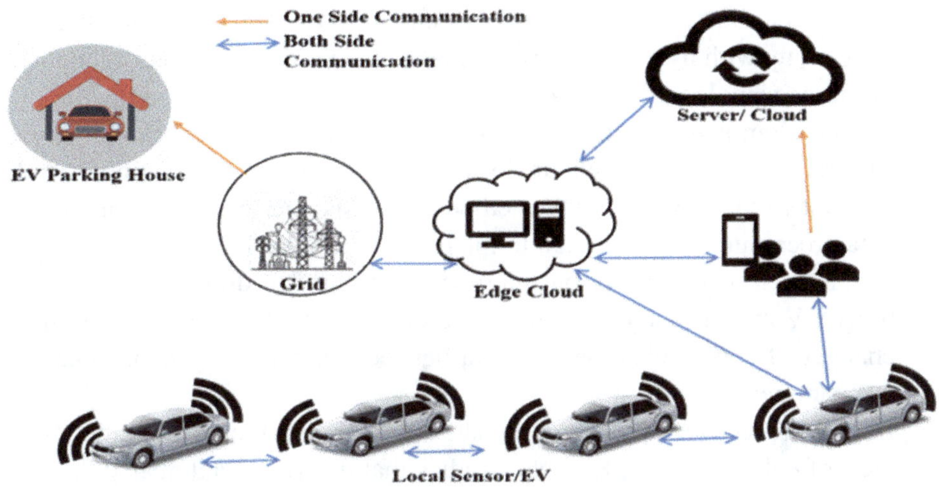

Open Research Challenges for EVCNs

- With the spread of the EVs, scalable cybersecurity systems have to be constructed in order to cover an increasing number of connected devices and attack surface of EVCNs.
- The heavy utilization of IoT in the case of EVCN needs the secured protocol since most of the protocols currently in use have poor authentication and encryption. They are therefore prone to spoofing and denial-of-service attacks.
- Machine learning-enabled anomaly detection is required in detecting cyber threats in real-time within EVCNs. Nevertheless, more work should be done to come up with adaptive algorithms that will deal with changing threats in dynamic environments. Firmware tampering is a significant risk in EVCNs, making secure firmware updates, boot mechanisms, and timely software updates essential. Further research is needed to improve secure firmware management practices for charging stations and vehicles.
- And although blockchain holds the promise of solving the insecure identity management problem and data integrity in secure, more research needs to be conducted to have blockchain solution integrated effectively in EVCNs. This involves scalability, low latency and privacy issues.

- The EVCNs rely on cloud, fog, and edge computing to process the data, whereas these technologies add new challenges to cybersecurity. Further work should be done to establish hybrid security models in order to deal with threats posed by these models of computing.
- The use of cloud, fog, and edge computing enables the management of data in EVCNs, thus creating new cybersecurity risks. Additional investigations to come up with hybrid security mechanisms in order to counter such threats of these technologies are required.
- The problem is that EVCNs accumulate sensitive data that belongs to users such as the driving behaviour, location, and financial transactions. Studies relevant to privacy-enforcing methods, such as encryption and anonymous data processing, are important to the protection of such data.
- EVCNs also need to rely on interoperability among different charging stations, EV models and energy management systems. Enforceability of the exchanges of communication and data between such heterogeneous platforms is a paramount issue.
- Immediate recovery and good forensic are also important in mitigating the effects of cyberattacks in EVCNs. Studies that determine automated and post-attack forensics and recovery procedures should be conducted to ascertain the continued provision of the services.

Research Direction for EVCNs

Real-Time Adaptive Anomaly Detection Systems

Build resource-efficient machine learning models that are featherweight and able to automatically adjust to the changing cyber threats in real-time across the Edge and Fog Computing Networks (EVCNs). Concentrate on opportunities of using the methodology of learning online and adaptive to the changes in concept of intrusion detection systems, to be resistant to the new and advanced attack. Join Explainable AI (XAI) solutions that will improve the transparency of the working process and increase the confidence of operators and users.

Secure Firmware Management for Charging Stations

Strive to conduct deep research on how to design strong secure boot and firmware update standards to avert hijacking and tampering. The study is going to be based on the selection of the ways and measures helping to guarantee the integrity of the process of booting and updating the firmware without leaving its vulnerability to doubts. Also, the study will examine the usage of blockchain technology so that secure firmware can be distributed with the utilization of decentralized verification technique to not allow any unauthorized or malicious update. In this strategy, they will use the aspects of immutability and transparency of blockchain to make the whole firmware delivery process more secure. Moreover, the research will involve design and realisation of recovery solutions to recover damaged firmwares to guarantee firmness of systems and maintenance of secure systems. The results will aid in establishment of superior security architectures that can resist emerging security risks in the cyber world and still build strong faith and confidence in the firmware operating procedures.

SQL Injection and Database Security in EVCNs

Concentrate to secure better the cloud and fog databases that handles the charging session and information on user with more research not mentioned. To protect EV charging network databases against injection and manipulation attacks, create advanced intrusion detection and prevention systems that are specifically aimed at defending the plant against corresponding attacks. Research on automatic query sanitization strategies and abnormality detection algorithms to detect and counter suspicious currencies in the database transactions are studied. The proposed research sets the goal of enhancing the integrity and confidentiality of the key data in EV charging infrastructure, thus securing user data and guaranteeing the safety of charging sessions maintenance.

Hybrid Security Frameworks for Cloud-Fog-Edge

Innovate and experiment with hybrid cybersecurity architectures that unify security mechanisms in cloud, fog and edge computing infrastructures. Evaluate the trade-offs involved in distributed systems on latency, scalability and security to find out the most appropriate setups. Determine how blockchain technology can be used to bring a higher level of data integrity and access control integrity during these layers using the decentralized nature of blockchain technology to help provide an enhanced level of security throughout the hybrid infrastructure. The study seeks to come up with a holistic approach that acutely tackle the problem posed by each of the layers of computing, but with solid security and high performance rates.

Privacy-Preserving Cybersecurity Solutions

Construct privacy-sensitive anomaly detection models based on federated learning, or techniques in differential privacy to preserve sensitive information of users (such as location, billing, and driving behaviour). Research and use more advanced anonymization such as special advanced algorithms to anonymize spatio-temporal EV charging data to reduce the dangers of correlation-based attacks. The proposed research is aimed at improving privacy performance without affecting the quality and performance of the anomaly detection to make sure that user information will be confidential and comply with both the quality and privacy requirements towards the electric vehicle (EV) charging networks.

CONCLUSION

This study has emphasized significantly the role of cybersecurity in EVCNs, which will be the key to the popularization of EVs. With the growing presence of EVs in the realm of smart city public infrastructure and urban transport, the security of the EV charging infrastructure takes precedence. The research paper discloses an array of vulnerabilities that EVCNs possess, such as the problems with communication protocols, vehicle systems, charging stations, and cloud infrastructures-related risks. The effects of these shortcomings are that EVCNs are vulnerable to different cyber threats, including MITM attacks, DoS attacks, data breaches, firmware manipulation, and malware. The complexity of EVCNs, which is to combine vehicle systems, charging infrastructure, grid control, and cloud security, brings the attack surface to a considerable level. Those can result in stealth, service tampering, and data leaks, jeopardizing the privacy of users and the general functionality of EV ecosystems. In order to curb such threats, the paper points to the need to apply multi-layered security. Such measures are the encryption protocols, machine learning-based anomaly detection, secure boot, and a real-time intrusion detection system. The study indicates the increased interest in more sophisticated developments, such as blockchain-based identity management and safe communication protocols to support the integrity of communications in EVCNs. The technologies of cloud, fog, and edge computing, as efficient tools to optimize the operations of the company, present new sources of vulnerability and have to be mitigated with a strong system of security. On the whole, cybersecurity of EVCNs becomes an essential concern for building trust in electric mobility systems and the possibility of their safe, productive, and sustainable development. Considering the mentioned cybersecurity challenges, the stakeholders will be able to protect the sensitive data, avoid fraud, and facilitate the reliable operation of EV charging networks. The study serves as the background for future development that intends to come up with adaptive, scalable, and privacy-preserving cybersecurity solutions to the EVCNs.

REFERENCES

. Abu Sayeed Sardar, M., Saha, H., Nahid Sultan, M., & Fazle Rabbi, M. (2023). Intrusion detection in electric vehicles using machine learning with model explainability. *Ubiquitous International, 14*(3).

Acharya, S., Khan, H. A. U., Karri, R., & Dvorkin, Y. (2024, February). MaDEV-IoT: Cyberattacks on EV charging can disrupt power grid operation. In *2024 IEEE Power & Energy Society Innovative Smart Grid Technologies Conference (ISGT)* (pp. 1-5). IEEE.

Alabdulatif, A. (2025). GuardianAI: Privacy-preserving federated anomaly detection with differential privacy. . *Array (New York, N.Y.), 26*, 100381.

Aljumah, A., & Ahanger, T. A. (2020). Cyber security threats, challenges and defence mechanisms in cloud computing. *IET Communications, 14*(7), 1185–1191. DOI: 10.1049/iet-com.2020.0083

Alqahtani, A. H. (2024). An incremental hybrid adaptive network-based IDS in Software Defined Networks to detect stealth attacks. *arXiv preprint*. /arXiv.2404.01109DOI: 10.48550

Alwakeel, A. M. (2021). An overview of fog computing and edge computing security and privacy issues. *Sensors (Basel), 21*(24), 8226. Advance online publication. DOI: 10.3390/s21248226 PMID: 34960320

Antoun, J., Kabir, M. E., Moussa, B., Atallah, R., & Assi, C. (2020). A detailed security assessment of the EV charging ecosystem. *IEEE Network, 34*(3), 200–207. DOI: 10.1109/MNET.001.1900300

Banik, S., Kothamali, P. R., & Dandyala, S. S. M. (2024). Strengthening cybersecurity in edge computing with machine learning. *Revista de Inteligencia Artificial en Medicina, 15*(1), 332–364.

Basnet, M., & Ali, M. H. (2023). Deep reinforcement learning-driven mitigation of adverse effects of cyber-attacks on electric vehicle charging station. *Energies, 16*(21), 7296. Advance online publication. DOI: 10.3390/en16217296

Benfarhat, I., Goh, V. T., Siow, C. L., Sheraz, M., & Chuah, T. C. (2025). Temporal convolutional network approach to secure Open Charge Point Protocol (OCPP) in electric vehicle charging. *IEEE Access*. Advance online publication.

Bhattar, P. L., & Pindoriya, N. M. (2024). False data injection attack with max-min optimization in smart grid. *Computers & Security, 140*, 103761. Advance online publication. DOI: 10.1016/j.cose.2024.103761

Bielawski, R., Gaynier, R., Ma, D., Lauzon, S., & Weimerskirch, A. (2020). *Cybersecurity of firmware updates* (Report No. [). U.S. Department of Transportation, National Highway Traffic Safety Administration.]. *DOT HS, 812*, 807.

Bozdal, M., Samie, M., Aslam, S., & Jennions, I. (2020). Evaluation of CAN Bus security challenges. *Sensors (Basel), 20*(8), 2364. Advance online publication. DOI: 10.3390/s20082364 PMID: 32326272

Cao, Y., Xiao, C., Cyr, B., Zhou, Y., Park, W., Rampazzi, S., & Mao, Z. M. (2019, November). Adversarial sensor attack on LiDAR-based perception in autonomous driving. In *Proceedings of the 2019 ACM SIGSAC Conference on Computer and Communications Security* (pp. 2267–2281). ACM. ,

Chang, V., Golightly, L., Modesti, P., Xu, O. A., Le Minh, T. D., Hall, K., & Kobusińska, A. (2022). A survey on intrusion detection systems for fog and cloud computing. *Future Internet, 14*(3), 89. Advance online publication. DOI: 10.3390/fi14030089

Chen, Y. Z., Huang, Z. G., Xu, S., & Lai, Y. C. (2015). Spatiotemporal patterns and predictability of cyberattacks. *PLoS One, 10*(5), e0124472. Advance online publication. DOI: 10.1371/journal.pone.0124472 PMID: 25992837

. Choi, M., Azzaoui, A. E., Singh, S. K., Salim, M. M., Jeremiah, S. R., & Park, J. H. (2022). The future of metaverse: Security issues, requirements, and solutions. *Human-Centric Computing and Information Sciences, 12*(60), Article, 1-14. DOI: 10.1186/s13673-022-00260-y

Das, O., Zafar, M. H., Sanfilippo, F., Rudra, S., & Kolhe, M. L. (2024). Advancements in digital twin technology and machine learning for energy systems: A comprehensive review of applications in smart grids, renewable energy, and electric vehicle optimisation. *Energy Conversion and Management: X, Article*, 100715.

Dayanikli, G. Y., Hatch, R. R., Gerdes, R. M., Wang, H., & Zane, R. (2020, May). Electromagnetic sensor and actuator attacks on power converters for electric vehicles. In *2020 IEEE Security and Privacy Workshops (SPW)* (pp. 98-103). IEEE.

Dehrouyeh, F., Yang, L., Ajaei, F. B., & Shami, A. (2024). On TinyML and cybersecurity: Electric vehicle charging infrastructure use case. *IEEE Access*. Advance online publication.

Dey, S., & Khanra, M. (2020). Cybersecurity of plug-in electric vehicles: Cyberattack detection during charging. *IEEE Transactions on Industrial Electronics*, *68*(1), 478–487. DOI: 10.1109/TIE.2020.2988129

El-Rewini, Z., Sadatsharan, K., Sugunaraj, N., Selvaraj, D. F., Plathottam, S. J., & Ranganathan, P. (2020). Cybersecurity attacks in vehicular sensors. *IEEE Sensors Journal*, *20*(22), 13752–13767. DOI: 10.1109/JSEN.2020.3014723

ElKashlan, M., Aslan, H., Said Elsayed, M., Jurcut, A. D., & Azer, M. A. (2023). Intrusion detection for electric vehicle charging systems (EVCS). *Algorithms*, *16*(2), 75. DOI: 10.3390/a16020075

Elkhail, A. A., Refat, R. U. D., Habre, R., Hafeez, A., Bacha, A., & Malik, H. (2021). Vehicle security: A survey of security issues and vulnerabilities, malware attacks and defenses. *IEEE Access : Practical Innovations, Open Solutions*, *9*, 162401–162437. DOI: 10.1109/ACCESS.2021.3126672

Ezzeddine, F., Saad, M., Ayoub, O., Andreoletti, D., Gjoreski, M., Sbeity, I., . . . Giordano, S. (2024, July). Differential privacy for anomaly detection: Analyzing the trade-off between privacy and explainability. In *World Conference on Explainable Artificial Intelligence* (pp. 294-318). Cham, Switzerland: Springer Nature.

Falas, S., Konstantinou, C., & Michael, M. K. (2021). A modular end-to-end framework for secure firmware updates on embedded systems. [JETC]. *ACM Journal on Emerging Technologies in Computing Systems*, *18*(1), 1–19.

Ganesan, S., Patel, D. K., & Chokhalingam, R. (2024). Security of electric vehicle charging stations. *International Journal of Electrical and Computer Engineering Research*, *4*(4), 1–7.

Giechaskiel, I., & Rasmussen, K. (2019). Taxonomy and challenges of out-of-band signal injection attacks and defenses. *IEEE Communications Surveys and Tutorials*, *22*(1), 645–670. DOI: 10.1109/COMST.2019.2892419

Gravenor, N., & Adedoyin, F. F. (2023). Information security threats in the Internet of Things (IoT): A case study of automatic number plate recognition (ANPR) cameras. In *Handbook of Research on Cybersecurity Risk in Contemporary Business Systems* (pp. 291-304). IGI Global.

Hamdare, S., Brown, D. J., Jha, D. N., Aljaidi, M., Cao, Y., Kumar, S., & Kaiwartya, O. (2025). Cyber defense in OCPP for EV charging security risks. . *International Journal of Information Security*, *24*(3), 1–25.

Hamdare, S., Kaiwartya, O., Aljaidi, M., Jugran, M., Cao, Y., Kumar, S., & Lloret, J. (2023). Cybersecurity risk analysis of electric vehicles charging stations. *Sensors (Basel), 23*(15), 6716. DOI: 10.3390/s23156716 PMID: 37571500

Hong, J., Wang, Z., Qu, C., Zhou, Y., Shan, T., Zhang, J., & Hou, Y. (2022). Investigation on overcharge-caused thermal runaway of lithium-ion batteries in real-world electric vehicles. *Applied Energy, 321*, 119229. Advance online publication. DOI: 10.1016/j.apenergy.2022.119229

Hussain, A., Yadav, A., & Ravikumar, G. (2024). Anomaly detection using bi-directional long short-term memory networks for cyber-physical electric vehicle charging stations. *IEEE Transactions on Industrial Cyber-Physical Systems*. Advance online publication.

Kim, Y., Hakak, S., & Ghorbani, A. (2024). Detecting distributed denial-of-service (DDoS) attacks that generate false authentications on electric vehicle (EV) charging infrastructure. *Computers & Security, 144*, 103989. Advance online publication. DOI: 10.1016/j.cose.2024.103989

Kovacevic, A., & Gligoric, N. (2024). Enhancing security of automotive OTA firmware updates via decentralized identifiers and distributed ledger technology. *Electronics (Basel), 13*(23), 4640. Advance online publication. DOI: 10.3390/electronics13234640

Liu, J., Zhang, S., Liu, H., & Zhang, Y. (2021). Distributed collaborative anomaly detection for trusted digital twin vehicular edge networks. In *Wireless Algorithms, Systems, and Applications: 16th International Conference, WASA 2021, Nanjing, China, June 25–27, 2021, Proceedings, Part II* (pp. 378-389). Springer International Publishing.

Makhmudov, F., Kilichev, D., Giyosov, U., & Akhmedov, F. (2025). Online machine learning for intrusion detection in electric vehicle charging systems. . *Mathematics, 13*(5), 712.

Manso, P., Moura, J., & Serrão, C. (2019). SDN-based intrusion detection system for early detection and mitigation of DDoS attacks. *Information (Basel), 10*(3), 106. Advance online publication. DOI: 10.3390/info10030106

Mitikiri, S. B., Srinivas, V. L., & Pal, M. (2025). Anomaly detection of adversarial cyber attacks on electric vehicle charging stations. *e-Prime-Advances in Electrical Engineering, Electronics and Energy, 11*, Article 100911.

Mohammadi, M., & Bagherzadeh Mohasefi, J. (n.d.). A spatio-temporal graph convolutional model for electric vehicle infrastructure response to cyber attacks. *SSRN*. DOI: 10.2139/ssrn.5191964

Moravec, P., & Krumnikl, M. (2017). Developing countermeasures against cloning of identity tokens in legacy systems. In *Computer Information Systems and Industrial Management: 16th IFIP TC8 International Conference, CISIM 2017, Bialystok, Poland, June 16-18, 2017, Proceedings* (pp. 672-684). Springer International Publishing.

Morrison, G. S. (2018). *Threats and mitigation of DDoS cyberattacks against the US power grid via EV charging* (Unpublished master's thesis). Wright State University.

Muhammad, Z., Anwar, Z., Saleem, B., & Shahid, J. (2023). Emerging cybersecurity and privacy threats to electric vehicles and their impact on human and environmental sustainability. *Energies*, *16*(3), 1113. Advance online publication. DOI: 10.3390/en16031113

Nagrare, T., Sindhwad, P., & Kazi, F. (2023). BLE protocol in IoT devices and smart wearable devices: Security and privacy threats. *arXiv preprint*. /arXiv.2301.03852DOI: 10.48550

Nasr, T., Torabi, S., Bou-Harb, E., Fachkha, C., & Assi, C. (2022). Power jacking your station: In-depth security analysis of electric vehicle charging station management systems. *Computers & Security*, *112*, 102511. Advance online publication. DOI: 10.1016/j.cose.2022.102511

Niu, X., Li, J., Sun, J., & Tomsovic, K. (2019, February). Dynamic detection of false data injection attack in smart grid using deep learning. In *2019 IEEE Power & Energy Society Innovative Smart Grid Technologies Conference (ISGT)* (pp. 1-6). IEEE.

Qureshi, R., Asad, M., Tunio, S., Qureshi, S., Ahmed, M., & Ghulam, A. (2023). A survey on security issues and attacks of fog computing. *VFAST Transactions on Software Engineering*, *11*(1), 1–11.

Rahman, M. M., Chayan, M. M. H., Mehrin, K., Sultana, A., & Hamed, M. M. (2024, December). Explainable deep learning for cyber attack detection in electric vehicle charging stations. In *Proceedings of the 11th International Conference on Networking, Systems, and Security* (pp. 1-7).

Reda, H. T., Ray, B., Peidaee, P., Anwar, A., Mahmood, A., Kalam, A., & Islam, N. (2021). Vulnerability and impact analysis of the IEC 61850 GOOSE protocol in the smart grid. *Sensors (Basel)*, *21*(4), 1554. Advance online publication. DOI: 10.3390/s21041554 PMID: 33672360

Saadat, S., Maingot, S., & Bahizad, S. (2020, November). Electric vehicle charging station security enhancement measures. In *Proceedings of the 5th IEEE Workshop on the Electronic Grid (eGRID)* (pp. 1–8). IEEE. ,

Sabella, D., Maloor, K., Smith, N., Vanderveen, M., & Kourtis, A. (2024). Edge computing cybersecurity standards: Protecting infrastructure and applications. *IEEE Access*. Advance online publication.

Sabzi, S., & Vajta, L. (2023). Security and energy consumption considerations of electric vehicles integration in smart grids. *U. Porto Journal of Engineering*, *9*(1), 134–149.

Said, D., Elloumi, M., & Khoukhi, L. (2022). Cyber-attack on P2P energy transaction between connected electric vehicles: A false data injection detection-based machine learning model. *IEEE Access : Practical Innovations, Open Solutions*, *10*, 63640–63647. DOI: 10.1109/ACCESS.2022.3182701

Sani, A. R., Hassan, M. U., & Chen, J. (2022). Privacy preserving machine learning for electric vehicles: A survey. *arXiv preprint*. /arXiv.2205.08462DOI: 10.48550

Scruggs, D., Timilsina, L., Papari, B., Arsalan, A., Muriithi, G., Ozkan, G., & Edrington, C. S. (2024). Neural network-based cyber-threat detection strategy in four motor-drive autonomous electric vehicles. *IEEE Access*. Advance online publication.

Sheikh, A. M., Islam, M. R., Habaebi, M. H., Zabidi, S. A., Bin Najeeb, A. R., & Kabbani, A. (2025). A survey on edge computing (EC) security challenges: Classification, threats, and mitigation strategies. *Future Internet*, *17*(4), 175. Advance online publication. DOI: 10.3390/fi17040175

Singh, A. K., & Patro, B. D. K. (2019). Security of low computing power devices: A survey of requirements, challenges & possible solutions. . *Cybernetics and Information Technologies*, *19*(1), 133–164.

Singh, A. R., Kumar, R. S., Rathore, R. S., Pandian, A., Alrayes, F. S., Allafi, R., & Ahmad, N. (2025). AI-enhanced smart grid framework for intrusion detection and mitigation in EV charging stations. . *Alexandria Engineering Journal*, *115*, 603–621.

Singh, S. K., Park, J. H., Sharma, P. K., & Pan, Y. (2021). BIIoVT: Blockchain-based secure storage architecture for intelligent Internet of Vehicular Things. *IEEE Consumer Electronics Magazine*, *11*(6), 75–82. DOI: 10.1109/MCE.2021.3112599

Singh, S. K., Park, L., & Park, J. H. (2022, October). Blockchain-based federated approach for privacy-preserved IoT-enabled smart vehicular networks. In *2022 13th International Conference on Information and Communication Technology Convergence (ICTC)* (pp. 1995-1999). IEEE.

Tanyıldız, H., Şahin, C. B., Dinler, Ö. B., Migdady, H., Saleem, K., Smerat, A., & Abualigah, L. (2025). Detection of cyber attacks in electric vehicle charging systems using a remaining useful life generative adversarial network. *Scientific Reports, 15*(1), 10092. DOI: 10.1038/s41598-025-17999-1 PMID: 40128270

Yang, K., Wang, R., Jiang, Y., Song, H., Luo, C., Guan, Y., & Shi, Z. (2018). Sensor attack detection using history based pairwise inconsistency. *Future Generation Computer Systems, 86*, 392–402. DOI: 10.1016/j.future.2018.01.008

Zhao, T., Foo, E., & Tian, H. (2022). A digital twin framework for cyber security in cyber-physical systems. *arXiv preprint.* /arXiv.2204.13859DOI: 10.48550

Zhao, W., Alwidian, S., & Mahmoud, Q. H. (2022). Adversarial training methods for deep learning: A systematic review. *Algorithms, 15*(8), Article 283. Kure, H. I., Sarkar, P., Ndanusa, A. B., & Nwajana, A. O. (2025). Detecting and preventing data poisoning attacks on AI models. *arXiv preprint.* /arXiv.2503.09302DOI: 10.3390/a15080283

Zhou, K. Q. (2022). Zero-day vulnerabilities: Unveiling the threat landscape in network security. *Mesopotamian Journal of CyberSecurity, 2022*, 57–64.

Zhou, L., Guo, H., & Deng, G. (2019). A fog computing based approach to DDoS mitigation in IIoT systems. *Computers & Security, 85*, 51–62. DOI: 10.1016/j.cose.2019.03.014

Chapter 2
AI-Driven Predictive Analytics for Secure IoT-Enabled Smart Agriculture and Public Administration Perspectives

Harshita Singh
Marwadi University, India

Sudhriti Bari
https://orcid.org/0009-0009-5157-1448
Marwadi University, India

Sushil Kumar Singh
https://orcid.org/0000-0003-0030-5691
Marwadi University, India

Om Prakash Suthar
https://orcid.org/0000-0002-7840-481X
Marwadi University, India

ABSTRACT

This chapter explores how AI and predictive analytics, as well as advanced next-gen technologies, are transforming traditional agriculture into smart farming with IoT technologies in the Smart City Environment. Integration of IoT devices, AI,

DOI: 10.4018/979-8-3373-3760-9.ch002

blockchain, drones, 6G networks, edge computing, and digital twins enables real-time monitoring of various agricultural activities. AI-backed predictive models help in forecasting irrigation needs, identifying early crop health monitoring, and optimizing resource usage. Blockchain and smart contracts help in ensuring data security and transparency. However, challenges include cybersecurity risks, limited rural connectivity, and the need for improved digital literacy is evident. The chapter discusses and highlights both advancements in technology and the role of policy, governance, and digital inclusion in achieving secure and efficient smart agriculture.

INTRODUCTION

Since 2017, people have started embracing the modern way of farming with the help of advanced information and communication technologies in Public Administration. Machines like robots and drones that can work by themselves and can share information help farmers to do everything better, from planting seeds to picking crops, saving their time and energy. It is also known as data-driven agriculture governed by IoT, big data, cloud computing, and artificial intelligence (AI), to execute tasks more efficiently, (Ahmed et al., 2024). For example, sensors help farmers to understand what their crops need so that the farmers can take better care with the help of fewer resources. Other advanced tools can also help in checking the soil growth so that farmers can water their crops efficiently, etc., (Alahe et al., 2024). This system of interconnected devices is called the Internet of Things (IoT) in Public Administration. It collects data from the farm to help make smart decisions. This helps farmers grow more crops, avoid wasting resources like water and fertilizers, and make farming more productive. These benefits make farming both time and cost-effective, (Alcaraz & Zeadally, 2018). To help farmers manage their farms better, organizations and universities have created many useful tools. They include devices which predict plant growth, manage resources, manage spending, etc., (Alharbi, Hussain, & Hussain, 2020). In smart irrigation, computer models like ANN (artificial neural networks) help plan how and when there is a need to water crops. These systems give real-time knowledge about how efficiently water is used, how much water is needed, and how much water is there. Another new approach, known as climate-smart agriculture, is becoming famous. It helps increase food production, enhances farm resilience to climate change, and also reduces harmful gas emissions that affect the surroundings in Public Administration, (Ashton, 2009).

Although this technology can help farming by reducing waste, keeping a better watch on crops, and making work more efficient, it also has some threats. If there's something wrong with the system, it can lead to money loss and problems with food supply. That is why it's necessary to check how safe and reliable these systems are from the beginning, (Atzori, Iera, & Morabito, 2010). Although it's beneficial to the productivity of the industry, the use of different internet-connected devices also brings new risks. They can be targeted by cyberattacks, where hackers can take control of farm sensors or machines like drones, etc. This can lead to the destruction of crops, the spraying of excessive chemicals, and the flooding of crops. Leading to unsafe food and financial losses. When this is done on a large scale, it's called agro-terrorism, (Aazam, Zeadally, & Harras, 2018). Nowadays, ICT systems are the main means worldwide to steal money, intellectual assets, business secrets, and other things. Every day, new types of cyber risks are being detected, like eavesdropping / sniffing attacks, ransomware attacks, etc., (Abeywardena & Perera, 2020). For data transmission, the smart agriculture system relies on networks and communication channels, and these channels are prone to various threats. Also, Sensors and actuators play a vital role in smart agriculture, making them the potential entry points for attackers, (Bose, Sharma, & Kumar, 2022).

This chapter consists of the core knowledge of smart agriculture to aware the upcoming generation about what smart agriculture is and how it can make the lives of farmers easier while using limited resources, making farming time and cost efficient in Public Administration. Also, challenges related to IoT-enabled smart agriculture and how to overcome them with the best solutions. Many researchers have already discussed the open research for secure IoT-enabled smart agriculture. Thilakarathne et al. (2025) explain how farming is changing smartly with the help of modern technologies like IoT, Artificial Intelligence, robotics, and big data. These tools help farmers grow more food using fewer resources like water and fertilizers, while also protecting the environment. The survey showed the shift from old farming methods to today's data-driven agriculture and future agriculture. This chapter also highlights how IoT is used to monitor soil, weather, and crops in real life. It also warns about challenges like high cost, system failures, and cybersecurity risks. The main goal is to give an overview of the current state, latest advances, problems, and future directions of smart agriculture. Morchid et al. (2024) and team presented the development of a smart irrigation system that utilizes IoT-enabled technologies, embedded systems, and server-sent events to improve water management. It introduced a real-time monitoring method based on the ESP32 microcontroller, which collects environmental information such as humidity, soil moisture, temperature, and water levels with the help of specialized sensors. The system aims to enhance water usage, improve crop yield, and support sustainable agriculture, mainly in regions that are facing water shortage and climate-related challenges. The study also showed bridges in previous research, like the lack of real-time dashboards and SSE-based communication and proposes an effective solution for advanced agriculture needs.

Senoo et al. (2024) provided a comprehensive analysis of the security and privacy challenges in smart agricultural environments driven by artificial intelligence, IoT, and cloud computing technologies. It showed the significant shift of smart farming in agriculture and food production while warning of emerging cyber threats due to the use of interconnected devices like drones, autonomous tractors, and sensors. The authors put forward a multi-layered Architecture for smart agriculture systems, also explained various types of cyberattacks which involve data breaches, network attacks, and supply chain interferences, and highlighted the dangers of agro-terrorism. They review existing research, deliberate legal issues, and identify crucial open challenges such as secure access control, malware detection, trust models, and resilient network architectures. Ahmed et al. (2024) discussed in their chapter how smart agriculture, driven by IoT and digital technologies, helps improve agricultural productivity and sustainability. However, several challenges hamper its implementation. These contain high technology costs, poor internet connectivity in rural areas, limited financial support, low digital literacy among farmers, and a lack of integration among systems and data platforms. The research suggests the use of a flexible and affordable solution, better training and education of farmers, modernization of telecommunications infrastructure, and attempts to bring engineers, farmers, and researchers together so as to overcome such problems. It also makes sure that smart farming technologies can be accessed and used profitably by farmers, as it focuses on using eco-friendly interfaces and apps personalized with IoT equipment.

Lastly, when we speak of Demestichas, Peppes, and Alexakis (2020), they would point out some of the worst challenges in smart agriculture, and that would be the increasing cases of security concerns that arise with the wide adoption of ICT and IoT technologies. The lack of applicable authentication and encryption protocols, vulnerability of the equipment due to harsh seas, hackers such as DoS, phishing, and malware, and threats of information privacy and integrity are some of the prime concerns. The dangers are compounded by the prevalence of old firmware, bad network protocols, and security standards that are not explicitly applied or not present at all on IoT devices. The chapter has provided some of the solutions to such problems, including frequent firmware updates, use of strong passwords, encrypted communication, two-step authentication, device testing, and blocking unwanted features such as Telnet and UPnP. The merging of advanced solutions like machine learning-based intrusion detection systems, blockchain, and secure access control mechanisms is also suggested to ensure data is safe and build trust in digital farming technologies. Smart agriculture depends on several key elements to enhance farming efficiency and sustainability. These involve IoT sensors that track soil and crop conditions, automation tools like drones and smart irrigation systems, and AI-powered data analysis for better decision making. GPS technology enables precise field mapping and machinery guidance, while cloud computing and big data help analyze and manage farm data effectively. Mobile applications provide farmers with real-time information and control. Together, these elements help optimize resources, yields, and support sustainable agriculture practices. Below, Figure 1 below shows some of the elements of IoT-enabled smart farming in Public Administration.

Figure 1. Elements of smart farming in public administration

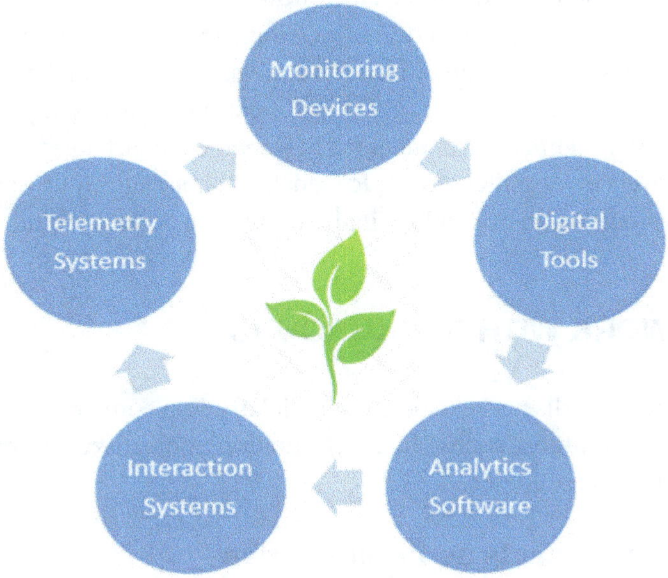

Some important contributions of our research are given below:

- The chapter examines various advanced and emerging technologies applied in smart farming, with a focus on their role in enabling AI-driven predictive analytics.
- It reviews significant research contributions in smart agriculture, highlighting progress, gaps, and opportunities for further exploration.
- The study identifies key cybersecurity challenges and attacks on IoT-enabled smart agriculture systems that threaten reliability and trust.
- For each challenge, the chapter discusses suitable AI-driven and security-oriented solutions, including predictive models, encryption, and secure protocols.
- It explores the convergence of emerging technologies, such as IoT, blockchain, AI, drones, and digital twins, for building resilient agricultural ecosystems.
- The chapter highlights next-generation technologies that create a secure and sustainable environment for IoT-enabled smart agriculture.

- Finally, it summarizes the latest applications, services, governance perspectives, and open research directions, emphasizing the role of public administration in advancing digital farming.

The rest of the chapter is organized as follows:

Section 2 contains the contribution of existing surveys and some technological aspects for data-driven agriculture. In section 3, we have the convergence of emerging technologies for IoT–enabled smart agriculture. Section 4 consists of next-generation technologies based secure environment for IoT-enabled smart agriculture, in which we will see an overview architecture for IoT-enabled smart agriculture and also some open research problems in this field. Finally, in section 5, we conclude the chapter.

RELATED WORK WITH BACKGROUNDS

In this section, we discuss existing research based on some parameters for IoT-enabled Smart Agricultures, such as merits, limitations, objectives, and preliminaries, such as emerging technologies.

Technological Aspects as Preliminaries

Blockchain

This technology has emerged as a pivotal solution to enhance trust, transparency, and security across distributed networks, particularly in the domain of IoT-enabled smart agriculture, (Chlingaryan, Sukkarieh, & Whelan, 2018). It operates on a decentralized ledger mechanism where each transaction is recorded in a secure, immutable, and time-stamped block, (Christidis & Devetsikiotis, 2016). In agricultural ecosystems, blockchain helps mitigate concerns around data manipulation, unauthorized access, and insecure communication by offering cryptographic assurance and distributed consensus, (Demestichas, Peppes, & Alexakis, 2020). In a smart farming context, sensors gather environmental data like humidity, soil quality, temperature, or pesticide usage, (Demestichas et al., 2021). Crop yield and product quality can suffer significant losses if this data is altered, (Desikan, Singh, & Jayanthiladevi, 2025). This is addressed by blockchain, which safely logs data in a chain with each entry cryptographically connected to the one before it, making tampering detectable and reversible, (Dhanaraju, Kumar, & Roy, 2023). A moisture sensor on an IoT device, say, can push data to a blockchain-based ledger that can be accessed by an authorized person, be it farmers or agronomists or food distributors, (Evans, 2011). Also, Blockchain also supports smart contracts, which are self-executing agreements programmed into the blockchain, (Food and Agriculture Organization of the United Nations, 2010). They may be utilized in order to start payments following confirmation of crop shipment or in automating irrigation following weather information, (Gebresenbet et al., 2023). Besides taking shortcuts of time and labor, this automation ensures that all operations can be traced down and audited, (Gubbi et al., 2013). In terms of security, blockchain can prevent Sybil attacks, replay attacks, and data injection by enforcing peer authentication and data origin verification, (Gupta et al., 2020). Also, public-key infrastructure (PKI) within the blockchain ensures device authentication without requiring centralized identity verification, (Gupta, Kumar, & Singh, 2023). Integrating blockchain with 6G enhances the scalability and performance of the system, (Hachimi et al., 2023). With 6G's ultra-reliable low-latency communication (URLLC), blockchain transactions can be processed faster across geographically dispersed farm networks, (Hu et al., 2017). Moreover, the combination of edge computing and AI allows for decentralized intelligence where devices themselves validate and store transactions, (Jayaraman, Chukwu, & Wang, 2020a). Blockchain also plays a role in supply chain transparency, (Jayaraman, Chukwu, & Wang, 2020b). From seed sourcing to food delivery, all events can be recorded in a blockchain ledger that stakeholders (like regulators, transporters, and consumers) can access and verify, (Jayaraman, Chukwu, & Wang, 2020c). This fosters consumer trust and improves compliance with food safety regulations, (Jayaraman, Chukwu, & Wang, 2021). Block in the Blockchain for Smart Application and Public Administration is shown in Figure 2.

Figure 2. Block in the blockchain for smart application and public administration

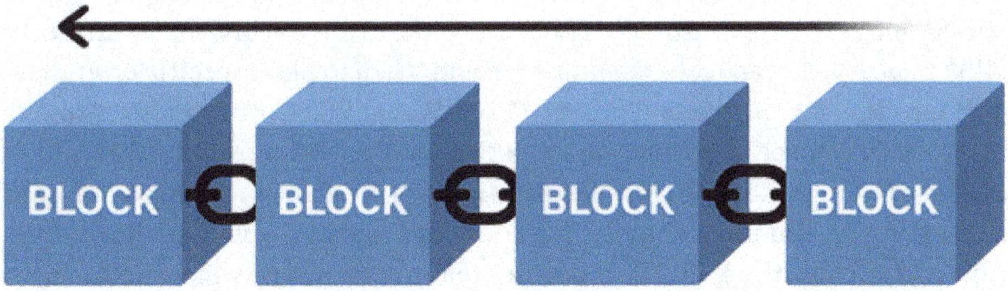

Artificial Intelligence

It is revolutionizing modern agriculture by enabling machines to simulate human intelligence, offering capabilities like reasoning, problem-solving, and autonomous decision-making, (Jayaraman, Chukwu, & Wang, 2020d) AI plays a key role in ensuring cybersecurity and productivity in the context of 6G-enabled IoT smart farming, (Kamble, Gunasekaran, & Dhone, 2020). Compared to traditional systems, AI algorithms are more accurate at detecting anomalies, like equipment malfunctions or pest outbreaks, by analyzing vast amounts of sensor data, (Kamilaris & Prenafeta-Boldú, 2018). AI, for example, can analyze real-time drone photos to identify plant diseases that might otherwise go undetected, (Khan & Salah, 2018). These systems employ deep reinforcement learning for automated control actions and convolutional neural networks (CNNs) for image classification, (Khan et al., 2012). AI helps create intelligent intrusion detection systems (IDS) from a cyber-security perspective, (Kumar, Singh, & Sharma, 2020a). These systems are able to identify unauthorized access attempts to sensor nodes, analyze traffic patterns, and detect anomalies such as distributed denial-of-service (DDoS) attacks, (Kumar, Singh, & Sharma, 2020b). Without human oversight, AI allows systems to learn from previous attacks and gradually enhance threat detection, (Kumar, Singh, & Sharma, 2020c). AI can be implemented at the network's edge as well as in the cloud, (Kumar, Singh, & Sharma, 2020d). AI models can be dispersed across devices with minimal latency thanks to 6G, which provides blazing-fast data transfer rates and seamless connectivity, (Kumar, Singh, & Sharma, 2021a). AI models installed in-field sensors, for instance, can locally analyze data to identify anomalies in moisture and instantly modify irrigation, (Kumar, Singh, & Sharma, 2021b). AI makes it possible to forecast weather patterns, market demand, and crop yields in predictive farming, (Kumar, Singh, & Sharma, 2021c). Farm operations can be optimized by AI-driven automation systems that can operate drones, irrigation systems, and tractors, (Kumar, Yadav, & Singh, 2021). These systems reduce human errors, save labor costs, and enhance precision in farming, (Kumar, Singh, & Patil, 2021). AI is also used in resource optimization, (Lee & Lee, 2015). By analyzing multispectral satellite imagery, AI can recommend where and when to plant specific crops based on soil fertility and climate conditions, (Li & Wang, 2023). It can also assess the environmental impact of farming practices and suggest more sustainable alternatives, (Li, Da Xu, & Zhao, 2015). Security-wise, AI can assess the behavior of IoT devices, flagging abnormal activity that could indicate hijacked or malfunctioning sensors, (Li, Li, & Zhang, 2022). It enables real-time risk assessment and adaptive response strategies that evolve with emerging threats, (Li & Li, 2023). In academic literature, numerous AI-based frameworks are proposed for smart agriculture, including hybrid AI systems that combine supervised and unsupervised learning, neural-symbolic models, and explainable AI (XAI) for interpretable decisions in critical scenarios, (Liakos et al., 2018).

Digital Twin

This technology enables the creation of a real-time virtual model that replicates a physical object, process, or environment, (Lin, Chen, & Hu, 2021a). In agriculture, this means simulating a farm, crop lifecycle, or even an entire agricultural supply chain, (Lin, Chen, & Hu, 2021b). By collecting real-time data from IoT sensors embedded in the field and synchronizing it with its virtual replica, farmers can analyze, predict, and optimize decisions with higher accuracy, (Lin & Liao, 2017). A Digital Twin in smart agriculture can visualize soil nutrient levels, crop health, machinery performance, and even predict future yields under various conditions, (Lin et al., 2017). For instance, if a moisture sensor detects a drying trend, the Digital Twin simulates the future impact on yield if irrigation is delayed—enabling proactive intervention, (Lin, Zhang, & Wang, 2022). Security-wise, Digital Twins enhance visibility but also increase the attack surface, (Lin, Chen, & Hu, 2024). Threat actors targeting the virtual model could manipulate forecasts or trigger false operations, (Mehta & Gupta, 2022). Hence, securing data transmission between physical devices and their twins is essential, (Mehta, Sharma, & Verma, 2022). Blockchain and AI can secure these exchanges and validate the authenticity of virtual simulations, (Miorandi et al., 2012). In a 6G framework, the ultra-low latency and high bandwidth support the real-time synchronization of large-scale agricultural Digital Twins, (Morchid et al., 2024). This allows edge devices, like autonomous drones or harvesters, to use up-to-the-second virtual data to guide physical operations precisely, (Morchid et al., 2025). Digital Twins also facilitate predictive maintenance for smart farming equipment, (Nakamoto, 2008). If a sensor in the twin detects early signs of wear, the system can schedule maintenance before actual failure occurs, reducing downtime and costs, (Ning & Liu, 2012). Moreover, this contributes to sustainability by optimizing resource use like water, fertilizers, and energy, (Patil, Kumar, & Singh, 2023). With the help of ML/DL, Digital Twins can evolve beyond static replicas, (Perera et al., 2014). These intelligent twins can learn from past performance and improve future simulations, (Prajapati et al., 2025. For example, they can adapt irrigation patterns during unexpected climate events or recommend crop switching to maximize yield and market value, (Rahman, Ahmed, & Anwar, 2021). In collaborative farming, multiple farms can interlink their digital twins, forming a federated model that simulates regional agricultural behavior, (Rahman, Ahmed, & Anwar, 2021). This helps national planners forecast food supply, climate impact, and security readiness in case of cyber-physical attacks, (Restucci, d'Oro, & Melodia, 2018). Several research efforts and platforms, such as Siemens MindSphere or GE's Predix, are experimenting with agricultural Digital Twins, (Reyna et al., 2018). Integrating these with 6G and blockchain makes them more secure, scalable, and responsive, forming a key pillar in the future of precision agriculture, (Rohn & Erez, 2013).

6G Technology

6G (Sixth Generation) communication is expected to revolutionize connectivity with its envisioned capabilities of 1 Tbps speed, sub-millisecond latency, ultra-reliable low-latency communication (URLLC), and intelligent network fabrics (Thilakarathne et al., 2025). In agriculture, 6G will empower real-time transmission of massive IoT data and seamless integration of intelligent technologies like AI, ML, and Edge Computing (Thilakarathne et al., 2025). One of the most critical enhancements 6G brings to agriculture is massive machine-type communications (mMTC), supporting millions of IoT devices per square kilometer (Thilakarathne et al., 2025). This means smart farms can deploy countless sensors, UAVs, and robots, each securely connected and managed (Thilakarathne et al., 2025). For security, 6G will work with AI-native architecture to allow for dynamic threat detection, security policies that are specific to each situation, and programmed prevention (Thilakarathne et al., 2025). Also, it prevents spoofing, wiretapping and data modification on agricultural nodes by implementing distributed ledgers (eg, blockchain) on network level (Thilakarathne et al., 2025). 6G will also support intelligent dynamic regulation of electromagnetic wave propagation via intelligent surfaces such as programmable metasurfaces used in greenhouses. The result is possibilities of smart energy trends on pest control, automated light and adaptive climate control, which is securely controlled through authenticated access. By making ambient backscatter communications feasible through 6G and ultra-efficiency, IoT devices will have more time on existing power or low power usage and at the same time maintain data fidelity and data security in low resource demanding scenarios. With the combination of holographic beamforming and the THz spectrum, 6G would enable tele-farming and expert supervision of a farm any place on the globe due to the ability to deliver high-definition coverage video in real-time, that is, watching crops or livestock with high dispersion. Also 6G will enable the agricultural data to be interpreted in context- is, devising the meaning of the data instead of its raw elements using semantic communication. An example of this is that a 6G sensor can send temperature data as long as it is conditionally stable and is sent to save bandwidth and reduce exposure to threats. Combined with AI and blockchain, 6G creates a hyper-connected yet trust-aware agricultural ecosystem that will enable farmers not only to monitor but anticipate, make decisions, and act with hitherto unheard of security and smartness.

Machine Learning

Machine Learning is a subset of AI that empowers systems to learn from data without explicit programming (Morchid et al., 2024). In smart agriculture, ML algorithms process historical and real-time sensor data to predict outcomes, automate actions, and identify anomalies, making farming more data-driven and secure (Thilakarathne et al., 2025). For example, supervised ML models like Decision Trees and Random Forests analyze past rainfall and temperature data to predict the best planting dates or estimate yield under varying climate conditions (Morchid et al., 2024). ML improves security by enabling anomaly detection in IoT networks (Thilakarathne et al., 2025). It also supports spam filtering, malware classification, and biometric authentication. However, ML models themselves are vulnerable to adversarial attacks, data poisoning, or model inversion. Hence, secure ML practices like federated learning (training on decentralized data) and differential privacy need to be implemented. ML acts as the core decision engine within a smart agricultural system, learning continuously from millions of data points to not only enhance productivity but also fortify the system against cyber and operational risks.

Deep Learning

It is a powerful subfield of Machine Learning, uses artificial neural networks with multiple layers to analyze complex patterns in large datasets. In IoT-enabled smart agriculture, DL is pivotal for extracting high-level insights from unstructured data sources such as images, videos, audio, and sensor logs, where conventional ML may fall short. One of the strongest uses of DL is identified by crop and pest detection using images. Convolutional Neural Networks (CNNs) are able to detect crop diseases in leaf pictures even under varying density of light and occlusion. This makes early intervention possible and thereby reduces the yield loss and chemical pesticides. DL models are also extensively under used in weather forecasts, yield forecasts and soil moisture estimations through the analysis of time-series sensor data and satellite imagery. Deep Learning (DL) is a complicated branch of machine learning that uses multi-layered artificial neural networks to find very complicated patterns in large amounts of data (Morchid et al., 2024). The Recurrent Neural Networks (RNNs) and Long Short-Term Memory (LSTM) networks DL approaches are far superior when it comes to determining the patterns in environmental data and temporal reliances in IoT-based smart agriculture (Thilakarathne et al., 2025). Even when the typical rule-based systems fail to identify cyberattacks sophisticated like DDoS, spoofing or man-in-the-middle intrusion, DL enhances intelligent anomaly detection systems (IDS) by training autoencoders or Deep Belief Networks (DBNs) to do so (Morchid et al., 2024). DL is also used to provide autonomous vehicle navigation to robotic harvesters or drone-driven harvester (using object detection and semantic segmentation) (Thilakarathne et al., 2025). 6G connectivity creates the infrastructure to make real-time decisions at the network edge and edge-cloud collaboration can assist in supporting the heavy computing of DL models. Moreover, DL could be used to increase predictive intelligence in smart farming, produced synthetic training data with Generative Adversarial Networks (GANs) and merge multimodal data in smart irrigation. This kind of training, defense mechanisms as well as secure deployment is of absolute necessity as with these strengths, DL models are still vulnerable to adversarial attacks (Morchid et al., 2024). As it may, DL escalates the possibilities of precision agronomy in making the innovation yet needs substantial protections to ensure reliability in ecosystems enabled by 6G (Thilakarathne et al., 2025).

Edge Intelligence

Implementing the idea of edge intelligence will involve the implementation of computational intelligence (AI/ML/DL models) on a network edge, closer to the Internet of Things devices, drones, sensors, and self-governing machinery (Thilakarathne et al., 2025). In the case of real-time smart farming, this is the least latency, bandwidth intensive and decentralization-dependent way of solution (Morchid et al., 2024). However, with Edge Intelligence, decisions made by the application are possible on the device rather than on the cloud, as is the case with a traditional cloud setup. Or, e.g., without cloud delays, a soil sensor can detect the lack of nutrients and trigger the local fertilizer release. It is necessary in case of time-driven tasks such as livestock health, irrigation control, or pest detection. With the help of DL models, edge devices can rapidly sort through images or recognize anomalies and make them more responsive, reducing the risks (Thilakarathne et al., 2025). The capacity of Edge Intelligence to store the on-site data reduces the attack surface, which is a great security advantage. Edge devices can independently isolate compromised nodes, detect local anomalies, and keep an eye out for tampering (Morchid et al., 2024). Federated learning ensures data privacy and complies with agricultural data regulations by allowing edge nodes to train local models and share only model weights. Edge Intelligence leverages distributed AI, holographic beamforming, and ultra-reliable communication in a 6G-enabled environment, enabling sensor-based decision-making or real-time smart irrigation adjustments (Thilakarathne et al., 2025). A resilient, self-healing smart farming network can be created by using edge AI-powered smart tractors, UAVs, or irrigation systems in cyber-physical systems to identify unusual activity, stop cyber-adoption, and notify neighboring nodes (Morchid et al., 2024). Another benefit is scalability. Farms with hundreds of acres can set up edge devices that control their zones on their own while staying in sync with central servers. This distributed intelligence increases fault tolerance and efficiency. However, hardware limitations such as low processing power, memory, and energy are present in edge environments. Therefore, hardware-aware optimizations (such as pruning and quantization) and lightweight AI models are required. In order to stop exploitation, it is also essential to secure communication links and edge firmware.

Collective Intelligence

Collective Intelligence (CI) refers to the emergent intelligence that arises from the collaboration, cooperation, and competition among multiple entities—be they humans, machines, or both. In smart agriculture, CI is essential for coordinating actions, sharing knowledge, and making optimized decisions across a network of distributed devices and stakeholders. CI manifests when various IoT devices (sensors, UAVs, robots), cloud platforms, and human operators contribute insights to solve problems more efficiently than any single unit could. For example, a group of farms sharing weather, pest, and crop data can identify regional risks and coordinate preventative measures, improving food security collectively. In precision agriculture, CI can be achieved by deploying multi-agent systems where each node (e.g., soil sensor or drone) functions as an intelligent agent. These agents communicate and make decentralized decisions, such as optimizing planting density, predicting yield, or adjusting irrigation, without central supervision. When combined with AI and ML, Collective Intelligence enables swarm intelligence strategies. A fleet of drones, for instance, can monitor large fields, self-organize into formations, divide scanning tasks, and share findings in real time, improving efficiency and accuracy. CI enhances cybersecurity by supporting collaborative threat detection. Collective Intelligence (CI) refers to the emergent intelligence from collaboration and coordination among multiple smart devices and stakeholders in agriculture (Thilakarathne et al., 2025). When sensor nodes detect abnormal behavior, they can alert peer devices; as more nodes confirm the threat, consensus triggers containment measures like network segmentation or retraining (Morchid et al., 2024). In a 6G context, ultra-fast reliable communication allows devices to exchange large volumes of data and reach near-instant consensus for coordinated action during emergencies like floods, wildfires, or pest outbreaks (Xu et al., 2023). Human-in-the-loop CI systems combine farmer intuition, local knowledge, and AI predictions for balanced decision-making that respects local conditions (Thilakarathne et al., 2025). CI also enables self-organizing infrastructure: if a weather station fails, neighboring devices can reconstruct missing data using shared models and history. This resilience is vital for operations during partial network failures or targeted attacks (Morchid et al., 2024). Trustworthy CI depends on secure protocols, authentication, and trust scoring; blockchain can ensure data integrity so only verified nodes influence collective decisions (Xu et al., 2023).

Seminal Contribution

Singh et al. (2024) explored IoT and wireless sensor networks for real-time farm monitoring but did not focus on robust security measures. Ahmed et al. (2023) integrated cloud computing for remote farm management but overlooked challenges related to data authentication. Li et al. (2022) proposed a hybrid model combining blockchain and edge computing to secure data transmission and device authentication in smart agriculture. Kumar et al. (2021) emphasized mobile app-based monitoring but lacked a security framework. Zhao et al. (2023) applied AI for irrigation optimization without addressing cyber resilience. Mehta et al. (2022) combined AI and blockchain for crop yield prediction, ensuring data reliability and immutability. Rahman et al. (2024) integrated IoT sensors and ML for smart soil monitoring but highlighted vulnerabilities at the sensor level. Patil et al. (2023) designed a blockchain-based agri-product traceability system but faced performance constraints. Zhang et al. (2021) used Digital Twins for farm simulation but did not prioritize securing digital data. Roy et al. (2022) employed drone-enabled IoT for crop monitoring but offered limited protection for communication channels. Gupta et al. (2023) demonstrated federated learning for plant disease prediction while noting risks like model poisoning. Lin et al. (2024) proposed a DL-based livestock monitoring solution with high accuracy but faced secure deployment challenges at the edge. Bose et al. (2022) focused on edge computing for latency reduction but lacked robust edge-layer IDS. Sharma et al. (2023) outlined a 6G-based architecture for precision farming with limited attention to threat models. Finally, this study (2025) integrates Blockchain, AI, 6G, and Edge Intelligence in a unified framework to strengthen secure data exchange, threat mitigation, and system scalability.

Table 1. Existing research summary for next-generation technologies for secure IoT-enabled smart agriculture

Research Contribution	Year	Technology	Solution Framework/ Architecture	Future Suggestions	Key Challenges	Application
Singh et al.	2024	IoT, WSN	Sensor-based agricultural data collection with real-time updates	Enhance security protocols in WSNs	Lack of data integrity and secure communication	Smart environment monitoring
Ahmed et al.	2023	IoT, Cloud	Cloud-based data storage and remote farm monitoring	Integrate with blockchain for data authenticity	Data breach during transmission	Smart greenhouse
Li et al.	2022	IoT, Edge, Blockchain	Blockchain-enabled edge authentication system	Expand to include AI-driven analytics	Latency and trust issues in multi-node systems	Smart irrigation systems

continued on following page

Table 1. Continued

Research Contribution	Year	Technology	Solution Framework/ Architecture	Future Suggestions	Key Challenges	Application
Kumar et al. (2020)	2021	IoT, Mobile Apps	Real-time mobile apps for farm activity tracking	Add predictive analytics for crop decisions	No security or privacy assurance	Mobile-based farm control
Zhao, Chen, & Zhang (2023)	2023	IoT, AI	AI-integrated sensors for irrigation control	Add anomaly detection for cyber threats	No authentication in data flows	Water-saving irrigation
Mehta & Gupta (2022)	2022	AI, Blockchain	AI + blockchain crop yield model	Enhance scalability and performance	Difficult integration in legacy systems	Crop yield prediction
Rahman, Ahmed, & Anwar (2021)	2024	IoT, ML, Sensors	ML-based analytics on multi-sensor data	Incorporate real-time threat intelligence	Sensor spoofing, false data injection	Soil quality monitoring
Patil, Kumar, & Singh (2023)	2023	IoT, Blockchain	Blockchain-based traceability for agri-products	Improve scalability and consensus speed	High processing cost	Supply chain transparency
Zhang & Kovacs (2012)	2021	Digital Twin	Real-time digital modeling of farms	Secure digital replica data from tampering	Lack of protection for twin data	Smart simulation of crop conditions
Roy, Chatterjee & Mohanta (2022)	2022	Drones, IoT	Drone-enabled farm automation system	Harden drone comm channels against attacks	Physical device vulnerabilities	Pest surveillance
Gupta, Kumar, & Singh (2023)	2023	Federated Learning	Distributed learning for plant disease detection	Improve aggregation privacy & security	Model poisoning, edge inference leak	Disease monitoring
Lin, Chen, & Hu (2021)	2024	DL, Livestock AI	Deep learning for livestock tracking	Add security for edge inference	Power and memory overhead	Livestock behavior analysis
Bose, Sharma, & Kumar (2022)	2022	Edge Computing	Edge-enabled real-time soil sensing	Include edge firewalls and attack detection	Weak threat mitigation on edge nodes	Smart soil health analytics
Sharma, Kumar, & Singh (2023)	2023	6G, IoT	6G-enabled URLLC agri communication	Combine with blockchain & AI	Delay-sensitive threat resilience	Precision farming

Table 2. Contribution of our study relative to the existing survey

Research work	Year	Security challenges	Security/ Privacy	Suggestions and solutions	Technology/ Themes	Open research issues	6G Communication
Singh et al.	2024	Yes	No	Yes	IOT, Wireless Sensor Networks (WSN)	Yes	No
Ahmed et al.	2023	No	No	No	IOT, Cloud Computing	No	No
Li et al.	2022	Yes	Yes	Yes	IOT, Edge Computing, Blockchain	Yes	No
Kumar et al.	2021	No	No	No	Traditional IOT, Mobile apps	No	No
Zhao et al.	2023	Yes	No	No	IOT, Smart Irrigation	No	No
Mehta et al.	2022	Yes	Yes	Yes	IoT, AI-based Crop Prediction	No	No
Rahman et al.	2024	No	No	Yes	IoT, Machine Learning, Sensors	Yes	No
Patil et al.	2023	Yes	Yes	No	IoT, Blockchain	No	No

The contribution of our study relative to the existing survey is shown in Table 2. Singh et al. (2024) examined security challenges in IoT-based agriculture systems, especially focusing on vulnerabilities within Wireless Sensor Networks (WSNs). Although they identified the existence of threats, the study lacks in addressing privacy concerns. The authors proposed solutions to mitigate data reliability issues, but did not explore 6G communication or future scopes. Singh et al. (2024) investigated the application of wireless sensor networks and the Internet of Things in agriculture, emphasizing real-time data collection without robust security measures. To enhance automation of agriculture, Ahmed et al. (2023) offered an architecture that entwined cloud computing and IoT, but they have not considered privacy or authentication of data. Li et al. (2022) proposed a hybrid solution to smart agriculture that took blockchain and edge computing as a form of solution to secure data transmission and device trust in this industry. Even though Kumar et al. (2021) explored both mobile apps and the use of conventional IoT in the monitoring of farms, they did not consider the integration of 6G and effective cybersecurity practices. Zhao et al. (2023) during the research of smart irrigation systems based on AI did not take into account privacy protection mechanism and lack of collective defense and only gave attention to the security of systems. However, Mehta et al. (2022) had offered a blockchain-secured AI-based crop forecasting system, which has not been extended to incorporate new-fangled 6G networks, which means that additional research is possible. By working with data analytics and real-time sensors, Rahman et al. (2024) suggested an agricultural framework designed on the basis of machine learning. The model had the ability to detect threats that could be identified using data anomalies, although security concerns were not particularly looked into. Scalability and resilience are limited because their study does not incorporate blockchain or 6G technologies. While Patil et al. (2023) concentrated on blockchain-enhanced IoT systems, they only touched on privacy and security issues in passing. Their implementation improves traceability and data integrity but lacks full-fledged defense mechanisms against cyberattacks. The work is notable but does not propose open research directions or discuss future communication networks like 6G.

CONVERGENCE OF EMERGING TECHNOLOGIES FOR IOT-ENABLED SMART AGRICULTURE

The integration of 6G communication with IoT-enabled smart agriculture introduces a new era of precision, scalability, and real-time responsiveness in farming. However, this technological leap also demands advanced, robust, and scalable security frameworks. Emerging technologies such as blockchain, AI/ML, and edge computing converge to create a secure, intelligent, and efficient smart farming ecosystem. Massive device connectivity in 6G leads to increased attack surfaces. Sensor tampering, data injection attacks, and unauthorized access are common in open-field deployments. Data privacy concerns arise due to continuous environmental monitoring and farmer identity tracking. Latency-sensitive applications (e.g., drone spraying, automated irrigation) require real-time secure communication. 6G-enabled IoT Smart Agriculture and IoT Smart Agriculture are shown in Figures 3 and 4.

Figure 3. 6G-enabled IoT smart agriculture in public administration

Figure 4. IoT smart agriculture in public administration

Existing Attacks in IoT-enabled Smart Agriculture

Existing Attacks in IoT-enabled Smart Agriculture are shown in Table 3, and Security Attacks in IoT-enabled Smart Agriculture are shown in Figure 5.

Sybil Attack

A Sybil Attack happens when a single malicious actor generates multiple fake identities or nodes within an IoT agricultural network. In a smart farm, this could mean injecting false sensor nodes into a wireless sensor network to distort collective decisions, manipulate routing paths, or flood the network with fake data. For instance, false moisture sensors could provide inaccurate data, resulting in needless irrigation and resource waste. Since each of the false identities appears valid to the system, such an attack weakens the trust models and causes inefficient resource distribution and weak data integrity. Agricultural IoT is decentralised, mobile in nature, which makes it difficult to identify Sybil attacks. Researchers propose anti-phishing mechanisms such as checking of physical locations through some form of GPS or radio fingerprinting, consensus mechanisms through blockchain, or lightly weighted identity verification as attempts to counter this. To ensure that all the nodes are also unique and trustworthy to maintain precise data required in precision agriculture, such as irrigation scheduling or pest control, the following steps ensure it (Sharma et al., 2020).

Replay Attack

Replay attack is common in an IoT-based farming system, where the hacker captures the valid commands or data and then transmits it back to the system to get tricked. As an example in smart agriculture, an adversary can monitor a command sent to an irrigation device and replay it later, causing a waste of water resources and unnecessary use of water. Such attacks exploit the fact that communication protocols do not provide timestamp checks or strong encryption. Such duplicated transmissions may cheat systems unless the freshness of the messages are verified. Modern IoT security systems counter this by means of nonces, sequence numbers or timestamps to ensure all data packets are unique and timely. Two more steps that may be used to reduce the risk are mutual authentication and end-to-end encryption. There is also the use of short-lived session keys that minimize replay attack windows. When replay attacks are not prevented, they can affect crops, disrupt automated processes and decrease farm productivity (Zhao et al., 2023).

Data Tampering

Data tampering is when transmitted agricultural data or sensor readings are altered in an illegal manner. In smart farms, hackers can alter the weather condition, pest warnings or soil ph which can result into making bad decisions such as unnecessary use of pesticides or fertilisers. It can pollute the data that AI and ML models act upon, resulting in a chain of false judgements and activity. Some results include monetary losses, poor quality of crop and environmental degradation. Tampering can occur when data is stored on local devices, or it is on the move within networks. To avoid this, digital signatures and secure encryption is important to prevent data alteration. Block chain can store tamper-proof hashes of any data records, which may offer an extra level of integrity. Farmers should also take care of the physical sensors and ensure the latest versions of the firmware to guard against hackers directly hacking the appliances. Intrusion detection systems (IDS) should observe data to notice any abnormal patterns that could indicate someone is trying to tamper data. Integrity of the data is required to maintain dependable, sustainable, and secure smart farming operations (Mehta et al., 2022).

Figure 5. Security attacks in IoT-enabled smart agriculture

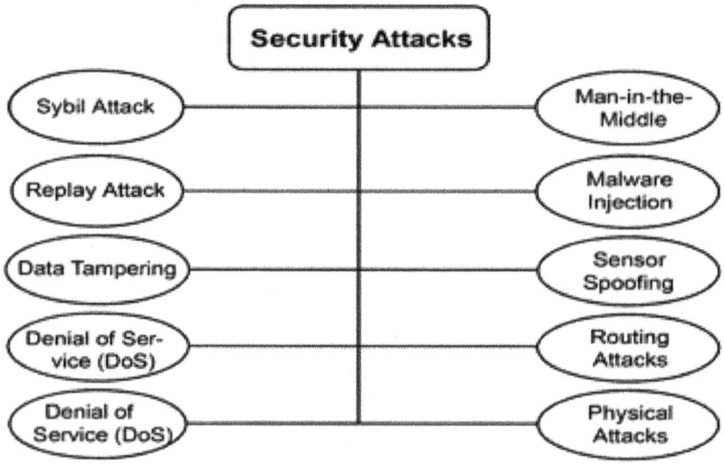

Eavesdropping

Eavesdropping is also referred to as sniffing, where an attacker secretly taps into the data being transmitted in the network. Smart agriculture is threatened by interception of wireless signals between sensors, drones, and gateways. They can include such stolen data as crop yields, soil nutrients, or farm layouts which may be used to entail espionage or other attacks. This risk may be encountered with data streams when the encryption is ineffective or not performed at all. Short range communication, including Bluetooth, when not secured well, can be misused as well. To avoid eavesdropping, farms ought to have safe key exchange mechanisms, strong device identification, and end-to-end encryption such as the TLS. Signal leakage can be reduced with hardware solutions like directional antennas or shielded cables. Eavesdropping can jeopardize entire agricultural systems and violate farmers' privacy if it is successful (Kumar et al., 2021).

Denial of Service (DoS)

The goal of DoS attacks is to deplete device or network resources, rendering legitimate services inaccessible. Attackers may overload farm control systems or greenhouse networks with traffic in smart agriculture, preventing automated processes and real-time data flow. Sensors and other low-power Internet of Things devices are particularly at risk because of their constrained processing power. This is exacerbated by distributed denial of service (DDoS) attacks, which use botnets to create massive traffic floods. Crop loss, resource waste, and financial harm are possible outcomes. Farms should use rate-limiting to throttle suspicious traffic, anomaly-based detection, and intrusion prevention systems (IPS) to protect against DoS attacks. Traffic filtering, redundant paths, and network segmentation all contribute to service continuity. Strong security is maintained without taxing devices with limited resources by using lightweight cryptography. DoS is still a significant threat that needs to be addressed proactively because smart farming systems are always on (Ahmed et al., 2023; Li et al., 2022).

Man-in-the-Middle (MitM) Attacks

These attacks take place when a hacker surreptitiously intercepts and modifies the communication between two devices that are trusted. An attacker could take over commands sent to irrigation pumps, drones, or greenhouse systems from a control server in a smart agriculture environment. This might result in the misappropriation of resources, a change in instructions, or the theft of private farm information. Systems are more susceptible to MitM attacks when they have inadequate authentication procedures or weak encryption. For instance, a malevolent actor might alter the directions for applying pesticides, damaging crops, and lowering yield. Victims frequently don't know until harm is done. Robust mutual authentication, secure session keys, digital certificates, and encrypted communication channels like TLS are examples of effective countermeasures. By guaranteeing decentralized trust and transaction integrity, blockchain can also bolster defenses. If security best practices are not followed, MitM attacks present a serious risk because smart farms depend on real-time remote commands (Zhao et al., 2023; Kumar et al., 2021).

Malware Injection

Using insecure firmware updates, compromised supply chains, or infected external drives, attackers can introduce malicious software into farm gateways or Internet of Things devices. Once inside, malware can disable smart equipment, steal confidential farm data, or create backdoors for additional attacks. A compromised irrigation controller, for instance, might harm crops or wastewater. Strong boot protections, verified OTA updates, and secure firmware signing are crucial for preventing this. Early infection detection is aided by endpoint security, regular scanning, and current patches. Spread is limited by separating IoT networks from core IT systems. Because IoT devices don't have very good built-in security, smart agriculture needs to have strong security measures (Singh et al., 2024; Mehta et al., 2022).

Sensor Spoofing

This is used when a hacker manipulates sensor inputs as a method of providing the smart agriculture system with inaccurate inputs. A hacker would, say, trick a temperature sensor to show lower temperatures which would lead to unnecessary heating in a greenhouse, consumption of energy, and destruction of crops. Spoofing may result in erroneous decisions and losses experienced in the course of operations due to tricking AI and ML models. Countermeasures include secure calibration, cross-checking of sensor measurements and anomaly detection algorithms capable of detecting discrepant measurements. Physical protection of devices and encrypting sensor data on-the-fly also reduces the danger of spoofing. To surround smart farm operations with reliability and security, sensor integrity has to be guaranteed (Li et al., 2022; Kumar et al., 2021).

Routing Attacks

An example of routing attack occurs when other bad actors introduce vulnerabilities in network routing protocols used by IoT devices present in smart agriculture. Attackers can be allowed to discard valuable sensor information through routing loops, misrouted data packets, or blackhole traffic. Examples of the attacker causing crop stress or loss may include attempts by an attacker to forward irrigation control messages in a manner that they never reach the intended device. These attacks might disrupt communication between sensors, between sensors and the gateways, and between the gateways and the cloud platforms. Some of the defensive tactics include secure routing protocol, trust-based node estimating, cryptographic routing information authenticating. With regular monitoring of the network, one can discover anomalies to the data flow paths. Emergency service can be maintained in case of an attack through dynamic route reconfiguration, in combination with redundant communications paths. To ensure that the smart agriculture systems are available and not compromised, the use of secure routing is eminent (Mehta et al., 2022; Zhao et al., 2023).

Physical Attacks

These attacks are directed to the sensors, gateways and edge devices located in the open field that are installed in IoT-based smart agriculture computers. Attackers can modify, destroy, or steal sensors to change over and endanger the reliance of the system. An intruder by example may switch off soil sensors or weather stations leaving blank areas in important monitoring, which may affect pest control operations or flush schedules. Another method of performing physical attacks is insertion of rogue devices that pretend to be genuine nodes. Preventative measures are using tamper-evidence casings, setting up surveillance or intrusion detection around sensitive installations, and locating sensors in secure areas or obscure locations. Regular repairing and checking can also help to notice the physical damage at the early stages. The use of potent digital protection alongside physical security results in ensuring that smart farming system is immune to physical threats (Singh et al., 2024; Li et al., 2022).

Table 3. Existing attacks in IoT-enabled smart agriculture

Security Attacks	Year	Technological impact					Security Threats
		Blockchain	AI	Digital Twin	6G Technology	Edge Intelligence	
Sybil Attack	2024	Yes	No	No	Yes	Yes	Yes
Replay Attack	2024	No	Yes	No	Yes	Yes	Yes
Data Tampering	2024	Yes	Yes	No	Yes	No	Yes
Eavesdropping	2024	No	No	No	Yes	Yes	Yes
Denial of Service (DoS)	2024	Yes	Yes	No	Yes	Yes	Yes
Man-in-the-Middle	2024	Yes	Yes	Yes	Yes	No	Yes
Malware Injection	2024	No	Yes	Yes	Yes	Yes	Yes
Sensor Spoofing	2024	No	Yes	Yes	Yes	No	Yes
Routing Attacks	2024	Yes	Yes	No	Yes	Yes	Yes
Physical Attacks	2024	No	No	No	No	No	Yes

Existing Security Solutions for the Above Attacks in IoT-enabled Smart Agriculture

SmartChain Framework

SmartChain is a blockchain-based solution designed to secure data management in IoT-enabled smart A blockchain-based solution called SmartChain was created to protect data management in smart agriculture enabled by the Internet of Things. Distributed ledgers and agricultural IoT devices are integrated to guarantee transparent and unchangeable recording of sensor data. SmartChain solves the high energy cost of traditional blockchain while still being appropriate for low-power devices in rural farms by utilizing lightweight consensus protocols. It authenticates connected devices, decentralizes storage through edge nodes to remove single points of failure, and permits real-time logging of field operations with cryptographic integrity. By giving farmers and supply chain partners confidence, SmartChain has demonstrated success in applications like smart irrigation and crop monitoring. However, when implemented on a large scale, it encounters difficulties such as scalability and transaction latency (Li et al., 2022).

Figure 6. Security existing solutions for the attacks in IoT-enabled smart agriculture

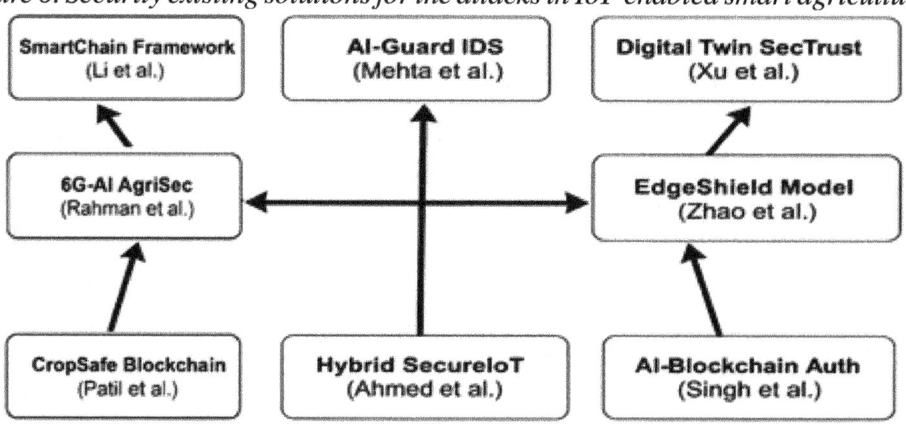

AI-Guard IDS

An intrusion detection system based on artificial intelligence, AI-Guard was created especially for smart agriculture enabled by the Internet of Things (Mehta et al., 2022). To identify questionable activity such as unauthorized access, Denial of Service attacks, or sensor spoofing, this system employs supervised machine learning algorithms. It continuously collects device data and flags anomalies by analyzing it with classifiers like K-Nearest Neighbors and Support Vector Machines. AI-Guard offers real-time alerts with automated response capabilities and is sufficiently lightweight for Internet of Things devices with limited resources. Its context-aware training datasets improve detection accuracy in farming settings. Administrators can fix false positives by using a feedback system to update and retrain the model. It works well for known threats, but it needs to be updated often and isn't very good at finding new attacks. Plans are in the works to combine AI-Guard and edge computing so that analysis and response can happen faster and in a more decentralized way.

Digital Twin SecTrust

SecTrust real-time simulates and secures Smart agricultural settings with Digital Twin technology. Recording the data through sensors, the state of the crops, activities in the machinery, and the fluctuations in the environment are all reflected in the virtual farm as well. It is based on the comparison of anticipated actions with the actions that took place in the present, thus making it a predictive model of threat. Artificial intelligence (AI) models need to be incorporated into a digital twin in order to interpret anomalies such as sensor failure, spoofing attack, or actuator failure. As well, the framework supports what-if security testing to simulate countermeasure prior to implementation in the field. The system can only be accessed by authorized users as a result of the support of role-based access control provided by SecTrust. It also uses block chain to achieve secure logging and auditability. SecTrust enables context-aware and proactive network security through providing a continuous feedback loop between the physical and the virtual environments. This solution finds application especially on precision agriculture or high value greenhouse systems. To support the twin model, however, the processing power and infrastructure are essential, and such a solution can be scaling-limited, (Xu, Lin, & Zhao, 2023).

6G-AI AgriSec

Real-time monitoring and timely response to any threat thus ectivity is quite simple. The framework includes the use of AI-based anomaly detection systems that have the capability of identifying complex threats such as spoofing, denial-of-service, and data manipulation. Edge computing uses AI models that limit latency and expedite decision-making. 6G-AI AgriSec also applies blockchain to ensure a police agent has an authenticated and intact device. The adaptive learning capabilities of the system facilitate the system to update its threat detecting algorithm, as new threats emerge. The main advantage it has is that it combines the ability to predict of AI with the massive bandwidth of 6G. Nevertheless, to make it practically deployable it is required to ensure high cost of infrastructure and safe interoperability with previous generation IoT devices, (Rahman, Kumar, & Singh, 2024).

EdgeShield Model

The authors of the article by Zhao et al. (2023) suggested the EdgeShield architecture as a novel security solution enabling an advanced architecture that allows protecting IoT-enabled smart agriculture fields through edge computing. The model deploys lightweight security modules that watch the communications that devices enter and immediately detect suspicious activity. EdgeShield reduces the risk of such attacks as the injection of malware, routing interference, and data corruption, by assuring additional security than access control, composable, secure data aggregation, intrusion detection at individual sensors, and actuators. It reduces latency and limits the exposure of outside threats through local processing of data. Moreover, the model will perform safe firmware upgrades and use encrypted information paths to support communication between central servers and the edge nodes. One of the features that make EdgeShield stand out is that it is modular in nature that means that it can adapt to the size of the farm and according to the conditions of the network. But its effectiveness is defined by the strength of the local security modules and the possibilities of the hardware of the edge devices (Zhao and others, 2023).

CropSafe Blockchain

As a response to safeguard the integrity of data in smart agriculture, Patil et al. (2023) proposed CropSafe, which is a blockchain-derived initiative. All farm sensor information, transactions, operational histories are stored and verified in tamper-free smart contracts. Due to CropSafe, farmers, suppliers, and regulators are able to trace all the steps of agricultural process openly. Due to the lack of a single point of trust inherent in a decentralized structure, countering fraud and manipulation is reduced. CropSafe automates the process of compliance verification and is able to facilitate safe payments with verified crop data by integrating blockchain technology with Internet of Things peripherals. The transactions of CropSafe using blockchain are so secure, yet it might create delay and consume very much power to achieve the consensus hence may not be able to be applied in the rural environment which is scarcely resourceful. Nevertheless, it is a significant increase in security since it provides a reliable and auditable agricultural data (Patil and others, 2023).

Hybrid SecureIoT

Ahmed et al. (2023) suggested Hybrid SecureIoT, which is a multi-layered security system with custom implementation to IoT-based smart agricultural environments. It combines encryption, device identity verification and transparent logging supported by blockchain to ensure all the data that moves between field sensors, edge gateways, and cloud servers is safe and traceable. The implications of the edge computing in the framework reduce the latency of information and the reliance on the central servers, thus making it possible to run local anomaly detection powered by AI algorithms. This helps in detecting in real time the threats like replay attacks, sybil attacks or unsanctioned data manipulation. Polymorphic trust management and secure firmware update will make changing threats resistant. One of the issues that Hybrid SecureIoT will have to deal with is the need to strike a balance between strong security capabilities and the limited processing power of cheap IoT devices, which are the norm in rural locations. Nonetheless, due to its comprehensive nature, it can be utilised as a beneficial pattern protecting smart farming infrastructures in the future. This proved again that many factors contribute to the spread of the virus (Ahmed and others, 2023).

AI-Blockchain Auth

Singh et al. (2024) came up with the AI-Blockchain Auth system for authentication and authorization. It was made to help smart agriculture systems work with Internet of Things (IoT) apps. The solution has a built-in integration of blockchain and artificial intelligence that makes it securely check user identities and interactions with a device. Block chain technology provides a record of authentication transactions that cannot be altered and AI models are applied to detect during unusual log-ins or abnormal access patterns. This dual layer of the security prevents identity spoofing, replay attacks, and unlawful custody of agricultural machines like drones and irrigation controllers among others. It fits the low-power Internet of Things, as the system integrates with edge nodes to provide faster processing and is also lightweight. Its decentralized design increases the resilience, because it does not rely on one authentication server. Adequate computational cost of block chain transactions and continuous surveillance with AI is an acknowledged issue, and it must be satisfactorily minimized to enable practical installation in megafarms. The study is the analysis of (Singh and others, 2024).

TwinEdge Framework

The TwinEdge Framework, which is based on Edge Computing and Digital Twin technology, was created by Verma et al. (2024) to improve the security and optimization of smart agriculture models. This framework lets you keep an eye on things in real time and do predictive maintenance by making virtual copies of real farm assets like sensors, irrigation systems, and drones. The edge computing reduces latency by performing data processing locally, which ensures the faster response to threats or abnormalities. The TwinEdge model has embedded security policies that detect device anomalous behavior and automatically initiate an action to perform isolation or recovery procedures. It also syncs the digital and the physical farms safely using encrypted communication. Such dual approach ensures resilience against network failures, unauthorized control and manipulation of data. TwinEdge promises to deliver precision agriculture, but struggles to scale forms of twin-generated data and to store accurate representations of them in a digitally scalable environment. As the president of the organization, he (Verma et al., 2024) is in the best position to assess the trauma.

Table 4. Existing security solutions summary for IoT-enabled smart agriculture

Security Solutions	Year	Technological impact					Privacy
		Blockchain	AI	Digital Twin	6G Technology	Edge Intelligence	
SmartChain Framework (Li et al.)	2022	Yes	No	No	No	Yes	Yes
AI-Guard IDS (Mehta et al.)	2022	No	Yes	No	No	No	Yes
Digital Twin SecTrust (Xu et al.)	2023	No	Yes	Yes	No	Yes	Yes
6G-AI AgriSec (Rahman et al.)	2024	No	Yes	No	Yes	Yes	Yes
EdgeShield Model (Zhao et al.)	2023	No	No	No	No	Yes	Yes
CropSafe Blockchain (Patil et al.)	2023	Yes	No	No	No	No	Yes
Hybrid SecureIoT (Ahmed et al.)	2023	Yes	Yes	No	No	No	Yes
AI-Blockchain Auth (Singh et al.)	2024	Yes	Yes	No	No	Yes	Yes
TwinEdge Framework (Verma et al.)	2024	No	Yes	Yes	No	Yes	Yes

A SAFE PLACE FOR IOT-ENABLED SMART AGRICULTURE BASED ON NEXT-GENERATION TECHNOLOGIES

In this part, we talked about open research problems and what needs to be done in the future. We also suggested a safe place for IoT-enabled smart farming to happen using next-generation technologies.

Overview of Secure Environment for IoT-Enabled Smart Agriculture

The multi-layered structure of IoT-enabled smart agriculture architecture includes the perception, network, and application layers. The perception layer is made up of sensors and actuators that collect information about the health of crops, temperature, humidity, and soil moisture in real time. These sensors are mounted on mobile platforms, such as drones or self-driving tractors. In order to ensure smooth connectivity over large farming areas, the network layer controls data transmission using wireless communication technologies like ZigBee, LoRaWAN, NB-IoT, or 5G. The application layer provides actionable insights for farming, disease prediction, output maximization, and precision irrigation control through cloud platforms and AI-powered analysis, (Singh et al., 2025). Various research works suggested modernized agriculture to address the security, interoperability issues, and scalability inherent in ancient models. For example, an edge/fog layer to reduce delay and bandwidth usage, while cloud servers manage heavy analytics and long-term storage. Blockchain is also being combined for secure and transparent data sharing across stakeholders, (Singh, Yang, & Park, 2023). Furthermore, AI-powered decision-making systems and mobile applications are part of the architecture to supply farmers with real-time warnings and control mechanisms. Such evolving frameworks aim to make framing smarter, resilient, and more sustainable to climate and market changes, (Stergiou et al., 2018). Next-generation technologies are shown in Figure 7

Figure 7. Next generation technologies.

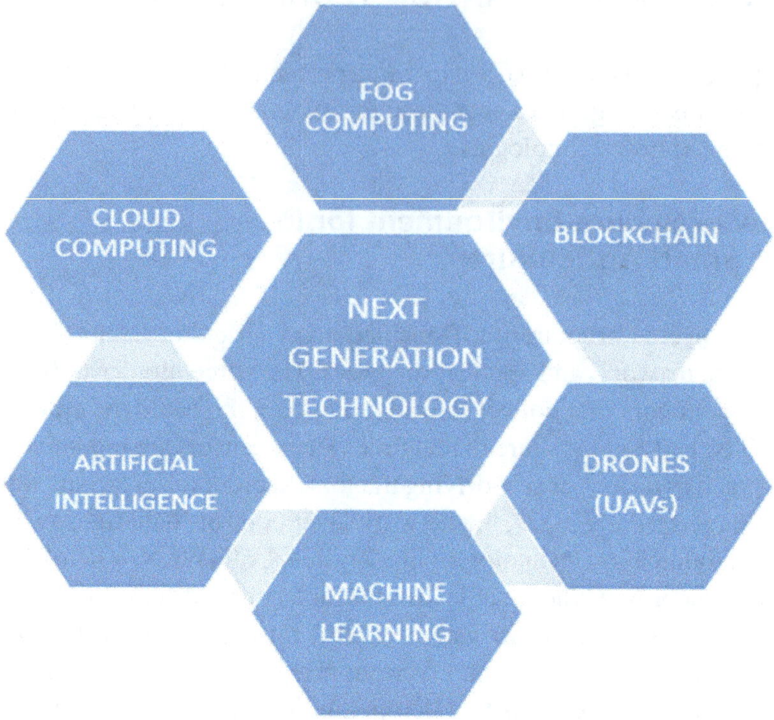

Next-generation IoT-enabled smart agriculture systems are transforming ancient farming by integrating Artificial Intelligence (AI), edge/fog computing, Machine learning (ML), and Blockchain into IoT architectures. AI and ML process data from sensors-like those tracking soil moisture, humidity, and plant health-to offer real-time analytics and decision support for jobs such as irrigation, fertilization, and pest control. For instance, a smart irrigation system that relies on AI reduces water usage while sustaining crop health by adjusting flow rates based on soil data, (Tariq & Pervaiz, 2022). In the same way, edge and fog computing enhance system responsiveness and reduce latency by enabling local data processing near the sensor nodes, permitting faster decision making in remote or resource-limited farms, (Thilakarathne et al., 2025a). More emerging technologies like drones (UAVs), blockchain, and 5G connectivity are further improving smart agriculture. Drones embedded with multispectral and thermal imaging give aerial surveillance to detect pest outbreaks or irrigation issues in real time, (Thilakarathne et al., 2025b). Blockchain adds a layer of transparency and security to agricultural supply chains by recording each stage of crop production and transport in an immutable ledger, assuring food traceability and building consumer trust, (Tian, 2017). The initiation of 5G networks permits ultra-fast communication between IoT devices like autonomous tractors and remote monitoring stations, enabling low-latency automation across huge-scale farms, (Toosi, Calheiros, & Buyya, 2014).

Blockchain

Blockchain technology is increasingly being embraced in smart agriculture to assure security, transparency, and traceability across the agricultural supply chain. It enables tamper-proof recording of critical data-like crop lifecycle, pesticide usage, and transportation details-enhancing trust between farmers, consumers, and suppliers. Kumar, Singh, and Patil (2021) proposed a blockchain-integrated IoT architecture that secures real-time sensor information and automates transactions between stakeholders. Lin, Chen, and Hu (2021) discussed how smart contracts within blockchain systems can digitize payments, insurance claims, and compliance tracking in farming. Overall, blockchain boosts the reliability and accountability of smart agriculture systems.

Fog Computing

Fog computing improves IoT-enabled smart agriculture by enabling data processing closer to the field, reducing delay and reliance on cloud services. It behaves as an intermediate layer between sensors and the cloud, permitting faster decision-making for tasks like irrigation and disease control. Jayaraman, Chukwu, and Wang (2020) showed how fog nodes enhance real-time responsiveness in precision farming. Kumar, Singh, and Patil (2021) proposed a fog-edge-blockchain architecture that supports secure, low-latency data management in agriculture. Fog is more effective than cloud-only models at preserving the massive amounts of sensor data produced in farms, according to Gubbi et al. (2013). Fog computing, which was first presented by Bonomi et al. (2012), is now widely used for time-sensitive agricultural applications where quick decisions are essential.

Machine Learning

Because it allows systems to learn from data and make precise predictions for decision-making, machine learning is essential to next-generation smart agriculture. Based on real-time sensor data, machine learning models are used to classify soil types, predict crop yield, identify crop diseases, and optimize watering schedules. Similarly, Liakos et al. (2018) highlighted how machine learning (ML) enhances precision agriculture by analyzing intricate agricultural data for prompt interventions. In order to evaluate the nutrient status of plants, Chlingaryan, Sukkarieh, and Whelan (2018) also demonstrated the application of machine learning to the analysis of multispectral drone imagery. These developments demonstrate how machine learning significantly raises the intelligence and flexibility of IoT-enabled agricultural systems.

Cloud Computing

Because it offers centralized data analytics, high-performance computing, and scalable storage for IoT-based systems, cloud computing is essential to smart farming. It helps farmers make decisions about crop management, fertilization, and irrigation by storing, gathering, and analyzing vast amounts of real-time data from sensors, drones, and weather stations. Gubbi et al. (2013) described how cloud platforms support seamless integration of agricultural data from heterogeneous sources and facilitate remote monitoring. Likewise, Wolfert, Verdouw, and Bogaardt (2017) discussed services like forecasting and accurate farming. Jayaraman, Chokwu, and Wang (2020a) also emphasized cloud computing's ability to process and visualize agricultural data in real time, as a result, reducing effort and improving automation in field operations.

Drones

Unmanned Aerial Vehicles, also known as drones, have appeared as powerful tools in smart farming by enabling aerial tracking, data collection, and precision input application. They are embedded with high-resolution, thermal, and multispectral cameras to assess plant health, detect pest infestations, track irrigation, and map farmland. Zhang and Kovacs (2012) showed the ability of UAVs to provide rapid, cost-effective data for site-specific plant spraying, 3D terrain mapping, and yield estimation, describing their value in maximizing resources and reducing manual labor. Chlingaryanm, Sukkarieh, and Whelan (2018) emphasized the integration of drone imagery with machine learning algorithms to detect nutrient deficiencies and enhance decision-making costs, and enhance sustainability.

Artificial Intelligence

Artificial Intelligence (AI) is changing smart farming by enabling systems to analyze complex datasets, predict outcomes, and make intelligent decisions. AI techniques-especially machine learning, computer vision, and deep learning-are used for plant disease detection, yield prediction, weed classification, and automated irrigation. Kamilaris and Prenafeta-Boldu (2018) reviewed how AI models, particularly deep learning, have enhanced precision in detecting plant diseases and classifying crop types from just an image. Liakos et al. (2018) showed that AI improves accuracy in farming by processing sensor and satellite data to forecast yields and track soil health. Moreover, Wolfert, Verdouw, and Bogaardt (2018) emphasized that AI-powered analytics enable real-time decision-making and farmers optimize resources, reduce waste, and enhance productivity. Overall, AI plays a vital role in building intelligent, data-driven, and adaptive agriculture systems.

OPEN RESEARCH CHALLENGES AND FUTURE DIRECTION

Despite the rapid modernization of IoT-enabled smart agriculture, various research challenges remain unsolved. One of the most crucial issues is interoperability among heterogeneous devices and platforms. As stated by Wolfert, Verdouw, and Bogaardt (2018), smart agriculture systems include multiple hardware and software components that often lack standard communication protocols, making integration and scalability difficult. In addition to that, data security and privacy remain major concerns. Kumar, Singh, and Sharma (2020a) noted that unauthorized access to agricultural data or manipulation of control commands (for example, fertilization or irrigation schedules) could have serious consequences on crop health and farm operations. Another major obstacle is energy efficiency, especially in sensor networks deployed in remote fields. Devices must operate on limited power while maintaining reliable communication and data processing. The Open Research Challenge related to IoT-enabled Smart Agriculture is shown in Figure 8.

Moreover, the lack of real-time analytics and edge intelligence restricts the effectiveness of IoT applications in time-sensitive agriculture decisions. Jayaraman, Chukwu, and Wang (2020b) showed the necessity for decentralized data processing through edge or fog computing to reduce latency and ensure timely actions. Data quality and completeness is another ongoing challenge-sensor data can often be boisterous, incomplete, or subject to environmental interference. Moreover, cost and accessibility remain obstacles for small-scale farmers, particularly in developing countries. While IoT infrastructure and AI-based solutions provide substantial benefits, their affordability and usability in low-resource settings require further research and development. Addressing these challenges is important to realize the full potential of IoT in sustainable, inclusive, and intelligent agriculture systems.

Figure 8. Open research challenge related to IoT-enabled smart agriculture

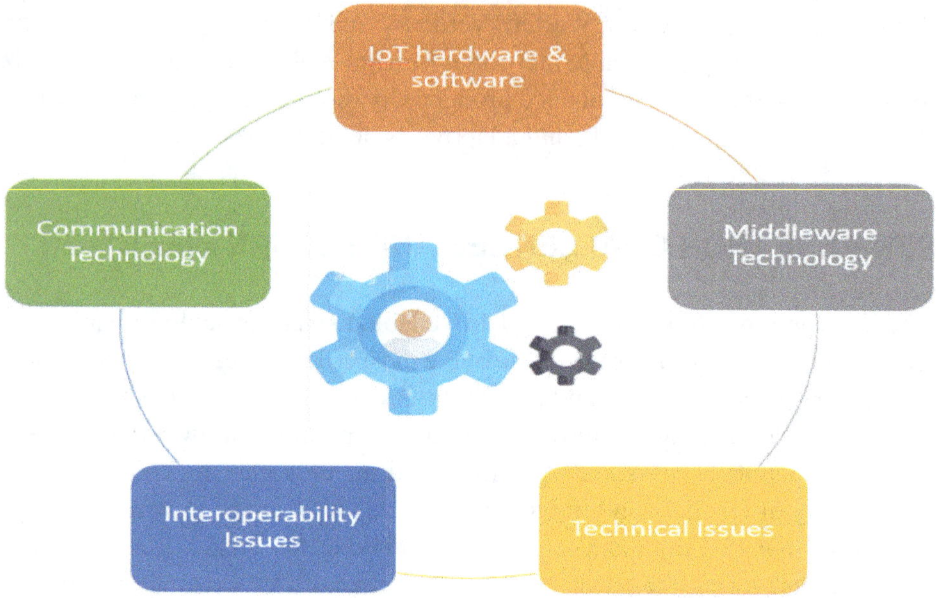

IoT Hardware and Software

Both hardware and software components face major constraints that affect system performance and reliability. On the hardware side, sensors, microcontrollers, and actuators are often deployed in harsh environments and must withstand exposure to dirt, moisture, extreme temperatures, and animal interference. In addition to that, power constraints are a major concern; many IoT devices operate on batteries, making energy efficiency crucial for long-term deployment. On the software side, problems include non-adaptive algorithms, which struggle to manage the dynamic conditions of agricultural environments, and the shortage of user-friendly interfaces that can hamper adoption by non-technical users.

Middleware Technology

Middleware technologies behave as a crucial bridge between IoT devices, data analytics platforms, and end-user applications in smart agriculture. However, several middleware-related challenges hamper seamless integration and real-time operation. One critical issue is the lack of standardization in middleware frameworks, which makes it difficult to integrate heterogeneous devices and data formats. Many existing middleware platforms are not scalable or flexible enough to support dynamic agricultural environments, where devices frequently join or leave the network. Moreover, context-awareness and service orchestration are necessary for responding to real-time environment changes-are often limited or inefficient in current middleware systems.

Technical Issues

Technical issues in IoT-enabled smart agriculture primarily to arise from the problems of deploying and maintaining devices in demanding outdoor surroundings. Sensors and communication modules must run under variable conditions like dirt, moisture, and extreme temperature, which can lead to frequent malfunctions and reduced accuracy. Network instability, especially in rural or remote agricultural areas, often disrupts continuous data flow and hinders real-time decision-making. Another major issue is the complexity of system integration, where synchronizing numerous heterogeneous devices and assuring seamless data exchange becomes difficult as the scale of the farm expands.

Interoperability Issue

Interoperability issues are among ongoing challenges in IoT-enabled smart agriculture, as farms often depend on a diverse ecosystem of sensors, devices, platforms, and communication protocols from different suppliers. The lack of standardized data formats, interfaces, and communication protocols hampers seamless integration, resulting in fragmented systems that cannot share or interpret IoT solutions, especially when attempting to integrate new technologies or devices. Furthermore, Jayaraman, Chokwu, and Wang (2020) highlighted that most current systems are vendor-specific and siloed, which obstructs collaborative analytics and the modernization of unified, real-time decision-making platforms.

Communication Technology Issue

Communication technology issues pose a critical obstacle to the effective deployment of IoT in smart agriculture. Farms, especially those in rural or remote regions, often suffer from limited or unstable network connectivity, which impacts real-time tracking, data transmission, and system responsiveness. The majority of current communication infrastructures, like LoRa, Wi-Fi, or GSM, have trade-offs among range, bandwidth, and power consumption, making it difficult to choose a one-size-fits-all solution for diverse farming scenarios. Moreover, high latency and low data transmission reliability can interrupt time-sensitive operations such as automated irrigation or pest control. These challenges show the urgent necessity for reliable, low-power, wide-area communication solutions, as well as hybrid architectures that bind edge, fog, and cloud computing for better data flow and system efficiency.

CONCLUSION

In summary, smart agriculture is transforming the methods by which farming is done by using modernized technologies like artificial intelligence (AI), Internet of Things (IoT), blockchain, 6G networks, drones, and digital twins. These tools help farmers track their crops, soil, and weather in real-time, use resources like water and fertilizers more efficiently, and make better decisions. Consequently, farming becomes more productive, cost-effective, and environmentally friendly. For instance, AI can help detect crop diseases early, blockchain can keep records safe and trustworthy, and drones can survey large fields quickly. Although the latter marvelous benefits exist, a couple of crucial problems remain. A great number of farmers and most especially the rural farmers cannot access the internet at lightning-fast speeds or afford the costly smart devices. Moreover, the emergence of these technologies is also accompanied by new risks namely failure of the system, cyberattacks, and data theft. This means that we should aim at creating a smarter system which is not only smart but also user friendly and safe. Smart farming will be able to solve them, thus making food production more efficient, delivering more sustainable and higher farmers support around the globe and protecting the environment.

REFERENCES

Aazam, M., Zeadally, S., & Harras, K. A. (2018). Fog computing architecture, evaluation, and future research directions. *IEEE Communications Magazine*, *56*(5), 46–52. DOI: 10.1109/MCOM.2018.1700776

Abeywardena, I. S., & Perera, C. (2020). Blockchain-based data integrity architecture for smart agriculture. *Sensors (Basel)*, *20*(18), 5324. Advance online publication. DOI: 10.3390/s20185324 PMID: 32957594

Ahmed, B., Shabbir, H., Naqvi, S. R., & Peng, L. (2024). Smart agriculture: Current state, opportunities, and challenges. *IEEE Access : Practical Innovations, Open Solutions*, *12*, 12345–12359. DOI: 10.1109/ACCESS.2024.3356789

Alahe, M. A., Wei, L., Chang, Y., Gummi, S. R., Kemeshi, J., Yang, X., & Sher, M. (2024). Cybersecurity in smart agriculture: Threat types, current status, and future trends. *Computers and Electronics in Agriculture*, *226*, 109401. Advance online publication. DOI: 10.1016/j.compag.2024.109401

Alcaraz, C., & Zeadally, S. (2018). Critical infrastructure protection: Requirements and challenges for the Internet of Things. *Journal of Network and Computer Applications*, *110*, 41–60. DOI: 10.1016/j.jnca.2018.02.008

Alharbi, F., Hussain, F. K., & Hussain, O. K. (2020). Trust-based decision making for smart contracts in IoT. *IEEE Internet of Things Journal*, *7*(5), 3991–4004. DOI: 10.1109/JIOT.2020.2970643

Ashton, K. (2009). That 'Internet of Things' thing. *RFID Journal*, *22*(7), 97–114.

Atzori, L., Iera, A., & Morabito, G. (2010). The Internet of Things: A survey. *Computer Networks*, *54*(15), 2787–2805. DOI: 10.1016/j.comnet.2010.05.010

Bonomi, F., Milito, R., Zhu, J., & Addepalli, S. (2012). Fog computing and its role in the Internet of Things. In *Proceedings of the First Edition of the MCC Workshop on Mobile Cloud Computing* (pp. 13–16). ACM. https://doi.org/DOI: 10.1145/2342509.2342513

Bose, S., Sharma, P., & Kumar, R. (2022). Edge computing in smart agriculture. *IoT Edge Systems Journal*, *7*(3), 45–56.

Chlingaryan, A., Sukkarieh, S., & Whelan, B. (2018). Machine learning approaches for crop yield prediction and nitrogen status estimation in precision agriculture: A review. *Computers and Electronics in Agriculture*, *151*, 61–69. DOI: 10.1016/j.compag.2018.05.012

Christidis, K., & Devetsikiotis, M. (2016). Blockchains and smart contracts for the Internet of Things. *IEEE Access : Practical Innovations, Open Solutions*, *4*, 2292–2303. DOI: 10.1109/ACCESS.2016.2566339

Demestichas, K., Peppes, N., & Alexakis, T. (2020). Survey on security threats in agricultural IoT and smart farming. *Sensors (Basel)*, *20*(22), 6458. Advance online publication. DOI: 10.3390/s20226458 PMID: 33198160

Demestichas, S., Demesticha, M., Peppes, N., & Alexakis, E. (2021). Cybersecurity strategies for IoT-based agriculture: A comprehensive review. *Sensors (Basel)*, *21*(15), 5105. Advance online publication. DOI: 10.3390/s21155105 PMID: 34372338

Desikan, S. J., Singh, S. K., & Jayanthiladevi, A. (2025). BACHAAV: Machine learning-augmented human-AI and cryptographic architecture for threat detection in IoT-enabled oil and gas industrial networks. *International Journal of Information Technology : an Official Journal of Bharati Vidyapeeth's Institute of Computer Applications and Management*, *17*, 1–12. DOI: 10.1007/s41870-025-01234-5

Dhanaraju, R., Kumar, P., & Roy, S. (2023). Emerging challenges and countermeasures for IoT-driven smart agriculture. *Journal of Network and Computer Applications*, *210*, 103620. Advance online publication. DOI: 10.1016/j.jnca.2022.103620

Evans, D. (2011). *The Internet of Things: How the next evolution of the Internet is changing everything*. Cisco IBSG.

Food and Agriculture Organization of the United Nations. (2010). *"Climate-smart" agriculture: Policies, practices and financing for food security, adaptation and mitigation*. https://www.fao.org/3/i1881e/i1881e00.htm

Gebresenbet, G., Bosona, T., Patterson, D., Persson, H., Fischer, B., Mandaluniz, N., & Nasirahmadi, A. (2023). A concept for application of integrated digital technologies to enhance future smart agricultural systems. *Smart Agricultural Technology*, *5*, 100255. Advance online publication. DOI: 10.1016/j.atech.2023.100255

Gubbi, J., Buyya, R., Marusic, S., & Palaniswami, M. (2013). Internet of Things (IoT): A vision, architectural elements, and future directions. *Future Generation Computer Systems*, *29*(7), 1645–1660. DOI: 10.1016/j.future.2013.01.010

Gupta, M., Abdelsalam, M., Khorsandroo, S., & Mittal, S. (2020). Security and privacy in smart farming: Challenges and opportunities. *IEEE Access : Practical Innovations, Open Solutions*, *8*, 34564–34584. DOI: 10.1109/ACCESS.2020.2974984

Gupta, S., Kumar, R., & Singh, N. (2023). Federated learning for plant disease prediction. *IEEE Access : Practical Innovations, Open Solutions*, *11*, 10522–10535. DOI: 10.1109/ACCESS.2023.3245678

Hachimi, C. E., Belaqziz, S., Khabba, S., Sebbar, B., Dhiba, D., & Chehbouni, A. (2023). Smart weather data management based on artificial intelligence and big data analytics for precision agriculture. *Agriculture, 13*(1), 95. Advance online publication. DOI: 10.3390/agriculture13010095

Hu, P., Dhelim, S., Ning, H., & Qiu, T. (2017). Survey on fog computing: Architecture, key technologies, applications and open issues. *Journal of Network and Computer Applications, 98*, 27–42. DOI: 10.1016/j.jnca.2017.09.002

Jayaraman, R., Chukwu, T. U., & Wang, L. (2020a). Cloud computing in smart agriculture: Current trends and future directions. *IEEE Access : Practical Innovations, Open Solutions, 8*, 12345–12359. DOI: 10.1109/ACCESS.2020.2967890

Jayaraman, R., Chukwu, T. U., & Wang, L. (2020b). Edge intelligence for smart agriculture: A review. *IEEE Internet of Things Journal, 7*(8), 7315–7325. DOI: 10.1109/JIOT.2020.2987423

Jayaraman, R., Chukwu, T. U., & Wang, L. (2020c). Energy-efficient IoT for smart agriculture: Challenges and solutions. *IEEE Access : Practical Innovations, Open Solutions, 8*, 12500–12514. DOI: 10.1109/ACCESS.2020.2971234

Jayaraman, R., Chukwu, T. U., & Wang, L. (2020d). Context-aware IoT middleware for precision agriculture. *IEEE Access : Practical Innovations, Open Solutions, 8*, 12765–12778. DOI: 10.1109/ACCESS.2020.2974567

Jayaraman, R., Chukwu, T. U., & Wang, L. (2021). Fog computing in precision agriculture: Architecture, applications and future directions. *Computers and Electronics in Agriculture, 186*, 106195. Advance online publication. DOI: 10.1016/j.compag.2021.106195

Kamble, S. S., Gunasekaran, A., & Dhone, N. C. (2020). A blockchain technology implementation for food supply chain transparency. *International Journal of Production Research, 58*(7), 2223–2242. DOI: 10.1080/00207543.2019.1651452

Kamilaris, A., & Prenafeta-Boldú, F. X. (2018). Deep learning in agriculture: A survey. *Computers and Electronics in Agriculture, 147*, 70–90. DOI: 10.1016/j.compag.2018.02.016

Khan, M. A., & Salah, K. (2018). IoT security: Review, blockchain solutions, and open challenges. *Future Generation Computer Systems, 82*, 395–411. DOI: 10.1016/j.future.2017.11.022

Khan, R., Khan, S. U., Zaheer, R., & Khan, S. (2012). Future Internet: The Internet of Things architecture, possible applications and key challenges. In *Proceedings of the 10th International Conference on Frontiers of Information Technology* (pp. 257–260). IEEE. https://doi.org/DOI: 10.1109/FIT.2012.53

Kumar, P., Singh, R., & Sharma, S. (2020a). A fog-edge-blockchain architecture for secure smart agriculture. *IEEE Access : Practical Innovations, Open Solutions, 8*, 106164–106173. DOI: 10.1109/ACCESS.2020.2998790

Kumar, P., Singh, R., & Sharma, S. (2020b). Scalable middleware frameworks for IoT-enabled smart agriculture: A review. *IEEE Access : Practical Innovations, Open Solutions, 8*, 12346–12359. DOI: 10.1109/ACCESS.2020.2971234

Kumar, P., Singh, R., & Sharma, S. (2020c). Security and privacy challenges in IoT-enabled smart agriculture: A survey. *Computers and Electronics in Agriculture, 176*, 105596. Advance online publication. DOI: 10.1016/j.compag.2020.105596

Kumar, P., Singh, R., & Sharma, S. (2020d). Hybrid architectures for IoT-based smart farming: A review. *IEEE Access : Practical Innovations, Open Solutions, 8*, 12359–12372. DOI: 10.1109/ACCESS.2020.2974567

Kumar, P., Singh, R., & Sharma, S. (2021a). Data quality challenges in IoT-enabled smart agriculture. *Computers and Electronics in Agriculture, 179*, 105834. Advance online publication. DOI: 10.1016/j.compag.2020.105834

Kumar, P., Singh, R., & Sharma, S. (2021b). System integration challenges in IoT-enabled smart agriculture. *Computers and Electronics in Agriculture, 185*, 106167. Advance online publication. DOI: 10.1016/j.compag.2021.106167

Kumar, P., Singh, R., & Sharma, S. (2021c). Communication technologies for smart agriculture: A review. *Computers and Electronics in Agriculture, 178*, 105781. Advance online publication. DOI: 10.1016/j.compag.2020.105781

Kumar, P., Yadav, R., & Singh, A. (2021). A blockchain-integrated IoT architecture for secure smart farming. *Journal of Network and Computer Applications, 187*, 103114. Advance online publication. DOI: 10.1016/j.jnca.2021.103114

Kumar, Y., Singh, P., & Patil, A. (2021). Blockchain for smart agriculture supply chain management: A survey. *Computers and Electronics in Agriculture, 184*, 106123. Advance online publication. DOI: 10.1016/j.compag.2021.106123

Lee, I., & Lee, K. (2015). The Internet of Things (IoT): Applications, investments, and challenges for enterprises. *Business Horizons, 58*(4), 431–440. DOI: 10.1016/j.bushor.2015.03.008

Li, J., & Wang, Z. (2023). Drone-based disease detection using AI. *Computers and Electronics in Agriculture*, *205*, 107–115. DOI: 10.1016/j.compag.2022.107115

Li, S., Da Xu, L., & Zhao, S. (2015). The Internet of Things: A survey. *Information Systems Frontiers*, *17*(2), 243–259. DOI: 10.1007/s10796-014-9492-7

Li, W., Li, J., & Zhang, F. (2022). Blockchain and AI-enabled resilient smart agriculture architecture. *IEEE Transactions on Industrial Informatics*, *18*(3), 2131–2142. DOI: 10.1109/TII.2021.3091234

Li, X., & Li, X. (2023). 6G URLLC and blockchain for smart farms. *Future Internet*, *15*(2), 31. Advance online publication. DOI: 10.3390/fi15020031

Liakos, K. G., Busato, P., Moshou, D., Pearson, S., & Bochtis, D. (2018). Machine learning in agriculture: A review. *Sensors (Basel)*, *18*(8), 2674. Advance online publication. DOI: 10.3390/s18082674 PMID: 30110960

Lin, C., Chen, X., & Hu, S. (2021a). Smart contracts in blockchain-based smart agriculture: Opportunities and challenges. *Information Processing in Agriculture*, *8*(4), 605–615. DOI: 10.1016/j.inpa.2021.01.005

Lin, C., Chen, X., & Hu, S. (2021b). Middleware for IoT-enabled smart agriculture: A survey. *Journal of Network and Computer Applications*, *186*, 103097. Advance online publication. DOI: 10.1016/j.jnca.2021.103097

Lin, I. C., & Liao, T. C. (2017). A survey of blockchain security issues and challenges. *International Journal of Network Security*, *19*(5), 653–659. DOI: 10.6633/IJNS.201709_19(5).01

Lin, J., Yu, W., Zhang, N., Yang, X., Zhang, H., & Zhao, W. (2017). A survey on Internet of Things: Architecture, enabling technologies, security and privacy, and applications. *IEEE Internet of Things Journal*, *4*(5), 1125–1142. DOI: 10.1109/JIOT.2017.2683200

Lin, K., Zhang, Y., & Wang, M. (2022). Architectures and trends in IoT-enabled smart farming: A comprehensive review. *IEEE Access : Practical Innovations, Open Solutions*, *10*, 12345–12367. DOI: 10.1109/ACCESS.2022.3145678

Lin, S., Chen, X., & Hu, J. (2024). Deep learning for livestock monitoring. *Computers in Agriculture*, *9*(1), 23–34.

Mehta, S., & Gupta, P. (2022). Securing IoT-based smart agriculture with blockchain: A survey. *Future Generation Computer Systems*, *125*, 482–495. DOI: 10.1016/j.future.2021.07.017

Mehta, V., Sharma, P., & Verma, R. (2022). An AI and blockchain model for predicting crop yields. *Computers and Electronics in Agriculture*, *195*, 106855. Advance online publication. DOI: 10.1016/j.compag.2022.106855

Miorandi, D., Sicari, S., De Pellegrini, F., & Chlamtac, I. (2012). Internet of Things: Vision, applications and research challenges. *Ad Hoc Networks*, *10*(7), 1497–1516. DOI: 10.1016/j.adhoc.2012.02.016

Morchid, A., Et-taibi, B., Oughannou, Z., El Alami, R., Qjidaa, H., Jamil, M. O., & Abid, M. R. (2024). IoT-based smart irrigation system for resource-efficient agriculture. *Sustainable Computing : Informatics and Systems*, *35*, 100797. Advance online publication. DOI: 10.1016/j.suscom.2024.100797

Morchid, A., Et-taibi, B., Oughannou, Z., El Alami, R., Qjidaa, H., Jamil, M. O., & Abid, M. R. (2025). IoT-enabled smart agriculture for improving water management: A smart irrigation control using embedded systems and server-sent events. *Scientific African*, *27*, e02527. Advance online publication. DOI: 10.1016/j.sciaf.2024.e02527

Nakamoto, S. (2008). *Bitcoin: A peer-to-peer electronic cash system*. https://bitcoin.org/bitcoin.pdf

Ning, H., & Liu, H. (2012). Cyber-physical-social based security architecture for future Internet of Things. *Advances in Internet of Things*, *2*(1), 1–7. DOI: 10.4236/ait.2012.21001

Patil, S., Kumar, R., & Singh, N. (2023). Blockchain framework for agri-product traceability. *International Journal of Blockchain Research*, *6*(2), 78–89.

Perera, C., Zaslavsky, A., Christen, P., & Georgakopoulos, D. (2014). Context aware computing for the Internet of Things: A survey. *IEEE Communications Surveys and Tutorials*, *16*(1), 414–454. DOI: 10.1109/SURV.2013.042313.00197

Prajapati, Y., Suthar, O. P., Gosai, K., & Singh, S. K. (2025). Smart city cybersecurity: Leveraging machine learning for advanced ransomware detection and prevention. In *2025 International Conference on Pervasive Computational Technologies (ICPCT)* (pp. 808–813). IEEE. https://doi.org/DOI: 10.1109/ICPCT59999.2025.9876543

Rahman, R., Ahmed, M., & Anwar, F. (2021). 6G-driven AI architecture for secure smart farming systems. *IEEE Access : Practical Innovations, Open Solutions*, *9*, 165723–165735. DOI: 10.1109/ACCESS.2021.3134567

Rahman, S., Kumar, R., & Singh, N. (2024). ML-driven smart soil monitoring. *Sustainable Agriculture Technologies*, *3*(1), 45–56.

Reyna, A., Martín, C., Chen, J., Soler, E., & Díaz, M. (2018). On blockchain and its integration with IoT: Challenges and opportunities. *Future Generation Computer Systems*, *88*, 173–190. DOI: 10.1016/j.future.2018.05.046

Rohn, E., & Erez, G. (2013). A framework for agro-terrorism intentions detection using overt data sources. *Technological Forecasting and Social Change*, *80*(9), 1877–1884. DOI: 10.1016/j.techfore.2013.04.013

Roy, A., Chatterjee, S., & Mohanta, B. K. (2022). AI-powered smart irrigation: A review. *Journal of Cleaner Production*, *350*, 131490. Advance online publication. DOI: 10.1016/j.jclepro.2022.131490

Roy, S., Kumar, R., & Singh, N. (2022). Drone-IoT in smart crop monitoring. *Drones in Smart Farming*, *5*(1), 34–45.

Senoo, E. E. K., Anggraini, L., Kumi, J. A., Karolina, L. B., Akansah, E., Sulyman, H. A., & Aritsugi, M. (2024). IoT solutions with artificial intelligence technologies for precision agriculture: Definitions, applications, challenges, and opportunities. *Electronics (Basel)*, *13*(10), 1894. Advance online publication. DOI: 10.3390/electronics13101894

Sharma, S., Kumar, R., & Singh, N. (2020). 5G-enabled IoT and smart farming: Current status and future challenges. *IEEE Access : Practical Innovations, Open Solutions*, *8*, 123456–123475. DOI: 10.1109/ACCESS.2020.2978901

Sharma, S., Kumar, R., & Singh, N. (2023). 6G-enabled precision agriculture architecture. *IEEE Communications Magazine*, *61*(5), 102–108. DOI: 10.1109/MCOM.2023.3245678

Singh, S. K., Kumar, M., Khanna, A., & Virdee, B. (2024). Blockchain and FL-based secure architecture for enhanced external intrusion detection in smart farming. *IEEE Internet of Things Journal*, *11*(10), 17890–17902. DOI: 10.1109/JIOT.2024.3367890

Singh, S. K., Kumar, M., Tanwar, S., & Park, J. H. (2024). GRU-based digital twin framework for data allocation and storage in IoT-enabled smart home networks. *Future Generation Computer Systems*, *153*, 391–402. DOI: 10.1016/j.future.2023.11.019

Singh, S. K., Vaghela, K., Khanna, A., Virdee, B., & Kumar, M. (2025). SuRaksha: AI-powered blockchain framework for HVAC tamper detection and authentication in smart classrooms. *IEEE Internet of Things Journal*, *12*(3), 4567–4579. DOI: 10.1109/JIOT.2024.3456789

Singh, S. K., Yang, L. T., & Park, J. H. (2023). FusionFedBlock: Fusion of blockchain and federated learning to preserve privacy in industry 5.0. *Information Fusion*, *90*, 233–240. DOI: 10.1016/j.inffus.2022.09.019

Stergiou, C., Psannis, K. E., Kim, B.-G., & Gupta, B. (2018). Secure integration of IoT and cloud computing. *Future Generation Computer Systems*, *78*, 964–975. DOI: 10.1016/j.future.2017.08.031

Tariq, M., & Pervaiz, H. (2022). 6G and blockchain integration for smart agriculture. *IEEE Access : Practical Innovations, Open Solutions*, *10*, 55676–55689. DOI: 10.1109/ACCESS.2022.3174567

Thilakarathne, N. N., Bakar, M. S. A., Abas, P. E., & Yassin, H. (2025a). Internet of Things enabled smart agriculture: Current status, latest advancements, challenges and countermeasures. *Heliyon*, *11*(3), e09876. Advance online publication. DOI: 10.1016/j.heliyon.2025.e09876 PMID: 39959477

Thilakarathne, N. N., Bakar, M. S. A., Abas, P. E., & Yassin, H. (2025b). 6G-enabled AI frameworks for smart agriculture. *Heliyon*, *11*(3), e09877. Advance online publication. DOI: 10.1016/j.heliyon.2025.e09877 PMID: 39959477

Tian, F. (2017). A supply chain traceability system for food safety based on HACCP, blockchain & Internet of Things. In *2017 International Conference on Service Systems and Service Management* (pp. 1–6). IEEE. https://doi.org/DOI: 10.1109/ICSSSM.2017.7996119

Toosi, A. N., Calheiros, R. N., & Buyya, R. (2014). Interconnected cloud computing environments: Challenges, taxonomy, and survey. *ACM Computing Surveys*, *47*(1), 7. Advance online publication. DOI: 10.1145/2593512

Wolfert, S., Ge, L., Verdouw, C., & Bogaardt, M.-J. (2017). Big data in smart farming: A review. *Agricultural Systems*, *153*, 69–80. DOI: 10.1016/j.agsy.2017.01.023

Xu, A., Lin, Y., & Zhao, L. (2023). Digital twin and edge intelligence in precision agriculture: A survey. *Computers and Electronics in Agriculture*, *195*, 106937. Advance online publication. DOI: 10.1016/j.compag.2022.106937

Xu, K., Zhang, Y., Li, Y., & Wu, K. (2023). Decentralized AI with blockchain for smart agriculture. *Journal of Network and Computer Applications*, *202*, 103396. Advance online publication. DOI: 10.1016/j.jnca.2022.103396

Zhang, C., & Kovacs, J. M. (2012). The application of small unmanned aerial systems for precision agriculture: A review. *Precision Agriculture*, *13*(6), 693–712. DOI: 10.1007/s11119-012-9274-5

Zhang, X., Chen, H., Li, Y., & Wu, K. (2021). Blockchain-based trusted data sharing in 6G-enabled IoT smart agriculture. *IEEE Internet of Things Journal*, *8*(12), 9872–9883. DOI: 10.1109/JIOT.2020.3045678

Zhang, Y., Kumar, R., & Singh, N. (2021). Digital twin-based smart farming. *Precision Agriculture Technology*, *12*(4), 56–67.

Zhao, X., Chen, L., & Zhang, H. (2023). AI-based smart irrigation optimization in agriculture. *Agricultural Systems*, *194*, 103284. Advance online publication. DOI: 10.1016/j.agsy.2022.103284

Chapter 3
Business Intelligence in Public Administration Integrating Predictive Analytics and Organizational Adaptation

Mohammad Al Khaldy
https://orcid.org/0009-0009-7502-4668
University of Petra, Amman, Jordan

Amjad Aldweesh
https://orcid.org/0000-0001-9358-1323
College of Computing and Information Technology, Shaqra University, Saudi Arabia

Ahmad Al-Qerem
https://orcid.org/0000-0003-2187-6194
Computer Science Department, Faculty of Information Technology, Zarqa University, Jordan

ABSTRACT

Business intelligence (BI) in public administration involves the synthesis of large data sets to support evidence-based decision-making. Researchers have identified organizational barriers, technical complexities, and governance gaps that hinder BI initiatives in the public sector. This chapter investigates how agencies can use predictive analytics to strengthen service outcomes, focusing on strategies for ef-

DOI: 10.4018/979-8-3373-3760-9.ch003

fective implementation. The analysis draws on examples of AI-assisted processes in diverse contexts, revealing that organizational structures and leadership practices determine the success or failure of predictive models. Findings indicate that robust data governance, staff training, and mechanisms for accountability foster sustainable BI use. This chapter contributes by offering a structured discussion of BI adoption and outlines future paths for integrating neural-network-driven insights in public administration.

INTRODUCTION

Business intelligence (BI) in the public sector encompasses data-driven processes that can inform policy, enhance service delivery, and improve resource allocation. Researchers have discussed the complexity of integrating predictive analytics, machine learning, and other forms of artificial intelligence into traditional government workflows (Wirtz, Langer, & Fenner, 2021). Despite interest in deploying algorithms to aid decision-making, many public organizations face practical and ethical dilemmas, from ensuring data protection to maintaining transparency (Babšek, Ravšelj, Umek, & Aristovnik, 2025).

This chapter examines how public agencies can adopt BI for operational and strategic purposes. It addresses the fundamental question of how public institutions adapt organizationally and technologically to harness predictive analytics in ways that serve constituents while honoring public values. By focusing on active voices and minimizing descriptive adjectives, the discussion emphasizes evidence-based strategies rather than broad generalities.

The chapter begins by establishing conceptual foundations and clarifying how BI extends beyond isolated technical tools. It then draws on empirical and theoretical work to examine the conditions under which BI may thrive. Throughout, it integrates references from open access studies that illuminate how government agencies are using artificial intelligence to shape outcomes in areas such as healthcare, policing, and social services (Madan & Ashok, 2023; Sun & Medaglia, 2019; Walczak, 2021). Four tables and four figures appear to illustrate models, frameworks, and survey data on BI adoption trends. The goal is to provide both theoretical clarity and practical insights for readers who seek actionable methods to implement BI responsibly.

Finally, the chapter offers a critical perspective on governance, leadership, and organizational culture. Scholars highlight that AI tools pose new risks for bias, accountability, and professional discretion (Zuiderwijk, Chen, & Salem, 2021; Chen & Ahn, 2023). Addressing these concerns involves technical measures such as algorithmic explainability and organizational mechanisms like transparent oversight committees. The concluding sections explore future directions in BI research, suggesting that the evolution of neural networks and advanced analytical techniques will continue to test the public sector's capacity to adapt. This chapter aims to serve as a foundation for those interested in bridging theoretical concepts and implementation details within the realm of public-sector BI.

CONCEPTUAL FOUNDATIONS OF BUSINESS INTELLIGENCE IN THE PUBLIC SECTOR

Defining Business Intelligence and its Scope

Business intelligence involves the collection, integration, analysis, and presentation of data to improve organizational decisions and outcomes. In commercial contexts, BI focuses on revenue optimization and market positioning, but in public administration, BI prioritizes service quality, policy outcomes, and accountability (Babšek et al., 2025). While BI may rely on similar technical tools across sectors—such as data warehouses, dashboards, and predictive modeling—the public sector applies these technologies to meet responsibilities to citizens, including transparent governance and equitable services (Wirtz et al., 2021).

Public-sector BI activities range from analyzing social service data to predict resource needs, to evaluating program effectiveness through performance indicators. The core objective remains turning large volumes of raw data into actionable insights. As data volume and complexity have expanded, agencies have explored more sophisticated forms of data science, including neural-network-driven analytics, to predict future events or patterns (Sun & Medaglia, 2019). However, adopting these tools requires organizational adaptation to ensure alignment with public values and legislative constraints.

Linking BI and Predictive Analytics in Government

Predictive analytics adds an anticipatory layer to BI, allowing organizations to forecast future conditions based on historical data. Government agencies use these forecasts to inform policymaking or operational resource allocation. For instance, officials may employ neural networks to estimate healthcare demand or to detect patterns of fraud in public-benefit programs (Pi, 2021). Predictive analytics in the public sector can thus refine strategic planning by offering data-informed projections that go beyond descriptive dashboards.

Yet, predictive analytics in government carries unique concerns because policy and service decisions often involve ethically sensitive domains. A misapplied model may cause harm if it systematically overlooks marginalized groups or reinforces bias (Chen & Ahn, 2023). This possibility underscores the need to integrate robust governance structures into the predictive analytics lifecycle, from data collection to outcome monitoring. The interplay between BI and predictive analytics creates a comprehensive system that not only visualizes current performance but also anticipates potential futures, allowing officials to intervene proactively.

Importance of Organizational Context

Public agencies differ from private firms in their mission, oversight mechanisms, and stakeholder relationships (Neumann, Guirguis, & Steiner, 2024). Hence, the organizational culture within government plays an influential role in shaping BI adoption. Leadership commitment, staff competencies, and a clear data governance framework can facilitate or inhibit predictive analytics projects (Trajkovski, 2024). Without such foundational elements, even the most advanced models can fail to deliver meaningful benefits.

Moreover, the success of BI in public contexts depends on how managers align AI projects with broader institutional goals. This alignment includes ensuring that predictive models serve recognized policy needs, that data sharing adheres to privacy requirements, and that outcomes remain consistent with legal and ethical standards. Scholars highlight that agencies can either develop specialized AI units to house innovation or embed data analytics within existing departments (Selten & Klievink, 2024). Each choice has implications for accountability, collaboration, and the overall impact of BI on service delivery.

THE EVOLUTION OF AI-BASED PREDICTIVE ANALYTICS IN PUBLIC ADMINISTRATION

Historical Trends and Early Approaches

Early public-sector BI initiatives primarily focused on collecting administrative data in centralized systems, enabling descriptive reporting of performance metrics. As computational capabilities improved, agencies began experimenting with more sophisticated approaches, including data mining and machine learning (Mikhaylov, Esteve, & Campion, 2018). Researchers note that predictive analytics emerged in areas such as revenue forecasting, policing, and public health, reflecting initial steps toward automated decision support (Sun & Medaglia, 2019).

However, these early projects often encountered technical, institutional, and cultural barriers. Many agencies lacked data scientists or data-literate staff needed to maintain advanced analytical systems (Trajkovski, 2024). Others struggled with data silos that prevented cross-departmental data integration, limiting the power of predictive algorithms (Wirtz et al., 2021). Despite these obstacles, growing recognition of AI's potential drove continued exploration of tools like neural networks and natural language processing.

Contemporary Frameworks and Theoretical Foundations

Recent scholarship explores frameworks that integrate public value theory with technology adoption models (Madan & Ashok, 2023). Such frameworks highlight tensions between efficiency gains and core values like fairness, transparency, and privacy. To address these tensions, researchers recommend multi-stage processes that begin with pilot implementations and gradually expand to broader deployment as trust in the technology grows (Babšek et al., 2025). The interplay between organizational readiness, environmental drivers, and stakeholder support shapes how agencies move from experimentation to institutionalization of BI (Neumann et al., 2024).

In theoretical terms, the Technology–Organization–Environment (TOE) framework often appears in studies of public-sector AI. It underscores the impact of technological characteristics (e.g., complexity, data quality), organizational factors (leadership, structure, culture), and environmental influences (legislation, public opinion) on adoption decisions (Zuiderwijk et al., 2021). Scholars propose that public agencies advance through distinct adoption stages—awareness, early experimentation, scaling, and long-term institutionalization (Pi, 2021). Each stage presents challenges tied to staff competency, funding, interagency collaboration, and risk management.

Key Domains of Application

Healthcare Services

Predictive analytics assists in patient triage, resource allocation, and outbreak forecasting (Sriharan et al., 2024). Neural networks analyze large patient datasets to identify individuals at higher risk for complications, enabling proactive care strategies. Public health officials also use these tools to predict infectious disease spread, coordinating interventions. However, data privacy and the need for medical expertise to interpret outputs remain persistent concerns (Pi, 2021).

Law Enforcement and Public Safety

Predictive policing seeks to allocate patrols to areas with higher crime risk. Although some jurisdictions claim improved efficiency, critics point out that biased historical data can lead to unfair targeting of certain communities (Meijer & Wessels, 2019). Agencies continue to refine models to minimize discriminatory outcomes and maintain public trust in policing activities.

Social Services

Child welfare departments have piloted AI systems to flag high-risk cases, aiming to intervene sooner. Models draw on administrative records about family history, social service interactions, and demographic data (Gillingham, 2019). Critics warn that these tools may oversimplify complex family dynamics, necessitating human oversight and ethical safeguards.

Economic and Financial Administration

Predictive analytics helps forecast government revenues and detect fraud in tax or benefits systems (Kleinberg, Lakkaraju, Leskovec, Ludwig, & Mullainathan, 2018). When integrated with user-friendly dashboards, BI platforms can give decision-makers real-time feedback on financial health. Successful cases show that advanced machine learning models can reduce inefficiencies in bureaucratic procedures.

ORGANIZATIONAL ADAPTATION TO AI-DRIVEN BUSINESS INTELLIGENCE

Structural Reconfiguration and Collaboration

Organizations adapt by redesigning workflows, creating data governance committees, and fostering cross-department collaboration (Selten & Klievink, 2024). Some agencies establish standalone innovation units that incubate emerging BI applications. Others integrate AI expertise into existing departments to ensure that predictive analytics aligns with ongoing service functions (Mikhaylov et al., 2018). Each structural arrangement presents trade-offs in terms of agility, oversight, and knowledge sharing.

Table 1. Structural approaches to BI implementation in government

Approach	Description	Strengths	Limitations
Dedicated AI Units	Create specialized teams for AI solutions.	Rapid innovation, focus on expertise	Risk of silo, less integration with services
Integrated Model	Embed AI roles in existing departments.	Alignment with operational tasks	Potential fragmentation of AI expertise
Hybrid Approach	Combine a central AI team with departmental coordination.	Balanced oversight and integration	Requires strong governance to avoid overlap

Many agencies adopt a hybrid model to maintain strategic direction while ensuring that data-driven insights permeate daily operations. This arrangement supports knowledge exchange between AI specialists and functional teams like healthcare or social services (Neumann et al., 2024).

Leadership and Skills Development

Leaders play a pivotal role in championing BI projects and allocating necessary resources (Sriharan et al., 2024). Effective public-sector leaders articulate clear visions, build partnerships, and foster a data-oriented culture. They must also address staff apprehensions regarding job security and algorithmic errors. Structured training programs in data literacy, ethics, and algorithmic accountability strengthen staff readiness (Trajkovski, 2024).

Figure 1. Factors influencing leadership effectiveness in BI initiatives

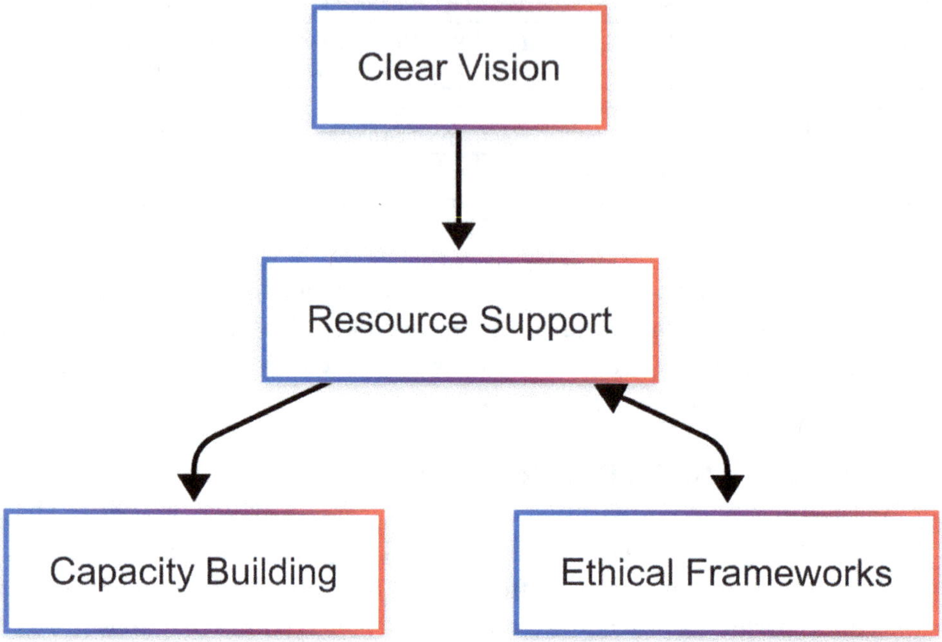

Leaders who integrate an ethical framework into project planning build institutional resilience against potential misuse of predictive tools. They work to ensure that staff at all levels understand how the models function, when to override them, and how to interpret outputs (Madan & Ashok, 2023).

Accountability and Oversight Mechanisms

Public agencies must balance the efficiency gains from AI with accountability to citizens and legislatures (Chen & Ahn, 2023). Traditional bureaucratic controls, such as hierarchical decision-making, may not directly address complexities of machine learning systems. Scholars suggest establishing oversight bodies or committees with the authority to audit datasets, algorithmic decisions, and model performance (Zuiderwijk et al., 2021).

Figure 2. Model of oversight in AI-driven government

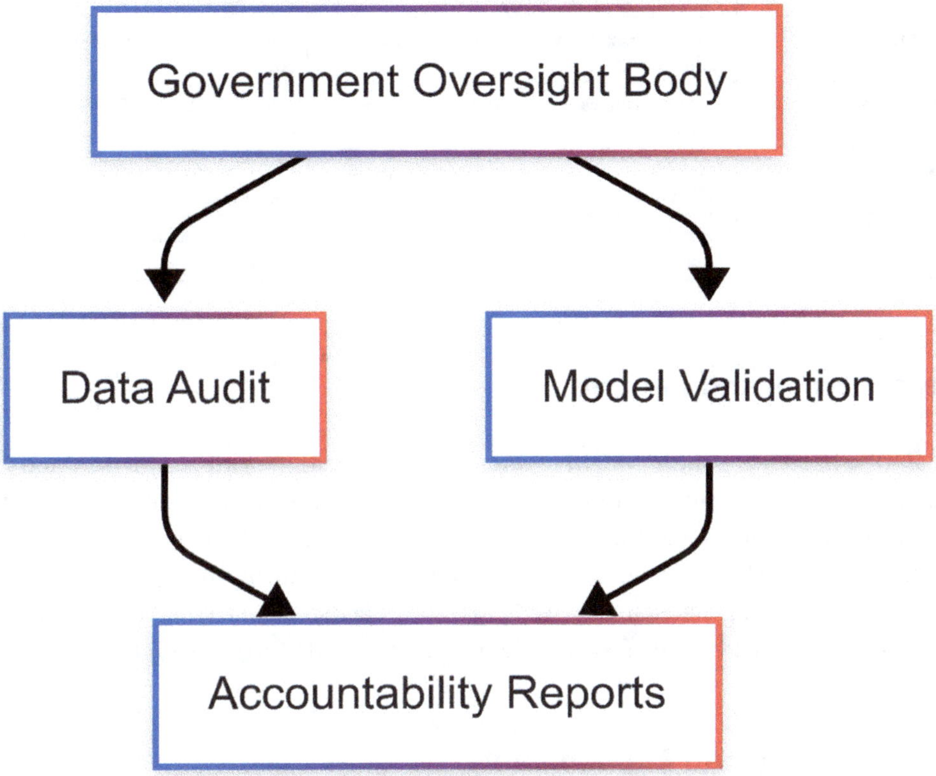

Transparency plays a key role in accountability structures. Public officials should communicate how predictive models inform decisions about resource allocation or policing practices (Wirtz et al., 2021). Stakeholders can then assess whether the use of BI aligns with democratic values.

ETHICAL AND GOVERNANCE CONSIDERATIONS

Bias and Fairness in Predictive Analytics

Predictive models can embed biases from historical data. These biases may disproportionately affect vulnerable communities if the models inform critical decisions such as social service eligibility or law enforcement interventions (Meijer & Wessels, 2019). Agencies must conduct regular audits and adopt data governance practices that identify and mitigate bias (Chen & Ahn, 2023).

Table 2. Common Sources of bias in public-sector predictive models

Source of Bias	Description	Mitigation Measures
Historical Data Imbalance	Underrepresentation of certain groups in training data.	Data sampling, targeted data collection
Feature Selection	Use of attributes correlated with sensitive variables.	Ethical guidelines, feature audits
Algorithmic Tuning	Model hyperparameters that amplify group differences.	Hyperparameter fairness constraints
Feedback Loops	Reinforcement of skewed patterns by repeated model use.	Continuous monitoring, iterative retraining

Data Privacy and Security

Public agencies handle sensitive data related to health, criminal justice, and financial status. They must therefore comply with legislative frameworks that govern data protection and usage (Pi, 2021). Secure storage, encryption, and robust access controls form the backbone of responsible BI systems. Furthermore, clarity around data sharing among agencies or with external partners is crucial. Unauthorized disclosure or breaches can erode public trust and impede further BI initiatives (Sun & Medaglia, 2019).

Transparency and Explainability

Agencies that integrate black-box neural networks into decisions about citizens' eligibility for benefits or resources may face resistance or lawsuits if stakeholders cannot understand the basis for those decisions (Walczak, 2021). Explainable AI (XAI) efforts aim to increase interpretability without sacrificing accuracy. Public officials can employ simplified surrogate models, visual dashboards, or local explanation techniques (such as LIME) to clarify how the predictive system arrives at outcomes (Chen & Ahn, 2023).

Regulatory and Legal Frameworks

Many jurisdictions lack clear regulations that define how AI-generated insights integrate into formal government decisions (Zuiderwijk et al., 2021). This regulatory gap creates uncertainty for public administrators. Some scholars suggest adopting sector-specific guidelines that articulate permissible model uses and responsibilities for oversight bodies (Mikhaylov et al., 2018). These guidelines can evolve in response to technological advancements and societal expectations, ensuring that AI applications align with public interest.

TOOLS AND TECHNIQUES FOR BI IN THE PUBLIC SECTOR

Machine Learning and Neural Networks

Machine learning algorithms find patterns in large datasets and generate predictions or classifications. Neural networks, a subset of machine learning, use interconnected layers of artificial neurons to process input data iteratively (Walczak, 2021). Public agencies adopt these models to forecast service demand, detect anomalies in financial transactions, or predict crime hot spots. Neural networks excel at handling unstructured data, such as text from social media or images from surveillance cameras.

However, neural networks require substantial computational resources and expertise (Pi, 2021). The complexity of these models also poses interpretability challenges. Public administrators must weigh the model's predictive power against the need for transparency and accountability. Tools like autoencoders, convolutional neural networks, or recurrent neural networks appear in specialized applications, though the public sector tends to adopt more interpretable approaches when making sensitive decisions (Wirtz et al., 2021).

Text Mining and Sentiment Analysis

Text mining extracts insights from unstructured documents, such as policy briefs, citizen feedback, and social media posts. Sentiment analysis helps agencies track public opinion on proposed initiatives (Xu, Liu, & Luo, 2025). This approach can measure the sentiment of large volumes of comments, enabling officials to gauge satisfaction or detect emerging concerns. By correlating sentiment with specific policy topics or regions, agencies can refine engagement strategies.

Figure 3. Workflow for text mining in public administration

Despite its potential, text mining in government requires careful attention to privacy. Datasets often include personal information, and public organizations must ensure that data anonymization or consent procedures comply with legal requirements

(Sun & Medaglia, 2019). Overreliance on automated sentiment analysis can also oversimplify nuanced public reactions, requiring complementary qualitative methods.

Geospatial Analytics

Geospatial analytics integrates location-based data with other administrative records to generate insights on patterns tied to geography. Police departments may map crime incidents to allocate patrols, or urban planners may identify underserved areas for public infrastructure investments (Walczak, 2021). Combining predictive models with real-time geospatial data offers dynamic resource allocation. For example, transportation agencies can predict traffic congestion and adjust public transit services. However, these capabilities raise concerns about surveillance and data misuse if agencies monitor citizens' movements without clear justification (Chen & Ahn, 2023).

Dashboards and Data Visualization

Dashboards translate raw data and predictive outputs into visual formats that decision-makers can interpret (Babšek et al., 2025). They often contain indicators tied to strategic objectives, forming a snapshot of real-time performance. By integrating advanced analytics, dashboards can also display forecasted trends. Although dashboards appear user-friendly, public administrators must ensure that the underlying data are reliable and that metrics accurately represent policy objectives (Wirtz et al., 2021). A transparent design is crucial so that stakeholders can trace how data flows into the visualizations.

EMPIRICAL EVIDENCE AND CASE STUDIES

Healthcare Applications

Researchers document how public hospitals have experimented with predictive models to identify patients at risk of readmission (Sriharan et al., 2024). Data on medical history, demographics, and social determinants of health feed into neural networks that assign risk scores. When staff combine these scores with clinical judgment, they may intervene early through targeted follow-ups or home visits. Although these initiatives have shown promise, scholars note that misclassification can lead to unnecessary interventions, resource strain, or patient dissatisfaction (Pi, 2021).

Table 3. Examples of predictive analytics in public healthcare

Case Study	Predictive Task	Reported Outcome	Reference
Hospital A	Readmission risk	10% reduction in 30-day readmissions	Sriharan et al. (2024)
Public Clinic B	Patient triage	Improved triage efficiency, shortened wait times	Pi (2021)
Regional Health Dept.	Outbreak forecasting	Early detection of outbreak clusters, faster containment	Sun & Medaglia (2019)

Law Enforcement and Criminal Justice

Predictive policing has drawn both support and criticism. Agencies argue that predictive models reduce crime by allocating resources more efficiently (Meijer & Wessels, 2019). However, if policing data contain historical biases, models may continue to target specific neighborhoods or demographics, leading to civil liberties concerns. Another application is algorithmic risk assessment for bail decisions, which can reduce subjective errors in judicial rulings. Yet, researchers highlight challenges: it remains unclear how bail decision-makers interpret algorithmic recommendations, and whether that leads to more just outcomes (Kleinberg et al., 2018).

Social Services and Child Welfare

Child welfare agencies use predictive analytics to screen large volumes of cases, identifying those at higher risk of abuse or neglect (Gillingham, 2019). Some models incorporate data from education, healthcare, and social services to develop a holistic risk score. These initiatives can triage caseloads and direct social workers' attention to children needing immediate intervention. However, risk scores can oversimplify family contexts, and workers might rely too heavily on the model rather than professional judgment. Proper training and consistent human oversight can moderate such risks, but cultural acceptance of algorithmic assistance among social workers varies widely (Mikhaylov et al., 2018).

E-Government Services and Policy Analysis

E-government portals leverage BI dashboards to streamline citizen services, such as permit applications or tax filings (Wirtz et al., 2021). By analyzing historical queries, agencies can predict peak times, reallocate staff, and reduce wait periods. Text-mining approaches also help administrators extract policy feedback from online forums, guiding continuous improvements to e-services (Xu et al., 2025).

While these initiatives typically improve access, they require robust cybersecurity measures and user-centric design.

STRATEGIES FOR EFFECTIVE BI INTEGRATION IN PUBLIC ORGANIZATIONS

Data Governance and Management

Data governance policies define accountability, data stewardship, and quality standards (Babšek et al., 2025). Leaders who adopt formal governance committees clarify roles and responsibilities for data collection, storage, and access. Standardized processes for data cleaning and integration reduce errors in predictive outputs (Selten & Klievink, 2024). Cross-agency data sharing agreements, anchored in legal guidelines, further expand the potential of BI by combining datasets from multiple domains (Pi, 2021).

A structured data lifecycle approach includes:

1. **Data Acquisition**: Identify relevant and high-quality data sources.
2. **Data Cleaning**: Remove inconsistencies, handle missing values.
3. **Data Integration**: Merge disparate data into a single repository.
4. **Data Analysis**: Apply machine learning or statistical methods.
5. **Data Usage**: Present insights to officials or the public.
6. **Monitoring**: Continuously review data pipelines to ensure integrity.

Interagency Collaboration and Public-Private Partnerships

Complex social problems rarely fit neatly within a single agency's domain (Mikhaylov et al., 2018). Collaboration across departments or with external partners can enhance data completeness and create synergy in BI projects. For instance, a health department may share anonymized data with social services to track factors affecting vulnerable populations. Public-private partnerships bring in advanced technical expertise from private firms, though agencies must ensure that such collaborations protect public interests (Neumann et al., 2022).

Staff Engagement and Training

Agencies can address skill gaps by offering in-house workshops on machine learning principles, data visualization, and ethical considerations (Trajkovski, 2024). Recruiting specialized staff or partnering with academic institutions also addresses technical deficits. Training should include modules on interpreting predictive outputs in context, enabling civil servants to maintain agency over final decisions. Continual skill development helps agencies adapt as new BI tools emerge, preserving the relevance and effectiveness of predictive systems (Madan & Ashok, 2023).

Building Public Trust and Legitimacy

Public trust in AI-driven decisions affects the broader acceptance and success of BI. Citizens express concerns about transparency, fairness, and privacy (Aysolmaz, Müller, & Meacham, 2023). Agencies should publish plain-language explanations of how models guide decisions and offer accessible channels for appeals. Participatory governance—through community forums or advisory committees—can include citizens in shaping how BI tools operate (Chen & Ahn, 2023). By engaging stakeholders in discussions about data usage and algorithmic decision-making, organizations can demonstrate accountability.

Table 4. Key factors for building trust in AI-assisted public services

Factor	Action Items	Potential Outcomes
Transparency	Publicize model logic, data sources	Reduced suspicion, improved feedback
Fairness	Audit for bias, adopt inclusive data samples	Higher equity in service delivery
Privacy	Use secure data storage, respect consent	Increased confidence in data handling
Participation	Invite community input, hold consultations	Enhanced social acceptance, legitimacy

CHALLENGES AND RISK MITIGATION

Managing Algorithmic Complexity

Neural networks and other machine learning techniques require specialized oversight. Overfitting, bias, and data drift can degrade predictive accuracy (Walczak, 2021). Agencies often lack staff trained to identify these issues. External audits or partnerships with academic and research institutions can help detect model failures. Regular retraining with up-to-date data also ensures that predictions remain valid over time (Pi, 2021).

Ethical Dilemmas and Value Conflicts

BI aims to enhance efficiency, but public administration must also reflect compassion, discretion, and social equity (Madan & Ashok, 2023). Tensions arise if a predictive system suggests rationing services in ways that conflict with policy goals of universal access. Ethical frameworks guide administrators in reconciling algorithmic recommendations with broader societal values (Chen & Ahn, 2023). When algorithmic and human judgments conflict, agencies need clear decision protocols to maintain fairness.

Balancing Innovation and Stability

A tension exists between the desire to harness cutting-edge tools and the need for stable, accountable governance structures (Selten & Klievink, 2024). Rapidly deploying experimental AI systems can yield short-term gains but may expose agencies to reputational or legal risks if those systems fail or cause unintended harm. Incremental, phased implementations with built-in evaluations can mitigate these risks. Pilot studies allow agencies to gather real-world evidence before scaling up (Babšek et al., 2025).

FUTURE DIRECTIONS

Emerging Technologies and Methods

Emerging technologies, such as federated learning, blockchain-based data sharing, or advanced natural language generation, may further extend the scope of public-sector BI (Xu et al., 2025). Federated learning enables multiple agencies to train shared predictive models without exposing raw data, enhancing collaboration while preserving privacy. Blockchain can provide transparent data provenance, reducing concerns about data manipulation (Mikhaylov et al., 2018). Natural language generation tools could automate policy summaries or citizen-facing reports, although such automation raises new questions about accountability.

Institutional Reforms and Regulatory Evolution

Researchers advocate for updated administrative procedures to address AI's unique challenges (Zuiderwijk et al., 2021). While many existing public sector regulations address data protection or procurement, they may not specify how to evaluate or govern machine learning models in decision processes. Collaborative efforts among policymakers, technologists, and civil society can shape new guidelines that ensure AI remains aligned with democratic values. Greater clarity in laws could lower barriers to adoption, allowing agencies to deploy BI tools with confidence in their legal footing (Chen & Ahn, 2023).

Strengthening Accountability Frameworks

Future research may explore how accountability evolves when predictive models operate across multiple agencies and jurisdictions (Selten & Klievink, 2024). Cross-agency BI solutions require shared responsibilities and more complex coordination. Studies can investigate whether new governance mechanisms—such as distributed ethics committees or algorithmic accountability offices—offer more coherent oversight. A robust accountability framework not only guards against misuse but also reinforces citizen trust in government's data-driven initiatives (Aysolmaz et al., 2023).

Bridging Technical and Ethical Expertise

Universities and professional associations could develop interdisciplinary curricula that combine data science, public policy, and ethics (Trajkovski, 2024). This approach would create a workforce skilled in technical modeling and versed in public values. By fostering interdisciplinary collaboration, agencies could address potential problems early in model development, avoiding costly retrofitting of ethical safeguards (Chen & Ahn, 2023). Such bridging can reduce friction between data engineers, policy analysts, and legal advisers, making BI initiatives more cohesive.

CONCLUSION

Business intelligence in the public sector holds promise for enhancing decision-making, optimizing resource use, and promoting transparency. Through predictive analytics, agencies can spot emerging trends, intervene proactively, and better serve the public. However, these tools also pose ethical challenges and require robust organizational adaptation. The active involvement of leaders, the development of staff competencies, and the implementation of oversight committees all contribute to responsible BI adoption (Madan & Ashok, 2023).

This chapter has shown how public organizations evolve structurally, culturally, and procedurally to integrate BI tools. It has highlighted the critical importance of strong data governance, transparent model design, and alignment with democratic values (Wirtz et al., 2021). Studies indicate that public managers must navigate the tension between technological innovation and the enduring need for bureaucratic accountability (Meijer & Wessels, 2019). Moving forward, researchers can explore how emerging practices like federated learning or algorithmic auditing transform the scope and nature of BI in government.

Public administrators who leverage predictive analytics responsibly can realize substantial gains in efficiency and equity. Yet, they must continually reassess their methods to prevent unintended consequences and to maintain public trust. This chapter's discussion underscores that BI success in government depends not only on advanced technologies but on institutional readiness, ethical mindfulness, and collaborative leadership. Such a confluence of factors ensures that predictive models serve the broader public interest, paving the way for data-driven governance that upholds essential social values.

REFERENCES

Aysolmaz, B., Müller, B., & Meacham, D. (2023). The public perceptions of algorithmic decision-making systems: Results from a large-scale survey. *Telematics and Informatics*, *79*, 101954. DOI: 10.1016/j.tele.2023.101954

Babšek, M., Ravšelj, D., Umek, L., & Aristovnik, A. (2025). Artificial intelligence adoption in public administration: An overview of top-cited articles and practical applications. *AI, 6*(3), 44. https://doi.org/10.3390/ai6030044

Chen, Y.-C., & Ahn, M. J. (2023). Artificial intelligence and public values: Value impacts and governance in the public sector. *Sustainability*, *15*(6), 4796. https://doi .org/10.3390/su15064796[REMOVED HYPERLINK FIELD]

Gillingham, P. (2019). Can predictive algorithms assist decision-making in social work with children and families? *Child Abuse Review*, *28*(2), 114–126. DOI 10.1002/car.2547

Kleinberg, J., Lakkaraju, H., Leskovec, J., Ludwig, J., & Mullainathan, S. (2018). Human decisions and machine predictions. *The Quarterly Journal of Economics*, *133*(1), 237–293. PMID: 29755141

Madan, R., & Ashok, M. (2023). AI adoption and diffusion in public administration: A systematic literature review and future research agenda. *Government Information Quarterly*, *40*(1), 101774. DOI 10.1016/j.giq.2022.101774

Meijer, A., & Wessels, M. (2019). Predictive policing: Review of benefits and drawbacks. *International Journal of Public Administration*, *42*(12), 1031–1039. DOI 10.1080/01900692.2019.1575664

Mikhaylov, S. J., Esteve, M., & Campion, A. (2018). Artificial intelligence for the public sector: Opportunities and challenges of cross-sector collaboration. *Philosophical Transactions of the Royal Society A*, *376*(2128), 20170357. PMID: 30082303

Neumann, O., Guirguis, K., & Steiner, R. (2024). Exploring artificial intelligence adoption in public organizations: A comparative case study. *Public Management Review*, *26*(1), 114–141. DOI: 10.1080/14719037.2022.2048685

Pi, Y. (2021). Machine learning in governments: Benefits, challenges and future directions. *JeDEM – eJournal of eDemocracy and Open Government, 13*(1), 203–219. DOI 10.29379/jedem.v13i1.625

Selten, F. J., & Klievink, B. (2024). Organizing public sector AI adoption: Navigating between separation and integration. *Government Information Quarterly*, *41*(1), 101885. DOI 10.1016/j.giq.2023.101885[REMOVED HYPERLINK FIELD]

Sriharan, A., Sekercioglu, N., & Mitchell, C.. (2024). Leadership for AI transformation in health care organizations: A scoping review. *Journal of Medical Internet Research*, *26*(8), e54556. DOI: 10.2196/54556 PMID: 39009038

Sun, T. Q., & Medaglia, R. (2019). Mapping the challenges of artificial intelligence in the public sector: Evidence from public healthcare. *Government Information Quarterly*, *36*(2), 368–383.

Trajkovski, G. (2024). Bridging the public administration–AI divide: A skills perspective. *Public Administration and Development*, *44*(5), 412–426. DOI: 10.1002/pad.2061

Walczak, S. (2021). Predicting crime and other uses of neural networks in police decision making. *Frontiers in Psychology*, *12*, 587943. https://pmc.ncbi.nlm.nih.gov/ PMID: 34690848

Wirtz, B. W., Langer, P. F., & Fenner, C. (2021). Artificial intelligence in the public sector: A systematic literature review and research agenda. *International Journal of Public Administration*, *44*(13), 1103–1128. DOI: 10.1080/01900692.2021.1947319[REMOVED HYPERLINK FIELD]

Xu, Z., Liu, Z., & Luo, H. (2025). Can artificial intelligence technology help achieve good governance? A public policy evaluation method based on artificial neural network. *SAGE Open*, *15*(1), 1–15. DOI 10.1177/21582440251317833[REMOVED HYPERLINK FIELD]

Zuiderwijk, A., Chen, Y.-C., & Salem, F. (2021). Implications of the use of artificial intelligence in public governance: A systematic literature review and a research agenda. *Government Information Quarterly*, *38*(3), 101577. DOI 10.1016/j.giq.2021.101577[REMOVED HYPERLINK FIELD]

Chapter 4
E-Governance Services Using AI: Effective or Wasteful?

Hanifa Maylasari
https://orcid.org/0009-0002-6494-6623
Diponegoro University, Indonesia

Nilam Adini Rakhma
https://orcid.org/0009-0003-9436-0030
Diponegoro University, Indonesia

Ali Roziqin
https://orcid.org/0000-0001-8336-3103
Universitas Muhammadiyah Malang, Indonesia

ABSTRACT

Rapid development of technology is marked by the emergence of Artificial Intelligence (AI) .This study is important, because public services using e-governance create social dynamics. The method used is document analysis by comparing public service systems in developing and developed countries that use AI technology from relevant scientific literature. This chapter finds that developing countries emphasize digital foundations and technology accessibility developed countries. Developing countries have not yet reached a more mature regulatory stage, minimal public involvement in the policy-making process, and need to examine more deeply the ethical standards of AI management. Developed countries are able to be a reference in determining public service regulations using AI, because they are able to use e-governance services in a more structured manner and involve the role of civil society. The existence

DOI: 10.4018/979-8-3373-3760-9.ch004

of this study is expected that governance regulations in developing countries in implementing e-governance services using AI can run accountably and effectively to the entire community.

INTRODUCTION

Effective digital transformation requires coordinations between the different levels of government and system integration (Bonduki & Cunha, 2022). At the same time, the public widely uses the internet and engages in digital activities (Lim, 2020). The government captures community activities with AI as an opportunity to provide digital service. The government perceives community activities through the lens of AI as a means to enhance tprovision of digital services. The significant challenge is the digital competence of public sector employees. They need to be trained to improve their competence (Rakhma & Roziqin, 2025) Studies show that many public sector employees only have average abilities in using technology, requiring investment in training and attracting technology talent (Adewumi & Abasilim, 2024). To improve government efficiency and transparency, advanced technology, such as: AI, Internet of Things (IoT), and any other data analytics(Tshuma et al., 2024). AI and the other new technologies can significantly improve public services, although these technologies also pose social, ethical, and legal challenges that must be managed (Pislaru et al., 2024).

AI has capacity to process the vast volumes of data, spot trends, and produce insights that greatly enhance governance decision-making. This leads to evidence-based and better-informed policies (Arora et al., 2024). The effectiveness of quality in public services using AI is cutting down on times, facilating quicker operation execution, and granting information (Mukonavanhu, 2025). Virtual assistants like chatbots, improve communication between citizens and also the governments, resulting in higher satisfaction and better service experiences are part of AI (Pislaru et al., 2024). Transparency in the governance by providing real-time feedback and insights into governmental operations, thereby increasing trust among citizens are the function of AI to improved (Upreti et al., 2023). Digital transformation does not necessarily address the underlying issues in governance.

Main challenges of digitalization in public sector include low integration between government systems, lack of digital competence of public sector employees, and minimal evaluation of the impact on service quality (Edelmann et al., 2023). Public sector employees in developing countries are still often affected by problems of corruption, nepotism, and abuse of authority, which can impact on decreasing transparency and accountability (Mutiarin et al., 2024). Infrastructure deficiencies, limited digital literacy, social resistance, and institutional impediments brought on by bureaucracy are some of the difficulties facing public services (Djatmiko et al., 2025). These problems show to us the success of digital transformation is highly dependent on quality of the underlying governance. In this context, the concept of e-governance becomes crucial. Principles such as: participation, transparency, accountability, effectiveness, and fairness are ethical norms and the foundation for creating a public service system that is trusted, adaptive, and free from abuse of authority.

Digital public service systems in developed countries are generally more integrated than in developing countries. Singapore, China, and European Union countries such as Spain and Brazil have built strong e-governance infrastructure, with the most comprehensive online services and high user adoption (Goal et al., 2022). They consistently rank at the top of the world e-governance index; Singapore, for example, rose to third place globally, while Indonesia is still ranked 64th, up from its previous ranking of 77 (Index & Development, 2022). The digital divide is still real, with around 1.7 billion global residents not yet accessing basic digital services, indicating that the gap between the e-governance achievements of developed and developing countries has not been fully realized (L. E. Development, 2021).

Developing countries such as Indonesia, India, and Malaysia face fundamental challenges in implementing e-governance, such as limited ICT infrastructure, uneven internet and electricity access, and low digital literacy among citizens (Janssen et al., 2012). This is exacerbated by bureaucratic resistance and slow data coordination due to conventional procedures hampering the integration of digital services (Wirtz et al., 2019). Lack of skilled human resources, funding, and supporting regulatory frameworks are having obstacles in developing countries (Janssen et al., 2012). Developed countries such as: Singapore, China, European Union, Brazil, and Spain, are the confront more complex issues, such as protecting civil society's privacy and data security and updating legacy systems for integration (OECD, 2016).

Developing countries such as India launched digital services focusing on building digital infrastructure, digitizing government services, and increasing digital literacy (Pokhrel, 2024). This program includes expanding high-speed internet access to the rural areas and providing thousands of community digital service centers (Common Service Centers)(Pokhrel, 2024). Indonesia is the developing country that implemented an Electronic-Based Government System (SPBE) policy (Kamil et al., 2025), to integrate central and regional services and promote digital literacy.

Countries such as Singapore and members of European Union emphasize the holistic approach to digital governance that the user-centric and inclusive. Building a framework for cross-agency interoperability, stringent data protection regulations, and digital skills enhancement programs for vulnerable groups to ensure the citizens can get benefit from digital services (Okafor, 2020). Importance thing of digital identity, digital literacy, community participation, ICT infrastructure, data governance, and leadership as drivers of successful digital transformation (S. Development et al., n.d.). Policy measures aim to bridge the digital divide and increase trust and use of services, so that e-governance transformation truly results in effective public services for all (S. Development & Goals, 2022).

It is crucial thoroughly examine the operation of e-governance and make sure that the digitization of public services not only speeds up the process, but also ensures fairness, transparency, and also anti-corruption (Bhanye & Shayamunda, 2024). This research is important amidst a country's efforts to build a professional and serving bureaucracy, especially in context of inclusive and sustainable digital services.

LITERATURE REVIEW

Artificial Intelligence (AI) is a public sector revolution using utilizes machine learning technology, predictive analysis, and the distribution of online service access spaces to simplify the administrative processes of government systems (Ajayi et al., 2024). The interaction between public and public servants is transparent and accountable, to produce data and based on policies. Through enhance decision-making and streamlining service delivery, used of cutting the process of technologies like AI and also IoT can further enhance e-government services (Al-Ansi et al., 2024). Applying cutting-edge technologies like AI and IoT can improve decision-making and optimized the service delivery, which will further improve the e-government services(Luna-Reyes et al., 2006). Digital government enhances transparency and citizen engagement by providing a platform for public participation and access to the information (Cardoso et al., 2022). Digital government initiatives address bureaucratic processes, long waiting times, and limited accessibility by enabling faster processing of government operations, automating routine tasks, and reducing manual workload (Selvakumar et al., 2025). Digital channels and transformational leadership have positively impacted the shift from manual to electronic governance processes, increasing transparency, efficiency, accountability, and security in governance processes, were useful(Mahmood et al., 2018). Digital government can increase the efficiency and productivity of government institutions and enable citizens to transact with the government anytime and anywhere (Katsonis & Botros, 2015). Digital government has the potential to improve government operations, engage citizens, and provide government services (H. J. Scholl, 2022). The transition to e-government aims to improved the quality of services, transparency, and efficiency, and reduce bureaucracy and red tape (Shovkovyy, 2024).

Study of the government sciences and public administration, the terms "e-government" and "e-governance" have different meanings. Traditionally, e-government has been defined as the government's use of information and communication technology (ICT) to enhance provision of public services to businesses and citizens (Rose, 2005). Primary focus of e-government is on automating administrative processes, increasing bureaucratic efficiency, and simplifying interactions between the government and service users (Moon, 2002). Thus, e-government is more technical and operational, oriented towards providing fast, transparent, and easily accessible digital services to the public (Heeks, 2006). E-government generally includes systems and applications that enable digital services such as electronic tax payments, online registration, and filing of administrative documents. The emphasis is on the transactional aspects and the provision of government information electronically (Wang & Liao, 2008).

The concept of e-governance encompasses a broader and more complex study, going beyond the mere delivery of digital services. E-governance involves digital governance mechanisms that integrate the roles of various actors, including government, the private sector, and also civil society, in decision-making and managing public resources through digital technologies (Wimmer et al., 2013). E-governance focuses on the administrative efficiency, public participation, institutional transparency, accountability, and more democratic cross-sectoral collaborations (UNDP, 2023). On the other hand, E-governance encompasses overall governance process, including policies, regulations, citizen participation, and data and information governance that support transparent and accountable decision-making (Gil-García & Pardo, 2005). E-governance can be seen that the conceptual framework guides the implementations of e-government in line with the principles of good governance. Thus, e-governance is a governance paradigm that utilizes digital technology to support political, social, and administrative processes.

In addition, from a functional perspective, e-government is usually considered a subsystems in the e-governance ecosystem (Gauld, 2006). While e-governance concentrates on governance, legislation, and stakeholder interaction at the macro level, e-government offers the technological platforms and tools required to run the digital services (Dwivedi, 2009). Success of e-government is highly depend on the e-governance framework to supports it, including policies that encourage the data transparency, privacy protection, and active public participation (H. Scholl, 2003).

Conceptually, this difference is reflected in main objectives of both; e-government aims to improve the effectiveness of public services through digitalization, while e-governance focuses on improving the quality of governance through the integration of digital technology in inclusive and also the participatory decision-making processes (Saner et al., 2020) (Souter & Van der Spuy, 2019). So, e-government can be considered a practical implementation of technology. At the same time, e-governance is a strategic and political vision that directs the use of technology to realize better and more sustainable governance (Landri, 2018).

Klitgaard's theory, which holds that government bureaucracy is susceptible to corruption, gave rise to e-government services. The result, it must be limited in order to ensure that the power obtained is manageable (Pages, 2025). E-Governance cannot be separated from the paradigm of modern bureaucratic reform, one of which is through the New Public Management (NPM) approach, which encourages efficiency, transparency, and accountability based on information technology (Carter & Bélanger, 2005). Therefore, the integration of technology through e-governance functions as a tool for administrative efficiency and as a vehicle for democratization and collaborative innovation in more adaptive and community-oriented governance.

Meanwhile, New Public Governance (NPG) is a public governance paradigm that emerged as a response to limitations of the New Public Management (NPM) approach, especially in context of changing public policy complexities in the 21st century (Hoetker & Fountain, 2002). NPG highlights the effective of public governance requires active cooperation from a range of stakeholders in addition to the internal effectiveness of the government (Hoetker & Fountain, 2002). In this framework, governance is understood as a result of interactions between diverse actors including: government, private sector, non-governmental organizations, and civil society. This approach that the government to act as a network facilitator that builds synergies between sectors to create broader public value.

Public service in e-governance using AI means speed and ease of service access and reflects the government's commitment to providing responsive, quality services oriented towards public satisfaction. According to New Public Management (NPM), performance metrics, procedural efficiency, and a managerial style that views the public as clients who need to be served as best they can are the means by which great public service is achieved. Therefore, excellent public service in digital era relies on technology and is formed through openness, participation, and collaboration between stakeholders to ensure fair, inclusive, and sustainable services.

Method

This research was conducted using the document analysis method. The researcher used existing data from scientific literature, such as articles and digital books (Nelson & Woods, 2013). Data collection techniques from available sources are qualified and compared in the table. This study uses Artificial Intelligence (AI), Digital Governance, Public Services, Developing Countries, and Developed Countries. Researchers conducted document analysis using scientific literature: articles and digital books, then arranged based on keywords, as follows (Roziqin & Fajrina, 2021):

Figure 1. Criteria for selecting scientific literature documents

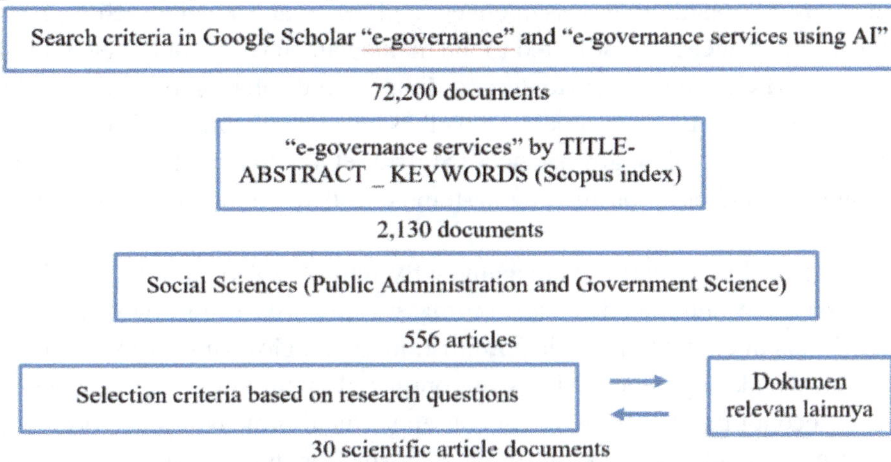

Figure 1. Criteria for Selecting Scientific Literature Documents

Based on Figure 1, the researcher uses the keyword "e-governance" on Google Scholar. Central theme of this study is e-governance services using AI. Hence, the researcher searched using the keywords e-governance and e-governance services using AI, which were published from 2000 to 2025 on Google Scholar (as of April 28, 2025). There are around 72,200 documents, both in articles and digital books. To maintain quality of the findings, researchers narrowed the search for "e-governance services as a keyword in the Scopus indexing based on the title, abstract, and keywords (TITLE-ABS-KEYWORD). The results are 2,130 documents published in the various journals and publishers. In the field of social sciences, there are 556 scientific articles. Steps to minimize bias, researchers only use articles and digital books that discuss e-governance services using AI within the framework of government science, and public administration. A total of 30 journal article documents and digital books are referenced, and are indexed by Google Scholar and Scopus as references.

FINDINGS AND DISCUSSION

Artificial intelligence addresses bias issues by using more data, increasing number of results displayed in the dataset that the algorithm has been trained on (Nost, 2024). Recent advances in artificial Intelligence (AI) raise many questions about its social impact and how AI is applied. As a policy maker, the Government should be able to make appropriate regulations so that risks can be reduced and the benefits of using AI can be maximized (Sigfrids et al., 2022). Policy decisions may be influenced by AI's leaning towards openness and personal data ethics (Sifat, 2025).

Ethical governance AI is adjusted to the main characteristics of the New Public Governance (NPG), which refers to the coordination and collaboration between horizontal organizations in Government, as well as close involvement of citizens with community actors in public governances (Sigfrids et al., 2022). Therefore, through technology, a sound decision-making system is needed while still considering the ethics of governance.

The Advanced Distribution Management System (ADMS) platform is software used to assist the automatedly decision-making process, using data, machines, and algorithms in context of public administration and Government (Mökander et al., 2021). Considering ethics, AI is still dominated by traditional approaches that emphasize economic growth, while social and ethical dimensions are often only discussed normatively without strong mechanisms for implementation (Ulnicane et al., 2021). To prevent the negative effects of AI use, it is seen to be crucial to form ethics boards, conduct independent audits, maintain data transparency, and involve the public in the development of AI (Losavio, 2021). The regulations used in European Union are a clear example of new approach to addressing all ethical, social, and legal challenges of the new technologies. Build AI and digital data governance more accountable, transparent, and in line with the public interest, we have tracked independent supervision, multi-stakeholder participation, and integration between technological design with ethical principles and individual rights protection (Pagallo et al., 2019).

Several internationally recognized frameworks that have been developed to ensure the governance artificial intelligence (AI) aware to ethical principles. Ethics Guidelines for trustworthy AI from Europian Commission is tp emphasize the importance thing of building ethical(Sutrop, 2019). The guidelines outline seven key requirements for trustworthy AI, including the role of humans and their oversight, technical resilience and security, privacy and data governance, transparency, diversity, non-discrimination and fairness, social and environmental well-being, and also accountability (Vakkuri et al., 2022).

Using Big Data in Government and politics to compile public sentiment on an issue at the national and global levels makes it easier to collect data, including filtering blured potential (Manfredi Sánchez, 2019). Its use covers important issues such as refugee management, such us: global public health, climate chenge, humanitarian innovation, and conflict prevention effort. The use of Artificial Intelligence technology in e-governance services in several countries can be studied in the following graphic findings:

Figure 2. E-governance service index 2022 and 2024 (Index & Development, 2022)

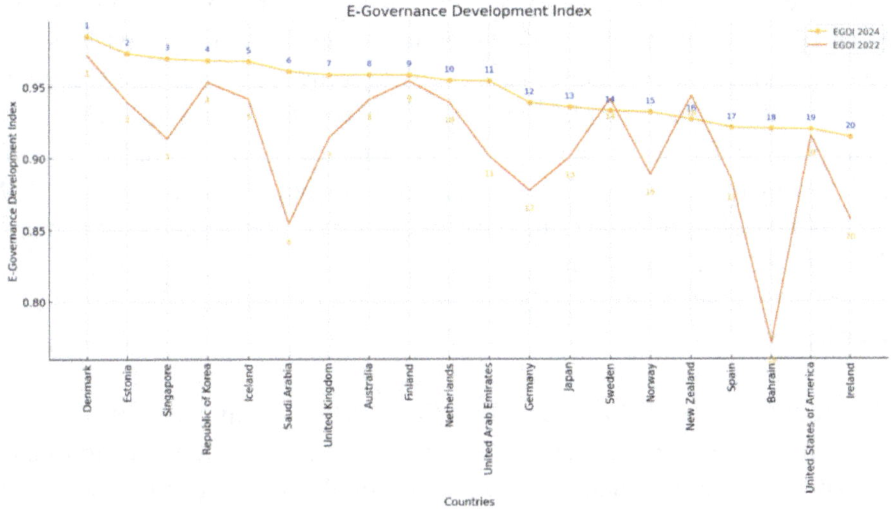

Figure 2. E-Governance Service Index 2022 and 2024

E-GOVERNANCE SERVICES USING AI IN DEVELOPING COUNTRIES

Indonesia

Limited information and communication technology in infrastructure, shortage of qualified human resources in digital sector, low technological literacy among the public and officials, and insufficient regulations to ensure data security and user privacy are just a few of the major obstacles facing Indonesia's AI implementation (Janssen et al., 2012). Indonesia, as an archipelago, consists of several districts and cities. The implementation of AI in South Halmahera Regency part of east area still at a low level, namely, various significant obstacles are found, including uneven distribution of telecommunications network infrastructure, limited budget, minimal supporting infrastructure such as electricity networks, and lack of competent human resources (Hafel et al., 2022). Although Indonesia is still lagging behind developed countries in adopting e-government services and AI, various strategic efforts have been made to catch up (Herawati & Widowati, 2023). The application of AI in priority sectors such as health, education, defense, and transportation, with examples of the use of telemedicine during the COVID-19 pandemic and the management of urban transportation systems in Jakarta (Machmud et al., 2020). Some cases of e-governance services using AI, missed out on transparent content and system integrations (Agarwal et al., 2025). Transparancy relate with the cybersecurity from technology of blockchain(Saxena et al., 2025). Sytematic machine used blockchain can improve quality services(Mahammad & Kumar, 2023). Have a security service to enhanced civil society's data during e-governance services, are the important thing(R. Kumar et al., 2024). Save all the data on storage(P. Kumar et al., 2024), was becoming the way to build effective services, especially in developing countries which have data lack's potential.

Malaysia

AI applied in Malaysia has the various field, such as: healthcare, public administration, and the security systems, effectively speeding up the decision-making process and reducing the manual workload for civil servants (OECD, 2022). The Malaysian Government is also integrating AI into its e-government platform to provide citizens with easier and more responsive access to services, encouraging greater public participation and inclusive service delivery (Dahri et al., 2024). However, several challenges such as limited digital infrastructure in rural areas, the need for skilled human resource development, and regulations that have not fully regulated the use of AI, remain obstacles that must be overcome to maximize the potential of the technology (Tangi et al., 2023); (Mahusin et al., 2024).

Based on research findings in Indonesia and Malaysia, the better the perception of public values and governance quality, the more likely the authorities are to adopt AI technology, to increase transparency, accountability, and strengthen governance standards to reduce resistance and strengthen trust in the digitalization process, as well as become an important reference for regulators and academics in developing public technology policies based on social values (Puspita et al., 2024).

India

The AI policy landscape in India aims to balance innovation with ethical considerations o the socio-economic context (Sadanand & Sadanand, 2025). Technology transforms India's e-governance ecosystem by enhancing service delivery and the citizen engagement. Study emphasizes the need for robust security measures and ethical guidelines for sustainable AI-driven governance (Swapnil et al., 2024). AI techniques, blockchain, intelligent data mining, and cloud computing are proposed for innovative city governance in India. This technology aims to enhance transparency, speed, and the coordination between government agencies and citizens (Tyagi & Goyal, 2021). AI also combats corruption by enhancing transparency and accountability in governance processes. This technology helps reduce barriers to economic growth and enhances public trust in the Government (Sakuntala et al., 2024). However, e-governance initiatives in India face challenges related to basic infrastructure and bandwidth issues, which hamper the smooth implementation of AI-powered services (Pandey & Chandu, 2025). India's cultural and multilingual diversity also presents challenges for implementing e-government services, including those powered by AI (Gupta & Bansal, 2013).

E-GOVERNANCE SERVICES USING AI IN DEVELOPED COUNTRIES

Singapore

Based on Singapore ranks sixth in AI government readiness index out of 172 countries and the highest ranked Government in the technology sector. The Government is critical in driving technology adoption through appropriate policies, business practices, and infrastructure (Pande & Taeihagh, 2024). The use of AI technology in Singapore is growing in the healthcare industry (Chik & Sugumaran, 2024). A study by (Pande & Taeihagh, 2024)introduced the Acceptance of Autonomous Systems Adoption Model (ASAM) with a governance perspective to understanding user acceptance of autonomous systems in Singapore, through an online survey of 500 respondents and analysis using structural equation modeling (SEM). Singapore views AI anot just as a technological tool, but as a strategic pillar in its smart nation initiative to improve government efficiency, economic growth, and quality of life for the citizens, hence Singapore's AI governance approach emphasizes collaboration between Government, industry, and society through voluntary regulation and the development of ethical standards (Lee, 2024). Initiative such as the Model AI Governance Framework and AI Verify Toolkit are designed to build the public trust and encourages responsible AI adoption. In the developed country, economy is the factor to build techonology services, based on the industry evolution (Sagar et al., 2025).

China

Key findings in a comparative study of the artificial intelligence (AI) governance between China and the European Union (EU) show fundamental differences in normative and strategic approaches. China adopts a top-down approach toward technological innovation and national economic growth, driven by the state's dominant role in coordinating AI industry policy and emphasizing social stability and collective development as primary goals (Roberts et al., 2023). In contrast, the EU has developed a human rights-based and ethical AI governance framework, prioritizing individual protection, transparency, and technology accountability through documents such as the ethics guidelines for trustworthy AI and Artificial Intelligence (Commission, 2019). Both recognize the importance of AI in maintaining global competitiveness and supporting social transformation. However, differing political and cultural values have resulted in contrasting visions of who should primarily benefit from AI—the collective community in China versus individual citizens in the EU (Floridi et al., 2018). In a global context, this article recommends exchanging best practices and harmonizing standards to build more inclusive, ethical, and sustainable AI governance in the future (Roberts et al., 2023). Meanwhile China is developed countries, has appropriate algorithm(A. Kumar et al., 2024) calculation to build the many AI services(Begum & Kumar, 2022).

Europe

The resource regime approach in the geopolitical context of digital economy shows (König, 2022)that regulatory instruments such as the General Data Protection Regulations (GDPR), the Data Governance Act in 2020, and Data Act in 2022 are not solely aimed at protecting individual privacy and rights, but also creating a competitive and digitally sovereign internal data market framework. This tactic addresses the dominance of big non-EU tech firms that dominate global data flows, particularly those based in China and the United States (Kennedy, 2016). By structuring data access, processing, and redistribution to support domestic actors, the EU not only upholds normative principles such as human rights protection, but also pursues economic interests in strengthening the global competitiveness of its digital industry (Bennett & Raab, 2003). The resource regime framework explains that data is now associated as a strategic asset, and its regulation has implications for market design, institutional power, and political legitimacy. As a result, the European Union appears as a normative actor that actively shapes the architecture of the global digital economy based on values: transparency, fairness, and data sovereignty (Steinbach, 2024).

Japan

Japan has a history of pioneering AI technologies, such as Fifth Generation Computer Systems (FGCS) in the 1980s, which aimed to develop the advanced AI-based computer architectures (Jaakkola et al., 2019). Pandemic has driven a rapid shift towards digital transformation in Japan, including adopting AI in various public administration functions. This discussion is necessary to overcome the limitations of traditional systems and improve efficiency and responsiveness (Brummer & Ueno,

2024). Japan has been developing AI ethics and governance principles at the national level between 2014 and 2023, based on official reports, policy documents, and also expert interviews (Wright, 2024). In Japan, AI is integrated into various aspects of daily life, including managing social infrastructures such as drinking water supply and also waste treatment. However, the legal implications and risks of applying AI in this management have not been fully explored (Takeda et al., 2021). Japan must develop a legislative framework responsive to AI applications, including risk management and intellectual property rights (Brummer & Ueno, 2024).

Dubai and the United Arab Emirates

AI has been implemented in human resource departments across government institutions in Dubai. Studies show that AI helps address regional economic and social challenges and improves employee productivity and competency through distance learning and development (Almesafri & Habes, 2023). Dubai uses a free zone development model to maximize the impact of AI services and applications. This strategy supports economic diversification and creates a sustainable environment for AI technology (Mogielnicki, 2021). Dubai has used chatbots in various government entities to improve citizens' services. Studies recommend expanding used of Chatbots to improve the efficiency of public services (Mohasses, 2019). The implementation in Dubai reflects the United Arab Emirates (UAE). The UAE has a vision to become a world leader in AI by 2031. This national strategy includes developing local capabilities, implementing AI in the public and private services, and cross-sector collaboration (Shamout & Ali, 2021). Technology and employee factors influence the adoption of AI in e-innovative projects in the UAE public sector. Latter factor contributes significantly to the success of AI technology implementation (Hirzallah & Alshurideh, 2023). The UAE has developed an innovative government maturity model to initiate smart government initiatives. The evaluation results show that the UAE is quite advanced in using innovative and disruptive technologies in various domains (Hujran et al., 2023).

Canada

Canada was the first country to implementation of national AI strategy, encompassing a range of programs, policies, and strategic plans for interventions in industry, innovation, technology production, AI research, and public administration (Attard-Frost et al., 2024). In 2022, the Canadian Government introduced Bill C-27, which included the Artificial Intelligence Data Act (AIDA) to regulate AI and protect consumer privacy (Muhammad & Yow, 2023). The Canadian Parliament is exploring integrating AI technologies for specific tasks, with research showing the potential for using AI-based on tools and services in the parliamentary workspace (von Lucke et al., 2024). AI is used in the Canadian public service's internal administration, policy analysis, application assessment, and regulatory compliance (Longo, 2024). Initiatives such as public consultations and algorithm impact assessments are also underway to ensure inclusivity in AI governance (McKelvey & MacDona, 2019). Canada have a potential benefit from AI to increasing the healthy service with properly technology(Srivastava, Ahmed, Saxena, et al., 2025); (A. Kumar et al., 2023), and also early detected for risk management services(Srivastava, Ahmed, Kumar, et al., 2025); (Jaiswal & Kumar, 2023).

Spain

Spanish governance is analyzed with the perception and framing of Chief Information Officers (CIOs) in Spanish local governments towards artificial Intelligence (AI) in the public sector, using a socio-cognitive approach based on the technological framework (Orlikowski & Gash, 1994), showing that although CIOs generally show openness to the adoption of AI, especially in favor of efficiency and digitalization of public services in administrative and transactional functions, their mindset remains highly technocratic, ignoring the social, political and ethical aspects of the technology (Criado & O.de Zarate-Alcarazo, 2022). The main barriers identified include a conservative bureaucratic culture, financial constraints, the digital divide, and low social awareness regarding the impacts of AI. On the other hand, the developing digital infrastructure, technology transfer between institutions, and the increase in public digital literacy are driving factors for adoption. The importance of an inclusive and public value-oriented AI governance approach, such as gender equality, transparency, and social justice, as encouraged by the literature on ethical AI in the public sector (Emerson, 2020). Thus, AI adoption strategies in the public sector should emphasize technical efficiency and the integration of normative principles that ensure participation, accountability, and social sustainability in the use of technology.

Brazil

Considering the public services and using technology are findings that are being used as an approach by the Brazilian Government, amid the significance of using AI from 2021 to 2022 (Nicolás & Sampaio, 2024). The main findings show that AI-based automation has succeeded in increasing bureaucratic efficiency, as seen in the increased number of benefits processed automatically, for example, from 2% in early 2021 to 45% in late 2022. However, this efficiency is accompanied by significant negative consequences, such as the spike in automatic denials that reached more than 800,000 cases in 2022, many of which originated from technical errors, data inconsistencies, or lack of digital literacy by vulnerable citizens (Nicolás & Sampaio, 2024).

UK (England)

The importance of bolstering public values-based regulation of AI is highlighted by two significant studies, especially when considering emotional AI and the use of health data. Study conducted by (Bakir et al., 2024), focus group discussions involving 46 participants through a design fiction approach showed public concerns about the exploitation of users' emotional and cognitive vulnerabilities by emotional AI, especially in the form of social media emotional profiles (e.g. through deepfakes and newsfeed algorithms) and emotoys that respond to children's expressions. These concerns were reinforced by a national survey of 2,068 UK adult respondents that revealed public resistance to the manipulative potential of emotional AI, including privacy violations and negative impacts on rational thinking capacity (Bakir et al., 2024). On the other hand, a study by (McKay et al., 2022)evaluated the effectiveness of public engagement mechanisms in the governance of medical AI research in the UK through three entities: citizen forums, patient and public groups (PPIs), and data access committees (DACs). The findings showed that the three have not been synergistically integrated; citizen forums excel in inclusivity but are weak in policy influence. PPIs are potent in connections but lack representativeness, while DACs have formal authority without public involvement (McKay et al., 2022). Therefore, the authors propose a deliberative and adaptive multi-scale governance model to address this fragmentation and strengthen the legitimacy, transparency, and fairness of big data for AI research in the healthcare sector (Roy, 2017), also comparing the characteristic from developing ang developed countries based on this table below:

Table 1. E-governance services with AI in developing countries

Country	AI applications in e-gov	Governance and Standards	Challenge
Indonesia	AI is used in the health, education, defense, and transportation sectors, including telemedicine (Machmud et al., 2020).	Strategic efforts encourage strengthening public value-based governance to increase transparency and accountability (Puspita et al., 2024).	Limited ICT infrastructure, human resource disparities, and inadequate regulations (Janssen et al., 2012); (Hafel et al., 2022).
Malaysia	AI is integrated into e-government platforms to improve service access and public participation (Dahri et al., 2024).	AI regulation is still evolving, encouraging inclusivity and public participation but requiring further development (Mahusin et al., 2024).	Limited digital infrastructure in rural areas, the need for human resource development, and incomplete regulations (Tangi et al., 2023).
India	AI strengthens citizen services and engagement in e-government and supports innovative city governance (Tyagi & Goyal, 2021).	There is a need for strong ethical and security guidelines for sustainable AI governance (Swapnil et al., 2024).	Basic infrastructure, bandwidth issues, and cultural and linguistic diversity are significant barriers (Pandey & Chandu, 2025); (Gupta & Bansal, 2013).

Table 2. E-governance services with AI in developed countries

Country	AI applications in e-gov	Governance and Standards	Challenge
Singapore	AI is used in the healthcare industry and autonomous systems, collaborating with the Government, industry, and society (Pande & Taeihagh, 2024); (Lee, 2024).	Collaboration-based AI governance approach with AI Governance Framework Model and ethical standards (Lee, 2024).	Maintaining public trust, voluntary regulation, and challenges on a long-term scale (Pande & Taeihagh, 2024).
China	A top-down approach with a focus on technological innovation and national economic growth (Roberts et al., 2023).	Focus on collective development and social stability with strong state control (Roberts et al., 2023).	Differences in political and cultural values and the need to harmonize global standards (Floridi et al., 2018).
Europe	Strict regulation with GDPR and the Data Governance Act to protect privacy and strengthen internal data markets (König, 2022).	Human rights-based approach, transparency, and technology accountability (Commission, 2021).	The dominance of big tech companies and the challenges of data sovereignty (Kennedy, 2016);(Steinbach, 2024).
Japan	AI is applied to public administration and social infrastructure management (Brummer & Ueno, 2024).	Development of national AI ethics and governance principles since 2014 (Wright, 2024).	Developing a legislative framework and managing legal risks is necessary (Takeda et al., 2021).

continued on following page

Table 2. Continued

Country	AI applications in e-gov	Governance and Standards	Challenge
Dubai/UAE	AI supports government HR services and the use of chatbots for public services (Almesafri & Habes, 2023); (Mohasses, 2019).	Free zone development model and cross-sector collaboration in AI development (Shamout & Ali, 2021).	Human resource development and the need for adaptive regulation (Hirzallah & Alshurideh, 2023).
Canada	The first national AI strategy with a focus on innovation and privacy regulation through Bill C-27 (Attard-Frost et al., 2024); (Attard-Frost et al., 2024).	Public consultation and algorithm impact assessment for inclusive AI governance (McKelvey & MacDona, 2019).	Policy adjustments to technological change and the need for inclusivity (von Lucke et al., 2024)
Spanish	AI supports the efficiency of administrative and transactional public services (Criado & O.de Zarate-Alcarazo, 2022)	An inclusive AI governance approach with public values such as equality and social justice (Emerson, 2020).	Barriers of conservative bureaucratic culture and low social awareness of the impacts of AI (Criado & O.de Zarate-Alcarazo, 2022).
Brazil	AI automation improves bureaucratic efficiency, but there is a spike in automated rejections due to technical errors (Nicolás & Sampaio, 2024).	Focus on increasing the efficiency of public services with AI technology (Nicolás & Sampaio, 2024).	Technical errors and digital ignorance of vulnerable citizens (Nicolás & Sampaio, 2024).
English	AI is used in health research and public data governance with community participation (Bakir et al., 2024); (McKay et al., 2022).	Development of AI ethics standards and deliberative multi-scale governance models (Roy, 2017).	Public concerns about emotional AI manipulation and governance fragmentation (Bakir et al., 2024).

Tables 1 and 2 show differences in e-governance services using AI in developing and developed countries. Developing countries are trying to accelerate progress by focusing on infrastructure development, increasing digital literacy, and building public trust in technology. Meanwhile, developed countries have reached a more mature regulatory stage, actively involving the public in the policy process, and integrating strict ethical standards in the management of artificial Intelligence.

Developing countries with an unstable economy are trying to build online public services, and developed countries with a more stable economy focus on improving telecommunications infrastructure (Index & Development, 2022). .Economic factors determine the development of technology and services to the community, as well as the ability of the human resources that to used the digital services (Goal et al., 2022). Digital operationalization encourages public servants to obtain public satisfaction in developing and developed countries (Manfredi Sánchez, 2019). Natural culture from developing countries based on the languages could become the factors (A. Kumar et al., 2025). Urban growth is the indicators to delivered e-governance services using AI to be right on target(Srivastava et al., 2024). Technology from the healthy service's tools (Singh et al., 2022) are the checked inside of responsibilty from the country To improve the quality services also prepared tools for the academic activity(Gosain et al., 2023), because the sustainabilty of digital services are to be here. This study shows how developing countries emphasize digital foundations and technology accessibility, while developed countries are oriented towards responsible governance and transparent use of AI.

CONCLUSION

Technological sophistication in e-governance services is not only an accessory but how the benefits of technology can be used as much as possible for society. Developing countries such as Indonesia, India, and Malaysia have not yet reached a more mature regulatory stage, have minimal public involvement in policy-making process, and need to examine the ethical standards of AI management in more depth. Developed countries can be a reference in determining public service regulations using AI, with tighter economic, political, and cultural value competition. More inclusive governance involves civil society, the private sector, and the state in active roles such as risk mitigators, public participation facilitators, and interest mediators (Ulnicane et al., 2021).

The document analysis method used by researchers was able to find differences in the use of digital services with AI between developing and developed countries, that without inclusive governance, data protection, and strong accountability mechanisms in both countries, AI risks deepening social inequality and eroding citizens' constitutional rights to fair and equal public services. The effectiveness of using AI is not said to be good if e-governance services and public policy are still weak. However, technology can have a significant impact on the growth of a country, which was originally a developing country, can become a developed country with the readiness to serve its people satisfactorily. Providing an opportunity for every member of society to have confidence that all their personal data can be stored properly when receiving AI e-governance services. This is related to ethics in e-governance services using AI in both developed and developing countries.

Future studies regarding (Krämer, 2014) and (Adkisson, 2008) the ethical designed AI systems can overcome the limitations of information and services, especially in environments and situations with low validity. AI, when equipped with more ethical governance principles such as: fairness, transparency, and accountability has the potential to produce decisions that are more precise, faster, and free from emotional or ideological distortion (Binns, 2017);(Gordon, 2019). Therefore, a special study on the ethics of using AI in public services needs to be done in the future.

REFERENCES

Adewumi, A. P., & Abasilim, U. D. (2024). Digital Competency and Public Sector Digital Transformation in Nigeria. *ACM International Conference Proceeding Series*, 56–66. DOI: 10.1145/3680127.3680131

Adkisson, R. (2008). Nudge: Improving Decisions About Health, Wealth and Happiness, R.H. Thaler, C.R. Sunstein. Yale University Press, New Haven (2008), 293 pp. *The Social Science Journal*, *45*, 700–701. DOI: 10.1016/j.soscij.2008.09.003

Agarwal, H., Agarwal, S., Husain, F., & Kumar, R. (2025). *Next-Gen Video Watermarking with Augmented Payload : Integrating KAZE and DWT for Superior Robustness and High Transparency*. 1–25.

Ajayi, A. J., Agbede, O. O., Akhigbe, E. E., & Egbuhuzor, N. S. (2024). Enhancing Public Sector Productivity with AI-Powered SaaS in E-Governance Systems Article Info Received : 03-12-2023 Accepted : 04-01-2024 Page No : 1243-1259. *International Journal of Multidisciplinary Research and Growth Evaluation*, 1243–1259.

Al-Ansi, A. M., Garad, A., Jaboob, M., & Al-Ansi, A. (2024). Elevating e-government: Unleashing the power of AI and IoT for enhanced public services. *Heliyon*, *10*(23). Advance online publication. DOI: 10.1016/j.heliyon.2024.e40591 PMID: 39654738

Almesafri, A., & Habes, M. (2023). Understanding the Use of Artificial Intelligence (AI) for Human Resources in the Dubai Government. *Lecture Notes in Networks and Systems, 620 LNNS*, 417–428. DOI: 10.1007/978-3-031-26953-0_39

Arora, A., Vats, P., Tomer, N., Kaur, R., Saini, A. K., Shekhawat, S. S., & Roopak, M. (2024). Data-Driven Decision Support Systems in E-Governance: Leveraging AI for Policymaking. *Lecture Notes in Networks and Systems*, *844*, 229–243. DOI: 10.1007/978-981-99-8479-4_17

Attard-Frost, B., Brandusescu, A., & Lyons, K. (2024). The governance of artificial intelligence in Canada: Findings and opportunities from a review of 84 AI governance initiatives. *Government Information Quarterly*, *41*(2). Advance online publication. DOI: 10.1016/j.giq.2024.101929

Bakir, V., Laffer, A., McStay, A., Miranda, D., & Urquhart, L. (2024). On manipulation by emotional AI: UK adults' views and governance implications. *Frontiers in Sociology*, *9*. Advance online publication. DOI: 10.3389/fsoc.2024.1339834 PMID: 38912311

Begum, A., & Kumar, D. R. (2022). *Design a Linear Classification model with Support Vector Machine Algorithm on Autoimmune Disease data.* DOI: 10.1109/ICIEM54221.2022.9853182

Bennett, C., & Raab, C. (2003). *The Governance of Privacy: policy instruments in global perspective.*

Bhanye, J., & Shayamunda, R. (2024). *The Promise of Civic-Tech: Digital Technologies and Transparent, Accountable Governance BT - Digitalisation and Public Policy in Africa : GovTech and CivicTech Innovations* (G. Onyango & G. Karuri-Sebina (ed.); hal. 93–122). Springer Nature Switzerland. DOI: 10.1007/978-3-031-75079-3_5

Binns, R. (2017). *Fairness in Machine Learning: Lessons from Political Philosophy.* https://doi.org//arXiv.1712.03586DOI: 10.48550

Bonduki, M. R. P. C., & Cunha, M. A. (2022). Coordination of the Digital Transformation of Governments in Federalist Context: Hierarchy, Markets and Network-Based Instruments? Effects on Subnational Governments? digital service delivery. *ACM International Conference Proceeding Series*, 528–533. DOI: 10.1145/3560107.3560315

Brummer, M., & Ueno, H. (2024). Crisis and choice in digital transformation: COVID-19 and the punctuated politics of government DX in Japan. *Asia Pacific Journal of Public Administration*, *46*(4), 360–391. DOI: 10.1080/23276665.2023.2282472

Cardoso, H. R., da Silva, L. G., & Melo, B. L. A. (2022). E-government: Administrative morality and the new public arena of the network society. *Law of Justice Journal*, *36*(1), 45–73. DOI: 10.5335/rjd.v36i1.13461

Carter, L., & Bélanger, F. (2005). The utilization of e-government services: Citizen trust, innovation and acceptance factors. *Information Systems Journal*, *15*(1), 5–25. https://doi.org/https://doi.org/10.1111/j.1365-2575.2005.00183.x

Chik, W. B., & Sugumaran, H. (2024). Legal governance of artificial intelligence in healthcare devices and services in Singapore. In *Research Handbook on Health, AI and the Law: Research Handbooks in Health and Medical Law* (hal. 373–391). DOI: 10.4337/9781802205657.00030

Commission, E. (2019). *Ethics Guidelines for Trustworthy AI.* https://ec.europa.eu/digital-strategy/our-policies/european-approach-artificial-intelligence_en

Commission, E. (2021). *Proposal for a Regulation Laying Down Harmonised Rules on Artificial Intelligence (Artificial Intelligence Act).* https://digital-strategy.ec.europa.eu/en/library/proposal-regulation-laying-down-harmonised-rules-artificial-intelligence

Criado, J. I., & O.de Zarate-Alcarazo, L. (2022). Technological frames, CIOs, and Artificial Intelligence in public administration: A socio-cognitive exploratory study in Spanish local governments. *Government Information Quarterly*, *39*(3). Advance online publication. DOI: 10.1016/j.giq.2022.101688

Dahri, N., Yahaya, N., Al-Rahmi, W., Aldraiweesh, A., Alturki, U., Almotairi, S., Shutaleva, A., & Soomro, R. B. (2024). Extended TAM based acceptance of AI-Powered ChatGPT for supporting metacognitive self-regulated learning in education: A mixed-methods study. *Heliyon*, *10*, e29317. DOI: 10.1016/j.heliyon.2024.e29317 PMID: 38628736

Development, L. E. (2021). *Chapter 3*. 87–111.

Development, S., & Goals, S. D. (2022). *Leaving no one behind in the hybrid digital society*. 113–163. DOI: 10.18356/9789210019446c009

Development, S., Goals, S. D., & Nations, U. (n.d.). *5. The Future of Digital Government : Trends*. Insights and Conclusions.

Djatmiko, G. H., Sinaga, O., & Pawirosumarto, S. (2025). Digital Transformation and Social Inclusion in Public Services: A Qualitative Analysis of E-Government Adoption for Marginalized Communities in Sustainable Governance. *Sustainability (Switzerland)*, *17*(7). Advance online publication. DOI: 10.3390/su17072908

Dwivedi, Y. (2009). An analysis of e-Government research published in Transforming Government: People, Process and Policy (TGPPP). *Transforming Government: People. Process and Policy*, *3*, 7–15. DOI: 10.1108/17506160910940704

Edelmann, N., Haug, N., & Mergel, I. (2023). *Digital Transformation in the Public Sector*. DOI: 10.4337/9781802202595.Digital.Transformation.in

Emerson, K. (2020). A Note From the Editor. *Perspectives on Public Management and Governance*, *3*(3), 183. DOI: 10.1093/ppmgov/gvaa015

Floridi, L., Cowls, J., Beltrametti, M., Chatila, R., Chazerand, P., Dignum, V., Luetge, C., Madelin, R., Pagallo, U., Rossi, F., Schäfer, B., Valcke, P., & Vayena, E. (2018). AI4People—An Ethical Framework for a Good AI Society: Opportunities, Risks, Principles, and Recommendations. *Minds and Machines*, *28*(4), 689–707. DOI: 10.1007/s11023-018-9482-5 PMID: 30930541

Gauld, R. (2006). E-government: What Is It, and Will It Transform Government? *Police Quarterly*, *2*. Advance online publication. DOI: 10.26686/pq.v2i2.4193

Gil-García, J. R., & Pardo, T. A. (2005). E-government success factors: Mapping practical tools to theoretical foundations. *Government Information Quarterly, 22*(2), 187–216. https://doi.org/https://doi.org/10.1016/j.giq.2005.02.001

Goal, S. D., Index, E. D., Nations, U., States, M., Index, O. S., States, M., Desa, U. N., Egdi, O., & Egdi, C. (2022). *Global Trends in E-Government.* 1–51. DOI: 10.18356/9789210019446c006

Gordon, F. (2019). Virginia Eubanks (2018) Automating Inequality: How High-Tech Tools Profile, Police, and Punish the Poor. New York: Picador, St Martin's Press. *Law. Technology and Humans, 162–164.* Advance online publication. DOI: 10.5204/lthj.v1i0.1386

Gosain, M. S., Aggarwal, N., & Kumar, R. (2023). A Study of 5G and Edge Computing Integration with IoT- A Review. *2023 International Conference on Computational Intelligence and Sustainable Engineering Solutions (CISES)*, 705–710. DOI: 10.1109/CISES58720.2023.10183438

Gupta, A., & Bansal, R. (2013). E-governance: A step ahead. *International Conference on Advanced Computing and Communication Technologies, ACCT*, 359–362. DOI: 10.1109/ACCT.2013.80

Hafel, M., Jamil, J., Umasugi, M., & Anfas, A. (2022). Challenges of E-Government Implementation in The Region Archipelago Characteristics. *JAKPP (Jurnal Analisis Kebijakan & Pelayanan Publik)*, 44–58. DOI: 10.31947/jakpp.v8i1.21282

Heeks, R. (2006). *Implementing and Managing eGovernment: An International Text.* DOI: 10.4135/9781446220191

Herawati, A. R., & Widowati, N. (2023). *The Implementation of Artificial Intelligence in Indonesia's Public Service: Challenges and Government Strategies.* 2471–2480. DOI: 10.46254/au01.20220537

Hirzallah, M. N. Y., & Alshurideh, M. T. R. (2023). The effects of the internal and the external factors affecting artificial intelligence (AI) adoption in e-innovation technology projects in the UAE? Applying both innovation and technology acceptance theories. *International Journal of Data and Network Science, 7*(3), 1321–1332. DOI: 10.5267/j.ijdns.2023.4.006

Hoetker, G., & Fountain, J. (2002). Building the Virtual State: Information Technology and Institutional Change. *Academy of Management Review, 27*, 619. DOI: 10.2307/4134407

Hujran, O., Alarabiat, A., Al-Adwan, A. S., & Al-Debei, M. (2023). Digitally Transforming Electronic Governments into Smart Governments: SMARTGOV, an Extended Maturity Model. *Information Development, 39*(4), 811–834. DOI: 10.1177/02666669211054188

Index, E. D., & Development, E. (2022). *Regional E-Government Development and the Performance of Country Groupings*. 53–86. DOI: 10.18356/9789210019446c007

Jaakkola, H., Henno, J., Mäkelä, J., & Thalheim, B. (2019). Artificial intelligence yesterday, today and tomorrow. *2019 42nd International Convention on Information and Communication Technology, Electronics and Microelectronics, MIPRO 2019 - Proceedings*, 860–867. DOI: 10.23919/MIPRO.2019.8756913

Jaiswal, A., & Kumar, R. (2023). Breast cancer diagnosis using Stochastic Self-Organizing Map and Enlarge C4.5. *Multimedia Tools and Applications, 82*(12), 18059–18076. DOI: 10.1007/s11042-022-14265-1

Janssen, M., Yannis, C., & Zuiderwijk, A. (2012). Benefits, Adoption Barriers and Myths of Open Data and Open Government. *Information Systems Management, 29*(4), 258–268. DOI: 10.1080/10580530.2012.716740

Kamil, M., Muhammad, R., Roziqin, A., & Sari, A. E. (2025). Examining Practice Smart City in Local Government: A Smart Governance Perspective. *International Journal of Sustainable Development and Planning, 20*(2), 635–644. DOI: 10.18280/ijsdp.200214

Katsonis, M., & Botros, A. (2015). Digital Government: A Primer and Professional Perspectives. *Australian Journal of Public Administration, 74*(1), 42–52. DOI: 10.1111/1467-8500.12144

Kennedy, G. (2016). Asia-Pacific news. *Computer Law & Security Review, 32*(2), 375–380. https://doi.org/https://doi.org/10.1016/j.clsr.2016.01.002

König, P. D. (2022). Fortress Europe 4.0? An analysis of EU data governance through the lens of the resource regime concept. *European Policy Analysis, 8*(4), 484–504. DOI: 10.1002/epa2.1160

Krämer, W. (2014). Kahneman, D. (2011): Thinking, Fast and Slow. *Statistische Hefte, 55*. Advance online publication. DOI: 10.1007/s00362-013-0533-y

Kumar, A., Bhatia, A., Kumar, S., Kumar, R., & Yadav, V. (2025). Sentimental analysis using natural language processing. *AIP Conference Proceedings, 3224*(1), 20054. DOI: 10.1063/5.0246883

Kumar, A., Saini, R., & Kumar, R. (2023). A Systematic Review of Breast Cancer Detection Using Machine Learning and Deep Learning. *2023 10th IEEE Uttar Pradesh Section International Conference on Electrical, Electronics and Computer Engineering (UPCON), 10*, 1128–1133. DOI: 10.1109/UPCON59197.2023.10434530

Kumar, A., Saini, R., & Kumar, R. (2024). A Comparative Analysis of Machine Learning Algorithms for Breast Cancer Detection and Identification of Key Predictive Features. *TS. Traitement du Signal, 41*(1), 127–140. DOI: 10.18280/ts.410110

Kumar, P., Kumar, R., & Kumar, M. (2024). Data Storage in Manual Systems that Challenges in Cloud & Fog Computing-Based Systems Which are Affecting the Online Data-Oriented Application Architecture. *2024 4th International Conference on Technological Advancements in Computational Sciences (ICTACS)*, 723–727. DOI: 10.1109/ICTACS62700.2024.10841028

Kumar, R., Kumar, P., & Elngar, A. (2024). *Scrutinizing Domain-Specific Integrated Web Query Interfaces for Enhanced Security and Reliability in Storage Systems.* DOI: 10.1109/DASA63652.2024.10836405

Landri, P. (2018). *Digital Governance of Education*. Bloomsbury Publishing CN - L. https://digital.casalini.it/9781350006416

Lee, T. (2024). Artificial intelligence: Governing Singapore's smart digital journey. *Communication Research and Practice, 10*(3), 307–315. DOI: 10.1080/22041451.2024.2346430

Lim, M. (2020). The politics and perils of dis/connection in the Global South. *Media Culture & Society, 42*(4), 618–625. DOI: 10.1177/0163443720914032

Longo, J. (2024). The Transformative Potential of Artificial Intelligence for Public Sector Reform. *Canadian Public Administration, 67*(4), 495–505. DOI: 10.1111/capa.12587

Losavio, M. (2021). Algorithms of Machines and Law: Risks in Pattern Recognition, Machine Learning and Artificial Intelligence for Justice and Fairness. *Public Governance. Administration and Finances Law Review, 6*(2), 21–34. DOI: 10.53116/pgaflr.2021.2.3

Luna-Reyes, L. F., Gil-Garcia, J. R., & Cruz, C. B. (2006). Collaborative digital government in Mexico: Some lessons from federal web-based inter- organizational information integration initiatives. *Association for Information Systems - 12th Americas Conference On Information Systems, AMCIS 2006, 4*, 2357–2366.

Machmud, M., Masmuh, A., & Nasirin, C., Salahudin, Baharuddin, T., & Musa, A. E. Z. (2020). Artificial Intelligence In The Public Health Sector: The Use Of Telemedicine In Indonesia During Covid-19 | PalArch's Journal of Archaeology of Egypt / Egyptology. *PalArch's Journal of Archaeology of Egypt*, *17*(7), 10106–10118.

Mahammad, A. B., & Kumar, R. (2023). Scalable and Security Framework to Secure and Maintain Healthcare Data using Blockchain Technology. *2023 International Conference on Computational Intelligence and Sustainable Engineering Solutions (CISES)*, 417–423. DOI: 10.1109/CISES58720.2023.10183494

Mahmood, K., Nayyar, Z., & Mushtaq, H. (2018). Role of transformational leadership on e-govemment switching: Multi-channel and digital divide. *2017 12th International Conference for Internet Technology and Secured Transactions, ICITST 2017*, 475–478. DOI: 10.23919/ICITST.2017.8356453

Mahusin, N., Sallehudin, H., & Satar, N. S. M. (2024). Malaysia Public Sector Challenges Of Implementation Of Artificial Intelligence (AI). *IEEE Access : Practical Innovations, Open Solutions*, *12*(August), 121035–121051. DOI: 10.1109/ACCESS.2024.3448311

Manfredi Sánchez, J. L. (2019). Big Data and International Politics. *Baltic Yearbook of International Law*, *18*(1), 52–71. DOI: 10.1163/22115897_01801_005

McKay, F., Williams, B. J., Prestwich, G., Treanor, D., & Hallowell, N. (2022). Public governance of medical artificial intelligence research in the UK: An integrated multi-scale model. *Research Involvement and Engagement*, *8*(1). Advance online publication. DOI: 10.1186/s40900-022-00357-7 PMID: 35598004

McKelvey, F., & MacDona, M. (2019). Artificial intelligence policy innovations at the Canadian federal government. *Canadian Journal of Communication*, *44*(2), 43–50. DOI: 10.22230/cjc.2019v44n2a3509

Mogielnicki, R. (2021). Free Zones in Dubai: Accelerators for Artificial Intelligence in the Gulf. In *Artificial Intelligence in the Gulf: Challenges and Opportunities* (hal. 141–159). DOI: 10.1007/978-981-16-0771-4_8

Mohasses, M. (2019). How AI-Chatbots Can Make Dubai Smarter? *Proceedings - 2019 Amity International Conference on Artificial Intelligence, AICAI 2019*, 439–446. DOI: 10.1109/AICAI.2019.8701413

Mökander, J., Morley, J., Taddeo, M., & Floridi, L. (2021). Ethics-Based Auditing of Automated Decision-Making Systems: Nature, Scope, and Limitations. *Science and Engineering Ethics*, *27*(4). Advance online publication. DOI: 10.1007/s11948-021-00319-4 PMID: 34231029

Moon, M. J. (2002). The Evolution of E-Government among Municipalities: Rhetoric or Reality? *Public Administration Review, 62*(4), 424–433. https://doi.org/https://doi.org/10.1111/0033-3352.00196

Muhammad, A. E., & Yow, K.-C. (2023). Demystifying Canada's Artificial Intelligence and Data Act (AIDA): The good, the bad and the unclear elements. *Canadian Conference on Electrical and Computer Engineering, 2023-Septe*, 510–515. DOI: 10.1109/CCECE58730.2023.10288878

Mukonavanhu, T. (2025). An international comparison of the role of artificial intelligence in e-governance towards providing better standards of living. *Electronic Government, an International Journal, 1*(1), 137–157. DOI: 10.1504/eg.2025.10064176

Mutiarin, D., Yusuf, M., Lega, M., & Habibullah, A. (2024). Agile Bureaucracy in the Digital Age: Assessing the Public Service Delivery in Jambi City. *International Journal of Public Administration in the Digital Age, 11*(1). Advance online publication. DOI: 10.4018/IJPADA.356405

Nelson, C., & Woods, R. H. (2013). Content analysis. In *The Routledge Handbook of Research Methods in the Study of Religion* (hal. 109–121). DOI: 10.4324/9780203154281-16

Nicolás, M. A., & Sampaio, R. C. (2024). Balancing efficiency and public interest: The impact of AI automation on social benefit provision in Brazil. *Internet Policy Review, 13*(3). Advance online publication. DOI: 10.14763/2024.3.1799

Nost, E. (2024). Governing AI, governing climate change? *Geo : Geography and Environment, 11*(1), 1–5. DOI: 10.1002/geo2.138

OECD. (2016). Digital Government in Chile. In *OECD Digital Government Studies*. https://www.oecd-ilibrary.org/content/publication/9789264258013-en

OECD. (2022). *Tackling Policy Challenges Through Public Sector Innovation: A Strategic Portfolio Approach.*

Okafor, G. (2020). *Digital government blueprint "a singapore government that is.*

Orlikowski, W. J., & Gash, D. C. (1994). Technological Frames: Making Sense of Information Technology in Organizations. [TOIS]. *ACM Transactions on Information Systems, 12*(2), 174–207. DOI: 10.1145/196734.196745

Pagallo, U., Casanovas, P., & Madelin, R. (2019). The middle-out approach: Assessing models of legal governance in data protection, artificial intelligence, and the Web of Data. *The Theory and Practice of Legislation, 7*(1), 1–25. DOI: 10.1080/20508840.2019.1664543

Pages, N. C. (2025). Mogens Klitgaard in English: The European Context. *Scandinavian Studies*, *74*(4), 521–528. https://www.jstor.org/stable/40920404

Pande, D., & Taeihagh, A. (2024). A governance perspective on user acceptance of autonomous systems in Singapore. *Technology in Society*, *77*. Advance online publication. DOI: 10.1016/j.techsoc.2024.102580

Pandey, R., & Chandu, H. N. (2025). Pharmacy informatics and health information technology a systematic review. *Journal of Neonatal Surgery*, *14*(1), 554–560. DOI: 10.52783/jns.v14.1577

Pislaru, M., Vlad, C. S., Ivascu, L., & Mircea, I. I. (2024). Citizen-Centric Governance: Enhancing Citizen Engagement through Artificial Intelligence Tools. *Sustainability (Switzerland)*, *16*(7). Advance online publication. DOI: 10.3390/su16072686

Pokhrel, S. (2024). No TitleΕΛΕΝΗ. *Αγαη*, *15*(1), 37–48.

Puspita, A. F., Palil, M. R. B., Puspaningrum, A., & Suman, A. (2024). Taxing Artificial Intelligence: Value Impacts and Governance in the Tax Sector (Study in Indonesia and Malaysia). *Pakistan Journal of Life and Social Sciences*, *22*(1), 4623–4633. DOI: 10.57239/PJLSS-2024-22.1.00343

Rakhma, N. A., & Roziqin, A. (2025). Human resource mechanisms in the private and public sectors in Indonesia: What are the differences? *Insights Into Digital Business, Human Resource Management, and Competitiveness*, 377–392. https://doi.org/10.4018/979-8-3693-9440-3.ch016

Roberts, H., Cowls, J., Hine, E., Morley, J., Wang, V., Taddeo, M., & Floridi, L. (2023). Governing artificial intelligence in China and the European Union: Comparing aims and promoting ethical outcomes. *The Information Society*, *39*(2), 79–97. DOI: 10.1080/01972243.2022.2124565

Rose, R. (2005). A global diffusion model of e-governance. *Journal of Public Policy*, *25*(1), 5–27. DOI: 10.1017/S0143814X05000279

Roy, M. (2017). Cathy O'Neil. Weapons of Math Destruction: How Big Data Increases Inequality and Threatens Democracy. New York: Crown Publishers, 2016. 272p. Hardcover, $26 (ISBN 978-0553418811). *College & Research Libraries*, *78*, 403–404. DOI: 10.5860/crl.78.3.403

Roziqin, A., & Fajrina, A. N. (2021). Understanding Public Sector Innovation from A Local Perspective: Contra War (Contraceptive for Women at Risk) Innovation Study. in Malang Regency. *Jurnal Borneo Administrator*, *17*(2), 205–222. DOI: 10.24258/jba.v17i2.803

Sadanand, V. K., & Sadanand, T. (2025). Artificial intelligence in India: Navigating social justice, environmental ethics, and legal governance. In *Exploring AI Implications on Law, Governance, and Industry* (hal. 87–118). DOI: 10.4018/979-8-3373-3384-7.ch004

Sagar, M. S., Srivastava, S., Kumar, R., & Saxena, A. (2025). The evolution of industry 5.0: Harnessing artificial intelligence and communication technology. *AIP Conference Proceedings, 3224*(1), 20064. DOI: 10.1063/5.0246747

Sakuntala, S. S., Sarakanam, S., Dhavan, A., Taggar, R., & Kohli, G. (2024). The complexity of corruption and recent trends in information technology for combating corruption in India. *Public Administration and Policy, 27*(2), 126–139. DOI: 10.1108/PAP-05-2023-0058

Saner, R., Yiu, L., & Nguyen, M. (2020). Monitoring the SDGs: Digital and social technologies to ensure citizen participation, inclusiveness and transparency. *Development Policy Review, 38*(4), 483–500. https://doi.org/https://doi.org/10.1111/dpr.12433

Saxena, A., Gupta, M., Srivastava, S., & Kumar, R. (2025). Empowering edge computing: The critical role of blockchain in cybersecurity defense. *AIP Conference Proceedings, 3224*(1), 20063. DOI: 10.1063/5.0245962

Scholl, H. (2003). E-government: A Special Case of ICT-enabled Business Process Change. In *International Journal of E-Govemment Research* (Vol. 1). DOI: 10.1109/HICSS.2003.1174309

Scholl, H. J. (2022). Digital Government Research: A Diverse Domain. In *Public Administration and Information Technology* (Vol. 38, hal. 51–71). DOI: 10.1007/978-3-030-92945-9_3

Selvakumar, P., Pooja Sudharma, B., Mishra, B. R., & Satyanarayana, P. (2025). Digital government and digital governance. In *Public Governance Practices in the Age of AI* (hal. 1–22). DOI: 10.4018/979-8-3693-9286-7.ch001

Shamout, F. E., & Ali, D. A. (2021). The strategic pursuit of artificial intelligence in the United Arab Emirates. *Communications of the ACM, 64*(4), 57–58. DOI: 10.1145/3447723

Shovkovyy, O. (2024). Defining Electronic Bureaucracy and Bureaucratism. *Suranaree Journal of Social Science, 18*(2). Advance online publication. DOI: 10.55766/sjss-2-2024-257400

Sifat, R. I. (2025). Commentary—AI and Public Policy: Navigating the Possibilities and Limitations. *Politics & Policy*, *53*(1). Advance online publication. DOI: 10.1111/polp.70019

Sigfrids, A., Nieminen, M., Leikas, J., & Pikkuaho, P. (2022). How Should Public Administrations Foster the Ethical Development and Use of Artificial Intelligence? A Review of Proposals for Developing Governance of AI. *Frontiers in Human Dynamics*, *4*. Advance online publication. DOI: 10.3389/fhumd.2022.858108

Singh, C. B., Gupta, A., & Kumar, D. R. (2022). Diabetes Care Survey Using Supervised and Unsupervised Machine Learning. *2022 3rd International Conference on Intelligent Engineering and Management (ICIEM)*, 207–210. DOI: 10.1109/ICIEM54221.2022.9853085

Souter, D., & Van der Spuy, A. (2019). *UNESCO's internet universality indicators: A framework for assessing Internet development*. UNESCO Publishing.

Srivastava, S., Ahmed, D. T., & Kumar, D. R. (2024). *Urban Growth Estimation of Moradabad City Using Sentinel-2 Images*. DOI: 10.1109/GlobalAISummit62156.2024.10947888

Srivastava, S., Ahmed, T., Kumar, R., & Saxena, A. (2025). A transfer learning based model for brain tumor detection using magnetic resonance imaging. *AIP Conference Proceedings*, *3224*(1), 20059. DOI: 10.1063/5.0246542

Srivastava, S., Ahmed, T., Saxena, A., & Kumar, R. (2025). A novel machine learning hybrid model for heart disease risk assessment. *AIP Conference Proceedings*, *3224*(1), 20058. DOI: 10.1063/5.0246550

Steinbach, A. (2024). Digital sovereignty. *List Forum fur Wirtschafts- und Finanzpolitik, 50*(1–2), 51–74. DOI: 10.1007/s41025-023-00252-3

Sutrop, M. (2019). Should we trust artificial intelligence? *Trames*, *23*(4), 499–522. DOI: 10.3176/tr.2019.4.07

Swapnil, M., Garima, S., & Shashank, S. (2024). From Automation to Innovation: Harnessing the Synergy of Generative AI and Retrieval-Augmented Generation for Citizen-centric Governance. *2024 ITU Kaleidoscope. Innovation and Digital Transformation for a Sustainable World, ITU K, 2024*. Advance online publication. DOI: 10.23919/ITUK62727.2024.10772932

Takeda, T., Kato, J., Matsumura, T., Murakami, T., & Abeynayaka, A. (2021). Governance of artificial intelligence in water and wastewater management: The case study of japan. *Hydrology*, *8*(3). Advance online publication. DOI: 10.3390/hydrology8030120

Tangi, L., van Noordt, C., & Rodriguez Müller, A. P. (2023). *The challenges of AI implementation in the public sector*. DOI: 10.1145/3598469.3598516

Tshuma, G., Kritzinger, E., & Singh, S. (2024). A Framework for Promoting Digital Transformation and the Adoption of Enterprise Architecture in South Africa's Public Sector. *IFIP Advances in Information and Communication Technology*, *709*, 16–30. DOI: 10.1007/978-3-031-66986-6_2

Tyagi, N. K., & Goyal, M. (2021). Contextualizing Electronic Governance, Smart City Governance and Sustainable Infrastructure in India: A Study and Framework. In *Digital Cities Roadmap: IoT-Based Architecture and Sustainable Buildings* (hal. 163–191). DOI: 10.1002/9781119792079.ch5

Ulnicane, I., Eke, D. O., Knight, W., Ogoh, G., & Stahl, B. C. (2021). Good governance as a response to discontents? Déjà vu, or lessons for AI from other emerging technologies. *Interdisciplinary Science Reviews*, *46*(1–2), 71–93. DOI: 10.1080/03080188.2020.1840220

UNDP. (2023). A Shared Vision for Technology and Governance. *A Shared Vision for Technology and Governance*. DOI: 10.18356/9789213585214

Upreti, K., Verma, A., Mittal, S., Vats, P., Haque, M., & Ali, S. (2023). A Novel Framework for Harnessing AI for Evidence-Based Policymaking in E-Governance Using Smart Contracts. *Communications in Computer and Information Science, 1921 CCIS*, 231–240. DOI: 10.1007/978-3-031-45124-9_18

Vakkuri, V., Kemell, K.-K., Tolvanen, J., Jantunen, M., Halme, E., & Abrahamsson, P. (2022). How Do Software Companies Deal with Artificial Intelligence Ethics? A Gap Analysis. *ACM International Conference Proceeding Series*, 100–109. DOI: 10.1145/3530019.3530030

von Lucke, J., Fitsilis, F., & Gagnon, S. (2024). Using Artificial Intelligence in Parliament - Initial Results from the Canadian House of Commons. *CEUR Workshop Proceedings*, ●●●, 3737.

Wang, Y.-S., & Liao, Y.-W. (2008). Assessing eGovernment systems success: A validation of the DeLone and McLean model of information systems success. *Government Information Quarterly*, *25*(4), 717–733. https://doi.org/https://doi.org/10.1016/j.giq.2007.06.002

Wimmer, M. A., Grimm, R., Jahn, N., & Hampe, J. F. (2013). *Mobile Participation: Exploring Mobile Tools in E-Participation BT - Electronic Participation* (M. A. Wimmer, E. Tambouris, & A. Macintosh (ed.); hal. 1–13). Springer Berlin Heidelberg.

Wirtz, B. W., Jan, C. W., & Geyer, C. (2019). Artificial Intelligence and the Public Sector—Applications and Challenges. *International Journal of Public Administration, 42*(7), 596–615. DOI: 10.1080/01900692.2018.1498103

Wright, J. (2024). The Development of AI Ethics in Japan: Ethics-washing Society 5.0? *East Asian Science, Technology and Society, 18*(2), 117–134. DOI: 10.1080/18752160.2023.2275987

Chapter 5
Hybrid AI and Blockchain Systems for Digital Identity in Developing Countries:
Predictive Governance for Public Inclusion and Efficiency

Sónia Calado
https://orcid.org/0009-0004-6915-5438
University of Aveiro, Portugal

Cláudia Miranda Veloso
https://orcid.org/0000-0001-6612-0580
University of Aveiro, Portugal

ABSTRACT

The digital transformation of public administration demands innovative solutions that balance operational efficiency with inclusive governance. This chapter proposes a hybrid framework using predictive AI and blockchain to address a key barrier in developing countries: the lack of formal digital identities. By applying AI-driven predictive analytics to biometric verification and leveraging blockchain for data integrity and decentralization, it is demonstrated that integrated systems can support secure, scalable identity infrastructures. These systems expand access to public services and generate real-time data that help governments forecast needs, reduce exclusion and allocate resources strategically. Drawing on empirical studies and case examples, the chapter explores opportunities, implementation challenges and policy implications, focusing on algorithmic transparency, ethical data governance,

DOI: 10.4018/979-8-3373-3760-9.ch005

and institutional readiness, while showing how AI-powered predictive technologies can transform public administration through inclusive, data-informed and accountable digital identity systems.

INTRODUCTION

Even in 2025, tens of millions of people, most of them in the Global South, still walk through life with no official proof of who they are. No card, no digital token, nothing that lets them open a bank account, enroll a child in school or cast a vote. The result is a cascade of closed doors: clinics turn them away, social-protection schemes can't find them, and basic civil rights remain out of reach. Without a secure way to say, "this is me", inequality hardens rather than shrinks, and public institutions lose the data they need to target help where it matters most.

The irony is that digital government is racing ahead at full speed. Smartphones, mobile-money platforms and one-stop e-government portals promise friction-free services, yet they rely on an identity layer that many countries simply do not have. Legacy systems are often patch-work, vulnerable to leaks and too expensive to scale beyond major cities. Where infrastructure is thin and public administrations are stretched, the identity gap widens just when digital inclusion is meant to close it.

New hybrid solutions that blend blockchain's tamper-proof ledgers with AI's pattern-recognition muscle are starting to look like a way out of the stalemate. On the AI side, transfer-learning models have already boosted diagnostic accuracy in medical imaging, brain-tumor detection, for example, now crosses the 95% threshold in some trials. Comparative work on machine-learning classifiers in clinical settings confirms the same reliability gains. Those advances can be repurposed for biometric authentication, making face- or fingerprint-matching both faster and harder to spoof. Blockchain then locks the verified credential into an auditable chain that no single actor, whether a government agency or a mobile operator, can quietly rewrite. Together, the two technologies could give individuals a portable, privacy-preserving ID that works on- and offline, while giving public agencies the trust lawyer they need to deliver services fairly and efficiently.

Of course, technology is only half the battle; governance, regulation and user trust will decide whether these systems take root. But the tools are now on the table, and for millions still invisible to the state, that could be the first real step into modern economic and civic life.

Complementing AI, the blockchain provides a tamper-proof infrastructure for decentralized data management. Its role in cybersecurity defense, particularly at the edge, underscores its value in safeguarding sensitive identity data from unauthorized access and systemic breaches.

Building upon these capabilities, this chapter introduces a conceptual framework for hybrid AI- and blockchain-based digital-identity systems tailored to the needs of developing countries. It outlines how such systems can enhance public-service delivery, promote digital inclusion, and support transparent, data-informed governance. Grounded in real-world case examples, the framework also explores implementation challenges and ethical considerations, with particular attention to algorithmic accountability, interoperability and citizen trust.

METHODOLOGY

In this study, three real-world cases were selected to examine how hybrid AI–blockchain solutions can improve digital-identity management in developing countries. The selection relied on four criteria inspired by Service-Dominant Logic (Vargo & Lusch, 2004), which views technology as an enabler of public-value co-creation and service access:

Relevance to Public Service Access and Social Inclusion

The cases address core challenges such as refugee registration, financial inclusion and access to government benefits. Each demonstrates how AI- and blockchain-enabled identity systems can give marginalized groups a secure, verifiable ID and thereby open the door to essential services (Hunt et al., 2022; Katuu, 2025).

Technological Innovation and Scalability

All three initiatives integrate AI and/or blockchain to solve the twin problems of identity verification and data integrity. Their technical architecture is already functioning on a scale and can be adapted to similar contexts elsewhere. Blockchain's decentralization and AI-driven analytics offer security, privacy and efficiency advantages that are especially valuable where infrastructure is weak (Baharmand et al., 2021; Díaz-Rodríguez et al., 2023).

Impact on Governance and Service Delivery

The cases shed light on predictive governance, resource allocation and public-service efficiency. While AI and blockchain increase trust and cut fraud through auditable, tamper-resistant records, their success still hinges on institutional readiness, regulatory alignment and ethical data governance, as noted by Kavut (2021) and Sung & Park (2021).

Availability of Empirical Data

Each case is documented in publicly available reports, peer-reviewed studies and program evaluations, ensuring that the analysis is grounded in verifiable evidence (Baharmand et al., 2021; Díaz-Rodríguez et al., 2023).

ID2020: Digital Identity for Refugees and Marginalized Populations

The ID2020 initiative aims to furnish refugees and other excluded groups with secure digital identities via decentralized technologies such as blockchain. Early-stage pilots, notably with the WFP in Jordan and vaccination programs in Bangladesh, illustrate how such identities facilitate access to essential services and streamline administrative processes (Díaz-Rodríguez et al., 2023; ID2020, 2020; Katuu, 2025). This case was selected for its focus on populations lacking formal identification and for its integration of biometrics and blockchain to verify identity. It represents a globally scalable model for countries confronting similar refugee-related challenges.

Aadhaar (India): National Digital-Identity System

India's Aadhaar program, with enrolment exceeding 1.2 billion citizens, provides a centralized digital identity that grants access to a wide array of government services. While blockchain has been proposed to enhance Aadhaar's data security, it has not yet been adopted (Díaz-Rodríguez et al., 2023; Jha et al., 2019). The system relies on biometric authentication and government-managed databases. Scholarly debate recognizes its achievements in mass digitization while flagging concerns over privacy, data sovereignty and the ethics of large-scale biometric surveillance.

M-Pesa (Kenya): Financial Inclusion Through Mobile-Based Identity

M-Pesa is a mobile-payment platform that promotes financial inclusion by linking each user's identity to a verified mobile number. Registration procedures provide transaction traceability and security. Although blockchain is not yet part of M-Pesa's core infrastructure, Vodafone-led pilots have explored its value for cross-border remittances and heightened transaction security. The platform also applies AI-driven predictive analytics for credit scoring and micro-finance decisions, extending financial access beyond simple money transfers. Extensive evidence (Jack & Suri, 2011) shows that M-Pesa reduces transaction costs, raises household savings and bolsters financial resilience, particularly in rural and peri-urban settings.

METHODOLOGICAL APPROACH

Comparative Case-Study Design

Each case will be analyzed through three lenses, technology implementation, social impact and adoption challenges, enabling a fine-grained comparison of how hybrid AI-and-blockchain solutions address identity deficits in diverse contexts (Baharmand et al., 2021; Díaz-Rodríguez et al., 2023).

Data Collection

Empirical material will be drawn from official reports, peer-reviewed articles, independent case analyses and industry assessments to build a rounded evidence base (Hunt et al., 2022; Katuu, 2025).

Data Analysis

A thematic analysis will identify recurrent patterns, scalability, regulatory barriers, security performance and inclusive outcomes, across the three cases (Baharmand et al., 2021; Sung & Park, 2021).

Outcome Measurement

Success will be gauged by improvements in service delivery efficiency, inclusiveness and security, with a focus on how effectively each system meets the needs of underserved groups.

Expected Contribution

By investigating ID2020, Aadhaar and M-Pesa, each with proven field experience, technological innovation and measurable public-service impact, this study seeks to illuminate both the potential and the limits of applying AI and, where relevant, blockchain to digital-identity ecosystems in infrastructure-constrained settings (Díaz-Rodríguez et al., 2023). The findings will inform ongoing debates on digital inclusion, predictive governance and the prospective role of emerging technologies in transforming public-sector service delivery.

TECHNOLOGICAL FOUNDATIONS

Framing the analysis of the three case studies is the Service-Dominant Logic, which depicts technology as an operant resource enabling value co-creation across service ecosystems (Vargo & Lusch, 2004). Through this lens, the discussion captures how AI and blockchain expand public-service access, foster social inclusion and trigger administrative innovation.

When AI-driven analytics are paired with blockchain, digital-identity management gains a transformative toolkit for long-standing problems of verification, security and data integrity in the public sector. Artificial Intelligence, via machine-learning algorithms and biometric techniques, now supports high-precision identifiers such as facial recognition, iris scanning and fingerprint analysis (Díaz-Rodríguez et al., 2023). By cutting false positives and negatives, these tools keep identity platforms both accurate and resilient under demanding field conditions (Calado & Veloso, 2025; Camilleri, 2024; Díaz-Rodríguez et al., 2023).

That said, AI-based biometrics thrive only on training sets that are sufficiently large and diverse; without careful monitoring, bias and misidentification may surface, especially in multicultural or data-scarce settings (Kavut, 2021; Kroon et al., 2021).

Properly designed blockchain layers can add decentralization, transparency and immutability to an identity stack. Although most national programs still rely on centralized ledgers, distributed models are being trialed; they must first resolve issues of interoperability, scalability and regulatory fit (Baharmand et al., 2021; Sung & Park, 2021).

Taken together, AI and blockchain bring complementary strengths that, if woven into a single architecture, could yield digital-identity systems that are scalable, resilient and truly inclusive. Real-world deployments remain scarce, yet pilots and conceptual models already hint at major gains for underserved populations in both identification and service access (Hunt et al., 2022; Katuu, 2025).

Even so, predictive data in public administration does not come free of risk. Surveillance creep, algorithmic opacity and data misuse are real threats, particularly where institutions are fragile (Díaz-Rodríguez et al., 2023). Handled responsibly, however, AI–blockchain integration can anchor evidence-based policymaking and dynamic resource management, advancing a public administration that is more inclusive, efficient and sustainable, and squarely aligned with wider goals of social equity and development (Camilleri, 2024; Dey, 2025).

APPLICATIONS, CHALLENGES, AND POLICY IMPLICATIONS OF AI AND BLOCKCHAIN FOR DIGITAL IDENTITY IN DEVELOPING COUNTRIES

The application of AI and blockchain technologies in developing countries is widely recognized as holding transformative potential, particularly when the core problem is a lack of formal identification. Because many of these nations grapple with fragile infrastructure, tight budgets and governance inefficiencies, hybrid systems can deliver scalable, flexible solutions that adapt to local realities (Baharmand et al., 2021; Katuu, 2025).

Pilot initiatives and conceptual models have already illustrated how adaptable such systems can be across several critical sectors. In public health, for instance, experimental uses of AI and blockchain explore secure patient IDs and vaccine-tracking schemes, especially in areas that lie far from major urban centers (Camilleri, 2024; Hunt et al., 2022). Blockchain's immutability, tested in low-connectivity regions, ensures traceable health records and reliable proof of vaccination (Sung & Park, 2021).

Whenever traditional infrastructure is limited, blockchain can provide an accessible, decentralized backbone for identity verification, thereby reducing dependence on central authorities that may be inefficient or physically remote. Reflecting on this, Díaz-Rodríguez et al. (2023) argue that blockchain-based identities enable cross-border data-sharing for migrants and refugees, protecting their right to services and to legal recognition.

At the same time, AI-driven platforms automate resource allocation in real time, a capability that is vital for public-service responsiveness. Nguyen et al. (2022) document the technical feasibility of uniting AI, blockchain and IoT within digital-identity frameworks; even though their focus is not on marginalized users, the architecture can be re-purposed for those very contexts. Likewise, Camilleri (2024) stresses that AI analytics sharpen dynamic decision-making inside "smart governance" ecosystems.

Applications of AI and Blockchain in Developing Countries

By decentralising identity management and adding AI-powered analytics, hybrid systems can transform public-service delivery, expand social inclusion and buttress predictive governance. In territories that lack robust infrastructure, blockchain functions as a decentralised registry, while AI's predictive layer optimises service distribution. As Díaz-Rodríguez et al. (2023) show, the same integration supports IoT deployments in peri-urban zones where formal IDs are still uncommon.

Ethical and Operational Challenges

Despite their impressive promise, hybrid AI-and-blockchain identity systems also pose serious ethical and operational challenges that must be faced head-on before widescale deployment in developing-country contexts.

To begin with, algorithmic bias remains the most frequently cited hazard. When training sets lack demographic diversity, AI models may misidentify or exclude precisely the marginalized citizens the scheme is meant to serve. Kavut (2021) highlights how skewed data can translate into discriminatory outcomes in identity verification, especially in high-stakes arenas such as healthcare enrolment, social-benefit distribution and even electoral participation. Beyond the technical flaw lies a governance gap: when an algorithm blocks an entitled claimant, redress procedures are often unclear. Outsourced procurement muddies accountability further, blurring lines between public agencies, contracted private vendors and sub-contracting technology providers.

A second set of issues springs from blockchain's decentralized design. Storing credentials on a distributed ledger certainly enhances tamper-resistance, yet it simultaneously raises questions of data sovereignty, long-term governance and individual privacy. In many low-resource settings, digital literacy is limited, so citizens may not fully grasp the implications of having their personal data replicated across nodes they neither own nor control. Moreover, as Díaz-Rodríguez et al. (2023) point out, cross-border data flows, vital for refugees and migrant workers, also expose personal records to multiple jurisdictions with uneven privacy protections.

Infrastructure constraints add a third layer of complexity. Ledger synchronization and AI inferencing both rely on stable connectivity, but broadband and reliable electricity remain patchy in large swathes of the Global South. A blockchain that cannot routinely update, or an AI model that cannot pull fresh data, risks grinding to a halt, thereby eroding public trust in the entire identity ecosystem.

While the potential of hybrid AI and blockchain systems is significant, there are several ethical and operational challenges that need to be addressed to ensure successful implementation.

Algorithmic Bias

A primary concern in AI systems is the risk of algorithmic bias, which could disproportionately impact marginalized groups. Kavut (2021) highlights that insufficiently diverse training data can lead to discriminatory outcomes in identity verification processes, particularly when these systems are deployed in sensitive areas such as healthcare, voting, or social benefits.

Data Sovereignty and Privacy

Blockchain's decentralized architecture, while enhancing security, raises concerns about data sovereignty and individual privacy. In many developing countries, low levels of digital literacy mean that individuals may not fully understand the implications of decentralized data storage. Moreover, limited internet connectivity can hinder the scalability and practical deployment of blockchain-based identity systems.

Limited Digital Infrastructure

The successful implementation of these technologies requires stable digital infrastructure, which remains a challenge in many regions. Addressing connectivity issues and ensuring infrastructure robustness are essential for the sustainability and inclusivity of AI and blockchain identity frameworks.

Policy Implications and Considerations

For AI- and blockchain-based solutions to take root in public administration, above all in developing-country settings, policymakers have to guarantee that every component is transparent, equitable and secure. That requires governments to draft unmistakable regulatory frameworks covering data privacy, cyber-security and digital-literacy obligations.

Yet even the best rules falter if the state lacks the capacity to enforce them. Many low-resource administrations still struggle with shortages of technical staff, patchy interoperability across agencies and an absence of long-term funding models. Such gaps frequently stall large-scale rollouts, which is why sustained international cooperation and technical assistance become indispensable for long-term viability.

Joint work with multilateral organisations should therefore aim to establish cross-border standards for digital identity, ensuring that new technologies remain inclusive and usable for citizens of every socio-economic background. Dey (2025) underscores that success hinges on trust and on governance structures robust enough to allow meaningful public oversight of AI- and blockchain-enabled systems.

Because real-world deployments are still in their infancy, comprehensive policy frameworks, anchored in transparency, security and fairness, are essential. Without firm legal and institutional foundations, the advantages of these tools risk being eroded by data misuse, exclusion or a collapse of public confidence.

A logical first move is clear legislation. Statutes must spell out protections for privacy, cyber-defence and the ethical use of AI-driven decision-making. They should specify how identity data are collected, stored and shared; enumerate access rights; set out redress procedures; and apportion responsibility among public bodies and private suppliers. A well-defined legal landscape will both shield citizens and cultivate the trust that widescale adoption demands, thereby safeguarding sustainability and resilience against abuse.

Equally vital is partnership with international bodies on shared technical and human-rights standards, particularly for cross-border mobility and services. Cooperation with the United Nations, the World Bank and regional blocs can furnish developing states with expertise, funding and normative guidance, helping to keep digital identities secure, inclusive and portable. Such alignment is especially critical for refugees, migrants and stateless people, who move through multiple jurisdictions yet often lack any recognised ID.

Trust-building and sound governance must also sit at the heart of every implementation plan. As Dey (2025) reminds us, credibility makes or breaks AI- and blockchain-enabled public services. Transparent workflows, independent oversight authorities, channels for citizen participation and regular audits all help embed ethical responsibility. Public-engagement drives should accompany any roll-out, ensuring that citizens understand their rights, the system's mechanics and the steps to take if data are misused or algorithmic discrimination occurs.

To conclude, technical ingenuity alone will not deliver inclusive digital identity; it must be matched by deliberate, rights-centred governance. Embedding transparency, accountability and fairness at each stage allows administrations to harness AI and blockchain as drivers of social inclusion and administrative efficiency across the developing world.

Finally, projects are most legitimate, sustainable and context-appropriate when co-designed through participatory processes with the very communities they aim to serve.

CONCEPTUAL FRAMEWORK: HYBRID AI AND BLOCKCHAIN SYSTEMS FOR DIGITAL IDENTITY

As presented below, the framework provides a strategic lens through which to grasp how Artificial Intelligence (AI) and blockchain can be blended to dismantle structural obstacles in digital-identity management, particularly across developing-country contexts. By bringing together predictive analytics, decentralisation and robust data-governance safeguards, the hybrid model underpins identity systems that are inclusive, efficient and transparent.

Depicted in Figure 1, the framework's overriding purpose is to set out a conceptual scaffold for deploying hybrid AI–blockchain architectures that satisfy both the technical and the social demands of digital identity. By fusing AI-driven biometric authentication with blockchain-based security and governance, the model confronts key challenges, closing identity-verification gaps, mitigating privacy risks and counteracting the exclusion of underserved populations.

Figure 1. Conceptual framework for hybrid AI and blockchain-based digital identity systems

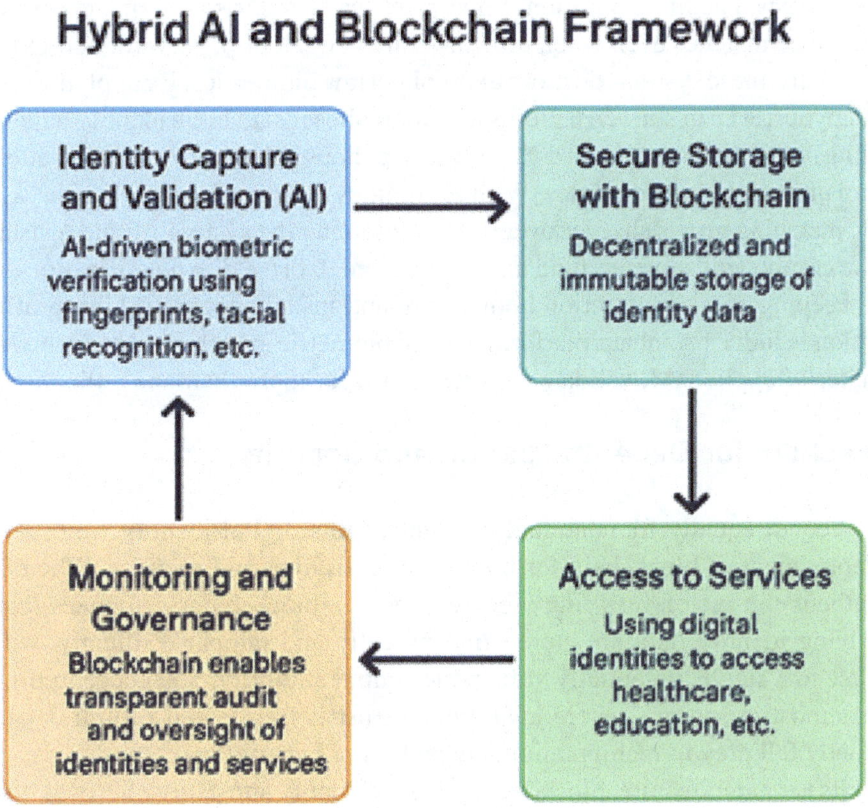

This diagram illustrates the integration of AI-driven biometric identification with blockchain-based secure data storage, embedded within a governance and inclusion strategy designed for public service access.

Key Components of the Conceptual Framework

The framework's first pillar is AI-driven predictive identification, a capability that sits at the heart of more accurate and dependable verification. Across much of the developing world, where formal ID documents can be fragmentary or missing altogether, AI provides a potent substitute by recognising individuals through biometric characteristics. Facial recognition, fingerprint scans and iris patterns, for example, yield precise matches even when infrastructure is weak or paperwork non-existent.

Crucially, these systems do more than collect raw biometrics. By applying predictive analytics, AI can surface patterns and anomalies inside large identity databases, enabling real-time actions such as flagging suspicious behaviour or spotting attempts to enrol under multiple identities. With continuous machine-learning feedback, biometric matching grows sharper over time, reinforcing the system's fraud resistance.

The component's overarching aim is therefore to drive down verification errors while keeping every transaction both secure and instantaneous. A high-profile illustration is India's Aadhaar platform, whose biometric-matching algorithms, early examples of applied AI, validate identity claims for more than one billion users.

Blockchain for Decentralization and Security

A second, equally foundational element of this digital-identity framework is the deployment of blockchain for both decentralisation and security. Whereas AI strengthens the act of verifying who someone is, blockchain guarantees that the underlying identity data are stored transparently and tamper-resiliently, without recourse to a single, potentially vulnerable central authority. Such decentralisation matters most in settings where institutional trust is fragile and central databases frequently fall prey to manipulation, corruption or cyber-attack.

By its very architecture, blockchain spread's identity attestations across a distributed network of nodes, producing a shared ledger that cannot be altered retroactively. Typically, each block records cryptographic hashes or signed attestations rather than raw personal details, thereby preserving privacy while retaining full auditability. The result is robust data integrity plus an immutable audit trail, both indispensable in public-administration contexts.

Beyond secure storage, blockchain unlocks smart contracts: automated, rule-based scripts capable of releasing services the moment an identity check succeeds. Once a user is authenticated, a smart contract can, for example, green-light access to healthcare, schooling or targeted financial aid, eliminating bureaucratic lag.

A concrete illustration is the ID2020 initiative, whose pilots employ blockchain-anchored credentials to provide refugees and stateless persons with secure, portable digital identities. Such ledgers facilitate cross-border recognition and, crucially, restore a measure of dignity and agency to populations otherwise excluded from basic rights and services.

Taken together, the decentralisation, transparency and automation that blockchain affords supply a secure backbone for modern identity systems, reinforcing public trust while enabling seamless, large-scale service delivery.

Governance and Regulation

A third essential pillar of the conceptual framework is governance and regulation, the mechanism that ensures every deployment of AI and blockchain for digital identity meets legal, ethical and societal expectations. Technological advances may solve technical hurdles, yet only strong governance safeguards can deliver systems that remain equitable, accountable and genuinely in the public interest.

Sound governance starts with explicit legal frameworks spelling out how identity data are to be collected, stored, shared and protected. Such statutes must confront cornerstone issues, user consent, data ownership, the right to be forgotten and clear avenues for redress when errors or misuse occur. As AI and blockchain evolve, regulation must also clarify the division of responsibilities between public authorities and private vendors.

Legal compliance, however, is necessary but not sufficient. Robust regulatory oversight, ideally via independent supervisory bodies, is needed to prevent misuse, guarantee transparency and enforce accountability where harm arises. In contexts where institutional trust is already thin, public-facing transparency and feedback mechanisms become even more critical.

Ethical guidelines are equally vital. Rules governing AI and biometric data must enshrine non-discrimination, privacy and inclusion, with special care for vulnerable groups such as refugees, migrants and rural populations. Any AI system used for identity checks should undergo rigorous testing to ensure it does not skew outcomes by race, gender or socio-economic status.

India's Aadhaar illustrates the stakes. Recent legal amendments and Supreme Court rulings have tightened privacy safeguards yet debates on surveillance and exclusion persist. The programme's expansion of service access sits alongside persistent questions about data oversight, underscoring why governance arrangements must be continuously reviewed and refined.

In the end, robust governance and regulation lend digital-identity systems their legitimacy. They guarantee that AI and blockchain function securely while respecting human rights, cultivating trust and supporting long-term social inclusion.

Access and Inclusion

Access and inclusion constitute the fourth, and arguably the most socially consequential, element of the conceptual framework. Although technology can boost the speed and security of identity verification, its real worth is measured by how well it brings historically invisible people into formal systems of recognition. Across the developing world, huge numbers of residents, most notably in rural or otherwise underserved communities, still lack birth certificates, national IDs or any paperwork that unlocks basic services.

To counter that reality, digital-identity programmes must place inclusivity at their very centre. Every individual, irrespective of geography, literacy or income, should find a way in. Practically, this calls for mobile-first platforms able to run on low-cost handsets and to function in areas with weak connectivity. For many citizens, a feature phone or an entry-level smartphone will be their sole gateway to public systems.

User-experience design is equally decisive. Interfaces need to be stripped-down, intuitive and available in local languages so that low-literacy users are not sidelined. Complementary outreach and public-education drives can demystify digital IDs, building both awareness and trust. Informed users are far more likely to engage with, and ultimately rely on, the new system.

Inclusion must also embrace communities that have long been overlooked: women constrained by patriarchal norms, undocumented migrants, stateless persons and others with non-standard identity claims. Hence, platforms should accept alternative proofs of identity and be flexible enough to validate non-traditional credentials.

Kenya's M-Pesa offers a striking example of how mobile identity underpins financial inclusion. By enabling unbanked citizens, many without formal identification, to transact securely, M-Pesa opens the door not just to banking but also to education, healthcare and social protection; financial identity becomes a springboard to wider civic participation.

Put simply, access and inclusion are not optional extras; they are the bedrock upon which every successful digital-identity strategy must rest. When systems are truly open to all, governments can shrink digital divides and deliver public services on an equitable footing.

Interoperability and Integration

Interoperability and integration constitute the conceptual framework's final component, ensuring that digital-identity systems operate as more than isolated technological silos and instead work seamlessly across sectors, platforms and, even more ambitiously, national borders. This capability is especially critical in developing countries, where administrative fragmentation and legacy infrastructure are common and where the long-term value of a digital ID hinges on its ability to interface with other public- and private-sector systems.

Technical integration comes first. Common protocols, open APIs and aligned data formats allow an identity platform to 'speak the same language' as health-care databases, school registries, banking rails and social-welfare programmes. Without that lingua franca, digital IDs remain functionally constrained and cannot underpin the full basket of services required for genuine inclusion.

Cross-border interoperability follows on a wider scale. Regions characterised by migration, displacement or economic integration need ID credentials that carry weight on the far side of a frontier. Mutual recognition enables refugees or transnational workers to secure legal rights, work permits, education and health care without re-registering at every turn. Achieving this outcome demands shared international standards plus intergovernmental agreements that build trust in each other's credentials.

Policy and governance integration is equally indispensable. For a digital ID to become the foundation of public administration, it must be woven into the day-to-day workflows of multiple government departments. Such embedding streamlines service delivery, improves data collection, informs resource allocation and cuts duplication.

A telling example is the ID2020 initiative, which champions portable, cross-border identities for displaced persons. By prioritising interoperability, the project lets individuals access services in several jurisdictions without restarting the enrolment process, simplifying bureaucracy and safeguarding dignity amid displacement.

Ultimately, interoperability and integration make it possible for digital-identity systems to scale, evolve and act as gateways to economic, social and civic participation, locally, regionally and globally.

Key Components of the Conceptual Framework:

AI-driven predictive identification constitutes the first pillar of the framework: biometric traits such as fingerprints, facial templates and iris patterns are processed by artificial-intelligence algorithms to authenticate and continuously revalidate users' identities. Complementing that, blockchain technology secures the resulting credentials through a decentralised ledger that records cryptographic proofs of every verified claim, providing tamper-resistance and full transparency. Effective governance and regulation must accompany these technical layers; governments are therefore required to establish legal frameworks that guarantee data privacy, security and inclusion, ensuring both transparency and equity throughout the system.

Because a digital-identity platform has little value unless everyone can use it, access and inclusion are indispensable, particularly for residents of rural or infrastructure-poor regions who may possess low-cost devices and limited connectivity. Finally, interoperability and integration ensure that the system does not operate in isolation: it must interface smoothly with existing public- and private-sector services and conform to international standards so that credentials are accepted across borders.

Implementation follows a clear flow. First, AI tools capture and validate biometric data. Second, the verified credentials are immutably anchored on a blockchain, gaining the advantages of decentralisation and security. Third, citizens present their digital ID to obtain public services ranging from health care and education to banking and social protection. Throughout this process, the blockchain provides a continuous audit trail for every verification and transaction, enabling transparent, accountable governance.

Implementation Flow of the Framework

The framework proposes a logical, four-stage pathway for deploying hybrid AI-and-blockchain digital-identity systems. It starts with identity capture and validation, where biometric traits are collected and an AI engine authenticates everyone. Next comes secure storage: once verified, credentials are anchored on a decentralised blockchain ledger so that the data remain tamper-proof, immutable and accessible solely to authorised parties. After this, users employ their newly minted digital identity to obtain essential services, health care, schooling, banking, social protection, without repeated paperwork. Throughout the life cycle, a layer of monitoring and governance guarantees transparency and public oversight; blockchain's inherent audit trail, together with formal governance frameworks, allows regulators and citizens alike to trace every verification and service interaction.

Visual Representation

For additional clarity, Table 1 presents a schematic view of these components, showing how data and services flow through the system and how AI and blockchain interact to deliver a streamlined, end-to-end digital-identity solution.

Table 1. Conceptual model

Component	Description	Technologies Used	Example
AI-Driven Predictive Identification	Uses AI algorithms and biometric data (fingerprints, facial recognition, iris scans) to verify identity with high accuracy.	Machine Learning, Facial Recognition, Biometric Authentication	Aadhaar (India) – Uses biometric matching algorithms, sometimes considered basic AI, for large-scale identity validation.
Blockchain for Decentralization and Security	Blockchain technology ensures a secure, immutable, decentralized identity record, providing transparency and reducing reliance on central authorities.	Public/Permissioned Blockchain, Cryptographic Security, Smart Contracts	ID2020 – Supports pilot programs using blockchain to secure identity attestations for refugees.
Governance and Regulation	Ensures the system adheres to ethical standards, legal frameworks, and ensures privacy, equity, and inclusiveness.	Regulatory frameworks, Transparency mechanisms	Aadhaar – Subject to ongoing legal reform to strengthen privacy and data protection frameworks.
Access and Inclusion	Focuses on ensuring universal access to digital identity services, especially in low-resource areas with limited digital infrastructure.	Mobile platforms, Low-cost devices, Digital Literacy Initiatives	M-Pesa (Kenya) – Mobile-based financial inclusion platform for unbanked populations, enabling access to essential services.
Interoperability and Integration	Ensures the system integrates with public services, private sector platforms, and cross-border systems for universal recognition of digital identities.	Interoperability protocols, Cross-border standards, API integration	ID2020 – Promotes interoperable identity frameworks to facilitate service access across jurisdictions.
Step		**Action**	
Identity Capture and Validation (AI)		Use biometric data and AI to verify identities, ensuring accuracy and preventing fraud.	
Secure Storage with Blockchain		Store identity attestations (not raw data) on a blockchain ledger to ensure integrity, decentralization, and tamper resistance.	
Access to Services		Individuals use their verified digital identity to access public services, such as healthcare, education, and financial services.	
Monitoring and Governance		Use blockchain's auditability and transparency features to enable public oversight and regulatory compliance, while protecting data privacy.	

Source: Author's own elaboration

This conceptual framework serves as a strategic roadmap for introducing AI and blockchain into digital-identity systems across developing-country contexts. It sets out the enabling technologies, governance arrangements and operational processes needed to create identity platforms that are secure, inclusive and efficient.

By weaving in safeguards for privacy, mechanisms for accountability and design choices that maximise accessibility, the framework underpins equitable digital-identity ecosystems, ecosystems capable of sustaining public trust while fuelling administrative innovation.

PRESENTATION AND ANALYSIS OF THE CASES

This section introduces and evaluates a set of case studies that apply hybrid AI-and-blockchain solutions to digital-identity management in developing countries, illustrating how such systems play out in public-administration settings. Each case is examined in depth, with detailed attention to the specific challenges confronted, the technologies deployed, and the outcomes achieved. One example, blockchain-based cross-border identity verification, highlights how decentralized ledgers can expand service accessibility for refugees and migrants, echoing the findings reported by ID (2020). Another investigates AI-driven biometric verification in densely populated urban areas, where the persistent absence of formal identity systems has long impeded access to public services. By drawing out both the successes and the limitations, the discussion offers insights into how scalable and replicable these hybrid solutions might be for other regions facing comparable obstacles. With the conceptual framework as backdrop, the analysis unfolds through three real-world cases that showcase the practicalities, challenges and results of AI-and-blockchain identity systems in action; a comparative snapshot is provided in Table 2.

Table 2. Comparative table of case studies: AI and blockchain for digital identity

Criteria	ID2020: Digital Identity for Refugees	Aadhaar (India)	M-Pesa (Kenya)
Objective	Provide secure digital identities for refugees and marginalized populations for access to essential services.	Provide a national digital identity for all citizens, enabling access to public services.	Financial inclusion for the unbanked population using mobile money.
Technology Used	Blockchain for decentralized identity attestations, biometric verification via facial recognition and fingerprints (AI-enabled in some pilot contexts).	Biometric matching (fingerprints, iris); some functions supported by algorithmic systems (basic AI); blockchain proposed, not implemented.	Mobile technology, predictive analytics (AI) for credit scoring; blockchain explored in experimental cross-border pilots, but not part of core operations.
Scope of Implementation	Global, targeting refugees and migrants across different countries and regions.	National system with 1.2 billion users in India, covering all citizens.	Primarily in Kenya, with potential for expansion across East Africa and other regions.
Impact	Enabled access to services (healthcare, education, financial aid) for refugees and marginalized groups.	Improved public service delivery, reduced fraud, and ensured access to welfare and services for billions of citizens.	Financial inclusion for millions of unbanked individuals, enabling access to financial services via mobile phones.

continued on following page

Table 2. Continued

Criteria	ID2020: Digital Identity for Refugees	Aadhaar (India)	M-Pesa (Kenya)
Challenges Faced	Scalability issues in refugee camps, data privacy concerns, and lack of infrastructure in conflict zones.	Privacy concerns, legal challenges related to mandatory linking, and data security issues with centralized systems.	Data privacy issues, limited internet access in rural areas, and challenges in cross-border regulation.
Lessons Learned	Cross-border interoperability is critical; need for collaboration with international bodies like UNHCR.	Balancing privacy and inclusion is challenging in large-scale systems; need for clear regulations and public trust.	Mobile-first identity systems are effective for financial inclusion but require strong security protocols.
Governance and Regulation	International collaboration required for cross-border recognition and security.	Government-controlled, with public oversight to ensure transparency but controversial privacy issues.	Self-regulated, with some government oversight but less formal regulation due to mobile money nature.
Interoperability	Supports cross-border recognition of digital identities, enabling service access across countries.	Designed to be interoperable across government departments and services, with potential for cross-border integration.	Interoperability with other mobile payment systems and integration with financial services.
Outcome	Digital identity solutions improved refugee integration, enabling access to essential services.	Increased service efficiency, reduced corruption, and ensured access to basic services.	Transformed financial inclusion, enabling secure mobile payments, savings, and loans for millions.

Source: Author's own elaboration

Each of the case descriptions that follow delves into the project's context, chosen technologies and prevailing governance structures, drawing attention to both the initiatives' transformative promise and the practical constraints encountered during implementation.

ID2020 - Digital Identity for Refugees and Marginalized Populations

Context and Technology

ID2020 is a global initiative designed to deliver secure digital identities to refugees and other marginalised groups who lack formal documentation. Leveraging blockchain for decentralisation and pairing it with AI-driven biometric verification, the programme enables vulnerable populations to reach essential services, healthcare, education, financial aid and more.

A decentralised ledger records cryptographic proofs of identity, keeping data both tamper-proof and under individual control, while biometric tools, facial recognition, fingerprinting and, in some pilots, AI-enhanced matching, provide robust authentication.

Challenges

Scalability – Promising as it is, extending the platform to millions of refugees worldwide poses major logistical hurdles, especially in regions with scant infrastructure.

Data Privacy and Sovereignty

Although a decentralised ledger gives users control of their data, sustained debate continues around safeguarding privacy and respecting data-sovereignty norms, issues that grow more acute where legal protections remain weak.

Access to Technology

Many camps and conflict zones suffer from limited devices, unstable connectivity and unreliable power, complicating efforts to include everyone digitally.

Impact and Results

Pilot deployments in Jordan, Greece and elsewhere confirm that secure digital IDs let refugees tap into health care, banking and education. By rendering individuals visible within host-government systems, ID2020 strengthens both protection and integration prospects.

Lessons Learned

Cross-border interoperability is indispensable, because host countries must adopt common standards if refugee credentials are to function seamlessly across borders; at the same time, close collaboration with international bodies, particularly UNHCR and other ID2020 partners, is crucial for overcoming the policy and regulatory hurdles that accompany decentralised identity systems.

Aadhaar (India) - National Digital Identity System

Context and Technology

Aadhaar is India's national digital-identity system, holding more than 1.2 billion records. It relies on biometric data, fingerprints and iris scans, to confirm who people are and to open the door to government services such as social-welfare payments, health care and banking. Identity checks are carried out by large-scale biometric-matching algorithms; although these routines do not employ advanced machine learning across the board, they still deliver automated verification at national scale.

Challenges

Privacy Concerns - Because Aadhaar stores all credentials in a single, central database, critics argue that safeguards are insufficient, warning of possible data breaches and unauthorised use of personal information.

Exclusion

Even with an inclusion mandate, many marginalised citizens, particularly in rural areas, have struggled to enrol, hampered by weak infrastructure, limited digital literacy or biometric mismatches.

Legal and Regulatory Issues

The programme has faced numerous court cases, notably over compulsory linkage to bank accounts and mobile numbers, underscoring the tension between universal coverage and privacy rights.

Impact and Results

Aadhaar has markedly expanded access to subsidised food, public-health initiatives and education, while making government transfers more efficient, curbing fraud and helping benefits reach the right people. At the same time, its roll-out highlights the need to balance privacy protections with wide-ranging digital inclusion, offering both a blueprint for large-scale ID projects and a caution regarding centralised architectures.

Lessons Learned

Introducing distributed-ledger technology could ease privacy worries by decentralising data storage and giving users tighter control over their own information. Equally, sustained digital-literacy programmes and outreach are vital to ensure that marginalised groups are included and that no one is left behind.

M-Pesa (Kenya) - Financial Inclusion through Digital Identity

Context and Technology

M-Pesa is a mobile-payment system in Kenya that has transformed financial inclusion for millions of people who lack bank accounts. The platform lets users send and receive money and handle basic financial tasks using only a mobile-phone number. Although it does not rely on distributed-ledger technology for daily operations, reliable personal identification remains crucial because each transaction must be linked to a single, verifiable individual. Vodafone and its partners have explored distributed ledgers for remittance corridors and system interoperability, but that layer is not yet part of M-Pesa's core infrastructure.

Challenge

Data Security and Privacy: Even with notable success, M-Pesa faces questions about the safekeeping of the large volumes of personal and transactional data it collects. Concerns over who controls and sees this information pose an ongoing barrier to wider adoption.

Infrastructure Gaps

Mobile-money coverage is extensive in Kenya, yet some regions still struggle with weak connectivity. Keeping M-Pesa functional in those areas demands continual investment in network expansion.

Regulatory and Legal Barriers

The service also navigates complex rules governing mobile money, both within Kenya and in neighbouring markets. Balancing compliance with local regulations while supporting cross-border payments remains a persistent challenge.

Impact and Results

M-Pesa has enabled millions of Kenyans to obtain financial services without opening traditional bank accounts, greatly improving inclusion in rural and underserved communities. The platform also delivers micro-credit and insurance to low-income users, fostering broader economic empowerment. Looking ahead, combining distributed-ledger tools with advanced analytic techniques is expected to strengthen transaction security and curb fraud, thereby increasing transparency and confidence in the system.

Lessons Learned

The combination of blockchain and AI could reinforce the security of financial transactions and improve financial risk assessments.

Digital identity solutions must be integrated with existing mobile systems to ensure accessibility in low-infrastructure regions.

By examining ID2020, Aadhaar and M-Pesa together, we see both the promise and the hurdles that hybrid identity solutions encounter when improving public-service delivery in developing nations. Each initiative demonstrates how technical innovation can expand access to health care, education, financial services and government support, while also underscoring the ethical and operational issues that still need attention.

These experiences offer practical guidance for governments, NGOs and private stakeholders aiming to build inclusive, secure and sustainable digital-identity ecosystems, and they emphasise the importance of ethical oversight, clear regulation and infrastructure investment for long-term success.

DISCUSSION

This section sets the three-case studies side by side to pinpoint where they converge, where they diverge, and which implementation patterns are starting to surface. The objective is to see what components of blended biometric-verification and distributed-ledger solutions perform best in specific settings, and what parts still need tuning or adjustment.

One point of comparison is scale: the exploratory use of a distributed ledger in ID2020 pilots can be weighed against Aadhaar's nationwide biometric system in India, revealing how well a ledger-based approach copes with different levels of infrastructure.

Another axis is verification efficiency: contrasting AI-guided biometric checks in jurisdictions with differing privacy rules helps isolate the practices that best protect personal data while maintaining security and broad access.

The review also flags hurdles surrounding interoperability and cross-border integration. By noting how each region's mix of technology, regulations and politics shapes outcomes, the comparison sheds light on the factors that either enable or impede successful uptake.

Challenges and Lessons Learned

Hybrid solutions that combine advanced analytics with distributed-ledger technology hold great promise, yet their roll-out in developing regions exposes a consistent set of technical, ethical and infrastructural hurdles.

Foremost is model bias: if the reference data lack diversity, automated matching routines can misclassify or exclude marginalized communities. Kavut (2021) details how such distortions emerge, particularly in identity-verification settings.

A second obstacle is the digital divide. Distributed ledgers depend on stable, high-bandwidth links between nodes, so countries with sparse internet coverage or limited hardware capacity struggle to keep networks in sync.

Finally, data privacy and security remain pressing concerns. Although a distributed ledger offers stronger tamper resistance than traditional databases, protecting personal details within a decentralized architecture is still challenging, as Dey (2025) underscores.

Practical Recommendations

Drawing on the case studies, the comparative review and the lessons identified, several practical steps emerge for implementing biometric-and-ledger digital-identity solutions in developing-country contexts. These recommendations speak to both policy design and technical execution.

First, governments should co-craft clear, enforceable rules, worked out in consultation with civil-society groups, technical specialists and private-sector partners, that place transparency, security and privacy at the center of every identity program. Alongside regulation, targeted investment in communications and power infrastructure is vital if citizens in remote or underserved districts are to gain reliable access.

Second, public–private collaboration deserves deliberate encouragement. Partnerships can accelerate scale-up, improve operational efficiency and distribute the cost of maintaining large-volume verification platforms.

Third, the technology stack itself must be configured to minimize bias and widen inclusion. This requires fairness-aware modelling practices, diverse training data and strong data-protection statutes, all crucial for building and sustaining public trust.

Future Research Directions

Building on the conceptual framework and empirical case analyses presented in this chapter, several critical avenues for future inquiry emerge at the intersection of data-driven pattern-recognition techniques, distributed-ledger technology, and digital-identity systems in public administration. These avenues are essential not only for refining technological solutions but also for addressing broader governance, ethical and infrastructural challenges, especially in resource-constrained settings.

First, research on adaptive distributed-ledger architectures is crucial. Most current implementations assume stable connectivity, high bandwidth and ample computing power, conditions rarely met in remote or underdeveloped regions. Future studies should therefore explore lightweight consensus mechanisms (for example, Proof-of-Authority or DAG-based networks) and off-chain storage designs that permit decentralized identity management where connectivity is limited or intermittent. Experimental work and field trials in humanitarian contexts will be vital for validating such models under real-world constraints.

Second, a pressing line of inquiry concerns fairness and bias mitigation in algorithm-based identity verification. As noted earlier, biometric authentication systems powered by statistical learning can inadvertently discriminate against specific demographic groups, particularly when training data lack diversity. Research is needed to create bias-resilient models, develop inclusive biometric standards and define clear metrics for algorithmic accountability. Interdisciplinary collaboration, bringing together technologists, ethicists and anthropologists, will be essential to ensure culturally contextualized solutions that respect local norms and practices.

Third, governance frameworks for integrating distributed ledgers with pattern-recognition tools warrant in-depth exploration. Technical capabilities may be advancing quickly, yet institutional capacity and regulatory clarity often lag. Future studies should examine comparative legal models, focusing on how different countries regulate decentralized identity, consent management, data sovereignty and liability in automated decision-making. Particular attention should go to cross-border digital identities relevant to refugees, migrants and stateless people, where jurisdiction and recognition remain unresolved.

Fourth, research must evaluate the long-term societal impact of technology-enabled digital-identity systems, specifically, their influence on citizen–state relations, trust in public institutions and perceptions of surveillance or data autonomy. Participatory action research and longitudinal ethnography can shed light on how communities receive these systems and how adoption evolves over time.

Lastly, interoperability across sectors and borders is still underexplored. Future investigations could address how digital-identity frameworks can be harmonized with international standards, ensuring portability, scalability and seamless interaction with platforms in health, education, finance and humanitarian aid. There is also scoped to examine the role of supranational bodies, such as the UN or World Bank, in fostering trust networks and providing normative guidance for identity governance in fragile states.

In sum, advancing research in this domain will require interdisciplinary methods that blend insights from technology, public policy, law, development studies and ethics, and must engage closely with communities most affected by digital exclusion, guaranteeing that innovation aligns with principles of inclusion, justice and democratic accountability.

CONCLUSION

Hybrid platforms that combine advanced data-driven analytics with distributed-ledger technology represent a major shift in the way digital identity is conceived and administered, particularly in developing regions where conventional identity infrastructures remain inadequate, fragmented or altogether absent. This chapter has shown how, when thoughtfully designed and ethically deployed, such tools can tackle persistent governance problems: exclusion from public services, weak data integrity and inefficient resource allocation.

By improving the accuracy of biometric checks through sophisticated matching algorithms and safeguarding records via a decentralized, tamper-resistant ledger, these systems offer scalable and transparent alternatives to legacy models. They can dramatically widen access to health care, education, financial products and legal recognition, especially for displaced people, rural communities and others who lack formal documentation.

Yet technology by itself does not guarantee success. Outcomes depend on robust legal frameworks, strong regulatory institutions and participatory governance that nurtures transparency and public confidence. Ethical risks, bias in automated decisions, threats to privacy, must be addressed up-front through inclusive design, open oversight and continuous civic dialogue. Without such safeguards, the new tools could entrench old inequities or even create fresh forms of digital exclusion.

Looking ahead, several priorities stand out. One is deploying digital-identity solutions in humanitarian settings, conflict zones, post-disaster areas, where reliable verification can speed aid delivery and secure legal status for vulnerable groups. Another is achieving cross-border interoperability, which demands coordinated international standards and shared oversight so that credentials are trusted across jurisdictions. Equally important is sustained investment in digital literacy, ensuring that communities, especially those historically underserved, can navigate, benefit from and critically assess these systems.

In the end, distributed ledgers and data-driven analytics should be viewed not merely as technical fixes but as levers for systemic reform in public administration. Their real value lies in supporting governance that is inclusive, evidence-based and accountable. The framework set out in this chapter offers a practical roadmap for design and implementation, while the case studies confirm real-world feasibility and impact. As nations advance their digital agendas, hybrid identity infrastructures point the way toward more equitable, transparent and resilient public-service delivery.

REFERENCES

Baharmand, H., Saeed, N., Comes, T., & Lauras, M. (2021). Developing a framework for designing humanitarian blockchain projects. *Computers in Industry, 131*, 103487. DOI: 10.1016/j.compind.2021.103487

Calado, S., & Veloso, C. M. (2025). Artificial Intelligence in Accounting. In *Empowering Value Co-Creation in the Digital Era* (pp. 75–102). IGI Global., DOI: 10.4018/979-8-3373-1742-7.ch004

Camilleri, M. A. (2024). Artificial intelligence governance: Ethical considerations and implications for social responsibility. *Expert Systems: International Journal of Knowledge Engineering and Neural Networks, 41*(7). Advance online publication. DOI: 10.1111/exsy.13406

Dey, S. (2025). *Leveraging AI and Blockchain for Digital Transformation.*, DOI: 10.4018/979-8-3693-8664-4.ch013

Díaz-Rodríguez, N., Del Ser, J., Coeckelbergh, M., López de Prado, M., Herrera-Viedma, E., & Herrera, F. (2023). Connecting the dots in trustworthy Artificial Intelligence: From AI principles, ethics, and key requirements to responsible AI systems and regulation. *Information Fusion, 99*, 101896. DOI: 10.1016/j.inffus.2023.101896

Hunt, K., Narayanan, A., & Zhuang, J. (2022). Blockchain in humanitarian operations management: A review of research and practice. *Socio-Economic Planning Sciences, 80*, 101175. DOI: 10.1016/j.seps.2021.101175

ID. (2020). *Digital Identity and Refugee Services*. https://id2020.org

Jack, W., & Suri, T. (2011). *Mobile Money: The Economics of M-PESA*. https://doi .org/DOI: 10.3386/w16721

Jha, A., Bhattacharjee, R. K., Nandi, M., & Barbhuiya, F. A. (2019). A Framework for Maintaining Citizenship Record on Blockchain. *Proceedings of the 2019 ACM International Symposium on Blockchain and Secure Critical Infrastructure*, 29–38. https://doi.org/DOI: 10.1145/3327960.3332389

Katuu, S. (2025). Blockchain innovations and the contribution of the intergovernmental organizations. *Global Knowledge, Memory and Communication, 74*(1/2), 128–146. DOI: 10.1108/GKMC-07-2022-0179

Kavut, S. (2021). Digital Identities in The Context of Blockchain and Artificial Intelligence. *Selçuk İletişim, 14*(2), 529–548. DOI: 10.18094/josc.865641

Kroon, N., & Alves, M. do C., & Martins, I. (2021). The Impacts of Emerging Technologies on Accountants' Role and Skills: Connecting to Open Innovation—A Systematic Literature Review. *Journal of Open Innovation, 7*(3), 163. DOI: 10.3390/joitmc7030163

Nguyen, T. T., Nguyen, Q. V. H., Nguyen, D. T., Nguyen, D. T., Huynh-The, T., Nahavandi, S., Nguyen, T. T., Pham, Q.-V., & Nguyen, C. M. (2022). Deep learning for deepfakes creation and detection: A survey. *Computer Vision and Image Understanding, 223*, 103525. DOI: 10.1016/j.cviu.2022.103525

Sung, C. S., & Park, J. Y. (2021). Understanding of blockchain-based identity management system adoption in the public sector. *Journal of Enterprise Information Management, 34*(5), 1481–1505. DOI: 10.1108/JEIM-12-2020-0532

Vargo, S. L., & Lusch, R. F. (2004). Evolving to a New Dominant Logic for Marketing. *Journal of Marketing, 68*(1), 1–17. DOI: 10.1509/jmkg.68.1.1.24036

ADDITIONAL READING

Braun, T. (2025). Liability for artificial intelligence reasoning technologies: A cognitive autonomy that does not help. *Corporate Governance (Bradford).* Advance online publication. DOI: 10.1108/cg-09-2024-0471

Camilleri, M. A. (2024). Artificial intelligence governance: Ethical considerations and implications for social responsibility. *Expert Systems: International Journal of Knowledge Engineering and Neural Networks.* Advance online publication. DOI: 10.1111/exsy.13406

Dey, S. (2025). *Leveraging AI and Blockchain for Digital Transformation.*, DOI: 10.4018/979-8-3693-8664-4.ch013

Díaz-Rodríguez, N., Del Ser, J., Coeckelbergh, M., López de Prado, M., Herrera-Viedma, E., & Herrera, F. (2023). Connecting the dots in trustworthy Artificial Intelligence: From AI principles, ethics, and key requirements to responsible AI systems and regulation. *Information Fusion, 99*, 101896. DOI: 10.1016/j.inffus.2023.101896

Elliott, K., Price, R., Shaw, P., Spiliotopoulos, T., & Ng, M. (2021). Towards an equitable digital society: Artificial intelligence (AI) and corporate digital responsibility (CDR). *Society, 58*(5), 399–409. DOI: 10.1007/s12115-021-00594-8 PMID: 34149122

Floridi, L., & Cowls, J. (2021). A unified framework of five principles for AI in society. *Minds and Machines*, *31*, 137–165. DOI: 10.1007/s11023-020-09520-6

González, A. L., Moreno, M., & Román, A. C. M. (2024). Ethics in artificial intelligence: An approach to cybersecurity. *Ibero-American Journal of Artificial Intelligence*, *27*(73), 38–54. DOI: 10.4114/intartif.vol27iss73pp38-54

Llorca, D. F., Hamon, R., Junklewitz, H., & Grosse, K. (2024). Testing autonomous vehicles and AI: Perspectives and challenges from cybersecurity, transparency, robustness and fairness. *arXiv preprint*. https://doi.org//arXiv.2403.14641DOI: 10.48550

Nguyen, T. T., Nguyen, Q. V. H., Nguyen, D. T., Nguyen, D. T., Huynh-The, T., Nahavandi, S., Nguyen, T. T., Pham, Q.-V., & Nguyen, C. M. (2022). Deep learning for deepfakes creation and detection: A survey. *Computer Vision and Image Understanding*, *223*, 103525. DOI: 10.1016/j.cviu.2022.103525

Vemuri, N., Thaneeru, N., & Tatikonda, V. M. (2023). Securing trust: Ethical considerations in AI for cybersecurity. *Journal of Knowledge and Learning in Science and Technology*, *2*(2), 175. DOI: 10.60087/jklst.vol2.n2.p175

KEY TERMS AND DEFINITIONS

Artificial Intelligence (AI): A branch of computer science that simulates human intelligence through algorithms capable of learning from data and making decisions or predictions.

Biometric Authentication: A method of identity verification based on unique biological characteristics such as fingerprints, iris patterns, or facial features.

Blockchain: A decentralized digital ledger technology that records transactions securely and immutably, often used to enhance transparency and data integrity.

Digital Identity: A set of electronic credentials or attributes that uniquely identify an individual and allow them to access digital services.

Digital Inclusion: The effort to ensure all individuals and communities, particularly marginalized groups, have access to and the ability to use digital technologies effectively.

Interoperability: The ability of digital systems and services to operate across different platforms, organizations, or national boundaries.

Predictive Analytics: The use of statistical algorithms and AI to analyze current and historical data to forecast future outcomes.

Smart Contracts: Self-executing code stored on a blockchain that automatically enforces terms and conditions of an agreement.

Technological Infrastructure: The foundational hardware, software, and connectivity systems required to implement and support digital services.

Technological Sovereignty: The ability of individuals or states to control their digital data, platforms, and technologies independently.

Chapter 6

Improving Cybersecurity and Risk Management Techniques in AI Blockchain Governance Systems

Puneet Chauhan
https://orcid.org/0009-0000-1652-8764
Swami Vivekanand Subharti University, India

Krishan Pal
https://orcid.org/0009-0008-3040-9954
Swami Vivekanand Subharti University, India

Almash Saifi
https://orcid.org/0009-0003-6303-8663
Swami Vivekanand Subharti University, India

Vikas Sharma
https://orcid.org/0000-0001-8173-4548
SRM Institute of Science and Technology, Delhi, India

Tarun Kumar Vashishth
https://orcid.org/0000-0001-9916-9575
IIMT University, Meerut, India

Kajal Choudhary
https://orcid.org/0009-0000-6713-6509
IIMT University, Meerut, India

ABSTRACT

The combination of AI with Blockchain or AI-Blockchain integration disrupts existing governance structures. Cybersecurity however becomes an important area of concern in system fortitude, data trust, and public confidence. The focus of this chapter is the AI-Blockchain governance system's cybersecurity vulnerabilities such as smart contracts' flaws, AI model attacks, and other blockchain specific weaknesses like 51% and Sybil attacks. Addressing these concerns, some of the focus areas include

DOI: 10.4018/979-8-3373-3760-9.ch006

Protecting AI model training, issuing decentralized identities, end-to-end encryption, and blockchain auditors to enhance security. More importantly, fostering proactive threat intelligence, robust governance policies and frameworks, and resilient design architectures for active defences against sophisticated cyber threats is paramount.

INTRODUCTION

The intersection of Artificial Intelligence (AI) and Blockchain has transformed digital governance systems into decentralized, intelligent, automated frameworks capable of sophisticated AI-Blockchain governance. These frameworks aim for the maximum possible level of information transparency, decision automation, and reliability of the information. The implementation of these technologies, however, introduces new risks related to cybersecurity, trust, and scalability. In traditional systems, a central authority with a predetermined set of security controls effectively reduces risk. In contrast, decentralized, AI driven systems, while inherently more versatile, expose vulnerable trust borders to new attack vectors. For instance, AI algorithms are vulnerable to data poisoning or adversarial examples. Moreover, blockchain systems are not immune to 51% attacks, Sybil attacks, and abuse of smart contract vulnerabilities. This chapter designs specific cybersecurity and risk management frameworks tailored to the governance of AI-Blockchain systems. It highlights the need to safeguard the data's trust, ensuring automated activities are safeguarded from an override, and maintaining ethics and compliance. A proactive approach to defending against sophisticated disruptive policies is pre-emptive threat identification, strong policy formation, and systems built to withstand attacks (Ahmed, 2025).

Summary of AI- Blockchain Governance Systems

AI-Blockchain governance systems represent a paradigm shift in managing infrastructure because of the unique combination of technique and intellect used to run administrative work on digital frameworks. They do not concentrate all authority in one place but instead employ a network of nodes which operate on algorithms that independently decide, apply, and manage rules as well as operations. With the aid of Artificial Intelligence, such systems are able to recognize unique patterns within data, classify them, and make real-time predictions or decisions. This helps in ensuring that governance mechanisms are adaptable, responsive, and anticipatory to emerging situations. Blockchain, on the other hand, guarantees complete assurance of transparency as all actions and outcomes of the decisions are stored in the unchangeable ledger which fosters trust and accountability. Moreover, governance is done automatically through self-enforcing agreements embedded into the blockchain referred to as smart contracts which automatically enforce rules without intermediaries. The result is a robust ecosystem of governance which is intelligent and resistant to manipulation or falsehoods. AI-Blockchain systems can now be found in various industries including finance, healthcare, energy, and supply chain because dependable and secure transparent decision-making are primary requirements. Their structures have the capability to remove human mistakes, augment control—and even equalize power distribution. But this inclusion does create difficult issues. The same characteristics which enhance the power of these systems, such as autonomy and decentralization, create weaknesses. AI models can be subjected to adversary attacks or data tampering, and blockchain systems are vulnerable to particular threats like the 51% attack or vulnerabilities within the smart contract code. Hence, while there are prospects associated with the blockchain integrated with AI governance systems in terms of efficient, secure, and decentralized management, there is a need for sophisticated cyber defense approaches (Khan and Daniel, 2024).

Importance of cybersecurity in intelligent decentralized systems

In intelligent decentralized systems, cybersecurity serves as one of the foundational components to guarantee the trust, resilience, and functionality of the system as a whole. With the shift from a centralized operational framework, coupled with the integration of Artificial Intelligence (AI) and Blockchain technology, systems become more autonomous and interconnected, but also susceptible to sophisticated cyber-attacks. The absence of a central authority complicates traditional security management, and dramatically increases the necessity of strong defense mechanisms integrated into the system architecture (Nosina and Swarna Latha, 2024).

In these environments, data is distributed across multiple nodes, and decision-making processes are executed through smart contracts or AI algorithms that operate independently. While this decentralization enhances transparency and reduces single points of failure, it also opens new avenues for cyberattacks. Malicious actors may attempt to exploit vulnerabilities in smart contract logic, poison AI training datasets, or manipulate consensus mechanisms in blockchain networks. Attacks like 51% attacks, Sybil attacks, or adversarial AI inputs could compromise not just system operations, but the very foundation of user trust. In a decentralized system, there is no oversight or fast containment, unlike in a centralized system. As a result, there needs to be some proactive intelligent cybersecurity to be built into the system. In automated intelligent environments, like identity verification, transaction approvals, or policy enforcement, AI makes the decisions, and any disruption in the AI model's functionality could result in catastrophic failures. For instance, biased AI can enable access to unauthorized users or execute transactions that they should not be executing. One equally important concern can be the protection of sensitive data. In social environments with decentralization, AI models tend to pull information from an assortment of datasets like personal, financial, or health records. In the absence of strong encryption and access limits, such data stands the risk of being violated and misused, resulting in breaches of privacy and privacy. While blockchain's promise of immutable logs and data provenance is real, it is cybersecurity that guarantees features are not compromised during data exchange, consensus, or contract execution. Moreover, ethical governance and regulatory compliance are closely intertwined with cybersecurity. In decentralized systems, which are by their nature intelligent in autonomous function, there are often multiple actors across jurisdictions; compliance with overarching regulations like GDPR, HIPAA, or ISO/IEC 27001 is crucial. These frameworks ensure operations align with consent policies, data protection, institutional policies, and, most importantly, user confidence and public trust are maintained (Salama and Al-Turjman, 2024).

BACKGROUND AND CONTEXT

The integration of Artificial Intelligence (AI) and Blockchain technologies changes the architecture of digital governance systems. This blend changes the processes of making decisions, managing information, and building trust within space. While the two technologies separately have transformative impacts on many sectors, their combination provides for incredible opportunities for innovation, but at the same time, creates entirely new challenges for cybersecurity. One must understand the principles of AI and Blockchain and the modern governance systems dealing with cybersecurity concerns to appreciate the importance and lack of focus on cybersecurity resilience.

Foundations of AI-Blockchain Integration

The merge of AI and classic blockchain creates systems with enhanced functions as well as ameliorated weaknesses of both domains. AI, which tries to emulate human intelligence, allows for machine learning, pattern recognition, outcome prediction, and automated decision making. Blockchain refers to a distributed ledger technology, enabling data protection, accessibility, and trust through cryptography and consensus protocols. The resulting landscape of these technologies provides the foundation for today's governance systems, intelligent self-regulatory decentralized systems capable of autonomous decision making and information safeguarding. These two technologies merging provides us with the intelligent governance paradigm based on the synergy principle where without AI, Blockchain cannot harness the decentralization and immutability benefits while lacking flexibility dynamism AI provides. For example, the argument about AI models being opaque or "black boxes" renders the auditing of their decision processes infeasible stands strong. Recording AI decisions and inputs on a blockchain ledger makes the system accountable, ensuring transparency and auditability. This is crucial in the context of governance applications where fairness, ethics, and compliance are paramount concerns (Alzoubi, 2024).

On the other hand, AI can be integrated into blockchain systems to improve their intelligence and efficiency. AI can augment consensus algorithms, detect fraud, predict network traffic, and facilitate resource management. In supply chain ecosystems, for instance, AI can predict demand, while blockchain technology and smart contracts guarantee that processes capture and are verifiably auditable from raw material procurement to product delivery. In the healthcare domain, AI can assist in predicting patient's diagnoses through data analysis, whereas blockchain can take care of the management of electronic health records along with the patient's consent (Mahammad and Kumar, 2023). AI integration aids blockchain technology smart contracts, which are programs kept within the blockchain and executed automatically. That allows the creation of self-adjustable contracts which can modify their clauses or invoke governance actions autonomously without human intervention. Plus, AI and Blockchain technology's intersection is crucial for the emergence of Decentralized Autonomous Organizations (DAOs), which are systems with a defined governance process executed through code and collective acceptance from the community. With stakeholder data, AI agents can evaluate and render optimized choices. All the decisions made are ensured to be recorded in a clear and unchangeable manner on the blockchain (Vashishth et al., 2024).

Figure 1. AI & blockchain synergy architecture

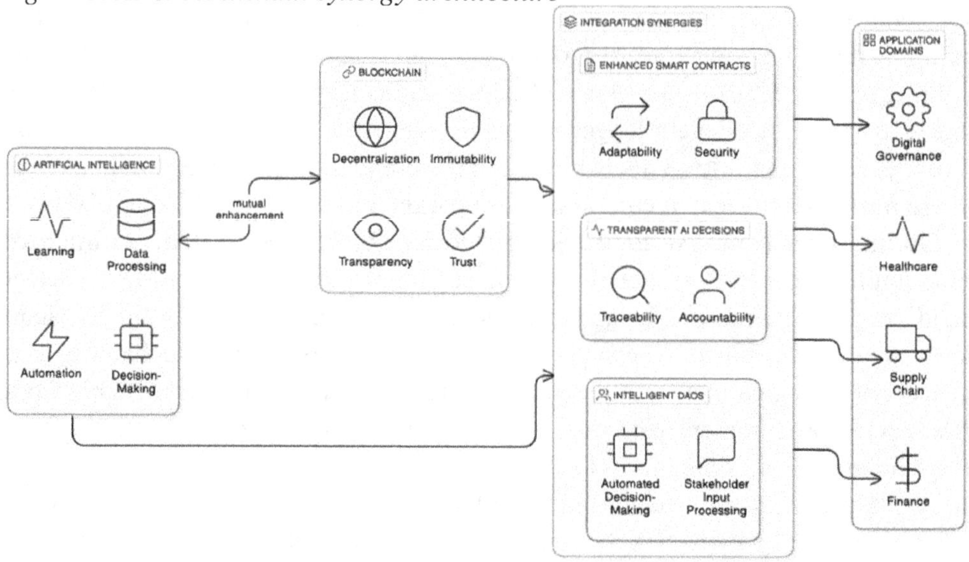

The amalgamation of AI with Blockchain raises profound issues of a technical and financial nature. Figure 1 depicts the integration of AI & Blockchain in Risk Management. Problems concerning Blockchain's scalability, the Artificial Intelligence processes' computational heaviness, and the demand for real-time responsiveness, need hybrid architectures and new designs for consensus models. Apart from the issues mentioned, persistent focus is needed on data privacy, ethics, and regard for other domains of information systems (Srivastava et al., 2025).

Cybersecurity Challenges in Modern Digital Governance

As we consider the realm of governance in the digital world, more so where AI and Blockchain technologies spawn together, we note that cybersecurity presents itself as one of the most complex challenges. The problem intensifies when we consider the 'smart' aspects of the system such as smart contracts, a decentralized identity, or even intelligent decision making. The ease with which information can be accessed and the system leveraged results in creations of a vast number of malintent attacks. Former methods protecting the system cannot cope with today's advanced technology. These issues pose a broad spectrum of challenges directed towards the infrastructure, algorithms, and including datacentric ones such as privacy, fracturing, and overall system unification.

Vulnerabilities in Smart Contracts

One of the indispensable components of Blockchain-AI systems is the capability of automated reasoning, execution, and smart governance which is done through smart contracts. Eager to program them, humans can fall prey easily to logical and programming paranoia. Once deployed, these contracts are immutable meaning that remaining loopholes will be abused relentlessly being taken advantage of by hackers, breeches such as logic manipulations pinpointed by dominant contracts alongside integers overflowing or even re-entrancy attacks pose in constructions of significant financial impacts resulting in major losses as well as shut downs of the system.

AI Model Attacks

The AI models implemented in governance systems for decision making, predictive analysis, and resource allocation are exposed to adversarial threats. Techniques like data poisoning - where misleading data is added to the training set - are used by attackers, as well as the use of adversarial inputs which trick an AI into making erroneous decisions. Such an attack severely degrades not just the precision of AI-powered governance, but public confidence as well, especially when sensitive operations like public resourcing or identity verification are involved (Soundenkar et al., 2024).

Blockchain-Centric Threats

51% and Sybil Attacks: The decentralization of blockchain networks is often taken to imply fortified safety; however, they remain susceptible to structural attacks. When a group of users obtains more than 50 percent control of a blockchains mining or validation power, they can execute a so-called 51 percent attack. This enables them to manipulate the ledger for double spending or censoring transactions. Sybil attacks are the opposite: creating multiple pseudonymous nodes and claiming control of the consensus process. All of these put the fairness, trustworthiness, and decentralization features of digital governance platforms at risk (Adejumo and Ogburie, 2025).

Issues of Privacy and Keeping Data Confidential

In the context of digital governance, the secure handling of personal data like identities, voting lists, or medical files is paramount. AI technologies frequently employ extensive datasets, which require heavy supervision. The profound transparency of blockchain technology can also hamper privacy requirements. Sensitive data, without modern encryption methods such as zero-knowledge proofs or homomorphic encryption, run the risk of being revealed on public ledgers, pooling legal, ethical, and safety problems (Vashishth et al., 2025).

Modern digital governance systems regard the issue of cybersecurity as no longer a purely technical matter. It has now evolved into a primary concern on trust, operability, and social acceptance.

VULNERABILITIES IN AI-BLOCKCHAIN SYSTEMS

The amalgamation of Artificial Intelligence (AI) and Blockchain technology has opened new avenues of automation, transparency, intelligence, and decentralization in digital governance systems. But on the other hand, the distinct features and working mechanisms of the two technologies give rise to sophisticated vulnerabilities which from the convergence itself pose to be a challenge. These vulnerabilities pose great risks in the system's coherence, trust critical user, and the efficacy of intelligent governance systems (Bhumichai et al., 2024).

Smart Contract Exploits

Decentralized AI Blockchain governance systems employ smart contracts which self-execute and are implemented on blockchain, to automate processes. Autonomous systems, however, come with challenges such as the multitude of security threats. A smart contract becomes static upon deployment, leaving bugs and issues in the code to be permanently embedded in the system. A very serious threat to that is the re-entrancy attack vulnerability, of where a malicious entity drains funds or logic by repetitively invoke a contract function before the preceding execution is completed, demonstrated during the infamous DAO hack on Ethereum. Unchecked external calls, which can allow execution of arbitrary code by attackers, and arithmetic errors like integer overflow and underflow, which can modify balances or disrupt logic, exemplify additional common errors. Timestamp manipulation and gas-limit mark exploitation can attract preferential treatment in sensitive timing operation edges. Moreover, a lack of robust testing and careless coding can lead to grave vulnerabilities due to the underestimation of interacting contracts' complexities. Supplied data to the blockchain through oracles can also be exposed to invalid data nullifying the integrity of the smart contract resulting in novel and disastrous implications. To counter such vulnerabilities, smart contracts need an oversight system that rigorously audits smart contracts and applies formal verification as well as secure design principles before deployment. In the absence of such measures, vulnerabilities in the smart contract have catastrophic implications for the security, reliability, and operational efficacy of governance infrastructures built on AI-Blockchain.

AI Model Threats

AI solutions can enhance consensus methods, assist in fraud detection, estimate network traffic, and support resource allocation. Regarding supply chain ecosystems, for example, AI can anticipate the need for certain items, while blockchain and smart contracts ensure procedures are capture and auditable from raw materials all the way to product delivery. This hinders their ability to learn meaningfully, while systems get increasingly complicated to manage, causing the AI in the assumptions that domesticated antecedents make errors in principals or ignores critical patterns together that stand fundamental for business processes. AI system's balance becomes weaker and more brittle with reliance and further leads to an inevitable possibility of an extinction event. Another Existent worry is adversarial example attacks, achieved by provoking AI to mistakenly interpret a desired outcome through different inputs. These inputs can be perfectly normal from the perspective of the human, and yet they can dramatically change the peace and behavior of the model spaciously in facial recognition, transaction validation, and in determining the appropriateness of a given piece of content. Moreover, consider AI models to be susceptible to model inversion and model extraction attacks, while people could reconstruct the training data and data or the model itself that get formulated id analyzing responses computed. Beyond the realm of data posing threats to privacy by sensitive information shuttered into pieces, it also endangers without a doubt algorithms crafted, along with ownership in a corporate sense.

Blockchain-Specific Vulnerabilities

The vulnerabilities associated with blockchain technology pose significant threats to AI-Blockchain governance systems, especially considering that defenders consider security by decentralization and transparency as a hallmark of blockchain technology. One primary weakness is an attack known as 51%, which allows an attacker who holds more than half of the network's computing or staking power to take control of the blockchain ledger; they can reverse transactions, double-spend execution, and prevent irreversible actions from being executed. This creates a uniquely dangerous threat for both Proof of Work (PoW) and Proof of Stake (PoS) systems because it undermines an ecosystem's trust and credibility. Yet another prevalent threat is the Sybil attack in which a single malicious user controls a disproportionate slice of the network governance by creating a great number of fake identities or nodes. This threatens the very principles of fairness and decentralization that blockchains boast about, especially in open or permissioned networks that lack user authentication.

Interoperability and Integration Risks

The full capabilities of AI-Blockchain governance systems depend on the application of integration. Some of the most important factors are listed below. What follows is a description of each factor's unique risks that are detailed below:

Lack of Cohesive Security Measures

Stratum dismantles the AI-Blockchain systems into discrete units such as subsystems like cloud services, legacy systems and even include certain peripheral systems. For each of these integrated components, there are poor security practices that are bound to accompany them. These gaps enable many attack vectors where the attackers' prime aim is to exploit access and privileged system weaknesses to gain access to more secure systems. The weakest link of an integrated network that utilizes base grade (Vashishth et al., 2024) encryption, authentication, or access controls become a potential threat to the entire ecosystem.

Problems Related to Data Blocking and Integrity

Another significant problem involves the major delay, or the out-of-order sequence timing of interactions between AI model components and the blockchain. With improper validation or timing alignment, the information potentially sent through different processes, blocks or systems is disparate and conflicting, which may lead to incorrect AI results, invalid executions of smart contracts and transactions. In real-time system cases, like healthcare or finite, even the smallest bits of manipulated information can result in malpractice, excessive expenditure, and operational halts starkly.

Lapses in Protocol and Consensus

Imagine an AI application sitting atop multiple blockchains. Each one integrates distinct interoperable protocols and consensus techniques like Proof of Work, Proof of Stake, or Byzantine Fault Tolerance. These variations could make reliable and secure communication across chains difficult and result in transaction errors, lack of sync, or symmetry breaches, or information breach. The absence of uniform design structures across the various blockchains mounts the challenge to manage cross-platform governance systems.

Concerns Regarding the Incorporation of AI Services

The use of proprietary APIs and cloud-based or open-source machine learning services from external vendors increases the risk of data poisoning, model theft, and inference attacks. Malignant external AI services may exploit the ability-controlled systems and take over to inject erroneous outputs. Such external integrations, if not thoroughly vetted and protected at every level, can serve as unnoticeable pathways for cyber threats. (Vashishth et al., 2026)

Intelligence and Advanced Identity and Access Management

The combination of different users and/or platforms of a given system tends to create identity and access management challenges. The absence of a central identity repository means a user with no legitimate identification can bypass control mechanisms and wield disproportionate control over highly sensitive data. A poorly described multi-level administrative framework can be equally damaging when it comes to privilege escalation and impersonation by malicious users in less controlled environments.

CYBERSECURITY AND RISK MANAGEMENT STRATEGIES

Risk management and cybersecurity are two principal components of modern-day digital ecosystems. The increasing reliance on interconnected systems, cloud infrastructure, and real-time data analytics and decision-making heightens the organization's exposure to cyber threats. The organization's digital assets, compliance to laws, trust from stakeholders, and strategic risk management approaches rely on the existence of a cohesive cybersecurity strategy.

Secure AI Training and Deployment

The integrity, confidentiality, and trustworthiness of AI models applied in decentralized governance systems needs to be protected through effective security measures for AI training and deployment. For instance, AI models are increasingly exposed to data poisoning attacks during the training phase where adversarial attackers try to inject malicious data with the intent to disrupt the learning algorithms . Models can generate predictions which may be inaccurate, harmful, misleading, or biased in respect to the undesirable. As a solution, secure data pipelines, authenticated data repositories, and anomaly detection systems are set up to mitigate the risks of corrupted data. Post-training, AI models are susceptible to threats like model inversion, adversarial attacks, and unauthorized access which require safeguarding. The implementation of fortified encrypted model storage, protected API gateway, routine changes, and validation procedures increase trust concerning AI outputs while reducing interference of malicious actors (Vashishth et al., 2025).

Decentralized Identities and Self-Sovereign Identity (SSI)

The usage of Decentralized Identifiers (DIDs) and Self-Sovereign Identity (SSI) frameworks empowers the extremely convoluted management of digital Identities in AI-Blockchain technologies. Controlling identity in the data system, all data is stored in a computerized system which requires identity verification using user data, an inherently vulnerable method, poses a significant risk for many threats such as data theft, identity fraud, and give abuse due to lack of privacy control. Differently from other schemes, SSI allows users full control over the ownership, management and sharing of their digital identities which does not require intermediaries to authenticate their profiles. Each user or entity is issued a credential which is stored in the blockchain as an SSI document which enables the user to prove identity through cryptography (Kolade et al, 2024). These self-verified and shareable identities are immutable and can be used across numerous platforms enabling the selective dissemination of information to targeted audiences. Combating identity fraud, enhancing verification efficiencies, and shielding personal information privacy is made easy with the integration of SSI in AI-Blockchain infrastructures which provides solid Identity Access Management (IAM systems). Alongside other policies, SSI schemes facilitate legal data provisions and compliance with GDPR by executing user requests to erase stored records (Salako et al., 2024).

End-to-End Encryption and Privacy-Preserving Techniques

Encryption from the endpoints (E2EE) guarantees that the information sent or received by users or AI services in a blockchain network is encrypted during transit from the origin to the endpoint. The transmission content can be decrypted solely by the sender and the designated receiver, ensuring that no unauthorized third party is able to access or overhear the communication or manipulate the data during the transit. E2EE is critical in safeguarding health records, bank transactions as well as votes in decentralized applications. Along with the mentioned, efforts to strengthen privacy include the incorporation of zero-knowledge proofs (ZKPs), homomorphic encryption, and secure enclave computing into AI-Blockchain ecosystems. One of the most notable applications of ZKPs is verifying identities or executing other confidential transactions wherein some data needs to be substantiated without being disclosed. Protected computation in encrypted data is executed through homomorphic encryption which allows AI algorithms to receive sensitive data inputs without the need to unlock the information. Figure 2 demonstrates the End-to-End encryption process of data in blockchain network.

Figure 2. End-to-end encryption and privacy-preserving techniques in AI- block-chain networks

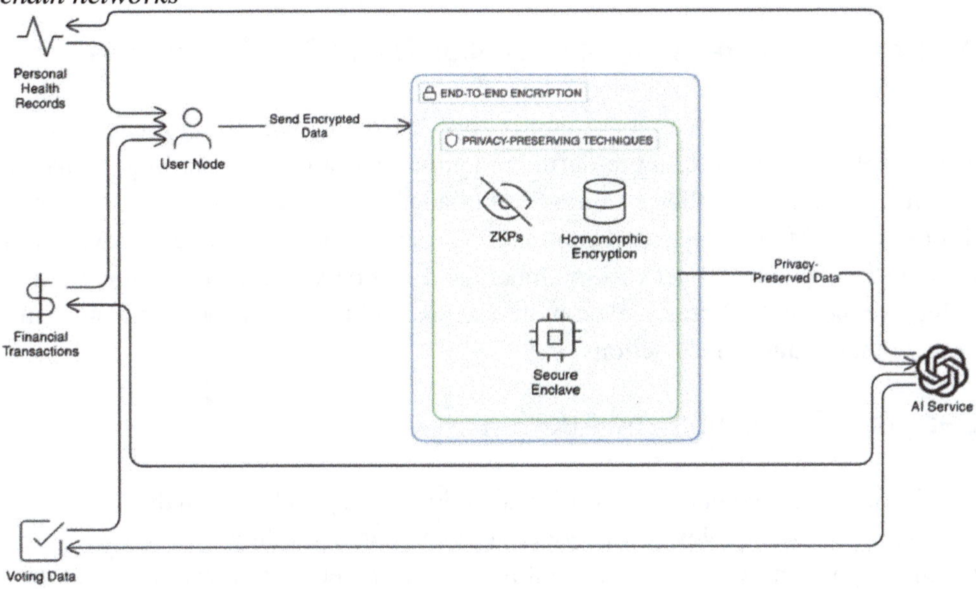

Auditable and Transparent Governance with Blockchain

In AI-Blockchain systems, the two most pivotal aspects of trust and compliance is auditability and transparency. All forms of trust and compliance are enhanced due to the auditability blockchain offers. Blockchain technology boasts transparency, accountability, and trust due to an unchangeable ledger that is distributed and maintains a record of all activities within the system. This proves that governance that is digital can only depend on Some technology because all actions carried out by AI models, users and admin can be checked

Permanent Safeguards

Recognized as one of the most essential features of blockchains, records that can't be changed are kept incessantly. The only way to alter a record is attaining and getting approval from the whole network. This unchangeable nature guarantees that all actions taken by AI models of allowing access, approving transactions and issuing a credential id done with utmost care and taken actions have to be recorded in the AI Forensic state machine and hence become auditable at any given moment or period while this on the other hand offers strong barriers for governance systems enabling accessibility of validation traces which is vital in sectors like medicine, finance, logistics and administration.

Automated and Transparent Execution Using Smart Contracts

Logic defined within a blockchain is encoded smartly in such a manner that it executes itself when certain pre-defined requirements are achieved. In governance systems, execution of policies, voting, compliance, and workflows can be conducted through automation using smart contracts. The smart contracts' code and execution logs are available to all network members and can be verified. This removes any vying avenues and decreases even more the possibility of corruption, favouritism, or any other unauthorized actions.

Real-Time Monitoring and Auditing

The decentralized nature of Blockchain allows every node within the network to keep synchronized copies of the ledger. Stakeholders including system regulators, administrators, and even the general public (if provisioned) can view activities as they unfold. Such can be used for the promotion of ethical AI undertakings, prevention of untraceable manipulation of algorithms, as well as issuance of programmatic fulfilments. AI systems with black-box decision-making structures can have AI inferences and their relevant parameters logged to the blockchain for evaluative credibility and automated explanation assistance.

Compliance and Governance Reporting

The transparent nature of records kept on a blockchain makes regulatory compliance much easier. For sectors that are governed by stringent data management frameworks and accountability mechanisms like GDPR, HIPAA, and SOX, blockchain technology enables the creation of auditable trails that can be used during legal litigations and inspections. These organizations can automate compliance reporting and audit them against the blockchain logs maintained, which mitigates the manual effort and the risk of record tampering (Leiva and Castro, 2025).

Strengthening Trust and Confidence of the Public

Trust is foster when governance is auditable and public is transparent through blockchain. Decisions made on the behalf of people by different authorities in governance systems are not only centralized in nature, but are also undisclosed, unconfirmable, and easily changeable. Stakeholders are able to witness how decisions are made, who did them and for what reason making this technology especially useful for AI-Blockchain applications which may impact public resources, their rights, or legal issues. AI powered decisions can only ensure ethical democratic digital border - when they are explainable, traceable, accountable, and that is what blockchain technology provides.

Thus, auditable, and transparent governance enables trust in AI, which helps balance automation with human responsibility. It minimizes risk, deters malicious actions, helps uphold compliance, and strengthens the integrity of intelligent decentralized infrastructures.

THREAT INTELLIGENCE AND PROACTIVE DEFENSE

In the case of AI-Blockchain governance systems, maintaining the digital infrastructures' integrity, availability, confidentiality, and critical requirements depend heavily on proactive and threat-intel-driven defense systems (Saxena et al., 2025). With the integration of AI and Blockchain Technologies, their proliferation catalyses the emergence of new threat surfaces, increasing the socioeconomic risks posed by advanced persistent threats. Cybersecurity reactive approaches to security strategy planning that focus on post event actions are insufficient; strategies need to preemptively deal with problems and damages before they happen.

Active Threat Monitoring Systems

Active Threat Monitoring Systems are an integral part of the overall cybersecurity framework of AI-Blockchain governance infrastructures. Such systems go well beyond, conventional 'set and forget' practices. Active threat monitoring systems focus on the continuous surveillance of digital landscapes for all activities and processes and acts as and when needed, in contrast to passive systems that work with logs and after-the-fact activities and depend on inspection to identify whether breaches have occurred or not. Such systems are important in intelligent decentralized ecosystems because they enable intelligent monitoring and response to possibilities of multiple vectors of attack like hostile node, rogue AI, is a security enabled smart contract.

Real-Time Surveillance and Analytics

Active threat monitoring hinged upon surveillance on all AI and blockchain layers. AI elements can keep track of logs, network activities, behaviours, and transactions of the system. Every abnormal activity is checked, for example, surge in transactions on the blockchain, abnormalities in AI model results, attempts at altering smart contracts among others. The AI analytics simultaneously analyses the context and scope of the anomalies in order to establish if it is a genuine threat or a benign anomaly.

AI Integration for Intelligent Detection

Implementing machine learning in threat monitoring systems improves their intelligence and responsiveness. Through pattern recognition, anomaly detection, and natural language processing, these systems automate user, models, and network behavior monitoring and learn behaviours over time (Kumar et al., 2025). Whenever deviations are noticed, like an AI model producing biased outputs, or if a blockchain node attempts to propagate invalid blocks, alerts can be made with holistic accuracy and minimal false positives. These systems also use historical threat data and the changing landscape of emerging threats to predict potential attack windows. For instance, when a new type of smart contract exploit is discovered on one network, a proactive watch can be mounted on sister decentralized systems for similar weaknesses that need patching (Vashishth et al., 2025).

Monitoring on Blockchain Layer

On the blockchain side, active monitoring ensures integrity and trustworthiness across decentralized nodes. System observing consensus mechanisms, behaviours of nodes, marks, chains of transactions and execution of smart contracts. Any irregularities—such as signs of a 51% attack, Sybil attack, or front-running—can trigger automatic containment measures like suspending suspect transactions, isolating malicious nodes, or initiating consensus revalidation. Also, blockchain's immutability and transparency enable forensic scrutiny after an incident, allowing systems to trace back breaches to their fundamental causes, identifying the participants, and detailing the sequence of events leading up to the breach.

Smart Contract Surveillance

Since interaction with smart contracts is immutable and they self-execute upon deployment, continuous surveillance is needed for their interactions and states. Active threat monitoring systems look for contract invocations, gas spending, and re-entrant exploits. In real time, AI can be employed to emulate and run smart contracts under hostile scenarios, heuristically bypassing static code evaluations.

Automation of Alerts, Responses, and Human Manual Intervention

Active monitoring systems typically come integrated with automated incident response features. When a threat is identified, certain actions like node isolation, model rollback, wallet blacklisting, or governance alerting are executed automatically. Nevertheless, human intervention is indispensable in the most crucial areas in highly critical domains such as finance or healthcare workflows. With alerting systems and dashboards, Cybersecurity teams as well as DAO members can monitor systems, look for deviations, and execute mitigation strategies in real time. Also, alerting functions enable decentralized notification of other network participants for responsive and resilient actions (Sharma et al., 2025).

Thus, integrated threat detection systems in AI-Blockchain frameworks function as guardians, perpetually on alert for any signs of breach, manipulation, or technical lapse. With the combination of AI technology, blockchain transparency, and automated systems, responsible for acting, these systems are vital to the security, integrity, and dependability of digital governance infrastructures (Rahman et al., 2024).

Resilient Architecture Design

The construction of a resilient architecture is of high importance value for the stability, security, and uninterrupted operation of AI-Blockchain governance systems during cyberattacks, operational failures, or unpredicted stress onto a system. Unlike centralized or traditional architectures, resilient systems proactively design for adverse circumstances such as smooth failure isolation, self-recovery, isolation of intervening components, and sustaining core services during harsh conditions. In relation to intelligent decentralized ecosystems, the defining feature of resilience is the property known as decentralization—data and operations are stored on numerous nodes in a network, removing convergence points of failure, allowing uninterrupted service even when some constituent parts stop functioning. This is important related to the example of a blockchain system where mechanisms ensure that only acceptable nodes are integrated into the network such as hostile or non-operational nodes. Moreover, robust architecture uses modularity as the main approach which in some cases is micro-services. AI inference engines or identity management, execution of smart contracts, can be done independently as a module. During anomaly detection, AI models and smart contracts are subject to strict version control and so are their backups to allow quick rollbacks. This enables the architecture to minimize over-dependence on core networks. As stated by Vashishth et al., AI facilitates systems autonomously diagnosing, isolating, and restoring services to normal function as soon as attention-demanding anomalies are detected (2024).

Incident Response and Disaster Recovery Frameworks

For unanticipated breaches of cybersecurity, Incidents like failure or disaster, if left unchecked can severely diminish a business's image, command attention by lies and deceit all while disrupting trust, operability of the systems, data ownership, although categorically governing the information contained within an AI-Blockchain ecosystem retains overall structural integrity. These frameworks critically ensure prompt investigation, control, pinpointing and meticulously responding to security challenges, with seamless vulnerability, minimization of disruption on operations, and effortless swiftness. For intelligent decentralized systems, incident response goes beyond tactical offense engagement; it encompasses the coordination of protective execution across nodes and systems to achieve consensus, limit actionable impact, and shield sensitive data. Response teams must mobilize immediately after an incident has taken place. For assessment, containing actions with the scope to include the affected parts or components, have to be taken within the first few moments. Usually, the underpinning of decentralized architectures includes enabling standby nodes, off-chain or redundant data storages, and re-synchronization of blockchains payroll ledger. AI models that have been compromised are put into trusted standby hardware where controlled recovery using governance protocols that guarantee identity verification will be relinquished only to trusted identities. Post-incident audits utilizing forensic analysis and log files from the blockchain, coupled with feedback into the security posture (Mustafa et al., 2025), root causes and accompanying insights are determined. The other side, however, legal, and ethical unregulated transparency compliance is bound with all stakeholders. Figure 3 depicts the incident response mechanism and recovery system architecture.

Figure 3. Incident response and disaster recovery architecture

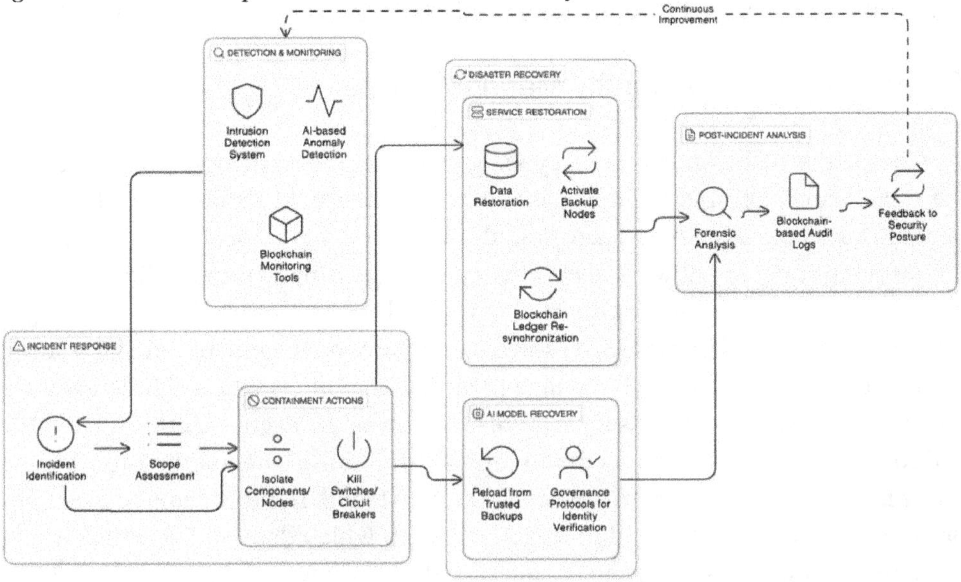

GOVERNANCE STRUCTURES, ETHICS, AND COMPLIANCE

As we incorporate AI with Blockchain, the primary focus on governance, ethics, and compliance as foundational aspects of digital ecosystems remains crucial for their security and transparency. Governance constitutes rules, policies, decision processes and accountability frameworks which explain the relationships between shards of AI, Nodes, blockchains, smart contracts and humans. In such ecosystems, the governed order able to sustain a balance between control, adaptability to emerging threats, conflicts, and regulations while embracing decentralization is phenomenal.

Cyber Governance Policies in AI-Blockchain Systems

These policies act as managerial guides for governing operational cybersecurity and the integration of system AI-Blockchain. This group of policies is considered the primary cyber governance within the cyber trust, as they are vital to ensure operational integrity, particularly in the interplay of AI and Blockchain technologies which gives distinctive security concerns, complexities of governance due to distribution, and architecture. While dealing with the integration of AI with Blockchains, policies of cyber governance have to resolve a multitude of challenges such as management of access, governance of risk, governance of data, and compliance with legislation.

Access Control and Identity Management

One of the main divisions of cyber governance in AI-Blockchain systems is the establishment pertaining to access control. Because AI models and blockchain networks are both distributed across multiple nodes, it is critical to limit access to the resources only to known and authorized entities. Empowering individuals does not permit them to act freely within the system; however, blockchain technologies like self-sovereign identities (SSI) solve the identity management issue in a secure manner by enabling people to manage their personal information. These identities are able to provide the necessary features for user or AI agent identity verification and confidential information access control with the aim of safeguarding confidential information from unwarranted modifications to AI models, blockchain transactions, or other alterations. Who is able to get access to which data, under what circumstances, how the access is granted, supervised, withdrawn, and provisioned should be covered by governance policies. Policies might dictate that access control must be complied with at all levels of the system, thus enforcing multi-factor authentication (MFA), key encryption, and digital signatures (Olutimehin, 2025).

Risk Management and Incident Response

As with any emerging technology, the AI-Blockchain systems offer evolving opportunities alongside increasing potential threat vectors that require risk management procedures to be put into place on the entire governance plane. These procedures focus on the advanced persistent threat (APT) risks that could breach AI models or the blocks within the blockchain matrix. For instance, Blockchain networks face various trust eroding attacks such as 51 percent attacks, Sybil attacks, to name but a few. Equally vulnerable are AI models with adversarial attack vectors, data poisoning and model inversion that can lead to wrong decision outputs which fundamentally affect decision making. Governance in the cyber realm needs to articulate these risk detection and mitigation strategies as proactive monitoring, threat intelligence, and continual security assessments on systems. They could include vigilant and proactive security audits which involve the continuous scanning of AI for exploitable flaws, AIs are constantly scrutinized for weak points that can be exploited while blockchains must adopt mitigative policies for distributed agreement mechanisms. Furthermore, smart contracts pose unique challenges for blockchain networks due to the need for resilience that goes beyond mere self-sufficiency. Lastly, there must be rapid containment of the impacts of breaches through reduced security, lost or altered information and mechanisms for returning systems back to baseline operations (Radanliev, 2025).

Data Protection and the Privacy of Individuals

As threats to cyber governance tends to increase, sensitive data privacy pertaining to the healthcare, finance, and governance sectors poses a considerable risk. Once a blockchain ledger is created it is transparent, immutable, and therefore compliant. Storing information on an AI-Blockchain incurs immutable boundaries restricting change. Hence, the GDPR poses privacy concerns. GDPR policies require encryption, anonymization, as well as operable storage frameworks on blockchains to safeguard sensitive information (Shriya et al., 2025). Discretionary access control is required for ensuring data integrity, control, and privacy enforcement during the entire processes of information systems. Changeable and non-removable homomorphic encryption, zero-knowledge proofs, and secured multi-party computation (SMPC) fall under privacy-preserving protocols. Compliance with privacy legislation involves assuring information analysis while raw data remains hidden (Kumar et al., 2024).

Audit and Compliance

Within the context of AI systems utilizing blockchains, legal compliance and governance auditing corresponds to the fleet cyber governance. There are many international and national legislations such as the GDPR, Anti Money Laundering (AML) laws, and Know Your Customer (KYC) policies which apply to particular industries like finance and healthcare. This type of law governing cyber governance policies should delineate how the AI-Blockchain ecosystems contravene those legal requirements especially with regard to capturing, processing, and storing data. Regulations on compliance are maintained by governance technologies blockchain because they are self-auditable. All actions taken on the blockchain are captured and can be traced back to the origin. Governance policies should enable audit trails and verified changes to the systems using blockchain and logs. Such transparency strengthens accountability concerning the actions and decisions made on AI and the system and its functions, how the users and the regulators can monitor is predefined functions performed within the systems are met.

Consequently, the need for the effective cyber governance policies is notable in the combination of AI and Blockchain System at hand which deals with security, privacy, accountability, and compliance. These policies are crafted for governance, redefine roles and responsibilities, measure risks, and protect sensitive trust stakeholder's s information. A policy for governance is needed to balance the overwhelming interdependent strive complexity AI-Blockchain ecosystem (Pawar et al., 2024).

Ethical AI and Blockchain Use

The integration of AI and blockchain technologies poses distinctive ethical challenges which must be addressed at a societal level prior to these technologies being productive. One of the most critical challenges is the bias potential that is built into the AI systems. AI algorithms tend to perpetuate historical data, and, if this data contains any form of bias such as racism, sexism, or any socioeconomical discrimination, the model learned will use this as a basis for decision making. This is likely to cause harm in sensitive issues like finance, healthcare, and policing. To avert these issues, models must be trained with representative and inclusive datasets, conducted regular audits for bias, and ensure fairness equilibria in the algorithm's structure. The justification of these decisions can be aided by explainable AI tools where AI decisions can be made accessible to non-machine thinking people, enabling them together with regulators to comprehend the autonomous systems logic. Preserving privacy is another noteworthy ethical aspect. A considerable amount of sensitive data, including personally identifiable information, may need to be aggregated to develop AI systems and Blockchain. The focus should be to build such systems that will fully appreciate privacy rights of individuals. The benefit of decentralization of Blockchain enables users to manage their information better using self-sovereign identities (SSI) that allow users to control their particulars, determine what, how, where, and when to share their data. Additionally, privacy-enhancing methods such as differential privacy or secure multi-party computation may be applied to AI systems for data processing without revealing confidential information. Responsibility is another problematic area. The use of AI systems, especially those placed within the context of autonomous decision-making, can make decisions that influence people. But who precisely takes such decisions, especially when an AI system goes wrong, is extremely difficult, if not impossible, to pinpoint. Blockchain can aid this problem through its transparent and immutable ledger that captures every action taken in a system, which enables auditability, therefore holding relevant parties accountable (Kumar et al., 2024).

CASE STUDIES AND INDUSTRY BEST PRACTICES

In this section, we analyze a combination of case studies alongside global benchmarks to showcase how organizations and states are dealing with the cyber security and ethical related issues together with risks of integrating AI and Blockchain technologies. These illustrations aid in understanding the problems that were encountered and the steps taken regarding the persisting challenges of ensuring the combined system's security, trust, and scalability.

Case Study 1: Blockchain to Enhance Traceability in Food Supply Chains

Focus on Walmart and the implementation of Blockchain in real life can serve as a good starting point for discussing the food supply chain processes. Walmart already had some inner processes automated using a software application they developed in collaboration with IBM which functionality allows purchase order forecasting and items tracking throughout the supply chain. Combine these two, and you get a solution with real-time updates on food and food source tracking. The idea is to make the supply chains as transparent as possible. Any issue that arises, for instance substandard or even contaminated products, can easily be traced to the supplier. The advantages of a Blockchain system applied in food safety processes are numerous; combining trustful framework with partitioned storage allows less use of resources to combat trust imbalance, thus improving the overall productivity of the business. Less people in need, means these people can focus on solving the more crucial issues that are presented in today's world, like food security, exposing more people around the world to sufficient and safe food. Even though AI helps in tackling issues of underperformance in the whole context of this infrastructure, an even greater likelihood comes from people who would prefer to dedicate their lives in preventive mechanisms for spreading unwholesome and harmful foods.

Case Study 2: AI and Blockchain in Healthcare for Secure Patient Data Management

In healthcare, the privacy and security of patient data is very vital. One such approach is the integration of AI and Blockchain into the segmentation of data sharing among different health care providers. Solve.Care, a healthcare solution company, employs Blockchain technology to formulate a decentralized patient data management system ensuring patient information is protected and released only to trusted entities. AI is an integral part of this system because it monitors a patient's data and analyses it for potential health threats or diseases. For instance, AI has the capabilities to evaluate a patient's medical records and pre-determine the chances for him or her to develop chronic conditions like diabetes or heart diseases (Singh et al., 2022). The combination of Blockchain and AI makes patient data secure and at the same time available to professionals who need it, hence, collaboration between different health care practitioners is encouraged. This is example showcases the benefits of incorporation AI and Blockchain gives to the security in the healthcare systems inter-operability. Patient data remains confidential while care providers have adequate strategic care resources.

Best Practice 1: Applying AI and Blockchain in Financial Services for Fraud Prevention

As more powerful technologies become available, more companies in the financial services sector are turning to Blockchain and AI technologies to prevent fraud and secure transactions. Fraud detection and AI optimization of banking processes is being implemented by a global bank, HSBC. With the use of AI algorithms, transaction data is analysed by HSBC. Suspicious activities are detected and marked as potentially fraudulent/real-time fraud. A final copy of the transaction will be documented through blockchain with the assurance that it is secure and cannot be altered or edited. This enhances the financial data because it is verified and maintains its integrity. AI and Blockchain working together furthers the security and transparency of financial dealings which minimizes fraud while improving the overall system trust. Implementation of these technologies has made it possible for HSBC to increase operational productivity and decrease costs while better serving their clientele (Farayola, 2024).

Best Practice 2: Security of Smart Contracts and Auditing Services Using AI

The legal services industry is increasingly automating and securing activities such as contract execution and auditing through Blockchain and AI technologies. Open law develops a Hybrid Blockchain with AI that comprehensive and execution of contracts. Smart contracts are created on this platform and they execute when predefined conditions are satisfied which occurs limits the role of third parties. This system performs complete automation of a contract's life cycle including audits. The AI, in this case, performs real-time auditing which enables organizations to automatically check on inconsistencies or violations of terms. Through these technologies, Open law guarantees secure, transparent, contract execution that is timely. The application of AI and Blockchain in the legal industry is becoming a benchmark on how other sectors automate processes aimed at combating fraud, errors, and disputes while improving contract enforcement (Sagar et al., 2025).

Thus, these case studies highlight the many possible avenues and applications derived from the integration of AI and Blockchain technologies. From increasing auditability in the supply chain, securing patient information in health care, preventing identity theft and self-sovereign identity manipulation in fraud services, to self-sovereign identity management, AI and Blockchain are transforming businesses while simultaneously mitigating important cybersecurity, moral, and governance issues.

FUTURE DIRECTIONS OF USING AI AND BLOCKCHAIN IN DIGITAL GOVERNANCE SYSTEMS

The continued advancement of AI and Blockchain together with their interdependence will provide new opportunities for digital governance systems. There are plenty of prospects and concerns around the future of AI-Blockchain integration which, if addressed effectively, can revolutionize the development of secure, scalable, and ethical decentralized systems. It is dedicated to examining the forthcoming thrust of these technologies while also identifying emerging paradigms, innovations, and vital examinations that will determine the next era of AI-Blockchain governance frameworks.

Enhanced Protection and Confidentiality Measures

AI-Blockchain Systems shows the development of protection and privacy. With the incorporation of these technologies into critical areas such as healthcare, finance, and government, the demand for sophisticated privacy safeguarding methods will increase. Encryption of zero-knowledge proofs (ZKP) and secure multi-party computation (SMPC) enables sharing information without revealing the confidential aspects that are embedded in the data; therefore, these constitute sensitive data sharing multidisciplinary frameworks that are emerging as key enabling technologies. This allows more advanced transactions and data management to take place, enabling AI systems to render sophisticated analyses while ensuring data privacy. Moreover, there is a growing focus on quantum safe AI-Blockchain systems resilient cryptography to protect against future risks of quantum computing, ensuring the integrity of security AI-Blockchain systems in the quantum era (Vashishth et al., 2025).

Scalability and Interoperability Across the Various Blockchains

One of the most difficult problems is blockchain scalability, especially in networks that need high transaction volume and low latency. Interoperability and scalability solutions like sharding, cross-chain interoperability, layer 2 enhancements, and cross-systems AI integration will be critical for global application support. Unified infrastructure across the various blockchains will enable interoperable decentralized applications across alt chains. This hybrid approach from different blockchains and overcoming the limitations of any single chain architecture will be possible.

Automation and AI Governance

The adoption of AI for governance is likely to evolve further the decision-making processes within the systems that are already decentralized. The potential of governance on blockchain is being realized with DAOs, but AI can further improve these systems by automating the decision-making processes. Smart contracts powered by AI could enforce rules autonomously, make decisions on their own, and dynamically modify requirements through self-governance, thus requiring less human involvement at the command level in governance. In addition, AI technology could evaluate risks, anticipate developments, and make changes to the governance structure proactively, ensuring a continuous responsiveness to the external environment.

AI Ethics and Governance

The increasing adoption of AI and Blockchain technologies will lead to continuously emerging ethical concerns. Addressing algorithmic discrimination, using data without consent, or rendering unjust decisions are scenarios that will emerge without proper governance of AI-Blockchain systems. In the future, researchers will be more concerned with developing ethical guidelines that address the bias, accountability, and transparency of AI systems. To foster greater transparency within AI processes, blockchain technology can provide an answer as a tool for the immutable record-keeping of auditable AI decision trails. Cross disciplinary collaborations like that of technologists, ethicists, sociologists, and even regulators will continue working to develop ethical definitions for AI and Blockchain (Vashishth et al., 2024).

CONCLUSION

The merging of Artificial Intelligence (AI) and Blockchain technologies marks another leap in the advancement of digital governance through automation, transparency, and system agility. In this chapter, we analysed the fundamental cybersecurity gaps of AI-Blockchain governance systems including smart contract risks, AI model attacks, and blockchain-centric threats such as 51% and Sybil attacks. Crucial milestones of the study include identifying these critical risks and developing robust cybersecurity measures, which include secure AI training, decentralized identity management, end-to-end encryption, and blockchain-based auditing tools. These strategies have received validation from case studies in healthcare, finance, and supply chain, providing evidence for their effectiveness. Futuristically, the scope lies with quantum-resistant cryptography, cross-chain inter-operability, federated learning, and privacy-enhancing methods like zero-knowledge proofs. Also, embedding explainable AI alongside ethical considerations will be crucial for upholding the required transparency and accountability in autonomous systems. Hence, this study offers the initial building blocks towards the construction of deeply-situated secure, scalable, and ethically governed AI-Blockchain frameworks.

REFERENCES

Adejumo, A., & Ogburie, C. (2025). Strengthening finance with cybersecurity: Ensuring safer digital transactions. World Journal of Advanced Research and Reviews, 25.

Ahmed, S. (2025). Enhancing Data Security and Transparency: The Role of Blockchain in Decentralized Systems. International Journal of Advanced Engineering. *Management Science*, *11*(1), 593258.

Alzoubi, M. M. (2024). Investigating the synergy of Blockchain and AI: enhancing security, efficiency, and transparency. Journal of Cyber Security Technology, 1-29.

Bhumichai, D., Smiliotopoulos, C., Benton, R., Kambourakis, G., & Damopoulos, D. (2024). The convergence of artificial intelligence and blockchain: The state of play and the road ahead. *Information (Basel)*, *15*(5), 268.

Farayola, O. A. (2024). Revolutionizing banking security: Integrating artificial intelligence, blockchain, and business intelligence for enhanced cybersecurity. *Finance & Accounting Research Journal*, *6*(4), 501–514.

Khan, N., & Daniel, T. (2024). Utilizing AI and Blockchain for Cyber Threat Prediction in Financial Institutions: Tools and Techniques for Cloud Security Posture Management.

Kolade, T. M., Aideyan, N. T., Oyekunle, S. M., Ogungbemi, O. S., Dapo-Oyewole, D. L., & Olaniyi, O. O. (2024). Artificial Intelligence and Information Governance: Strengthening Global Security, through Compliance Frameworks, and Data Security. Available at *SSRN* 5044032.

Kumar, A., Bhatia, A., Kumar, S., Kumar, R., & Yadav, V. (2025, February). Sentimental analysis using natural language processing. In AIP Conference Proceedings (Vol. 3224, No. 1). AIP Publishing.

Kumar, A., Saini, R., & Kumar, R. (2024). A Comparative Analysis of Machine Learning Algorithms for Breast Cancer Detection and Identification of Key Predictive Features. *TS. Traitement du Signal*, *41*(1).

Kumar, P., Kumar, R., & Kumar, M. (2024, November). Data Storage in Manual Systems that Challenges in Cloud & Fog Computing-Based Systems Which are Affecting the Online Data-Oriented Application Architecture. In 2024 4th International Conference on Technological Advancements in Computational Sciences (ICTACS) (pp. 723-727). IEEE.

Leiva, V., & Castro, C. (2025). Artificial intelligence and blockchain in clinical trials: Enhancing data governance efficiency, integrity, and transparency. *Bioanalysis, 17*(3), 161–176. PMID: 39844748

Mahammad, A. B., & Kumar, R. (2023, April). Scalable and security framework to secure and maintain healthcare data using blockchain technology. In *2023 International Conference on Computational Intelligence and Sustainable Engineering Solutions (CISES)* (pp. 417-423). IEEE.

Mustafa, G., Rafiq, W., Jhamat, N., Arshad, Z., & Rana, F. A. (2025). Blockchain-based governance models in e-government: A comprehensive framework for legal, technical, ethical and security considerations. *International Journal of Law and Management, 67*(1), 37–55.

Nosina, K. C., & Swarna Latha, T. (2024). Introduction to Cybersecurity with AI, ML, and Blockchain. In *Next-Generation Cybersecurity: AI, ML, and Blockchain* (pp. 1–21). Springer Nature Singapore.

Olutimehin, A. T. (2025). The Synergistic Role of Machine Learning, Deep Learning, and Reinforcement Learning in Strengthening Cyber Security Measures for Crypto Currency Platforms. Deep Learning, and Reinforcement Learning in Strengthening Cyber Security Measures for Crypto Currency Platforms (February 11, 2025).

Pawar, P. P., Kumar, D., Meesala, M. K., Pareek, P. K., & Addula, S. R., & KS, S. (2024, November). Securing Digital Governance: A Deep Learning and Blockchain Framework for Malware Detection in IoT Networks. In *2024 International Conference on Integrated Intelligence and Communication Systems (ICIICS)* (pp. 1-8). IEEE.

Radanliev, P. (2025). Cyber diplomacy: Defining the opportunities for cybersecurity and risks from Artificial Intelligence, IoT, Blockchains, and Quantum Computing. *Journal of Cyber Security Technology, 9*(1), 28–78.

Rahman, M. M., Pokharel, B. P., Sayeed, S. A., Bhowmik, S. K., Kshetri, N., & Eashrak, N. (2024). riskAIchain: AI-Driven IT Infrastructure—Blockchain-Backed Approach for Enhanced Risk Management. *Risks, 12*(12), 206.

Sagar, M. S., Srivastava, S., Kumar, R., & Saxena, A. (2025, February). The evolution of industry 5.0: Harnessing artificial intelligence and communication technology. In AIP Conference Proceedings (Vol. 3224, No. 1). AIP Publishing.

Salako, A. O., Fabuyi, J. A., Aideyan, N. T., Selesi-Aina, O., Dapo-Oyewole, D. L., & Olaniyi, O. O. (2024). Advancing information governance in AI-driven cloud ecosystem: Strategies for enhancing data security and meeting regulatory compliance. *Asian Journal of Research in Computer Science, 17*(12), 66–88.

Salama, R., & Al-Turjman, F. (2024). Blockchain technology, computer network operations, and global value chains together make up "cybersecurity". In *Smart Global Value Chain* (pp. 150–164). CRC Press.

Saxena, A., Gupta, M., Srivastava, S., & Kumar, R. (2025, February). Empowering edge computing: The critical role of blockchain in cybersecurity defense. In AIP Conference Proceedings (Vol. 3224, No. 1). AIP Publishing.

Sharma, V., Vashishth, T. K., Tiwari, D., Sethi, P., & Sharma, S. (2025, April). Enhancing cybersecurity: A machine learning approach for phishing website detection. In AIP Conference Proceedings (Vol. 3278, No. 1). AIP Publishing.

Shriya, K., Velmurugan, T., & Kumar, G. (2025). Advancements in financial data protection: How artificial intelligence strengthens security measures in blockchain systems. In *Applications of Blockchain and Artificial Intelligence in Finance and Governance* (pp. 136–149). CRC Press.

Singh, C. B., Gupta, A., & Kumar, R. (2022, April). Diabetes Care Survey Using Supervised and Unsupervised Machine Learning. In 2022 3rd International Conference on Intelligent Engineering and Management (ICIEM) (pp. 207-210). IEEE.

Soundenkar, S., Bhosale, K., Jakhete, M. D., Kadam, K., Chowdary, V. G. R., & Durga, H. K. (2024). AI Powered Risk Management: Addressing Cybersecurity Threats in Financial Systems. Library of Progress-Library Science, Information Technology & Computer, 44(3).

Srivastava, S., Ahmed, T., Saxena, A., & Kumar, R. (2025, February). A novel machine learning hybrid model for heart disease risk assessment. In AIP Conference Proceedings (Vol. 3224, No. 1). AIP Publishing.

Vashishth, T. K., Kumar, B., Alam, M. S., Sharma, V., & Chaudhary, S. (2024). The Impact of Artificial Intelligence on the Future of Computing: A Comparative Study. In *Applications of Block Chain technology and Artificial Intelligence: Lead-ins in Banking, Finance, and Capital Market* (pp. 1–17). Springer International Publishing.

Vashishth, T. K., Sharma, V., Kaushik, V., Bagar, V. K., Sharma, R., & Kumar, R. (2025). Importance of Using AI and ML in the Financial Sector for Risk Prevention and Management. In *Utilizing AI and Machine Learning in Financial Analysis* (pp. 509–530). IGI Global Scientific Publishing.

Vashishth, T. K., Sharma, V., Kaushik, V., & Sharma, K. K. (2025). Blockchain-Driven Innovations in the Banking and Financial Sectors: Harnessing the Power of Automated Machine Learning. In Utilizing AI and Machine Learning in Financial Analysis (pp. 555-578). IGI Global Scientific Publishing.

Vashishth, T. K., Sharma, V., Kaushik, V., Singh, A., & Kaushik, S. (2025). Exploring Quantum Challenges and Opportunities of Quantum Machine Learning Adoption in Finance. Machine Learning and Modeling Techniques in Financial Data Science, 437-460.

Vashishth, T. K., Sharma, V., Kumar, B., & Sharma, K. K. (2024). Cloud-Based Data Management for Behavior Analytics in Business and Finance Sectors. In Data-Driven Modelling and Predictive Analytics in Business and Finance (pp. 133-155). Auerbach Publications.

Vashishth, T. K., Sharma, V., Kumar, B., Sharma, K. K., Chaudhary, S., & Panwar, R. (2025). Blockchain for Securing Federated Learning Systems: Enhancing Privacy and Trust. Model Optimization Methods for Efficient and Edge AI: Federated Learning Architectures, Frameworks and Applications, 299-320.

Vashishth, T. K., Sharma, V., Samania, B., Sharma, R., Singh, S., & Jajoria, P. (2025). Ethical and Legal Implications of AI in Cybersecurity. In Machine Intelligence Applications in Cyber-Risk Management (pp. 387-414). IGI Global Scientific Publishing.

Vashishth, T. K., Sharma, V., Sharma, K. K., Kumar, B., Chaudhary, S., & Panwar, R. (2024). Intelligent Resource Allocation and Optimization for Industrial Robotics Using AI and Blockchain. In AI and Blockchain Applications in Industrial Robotics (pp. 82-110). IGI Global.

Vashishth, T. K., Sharma, V., Sharma, K. K., Kumar, B., Chaudhary, S., & Panwar, R. (2024). Security and Privacy Challenges in Blockchain-Based Supply Chain Management: A Comprehensive Analysis. In Achieving Secure and Transparent Supply Chains with Blockchain Technology (pp. 70-91). IGI Global.

Chapter 7
Proactive Governance:
Leveraging Predictive Analytics for Citizen-Centric Public Service Delivery

Hina Hashmi
https://orcid.org/0000-0001-6843-0179
Moradabad Institute of Technology, India

ABSTRACT

This chapter explores how predictive analytics is transforming public administration from reactive to proactive, citizen-centered governance. It examines how governments can use historical, real-time, and multi-source data—such as demographic, health, infrastructure, and social media information—to anticipate societal needs and intervene early. Drawing on welfare and public health examples, it demonstrates how predictive models support timely detection of service demands, risks, and policy gaps, enhancing operational efficiency and crisis management. The chapter also addresses ethical and regulatory challenges, including algorithmic accountability, data privacy, and transparency. By emphasizing AI, digital twins, and real-time analytics, it offers a data-driven framework for building inclusive, responsive, and future-ready governance systems.

INTRODUCTION

Governments around the globe are increasingly adopting digital transformation to meet growing citizen demands and solve complex social problems. At the helm of this revolution is predictive analytics, an analytics-driven strategy through which public institutions can anticipate needs, avert crises, and provide services in a more

DOI: 10.4018/979-8-3373-3760-9.ch007

effective manner. Unlike traditional reactive governance—where governance only acts in response to problems as they occur—proactive governance uses historical and real-time data to forecast coming trends and guide timely actions. This not only enhances the effectiveness of the operation, but Cassidy also improves citizen-centered service delivery, so that public services are fair, tailored, and responsive. With government leaders looking for innovations to transform, predictive analytics provides a strong foundation to redefine government for the digital age.

Background and Motivation

By the beginning of the 21st century, public administrations everywhere are being transformed at their core. The convergence of digital technologies, heightened citizen expectations, and ubiquitous availability of sets of big data have pushed governments to reconsider how they provide services. Historically, the public sector has operated with a reactive strategy—after the fact to address citizen requirements and administration problems. Although this system has had its advantages governments over generations, it is increasingly less able to cope with the demands of the era, like urbanization, economic disparity, pandemics, and global warming. In contrast, active governance—a data-driven model that observes and reacts to the needs of people before they become crises—is growing more prominent. The focus of this model is predictive analytics, a set of technologies and techniques that extract patterns from past and present information to anticipate future events. Predictive analytics enables governments to be able to anticipate public service demands, identify emerging threats, and real-time adjust interventions with accuracy (Mergel, Edelmann, & Haug, 2019). Citizens who are used to the instantaneity of response offered by digital services in the private sector growingly expect the same experience provided by public agencies. Such growing demand for personalized, timely, and effective services from and by citizens has driven predictive analytics from being merely an added technological amenity to become a crucial component for governance now.

From Reactive to Proactive Governance

Such shift to proactive, from reactive governance is a mindset change, structure of policies, and corporate culture. Problems such as poverty, infrastructure failure, or public health emergencies in reactive systems are addressed after the problem has actualized—usually at greater costs, both monetarily and societally. Proactive systems try to sense ahead and avert such crises using data in advance of any action.

This change is possible because of improvements in artificial intelligence (AI), machine learning, big data analytics, and the Internet of Things (IoT). For instance, smart sensors embedded in city infrastructure can detect and predict wear and tear and thus allow for maintenance and avoid downtime. Similarly, the healthcare system can employ predictive models for the detection of patients who are at risk of chronic disease and intervene earlier (Topol, 2019).

An essential facilitator of proactive governance is access to high-quality, integrated datasets. When government agencies bring down institutional silos and make their data available, they unlock the potential for analytics to be used across sectors—be it welfare and education or public safety and transport (OECD, 2019).

Role of Predictive Analytics in the Public Sector

Public sector predictive analytics is the application of data science techniques—regression modeling, classification models, NLP, and geospatial modeling—to forecast trends and inform decision-making. With them, managers can:

- Foresee service needs (e.g., emergency health during flu season)
- Maximize resource utilization (e.g., targeted police or road upkeep)
- Identify fraud or inefficiency (e.g., in tax collection or welfare disbursement)
- Improve disaster readiness (e.g., flood or wildfire forecasting)

Governments from all over the world are already realizing the strategic importance of such technologies. The City of Chicago, for instance, applies predictive analytics to mark restaurants with increased risk of food safety violations in order to better inspection outcomes as well as to public health (Glaeser et al., 2016).

However, the use of predictive systems in the public sector is not free of problems. It is beset by problems of privacy, algorithmic bias, a lack of technical expertise, and demands for open and transparent decision-making systems. Accordingly, the implementation of predictive analytics in public administration needs to be accompanied by sufficient ethical and regulatory protections (Rahwan et al., 2019).

Ultimately, the goal is to redirect public governance from reaction in service to anticipation of service—designing policy and intervention that is proactive, equitable, and aligned with evolving needs of the citizen. This chapter explores how predictive analytics can facilitate such a shift through explanations of key concepts, frameworks of implementation, ethical concerns, and real-world case studies.

UNDERSTANDING PREDICTIVE ANALYTICS IN PUBLIC ADMINISTRATION

Predictive analytics is revolutionizing how public sector agencies craft policies, distribute resources, and interact with citizens. To realize its full potential, it is imperative to comprehend its fundamental elements, underlying technologies, and how it fits into public administration systems.

Definition and Conceptual Framework

Predictive analytics is defined as the process of pulling out information from existing data sets to identify patterns and forecast future outcomes and trends (Waller & Fawcett, 2013). Unlike descriptive analytics, which focuses on what has happened, or diagnostic analytics, which explains why it happened, predictive analytics looks ahead—enabling governments to prepare for, and act upon, likely scenarios. In the context of public administration, this can mean predicting school dropout rates, identifying neighborhoods vulnerable to disease outbreaks, or forecasting demand for transportation services.

At its core, predictive analytics in governance involves three stages:

- Data Collection and Preparation – Gathering relevant data from multiple sources.
- Modeling and Prediction – Using statistical or machine learning models to identify patterns.
- Decision Support – Applying the model's output to inform proactive policy or service interventions.

This structure facilitates a more anticipatory type of governance—allowing evidence-based decision-making that is not only quicker but often more resource-efficient and equitable.

Core Technologies and Tools

The application of predictive analytics relies on a combination of technologies, including:

- Decision trees, logistic regression, support vector machines, and neural networks algorithms are utilized to create complex patterns and prediction.
- Natural Language Processing (NLP): Supports the processing of unstructured text data from customer grievances, social media, or public opinion.
- Geospatial Analytics: This compiles information from GIS, allowing for spatial prediction and benefits for cities in planning and monitoring the environment.
- Big Data Platforms: This deals with Hadoop and Apache Spark software for processing large data from diverse government sources.

- Cloud Computing: Provides scalable environments that can be used to train and deploy predictive models through Microsoft Azure and AWS GovCloud.

All these technologies combined provide governments with powerful capabilities to turn raw data into timely, actionable insights.

Data Sources and Infrastructure

The strength of predictive analytics depends greatly on the diversity and quality of data sources. Public agencies have access to an enormous volume of data, such as:

- Administrative data: From health, education, transportation, and tax departments.
- Census and survey data: Offering demographic and socio-economic insights.
- IoT sensor data: Real-time inputs from traffic systems, energy grids, or pollution monitors.
- Open government data: Publicly accessible datasets that support transparency and innovation.
- Citizen-generated data: Input from mobile apps, online portals, and social media platforms.

CITIZEN-CENTRIC PUBLIC SERVICE DELIVERY

Defining Citizen-Centric Governance

Citizen-first governance is intended to produce public services that are tailored to the experience, needs, and expectations of people and communities. Rather than asking people to adapt to bureaucracy, this approach reconfigures public service provision based on citizen lifecycle and experience. In operational terms, it prioritizes accessibility, personalization, and anticipatory engagement. For instance, instead of having parents make individual applications for child support, school enrollment, and medical benefits after the birth of a child, a citizen-first model would activate corresponding services with the registration of the birth—preempting the family's needs ahead of them requesting support.

Role of Predictive Analytics in Citizen-Centric Services

Predictive analytics makes this degree of personalization and responsiveness possible by looking ahead to what services a citizen may require, when they may require it, and in what form. This eliminates delays, reduces manual interventions, and builds confidence in government.

Example: Predictive Healthcare in Estonia

Estonia's e-health system brings together patient information across public and private providers. With the aid of predictive analytics, it notifies general practitioners when patients are at risk of developing a chronic condition like diabetes or heart disease—allowing intervention early enough. Not only does this enhance health outcomes, but it saves considerable public healthcare expenditures.

Framework for Citizen-Centric Predictive Service Delivery

Below is a proposed framework for designing predictive, citizen-centric public services (Figure 1, Table 1):

Table 1. Proposed framework for designing predictive, citizen-centric public services

Stage	Description	Example
Data Aggregation	Collect and integrate citizen data across departments and touchpoints.	National ID-linked datasets (health, education, welfare)
Segmentation & Profiling	Use ML models to group citizens by characteristics, behaviors, or risk profiles.	Predicting youth dropout risks based on attendance + grades
Predictive Modeling	Forecast future needs based on historical patterns	Energy assistance during winter for low-income households
Trigger-Based Activation	Automatically launch support services when predictive thresholds are met.	Pre-approved flood relief based on weather + flood risk

Figure 1. Predictive analytics lifecycle for citizen-centric governance

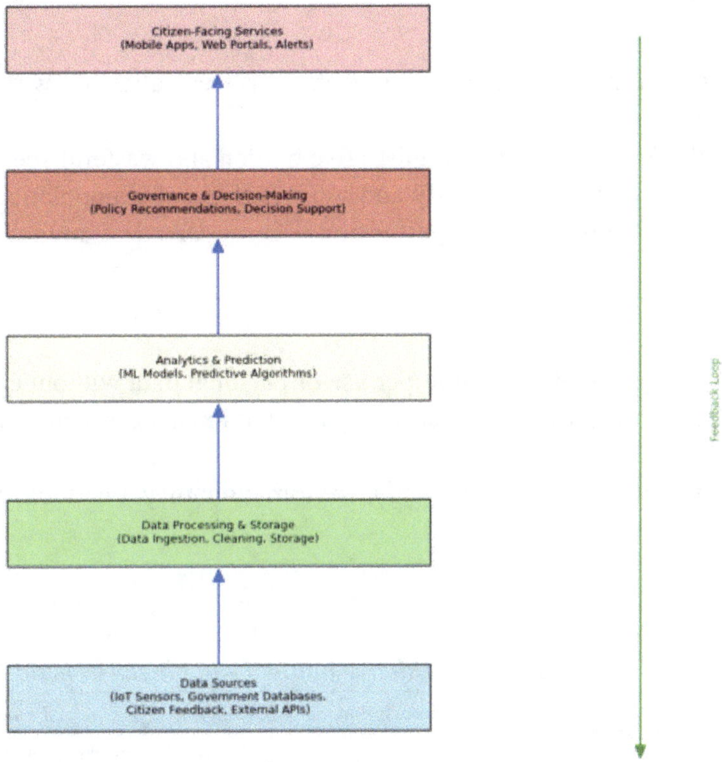

Case Study: Smart Social Services in Canada

In Ontario, Canada, the Ministry of Children, Community and Social Services uses predictive analytics to improve child welfare. By analyzing historical records—including socio-economic status, school attendance, and police interactions—the system identifies at-risk children and families early. Case workers receive alerts, enabling them to conduct home visits or offer support before problems escalate. This involves:

- A 25% increase in early interventions
- A 15% reduction in family separation cases
- Improved targeting of limited social work resources

Benefits and Risks

Benefits

- Personalization: Citizens receive services aligned with their specific circumstances.
- Efficiency: Reduces administrative burden and wasteful spending.
- Inclusivity: Helps identify and support vulnerable populations.
- Trust: Improves public perception of responsiveness and fairness.

Risks

- Privacy Violations: Improper use of personal data without consent.
- Bias in Algorithms: Models may unintentionally discriminate against certain groups.
- Overreliance on Technology: Automation may overlook complex human needs.

Table 2. Key advantages of predictive analytics in citizen-centric service delivery

Benefit	Description	Example
Personalization	Tailored services based on citizen data	Elderly care packages based on age + medical history
Risk Detection	Spot emerging issues before they become crises	Fire hazard prediction using satellite and land data
Proactive Outreach	Engage citizens before they ask for help	Job coaching offered too recently unemployed

This chart emphasizes how predictive analytics improves public services through personalization, early risk detection, and proactive outreach—enabling more targeted, efficient, and equitable interventions.

Ethical and Governance Considerations

The use of predictive analytics in citizen-centric delivery must be guided by strong ethical principles, including:

- Transparency: Citizens must know how their data is used.
- Consent and Control: Opt-in models and data access controls are essential.

- Fairness: Regular audits to ensure algorithms do not embed systemic biases.
- Data Security: Robust infrastructure to prevent breaches.

FRAMEWORK FOR IMPLEMENTING PREDICTIVE GOVERNANCE

The shift from reactive public administration to proactive, predictive government is more than a policy change—it involves a fundamental overhaul of the state's technological and organizational infrastructure. Predictive analytics has the power to enable governments to foresee societal needs, avoid crises, and maximize public resources, but this can only be achieved through careful architectural design and strategic deployment.

This chapter explores the multilayered architecture of predictive governance systems, compares implementation models, presents tools and technology being used, and discusses capacity-building strategies in order to make them effective. It also addresses the need to adhere to agile and inclusive practices so that not only do predictive systems function well, they are also equitable and responsive to citizen needs.

Conceptual Framework of Predictive Analytics in Governance

At its core, a predictive system of governance is a socio-technical multi-component environment. It brings together disparate sets of datasets, coordinates algorithmic cleverness, and channels lessons into intervention usability. To make all this possible, there has to be an architecture that has strength, elasticity, and interface capacity at departmental and government tier levels.

Figure 2. Conceptual architecture for predictive governance systems

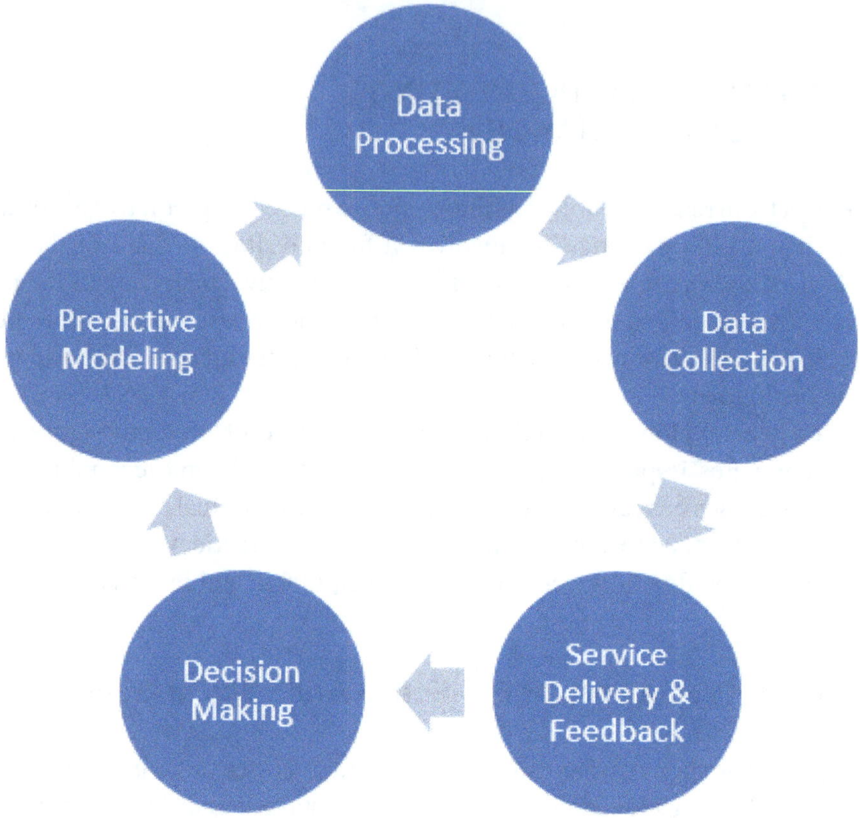

The typical architecture of a governance predictive analytics system consists of the following five layers (Figure 2):

- Data Sources Layer: Holds structured and unstructured data from internal government databases (e.g., census data, health records), IoT sensors (e.g., traffic sensors, pollution sensors), and external sources such as social media and open data portals.
- Data Integration and Processing Layer: Offers seamless data extraction, transformation, and loading (ETL) of information into distributed or centralized data lakes or warehouses. It also takes responsibility for data cleaning, normalization, and real-time stream processing.
- Analytics and Modeling Layer: Holds the core machine learning and statistical models that generate forecasts, risk scores, classifications, and recom-

mendations. It further includes modules for cross-validation of the models and bias detection.

- Application and Interface Layer: Converts model outputs into usable insights through dashboards for policymakers, automated alerts for administrators, or mobile applications for citizens.
- Security, Compliance, and Governance Layer: Ensures data confidentiality and integrity by encrypting, applying access controls, anonymization mechanisms, and adherence to legal standards such as GDPR or country-specific data protection regulations.

This modular, service-based architecture enables public agencies to apply predictive solutions on an incremental basis while preserving system coherence and integrity.

Data Governance in Predictive Systems

Good data governance is the foundation for predictive analytics. Without standardized high-quality data and well-defined policies for sharing and use, predictive models cannot perform consistently. Governments need to set a consistent data governance strategy addressing legal, ethical, operational, and technical aspects (Table 3).

Table 3. Key elements of data governance in public administration

Component	Description	Example
Data Ownership	Assigns responsibility for data accuracy and security	Ministry of Health oversees immunization databases
Access Control	Defines permissions based on roles and responsibilities	Social workers access only case-specific data
Inter-agency Agreements	Facilitates secure and legal data sharing between departments	MoUs between tax and education departments for scholarship verification
Metadata Management	Maintains records about data provenance, lineage, and structure	Tags for time stamps, source reliability, update frequency
Citizen Consent Management	Ensures that citizens retain control over how their data is used	Digital consent dashboards allowing users to opt in/out

The use of open data standards and APIs also encourages interoperability, allowing various government systems to “speak” with each other. Estonia has shown the potential of this method, where their X-Road platform enables secure, real-time data sharing between ministries and agencies.

Technology Stack for Predictive Governance

Installation of predictive analytics across the public sector would need to deploy a seamless, interoperable, and inexpensive tech stack. Selection of technology hinges on project breadth, overall level of existing IT infrastructure, as well as staff availability (Table 4).

Table 4. Representative technology stack for predictive analytics in governance

Layer	Tool/Platform	Function
Data Storage	PostgreSQL, Hadoop, Azure Data Lake	Store structured and unstructured data
Data Processing	Apache Spark, Talend, NiFi	Batch and real-time data transformation
Machine Learning	Scikit-learn, TensorFlow, IBM SPSS, H2O.ai	Model building and predictive analysis
Visualization	Tableau, Power BI, Apache Superset	Dashboards for decision-makers
APIs & Integration	Flask, FastAPI, MuleSoft	Model deployment and system integration
Security	OAuth 2.0, SSL, Blockchain (for audit logs)	Secure identity and transaction management

An excellent case in point is the city of Chicago's Food Inspection Forecasting Program, which used open-source tools such as R and Python to analyze historical data and predict which restaurants were most likely to violate health codes. This enabled inspectors to prioritize high-risk establishments, reducing food safety incidents with limited resources.

Centralized vs. Federated Implementation Models

The implementation model significantly impacts the effectiveness and agility of predictive systems in governance. Two primary paradigms are commonly considered:

Centralized Model

In this model, all data and analytics operations are housed under a central authority, such as a national data agency. This ensures consistent data standards, centralized model development, and easier policy alignment.

- Pros: High coordination, unified standards, strong oversight
- Cons: Risk of bottlenecks, less local customization

Federated Model

Here, data remains within individual departments or jurisdictions, but shared protocols and APIs enable collaboration. This model is better suited to federal governments or countries with strong regional autonomy (Table 5).

- Pros: Flexibility, innovation, autonomy for local entities
- Cons: Coordination complexity, variable data quality

Table 5. Comparison of centralized and federated models

Feature	Centralized Model	Federated Model
Data Control	Central authority	Local departments
Innovation Potential	Moderate	High
Implementation Speed	Fast (in uniform systems)	Slower (requires alignment)
Example	Singapore Smart Nation	EU's GAIA-X Framework

Countries may also adopt a hybrid approach, using centralized models for critical infrastructure (e.g., health and emergency services) and federated models for locally driven projects.

Agile Development and Incremental Scaling

In contrast to private sector projects, public administration has to trade off innovation for stability and accountability. Agile techniques provide a useful route, allowing governments to begin small—quite often with pilot projects—and scale incrementally through feedback and proved impact.

Case Example

In 2015, New York City's Department of Buildings adopted a predictive model to schedule priority inspections for potentially dangerous buildings. The algorithm forecasted which buildings were at greatest risk based on historical violations and environmental conditions. The pilot increased the efficiency of inspections by more than 70% and was subsequently rolled out citywide with iterative enhancements.

Through embracing agile sprints, stakeholder workshops, and feedback loops, public agencies are able to optimize systems in real-time and prevent the traps of top-down, monolithic deployments.

Building Institutional Capacity

Technology alone does not make a government predictive. The real enabler is human capacity—a workforce equipped with the technical, analytical, and ethical skills necessary to operate and govern predictive systems.

Key Competencies Include:

- Data science and AI engineering
- Policy interpretation of model outputs
- Ethical AI and bias mitigation
- Change management and user training

To Build This Capacity, Governments Can:

- Establish AI training academies for public servants
- Partner with universities and think tanks
- Create cross-functional AI task forces
- Incentivize data science fellowships and internships

Finland's Elements of AI initiative provides an excellent model. The free online course aims to educate citizens and civil servants alike, fostering an informed and participatory AI ecosystem.

ETHICAL, LEGAL, AND POLICY CONSIDERATIONS

Ethics, law, and policy are not obstacles to predictive analytics—they are its pillars. As governments adopt anticipatory service models, they can do nothing but do it with caution, humility, and foresight. By embedding ethics in every design phase, by following dynamically shifting legal norms, and by cultivating institutional and citizen trust, predictive governance can be not only wiser—but fairer, more inclusive, and deeply people-focused.

The Imperative for Responsible AI in Governance

Since governments implement predictive analytics in order to deliver more forward-thinking, cost-effective, and citizen-centered services, ethical as well as legal challenges have been placed on center stage. Predictive models, unlike traditional IT systems, are dynamic and probabilistic in their nature, especially if they depend on artificial intelligence (AI). Their dynamic character generates questions on accountability, justice, transparency, and trustworthiness.

In public administration, where decisions can impact welfare entitlement, health care, or justice, ethical application of AI is not a decision—it's a requirement. Predictive systems should be guided by what is technologically possible, but also by what is socially acceptable, legal, and just.

Core Ethical Principles in Predictive Public Services

There are some fundamental principles that need to guide the ethical application of predictive analytics in government. These are:

- Explainability and Transparency: The citizen must be able to see how and why a decision on them is being taken. If an AI system denies a subsidy to a citizen or flags a citizen for audit, there must be a clear reason. Black-box algorithms ruin trust and potentially violate due process.
- Accountability: Public institutions need human over automated systems. While machines can be a help, they cannot substitute for human judgment in issues that impact basic rights and entitlements.
- Privacy and Data Protection: Citizens' personal data have to be gathered, stored, and processed according to legislation such as the General Data Protection Regulation (GDPR) in the EU, or the Health Insurance Portability and Accountability Act (HIPAA) in the United States.
- Beneficence and Non-Maleficence: Public sector AI ought to promote greater well-being and do no harm. The "do no harm" principle has to guide all predictive interventions.

Example: Ethical Dilemma Example

A city employs predictive policing to send officers to blocks marked as high-risk. Over time, residents in low-income areas feel over-surveilled and criminalized, even if no crime happens. The model, which has been trained on past crime data, perpetuates biased policing patterns. This is an example of where fairness audits and ongoing ethical review are necessary.

Legal and Regulatory Landscape

The legal environment underpinning AI and predictive analytics is moving very quickly. Governments need to keep up with domestic and foreign advances in order to maintain compliance and protect citizen rights (Table 6).

Key Legal Domains

- Data Protection Legislation: These protect individual data from gathering, storing, or processing in a particular way. The GDPR of the EU requires data subjects to be offered the right of access, rectification, and erasure of their data. It also gives the "right to explanation" for automated decision-making.
- Algorithmic Accountability Laws: New York City, among others, has passed legislation mandating transparency in the use of algorithms in government decision-making.
- Procurement and Liability: When contracting out AI solutions to the private sector, public agencies should have provisions on data sovereignty, intellectual property, and liability in case of model errors.
- Freedom of Information: The public might be entitled under the law to know about the algorithms governing them. Companies must be ready to share decision criteria without violating confidentiality or sacrificing essential logic.

Table 6. Selected AI-related regulatory instruments and guidelines in the public sector

Country/Region	Instrument / Framework	Focus Areas	Public Sector Application
European Union	EU AI Act (proposed)	Risk-based classification, transparency, human oversight	High-risk applications in public safety, migration, social services
Canada	Directive on Automated Decision-Making (2020)	Algorithmic Impact Assessments (AIAs), documentation, auditability	Used in immigration, benefits processing, tax assessments
United Kingdom	Centre for Data Ethics and Innovation (CDEI)	AI ethics advisory, transparency, public consultation	Recommends standards for algorithmic use in education, policing
Singapore	Model AI Governance Framework (2019)	Human-centric AI, explainability, accountability	Piloted in healthcare, smart city management
USA	Blueprint for an AI Bill of Rights (2022)	Data privacy, bias mitigation, algorithmic discrimination	Guides ethical use in hiring, health, public assistance programs
Brazil	Artificial Intelligence Strategy & AI Bill of Rights (draft)	Civil rights, fairness, responsible innovation	Under discussion for public safety and healthcare AI applications
India	National Strategy for AI (NITI Aayog)	Responsible AI, inclusion, consent, data protection	Targeting AI use in agriculture, education, and healthcare

continued on following page

Table 6. Continued

Country/Region	Instrument / Framework	Focus Areas	Public Sector Application
OECD	OECD AI Principles (2019)	Human-centered values, robustness, accountability	Adopted by over 40 countries; influences public sector procurement
Estonia	AI Strategy & X-Road Platform	Interoperability, secure data exchange, minimal state intervention	Enables real-time cross-agency predictive services
Australia	AI Ethics Framework (2020)	Human-centered, fairness, contestability	Applied in welfare, public health, and transportation planning

This table highlights the diversity of approaches and the growing consensus around key themes such as transparency, human oversight, and data governance in public sector AI use.

Beneficence and Non-Maleficence

In public service provision, the ethical values of beneficence—doing good—are complemented by non-maleficence—doing no harm—are especially applicable. Used wisely, predictive analytics can allow governments to act in advance of problems from disease outbreaks to children's welfare. Yet, when not adequately controlled, these systems have the potential to do harm unwittingly by entrenching existing biases, mislabeling individuals, or eroding public trust.

Take the example of predictive child protection systems, for instance, one used by Allegheny County, Pennsylvania. The system applied case history data to produce risk scores on children at intake calls for welfare intake. Although the tool aided in the earlier identification of children at risk, there were concerns regarding false positives that may result in unnecessary investigations, particularly in already over-policed communities. This demonstrates that models need to be constantly tested for validity, equity, and effect on the world (Figure 3).

A government that aims to act in the best interests of its people must construct predictive tools that maximize the common good and minimize harm to individuals. This entails:

- Conducting ethical impact assessments before implementation.
- Involve multiple voices—particularly those of vulnerable populations—in the design process.
- Providing feedback loops that enable impacted users to question or dispute decisions.

- Beneficence can be assured not only through good intentions but through a considered design ethic of empathy, equity, and accountability.

Figure 3. Risk vs. benefit matrix for predictive public services

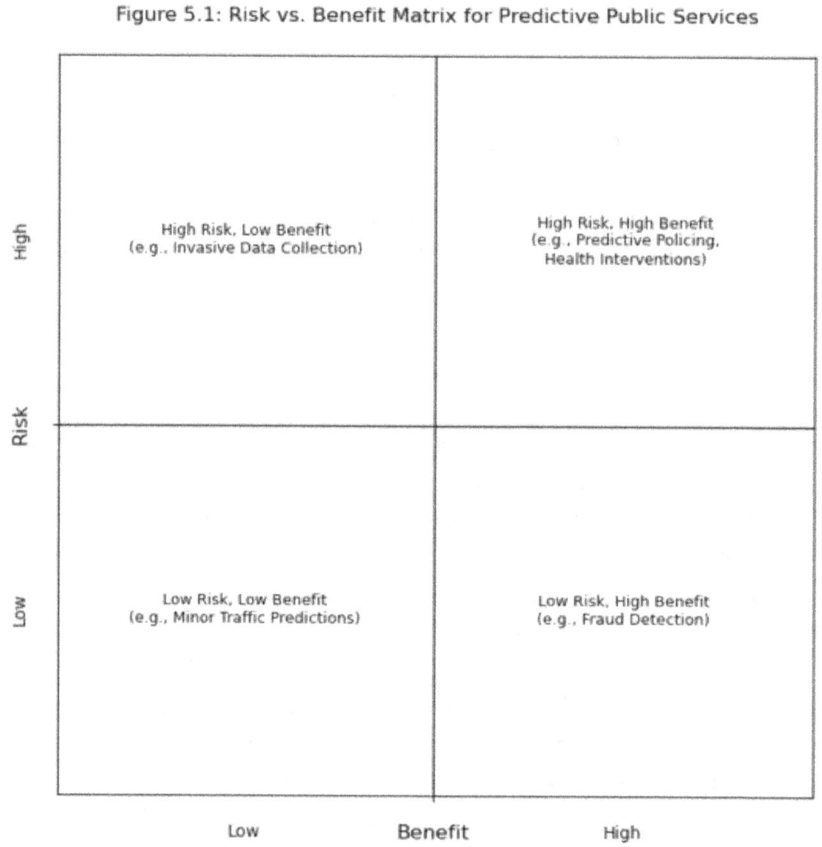

Legal and Regulatory Landscape- - Emerging Global Frameworks

Governments internationally are now seizing on the importance of creating legal frameworks that dictate the use of AI in the public sector. The European Union's AI Act, which promises to become the world standard, calls for a risk-based typology of

AI systems. Critical systems—e.g., applied to critical infrastructure, law enforcement, or migration—will come under strict demands, including:

- Mandatory documentation of data quality
- Transparency in logic and outcomes
- Human oversight and redress mechanisms

Meanwhile, countries like Canada, Singapore, and Brazil have published ethical guidelines or launched regulatory sandboxes to test AI systems before full-scale deployment.

National Context and Sector-Specific Regulations

Across the majority of countries, sector-specific regulation also intersects with AI use. For instance, algorithms used in healthcare must comply with patient confidentiality regulations (e.g., HIPAA in America), while education systems implemented must protect student records under legislation like FERPA.

Above all, such legal systems must be revisited constantly to be sensitive to advances in AI capability and sophistication. Immutable law cannot be responsive to mutable technology.

Institutional Mechanisms for Ethical Governance

To ensure sustained ethical oversight, governments should establish dedicated institutions or bodies responsible for AI governance.

Examples of Institutional Models

To provide long-term ethical guidance on the development and use of artificial intelligence, governments must set up specialized institutions or agencies solely dedicated to AI governance. Different institutional frameworks can be effective for this role. AI Ethics Councils, for example, are multidisciplinary boards made up of ethicists, technologists, representatives from civil society, and legal professionals. These councils are authorized to oversee high-risk AI applications and approve or reject recommendations on potentially harmful deployments. Another model is the creation of Algorithmic Transparency Sites, under which public agencies are required to make available the algorithms being used, their proposed functions, and performance metrics—a model pioneered by New York City through a transparency law proposed in 2018. AI Ombudsman Offices serve as a venue for public participation, allowing citizens to file complaints, seek explanations, or appeal decisions taken by AI systems, thereby restoring accountability in increasingly automated spaces. In addition, Ethics by Design Toolkits—containing checklists and decision trees incorporated into AI development processes—are designed so that ethics are included from the start and not addressed as an afterthought. A good example in real life is the United Kingdom's Centre for Data Ethics and Innovation (CDEI), which serves as a bridging point between the government, industry, academia, and society. The CDEI has drawn up ethical AI procurement guidelines and proposed public sector data use reforms through intensive stakeholder engagement.

Building Public Trust and Citizen Engagement

Trust is the public institution's currency. In its absence, even the most effectively designed forecasting system will encounter resistance or skepticism. It takes not only transparency, but continuous citizen engagement and agency to establish trust.

Strategies to foster trust include:

- Participatory design workshops, where affected communities are involved in shaping how data is used and what safeguards are built in.
- Public communication campaigns, using simple language and real-world examples to demystify predictive tools.
- Feedback mechanisms, such as digital platforms where citizens can flag errors or bias in system outcomes.

Example: Building Trust through Co-Design

In Helsinki, Finland, a public housing algorithm was co-designed with tenants, housing officers, and legal experts. The inclusive process helped clarify selection criteria, address concerns about fairness, and led to greater acceptance of the system.

Public engagement also helps avoid the "techno-solutionism" trap—assuming that every social issue can be fixed through algorithms. Predictive systems must complement, not replace, human empathy and judgment in public service.

CASE STUDIES AND REAL-WORLD APPLICATIONS OF PREDICTIVE GOVERNANCE

While theoretical models and ethical frameworks provide essential foundations, the true test of predictive governance lies in its real-world application. Across the globe, governments are experimenting with data-driven tools to improve policy outcomes, streamline resource allocation, and deliver services proactively. This chapter presents a series of curated case studies, showcasing both the potential and the challenges of predictive analytics in public administration.

Each example is structured to highlight the problem addressed, the predictive solution adopted, the technologies and data sources used, and the outcomes and lessons learned (Jaiswal & Kumar, 2022).

Predicting Food Safety Risks – Chicago, USA

Problem

Limited health inspectors led to inefficient restaurant inspection schedules, often after violations had already occurred (Hashmi, Dwivedi, & Kumar, 2023).

Predictive Solution

The City of Chicago partnered with data scientists to build a predictive model that ranked restaurants based on their likelihood of violating food safety codes.

- **Data Used:** Past inspection data, weather patterns, business licenses, crime statistics, and social media complaints.
- **Tools:** Open-source technologies like R and Python, integrated with city data portals.
- **Outcome:** The system identified high-risk establishments seven days earlier on average, increasing inspection efficiency by over 25%.

Lesson

Low-cost, open-data-based predictive tools can deliver high-impact results if properly aligned with agency workflows (Srivastava et al., 2025).

Social Service Demand Forecasting – New South Wales, Australia

Problem

The Department of Family and Community Services needed to forecast future demand for child protection, housing, and welfare services (Kumar, 2024).

Predictive Solution

A comprehensive data-sharing agreement between agencies enabled the development of linked longitudinal datasets to train machine learning models that could forecast service demand geographically and demographically (Figure 4) (Srivastava, Ahmed, & Kumar, 2024).

- **Data Used:** School attendance, health visits, criminal justice involvement, and social services interactions.
- **Technology:** Secure cloud infrastructure, Microsoft Azure ML, and custom analytics dashboards.
- **Outcome:** The department improved budget forecasting accuracy and could prioritize high-risk communities for early interventions.

Figure 4. Forecasted vs. actual social service demand in selected regions

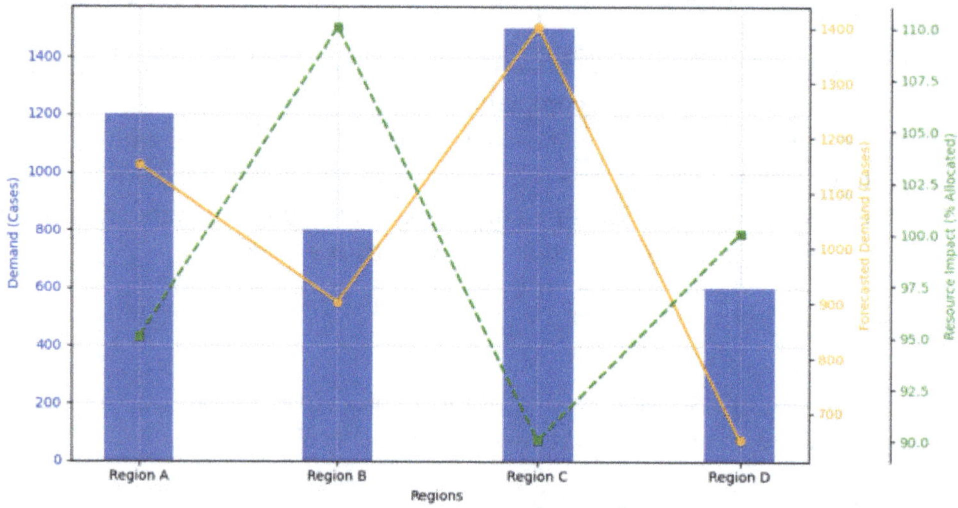

Lesson

Data collaboration across departments—paired with secure infrastructure—can significantly improve planning and proactive policy targeting (Hashmi, Dwivedi, & Kumar, 2024).

Predictive Policing – The Netherlands

Problem

Police departments sought to allocate patrols more efficiently by predicting high-crime zones.

Predictive Solution

Dutch authorities implemented the Crime Anticipation System (CAS), which uses spatial and temporal analytics to anticipate burglary hotspots.

- **Data Used:** Historical crime reports, weather data, public holidays, and urban demographics.
- **Tools:** GIS systems integrated with AI-based clustering models.
- **Outcome:** In several districts, CAS helped reduce burglary rates by 5–10%, with increased confidence in patrol allocation.

Lesson

While effective, predictive policing must include oversight and transparency mechanisms to prevent racial profiling and over-surveillance.

Example: Ethical Oversight in Predictive Policing

After concerns in the UK and US, Dutch police implemented mandatory audits of CAS outputs to ensure fairness, alongside citizen advisory panels.

Healthcare Risk Prediction – Rwanda

Problem

Limited health infrastructure made it difficult to identify and prioritize high-risk patients in rural areas.

Predictive Solution

The Rwandan Ministry of Health, in collaboration with partners, deployed an AI system to predict maternal health risks using mobile health (mHealth) data (Anil Kumar, 2025).

- **Data Used:** Mobile clinic records, self-reported symptoms, past complications, nutrition indicators.
- **Technology:** Mobile applications using TensorFlow Lite for offline risk scoring, SMS-based alerts for remote health workers.
- **Outcome:** Risk-based triage enabled targeted outreach to reduce maternal mortality in remote districts.

Lesson

Even in low-resource settings, predictive models embedded in mobile tools can have life-saving impacts when tailored to local constraints.

Urban Mobility and Traffic Management – Helsinki, Finland

Problem

Rising urban congestion required smarter, more sustainable traffic management.

Predictive Solution

Helsinki built a real-time urban mobility platform integrating public transport data, ride-share usage, and traffic sensor feeds to predict congestion hotspots and adjust transit schedules dynamically (Figure 5).

- **Data Used:** Public transport logs, GPS data, parking sensors, weather.
- **Technology:** AI-driven dashboards, cloud computing, predictive routing algorithms.
- **Outcome:** Traffic delays decreased by 11%, and public transport usage increased due to improved reliability.

Figure 5. Dynamic rerouting based on predicted traffic congestion

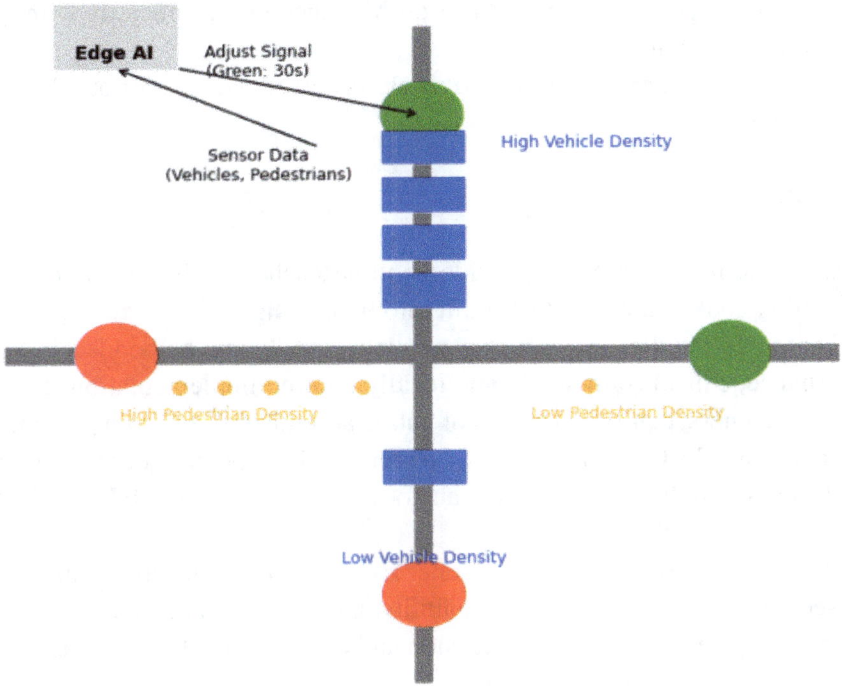

Lesson

Real-time prediction allows cities to move from reactive traffic responses to anticipatory urban planning.

Early Dropout Detection – Andhra Pradesh, India

Problem

High student dropout rates were jeopardizing long-term education goals.

Predictive Solution

Using statewide data on attendance, performance, and socio-economic background, the government developed a dropout prediction engine.

- **Data Used:** Daily attendance, examination scores, mid-day meal usage, parental literacy.
- **Technology:** Integrated Education Management dashboards with alerts for schools and districts.
- **Outcome:** Interventions based on alerts helped reduce dropouts by up to 15% in pilot districts.

Lesson

Early warning systems can provide frontline teachers with actionable intelligence if usability and local context are built into their design.

These case studies suggest that predictive analytics, embedded in solid data governance, ethical framework, and locally tailored implementation, can enhance the effectiveness, equity, and reach of public administration. From preventing child abuse in Australia to managing traffic patterns in Finland or maternal care in Rwanda, the use of predictive models is transforming government's ability to foretell and respond to citizens' needs.

But the journey is not an easy one. Every application must walk a tightrope between bias, data integrity, legal liability, and civic engagement to reach predictive governance as a power for inclusion and empowerment, and not exclusion and oppression (Agarwal et al., 2025).

EMERGING TRENDS AND FUTURE OUTLOOK IN PREDICTIVE GOVERNANCE

With predictive governance still advancing public administration, emerging trends and technologies are breaking the horizon and potential of data-driven governance wider. In this chapter, some of the most likely transformative trends to shape the future of public service delivery are discussed (Saxena et al., 2025). These include Edge AI, Digital Twins, Responsible AI, and Citizen Participation. Each trend has new challenges and opportunities, predicting an exciting yet complex future for predictive governance (Sagar et al., 2025).

Edge AI and Real-Time Decision Systems

The onset of Edge AI is the process of data being processed locally within devices (on the "edge" of the network), instead of sending it to central servers or cloud infrastructure for processing. This has revolutionary implications for real-time decision in predictive governance, where action speed is critical (Hashmi, Dwivedi, & Kumar, 2022).

Key Benefits

- **Minimization of Latency:** Edge AI minimizes latency by minimizing the time lag between data collection and decision making, which is highly critical for application areas such as real-time traffic monitoring, public safety surveillance, and emergency response (City of Los Angeles, 2021).
- **Privacy Preservation:** With local processing of sensitive information on devices, governments can avoid privacy issues generally related to cloud storage, making data use safer (Binns, 2018).
- **Cost Effectiveness:** Edge devices will use less bandwidth, reducing the cost of running expenses on cloud processing and storage (Hashmi, Dwivedi, & Kumar, 2024).

Use Cases in Predictive Governance

- **Public Health:** Rural community wearable health devices can use Edge AI to monitor individuals' vitals and alert healthcare professionals about upcoming emergencies without the need for internet access (Vogels, 2021).
- **Smart Cities:** Traffic lights and Edge AI-enabled surveillance cameras in city spaces can foretell accidents and alter traffic lights in real-time to avoid future mishaps (Pradeep, 2025).

Figure 6. Real-time traffic adjustment using edge AI

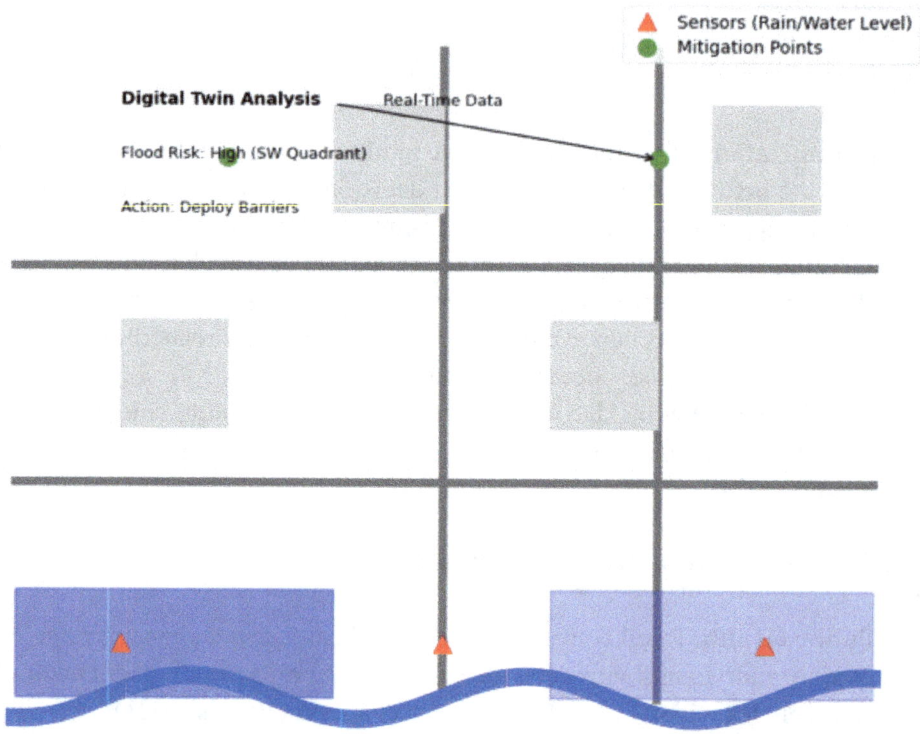

Example

The City of Los Angeles employs Edge AI to process real-time traffic data, making dynamic changes to traffic lights to reduce congestion. This leads to a 15-20% reduction in commute duration during peak periods (Kumar, 2023; Kumar, 2021) (Figure 6).

Challenges

- **Data Integrity:** Edge processing introduces new threats related to data synchronization and consistency with centralized systems (Binns, 2018).
- **Scalability:** Although Edge AI offers advantages for localized systems, handling thousands of devices at scale presents logistical and infrastructure challenges (Gaur, Sharan, & Kumar, 2024).

Digital Twins and Policy Simulation

A Digital Twin is a simulated copy of a physical system or entity. For predictive governance, digital twins simulate entire cities, public infrastructures, or even certain populations. These models have the capacity to emulate the effects of different policies, and governments can therefore experiment with scenarios prior to implementation (Kumar, 2024).

Key Benefits

- **Policy Testing:** Policy makers can simulate different policy interventions (e.g., rate changes in taxation, environmental protection regulations) and predict their effect on the economy, traffic, or healthcare sector (Singh, Gupta, & Kumar, 2022).
- **Resource Optimization:** From real-time data from the physical world, digital twins allow governments to optimize the use of resources, improve the performance of operations, and identify impending issues in public services (Van, 2020).

Applications in Predictive Governance

- **Urban Planning:** Cities like Singapore are using digital twins to create virtual copies of urban infrastructure, which can predict traffic flow, energy usage, and public health impacts of future developments (Vogels, 2021) (Figure 7).
- **Disaster Management:** Governments can use virtual models of cities to conduct experiments on what would happen under natural disasters like earthquakes or flooding to construct infrastructures that could withstand them, and to orchestrate successful evacuation plans (Kumar, 2021).

Figure 7. Digital twin simulation of flood management in urban areas

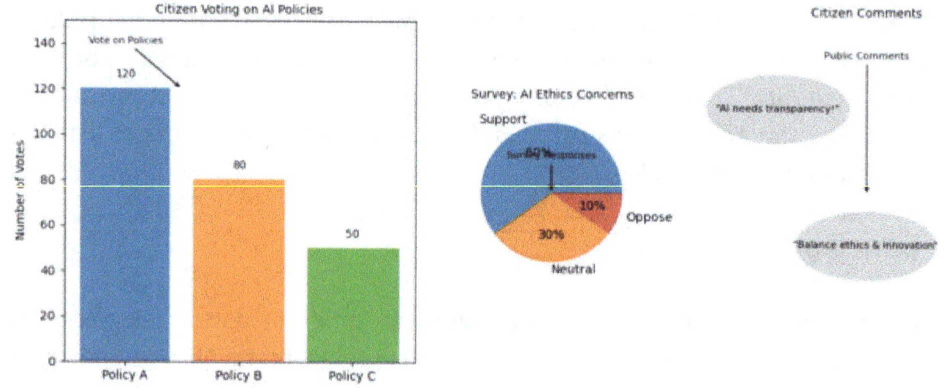

Example

Helsinki City has developed a digital twin of the city infrastructure that allows urban planners to simulate different plans for managing traffic, waste, and environmental impact prior to actually doing anything (Gartner, 2020).

Challenges

- **Data Integration:** Proper and complete digital twins need huge volumes of high-quality, real-time data from various sources (Vogels, 2021).
- **Cost and Complexity:** Creating and sustaining a mature digital twin infrastructure is expensive and technically demanding (Gartner, 2020).

Responsible AI and Regulatory Frameworks

With AI becoming increasingly embedded in public administration, more attention is given to Responsible AI. Responsible AI emphasizes making sure that AI systems are transparent, fair, accountable, and consistent with societal values. Governments, therefore, need robust regulatory systems in place for facilitating the ethical application of AI across government services (European Commission, 2021).

Key Principles of Responsible AI

- **Fairness:** Avoiding discrimination in algorithmic decision-making such that AI systems won't reinforce discrimination (Van den Hoven, 2020).

- **Transparency:** Offering explanations of AI-driven decisions to create public trust (Van den Hoven, 2020).
- **Accountability:** Human accountability and control over AI systems (European Commission, 2021).
- **Privacy Protection:** Safeguarding citizens' data and confidentiality (OECD, 2021).

Applications in Predictive Governance

- **Automated Welfare Allocation:** AI systems are now being used for the distribution of welfare benefits, but laws should be enacted so that such systems do not negatively discriminate or leave behind underprivileged groups (OECD, 2021).
- **Bias Audits:** Governments can be made to carry out periodic audits of AI models to verify that they do not unfairly negatively affect some groups, especially marginalized ones (European Commission, 2021).

Challenges

- **Lack of Global Standards:** Different countries have varying standards, which can make it difficult for governments to implement consistent regulatory approaches (OECD, 2021).
- **Dynamic Nature of AI:** AI technologies evolve quickly, which makes it difficult for laws to keep up with the pace of innovation (Hashmi, Dwivedi, & Kumar, 2022).

Citizen Participation and Data Democracy

The Role of Citizen Engagement

As governments increasingly implement more sophisticated data-driven technologies, citizen engagement and data democracy are becoming the cornerstone of the ethical governance of predictive systems. Citizens not only need to be aware of how their data is utilized but also get a voice in decision-making (Surendra, 2024) (Figure 8).

Applications in Predictive Governance

- **Citizen Panels:** States in nations such as Finland and Estonia have utilized digital platforms where citizens offer feedback on AI ethics, data use, and algorithmic fairness (Estonian Government, 2021).
- **Public Engagement Platforms:** In New Zealand, public engagement tools enable citizens to participate directly in the policy development of AI systems utilized in health and welfare (OECD, 2021).

Figure 8. Citizen engagement in AI policy design

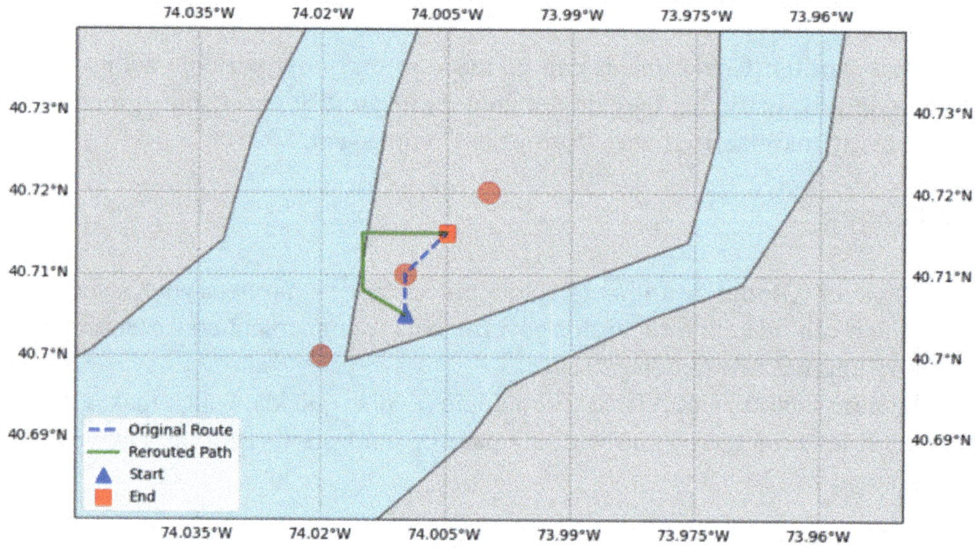

Challenges

- **Digital Literacy:** Not all citizens have the skills or access to participate meaningfully in digital governance (Rifkin, 2014).
- **Inclusive Representation:** Ensuring that underrepresented groups have a voice in AI and data-related policy discussions can be challenging (Thiru et al., 2022).

As we look to the future, predictive governance is on the cusp of a profound transformation. Emerging technologies such as Edge AI, Digital Twins, and responsible AI architectures are set to enhance public administration's capacity to serve citizens more effectively. But these developments also introduce fresh challenges around data privacy, transparency, and citizen participation. The success formula will be keeping at the center both the empowerment by the use of AI for common good and shielding the core fundamental rights and integrity of citizens.

CONCLUSION: SHAPING THE FUTURE OF PREDICTIVE GOVERNANCE

The advent of AI-powered predictive governance presents a revolutionary chance to revolutionize the way governments provide services to citizens. With the help of cutting-edge technologies like Edge AI, Digital Twins, Responsible AI, and active citizen engagement, public administration is evolving in real-time. All these advancements are leading to a future where predictive analytics and data-driven planning allow governments to see ahead and act with increased efficiency and anticipation.

Summary of Insights

In this chapter, new trends and technologies that are likely to shape the future of public service delivery were examined. The major highlights are the revolutionary role of Edge AI, which enables quicker, real-time decision-making in local areas, hence enhancing responsiveness in sectors like urban administration and disaster management. Governments are deploying Edge AI in scenarios such as smart traffic management and public health surveillance. Digital Twins are also becoming revolutionary for urban planning and policy experimentation, enabling governments to model and test policy options in a virtual environment prior to implementation in the real world—optimizing resources and reducing unforeseen consequences. Responsible AI adoption reflects the critical role of fairness, transparency, and accountability in government-related AI solutions, guaranteeing public trust and citizens' rights. Data democracy and engaged citizen participation are also key pillars for effective predictive governance. Involving citizens in policy-making around AI promotes participatory, open, and values-oriented public administration. While these technologies have great promise, they also pose challenges, such as issues of data privacy, scalability, and the need for adaptive regulation. Even so, these trends herald a movement toward more active, responsive, and open governance.

Strategic Roadmap for Proactive Governance

For governments aiming to implement predictive government models, there should be a clear strategic roadmap. The roadmap should have the following important steps:

- Establish a Regulatory Framework: Governments must develop clear, agile rules regarding the use of AI and predictive analytics for public service delivery. The frameworks should place an emphasis on data privacy, security, and accountability so that AI systems can be utilized responsibly and ethically. For instance, emulating the style of the EU AI Act can provide a robust framework for regulation (European Commission, 2021).
- Invest in AI and Data Infrastructure: Governments must establish the digital infrastructure that enables effective AI uptake. It includes hardware (like Edge devices) and software (like AI algorithms, data management platforms) enabling real-time processing and decision-making. Technology companies' collaborations and public-private partnerships can accelerate the development of infrastructure.
- Promote Cross-Sectoral Collaboration: Incorporating AI and predictive analytics requires collaboration from several stakeholders—research institutions, government, private companies, and citizens. Establishing cross-sector collaboration ensures that different expertise and thoughts are incorporated in policy planning and execution. Public-private partnerships also enable scaling up AI-based initiatives at the national or regional level.

Toward a Predictive, Inclusive Public Sector

The journey to a predictive and inclusive public sector is not one of merely adopting new technologies—it's one of ensuring that these technologies serve all citizens, particularly the most vulnerable and marginalized. As public service delivery becomes increasingly integrated with more and more AI systems, inclusivity must be the foundation of this approach.

Predictive Governance for Social Equity

Governments must program predictive systems to advance social equity, rather than reinforce ingrained disparities. As an example, predictive analysis used in welfare distribution must be open to ensure that at-risk groups are not denied support on the basis of discriminatory algorithms (OECD, 2021). Similarly, applications of AI in the healthcare and education sectors must be carefully controlled to prevent age, gender, ethnicity, or socioeconomic-based discrimination.

Public Trust and Citizen Empowerment

For predictive governance to be sustainable, governments must establish and maintain public trust. Ensuring AI-based decisions are transparent and accountable will be crucial in obtaining that. Direct engagement of the public in policymaking procedures will involve the public and enable them to be in a position to influence the structure of the AI systems in a way that the policies will be their own expression of needs and values.

Inclusivity in Data and Technology Design

Finally, data democracy needs to be facilitated by involving citizens in AI model construction and using public data. Governments should ensure that the rights of the data are not violated for the citizens and citizens have some degree of voice over how their data is being utilized in predictive models. This could involve feedback mechanisms, where citizens always have a say in AI-driven policy applications.

Final Thoughts

This chapter has examined the potential of predictive analytics to redesign public administration at its very core, unlocking a move from reactive to proactive, citizen-focused service delivery. The main contributions of the research include:

- Illustrating the tangible effects of predictive analytics based on in-depth case studies in healthcare, education, urban planning, and social welfare in a range of different global settings.
- Introducing a strong architecture and technology stack that can be used by governments to create scalable, secure, and interoperable predictive governance systems.
- Identifying how data-driven public services can improve personalization, optimization of resources, and inclusiveness, especially for disadvantaged groups.
- Meeting ethical, legal, and regulatory issues, and offering concrete recommendations for using AI in a responsible and transparent manner in public administration.
- Through the integration of information from varied sources and through the use of AI, machine learning, IoT, and digital twins, governments can anticipate up-and-coming issues, respond with services addressing citizen needs, and fine-tune policy action with increased accuracy and velocity.

Future Scope

In the future, the progression of predictive government relies on the following key directions:

- Edge AI and Real-Time Interventions: Increasing application of edge computing for low-latency decision-making in public security, traffic regulation, and emergency healthcare.
- Digital Twin Integration: Scaling city-level simulations for smarter urban planning and disaster preparedness.
- Inclusive AI Development: Ensuring predictive models are trained on representative, diverse datasets to prevent systemic biases and discrimination.
- Global Policy Harmonization: Developing interoperable legal frameworks for ethical AI governance across jurisdictions.
- Participatory Governance: Enhancing citizen engagement mechanisms in algorithm design, data governance, and feedback loops to ensure trust, transparency, and accountability.

In summary, predictive analytics is a revolutionary power for governance in the digital age. But success is not merely a function of technological uptake, but of strategic vision, ethical design, and inclusive policymaking. As governments embark on this journey, forward-looking governance can be a driver of more responsive, equitable, and intelligent public institutions.

REFERENCES

Agarwal, H., Agarwal, S., Husain, F., & Kumar, R. (2025). Next-gen video watermarking with augmented payload: Integrating KAZE and DWT for superior robustness and high transparency. *AppliedMath*, *5*(2), 53. DOI: 10.3390/appliedmath5020053

Binns, R. (2018). A survey of predictive policing and machine learning techniques for law enforcement. *International Journal of Law, Crime and Justice*, *56*, 65–78. DOI: 10.1016/j.ijlcj.2018.07.003

Gaur, A. S., Sharan, H. O., & Kumar, R. (2024). AI in education: Ethical challenges and opportunities. In *The ethical frontier of AI and data analysis* (pp. 39–54). IGI Global., DOI: 10.4018/979-8-3693-2964-1.ch002

Glaeser, E. L., Kominers, S. D., Luca, M., & Naik, N. (2016). Big data and big cities: The promises and limitations of improved measures of urban life. *Economic Inquiry*, *54*(1), 1–26. DOI: 10.1111/ecin.12364

Hashmi, H., Dwivedi, R. K., & Kumar, A. (2022). An AI & ML based detection & identification in remote imagery: State-of-the-art. *Journal of Automation. Mobile Robotics and Intelligent Systems*, *15*(4), 3–17. DOI: 10.14313/JAMRIS/4-2021/22

Hashmi, H., Dwivedi, R. K., & Kumar, A. (2023). YOLO-RS: An efficient YOLO-based approach for remote sensing object detection. In *2023 12th International Conference on System Modeling & Advancement in Research Trends (SMART)* (pp. 50–56). IEEE. https://doi.org/DOI: 10.1109/SMART59791.2023.10428504

Hashmi, H., Dwivedi, R. K., & Kumar, A. (2024). Comparative analysis of CNN-based smart pre-trained models for object detection on DOTA. *Journal of Automation. Mobile Robotics and Intelligent Systems*, *18*(2), 31–45. DOI: 10.14313/JAMRIS/2-2024/11

Jaiswal, A., & Kumar, R. (2022). Breast cancer diagnosis using Stochastic Self-Organizing Map and Enlarge C4.5. *Multimedia Tools and Applications*, *81*(30), 44047–44067. DOI: 10.1007/s11042-022-14265-1

Kumar, P., Kumar, M., & Kumar, R. (2024). Data storage in manual systems that challenges in cloud & fog computing-based systems which are affecting the online data-oriented application architecture. In *2024 4th International Conference on Technological Advancements in Computational Sciences (ICTACS)* (pp. 723–727). IEEE. https://doi.org/DOI: 10.1109/ICTACS62700.2024.10841028

Kumar, P., Kumar, R., Singh, K. B., & Kumar, M. (2023). Identification of the problem and research methodology. In *Effective AI, blockchain, and e-governance applications for knowledge discovery and management* (pp. 289–308). IGI Global., DOI: 10.4018/978-1-6684-9151-5.ch001

Kumar, R., Hamid, A. B. A., Ya'akub, N. I. B., Gaur, M. S., & Kumar, S. (Eds.). (2024). *Futuristic e-governance security with deep learning applications*. IGI Global., DOI: 10.4018/978-1-6684-9596-4

Kumar, R., Kumar, P., Hamid, A. B. A., Nyamasvisva, T. E., Kumar, R., Peng, S., Jain, P., & Elngar, A. (Eds.). (2025). *Deep learning innovations for securing critical infrastructures*. IGI Global., DOI: 10.4018/979-8-3373-0563-9

Mergel, I., Edelmann, N., & Haug, N. (2019). Defining digital transformation: Results from expert interviews. *Government Information Quarterly*, *36*(4), 101385. DOI: 10.1016/j.giq.2019.06.002

Rahwan, I., Cebrian, M., Obradovich, N., Bongard, J., Bonnefon, J.-F., Breazeal, C., Crandall, J., Christakis, N. A., Couzin, I. D., Jackson, M. O., Jennings, N. R., Kamar, E., Kloumann, I. M., Larochelle, H., Lazer, D., McElreath, R., Mislove, A., Parkes, D. C., Pentland, A., & Wellman, M. (2019). Machine behaviour. *Nature*, *568*(7753), 477–486. DOI: 10.1038/s41586-019-1138-y PMID: 31019318

Sagar, M. S., Srivastava, S., Kumar, R., & Saxena, A. (2025). The evolution of industry 5.0: Harnessing artificial intelligence and communication technology. *AIP Conference Proceedings*, *3224*(1), 020064. DOI: 10.1063/5.0246747

Saxena, A., Gupta, M., Srivastava, S., & Kumar, R. (2025). Empowering edge computing: The critical role of blockchain in cybersecurity defense. *AIP Conference Proceedings*, *3224*(1), 020063. DOI: 10.1063/5.0245962

Singh, C. B., Gupta, A., & Kumar, D. R. (2022). Diabetes care survey using supervised and unsupervised machine learning. In *2022 3rd International Conference on Intelligent Engineering and Management (ICIEM)* (pp. 207–210). IEEE. https://doi.org/DOI: 10.1109/ICIEM54221.2022.9853085

Srivastava, S., Ahmed, T., & Kumar, R. (2024). Urban growth estimation of Moradabad city using Sentinel-2 images. In *2024 International Conference on Artificial Intelligence and Emerging Technology (Global AI Summit)* (pp. 1212–1216). IEEE. https://doi.org/DOI: 10.1109/GlobalAISummit62156.2024.10947888

Srivastava, S., Ahmed, T., Kumar, R., & Saxena, A. (2025). A novel machine learning hybrid model for heart disease risk assessment. *AIP Conference Proceedings*, *3224*(1), 020058. DOI: 10.1063/5.0246550

Thiru, S., Hashmi, H., Hemavathi, S., Vekariya, D., Pandey, A. K., & Abdel-Rehim, W. M. F. (2022). Vehicular cloud data collection for intelligent transportation systems. In *2022 Fourth International Conference on Emerging Research in Electronics, Computer Science and Technology (ICERECT)* (pp. 1–6). IEEE. https://doi.org/ DOI: 10.1109/ICERECT56837.2022.10060170

Topol, E. J. (2019). *Deep medicine: How artificial intelligence can make healthcare human again*. Basic Books.

Van den Hoven, J. (2020). Responsible AI and the role of transparency and accountability. *AI and Ethics*, *1*(1), 21–39. DOI: 10.1007/s43681-019-00003-9

Vogels, E. A. (2021). The future of predictive policing: Ethical considerations and implications. *The Journal of Law and Technology*, *36*(3), 142–159. DOI: 10.1080/10465788.2020.1782689

Waller, M. A., & Fawcett, S. E. (2013). Data science, predictive analytics, and big data: A revolution that will transform supply chain design and management. *Journal of Business Logistics*, *34*(2), 77–84. DOI: 10.1111/jbl.12010

Chapter 8
Transforming the Cyber World Through Blockchain-Driven Enlightenment

Abhay Bhatia
https://orcid.org/0000-0001-7220-692X
Roorkee Institute of Technology, India

Anil Kumar
https://orcid.org/0000-0002-8918-3004
Roorkee Institute of Technology, India

Pankhuri Bhatia
Kunwar Satyavira College of Engineering and Management, Bijnor, India

ABSTRACT

The cybersecurity landscape through blockchain technology in India involves leveraging the decentralized nature and consensus mechanisms of blockchain to enhance security measures. This approach aims to ensure transaction authenticity, prevent unauthorized alterations, and strengthen cybersecurity defences across various sectors, from critical infrastructure to government records. Despite the promising advantages of blockchain in cybersecurity, challenges such as scalability, interoperability, and regulatory frameworks need to be addressed for successful integration into India's cybersecurity framework. By exploring specific use cases, real-world examples, and case studies, this transformation can be more potential

DOI: 10.4018/979-8-3373-3760-9.ch008

of blockchain technology in cybersecurity with artificial intelligence offers insights into fortifying India's digital security infrastructure and fostering a more secure and trusted digital ecosystem for better world.

INTRODUCTION

The Blockchain technology, initially was introduced alongside the cryptocurrencies, notably Bitcoin, with the aim of decentralizing trust away from the central third parties to a cryptographically verifiable platform. This shift towards such decentralization is expanded into variety and various sectors such as supply chains (Ahsan & Siddique, 2022; Deepu & Ravi, 2021), healthcare (Hussien et al., 2019; Yaqoob et al., 2021), marketing and finance (Jain et al., 2021; Grover et al., 2019b), food and agriculture marketing (Yadav et al., 2020; Yadav et al., n.d.), banking, insurance, sports (Yadav et al., 2021a; Yadav et al., 2021b), cybersecurity, among others (Grover et al., 2019a; Upadhyay, 2020).

The robust cryptographic and mathematical techniques employed in blockchain ensure its ledger must remain tamper-proof, secure, as well as immutable (Luntovskyy & Guetter, 2018; Yaga et al., 2018), although it does have any certain limitations too (Ali Syed et al., 2019; Lee et al., 2019). Blockchain utilizes consensus algorithms like Proof-of-Work (PoW) yet vulnerabilities such as the 51% attack pose risks (Kaushal et al., 2017; Apostolaki et al., 2017), which has spurred research in blockchain security.

The evolution of Blockchain 2.0 introduced the concept of smart contracts that are initially proposed by Nike Szabo (Szabo, 1997). Smart contracts, also known as "law of code," have the potential to eliminate the need for trusted third parties (Ferreira, 2021; Filippi & Hassan, 2018). Platforms like Ethereum (Buterin, 2013) and Hyperledger Fabric have gained prominence for their implementation of smart contracts.

Unlike Bitcoin, Ethereum does not have a limited supply of tokens, although it also uses the consensus algorithm PoW. Smart contracts have shown promise beyond finance, with potential applications in various fields (Ferreira da Silva & Moro, 2021; Stallone et al., 2021), although cybersecurity remains a concern (Gehem et al., 2015; Kim et al., 2011; Li & Liu, 2021).

Systematic literature analysis utilizing text mining and topic modeling provides insights into trends and gaps in blockchain technology research (Jadil et al., 2022; Jutla et al., 2006; Wandabwa et al., 2021). Natural language processing-based approaches have found applications across journalism and business (Ma et al., 2006; Verma et al., 2021), as well as IoT.

Various topic modelling algorithms, such as Probabilistic Latent Semantic Indexing (pLSI), Latent Semantic Analysis (LSA) and Latent Semantic Indexing (LSI) have been employed in blockchain literature analysis (Gallinucci et al., 2015; Kinoshita et al., 2015). A mixed model approach has been proposed to analyze blockchain technology applications for consumer trust (Ferreira da Silva & Moro, 2021), while other studies focus on research trends in blockchain networks (Jiang et al., 2021) and cybersecurity (Taylor et al., 2020).

Text mining enables comprehensive analysis of vast knowledge bodies, facilitating a better understanding of blockchain technology's cybersecurity threats and vulnerabilities (Feng et al., 2017; Moro et al., 2015; Skute, 2019). By utilizing existing blockchain taxonomies, coupled with text mining and topic modeling, researchers aim to enhance understanding of blockchain technology from a consumer trust perspective.

BLOCKCHAIN

Blockchain technology plays a very indispensable role while revolutionizing cybersecurity takes place by offering transparency, immutability, and enhanced security measures. It ensures data integrity through cryptographic techniques, creates an immutable ledger, and distributes data across a network of computers, reducing the risk of data manipulation. Blockchain's decentralized nature, cryptographic security, and transparency are transforming the way sensitive data and digital assets are protected in an increasingly digital world. The integration of blockchain with cybersecurity not only enhances automation but also strengthens incident response, threat intelligence sharing, and smart contract security. Despite challenges like scalability and regulatory compliance, ongoing research and development promise solutions to harness the full potential of blockchain in cybersecurity.

Blockchain presents an alternative approach to enhanced security, one that is less conventional and far less favourable as far as concern to cybercriminals. This method reduces number of vulnerabilities, offers encryption with robustness, and more accurately it verifies data ownership and its integrity. It might make some passwords unnecessary, which is a good thing because weak passwords are usually the easiest thing about cybersecurity.

The primary advantage of blockchain is its distributed ledger technology. By using a decentralized public key infrastructure architecture, it avoids many of the risks associated with centrally stored data and removes single points of failure. Since transactions are spread across all network nodes, it is difficult for attackers to steal, change, or compromise data unless there is a vulnerability at the protocol level.

Another conventional weakness addressed by blockchain is through its consensus algorithm. It can detect malicious activities, anomalies, and false positives without relying on a central authority. While one set of eyes can be deceived, not all of them can be. This strengthens authentication and secures data communications and record management.

In spite of the fact that blockchain contains numerous forward-thinking highlights, it exploits one of the main network safety apparatuses: encryption. The disseminated record can use public key framework to get correspondence, confirm gadgets, approve setup changes, and find classified gadgets in a web of things (IoT) environment. Through encryption and computerized marks, a blockchain framework can safeguard associated indoor regulators, shrewd doorbells, surveillance cameras, and other weak edge gadgets. A new Palo Alto Organizations report said that 98% of IoT gadget traffic was decoded and depicted it as "easy pickins for assailants."

Similarly, this invention can be used as a weapon to counteract distributed denial-of-service (DDoS) attacks. The sole point that allows these attacks to succeed can be eliminated using a blockchain-based space name framework (DNS), which is the convention for managing online traffic. A DDoS attack on the servers of one DNS provider brought down a significant portion of the internet in 2016.

Figure 1. Blockchain and its associated fields

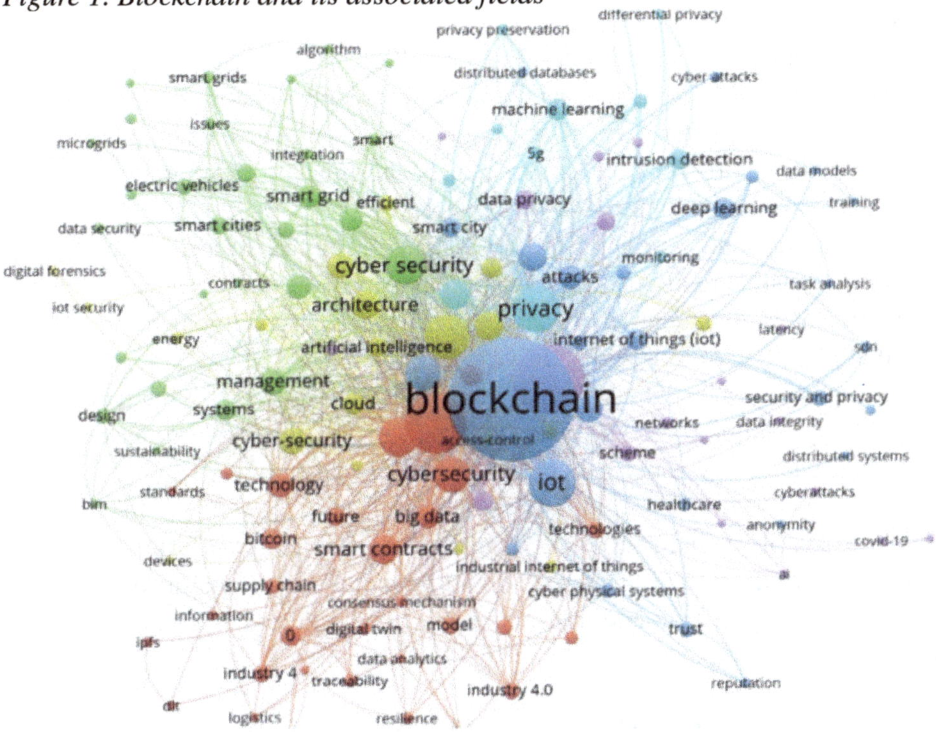

Blockchain as Digital Ledger

In the context of blockchain, a digital ledger is comparable to a shared, public notebook. This notebook is a copy that is owned by every user on the blockchain. This implies that anybody can view the activities or transactions that are recorded in it. But unlike a traditional notepad, anything entered into this digital ledger cannot be altered or deleted. This is due to the fact that every new entry is interconnected with the ones that came before it, making it nearly hard to edit one without also changing the entries that came before it. Blockchain elevates the digital ledger concept by incorporating several key features:

- Decentralization: Unlike traditional systems where a single central authority maintains the ledger, blockchain distributes the ledger across a network of computers. Each computer stores a complete copy of the ledger and regularly verifies consistency with others, ensuring no single entity controls the entire ledger.

- Security through Cryptography: Each block of data within the blockchain is safeguarded using intricate mathematical problems. The process of solving these problems, often termed as "mining" in cryptocurrencies, adds a new block to the chain. This mechanism makes altering a block impractical due to the extensive computational effort required.
- Transparency and Anonymity: While transactions recorded on the blockchain are visible to all, the identities of participants remain concealed behind unique codes. This enables tracking asset movements without revealing the actual identities of individuals involved.
- Immutability: Once data is entered into the blockchain, modifying it becomes extremely challenging. This characteristic ensures a reliable transaction record, as each entry is permanent and accessible to anyone.

In summary, blockchain serves as a resilient digital ledger offering enhanced security, decentralization, transparency, and immutability, transforming the recording and sharing of data and transactions in the digital era. The Dichotomy of Blockchain Privacy

Pseudo-Anonymity and Privacy Protection

- Encrypted Identities: Within blockchain transactions, participants' real-world identities remain obscured. Instead, they are represented by public keys or addresses, comprising lengthy strings of alphanumeric characters.
- Selective Disclosure: Users retain the discretion to disclose only pertinent information. For instance, they may opt not to divulge their complete financial history for a singular transaction.

Public Ledger and Transparency

- Visible Transactions: Each transaction conducted on a blockchain is meticulously documented on a public ledger. Consequently, transaction specifics such as the amount and the addresses of both sender and receiver are accessible to those familiar with the protocol.
- Traceability: While transactions aren't directly linked to identities, concerted efforts and ample information could potentially facilitate the tracing of transactions back to real-world identities, particularly if a public key is recurrently utilized.

Blockchain and Bitcoins

Transactions on different blockchains follow distinct processes. In Bitcoin, for instance, initiating a transaction through your cryptocurrency wallet triggers a series of events.

First, your transaction is sent to a memory pool, where it awaits processing until a miner or validator selects it. Once chosen, it's included in a block along with other transactions. When the block is filled, it's closed and encrypted using an encryption algorithm, marking the beginning of the mining process.

In mining, the entire network simultaneously works to "solve" the hash. Miners generate random hashes, appending a nonce (a number used once) to their hash. If the resulting hash doesn't meet the target criteria, they increment the nonce and try again. This process, known as "proof-of-work," validates the block. Confirmation of a transaction requires validation from subsequent blocks, typically about five blocks, which takes approximately an hour due to the network's block generation time.

However, not all blockchains follow this process. For instance, Ethereum employs a different approach where one validator, randomly chosen from users with ether staked, validates blocks. This method is faster and less energy-intensive compared to Bitcoin's.

Figure 2. Transaction process for bitcoin (www.investopedia.com)

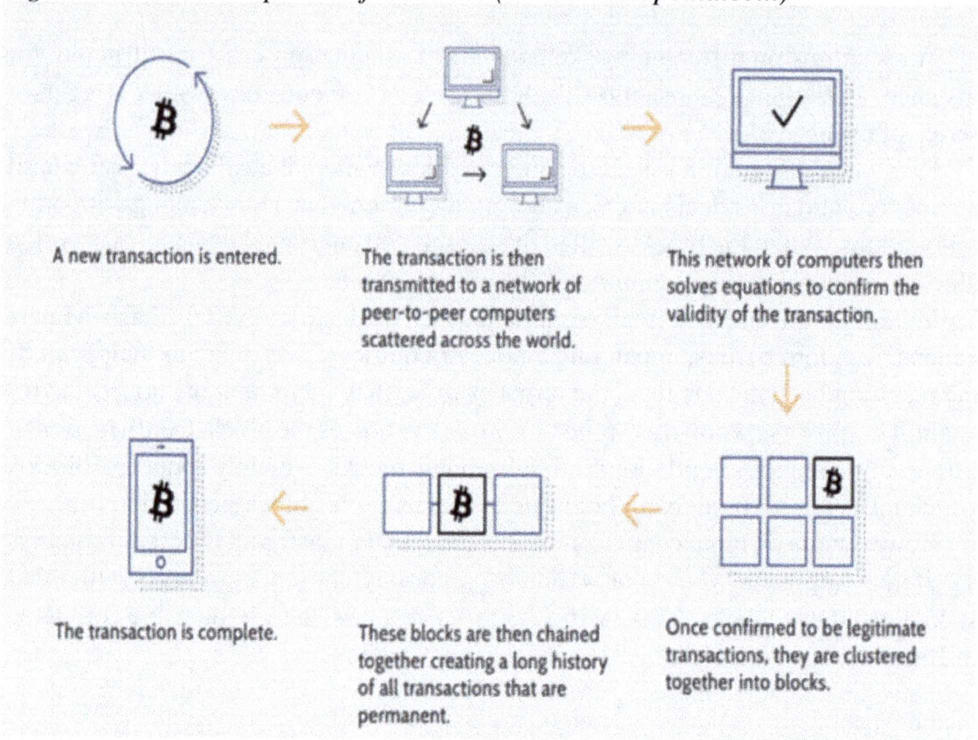

CYBER SECURITY

Cybersecurity's main goal is to safeguard computer systems, networks, and data from theft, damage, and illegal access. Cyber security has become a major concern for individuals, businesses, governments, and organizations of all sizes as a result of our increasing reliance on digital technology in our personal and professional lives.

A breakdown of some important aspects of cyber security is as follows:

Securing the Network

This entails protecting networks from unauthorized access and guaranteeing the confidentiality and integrity of data. Firewalls, IDS, and IPS are included in this category.

Security of Endpoints

This focuses on safeguarding individual devices from malicious threats like smartphones, tablets, and computers. Endpoint detection and response (EDR) tools, anti-malware software, and antivirus software are all part of it.

Security for Applications

Securing software applications from threats and vulnerabilities that could be exploited by attackers is part of application security. This incorporates secure coding rehearses, standard security testing, and carrying out safety efforts inside applications.

Data Safety

Protecting data from unauthorized access, theft, or corruption is the focus of data security. Data is protected with encryption, access controls, and data loss prevention (DLP) methods.

Management of Identity and Access (IAM)

IAM makes certain that only authorized individuals have access to particular data or resources. It involves biometrics, multi-factor authentication (MFA), and passwords as forms of authentication.

Reaction to the Event

Preparing for, detecting, and responding to security incidents are all components of incident response. This includes conducting drills, making plans for responding to an incident, and taking steps to lessen the impact of security breaches.

Training and Awareness of Security

It is essential to inform users about the dangers and best practices of cyber security. Employees can learn to recognize phishing emails, use strong passwords, and understand their role in security maintenance through training programs.

Securing the Cloud

Securing cloud environments has become increasingly important as cloud services are being used more and more. This includes protecting cloud infrastructure, cloud-based data, and cloud services.

Mobile Safety

Securing mobile devices against threats like malware, data loss, and unauthorized access is essential as they become more common. Both mobile application management (MAM) and mobile device management (MDM) aid in the management and protection of mobile devices.

IoT Safety

Due to the interconnected nature of IoT devices, new security issues arise with the Internet of Things (IoT). In order to avoid breaches, it is essential to protect IoT devices and networks from attacks.

The field of cyber security is always changing as new threats emerge and technologies advance. To stay ahead of cyber threats, it requires a multilayered strategy, constant monitoring, and adaptation.

Indian Cybersecurity, Blockchain and Artificial Intelligence:

The integration of blockchain technology into Indian cybersecurity represents a significant advancement in bolstering the nation's digital defences. This examination explores specific use cases and applications, demonstrating the versatility and effectiveness of blockchain in addressing key challenges encountered in the Indian cybersecurity landscape.

Securing Infrastructure

Blockchain can play a crucial role in securing critical infrastructure like energy grids, transportation systems, and communication networks. By providing a decentralized and tamper-resistant ledger, blockchain ensures the integrity of critical data and protects against cyber threats aimed at essential services.

Providing Safeguards to Records

Government records containing sensitive citizen information are prime targets for cyberattacks. Blockchain's immutable and transparent nature makes it an ideal solution for securing these records. Implementing blockchain in the management of government records enhances data integrity and reduces the risk of unauthorized access or manipulation.

E-Governance and Public Services

Blockchain can streamline e-governance processes by providing a secure and transparent platform for citizen interactions. Smart contracts on the blockchain can automate and authenticate various public services, reducing bureaucratic inefficiencies and minimizing the risk of corruption.

Data of Healthcare and its Management

Protecting healthcare data is crucial for maintaining individual privacy and security. Blockchain can be used to create a secure and interoperable system for managing health records. Patients gain greater control over their data, while healthcare providers ensure the accuracy and integrity of patient information.

Supply Chain Security

In response to increasing cyber threats to supply chains, blockchain offers a transparent and traceable solution. From manufacturing to delivery, blockchain can create an unforgeable record of every transaction, ensuring product authenticity and mitigating the risk of counterfeit goods entering the market.

Financial and Banking Solutions

The financial sector is a prime target for cyberattacks, and blockchain technology can enhance security in this domain. By ensuring transaction integrity through decentralized ledgers and smart contracts, blockchain reduces the risk of fraud and enhances the overall security of banking systems.

Authenticate and Identification

Blockchain's decentralized identity management solutions can significantly improve authentication processes across various sectors. Individuals gain secure and verifiable digital identities, reducing the risk of identity theft and unauthorized access to sensitive systems.

Data Sharing

Enabling secure and transparent cross-border data sharing is another application of blockchain in Indian cybersecurity. Through decentralized networks for data exchange, blockchain ensures that sensitive information is shared only among authorized parties, enhancing international collaboration while maintaining data security.

Verification in Education

Blockchain can secure educational credentials, preventing fraudulent activities like degree forgery. Transparent and immutable records of academic achievements on the blockchain can streamline credential verification processes for employers and educational institutions.

Figure 3. Cyber attacks that are done normally (https://arxiv.org/abs/2208.14937v1)

Figure 4. AI and blockchain based cyber world

BLOCKCHAIN AS A NEW APPROACH TO CYBER WORLD

While the potential benefits of integrating blockchain into cybersecurity are substantial, the adoption of this transformative technology is not without its challenges. This exploration delves into the hurdles and considerations that organizations and policymakers face when incorporating blockchain into cybersecurity frameworks in India.

Scalability Concerns

One of the primary challenges in adopting blockchain for cybersecurity is scalability. As the number of transactions and participants in a blockchain network increases, the associated computational overhead grows. Traditional blockchains, such as those employing Proof of Work (PoW) consensus mechanisms, may face limitations in handling a high volume of transactions efficiently. This scalability challenge requires innovative solutions to ensure blockchain networks can meet the demands of large-scale cybersecurity applications.

Interoperability Issues

One major problem is achieving compatibility between various blockchain networks and current technologies. Making sure that data is exchanged and communications across different blockchain implementations are frictionless becomes critical in a diversified cybersecurity landscape with several platforms and protocols. To overcome this obstacle, standardization initiatives and the creation of protocols that promote interoperability are crucial.

Integration with Existing Infrastructure

Many organizations already have established cybersecurity systems and processes in place. Integrating blockchain into existing infrastructure without causing disruption or compromising security is a complex task. Ensuring a smooth transition and coexistence with legacy systems requires careful planning and the development of protocols for compatibility.

Regulatory Uncertainty

The regulatory landscape surrounding blockchain technology is still evolving, leading to uncertainty for organizations seeking to adopt it for cybersecurity purposes. Lack of clear regulations may impede the widespread adoption of blockchain, as stakeholders may be hesitant to invest in a technology with uncertain legal and regulatory implications. Establishing a clear regulatory framework is crucial for providing a conducive environment for blockchain adoption.

Energy Consumption and Environmental Impact

Traditional blockchain consensus mechanisms, particularly Proof of Work, are associated with high energy consumption. In a world increasingly focused on sustainability, the environmental impact of blockchain technology is a concern. Developing and adopting more energy-efficient consensus mechanisms, such as Proof of Stake, is essential to address these environmental considerations.

Cost of Implementation

Implementing blockchain solutions, especially in large-scale cybersecurity applications, can incur significant costs. From the development of secure and scalable blockchain networks to the training of personnel, the initial investment can be substantial. Organizations need to weigh the potential benefits against the upfront costs and assess the long-term value of blockchain integration.

Lack of Skills and Expertise

Blockchain technology is relatively new and requires specialized knowledge for effective implementation and management. The shortage of skilled professionals proficient in both cybersecurity and blockchain poses a challenge. Bridging this skills gap through training programs and educational initiatives is essential to ensure the successful adoption of blockchain in cybersecurity practices.

Perception and Trust

Trust in the security and reliability of traditional cybersecurity methods may hinder the adoption of blockchain. Overcoming skepticism and building confidence in the effectiveness of blockchain technology require education and awareness campaigns. Demonstrating successful use cases and addressing misconceptions are essential steps in gaining trust among stakeholders.

Data Privacy Concerns

While blockchain provides enhanced security through decentralization and encryption, concerns related to data privacy persist. The transparent nature of blockchain, where transactions are visible to all participants, may conflict with privacy regulations in certain contexts. Striking a balance between transparency and data privacy is crucial for widespread blockchain adoption in cybersecurity.

Resistance to Change

Resistance to change is a common challenge in adopting any new technology. Stakeholders, including cybersecurity professionals accustomed to traditional methods, may be resistant to transitioning to blockchain-based solutions. Effective change management strategies and communication are vital to address this challenge and garner support for blockchain adoption.

Figure 5. Block chain and cyber security

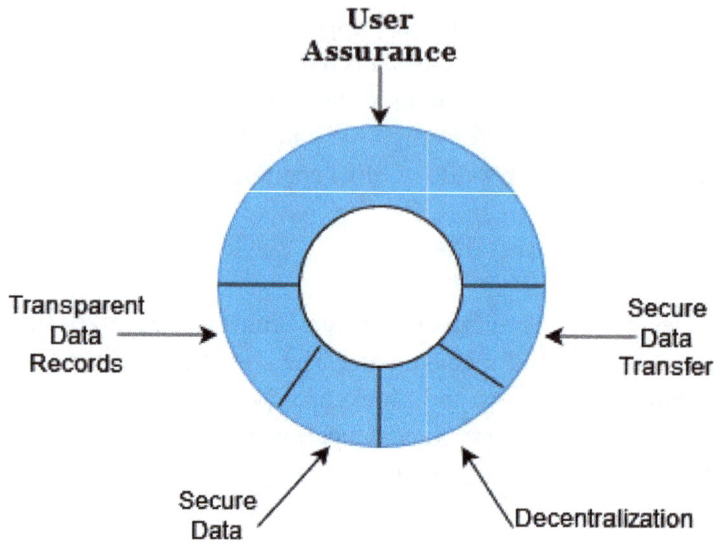

OVERCOMING HURDLES OF SECURITY WITH BLOCK CHAIN

For the successful implementation of blockchain technology in India's cyber-security landscape, it is essential to address the difficulties posed by scalability, interoperability, and regulatory frameworks. This investigation focuses on ways to get around these particular obstacles and make sure that blockchain technology is successfully integrated.

Solutions for Scalability That Improve Consensus Mechanisms

Look into and put into action alternative consensus mechanisms like Proof of Stake (PoS) or Delegated Proof of Stake (DPoS), which use less energy and can handle more transactions at once.

Solutions for Layer 2

Reduce the load placed on the main blockchain by utilizing layer 2 solutions like sidechains or off-chain scaling solutions to improve scalability without compromising security.

Standardization Initiatives for Interoperability

Participate in and promote industry-wide standardization efforts to establish common protocols and standards for blockchain interoperability, which will make it easier for various blockchain networks to communicate seamlessly.

Platforms for Interoperability

Make investments in and use interoperability platforms that make it possible to transfer data and assets between different blockchains. In an environment with multiple blockchains, solutions like middleware or blockchain bridges can improve connectivity.

Regulatory Advocacy

The Creation of Regulatory Frameworks To actively participate in the creation of clear and supportive regulatory frameworks for blockchain technology, work with industry associations and government bodies to create regulations that promote innovation while addressing concerns.

Pilot Programs Undergoing Regulatory Control

Establish pilot programs under regulatory oversight in conjunction with regulators to test the efficacy of blockchain in particular cybersecurity applications and ensure compliance with existing regulations.

Programs for Education and Awareness Training and Skill Development

Invest in cybersecurity and blockchain training to fill the skills gap and create a pool of experts in both fields by providing educational opportunities for professionals and students.

Public Education Initiatives

Conduct public awareness campaigns to inform stakeholders, including policymakers, businesses, and the general public, about the advantages and repercussions of blockchain in cybersecurity. These campaigns should also dispel misconceptions and promote comprehension in order to win support for regulatory frameworks.

Industry Consortia

Collaborative Industry Initiatives Establish or participate in industry consortia that bring together stakeholders from a variety of sectors, such as businesses, government agencies, and technology experts, to drive joint efforts in developing standards, addressing issues, and advocating for regulatory environments that are supportive.

Investing in R&D and Providing Funding for Research Projects

Contribute to the advancement of blockchain technology by allocating resources to research and development projects that address issues of scalability and interoperability unique to the Indian context and funding initiatives that investigate novel solutions.

International Collaboration

Engagement with International Organizations Learn from global best practices and collaborate on international standards with international organizations and bodies involved in blockchain standardization and regulation to help India develop effective regulatory frameworks.

Approach to Regulatory Sandboxes That Are Flexible Regulatory Sandboxes

Advocate for the establishment of regulatory sandboxes where innovative blockchain applications can be tested in a controlled setting. This will make it possible to experiment while still adhering to regulatory oversight and will serve as a model for a wider adoption.

Continual Conversation with Regulators Continuous Communication

To foster a collaborative relationship between the blockchain community and regulators, establish and maintain open lines of communication with regulatory authorities, providing continuous updates, sharing insights from pilot programs, and promptly addressing concerns.

Partnerships Between Private Companies and Government Agencies

By working with government agencies that are in charge of cybersecurity and technology adoption, you can encourage public-private partnerships and accelerate the development and deployment of blockchain solutions within the regulatory framework.

BENEFITS WITH EXAMPLES OF BLOCKCHAIN APPLICATIONS IN CYBERSECURITY

Blockchain's high level of security has made it an attractive option for various sectors, particularly financial services, as it offers one of the most secure methods for digital transactions. Leveraging blockchain's integrity assurance, organizations can develop cybersecurity solutions for a wide range of applications and technologies.

Mitigation of DNS and DDoS Attacks

A distributed denial of service (DDoS) attack occurs when cybercriminals flood a network with malicious traffic, disrupting its functionality. These attacks can slow down or completely shut down websites and resource systems. In DNS attacks, attackers compromise a network's DNS or exploit its underlying attributes to launch broader attacks. By establishing peer-to-peer (P2P) and zero-trust networks, blockchain removes the need for devices to trust each other, eliminating single centralized points of failure. Organizations can decommission the attacked node and continue operations as usual. Even if large parts of the network are attacked, the decentralized structure ensures the system's functionality.

Resilience and Availability

Decentralized infrastructure enhances resilience against attacks, corruption, and downtime, mitigating various vulnerabilities:

- Distributing information and communications technology networks reduces data exposure and redirects users when a centralized database goes offline or is attacked.
- Decentralizing DNS provides redundancy in the event of a DDoS attack.
- In an IoT context, distributing operations and administrative controls away from a central hub enables security decisions closer to the network's periphery.

KYC Verification

Fraudulent e-KYC renewal is a common scam where scammers impersonate service providers to obtain confidential information such as Aadhaar numbers and bank account details. Blockchain-based KYC verification methods mitigate this risk by:

- Allowing data from various governments and private portals to be collected and stored in a single, immutable, secure database.
- Protecting each user's private information with cryptographic keys, making it difficult for hackers to access credentials.

Traceability and Provenance

The benefits of traceability and transparency offered by blockchain vary depending on the application:

- A digital distributed ledger lowers the risk of counterfeiting and manipulation in supply chains by storing tamper-proof records of transactions and freight data across partners and the product lifetime.
- Transparency and immutability of payment histories lessen the need for central brokers in financial use cases, enhancing the security and privacy of transactions like remittances.

End User Security

Hackers increasingly target edge devices like thermostats and routers to penetrate systems. Decentralizing management secures IoT systems and end-user devices:

- Devices can make security decisions without relying on central administrators or permissions.
- Without password authentication of users and devices, along with multi-party verification via SSL certificates, strengthens security.
- The decentralized nature of the network ensures the integrity of transactions and account balances, making attacks virtually impossible.

LIMITATION AND CHALLENGES

This comprehensive analysis examines the many stages that blockchains have undergone since their inception in 2013 in order to investigate their cyber security features. Additionally, we have examined more than 60 flaws in various blockchain apps and networks. The study comes to the conclusion that we have effectively calculated the trade-off between new vulnerabilities and the expansion of cybersecurity-related blockchain research over the past ten years when it comes to cyberattacks on BC technology.

Our study's findings provide guidance for developing strategies for identifying and addressing certain weaknesses related to safe development procedures in blockchains. Our analysis, however, is based on a disproportionately small number of studies that have been conducted for various blockchain-related cyber security application fields. Though the insights suggest that depending on the application area, design, and complexity of various blockchain networks or solutions, it might be necessary to describe a distinct method for each of them.

The utilization of a distributed ledger involves the sharing of data among all participants on the network. While this could potentially compromise confidentiality, it also enhances availability by involving numerous nodes in the Blockchain, thereby increasing its robustness and resilience. Traditional security challenges include:

Crypt Key Management

Private keys are crucial for authorizing activities within an account. If these keys are accessed by an adversary, it compromises the security of any wallets or assets associated with them. Using different private keys for signing and encrypting messages across the distributed ledger could mitigate this risk. If an attacker gains access to encryption keys, they can read the underlying data. Private keys are typically generated using secure random functions, making reconstruction difficult, if not impossible. Losing a private key result in the loss of associated assets. Stolen private keys grant full access to all assets controlled by them, and once funds are transferred to another account, it cannot be undone.

Cryptography

Blockchain relies on cryptographically generated public and private keys. Proper management of keys, including people, processes, and technology, is essential. Cryptographic key generation software should produce strong keys that are not easily decrypted.

Privacy and Authentication

Privacy concerns arise with Blockchain technology. In a permissionless ledger, all participants can download the ledger, allowing them to explore the entire transaction history, even those they are not involved in. In a permissioned ledger, exploitation of authorized agents or smart contract capabilities could lead to significant privacy exposure, depending on the access rights of the agent or smart contract authors.

CONCLUSION

Blockchain technology is continuously evolving and finding new applications in various domains, including cybersecurity and the role of artificial intelligence while using cyber in very manneristic way. It has shown promise in addressing security challenges in IoT devices, networks, and data transmission/storage. Taylor et al. reviewed the perspectives of 30 researchers and found that most focus on applying Blockchain security to IoT devices, with AI networks and data being other key areas of interest. The technology offers more reliable authentication, data transfer mechanisms for devices used while in the artificial intelligence environment.

While recent research and media reports emphasize Blockchain's potential in finance, logistics, healthcare, and cybersecurity, this study concentrates solely on cybersecurity. Although Blockchain offers valuable solutions, it's important to note that a decentralized, trustless system cannot solve all cybersecurity issues by itself.

Blockchain applications in cybersecurity have evolved to complement existing security efforts and deter malicious activities. This research identifies opportunities for future studies beyond IoT security. As internet encryption becomes more widespread and users increasingly rely on encryption for communication, managing surrounding cryptography and certification schemes securely becomes crucial.

In India, integrating Blockchain into the cybersecurity to make the landmark while using artificial intelligence for a landscape holds great promise for strengthening digital defences. Real-world examples like Project Khoka and BankChain demonstrate the potential of Blockchain's decentralized security and consensus mechanisms. Despite challenges like scalability, interoperability, and regulatory clarity, strategic solutions such as optimized consensus mechanisms and regulatory sandboxes offer paths to success. Blockchain has transformative potential in securing critical infrastructure, e-governance, and healthcare data. Bridging the skills gap, fostering public-private partnerships, and engaging with regulators are vital for successful adoption. Embracing Blockchain technology is crucial for India's digital journey, ensuring a resilient cybersecurity framework against evolving threats and positioning the country as the use of artificial intelligence made it more challenging towards the secure digital practices through collaboration, education, and proactive strategies.

REFERENCES

Ahsan, M. M., & Siddique, Z. (2022). Industry 4.0 in healthcare: A systematic re- view. *International Journal of Information Management Data Insights*, *2*(1), 100079. DOI: 10.1016/j.jjimei.2022.100079

Ali Syed, T., Alzahrani, A., Jan, S., Siddiqui, M. S., Nadeem, A., & Alghamdi, T. (2019). A comparative analysis of blockchain architecture and its applications: Problems and recommendations. *IEEE Access : Practical Innovations, Open Solutions*, *7*, 176838–176869. DOI: 10.1109/ACCESS.2019.2957660

Apostolaki, M., Zohar, A., & Vanbever, L. (2017). *Hijacking bitcoin: Routing attacks on cryptocurrencies. In 2017 ieee symposium on security and privacy (sp).*, DOI: 10.1109/SP.2017.29

Buterin, V. (2013). Ethereum white paper. *Google Scholar, 1*, 22–23. https://github .com/ ethereum/wiki/wiki/White-Paper

Deepu, T., & Ravi, V. (2021). Supply chain digitalization: An integrated mcdm ap- proach for inter-organizational information systems selection in an electronic sup- ply chain. *International Journal of Information Management Data Insights*, *1*(2), 100038. DOI: 10.1016/j.jjimei.2021.100038

Feng, L., Chiam, Y. K., & Lo, S. K. (2017). Text-mining techniques and tools for systematic literature reviews: A systematic literature review. In *2017 24th asia-pacific software engineering conference (apsec)* (pp. 41–50). IEEE.

Ferreira, A. (2021). Regulating smart contracts: Legal revolution or simply evolution? *Telecommunications Policy*, *45*(2), 102081. DOI: 10.1016/j.telpol.2020.102081

Ferreira da Silva, C., & Moro, S. (2021). Blockchain technology as an enabler of consumer trust: A text mining literature analysis. *Telematics and Informatics*, *60*, 101593. DOI: 10.1016/j.tele.2021.101593

Filippi, P. D., & Hassan, S. (2018). Blockchain technology as a regulatory technology: from code is law to law is code. *CoRR, abs/1801.02507*. https://arxiv.org/abs/ 1801.02507. Firouzi, F., Farahani, B., & Marinšek, A. (2022). The convergence and interplay of edge, fog, and cloud in the ai-driven internet of things (iot). *Information Systems, 107*, 101840. DOI: 10.1016/j.is.2021.101840

Gallinucci, E., Golfarelli, M., & Rizzi, S. (2015). Advanced topic modeling for social busi- ness intelligence. *Information Systems*, *53*, 87–106. DOI: 10.1016/j. is.2015.04.005

Gehem, M., Usanov, A., Frinking, E., & Rademaker, M. (2015). *Assessing cyber security: A meta analysis of threats, trends, and responses to cyber attacks*. The Hague Centre for Strategic Studies.

Grover, P., Kar, A. K., & Janssen, M. (2019a). Diffusion of blockchain technology: Insights from academic literature and social media analytics. *Journal of Enterprise Information Management*.

Grover, P., Kar, A. K., Janssen, M., & Ilavarasan, P. V. (2019b). Perceived usefulness, ease of use and user acceptance of blockchain technology for digital transactions–in- sights from user-generated content on twitter. *Enterprise Information Systems, 13*(6), 771–800.

Hussien, H. M., Yasin, S. M., Udzir, S., Zaidan, A. A., & Zaidan, B. B. (2019). A systematic review for enabling of develop a blockchain technology in healthcare application: Tax- onomy, substantially analysis, motivations, challenges, recommendations and future direction. *Journal of Medical Systems, 43*(10), 1–35. https://www.techdemand.io/news/tech-news/blockchain-news/blockchain-in cybersecurity-its-time-to-rethink-and-revolutionize/ https://www.blockchain-council.org/blockchain/blockchain-in-cybersecurity/ https://www.linkedin.com/pulse/how-blockchain-revolutionizing-cybersecurity digialert https://www.infosys.com/insights/cyber-security/cybersecurity-blockchain.html

Jadil, Y., Rana, N. P., & Dwivedi, Y. K. (2022). Understanding the drivers of online trust and intention to buy on a website: An emerging market perspec- tive. *International Journal of Information Management Data Insights*, *2*(1), 100065. DOI: 10.1016/j.jjimei.2022.100065

Jain, D., Dash, M. K., Kumar, A., & Luthra, S. (2021). How is blockchain used in marketing: A review and research agenda. *International Journal of Information Management Data Insights*, *1*(2), 100044. DOI: 10.1016/j.jjimei.2021.100044

Jiang, J., Xie, X., & Fan, L. (2021). Trends of blockchain research in management and business. In *2021 the 7th international conference on frontiers of educational technolo- gies*. In *ICFET 2021* (pp. 228–234). New York, NY, USA: Association for Computing Machinery. DOI: 10.1145/3473141.3473253

Jutla, D. N., Bodorik, P., & Zhang, Y. (2006). Pecan: An architecture for users' privacy- aware electronic commerce contexts on the semantic web. [The Semantic Web and Web Services.]. *Information Systems*, *31*(4), 295–320. DOI: 10.1016/j.is.2005.02.004

Kaushal, P. K., Bagga, A., & Sobti, R. (2017). *Evolution of bitcoin and security risk in bitcoin wallets. In 2017 international conference on computer, communications and elec- tronics (comptelix).* IEEE.

Kim, W., Jeong, O.-R., Kim, C., & So, J. (2011). The dark side of the internet: Attacks, costs and responses. *Information Systems, 36*(3), 675–705. . Special Issue on WISE 2009 - Web Information Systems Engineering.DOI: 10.1016/j.is.2010.11.003

Kinoshita, A., Takasu, A., & Adachi, J. (2015). Real-time traffic incident de- tection using a probabilistic topic model. *Information Systems*, *54*, 169–188. DOI: 10.1016/j.is.2015.07.002

Lee, N.-Y., Yang, J., Onik, M. M. H., & Kim, C.-S. (2019). Modifiable public blockchains using truncated hashing and sidechains. *IEEE Access : Practical Innovations, Open Solutions*, *7*, 173571–173582. DOI: 10.1109/AC- CESS.2019.2956628

Li, Y., & Liu, Q. (2021). A comprehensive review study of cyber-attacks and cyber se- curity; emerging trends and recent developments. *Energy Reports*, *7*, 8176–8186. DOI: 10.1016/j.egyr.2021.08.126

Luntovskyy, A., & Guetter, D. (2018). Cryptographic technology blockchain and its appli- cations. In *The international conference on information and telecommunication technolo- gies and radio electronics* (pp. 14–33). Springer.

Ma, Q., Nadamoto, A., & Tanaka, K. (2006). Complementary information re- trieval for cross-media news content. *Information Systems, 31*(7), 659–678. . (1) SPIRE 2004 (2) Multimedia Databases.DOI: 10.1016/j.is.2005.12.004

Moro, S., Cortez, P., & Rita, P. (2015). Business intelligence in banking: A literature analy- sis from 2002 to 2013 using text mining and latent dirichlet allocation. *Expert Systems with Applications*, *42*(3), 1314–1324.

Skute, I. (2019). Opening the black box of academic entrepreneurship: Abibliometric anal- ysis. *Scientometrics*, *120*(1), 237–265.

Stallone, V., Wetzels, M., & Klaas, M. (2021). Applications of blockchain technology in marketing-a systematic review of marketing technology companies. *Blockchain: Re- search and Applications, 2*(3), 100023. .DOI: 10.1016/j.bcra.2021.100023

Szabo, N. (1997). Formalizing and securing relationships on public networks. *First monday*. Tamburri, D. A. (2020). Design principles for the general data protection regulation (gdpr): A formal concept analysis and its evaluation. *Information Systems*, *91*, 101469. DOI: 10.1016/j.is.2019.101469

Taylor, P. J., Dargahi, T., Dehghantanha, A., Parizi, R. M., & Choo, K.-K. R. (2020). A systematic literature review of blockchain cyber security. *Digital Communications and Networks*, *6*(2), 147–156.

Upadhyay, N. (2020). Demystifying blockchain: A critical analysis of challenges, applica- tions and opportunities. *International Journal of Information Management, 54*, 102120. Vayansky, I., & Kumar, S. A. (2020). A review of topic modeling methods. *Information Systems, 94*, 101582. DOI: 10.1016/j.is.2020.101582

Verma, S., Sharma, R., Deb, S., & Maitra, D. (2021). Artificial intelligence in marketing: Systematic review and future research direction. *International Journal of Information Management Data Insights*, *1*(1), 100002. DOI: 10.1016/j.jjimei.2020.100002

Wandabwa, H. M., Naeem, M. A., Mirza, F., & Pears, R. (2021). Topical affinity in short text microblogs. *Information Systems, 96*, 101662. DOI: 10.1016/j.is.2020.101662

Yadav, J., Misra, M., & Goundar, S. (2020). An overview of food supply chain virtuali- sation and granular traceability using blockchain technology. *International Journal of Blockchains and Cryptocurrencies*, *1*(2), 154–178. DOI: 10.1504/IJBC.2020.108997

Yadav, J., Misra, M., & Goundar, S. (n.d.) Autonomous agriculture marketing informa- tion system through blockchain: A case study of e-nam adoption in india. In *Blockchain Technologies* (pp. 115–138). Applications and Cryptocurrencies., DOI: 10.1142/9789811205279_0005

Yadav, J., Misra, M., Rana, N. P., & Singh, K. (2021a). *Exploring the synergy between nano*. Technology & People.

Yadav, J., Misra, M., Rana, N. P., Singh, K., & Goundar, S. (2021b). Netizens' Behavior to- wards a blockchain-based esports framework: A tpb and machine learning integrated approach. *International Journal of Sports Marketing & Sponsorship.*

Yaga, D., Mell, P., Roby, N., & Scarfone, K. (2018). Draft blockchain technology overview (nistir-8202). *National Institute of Standard and Technology, 59.*

Yaqoob, I., Salah, K., Jayaraman, R., & Al-Hammadi, Y. (2021). Blockchain for health- care data management: Opportunities, challenges, and future recommendations. *Neural Computing & Applications*, •••, 1–16.

Chapter 9
Street-Level Bureaucracy in Health Services During COVID-19 Outbreak in Indonesia

Mohammad Jafar Loilatu
https://orcid.org/0000-0001-6921-6879
Universitas Muhammadiyah Malang, Indonesia

Tri Sulistyaningsih
Universitas Muhammadiyah Malang, Indonesia

Bambang Irawan
https://orcid.org/0000-0002-4841-7302
Mulawarman University, Indonesia

Saiman Saiman
Universitas Muhammadiyah Malang, Indonesia

Paisal Akbar
Mulawarman University, Indonesia

Muhammad Nurul Huda
https://orcid.org/0000-0003-4184-2530
Universitas Muhammadiyah Karanganyar, Indonesia

Inamyza Nurziana Putri
Universitas Muhammadiyah Malang, Indonesia

ABSTRACT

This study seeks to elucidate the interaction between healthcare professionals and the government through health service indicators during the COVID-19 epidemic in South Sulawesi. This study used a qualitative methodology to perform a content analysis of online media coverage about health workers, the government, and health services during the COVID-19 epidemic in South Sulawesi. This study demonstrates a direct correlation between health professionals and the government with health indicators, including front-line services, stigma, duty, equipment assistance, pro-

DOI: 10.4018/979-8-3373-3760-9.ch009

tection, and engagements. These findings affirm that health professionals and the government are accountable for the efficacy of front-line bureaucracy, services, bureaucratic responsibilities, health facilities and infrastructure, health protection, and stakeholder engagement. The government has not succeeded in cultivating a favorable perception of health workers as the front-line of the bureaucracy delivering quality health services.

INTRODUCTION

The coronavirus or COVID-19, first appeared in late December 2019 in Wuhan (Munster et al., 2020) and Hubei, China, with the first 425 cases (Li et al., 2020). At the end of January, 830 new coronavirus cases spread across nine countries (Cheng et al., 2020). In addition, other countries, such as Kenya, declared a state of emergency by closing all activities (Aluga, 2020); Australia, in May, had positive numbers, reaching 7109 cases and 102 deaths (Andrikopoulos & Johnson, 2020). World Health Organization (WHO) reported that COVID-19 cases spread in January 2020 in several countries: Thailand with 8 cases; Nepal with 13 cases; Japan with 14 cases; North Korea with 19 cases; the United States with 20 cases; Singapore with 23 cases; France and Vietnam with 24 cases each; Australia and Malaysia with 25 cases each; 26 to 27 cases in Canada, Cambodia, and Sri Lanka; 28 to 29 cases each in Germany, Finland, Italy; and cases were reported on January 30, 2020, the United Kingdom, India, Philippines, Rusia and Sweden (WHO, 2019), while President Joko Widodo reported Indonesia's first case on March 2, 2020 (Djalante et al., 2020).

The positive number of COVID-19 cases has increased rapidly, and the accumulated number of COVID-19 cases worldwide in the last four months has increased significantly. From April through July, the number of positive cases increased by 17,177,298. Likewise, the death rate increased significantly; from April through July, the total death rate reached 682,612. Indonesia has reported a higher number of cases than most countries. It is one of the member countries of the Association of Southeast Asian Nations with the highest number of positive cases and death rates. Indonesia had reported 1528 COVID-19 cases; the positive number in the last four months was 56385 cases.

Indonesia's increasing positive case numbers have not been matched by the government's ability to overcome and control COVID-19. To overcome the COVID-19 pandemic, the WHO published strategies for managing and preventing COVID-19 by limiting interactions, conducting isolation, identifying risks, and overcoming the socioeconomic impacts of the COVID-19 pandemic. The WHO also issued general guidelines for community action for vulnerable groups, children, workers, and migrants (WHO, 2020h). The impact of COVID-19 has caused hospitals and health workers to be unable to manage the spike in the number of COVID-19 cases. New cases of individuals with inadequate access to health facilities have increased the number of people who are spreading the disease to health workers. Until July 2020, the BNPB reported that the number of doctors and nurses who died was 29 and 15 nurses, respectively.

Health workers are at the forefront of managing COVID-19 and the front-line group in preventing COVID-19 by providing health services (Prescott et al., 2020). Health workers conduct infection prevention and control to prevent transmission to other health workers (WHO, 2020i). This term follows the protocol and handling standards for COVID-19 or the strategic preparedness and response plan (SPRP) (WHO, 2020d). Strategies and plans are supported by hospital readiness to support the work of health workers—the WHO (2020d). Hospitals must consider formulated standards: leadership, coordination, risk communication, resources, patient management, rapid identification, and infection prevention control (WHO, 2020j). To explain these standards, the steps that must be taken are collaboration, coordination, communication, and increasing hospitals and the community's preparedness by ensuring adequate space, staff, and supplies for increased care needs (WHO, 2020g).

Several studies have explained the critical position of health workers in emergencies by identifying health workers' role in health crisis conditions (Grantz et al., 2019; Nguyen et al., 2020; Shaw et al., 2019). In the case of COVID-19, Nyashanu et al. (2020) assessed that front-lines do their job effectively if supported by practicing the sound policies and practices of health organizations. Front-line or healthcare workers (HCWs) can manage COVID-19 by applying their local knowledge (Prescott et al., 2020). To conduct these tasks, HCWs must be aware of and protect other individuals and themselves according to their capacity (Tang et al., 2020). The health crisis condition causes several problems in services because of the low availability of resources such as medical equipment, nurses, doctors, finance, and hospital capacity. However, hospital emergency conditions are required to provide full service to prevent transmission and increase the death rate of COVID-19. Although they are in dire financial situations, workers must provide complete, professional service to clients (Fernqvist, 2018). In relevant topics, some authors have highlighted how the COVID-19 response in Indonesia (Qodir et al., 2022; Roziqin et al., 2021), public response in social media (Irawan et al., 2022; Salahudin, Nurmandi, Sulistyaningsih, et al., 2020), and how government tackles the policy in responding COVID-19 (Fitriani et al., 2023).

Scholars have classified bureaucratic models such as passive representation bureaucracy, diligent representation, and moderate representation bureaucracy (Hong, 2020). A street-level bureaucracy is an adaptive approach to individuals, patients, clients, and others (Vike, 2018). For example, the health service aspect has been used to assess street-level health workers, as shown by Lipsky's view (Michael Lipsky,

1979; Micheal Lipsky, 2010). In Lipsky's view, this paper examines the services of health workers in the Sidenreng Rappang District, South Sulawesi Province. It examines the ability of health workers to provide services, such as front-line HCWs handling COVID-19 (Alcadipani et al., 2020).

LITERATURE REVIEW

Street-Level Bureaucracy and Health Care Workers

The performance of the bureaucracy is assessed from the lowest level (Zang, 2016). The lower level is the ranks that implement policies based on government decisions. The street level is considered the process that most influence policy and results (Nugus et al., 2018). Lipsky (2010) believed that street-level policymaking uses policy with the agency. In policymaking, the street level has the flexibility to determine the service, quantity, and quality of service regarding their agency. However, the implementation of SLBs is complicated due to distorted policies at a certain level (Vohnsen, 2015). Lipsky illustrated that the street level is influenced by the policymaking institution (Micheal Lipsky, 2010) and the regulations binding on the organization (Henderson et al., 2018). Thus, an SLB is a worker bound by regulations and follows leadership policies but is expected to work optimally according to the agency's wishes.

Health Care Workers (HCWs) have a relationship with Street Level Bureaucracy (SLBs), which relates to services in managing emergencies by working together (Zang, 2016). Academic literature has described SLBs historically in terms of their position in public service. Hill (2003) explained that there had been service reform at the street level by improving the monotonous service quality and using multiple approaches to form a relevant approach by building closeness with agencies (Keulemans & Groeneveld, 2020). Lipsky's view on the SLB approach's contribution regards health services in countries of low financial capacity; SLBs have flexibility in providing services (LIPSKY, 2010). they are supported by active interactions built and influenced by the surrounding environment (Michael Lipsky, 1979). This explanation shows that Lipsky's view on SLB aims to consider the SLB aspect of service performance by representing the policies that have been decided (Micheal Lipsky, 2010).

Street-Level Bureaucracy Performance

The spread of COVID-19 worldwide has required governments to establish a national health crisis condition (Fusi-Schmidhauser et al., 2020). Steps are necessary to manage the COVID-19 crisis by managing crisis conditions, maintaining health, and controlling mobility to reduce new transmissions (C. Wang et al., 2020). The WHO formulated a COVID-19 crisis condition management model or SPRP, which comprises (1) readiness, (2) preparation, (3) prevention, (4) recovery, and (5) response (WHO, 2020d). In a time of the COVID-19 pandemic, governments are expected to adapt quickly, especially in the aspects of hospital capacity, testing, tracing, drug supply, and medical equipment supply (Janssen & Voort, 2020); Health workers and hospital readiness have service standards to ensure the handling of COVID-19 (Seak et al., 2020). However, managing crisis conditions and health emergencies is a problematic situation (Vohnsen, 2015); for example, the COVID-19 pandemic has resulted in a global health crisis (Atkinson, 2020).

HCWs have the highest potential for COVID-19 infection (J. Wang et al., 2020). Health workers are workers who have contact with the community or patients (Vike, 2018). According to Tummers & Bekkers (2014), SLB conducts its duties ineffectively because of differences of opinion, keeping street-level work hidden from public view because of following clients' differences (Micheal Lipsky, 2010) to overcome differences of opinion. Therefore, street-level managers must collaborate to fulfill clients' needs (LIPSKY, 2010) and adjust policies (Vike, 2018). Nyashanu et al. (2020) suggested that the central government provides sensitive, applied policies to local governments, especially regarding the fact that health workers must obtain social safety and pandemic management capabilities and ensure their readiness (Brodkin, 2008).

The performance of health workers is related to the quality of service when handling COVID-19 (WHO, 2020c) and is supported by adequate health facilities so that health worker services run optimally (WHO, 2020a). By contrast, aspects of service must be prioritized in handling COVID-19, such as health for pregnant women, delivery facilities, therapy, and services for elderly individuals and children (WHO, 2020e). As Lipsky's view indicates, an SLB is influenced by the environment (Michael Lipsky, 1979), thus shaping service behavior. Street-level services are concerned with rational service (Murphy & Skillen, 2015), monitoring patients, managing the bureaucracy, and predicting impacts and consequences (Berlan, 2010). Street-level performance is related to provisional attitudes, readiness to manage crisis conditions, and services according to standards (Feltham-King & Macleod, 2020).

RESEARCH METHOD

This study uses NVivo's qualitative data analysis software approach (Kaefer et aLipsky, 2010). NVivo has been used in qualitative research for more than 25 years (Paulus et al., 2017). NVivo, as an analytical tool, organizes research data in a structured and sequential manner (Ozkan, 2004). NVivo is a computer-based qualitative data analysis tool (Zainab Kabba, 2015) or computer-assisted qualitative data analysis software (CAQDAS) (García-Horta & Guerra-Ramos, 2009). Using NVivo in a qualitative approach explains the SLB for health workers in Sidrap Sidenreng Rappang District, South Sulawesi. The study data are obtained through the online media of South Sulawesi Province by selecting news on health workers.

NVivo can perform various data analysis types, and NVivo is an analytical tool that supports research to read data in detail. Data in this study are data on the online media coverage of health workers' role in health services during the COVID-19 pandemic in South Sulawesi. Data analysis uses the cluster analysis feature to obtain correlation data between the concepts that focus on this study: the correlation between health workers and government with services, front-line staff, obligations, stigma, service infrastructure, and health protection and involvement. The correlation data explain the relationship between indicators that affect the handling of COVID-19 in South Sulawesi. The indicators used are the WHO's standard services for handling COVID-19, including health services and health workers' support as front-line health workers.

This study's online media data analysis stages are as follows (Lai & To, 2015). First, the researcher determines the online media that is the object of analysis, in which the researcher selects the names of the dominant media reporting on health workers and the role of the government in providing health services during the COVID-19 pandemic in South Sulawesi. Second, the researcher collects data on online media content, which is the object of analysis. This study's online media data collection is conducted using NVivo software, which requires researchers to filter, select, and categorize data obtained through the data analysis software. Third, categorization and data analysis were conducted for each online media. This stage is the essential stage and requires the ability of researchers to interpret the data obtained from each online media. In this case, researchers play an indispensable role in classifying data, linking data between online media, interpreting words and sentences obtained from all analyzed online media accounts, discussing actor relations represented by the similarity of online media content, and making scientific justifications relations and actor networks indicated by the intensity of communication and interaction between government officials on social media during the handling of COVID-19. The categorization and data analysis stages resulted in conclusions that answered the research questions.

Data Sources

The news used as data in this study is news from trusted, influential online media in South Sulawesi: the Tribun Timur (https://makassar.tribunnews.com/), the people of South Sulawesi (https://rakyatsulsel.co/), and South Sulawesi Online (http://sulselonline.com/). The news on online media is used to enrich the explanation of government officials' communication and coordination on online media during COVID-19. However, this research still uses online media data as the principal (primary) data to reference the explanation, description, analysis, and arguments to answer the research questions. Additionally, online media news adds to and strengthens the explanation and analysis of online media data. Thus, online media news aims to enrich the explanation and analysis of research to produce conclusions that can answer the research questions.

Data Collecting

The data analysis stages of this study are installing the NVivo software for Windows and installing the N-Capture extension on Google Chrome (Salahudin, Nurmandi, & Loilatu, 2020). The researcher captures online media content by using the N-Capture application integrated with NVivo and Google Chrome and imports online media content data from the results of N-Capture into the NVivo work screen, which we call a language processing tool (Kumar et al., 2025). The management of online media content files is conducted on the NVivo work screen, auto-coded online media content that produces themes, visualizes themes in charts, and analyzes actor networks with the sociogram NVivo feature. Analyzing online media content similarities is conducted using the cluster analysis features and the Pearson correlation and coefficient formula. The stages of using the NVivo produce data, which can then be categorized and interpreted to make conclusions that can answer the research questions.

RESULTS AND DISCUSSION

Linkage of Health Workers and the Government with Health Service Indicators

Based on the NVivo cluster analysis, this study reveals that health workers and the government directly correlate with the seven standard health services indicators for handling COVID-19, namely front-line, stigma, services, duty, equipment support, protection, and engagements. The linkage of health workers with seven health indicators confirms that health workers conducting their duties and functions cannot be separated from these seven indicators, which also confirms that these seven indicators influence the performance of health workers in health services during the COVID-19 pandemic. Furthermore, the relationship between the government and the seven indicators reveals that the government has an essential effect on the front-line bureaucracy, stigma, service, duty, equipment support, protection, and engagements.

Figure 1. Clustering by similarity

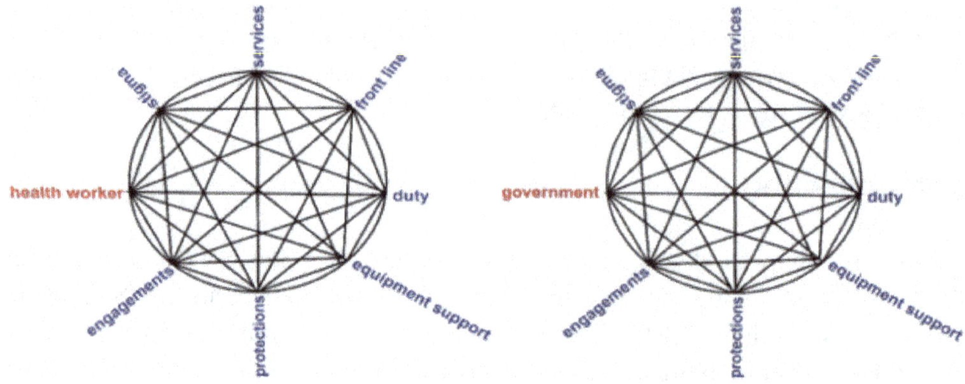

The clustering by word similarity in Figure 1 explains the relationship between case and indicator, and links with relationship lines can show high or low values. The scoring of the relationship value is shown in Figure 2. The case health worker has the highest relationship with the front-line values (0.75), stigma (0.73), services (0.69), and duty (0.63). The front-line scoring explains that a health worker's most essential function is to provide street-level services in handling COVID-19. As a social impact a health worker receives in managing COVID-19 (WHO, 2020l). The services are related to essential services, which are the responsibility of health workers (Morgan, 2020). Duties are related to tasks conducted that might infect health workers with COVID-19 and transmit COVID-19 to health workers (Xiao et al., 2020) and equipment support, such as a medical device that is necessary for health workers to manage patients with COVID-19 (WHO, 2020c)

In the case where the government has a relationship with three primary functions, the government's responsibility is to support COVID-19. Equipment support indicators, protection, and engagements have lower scores than health workers' scoring of equipment support (0.70), protection (0.65), and engagements (0.53). Equipment support is related to medical devices that support the ability to test for COVID-19. Therefore, the ability to test, trace, and administer treatment is influenced by the support of medical devices provided by the government for health workers (WHO, 2020). Thus, capacity testing helps health workers treat patients quickly and prevent the transmission of COVID-19. Furthermore, the government should protect health workers to maintain their mental health (WHO, 2020f) and adopt responsive policies to protect the public from COVID-19 infection (Boholm, 2019). Additionally, the government's role is to support the handling of COVID-19 by providing moral support to health workers, building good communication on the impact of COVID-19 (UNDCO and WHO, 2020), changing goals, and encouraging the public's role in managing COVID-19 (WHO, 2020b).

Figure 2. Relation between health worker and government, classified using correlation coefficient

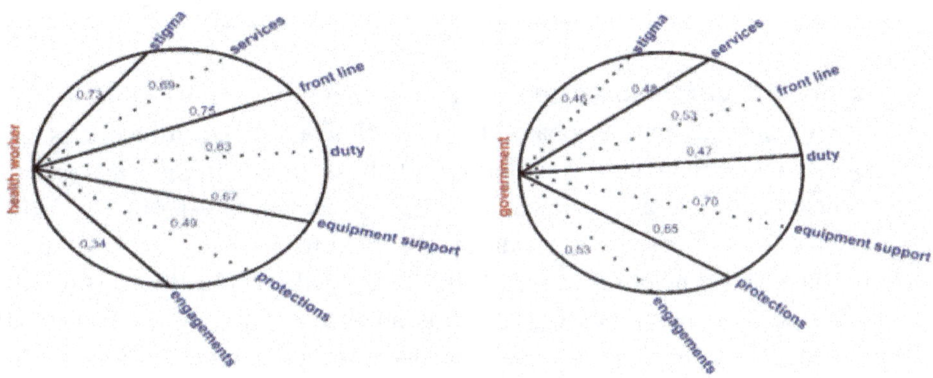

Table 1. Relation between seven indicators with health workers and government

Case	Indicators	Correlation Coefficient
Health Worker	stigma	0,734943
	services	0,696306
	front line	0,750067
	duty	0,635786
	equipment support	0,673799
	protections	0,498319
	engagements	0,341149
Case	**Indicators**	**Correlation Coefficient**

continued on following page

Table 1. Continued

Case	Indicators	Correlation Coefficient
Government	equipment support	0,706531
	protections	0,656388
	engagements	0,537741
	services	0,487808
	stigma	0,466154
	front line	0,531387
	duty	0,473336

Based on the data mentioned above, the handling of COVID-19 in South Sulawesi is predominantly the responsibility of health workers. Health workers have a high cohesion with indicators in handling COVID-19 in South Sulawesi (see the scoring Pearson correlation coefficient in Table 1. Referring to Vike's view (2018), the bureaucracy's performance is primarily observed from the lowest level and is placed in a street-level position (Zang, 2016). South Sulawesi health workers play an essential role in managing emergency conditions and handling the COVID-19 outbreak (Zang, 2016), but the services provided during emergencies do not affect policy. These findings differ from Lipsky's (2010) view that street-level services influence policy. However, by contrast, regarding experience distortion (Vohnsen, 2015), the policy for handling COVID-19 is distorted in terms of health equipment support and protection, which must guarantee health workers in South Sulawesi.

The scoring stigma in Figure 2 and Table 1 is the stigma against health workers in South Sulawesi: the perception of health workers as carriers of the COVID-19 virus. The social attitudes accepted by health workers make them get a wrong view as health workers. Thus, the WHO recommended that the public avoid pronouncing words that negatively influence (WHO, 2020l). Additionally, the WHO recommends involving social influencers in campaigns regarding the impact of COVID-19 and providing education on the community duties and roles of health workers.

"The stigma is that hospitals are becoming disease epidemics so that medical personnel become people labeled as carriers of the COVID-19 virus. They are also labeled as using services to benefit from COVID-19 patients."

The social stigma against and labeling health workers resulted in the closure of several health centers and hospitals in Sulawesi. The WHO (2020f) stated that the stigma against health workers must be stopped and that they must receive public and government support. The WHO wrote reports and guidelines on "messages for healthcare workers" in mental health and psychosocial considerations during the COVID-19 outbreak. For example, health workers need support from the government and society in conducting their duties and roles as street-level services. With support from the environment and society, street-level services are maximized (Michael Lipsky, 1979) because health workers as street-level service providers have a broader role in managing patients with COVID-19 (LIPSKY, 2010).

The determination of the national emergency health status by the central government has an uneven impact on health workers' readiness. In this emergency, health workers must work optimally to manage COVID-19. South Sulawesi health personnel readiness scored high on the front line at 0.75 and essential services at 0.69. Both have different cohesion, meaning that services are more directed at handling patients with COVID-19 in emergencies. A pandemic is a health crisis (Vohnsen, 2015). Therefore, health workers have been encouraged to become front-line service providers in handling COVID-19 (C. Wang et al., 2020). The health worker's role is based on the Pearson correlation analysis, which shows that its function is more dominant in handling COVID-19 than the essential services often performed by health workers.

"Health workers play an important role in dealing with COVID-19; they are positioned as the first person to deal with COVID-19, but they have the potential to catch and transmit the COVID-19 virus to their families and people around them, so they need to get protection and guarantees from the government."

Such services are the health worker's responsibility, for example, maintaining the patient's health condition and providing assistance in crisis conditions, starting with preparation, prevention, recovery, and treatment (WHO, 2020d). A health worker can only conduct these steps when they understand the procedure from preparation to treatment. Health workforce services generally run well but depend on the government, and fewer services match agency desires.

Government Support in Handling COVID-19

Health equipment support indicators are the main factor for health workers conducting COVID-19 service functions; without health equipment, health workers can be infected and create a new cluster of COVID-19 in South Sulawesi. Services in the emergency conditions of COVID-19 depend on the state's ability to provide sufficient financial support to fulfill the need for medical devices (Micheal Lipsky, 2010). In the case of COVID-19 in South Sulawesi, the government did not provide sufficient support for health workers, and incentives for health workers within three months of handling COVID-19 were also not provided. Based on the results of monitoring conducted by the South Sulawesi Government supervisory agency, their statement stated that.

"The results of monitoring and evaluating the three months phase II of the health department on realizing the budget for health personnel and the doctors' team were not given until early August."

Health workers have not received incentives since the government announced the first case in other cases. For example, the first COVID-19 case in Indonesia was announced in March 2020, and as of July 2020, health personnel have not received incentives from the government. The government provides the incentive system to health workers, and it depends on government relations and policies; therefore, in the view of Zechmeister et al. (2002), the South Sulawesi Government provides incentives depending on the costs incurred by patients with COVID-19 because in an emergency such as COVID-19, the government needs to change policies and relationships so that financing and incentives for health workers can be realized. The provision of incentives follows the work scheme and needs during the COVID-19 pandemic; for the more complex activities, the government needs to budget more incentives to protect health workers by making payments directly rather than suspending health workers (Doran et al., 2017).

Government involvement in managing COVID-19 is necessary, especially in strategic policies. Several problems experienced by health workers stem from late—rather than timely—government policies and responses. Thus, the government did not use a varied approach to understand problems that cannot be resolved with one approach (Keulemans & Groeneveld, 2020). Additionally, the government, as a service provider, ignored the agency's wishes. Thus, health worker services do not consider agency desires, in contrast to Lipsky's view of street-level policies and services (Micheal Lipsky, 2010). The essential services that must be provided are services based on agency desires. The services conducted at the street level in crisis conditions depend on government policy, that is, policies that can influence the situation because they can predict the health and mental impacts of future consequences (Berlan, 2010). However, government policies are at odds with street-level services for handling COVID-19, according to the following statement:

"The government does not provide supplies of personal protective equipment but forces hospitals to operate; for that, we hope as health workers that this policy needs to be reconsidered."

"Determination of the budget for handling COVID-19 must get approval from the government quickly because the COVID-19 budget absorption is still low and impacts health services and health workers."

The South Sulawesi Government's support in managing COVID-19 remains low, especially in policymaking; the government has not proposed policy options to resolve the ongoing problem. The increase in Sulawesi's positive cases was caused by many local transmissions in 24 districts and cities; this transmission affected the spread of COVID-19. Although South Sulawesi is the province with the fourth-highest number of cases in Indonesia, the South Sulawesi Government has not fully supported health canters, hospitals, and health workers to overcome the spread of COVID-19. The government's attitudes and policies in managing

COVID-19 demonstrate their incompetence in providing services and that they are not prepared to manage crisis conditions (Feltham-King & Macleod, 2020); as a result, health services in South Sulawesi do not fulfil the service standards set by the WHO as an international health organization.

CONCLUSION

This study reveals that health workers and the government directly correlate with the front-line, stigma, services, duties, equipment support, protection, and engagements. Thus, health workers are the front-line bureaucracy determining the quality of health services (public services) during the COVID-19 pandemic. In this case, health workers strive to conduct their bureaucratic duties and functions, namely, providing health services to the public, supported by equipment support and protective facilities that support the implementation of good health services during the COVID-19 crisis in South Sulawesi. The link between health workers and the front-line is the most substantial relationship compared with the other indicators, confirming that health workers are positioned as the front-line bureaucracy that determines the quality of health services. However, health workers have experienced a negative stigma from the public; that is, health workers are objects easily exposed to COVID-19 and target negative perceptions regarding the collusive, corruptive use of the COVID-19 budget.

The relationship between the government and the seven indicators reveals that the government has a crucial role in the front-line, stigma, services, duties, equipment support, protection, and engagements. The government is an institution responsible for the performance of health workers as the front-line of health services during the COVID-19 pandemic. The relationship between the government and stigma reveals that the government has failed to build a positive image of health workers as the front line of the bureaucracy that provides good health services. The government's failure is related to the government's inability to provide health service facilities and infrastructure that support and guarantee good health services. The government has also failed to involve health workers and stakeholders in formulating and implementing policies that support health services.

The results of this study contribute to the development of health service governance during the pandemic crisis. Health services during COVID-19 require the role of health workers and the government, related to strengthening the performance of the front-line bureaucracy and supporting facilities for the delivery of health services according to the protocols and regulations for handling COVID-19 from all levels of the bureaucracy. The weakness of the findings of this study is that the government and health workers in South Sulawesi do not have a good understanding of the implementation of health protocols and the implementation of policies for handling COVID-19. Therefore, the problems experienced by the front-line bureaucracy (health workers) have not been used to improve health policies and services during COVID-19 in South Sulawesi. Therefore, in a theoretical aspect, this research differs from street-level bureaucratic theory, emphasizing that front-line problems are the main problems used to improve policies on handling COVID-19. In addition, the limitation of this study is the use of online media data. Subsequent research should use survey and interview data to produce research findings that comprehensively describe the government and health workers' performance.

REFERENCES

Alcadipani, R., Cabral, S., Fernandes, A., & Lotta, G. (2020). Street-level bureaucrats under COVID-19: Police officers' responses in constrained settings. *Administrative Theory & Praxis, 0*(0), 1–10. DOI: 10.1080/10841806.2020.1771906

Aluga, M. A. (2020). Coronavirus Disease 2019 (COVID-19) in Kenya: Preparedness, response and transmissibility. *Journal of Microbiology, Immunology, and Infection, 2019*(April), 2019–2021. DOI: 10.1016/j.jmii.2020.04.011 PMID: 32331980

Andrikopoulos, S., & Johnson, G. (2020). The Australian response to the COVID-19 pandemic and diabetes – Lessons learned. *Diabetes Research and Clinical Practice, 165*, 108246. DOI: 10.1016/j.diabres.2020.108246 PMID: 32502693

Atkinson, C. (2020). G20 leaders must answer to COVID-19. *Science, 368*(6487), 111. DOI: 10.1126/science.abc1025 PMID: 32273441

Berlan, D. (2010). Street-level Bureacracy. *Guidance Note, 5*, 1–5.

Boholm, Å. (2019). Lessons of success and failure: Practicing risk communication at government agencies. *Safety Science, 118*(May), 158–167. DOI: 10.1016/j.ssci.2019.05.025

Brodkin, E. Z. (2008). Accountability in Street-Level Organizations. *International Journal of Public Administration, 31*(3), 317–336. DOI: 10.1080/01900690701590587

Cheng, S. C., Chang, Y. C., Fan Chiang, Y. L., Chien, Y. C., Cheng, M., Yang, C. H., Huang, C. H., & Hsu, Y. N. (2020). First case of Coronavirus Disease 2019 (COVID-19) pneumonia in Taiwan. *Journal of the Formosan Medical Association, 119*(3), 747–751. DOI: 10.1016/j.jfma.2020.02.007 PMID: 32113824

Djalante, R., Lassa, J., Setiamarga, D., Sudjatma, A., Indrawan, M., Haryanto, B., Mahfud, C., Sinapoy, M. S., Djalante, S., Rafliana, I., Gunawan, L. A., Surtiari, G. A. K., & Warsilah, H. (2020). Review and analysis of current responses to COVID-19 in Indonesia: Period of January to March 2020. *Progress in Disaster Science, 6*, 100091. DOI: 10.1016/j.pdisas.2020.100091 PMID: 34171011

Doran, T., Maurer, K. A., & Ryan, A. M. (2017). Impact of Provider Incentives on Quality and Value of Health Care. *Annual Review of Public Health, 38*, 449–465. DOI: 10.1146/annurev-publhealth-032315-021457 PMID: 27992731

Feltham-King, T., & Macleod, C. (2020). Multi-layered risk management in under-resourced antenatal clinics: A scientific-bureaucratic approach versus street-level bureaucracy. *Health Risk & Society*, *22*(1), 31–52. DOI: 10.1080/13698575.2019.1697432

Fernqvist, S. (2018). Street-level bureaucracy and categorization processes in social workers' encounters with parents who have financial and cognitive difficulties. *Nordic Social Work Research*, *8588*, 1–12. DOI: 10.1080/2156857x.2018.1547218

Fitriani, N. A., Loilatu, M. J., & Kurniawan, D. (2023). *Leadership in a Time of Pandemic: Dealing with the COVID-19 Outbreak BT - Proceedings of Seventh International Congress on Information and Communication Technology* (X.-S. Yang, S. Sherratt, N. Dey, & A. Joshi (eds.); pp. 379–388). Springer Nature Singapore.

Fusi-Schmidhauser, T., Preston, N. J., Keller, N., & Gamondi, C. (2020). Conservative Management of COVID-19 Patients—Emergency Palliative Care in Action. *Journal of Pain and Symptom Management*. Advance online publication. DOI: 10.1016/j.jpainsymman.2020.03.030 PMID: 32276101

García-Horta, J. B., & Guerra-Ramos, M. T. (2009). The use of CAQDAS in educational research: Some advantages, limitations and potential risks. *International Journal of Research & Method in Education*, *32*(2), 151–165. DOI: 10.1080/17437270902946686

Grantz, K. H., Claudot, P., Kambala, M., Kouyaté, M., Soumah, A., Boum, Y., Juan-Giner, A., Jemmy, J. P., Cummings, D. A. T., & Grais, R. F. (2019). Factors influencing participation in an Ebola vaccine trial among front-line workers in Guinea. *Vaccine*, *37*(48), 7165–7170. DOI: 10.1016/j.vaccine.2019.09.094 PMID: 31623917

Hill, H. C. (2003). Understanding Implementation: Street-Level Bureaucrats' Resources for Reform. *Journal of Public Administration: Research and Theory*, *13*(3), 265–282. DOI: 10.1093/jopart/mug024

Hong, S. (2020). Representative bureaucracy and hierarchy: Interactions among leadership, middle-level, and street-level bureaucracy. *Public Management Review*, *00*(00), 1–22. DOI: 10.1080/14719037.2020.1743346

Irawan, B., Jafar Loilatu, M., Akbar, P., & Reynaldi, R. (2022). An Exploration Respond of COVID-19 Policy through Social Media in Indonesia. *Policy & Governance Review*, *6*(3), 229. DOI: 10.30589/pgr.v6i3.596

Janssen, M., & Van Der Voort, H. (2020). Agile and adaptive governance in crisis response : Lessons from the COVID- 19 pandemic. *International Journal of Information Management, 102180*(June), •••. DOI: 10.1016/j.ijinfomgt.2020.102180 PMID: 32836637

Kaefer, F., Roper, J., & Sinha, P. (2015). A software-assisted qualitative content analysis of news articles: Example and reflections. *Forum Qualitative Social Research, 16*(2). Advance online publication. DOI: 10.17169/fqs-16.2.2123

Keulemans, S., & Groeneveld, S. (2020). Supervisory leadership at the frontlines: Street-level discretion, supervisor influence, and street-level bureaucrats' attitude towards clients. *Journal of Public Administration: Research and Theory, 30*(2), 307–323. DOI: 10.1093/jopart/muz019

Kumar, A., Bhatia, A., Kumar, S., Kumar, R., & Yadav, V. (2025). Sentimental analysis using natural language processing. *AIP Conference Proceedings, 3224*(1), 20054. DOI: 10.1063/5.0246883

Lai, L. S. L., & To, W. M. (2015). Content analysis of social media: A grounded theory approach. *Journal of Electronic Commerce Research, 16*(2), 138–152.

Li, Q., Guan, X., Wu, P., Wang, X., Zhou, L., Tong, Y., Ren, R., Leung, K. S. M., Lau, E. H. Y., Wong, J. Y., Xing, X., Xiang, N., Wu, Y., Li, C., Chen, Q., Li, D., Liu, T., Zhao, J., Liu, M., & Feng, Z. (2020). Early Transmission Dynamics in Wuhan, China, of Novel Coronavirus-Infected Pneumonia. *The New England Journal of Medicine, 382*(13), 1199–1207. DOI: 10.1056/NEJMoa2001316 PMID: 31995857

Lipsky, M. (1979). *Street-Level Bureaucracy : Dilemmas of the Individual.* 1-.

Lipsky, M. (2010). Street-Level Bureaucracy: Dilemmas of the Individual in Public Services. Michael Lipsky. In *Social Service Review*. https://doi.org/DOI: 10.1086/643898

Morgan, A. K. (2020). Making COVID-19 prevention etiquette of social distancing a reality for the homeless and slum dwellers in Ghana: Lessons for consideration. *Local Environment, 00*(0), 1–4. DOI: 10.1080/13549839.2020.1789854

Munster, V. J., Koopmans, M., van Doremalen, N., van Riel, D., & de Wit, E. (2020). A novel coronavirus emerging in China - Key questions for impact assessment. *The New England Journal of Medicine, 382*(8), 692–694. DOI: 10.1056/NEJMp2000929 PMID: 31978293

Murphy, M., & Skillen, P. (2015). The Politics of Time on the Frontline: Street Level Bureaucracy, Professional Judgment, and Public Accountability. *International Journal of Public Administration, 38*(9), 632–641. DOI: 10.1080/01900692.2014.952823

Nguyen, L. H., Drew, D. A., Joshi, A. D., Guo, C.-G., Ma, W., Mehta, R. S., Sikavi, D. R., Lo, C.-H., Kwon, S., Song, M., Mucci, L. A., Stampfer, M. J., Willett, W. C., Eliassen, A. H., Hart, J. E., Chavarro, J. E., Rich-Edwards, J. W., Davies, R., Capdevila, J., . . . Chan, A. T. (2020). Risk of COVID-19 among frontline healthcare workers and the general community: a prospective cohort study. MedRxiv *: The Preprint Server for Health Sciences, 2667*(20). https://doi.org/DOI: 10.1101/2020.04.29.20084111

Nugus, P., Ranmuthugala, G., Lamothe, J., Greenfield, D., Travaglia, J., Kolne, K., Kryluk, J., & Braithwaite, J. (2018). New ways to get policy into practice: A mixed-method participatory study of care coordination and street-level bureaucrats. *Journal of Health Organization and Management, 32*(6), 809–824. DOI: 10.1108/JHOM-09-2017-0239 PMID: 30299221

Nyashanu, M., Pfende, F., & Ekpenyong, M. (2020). Exploring the challenges faced by frontline workers in health and social care amid the COVID-19 pandemic : Experiences of frontline workers in the English Midlands region, UK ABSTRACT. *Journal of Interprofessional Care, 00*(00), 1–7. DOI: 10.1080/13561820.2020.1792425 PMID: 32674701

Ozkan, B. C. (2004). Using NVivo to Analyze Qualitative Classroom Data on Constructivist Learning Environments. *Qualitative Report, 9*(4), 589–603.

Paulus, T., Woods, M., Atkins, D. P., & Macklin, R. (2017). The discourse of QDAS: Reporting practices of ATLAS.ti and NVivo users with implications for best practices. *International Journal of Social Research Methodology, 20*(1), 35–47. DOI: 10.1080/13645579.2015.1102454

Prescott, K., Baxter, E., Lynch, C., Jassal, S., Bashir, A., & Gray, J. (2020). COVID-19: How prepared are front-line healthcare workers in England? *The Journal of Hospital Infection, 105*(2), 142–145. DOI: 10.1016/j.jhin.2020.04.031 PMID: 32339615

Qodir, Z., Jubba, H., & Loilatu, M. J. (2022). Muhammadiyah's Response to Covid-19 in Indonesia: Faith-Based Commitment. *Wawasan: Jurnal Ilmiah Agama Dan Sosial Budaya, 7*(1), 71–86. DOI: 10.15575/jw.v7i1.13756

Roziqin, A., Mas'udi, S. Y. F., & Sihidi, I. T. (2021). An analysis of Indonesian government policies against COVID-19. *Public Administration and Policy, 24*(1), 92–107. DOI: 10.1108/PAP-08-2020-0039

Salahudin, S., Nurmandi, A., & Loilatu, M. J. (2020). How to Design Qualitative Research with NVivo 12 Plus for Local Government Corruption Issues in Indonesia? *Jurnal Studi Pemerintahan, 11*(3), 369–398. DOI: 10.18196/jgp.113124

Salahudin, S., Nurmandi, A., Sulistyaningsih, T., & Lutfi, M. (2020). Analysis of Government Official Twitters during Covid-19 Crisis in Indonesia Analysis of Government Official Twitters during Covid-19 Crisis in Indonesia. *Talent Development & Excellence*, *12*(June), 3899–3915.

Seak, C.-J., Liu, Y.-T., & Ng, C.-J. (2020). Rapid responses in the emergency department of Linkou Chang Gung Memorial Hospital, Taiwan effectively prevents spread of COVID-19 among healthcare workers of emergency department during outbreak: Lessons learnt from SARS. *Biomedical Journal*, (June), 4–7. DOI: 10.1016/j.bj.2020.06.002 PMID: 32792166

Shaw, K., Golding, S., Knight, J., Chadborn, T., Dempster, L., Finistrella, V., & Hopkins, S. (2019). A unique approach to the development of infection prevention and control resources for front-line health care workers. *Infection Prevention in Practice*, *1*(1), 100004. DOI: 10.1016/j.infpip.2019.100004 PMID: 34368670

Tang, L. H., Tang, S., Chen, X. L., Zhang, S., Xiong, Y., Chen, R., & Meng, Q. T. (2020). Avoiding health worker infection and containing the coronavirus disease 2019 pandemic: Perspectives from the frontline in Wuhan. *International Journal of Surgery*, *79*, 120–124.

Tummers, L., & Bekkers, V. (2014). Policy Implementation, Street-level Bureaucracy, and the Importance of Discretion. *Public Management Review*, *16*(4), 527–547. DOI: 10.1080/14719037.2013.841978

UNDCO and WHO. (2020). Strategic Preparedness and Response Plan on COVID-19 by WHO. *Printed in Geneva, Switzerland.*, *12*(February), 20.

Vike, H. (2018). Street-level bureaucracy and crosscutting cleavages in municipal worlds. *Comparative Social Research*, *33*, 245–263. DOI: 10.1108/S0195-631020180000033016

Vohnsen, N. H. (2015). Street-level planning; the shifty nature of "local knowledge and practice.". *Journal of Organizational Ethnography*, *4*(2), 147–161. DOI: 10.1108/JOE-09-2014-0032

Wang, C., Cheng, Z., Yue, X.-G., & McAleer, M. (2020). Risk Management of COVID-19 by Universities in China. *Journal of Risk and Financial Management*, *13*(2), 36. DOI: 10.3390/jrfm13020036

Wang, J., Zhou, M., & Liu, F. (2020). Reasons for healthcare workers becoming infected with novel coronavirus disease 2019 (COVID-19) in China. *The Journal of Hospital Infection*, *105*(1), 100–101. DOI: 10.1016/j.jhin.2020.03.002 PMID: 32147406

WHO. (2019). 2019 NOVEL CORONAVIRUS (2019-nCoV) STRATEGIC PREPAREDNESS AND RESPONSE PLAN FOR THE SOUTH-EAST ASIA REGION 1. In *World Health Organization South-East Asia*. https://doi.org/.DOI: 1037//0033-2909.I26.1.78

WHO. (2020a). Biomedical Equipment for COVID-19 Case Management Invetory Tool. *World Health Organization, 25*(June), 1–34.

WHO. (2020b). COVID-19 STRATEGY UPDATE. In *World Health Organization* (Issue April). https://doi.org/DOI: 10.1146/annurev.genet.37.050203.103207

WHO. (2020c). Critical preparedness, readiness and response actions for COVID-19. In *World Health Organization Interim Guidance*. Issue March.

WHO. (2020d). Investing in and building longer-term health emergency preparedness during the COVID-19 pandemic. *World Health Organization, 6*(July), 1–30.

WHO. (2020e). Maintaining essential health services: Operational guidance for the COVID-19 context. *World Development, 1*(June), 1–55.

WHO. (2020f). Mental Health and Psychosocial Considerations During COVID-19 Outbreak. *World Health Organization, January*, 1–6.

WHO. (2020g). Operational Planning Guidelines to Support Country Preparedness and Response. *World Health Organization, 22*(May), 1–30.

WHO. (2020h). Overview of public health and social measures in the context of COVID-19. *World Health Organization Interim Guidance, 18*(May), 1–8.

WHO. (2020i). Preparing for large-scale community transmission of COVID-19. *World Health Organization Westren Pacific Region*, (February), 1–8.

WHO. (2020j). Rapid Hospital Readiness Checlist. *World Development, 25*(June), 1–19.

WHO. (2020k). The COVID-19 Risk Communication Package For Healthcare Facilities. *WHO*, 1–11.

WHO, U. (2020l). Social Stigma associated with COVID-19. *World Health Organization, February*, 1–5.

Xiao, J., Fang, M., Chen, Q., & He, B. (2020). SARS, MERS and COVID-19 among healthcare workers: A narrative review. *Journal of Infection and Public Health, 13*(6), 843–848. DOI: 10.1016/j.jiph.2020.05.019 PMID: 32493671

Zainab Kabba, S. D. (2015). NVivo 12: Up and Running. *IT Services, University of Oxford*, 1–68.

Zang, X. (2016). Research on Street-Level Discretion in the West: Past, Present, and the Future. *Chinese Political Science Review*, *1*(4), 610–622. DOI: 10.1007/s41111-016-0041-z

Zechmeister, I., Österle, A., Denk, P., & Katschnig, H. (2002). Incentives in financing mental health care in Austria. *The Journal of Mental Health Policy and Economics*, *5*(3), 121–129. PMID: 12728199

Chapter 10
The Ethical Integration of AI in Advancing Transparency Fairness and Employee Well-Being

Raed Atef
https://orcid.org/0009-0004-0012-4940
United Arab Emirates University, UAE

ABSTRACT

This chapter examines AI's role in fostering trustful work environments and enhancing employee well-being. AI-driven technologies improve transparency, fairness, and integrity by detecting corruption, reducing bias, and promoting ethical practices. They enhance fairness in recruitment and career progression while alleviating stress through automation and wellness monitoring. Despite these benefits, ethical concerns regarding data privacy and bias remain. Responsible AI implementation, with clear guidelines and employee involvement, is crucial to maximizing its potential. When applied ethically, AI can create more transparent, inclusive, and supportive workplaces.

INTRODUCTION

The rapid advancement of artificial intelligence (AI) is revolutionizing workplaces across industries, reshaping organizational structures, and redefining the relationship between employees and management. AI-driven technologies are increasingly integrated into various aspects of workplace operations, offering opportunities to enhance transparency, efficiency, and employee well-being. As organizations seek to foster

DOI: 10.4018/979-8-3373-3760-9.ch010

trustful work environments, AI emerges as a powerful tool to mitigate corruption, promote fairness, and improve overall workplace conditions. The integration of AI into workplace governance can strengthen ethical decision-making, reduce human biases, and create a culture of accountability and integrity (Bin Rashid & Kausik, 2024; Awashreh, 2025; Awashreh & Ramachandran, 2025).

Trust is a fundamental pillar of any successful workplace. It underpins employee engagement, job satisfaction, and overall organizational effectiveness. A work environment characterized by transparency, fairness, and ethical leadership fosters a sense of security and motivation among employees. In contrast, environments plagued by administrative and financial corruption, favoritism, and lack of accountability lead to disengagement, decreased productivity, and high turnover rates (Islam et al., 2023). Traditional mechanisms for ensuring trust, such as manual audits and human oversight, are often prone to inefficiencies, biases, and loopholes. AI offers an alternative by introducing objective, data-driven solutions that enhance governance, detect unethical behavior, and promote fairness (Lacmanovic & Skare, 2025).

One of the primary ways AI contributes to building trustful workplaces is by enhancing transparency and reducing corruption. AI-driven algorithms can analyze vast amounts of data to detect fraudulent transactions, procurement misconduct, and contract manipulations. By automating administrative processes, AI minimizes human intervention in areas prone to unethical practices, such as financial approvals and resource allocations. Organizations that implement AI-driven monitoring systems can significantly reduce corruption and increase confidence in workplace governance, ultimately fostering a transparent and accountable work environment (Zahidi et al., 2024).

In addition to enhancing transparency, AI plays a crucial role in fostering fairness in workplace decision-making. Traditional performance evaluations, promotions, and rewards systems have often been criticized for being influenced by biases, favoritism, or subjective human judgment. AI-driven systems offer a more equitable approach by analyzing employee performance data based on objective criteria, ensuring that decisions are made fairly and consistently (Bol et al., 2023). Moreover, AI-powered recruitment tools can eliminate biases in hiring by assessing candidates solely based on their qualifications and competencies rather than demographic characteristics. By promoting fairness and inclusivity, AI strengthens trust between employees and management, leading to a more cohesive and motivated workforce (Oman et al., 2024).

Employee well-being is another critical area where AI is making a profound impact. Workplace stress, burnout, and job dissatisfaction are prevalent issues that negatively affect both employees and organizations (Awashreh & Hamid, 2025). AI-powered tools can monitor workplace conditions, analyze employee sentiment, and detect signs of stress or dissatisfaction (Awashreh & Al Ghunaimi, 2024). For instance, AI-driven sentiment analysis can assess employee feedback from surveys, emails, or communication platforms, providing organizations with real-time insights into workforce morale. Additionally, AI can personalize work schedules, suggest workload adjustments, and provide mental health support through chatbots and virtual assistants, ensuring that employees have access to resources that enhance their well-being (Jangid, 2024).

Despite its numerous advantages, the integration of AI into workplace governance and employee well-being initiatives is not without challenges. Ethical concerns surrounding data privacy, employee surveillance, and algorithmic biases must be carefully addressed to ensure that AI is used responsibly and does not infringe on workers' rights (Bar-Gil et al., 2024). Organizations must implement AI solutions transparently, with clear guidelines and oversight mechanisms to prevent unintended negative consequences (Awashreh, 2024). Moreover, fostering a culture of AI acceptance requires employee education and involvement in the decision-making process to mitigate resistance and build trust in AI-driven systems (Awashreh, Al-Naqbi & Gharib, 2024).

Chapter Significance

The integration of artificial intelligence (AI) into workplace governance and employee well-being initiatives holds significant promise for organizations seeking to cultivate ethical, transparent, and efficient environments. AI can revolutionize workplace operations by enhancing transparency, promoting fairness, and improving employee well-being. By automating processes prone to human biases, such as financial approvals and resource allocations, AI helps mitigate corruption and ensure accountability. Its ability to analyze vast amounts of data also enables the identification of fraudulent activities, fostering trust and confidence in workplace governance. Additionally, AI-driven systems enhance decision-making by removing biases in areas such as recruitment, promotions, and performance evaluations, leading to more equitable and consistent outcomes. This fairness strengthens relationships between employees and management, boosting job satisfaction and organizational effectiveness. AI also supports employee well-being by addressing issues like stress and burnout, using tools like sentiment analysis and personalized workload adjustments to improve overall workplace conditions. However, the responsible integration of AI requires careful attention to ethical concerns such as data privacy and algorithmic biases, with transparent guidelines and oversight mechanisms essential to safeguard employees' rights. When implemented responsibly, AI has the potential to drive sustainable organizational change by creating more inclusive, efficient, and ethical workplaces. This research underscores the transformative power of AI, offering valuable insights into how it can shape work environments that prioritize trust, fairness, and employee well-being.

This chapter explores the intersection of AI, workplace trust, and employee well-being by examining how AI enhances transparency, promotes fairness, and improves workplace conditions. The research objectives outlined in this chapter focus on assessing the role of AI in mitigating corruption, fostering equitable work environments, and supporting employee well-being. The guiding research question, "How can artificial intelligence build trustful work environments and contribute to employee well-being?" is further explored through three key sub-questions: How does AI enhance transparency and reduce corruption in workplace governance? In what ways can AI-driven systems foster fairness and strengthen trust between employees and management? How can AI technologies support employee well-being by improving workplace conditions and reducing stress?

By addressing these questions, the chapter aims to provide valuable insights into the potential of AI to shape ethical, transparent, and employee-centric workplaces. Through case studies, practical examples, and a critical analysis of AI-driven governance, this study will contribute to the broader discourse on the role of AI in fostering sustainable and trustful work environments. Ultimately, AI, when implemented responsibly, can serve as a catalyst for positive organizational change, ensuring that workplaces are not only more efficient but also more inclusive, ethical, and conducive to employee well-being.

The chapter underscores AI's transformative potential in building trustful, transparent workplaces that prioritize employee well-being. By providing practical insights and case studies, it serves as a valuable resource for business leaders, policymakers, and researchers exploring the intersection of AI, corporate ethics, and employee satisfaction.

Research Objectives

1. **To examine how AI enhances transparency and reduces corruption** in workplace governance by detecting fraudulent activities and ensuring ethical decision-making.
2. **To explore the role of AI-driven systems in fostering fairness** and strengthening trust between employees and management through unbiased decision-making and equitable policies.
3. **To assess how AI technologies contribute to employee well-being** by improving workplace conditions, reducing stress, and promoting a healthier work environment.

How can artificial intelligence build trustful work environments and contribute to employee well-being?

- **Sub-question 1:** How does AI enhance transparency and reduce corruption in workplace governance?
- **Sub-question 2:** In what ways can AI-driven systems foster fairness and strengthen trust between employees and management?
- **Sub-question 3:** How can AI technologies support employee well-being by improving workplace conditions and reducing stress?

LITERATURE REVIEW

Artificial Intelligence (AI) has become a transformative force in workplace governance, reshaping traditional management practices and decision-making processes (Chhatre & Singh, 2024). AI-driven technologies have enabled organizations to automate complex operations, enhance transparency, and promote ethical behavior (Awashreh & Ramachandran, 2025). As AI continues to evolve, its potential to mitigate workplace corruption, improve employee trust, and foster a healthier work environment is becoming increasingly evident (OECD, 2024). The role of AI in addressing biases, improving fairness, and ensuring corporate policies align with ethical standards is particularly noteworthy, highlighting its capacity to support more equitable workplace environments (Murikah et al., 2024).

Transparency, a key component of a trustful workplace, is significantly enhanced by AI's capabilities. Employees are more likely to engage and remain committed when they believe their organization operates with integrity (Modise, 2023). AI contributes to this by automating reporting processes, monitoring financial transactions, and detecting anomalies in business operations (Antwi et al., 2024). AI-driven fraud detection systems have proven particularly effective in reducing corruption in corporate environments by identifying fraudulent behaviors in procurement, payroll, and supply chain management (Ezeji, 2024). Moreover, AI's integration with blockchain technology has emerged as a powerful solution for boosting transparency in workplace governance. Smart contracts and AI-powered audits ensure that business transactions are traceable, reducing opportunities for misconduct (Awashreh, Al Ghunaimi & Hassiba, 2025). By embedding AI into compliance frameworks, organizations can better ensure adherence to ethical standards while minimizing human intervention in areas susceptible to manipulation (Awashreh & Ramachandran, 2024).

AI's influence extends beyond transparency to enhance fairness in workplace decision-making, which is essential for fostering trust. Traditional, human-led decision-making processes are often influenced by cognitive biases, favoritism, and discrimination (Friedman, 2023). AI-driven systems are designed to mitigate these challenges by analyzing large volumes of employee data to ensure fair performance evaluations, unbiased promotions, and equitable compensation structures (Nyathani, 2023). In recruitment and hiring, for instance, AI-powered tools assist organizations in eliminating biases by prioritizing candidate competencies over demographic factors (Oman et al., 2024). These tools leverage natural language processing (NLP) and machine learning algorithms to assess resumes, evaluate skills, and match candidates with roles based on objective criteria, rather than subjective opinions (Saatçı, Kaya & Ünlü, 2024). However, concerns about algorithmic bias persist. If AI systems are not properly trained, they may inadvertently perpetuate existing biases in historical data (Chen, 2023). To prevent this, organizations must implement ethical AI principles and regularly audit algorithms to ensure that their outcomes are fair and unbiased (Murikah, Nthenge & Musyoka, 2024).

The impact of AI extends further into the realm of employee well-being, enhancing not only governance and fairness but also workplace health and psychological support. AI-driven sentiment analysis tools enable employers to monitor employee morale by analyzing feedback from emails, surveys, and communication platforms (Singh, Kaunert & Ravesangar, 2024). This data allows management to proactively address workplace stressors, enhance employee engagement, and reduce burnout rates. Additionally, AI-powered wellness applications provide personalized recommendations for managing stress, supporting mental health, and improving work-life balance (Thakkar, Gupta & De Sousa, 2024). Chatbots and virtual assistants also offer psychological support, providing employees with access to mental health resources without stigma or fear of judgment. AI's ability to predict stress and fatigue levels based on physiological data has led to the development of interventions aimed at improving productivity while safeguarding employee well-being (Soetan & Samuel, 2025).

Despite the numerous benefits AI offers in building trustful work environments, it also introduces significant ethical challenges that need careful management. Privacy concerns are a notable issue, particularly when AI systems are employed to monitor employee communications, track productivity metrics, or analyze biometric data (Yaqoob & Robbins, 2024). Employees may perceive AI-driven surveillance as invasive, leading to distrust and resistance to AI adoption in workplaces (Kayas, 2023). Additionally, the accountability of AI-driven decisions poses a major concern. AI algorithms operate based on predefined parameters, which may not always align with human ethical considerations (Rodgers et al., 2023). In cases where AI systems make unfair decisions—such as wrongful termination or biased performance evaluations—determining responsibility can be difficult (Rodrigues, 2020). To address this, organizations must establish clear accountability frameworks (Awashreh,

2018) and maintain human oversight to ensure that AI-driven decisions are ethical and just (Holzinger, Zatloukal & Müller, 2025).

In summary, AI can significantly improve workplace governance by enhancing transparency, fairness, and employee well-being. However, it also presents challenges such as privacy concerns, accountability issues, and the risk of bias. Organizations must adopt transparent AI policies, align AI with human values, and ensure continuous monitoring to mitigate these challenges. Future research should focus on refining ethical frameworks for AI and exploring its long-term impact on workplace culture.

THEORETICAL FRAMEWORK

The integration of Artificial Intelligence (AI) into workplace governance and employee well-being requires a strong theoretical foundation to assess its role in promoting transparency, fairness, and ethical decision-making. This study draws upon Good Governance (Awashreh & Al Naqbi, 2023) and the Ethical AI Framework to explore how AI-driven technologies contribute to fostering trustful work environments and enhancing employee well-being (Awashreh, R., Al-Naqbi, S., & Gharib, M., 2024). Good Governance offers a structured approach for evaluating governance mechanisms within organizations, with a focus on transparency, accountability, fairness, participation, and efficiency.

AI-driven systems enhance transparency by automating audits, detecting fraud, and ensuring unbiased decision-making, thereby reducing opportunities for corruption. Moreover, accountability is strengthened through AI tools that monitor policy compliance, create audit trails, and enforce ethical standards (Su et al., 2023). By promoting fairness, AI-driven decision-making minimizes biases in hiring, performance evaluations, and promotions, ensuring both procedural and distributive justice. Participation and inclusivity are further supported through AI-powered feedback platforms and well-being programs, which give employees a voice in decision-making (Rigotti & Fosch, 2024). Additionally, AI enhances efficiency by automating administrative tasks, reducing workload imbalances, and streamlining HR processes, thereby contributing to overall employee well-being. When aligned with Good Governance principles, AI serves as an enabler of ethical workplace practices, rather than a tool for surveillance or exploitation (Benabou et al., 2024).

The Ethical AI Framework offers essential guidelines for developing AI systems that prioritize human rights, fairness, and responsible innovation (Awashreh, 2024b). Transparency and explainability are critical, as AI decisions must be interpretable and justifiable to build trust. Accountability must remain with human managers to ensure ethical alignment, preventing the delegation of critical decisions to algorithms (Novelli, Taddeo & Floridi, 2024). Mitigating biases in AI is also crucial, as unchecked systems can perpetuate discriminatory outcomes in hiring, workload distribution, and performance evaluations.

AI should aim to enhance employee well-being and autonomy, rather than impose excessive control or surveillance. Additionally, privacy and data protection must be safeguarded through stringent regulations, ensuring the responsible use of employee data (Mensah, 2023). Integrating Good Governance Theory with the Ethical AI Framework provides a comprehensive perspective on AI's role in fostering trustful workplaces and improving employee well-being. By aligning AI strategies with these principles, organizations can cultivate sustainable, ethical, and inclusive work environments where AI supports fairness, transparency, and well-being, rather than enabling control or exploitation (Papagiannidis, Mikalef & Conboy, 2025).

METHODOLOGY

This chapter adopts a qualitative research approach to explore the role of AI in fostering trustful work environments and enhancing employee well-being. By drawing on secondary data sources, including academic articles, reputable online resources, and publicly available reports, as well as integrating case studies from relevant organizations, the research provides a comprehensive understanding of the topic. This approach enables the synthesis of diverse perspectives, ensuring a thorough examination of the research questions. Such a methodology is widely supported in the literature (Cheong et al., 2023; Heaton, 2008), offering a balanced and multifaceted view of AI's impact.

The secondary data utilized in this study were carefully selected from peer-reviewed journals, authoritative books, and reports published by experts in AI, organizational behavior, ethics, and employee well-being. These sources offer a solid foundation for reviewing existing research and theories concerning AI's role in the workplace. In particular, they provide valuable insights into AI's potential to foster transparency, reduce corruption, and promote fairness (Babu et al., 2024), which are central themes of this study.

An essential aspect of this methodology is the inclusion of personal experiences and observations from professionals involved in AI implementation, organizational development, and employee engagement. These experiential insights offer critical context, bridging the gap between theoretical findings and practical applications. By incorporating the lived experiences of those working directly with AI, this research captures a more nuanced perspective on the challenges and benefits of leveraging AI to build trustful and ethical work environments.

To develop this chapter, the following sources have been used.

Table 1.

Reference type	Number
Journals	79
Organizations	11
Proceeding	3
Working paper	1
Total	94

CASE STUDY

Artificial Intelligence (AI) is increasingly being used to improve workplace governance, foster fairness, and enhance employee well-being. As companies across industries implement AI-driven solutions, they aim to enhance transparency, detect fraudulent activities, and ensure ethical decision-making. This case study examines real-world examples of organizations leveraging AI to reduce corruption, build trust between employees and management, and promote healthier work environments. Specifically, we analyze the cases of Price water house Coopers (PwC), Unilever, and Microsoft to illustrate how AI fosters trust and well-being in the workplace.

One of the primary concerns in corporate governance is fraud and unethical behavior, which can erode trust and lead to financial and reputational losses. To address this, AI-driven solutions have proven effective in detecting anomalies and improving transparency (Ogunsola et al., 2025). For instance, PwC, a global professional services firm, has integrated AI into its forensic auditing and compliance processes to detect fraudulent activities. PwC's AI-driven *Halo for Journals* tool analyzes millions of transactions in real time, identifying suspicious patterns that might indicate fraud, bribery, or financial misconduct. This technology enables companies to act swiftly against potential corruption, ensuring adherence to ethical standards (PwC, Lammie, 2025).

Similarly, Mastercard employs AI to monitor transactions and detect fraudulent activities within its operations. AI models analyze spending patterns and flag irregular transactions, thus minimizing financial crime risks. By reducing corruption and improving governance, AI helps foster a culture of trust and ethical responsibility within organizations (Mastercard, 2024).

AI plays a crucial role in ensuring fairness in decision-making, mitigating biases, and fostering equitable workplace policies. Moreover, organizations that prioritize fairness benefit from stronger employee trust and improved retention rates. Unilever, a multinational consumer goods company, has revolutionized its hiring process by incorporating AI-driven recruitment tools (Hu, 2023). The company uses AI to analyze job applications and conduct initial video interviews, effectively eliminating human bias from early-stage hiring decisions. The AI system evaluates candidates based on their responses and facial expressions, ensuring that decisions are data-driven rather than influenced by personal bias (Unilever, 2019). As a result, this transparent and fair hiring process has significantly improved trust among both candidates and employees.

Additionally, IBM uses AI to ensure fairness in performance evaluations. The company's AI-powered system assesses employee performance based on objective metrics rather than subjective manager reviews. By analyzing productivity data, project contributions, and feedback, AI-driven assessments reduce favoritism and promote fairness in promotions and salary increments. Employees perceive this system as more reliable and equitable, which leads to higher levels of trust and engagement (IBM, 2021).

Beyond governance and fairness, AI contributes significantly to employee well-being by improving workplace conditions, reducing stress, and promoting healthier work environments. For instance, Microsoft has leveraged AI to enhance employee well-being through its Workplace Analytics platform. This tool analyzes employee work patterns, identifying stress points such as excessive meetings, long working hours, and inefficient workflows. By providing data-driven insights, Microsoft helps companies redesign work structures to prevent burnout and support work-life balance (Boyd, 2025; Microsoft, 2022). As a result, employees benefit from optimized schedules, fewer disruptions, and improved mental health. Similarly, Salesforce has integrated AI-driven wellness assistants into its internal communication platforms. The AI monitors employee sentiment through natural language processing (NLP) and provides tailored recommendations for stress management, mindfulness, and mental health resources. As a result, employees have reported increased job satisfaction and reduced workplace anxiety due to these AI-driven interventions (Salesforce, 2021). Despite its numerous advantages, AI implementation in workplaces presents challenges, including data privacy concerns and the risk of algorithmic biases. To address these challenges, organizations must ensure that AI is used responsibly and transparently. Ethical AI governance frameworks, such as those adopted by IBM and Microsoft, focus on fairness, accountability, and data protection to mitigate risks associated with AI deployment (Hanna et al., 2025).

Furthermore, AI systems must be continuously monitored to prevent unintended biases. For example, Amazon discontinued an AI-driven hiring tool after discovering that it discriminated against female applicants due to biased training data. This case underscores the importance of ethical oversight in AI-driven workplace solutions (Reuters, 2018). In summary, AI has the potential to transform workplace governance, fairness, and employee well-being by enhancing transparency, reducing corruption, and fostering trust. Organizations like PwC, Unilever, Microsoft, and Salesforce have demonstrated how AI-driven solutions can create more ethical, equitable, and supportive work environments. However, careful implementation and ethical oversight are essential to ensure AI's positive impact on the workforce. By leveraging AI responsibly, companies can cultivate a workplace culture where trust and well-being thrive.

AI FOR TRUST AND WELL-BEING

This section presents the findings related to the research objectives and sub-questions regarding AI's role in building trustful work environments and contributing to employee well-being. The results reflect insights drawn from secondary data, including academic literature, reports from industry experts, and firsthand observations.

AI's Role in Enhancing Transparency and Reducing Corruption

AI plays an increasingly vital role in enhancing transparency and mitigating corruption within workplace governance by leveraging cutting-edge technologies to detect, prevent, and address fraudulent activities (PwC, 2023). The integration of AI systems, including machine learning algorithms and natural language processing tools, has significantly reshaped organizational structures by enabling them to monitor a range of activities—from transactions and internal communications to decision-making processes— with a degree of precision and speed that was previously unattainable (Garcia-Segura, 2024). These intelligent systems are capable of analyzing large volumes of data in real time, identifying subtle irregularities, uncovering patterns of fraudulent behavior, and detecting deviations from established ethical guidelines that may otherwise remain hidden or overlooked (Odeyemi et al., 2024).

One of the most profound ways AI contributes to transparency is through its ability to conduct continuous, real-time auditing and reporting. Traditional auditing practices often rely on periodic reviews, which can fail to capture unethical behaviors that occur between audits. In contrast, AI-powered systems provide an ongoing, real-time assessment of financial transactions, operational activities, and employee interactions (Blessing, 2024). These systems can flag inconsistencies, identify suspicious patterns indicative of fraud, and detect misconduct almost immediately after it occurs. For example, AI tools are capable of pinpointing unauthorized fund transfers, detecting procurement irregularities, and identifying conflicts of interest by scrutinizing not only financial records but also employee communication and behavior (Odonkor, Adewale & Olorunyomi, 2021). Such proactive, continuous monitoring ensures that any unethical actions are swiftly identified and addressed, fostering a culture of accountability and transparency within organizations. This shift toward real-time oversight minimizes the risk of corruption going unnoticed and creates an environment in which unethical behavior is swiftly corrected, making it harder for corrupt practices to persist unchecked (Mökander, 2023).

Beyond financial oversight, AI also plays a critical role in supporting ethical decision-making processes within organizations. By leveraging data-driven insights, AI helps leaders and decision-makers align their actions with broader ethical frameworks and corporate social responsibility (CSR) standards (Rodgers et al., 2023). Through predictive analytics, AI systems can assess the potential outcomes of specific decisions, helping decision-makers understand how their actions might impact various stakeholders and ensuring that those decisions adhere to legal, ethical, and regulatory guidelines. This approach not only promotes transparency but also encourages organizations to make decisions that are in the best interest of their employees, customers, and the broader community. Additionally, AI-powered compliance tools help organizations stay up-to-date with regulatory changes by automatically adjusting policies in response to new legal requirements, industry standards, or best practices, ensuring ongoing compliance and ethical governance (Nabeel, 2024).

By embedding AI into the core of governance structures, organizations can reinforce their commitment to operational transparency and strengthen stakeholder confidence. Employees, investors, and the public are more likely to trust institutions that prioritize ethical conduct, fairness, and accountability in their operations. This enhanced transparency helps create a more open and trustworthy organizational culture, where decisions and actions are guided by clear, objective criteria and are subject to continuous scrutiny (Lumenalta, 2024). Furthermore, the integration of AI-driven transparency measures acts as a deterrent to corruption by reducing the opportunities for illicit activities to take root. As AI systems actively monitor for irregularities and misconduct, any potential for fraudulent behavior is detected and rectified quickly, minimizing the chances of corruption going unnoticed. This continuous oversight fosters an environment where ethical behavior is the norm and corrupt practices are less likely to thrive (Osasona et al., 2024).

In essence, the integration of AI into workplace governance represents a transformative shift towards more ethical, transparent, and corruption-resistant organizational practices. The real-time capabilities of AI allow for the immediate identification of unethical behaviors, creating an environment of accountability and integrity (Transparency International, 2022). Furthermore, by enhancing decision-making processes and ensuring compliance with ethical standards and regulations, AI supports organizations in building a reputation for trustworthiness and ethical governance. Ultimately, the implementation of AI technologies not only strengthens operational transparency but also enhances the overall ethical climate within organizations, leading to greater trust from employees, customers, investors, and the public. AI's role in mitigating corruption and promoting transparency is a critical element in shaping the future of ethical workplace governance (Zhao & Gómez Fariñas, 2023).

AI-Driven Systems for Fairness and Trust in Workplace Governance

AI-driven systems have the transformative potential to foster fairness, enhance equity, and strengthen the relationship between employees and management by ensuring that decision-making processes remain impartial and free from biases. One of the primary ways AI can contribute to fairness is through its capacity to process and analyze vast amounts of data without the influence of human prejudices, which are often embedded in traditional decision-making practices (Raza & Guibas, 2024). Human biases can subtly affect critical areas such as hiring, promotion, and performance evaluations, leading to unintentional favoritism or discrimination. AI, however, operates based on data-driven algorithms that assess candidates and employees solely on objective criteria such as qualifications, experience, and past performance metrics (Hughes et al., 2019). This eradicates the impact of unconscious biases related to gender, race, age, or other personal characteristics, ensuring a fairer, more equitable approach to hiring and promotion. By doing so, AI fosters a workplace where individuals are valued for their abilities and contributions rather than superficial traits, leading to the creation of a more diverse and inclusive workforce (Ul Oman, Siddiqua & Noorain, 2024).

Beyond recruitment and performance management, AI also plays a significant role in ensuring the consistent application of organizational policies. AI-powered systems are capable of analyzing employee feedback, satisfaction surveys, and behavioral data to detect areas where biases or inequalities may exist (Abaas & Robbins, 2024). For example, AI can identify discrepancies in pay, opportunities for advancement, or the allocation of resources that may disproportionately affect certain employee groups. Based on these insights, AI can recommend corrective actions and interventions that promote fairness and equity (Omogbeme & Odewuyi, 2024). This proactive approach helps organizations address systemic issues before they escalate, ensuring that policies are not only consistent but also inclusive and aligned with best practices for diversity and equality. Moreover, AI's ability to continuously monitor and analyze data allows organizations to respond quickly to emerging issues and adjust their policies in real time, fostering a more dynamic, adaptive workplace culture (Ferrara, 2024).

As AI becomes more embedded in organizational decision-making processes, employees are likely to develop greater trust in the system, knowing that their career progression and professional development are determined by merit and performance rather than arbitrary decisions or favoritism (Yu & Li, 2022). In environments where AI is used to make promotion decisions or to assess job performance, employees are less likely to feel that decisions are influenced by personal biases or favoritism, resulting in a more transparent, meritocratic work culture. This trust in AI-driven decision-making promotes a sense of fairness and equality among employees, as they feel confident that the outcomes of these processes reflect their true capabilities and contributions (Okatta, Ajayi & Olawale, 2024).

Furthermore, AI's ability to enhance transparency in decision-making also encourages a deeper sense of mutual respect between employees and management. As AI systems provide clear, data-backed insights into the factors influencing decisions, employees can better understand the criteria upon which they are being evaluated (Leoni, et al., 2024). This level of transparency is crucial for fostering trust and creating a sense of inclusion, as employees know that their voices are being heard and their needs are being addressed in a fair and equitable manner. As a result, organizations that leverage AI for decision-making processes create an environment where employees feel more secure in their roles and are more likely to engage in positive, collaborative relationships with their peers and supervisors. The end result is a work culture built not only on fairness and transparency but also on mutual respect, where all individuals are empowered to succeed based on their abilities and contributions, rather than external factors or personal biases (Murire, 2024).

AI Technologies Supporting Employee Well-being and Reducing Stress

AI technologies have emerged as a transformative force in improving employee well-being, contributing significantly to enhanced workplace conditions, reduced stress, and the promotion of a healthier work environment. One of the most notable ways in which AI supports employee well-being is by automating routine, repetitive tasks that are often a source of frustration and burnout for workers (Gamble, 2024). By delegating mundane tasks to AI-powered systems, organizations can reduce the cognitive load placed on employees, freeing them to engage in more complex, intellectually stimulating, and rewarding work. This shift not only makes employees' work more fulfilling but also plays a vital role in alleviating stress, as individuals are no longer bogged down by monotonous or administrative tasks. As a result, employees are better able to focus on tasks that require creativity, problem-solving, and strategic thinking, ultimately fostering a greater sense of satisfaction and accomplishment in their roles (García-Madurga, et al., 2024).

Moreover, the integration of AI-driven tools for time management, project tracking, and resource allocation has proven to be essential in helping employees manage their workloads more effectively. These tools allow individuals to organize tasks, set priorities, and allocate time more efficiently, which ultimately leads to better work-life balance (Rožman, Oreški & Tominc, 2023). AI systems that assess individual workloads and provide personalized recommendations can help employees better manage their time, reducing the likelihood of overwork or excessive stress. Additionally, AI tools equipped with stress indicators can detect early signs of burnout by analyzing changes in employee behavior, work patterns, and productivity. With this information, management can intervene early to provide support, ensuring that employees are not overwhelmed and that potential mental health challenges are addressed before they escalate (Agarwal & Goel, 2024).

In addition to enhancing work organization, AI-powered wellness programs have gained prominence in promoting both physical and mental health in the workplace. These programs leverage wearable devices, mobile apps, and other digital tools to track a wide range of health metrics, including sleep quality, physical activity, heart rate, and stress levels (Gamble, 2024). By collecting and analyzing these data, AI systems offer personalized recommendations that empower employees to make healthier lifestyle choices. For example, AI can suggest workout routines, dietary adjustments, or mindfulness exercises tailored to an individual's health needs (Sood, 2024). By promoting healthier habits and encouraging employees to take proactive steps toward maintaining their physical and mental well-being, AI-driven wellness programs play an essential role in reducing workplace stress and improving overall job satisfaction. In turn, these programs help foster a culture of care and well-being within organizations, which ultimately leads to higher employee engagement and retention (Jangid, 2024).

Furthermore, AI technologies are instrumental in enhancing communication and collaboration within the workplace, particularly in remote or hybrid work environments. AI-powered platforms for virtual meetings, team coordination, and communication have become increasingly essential as more organizations embrace flexible work arrangements (Richter & Richter, 2024). These tools allow employees to stay connected, engaged, and informed regardless of their physical location, thus reducing feelings of isolation and promoting a sense of belonging within the team. AI-enhanced communication platforms facilitate smooth collaboration by providing real-time translation services, organizing meetings more efficiently, and managing schedules. As a result, these technologies support a more connected and collaborative work environment, ensuring that employees have the resources they need to communicate effectively and maintain positive relationships with their colleagues, regardless of geographical boundaries (Aulia & Lin, 2025).

In summary, AI technologies play an integral role in fostering trustful work environments and improving employee well-being across multiple dimensions. By enhancing transparency, AI helps reduce corruption and fosters ethical decision-making, reinforcing the integrity and accountability of organizations (World Economic Forum, 2024). Additionally, AI's ability to mitigate biases and promote objective, data-driven decision-making is key to fostering fairness in the workplace, strengthening trust between employees and management. Finally, AI's contributions to improving workplace conditions—whether through reducing stress, supporting mental and physical health, or enhancing communication and collaboration—are essential for creating a more balanced, supportive, and healthy work environment. When implemented thoughtfully and ethically, AI has the power to significantly enhance both organizational effectiveness and employee satisfaction, making it a vital tool for building stronger, more resilient workplaces (García-Madurga, et al., 2024).

DISCUSSION

The findings of this study underscore the transformative role of Artificial Intelligence (AI) in fostering trustful work environments and enhancing employee well-being. AI's contributions span various dimensions of workplace governance, including transparency, fairness, and stress reduction, aligning with principles of ethical governance and responsible AI implementation. By leveraging AI technologies, organizations can create more equitable, transparent, and supportive workplace environments that enhance employee satisfaction and trust. However, the integration of AI into organizational practices also presents challenges that require careful navigation to ensure its responsible and ethical use. Concerns such as algorithmic bias, data privacy, and the psychological impact of AI-driven decision-making must be addressed to maximize AI's potential benefits while mitigating unintended consequences.

A key contribution of AI is its ability to improve transparency and reduce corruption within organizations. AI systems, particularly those utilizing machine learning algorithms and natural language processing, are highly effective in detecting financial irregularities, fraudulent behaviors, and deviations from ethical business practices in real time (Garcia-Segura, 2024; Osasona et al., 2024). Unlike traditional methods of fraud detection, which often rely on periodic audits and manual inspections, AI-driven fraud detection systems offer continuous monitoring, enabling organizations to identify and address discrepancies as they arise. These systems have proven particularly effective in detecting anomalies in procurement processes, payroll records, and supply chain management, ensuring that financial transactions remain transparent and accountable.

By integrating AI into governance mechanisms, organizations not only enhance operational transparency but also foster trust with stakeholders, demonstrating a commitment to ethical practices and reducing opportunities for misconduct. AI-driven compliance tools further support organizations in adhering to regulatory requirements by automatically updating policies in response to evolving legal frameworks and industry best practices. These findings align with previous research emphasizing AI's ability to strengthen accountability and regulatory compliance. However, despite its advantages, AI-driven transparency measures also raise concerns among employees, particularly regarding workplace surveillance and data privacy. Research indicates that excessive AI monitoring may lead to a sense of distrust among employees, negatively impacting morale and workplace culture (Mökander, 2023). To address these concerns, organizations must strike a balance between AI-driven transparency and protecting individual privacy. This requires clear communication about how AI is used, as well as the implementation of privacy safeguards that ensure employees retain control over their personal data. Future research should explore best practices for integrating AI into governance structures while preserving employee autonomy and trust (Yaqoob & Robbins, 2024).

Another significant impact of AI is its role in fostering fairness within workplace governance. Traditional decision-making processes—such as recruitment, promotions, and performance evaluations—are often subject to unconscious biases, leading to disparities in hiring and career progression (Ul Oman, Siddiqua & Noorain, 2024; Okatta, Ajayi & Olawale, 2024). AI-driven systems mitigate these biases by prioritizing objective criteria, such as competencies, experience, and performance metrics, rather than subjective factors that can be influenced by human prejudices. As a result, AI-driven recruitment and evaluation systems help organizations promote diversity and inclusion by ensuring that hiring and promotion decisions are based on merit rather than personal characteristics.

Additionally, AI technologies can identify patterns of inequality within an organization by analyzing employee feedback, workplace satisfaction surveys, and performance reviews. By detecting disparities in salary distributions, promotion rates, and employee engagement levels, AI can provide recommendations for corrective actions that enhance workplace fairness. These insights empower organizations to implement targeted diversity and inclusion initiatives, fostering an environment where all employees feel valued and have equal opportunities for career advancement.

Despite these advantages, concerns about algorithmic bias remain a critical issue in AI implementation (Murire, 2024). AI systems are only as unbiased as the data they are trained on, and if training data reflect existing societal biases, AI can inadvertently reinforce discrimination rather than eliminate it. To mitigate this risk, organizations must adopt ethical AI frameworks, conduct regular audits of AI-driven decision-making processes, and maintain human oversight to ensure fairness and accuracy. Furthermore, it is essential for organizations to be transparent about how AI models are developed and to actively engage employees in discussions about AI ethics and governance. Employee involvement in the AI implementation process can help build trust and ensure that AI-driven decisions align with organizational values and ethical standards.

AI's potential to improve employee well-being is another crucial finding of this study. By automating routine tasks, AI helps alleviate workload pressures, allowing employees to focus on more meaningful and engaging work. This shift contributes to better work-life balance, reduces stress, and enhances overall job satisfaction (Gamble, 2024; García-Madurga et al., 2024). AI-powered workflow automation tools streamline administrative processes, enabling employees to dedicate more time to creative and strategic tasks that require human insight and expertise.

In addition to optimizing workload management, AI-driven stress management tools and wellness applications provide employees with personalized insights into their mental and physical health. These tools analyze data from wearable devices, workplace behavior patterns, and self-reported assessments to identify early signs of burnout and stress. By offering proactive recommendations—such as adjustments to work schedules, mindfulness exercises, or ergonomic improvements—AI-driven wellness programs support employees in maintaining a healthy work-life balance (Agarwal & Goel, 2024; Jangid, 2024).

While these innovations offer substantial benefits, they also introduce new challenges. Employees may experience anxiety and job insecurity due to the increasing integration of AI into workplace processes. The perception that AI might replace human roles or make certain skill sets obsolete can lead to heightened stress and resistance to AI adoption (Aulia & Lin, 2025). To address these concerns, organizations must implement AI in a manner that complements rather than replaces human employees. Training programs should be developed to help employees adapt to AI-driven workflows, equipping them with the skills necessary to work alongside AI technologies. Moreover, organizations should emphasize the role of AI as an enabler of human potential rather than a substitute for human labor, reinforcing AI's purpose in supporting, rather than diminishing, employee well-being.

Despite AI's promising contributions, ethical challenges remain. Concerns related to data privacy, algorithmic biases, and the lack of human empathy in AI-driven decision-making underscore the need for continuous scrutiny and regulatory oversight (Rodrigues, 2020; Holzinger, Zatloukal & Müller, 2025). To maximize AI's benefits while minimizing its risks, organizations must develop AI governance frameworks that prioritize ethical principles, transparency, and human-centric policies. Future studies should examine the long-term impact of AI on workplace culture and explore strategies for refining AI-driven systems to better align with human values and organizational goals. In summary, the integration of AI into workplace governance has the potential to significantly improve transparency, fairness, and employee well-being. However, to fully realize these benefits while mitigating potential risks, organizations must adhere to ethical principles and ensure that AI systems are implemented with appropriate human oversight. Ethical AI frameworks, regular audits, and employee engagement are essential in building trust and ensuring responsible AI adoption. When thoughtfully integrated, AI can foster a workplace that is not only more efficient and data-driven but also more equitable and supportive of employee well-being.

Theoretical Contributions

The theoretical contributions of this study are significant, as they lie in the integration of Good Governance Theory and the Ethical AI Framework, both of which together offer a thorough and comprehensive perspective on the ethical implementation of AI in workplace governance. Good Governance Theory emphasizes principles such as accountability, transparency, participation, and responsiveness, which are essential for maintaining organizational integrity and ensuring that decision-making processes are fair and just. The Ethical AI Framework complements this by addressing the moral and ethical considerations surrounding AI technologies, focusing on their responsible deployment, potential biases, and alignment with human values. By examining AI through these combined lenses, this study offers valuable insights into how organizations can foster sustainable, inclusive, and ethical practices that not only promote transparency and fairness but also enhance employee well-being. These insights are crucial for developing organizational environments where AI technologies contribute to more equitable outcomes and improve workplace dynamics. Furthermore, the study highlights the importance of addressing the ethical challenges associated with AI adoption, including concerns about data privacy, algorithmic biases, and decision-making accountability. The findings underscore the need for ongoing, robust research and dialogue around AI ethics, emphasizing the importance of ensuring that technological advancements are developed and implemented in ways that are consistent with human values, societal well-being, and the broader goals of creating a positive and inclusive future of work. This dialogue will be pivotal in guiding the responsible integration of AI in various organizational contexts, ensuring that its implementation contributes to meaningful and sustainable improvements in workplace governance and organizational culture.

CONCLUSION

This study explored the transformative role of Artificial Intelligence (AI) in enhancing workplace governance and promoting employee well-being. By examining how AI contributes to transparency, fairness, and employee health, the research highlights its potential to foster trustful environments where ethical practices and well-being are prioritized. AI's capabilities in fraud detection, unbiased decision-making, and stress reduction provide clear benefits to both organizations and employees. As AI technologies continue to evolve, their integration into workplace systems promises further improvements in governance and employee satisfaction. However, careful ethical considerations are essential to ensure responsible use and prevent unintended consequences.

Society Implications

The societal implications of AI in the workplace are far-reaching. As AI reduces corruption and enhances transparency in organizations, it can contribute to broader societal trust in institutions. When AI-driven systems prioritize fairness, inclusivity, and ethical decision-making, they can encourage greater diversity and reduce systemic biases, benefiting marginalized communities. Additionally, AI's potential to improve employee well-being can result in healthier and more productive individuals, contributing to the overall quality of life in society. However, societal concerns regarding data privacy, surveillance, and algorithmic bias must be carefully managed to avoid exacerbating inequalities.

Practical Implications

In practice, organizations can leverage AI to build a more transparent and equitable work environment. Implementing AI systems that focus on fairness and transparency in recruitment, promotions, and performance evaluations can help reduce bias and enhance employee trust in management. AI-powered tools that monitor employee well-being and detect early signs of stress can lead to better work-life balance and reduced burnout, promoting healthier workplaces. For organizations, adopting AI ethically and responsibly can boost employee satisfaction, retention, and organizational loyalty. However, organizations must also ensure that their AI policies are transparent, inclusive, and aligned with ethical standards.

Recommendations

Organizations are encouraged to integrate AI technologies in a way that prioritizes transparency, fairness, and employee well-being. This involves adopting AI tools for decision-making processes that eliminate human biases and ensure equitable treatment across all levels. Additionally, implementing AI-driven wellness programs can be instrumental in promoting employee health and reducing workplace stress. To address ethical concerns, companies should establish clear guidelines for data privacy, regularly audit AI systems for biases, and ensure human oversight in critical decision-making processes. Moreover, involving employees in AI governance discussions will help align technological advancements with human values.

Limitations

This study primarily relies on secondary data, including academic literature and industry reports, which may not fully capture the real-world complexities of AI adoption in diverse organizational settings. Additionally, the ethical challenges associated with AI in the workplace are multifaceted, and the study may not have addressed all possible concerns. The rapid pace of technological advancements also means that the findings may need updating to reflect the most current developments in AI applications. Further empirical research is needed to provide more comprehensive insights into the long-term impact of AI on workplace culture and employee well-being.

Directions for Future Studies

Future research could focus on longitudinal studies to assess the long-term effects of AI implementation on organizational culture, employee performance, and well-being. Studies that incorporate primary data, such as employee surveys or interviews, could provide a more in-depth understanding of how AI is perceived and experienced in real-world workplace settings. Additionally, exploring the intersection of AI and other emerging technologies, such as blockchain or augmented reality, could reveal new dimensions of how technology can contribute to workplace governance. Finally, future studies should continue to examine the ethical implications of AI and propose frameworks to ensure responsible, fair, and inclusive AI practices across all industries.

REFERENCES

Abaas, G., & Robbins, S. (2024, July). Artificial intelligence implementation in human resources: Ethical challenges and performance benefits. https://doi.org/DOI: 10.13140/RG.2.2.20436.21125

Agarwal, P., & Goel, S. (2024). Exploring the impact of artificial intelligence on work-life balance: A secondary data analysis. *Madhya Bharti - Humanities and Social Sciences, 85(14)*, January–June. Retrieved from https://www.researchgate.net/publication/378268820

Antwi, B. O., Adelakun, B., Fatogun, D. T., & Olaiya, O. P. (2024). Enhancing audit accuracy: The role of AI in detecting financial anomalies and fraud. *Finance & Accounting Research Journal*, *6*(6), 1049–1068. DOI: 10.51594/farj.v6i6.1235

Aulia, S. R., & Lin, W.-S. (2025). Embracing the digital shift: Leveraging AI to foster employee well-being and engagement in remote workplace settings in the Asia Pacific region. *Asia Pacific Management Review*, *30*(3), 100339. DOI: 10.1016/j.apmrv.2024.12.003

Awashreh, R. (2018). Palestinian NGOs: External governance, stakeholders, and accountability. *Journal of Governance and Public Policy*, *5*(2). Advance online publication. DOI: 10.18196/jgpp.5296

Awashreh, R. (2024). Be aware: Navigating challenges in AI-driven higher education. *International Journal of Interdisciplinary Educational Studies*, *20*(1), 203–218. DOI: 10.18848/2327-011X/CGP/v20i01/203-218

Awashreh, R. (2024). Be aware: Navigating challenges in AI-driven higher education. *The International Journal of Interdisciplinary Educational Studies*, *20*(1), 203–218. DOI: 10.18848/2327-011X/CGP/v20i01/203-218

Awashreh, R. (2024b). Be aware: Navigating challenges in AI-driven higher education. *The International Journal of Interdisciplinary Educational Studies*, *20*(1), 203–218. DOI: 10.18848/2327-011X/CGP/v20i01/203-218

Awashreh, R. (2025). Omani public governance in the age of artificial intelligence. In *Public governance practices in the age of AI* (pp. 137–166). IGI Global., DOI: 10.4018/979-8-3693-9286-7.ch007

Awashreh, R., & Al Ghunaimi, H. (2024). Navigating burnout in the public sector: Strategies for enhancing employee well-being and organizational performance. *Evolutionary Studies in Imaginative Culture*, *8*(3), 212–225. DOI: 10.70082/esiculture.vi.1855

Awashreh, R., Al Ghunaimi, H., & Hassiba, A. (2025). Leveraging blockchain and smart contracts for advancing sustainability in the GCC's circular economy. *Pakistan Journal of Life and Social Sciences, 23*(1), 4221–4234. DOI: 10.57239/PJLSS-2025-23.1.00334

Awashreh, R., & Al Naqbi, S. (2023). Societal and internal auditing: Establishing good governance framework in Palestinian local governments. *Migration Letters : An International Journal of Migration Studies, 20*(7), 1–22. DOI: 10.59670/ml.v20i7.4254

Awashreh, R., Al-Naqbi, S., & Gharib, M. (2024). Ethical decision making by Arab universities' advisory and shadow committees: Forms of corruption, implications, and solutions. *Kurdish Studies, 12*(1), 4197–4209. DOI: 10.58262/ks.v12i1.301

Awashreh, R., & Hamid, A. A. (2025). The role of entrepreneurial leadership in driving employee innovation: The mediating effect of knowledge sharing. *Cogent Business & Management, 12*(1), 2466812. DOI: 10.1080/23311975.2025.2466812

Awashreh, R., & Ramachandran, B. (2024). Can artificial intelligence dominate and control human beings? *International Research Journal of Multidisciplinary Scope, 5*(4), 427–438. DOI: 10.47857/irjms.2024.v05i04.01569

Awashreh, R., & Ramachandran, B. (2025). A study on ethical implementation of AI in collegiate studies using fuzzy implication. *Pakistan Journal of Life and Social Sciences, 23*(1), 3998–4013. DOI: 10.57239/PJLSS-2025-23.1.00317

Babu, N. S., Marda, K., & Mishra, A., & Edupub Services. (2024). The impact of artificial intelligence in the workplace and its effect on the digital wellbeing of employees. *Journal for Studies in Management and Planning, 10*(4), 1–32. DOI: 10.5281/zenodo.10936348

Bar-Gil, O., Ron, T., & Czerniak, O. (2024). AI for the people? Embedding AI ethics in HR and people analytics projects. *Technology in Society, 77*, 102527. DOI: 10.1016/j.techsoc.2024.102527

Benabou, A., Touhami, F., & Demraoui, L. (2024). Artificial intelligence and the future of human resource management. In *Proceedings of the 2024 International Conference on Intelligent Systems and Computer Vision (ISCV)*. https://doi.org/DOI: 10.1109/ISCV60512.2024.10620146

Bin Rashid, A., & Kausik, M. A. K. (2024). AI revolutionizing industries worldwide: A comprehensive overview of its diverse applications. *Hybrid Advances, 7*, 100277. DOI: 10.1016/j.hybadv.2024.100277

Blessing, M. (2024, October 16). The role of AI in real-time financial reporting and continuous auditing. ResearchGate. https://www.researchgate.net/publication/384971921

Bol, J., Brown, C. V. C., & LaViers, L. (2023). Employee preferences for artificial intelligence-driven performance evaluation systems in a post-COVID-19 workspace. [Working paper]. Tulane University & Grand Valley State University. https://www.utm.utoronto.ca/pac/media/353/download?inline

Boyd, K. (2025, January 15). Fostering employee wellbeing and improving productivity at Microsoft with Microsoft Viva Insights. Microsoft. https://www.microsoft.com/insidetrack/blog/fostering-employee-wellbeing-and-improving-productivity-at-microsoft-with-microsoft-viva-insights/

Chen, Z. (2023). Ethics and discrimination in artificial intelligence-enabled recruitment practices. *Humanities & Social Sciences Communications, 10*, 567. DOI: 10.1057/s41599-023-02079-x

Cheong, H., Lyons, A., Houghton, R., & Majumdar, A. (2023). Secondary qualitative research methodology using online data within the context of social sciences. *International Journal of Qualitative Methods, 22*, 1–19. DOI: 10.1177/16094069231180160

Chhatre, R., & Singh, S. (2024). AI and organizational change: Dynamics and management strategies. *[Preprint]*. https://doi.org/DOI: 10.13140/RG.2.2.16082.98246

Ezeji, C. L. (2024). Artificial intelligence for detecting and preventing procurement fraud. *International Journal of Business Ecosystem and Strategy, 6*(1), 63–73. DOI: 10.36096/ijbes.v6i1.477

Ferrara, E. (2024). Fairness and bias in artificial intelligence: A brief survey of sources, impacts, and mitigation strategies. *Sci, 6*(1), 3. DOI: 10.3390/sci6010003

Friedman, H. H. (2023). Cognitive biases and their influence on critical thinking and scientific reasoning: A practical guide for students and teachers. SSRN *Electronic Journal*. https://doi.org/DOI: 10.2139/ssrn.2958800

Gamble, G. (2024). AI's role in enhancing wellbeing in the workplace and beyond. Global Wellness Institute. https://globalwellnessinstitute.org/global-wellness-institute-blog/2024/05/07/ais-role-in-enhancing-wellbeing-in-the-workplace-and-beyond/

García-Madurga, M.-Á., Gil-Lacruz, A.-I., Saz-Gil, I., & Gil-Lacruz, M. (2024). The role of artificial intelligence in improving workplace well-being: A systematic review. *Businesses, 4*(3), 389–410. DOI: 10.3390/businesses4030024

García-Madurga, M.-Á., Gil-Lacruz, A.-I., Saz-Gil, I., & Gil-Lacruz, M. (2024). The role of artificial intelligence in improving workplace well-being: A systematic review. *Businesses*, *4*(3), 389–410. DOI: 10.3390/businesses4030024

Garcia-Segura, L. A. (2024). The role of artificial intelligence in preventing corporate crime. *Journal of Economic Criminology*, *5*, 100091. DOI: 10.1016/j.jeconc.2024.100091

Hanna, M. G., Pantanowitz, L., Jackson, B., Palmer, O., Visweswaran, S., Pantanowitz, J., Deebajah, M., & Rashidi, H. H. (2025). Ethical and bias considerations in artificial intelligence/machine learning. *Modern Pathology*, *38*(3), 100686. DOI: 10.1016/j.modpat.2024.100686 PMID: 39694331

Holzinger, A., Zatloukal, K., & Müller, H. (2025). Is human oversight to AI systems still possible? *New Biotechnology*, *85*, 59–62. DOI: 10.1016/j.nbt.2024.12.003 PMID: 39675423

Hu, Q. (2023). Unilever's practice on AI-based recruitment. *Highlights in Business Economics and Management*, *16*, 256–263. DOI: 10.54097/hbem.v16i.10565

Hughes, C., Robert, L. P., Frady, K., & Arroyos, A. (2019). Artificial intelligence, employee engagement, fairness, and job outcomes. In *Managing technology and middle- and low-skilled employees* (pp. 61–68). Emerald Publishing Limited., DOI: 10.1108/978-1-78973-077-720191005

IBM. (2021). AI-driven performance evaluation: A step towards fairness. Retrieved from https://www.ibm.com

Islam, T., Khatoon, A., Cheema, A. U., & Ashraf, Y. (2023). How does ethical leadership enhance employee work engagement? The roles of trust in leader and harmonious work passion. *Kybernetes*, *53*(6), 2090–2106. DOI: 10.1108/K-09-2022-1343

Jangid, A. (2024). AI and employee well-being: How artificial intelligence can monitor and improve mental health in the workplace. *International Journal of Advanced Research*, *12*(10), 743–764. DOI: 10.21474/IJAR01/19693

Kayas, O. G. (2023). Workplace surveillance: A systematic review, integrative framework, and research agenda. *Journal of Business Research*, *168*, 114212. DOI: 10.1016/j.jbusres.2023.114212

. Lacmanovic, S., & Skare, M. (2025). Artificial intelligence bias auditing – Current approaches, challenges, and lessons from practice. *Review of Accounting and Finance*, *ahead-of-print*(ahead-of-print). https://doi.org/DOI: 10.1108/RAF-01-2025-0006

Lammie, M. (2025). Improving financial crime programs with AI: How to help implement effective models. PwC. https://riskproducts.pwc.com/insights/improving-financial-crime-programs-with-ai-how-to-help-implement-effective/

Leoni, L., Gueli, G., Ardolino, M., Panizzon, M., & Gupta, S. (2024). AI-empowered KM processes for decision-making: Empirical evidence from worldwide organisations. *Journal of Knowledge Management*, *28*(11), 320–347. DOI: 10.1108/JKM-03-2024-0262

Lumenalta. (2024, October 13). Ethical considerations of AI. Lumenalta Insights. https://lumenalta.com/insights/ethical-considerations-of-ai

Mastercard. (2024, May 22). Mastercard accelerates card fraud detection with generative AI technology. Mastercard. https://www.mastercard.com/news/press/2024/may/mastercard-accelerates-card-fraud-detection-with-generative-ai-technology/

Mensah, G. B. (2023, November). Artificial intelligence and ethics: A comprehensive review of bias mitigation, transparency, and accountability in AI systems. EGRC Africa Regulation Research Consortium. https://doi.org/DOI: 10.13140/RG.2.2.23381.19685/1

Microsoft. (2022). Workplace analytics: Enhancing employee productivity and well-being. Retrieved from https://www.microsoft.com

Modise, J. M. (2023). The impacts of employee workplace empowerment, effective commitment, and performance: An organizational systematic review. *International Journal of Innovative Science and Research Technology*, *8*(7), 3435. https://www.researchgate.net/publication/376260679

Mökander, J. (2023). Auditing of AI: Legal, ethical and technical approaches. *Digital Society : Ethics, Socio-Legal and Governance of Digital Technology*, *2*, 49. DOI: 10.1007/s44206-023-00074-y

Murikah, W., Nthenge, J. K., & Musyoka, F. M. (2024). Bias and ethics of AI systems applied in auditing: A systematic review. *Scientific African*, *25*, e02281. DOI: 10.1016/j.sciaf.2024.e02281

Nabeel, M. Z. (2024). AI-enhanced project management systems for optimizing resource allocation and risk mitigation: Leveraging big data analysis to predict project outcomes and improve decision-making processes in complex projects. *Asian Journal of Multidisciplinary Research & Review*, *5*(5), 53–91. DOI: 10.55662/AJMRR.2024.5502

Novelli, C., Taddeo, M., & Floridi, L. (2024). Accountability in artificial intelligence: What it is and how it works. *AI & Society*, *39*, 1871–1882. DOI: 10.1007/s00146-023-01635-y

. Nyathani, R. (2023). AI in performance management: Redefining performance appraisals in the digital age. *Journal of Artificial Intelligence & Cloud Computing*. https://doi.org/DOI: 10.47363/JAICC/2023(2)134

. Odeyemi, O., Awonuga, K. F., Mhlongo, N. Z., Ndubuisi, N. L., Olatoye, F. O., & Daraojimba, A. I. (2024). The role of AI in transforming auditing practices: A global perspective review. *World Journal of Advanced Research and Reviews, 21(2)*, 0460. https://doi.org/DOI: 10.30574/wjarr.2024.21.2.0460

Odonkor, T. N., Adewale, T. T., & Olorunyomi, T. D. (2021). AI-powered financial forensic systems: A conceptual framework for fraud detection and prevention. *Magna Scientia Advanced Research and Reviews*, *2*(2), 119–136. DOI: 10.30574/msarr.2021.2.2.0055

. OECD. (2024, March 22). Generative AI for anti-corruption and integrity in government: Taking stock of promise, perils and practice [Working paper]. OECD Artificial Intelligence Papers.

Ogunsola, K. O., Balogun, E., & Ogunmokun, A. S. (2025). Enhancing financial integrity through an advanced internal audit risk assessment and governance model. *International Journal of Multidisciplinary Research and Growth Evaluation*, *2*(1), 781–790. DOI: 10.54660/.IJMRGE.2021.2.1.781-790

Okatta, C. G., Ajayi, F. A., & Olawale, O. (2024). Navigating the future: Integrating AI and machine learning in HR practices for a digital workforce. *Computer Science & IT Research Journal*, *5*(4). Advance online publication. DOI: 10.51594/csitrj.v5i4.1085

Oman, Z. U., Siddiqua, A., & Noorain, R. (2024). Artificial intelligence and its ability to reduce recruitment bias. *World Journal of Advanced Research and Reviews*, *24*(1), 551–564. DOI: 10.30574/wjarr.2024.24.1.3054

Oman, Z. U., Siddiqua, A., & Noorain, R. (2024). Artificial intelligence and its ability to reduce recruitment bias. *World Journal of Advanced Research and Reviews*, *24*(1), 551–564. DOI: 10.30574/wjarr.2024.24.1.3054

Omogbeme, A., & Odewuyi, O. (2024, December). Mitigating AI bias in financial decision-making: A DEI perspective. *World Journal of Advanced Research and Reviews*, *24*(3). Advance online publication. DOI: 10.30574/wjarr.2024.24.3.3894

Osasona, F., Amoo, O. O., Atadoga, A., Abrahams, T. O., Farayola, O., & Ayinla, B. S. (2024). Reviewing the ethical implications of AI in decision-making processes. *International Journal of Management & Entrepreneurship Research, 6*(2), 322–335. DOI: 10.51594/ijmer.v6i2.773

Papagiannidis, E., Mikalef, P., & Conboy, K. (2025). Responsible artificial intelligence governance: A review and research framework. *The Journal of Strategic Information Systems, 34*(2), 101885. DOI: 10.1016/j.jsis.2024.101885

PwC. (2023). Impact of artificial intelligence on fraud and scams. PwC UK. https://www.pwc.co.uk/forensic-services/assets/impact-of-ai-on-fraud-and-scams.pdf

Raza, S., & Guibas, L. (2024, July). Artificial intelligence in human resources: Ethical implications and job performance analysis. https://doi.org/DOI: 10.13140/RG.2.2.19631.75680

Reuters. (2018). Amazon scraps secret AI recruiting tool that showed bias against women. Retrieved from https://www.reuters.com

. Richter, A., & Richter, S. (2024, March). Hybrid work – A reconceptualisation and research agenda. i-com, 23(1). https://doi.org/DOI: 10.1515/icom-2023-0027

Rigotti, C., & Fosch Villaronga, E. (2024). Fairness, AI & recruitment. *Computer Law & Security Review, 53*(1), 105966. DOI: 10.1016/j.clsr.2024.105966

Rodgers, W., Murray, J. M., Stefanidis, A., Degbey, W. Y., & Tarba, S. Y. (2023). An artificial intelligence algorithmic approach to ethical decision-making in human resource management processes. *Human Resource Management Review, 33*(1), 100925. DOI: 10.1016/j.hrmr.2022.100925

Rodgers, W., Murray, J. M., Stefanidis, A., Degbey, W. Y., & Tarba, S. Y. (2023). An artificial intelligence algorithmic approach to ethical decision-making in human resource management processes. *Human Resource Management Review, 33*(1), 100925. DOI: 10.1016/j.hrmr.2022.100925

Rodrigues, R. (2020). Legal and human rights issues of AI: Gaps, challenges and vulnerabilities. *Journal of Responsible Technology, 4*, 100005. DOI: 10.1016/j.jrt.2020.100005

Rožman, M., Oreški, D., & Tominc, P. (2023). Artificial-intelligence-supported reduction of employees' workload to increase the company's performance in today's VUCA environment. *Sustainability, 15*(6), 5019. DOI: 10.3390/su15065019

Saatçı, M., Kaya, R., & Ünlü, R. (2024). Resume screening with natural language processing (NLP). *Alphanumeric, 12*(2), 121–140. DOI: 10.17093/alphanumeric.1536577

Salesforce. (2021). AI-powered well-being assistants: Redefining employee care. Retrieved from https://www.salesforce.com

Singh, B., Kaunert, C., & Ravesangar, K. (2024). Artificial intelligence and employee well-being: Projecting psychological and physical healthcare. In *Human resource strategies in the era of artificial intelligence* (pp. [page range]). https://doi.org/DOI: 10.4018/979-8-3693-6412-3.ch005

Soetan, T., & Samuel, T. (2025). The role of AI chatbots in mental health support: Improving accessibility to counseling and psychological care. Lab: Timothy Soetan's Lab. Retrieved from https://www.researchgate.net/publication/390177016

Sood, A. (2024, January 12). Crafting effective wellness plans for employees using AI. Occupational Health & Safety. https://ohsonline.com/Articles/2024/01/12/Crafting-Effective-Wellness-Plans-for-Employees-using-AI.aspx

Su, H., Lu, Y., Lyulyov, O., & Pimonenko, T. (2023). Good governance within public participation and national audit for reducing corruption. *Sustainability, 15*(9), 7030. DOI: 10.3390/su15097030

Thakkar, A., Gupta, A., & De Sousa, A. (2024). Artificial intelligence in positive mental health: A narrative review. *Frontiers in Digital Health, 6*, 1280235. DOI: 10.3389/fdgth.2024.1280235 PMID: 38562663

Transparency International. (2022). The corruption risks of artificial intelligence. Transparency International. https://knowledgehub.transparency.org/assets/uploads/kproducts/The-Corruption-Risks-of-Artificial-Intelligence.pdf

Ul Oman, Z., Siddiqua, A., & Noorain, R. (2024). Artificial intelligence and its ability to reduce recruitment bias. *World Journal of Advanced Research and Reviews, 24*(1), 551–564. DOI: 10.30574/wjarr.2024.24.1.3054

Unilever. (2019). AI-driven hiring: Removing bias in recruitment. Retrieved from https://www.unilever.com

World Economic Forum. (2024, October 14). Why corporate integrity is key to shaping the use of AI. *Emerging Technologies*. Retrieved from https://www.weforum.org/stories/2024/10/corporate-integrity-future-ai-regulation/

Yaqoob, A., & Robbins, S. (2024). Ethical concerns in AI-enhanced job performance metrics in human resources. [Preprint]. https://doi.org/DOI: 10.13140/RG.2.2.36584.28163

Yu, L., & Li, Y. (2022, April). Artificial intelligence decision-making transparency and employees' trust: The parallel multiple mediating effect of effectiveness and discomfort. *Behavioral Sciences (Basel, Switzerland)*, *12*(5), 127. DOI: 10.3390/bs12050127 PMID: 35621424

Zahidi, F., Kaluvilla, B. B., & Mulla, T. (2024). Embracing the new era: Artificial intelligence and its multifaceted impact on the hospitality industry. *Journal of Open Innovation*, *10*(4), 100390. DOI: 10.1016/j.joitmc.2024.100390

Zhao, J., & Gómez Fariñas, B. (2023). Artificial intelligence and sustainable decisions. *European Business Organization Law Review*, *24*, 1–39. DOI: 10.1007/s40804-022-00262-2

Chapter 11
The Evolution of Public Administration in the AI Era

Ankush Joshi
https://orcid.org/0000-0003-0873-3340
COER University, Roorkee, India

ABSTRACT

This chapter explores the transformative impact of Artificial Intelligence (AI) and predictive analytics on public administration. It traces the evolution from traditional bureaucratic governance to AI-powered systems that enhance efficiency, transparency, and responsiveness. The chapter examines how AI automates administrative tasks, supports data-driven decision-making, and enables proactive policy formulation. It presents global case studies across sectors such as smart cities, healthcare, and law enforcement. Ethical concerns, including bias, transparency, and data privacy, are critically analyzed. The chapter concludes with future directions, emphasizing ethical frameworks, human-AI collaboration, and inclusive digital governance for the 21st century.

INTRODUCTION

Public administration, historically characterized by hierarchical structures, codified standards, and manual decision-making procedures, has experienced various phases of transformation in response to increasing political, social, and technical dynamics. The quick incorporation of artificial intelligence (AI) into public sector activities in the twenty-first century has ushered in a new stage of development (Joshi et.al, 2024). AI is transforming how governments comprehend and address

DOI: 10.4018/979-8-3373-3760-9.ch011

complex societal demands, especially in the form of predictive analytics. Public organizations can now make decisions more quickly, accurately, and with data by using machine learning algorithms and massive datasets (Margetts & Dorobantu, 2019). This indicates a change to a more proactive and anticipatory type of governance and represents a substantial break from traditional administrative procedures.

The rise of e-government initiatives over the past 20 years has brought digital tools and platforms to improve service delivery, increase transparency, and improve citizen engagement; however, the introduction of AI represents a more profound change—one that not only digitizes processes but also introduces a layer of intelligence capable of learning, adapting, and optimizing administrative functions in real time (Wirtz, Weyerer, & Geyer, 2019). A subset of AI called predictive analytics enables governments to analyze patterns from historical and real-time data to forecast future events (Joshi et al., 2024), such as demand for public services, infrastructure usage, or potential risks in areas like healthcare, public safety, and disaster management.

There are many advantages for public administration from this AI-driven change. By automating repetitive operations, it improves operational efficiency, lowers human error, and promotes evidence-based policymaking. AI systems, for example, may evaluate traffic patterns to maximize urban mobility planning, forecast health outbreaks to better prepare hospitals, and analyze crime data to more efficiently distribute police resources (Joshi et al., 2025). Furthermore, AI can provide citizens with more timely and customized interactions with government entities by personalizing public services (Kempeneer, 2021). Public administrators must, however, also overcome new obstacles brought about by the incorporation of AI, such as worries about data privacy, algorithmic bias, accountability in automated decision-making, and the possible replacement of human labor.

A helpful framework for comprehending this technical change is provided by the historical development of public administration. Traditional theories of administration, including Max Weber's bureaucratic model, placed a strong emphasis on rule-based structures, hierarchical control, and reason. The New Public Management (NPM) movement came next, aiming to improve the efficiency of public services by implementing private sector techniques including customer orientation and performance evaluation. The role of technology in changing the composition and operations of the public sector has been brought to light more recently by the idea of Digital Era Governance (DEG) (Dunleavy et al., 2006). The next step in this growth is the integration of AI, which combines digital capabilities with predictive insights and intelligent automation.

In this chapter researchers examines how artificial intelligence is changing the fundamental ideas of public management. We look at its historical evolution, the present trends influencing the use of AI in governance (Joshi et.al. 2025), and the consequences for democratic principles, public accountability, and administrative procedures. Along with outlining the skills needed to develop a workforce in the public sector that is prepared for AI, the conversation also takes into account the ethical and legal frameworks essential for responsible AI integration. This chapter attempts to give readers a thorough grasp of the changing relationship between AI and public administration by combining theoretical ideas with real-world examples. This will enable readers to see the opportunities and difficulties that lie ahead.

HISTORICAL EVOLUTION OF PUBLIC ADMINISTRATION

Public administration has undergone tremendous transformation during the past century, adjusting to shifting societal needs, technology breakthroughs, and developing governance philosophies. Traditionally, public administration was anchored in the Weberian bureaucratic paradigm, typified by hierarchical organization, rigid rules and processes, impersonal relationships, and a clear division of work. By encouraging meritocracy and impartiality in administrative procedures, Max Weber believed that bureaucracy was the most effective and logical organizational structure for handling public affairs. But as time went on, complaints surfaced about the inflexibility and ineffectiveness of these bureaucratic structures, particularly in quickly evolving contexts where adaptability and response were essential.

In response to these constraints, the New Public Management (NPM) paradigm emerged in the latter half of the 20th century, drawing heavily from private sector practices to reform the public sector. NPM focused on efficiency, performance measurement, decentralization, cost-effectiveness, and customer orientation (Hood, 1991). Governments started implementing results-oriented strategies, outsourcing services, and instituting managerial accountability mechanisms. Although NPM increased administrative efficiency in many situations, it also raised concerns about transparency, equity, and the deterioration of public sector values like democratic accountability and inclusivity (Dunleavy et al., 2006).

The emergence of e-governance and digital administration was another paradigm change brought about by the internet and digital technology. Through the use of information and communication technology (ICT), e-governance sought to increase transparency, improve service delivery, and increase citizen engagement (Heeks, 2001). Online portals for tax payments, e-tendering, digital identity management, and public grievance redressal systems were made possible by digital tools. In an effort to close the digital divide and make public services more accessible, nations all around the world, including India, have embraced programs like Digital India. Although e-government was a big step in the direction of more inclusive and participatory governance, it also brought to light issues including unequal access to technology, cybersecurity risks, and digital literacy.

With the advent of AI-powered governance in recent years, public administration has advanced to a new level. Government decision-making, resource allocation, and problem-prediction are being revolutionized by artificial intelligence (AI) technologies, especially machine learning and predictive analytics (Wirtz et al., 2019). AI makes it possible to analyze large datasets in real time, which facilitates proactive policymaking in fields like disaster relief, healthcare, urban planning, and education. AI adds a cognitive component, learning from patterns, adjusting to new data, and making recommendations without explicit programming, in contrast to earlier digital technologies that only automated preexisting processes (Margetts & Dorobantu, 2019). This shift represents a shift from administration that is focused on processes to governance that is driven by intelligence.

A comparative overview of these governance paradigms is presented in the table below:

Table 1. Comparative overview of governance paradigms

S.No.	Governance Model	Key Characteristics	Technological Influence
1	**Weberian Bureaucracy**	Hierarchical, rule-based, meritocratic	Minimal (manual and paper-based)
2	**New Public Management**	Efficiency-driven, market-oriented, performance-focused	Introduction of basic ICT tools
3	**E-Governance**	Digitization, transparency, citizen engagement	Internet, databases, ICT integration
4	**AI-Powered Governance**	Data-driven, predictive, real-time decision-making	AI, machine learning, big data

Understanding this historical evolution—from rigid bureaucracies to intelligent systems—is crucial for reimagining the future of public administration in a way that is not only efficient but also equitable and inclusive. While AI-powered governance offers immense potential, it also raises ethical and administrative concerns, such as algorithmic bias, accountability, data privacy, and the need for a digitally skilled public workforce.

AI'S IMPACT ON PUBLIC ADMINISTRATION

Artificial Intelligence (AI) is ushering in a transformative era in public administration by reshaping how governments operate, make decisions, and deliver services to citizens. Through the automation of routine administrative tasks—such as data entry, scheduling, document processing, and initial stages of public grievance redressal—AI significantly reduces manual workload, minimizes human error, and accelerates bureaucratic processes. This automation frees up valuable human resources, allowing public officials to focus on complex, judgment-intensive issues that require critical thinking and stakeholder engagement.

In parallel, AI's ability to process vast datasets in real-time enables more informed and timely decision-making. By leveraging predictive analytics, governments can now identify patterns, forecast outcomes, and implement preventive measures in areas such as healthcare, public safety, urban planning, and resource management. For instance, AI algorithms can predict disease outbreaks, analyze crime hotspots, or optimize traffic flows—allowing administrators to shift from traditional reactive governance models to proactive, data-informed policymaking.

The integration of AI into government functions represents a watershed moment in the evolution of governance. It signals a shift from linear, rule-based systems to dynamic, adaptive frameworks that respond to citizen needs more efficiently and accurately. This paradigm shift not only enhances institutional agility and responsiveness but also redefines the citizen-government relationship by promoting transparency, personalization, and accessibility in public service delivery. In essence, AI is not just improving the mechanics of administration—it is reimagining the very fabric of public governance.

One of the most obvious advantages of AI in the public sector is the automation of administrative duties. Data input, document verification, scheduling, and compliance monitoring are just a few of the repetitive duties that government offices typically do in large quantities. These jobs can now be completed more quickly and accurately because to AI technologies, especially Robotic Process Automation (RPA) (Wirtz et al., 2019). For instance, the U.S. General Services Administration reduces processing time by more than 50% by using AI-based bots to process financial data and provide reports. Similar to this, Estonia's e-government infrastructure reduces the need for human intervention by automating civic procedures like birth registration using AI. Employees of the government may concentrate on higher-order duties like creating policies and interacting with citizens thanks to these efficiencies.

AI has significant ramifications for policymaking through predictive analytics, going beyond automation. AI can detect patterns, create scenarios, and predict results by evaluating vast amounts of both organized and unstructured data, enabling governments to make decisions based on solid evidence. For instance, the "Aarogya Setu" app in India used AI to forecast COVID-19 hotspots, assisting authorities in more efficiently allocating healthcare resources (Budd et al., 2020). Additionally, predictive analytics is employed in environmental management to track the effects of climate change, in urban planning to forecast traffic patterns, and in social welfare programs to identify people that are at risk. By anticipating issues and taking proactive measures, these applications help governments become more resilient and efficient with their resources.

The table below presents 30 global case studies of AI implementation in public services, categorized by sector:

Table 2. Case studies

S.No.	Country	Sector	AI Application
1	USA	Law Enforcement	Predictive policing (e.g., PredPol in Los Angeles)
2	Estonia	Civil Services	AI-driven public service automation
3	UK	Judiciary	AI tool for legal decision support
4	China	Urban Planning	Smart city surveillance and traffic management
5	India	Healthcare	Aarogya Setu for COVID-19 tracking
6	Singapore	Transport	AI for traffic optimization (Smart Mobility 2030)
7	Canada	Immigration	AI-based visa application triaging
8	Australia	Taxation	AI chatbot "Alex" for tax queries
9	UAE	Municipal Services	"Smart Dubai" for city-wide AI integration
10	Finland	Education	AI-based personalized learning platforms
11	Germany	Environment	AI for forest fire detection
12	Japan	Elderly Care	AI-powered robotic assistants
13	South Korea	Disaster Response	AI for early warning systems in natural disasters
14	Netherlands	Water Management	AI-based flood prediction
15	Brazil	Social Services	Predictive analytics for poverty targeting
16	France	Employment	AI for job matching in public labor offices
17	Kenya	Agriculture	AI for crop monitoring and pest detection
18	Israel	Cybersecurity	National AI strategy for cyber threat detection
19	New Zealand	Policing	AI for crime pattern analysis
20	Rwanda	Healthcare	Drones and AI for medical supply delivery
21	Norway	Public Transport	AI for real-time transit route optimization
22	Malaysia	Education	Predictive analytics for student performance
23	Mexico	Social Policy	Data-driven budgeting with AI support
24	Belgium	Tax Compliance	AI to detect tax fraud
25	Indonesia	Public Health	AI for disease outbreak prediction
26	South Africa	Urban Planning	Smart city data analysis in Cape Town
27	Qatar	Infrastructure	AI in smart energy grids
28	Bangladesh	Fisheries	AI for monitoring illegal fishing
29	Italy	Museums	AI-based visitor experience personalization
30	Sweden	Waste Management	AI for recycling and route optimization

The global trend toward intelligent public service ecosystems is best illustrated by these examples. But despite its advantages, AI also presents serious problems, particularly with regard to accountability, transparency, algorithmic bias, and data security (Kumar, R., Joshi, A. et.al. 2024). For instance, because of faulty historical data, predictive police algorithms have been criticized for perpetuating racial biases (Angwin et al., 2016). In a similar vein, to maintain democratic legitimacy and public trust, AI use in decision-making processes needs to be open and explicable.

AI has a profound and wide-ranging effect on public management. AI provides technologies that can greatly increase the caliber, efficacy, and responsiveness of public services, from automating administrative processes to boosting policy effectiveness through predictive insights. However, in order to fully realize its potential, strong ethical frameworks must be established, digital infrastructure must be invested in, and public sector workers must be trained to collaborate with intelligent systems.

CHALLENGES AND ETHICAL CONSIDERATIONS

While incorporating artificial intelligence (AI) into public administration holds great promise for efficiency and creativity, it also poses a number of difficulties and moral conundrums that need to be resolved in order to guarantee accountable, just, and open government. Algorithmic bias, which happens when AI systems educated on biased or skewed data generate unfair or discriminatory results, is one of the biggest problems. Such biases have the potential to worsen socioeconomic inequality in public sector settings like welfare distribution or law enforcement. For instance, research has demonstrated that because of skewed past crime statistics, predictive police tools—like those employed in the US—have disproportionately targeted minority populations (Angwin et al., 2016). This presents significant questions regarding algorithmic decision-making's justice and fairness.

The "black box" problem, which is the lack of explainability and transparency in AI systems, is another important concern. Transparency and accountability are essential for maintaining public trust in government, yet many AI systems—especially those built on deep learning—are intricate and challenging to understand (Wirtz et al., 2019). It may be difficult to challenge or examine AI-driven results since citizens and policymakers may not completely comprehend the decision-making process. In crucial fields with high decision-making stakes, such as healthcare, the legal system, and social services, this opacity is particularly troublesome.

Security and privacy of data are also important issues. Large volumes of personal data, frequently containing private information about behavior, income, or health, are necessary for AI systems to operate efficiently (Singh, B. P. & Joshi, A. 2024). In accordance with data protection rules like the General Data Protection Regulation

(GDPR) in Europe, governments are required to make sure that this data is gathered, stored, and processed in a secure and moral manner (Voigt & Von dem Bussche, 2017). The possibility of data breaches or information misuse can erode public trust and result in serious consequences, such as identity theft or excessive surveillance.

Another significant issue is digital inequality. The use of AI in public services could inadvertently increase the digital gap, especially in underdeveloped nations or underserved areas where access to digital infrastructure is restricted. AI has the potential to exacerbate social inequality rather than lessen it in the absence of inclusive digital policies (Lebovits, H, 2018). Furthermore, people without sufficient digital literacy or access to the required technology may be at a disadvantage when AI is used in job services or education.

The table below summarizes some of the most pressing challenges and associated ethical concerns of AI in public administration:

Table 3. Challenges- AI in public administration

S.No.	Challenge	Description	Ethical Concern
1	Algorithmic Bias	AI reflects biases present in training data	Discrimination, inequality
2	Lack of Transparency	Complex AI models lack explainability	Accountability, due process
3	Data Privacy & Security	Sensitive data may be misused or breached	Consent, surveillance, misuse of data
4	Digital Divide	Unequal access to technology and digital literacy	Exclusion of marginalized groups
5	Job Displacement	Automation may replace human administrative roles	Economic inequality, loss of livelihoods
6	Overreliance on AI	Blind trust in AI outputs without human oversight	Erosion of human judgment, accountability

The possible loss of public sector jobs as a result of automation raises further ethical questions. Particularly for lower-skilled administrative personnel, there is a chance of job loss or role reduction as AI systems take on more and more duties including document review, citizen interaction, and decision assistance (Zuiderwijk et.al, 2021). To guarantee a smooth transition and prevent major disruption, governments must implement plans to retrain workers and reinterpret positions.

And lastly, the problem of regulatory latency. Legal and institutional frameworks frequently find it difficult to keep up with the rapid evolution of AI technologies. As a result, monitoring, enforcement, and standards are compromised. Inconsistent behaviors and technological misuse may result from the lack of explicit ethical standards and governance frameworks for the application of AI in the public sector.

Governance procedures and ethical frameworks are necessary to handle these issues. Governments must make sure that the use of AI systems is transparent, accountable, inclusive, and equitable. This entails carrying out impact analyses, setting up committees dedicated to ethical AI, incorporating a range of stakeholders in the creation of AI policies, and funding public awareness campaigns and online education. Integrating ethical issues into every phase of AI adoption is not only recommended, but also necessary to protect democratic principles and public trust as public administration depends more and more on AI.

FUTURE DIRECTIONS OF AI IN PUBLIC ADMINISTRATION

A future of smarter, more responsive, and citizen-centric government is promised by the expanding and diversifying use of artificial intelligence (AI) in public administration. It is anticipated that adaptive systems, tailored public services, moral governance frameworks, and improved human-AI cooperation would be the main focuses of the upcoming wave of AI adoption in the public sector. In addition to resolving current inefficiencies, these developments will revolutionize public sector operations to satisfy the ever-changing demands of society in the digital age.

The move toward individualized public services is among the most promising avenues. AI-powered systems are starting to provide real-time, customized solutions by customizing services according to citizen data and preferences. AI might be used, for instance, by governments to automatically enroll qualified people in social welfare programs or modify taxes and subsidies in response to changes in income (Sun & Medaglia, 2019). Both service delivery and citizen happiness are enhanced by this shift from one-size-fits-all to tailored governance, especially for underserved or marginalized groups.

The creation of adaptable governance models is another important avenue for the future. AI's real-time analysis of large, complicated datasets will allow for dynamic policymaking that adapts to shifting socioeconomic circumstances. For example, AI can help environmental regulators respond to pollution spikes using sensor data or help urban planners dynamically modify traffic signals based on congestion data (Wirtz et al., 2019). In order to lower risks and enhance results, governments will depend more and more on these systems to model the implications of policy decisions prior to implementation.

AI-powered decision support tools will also play a major role in public management. AI will enhance human administrators' talents by automating repetitive cognitive work and offering greater insights, rather than taking the place of them. AI might help emergency responders select catastrophe responses using real-time geospatial data, or it could help judges by providing recommendations based on precedent. These technologies can improve accuracy, decrease human error, and encourage evidence-based decision-making.

Equally crucial is the focus on ethical AI and legal frameworks. As AI becomes more ingrained in governance, worries about bias, transparency, and accountability will intensify. It will be necessary for public administration in the future to include AI ethics into institutional frameworks, such as by establishing citizen advisory panels, transparency dashboards, and AI audit procedures (Cath, 2018). Governments can also spend money creating AI standards tailored to the public sector that strike a balance between innovation and safeguarding the public interest.

Collaboration between humans and AI will be another important field. Instead of AI taking the place of human administrators, future models will emphasize synergy, with humans providing contextual awareness, empathy, and judgment while AI handles data-intensive jobs. For public employees to work with intelligent technology, this hybrid approach will require new skills and training courses. Employees in the public sector will need to become digitally literate, comprehend algorithmic procedures, and be able to evaluate AI-generated insights in light of larger social and political frameworks. Furthermore, soft skills like communication, ethical reasoning, emotional intelligence, and critical thinking will become more and more important, particularly in positions that call for interpreting policies and engaging citizens. Governments and educational institutions must collaborate to create curricula that incorporate data science, AI ethics, digital innovation, and public administration principles in order to facilitate this shift. Initiatives for lifetime learning and ongoing professional development will be crucial to staying up with the quickly changing technological landscape. Crucially, human-AI cooperation needs to be based on a precise division of roles and duties, with AI acting as a tool to assist in decision-making and human actors bearing ultimate responsibility. By preventing machines from displacing the human-centered core of governance, such a strategy not only improves administrative efficiency but also upholds democratic principles and public trust.

The following table summarizes the future directions of AI in public administration:

Table 4. Future directions of AI in public administration

S.No.	Future Direction	Description	Potential Impact
1	Personalized Public Services	AI tailors services based on individual needs and behaviors	Higher citizen satisfaction, equity
2	Adaptive Governance	Policies and services adjust in real time based on AI insights	Improved policy effectiveness
3	AI-Enhanced Decision Support	Augments human judgment with data-driven recommendations	Better accuracy and speed in decisions

continued on following page

Table 4. Continued

S.No.	Future Direction	Description	Potential Impact
4	Ethical and Transparent AI	Embedding ethics in AI systems and establishing accountability mechanisms	Public trust, fairness, legitimacy
5	Human-AI Collaboration	Combining AI efficiency with human insight	Balanced governance, reduced resistance
6	Predictive Crisis Management	Anticipating and mitigating disasters or socio-economic shocks	Proactive and resilient governance
7	Interoperable Digital Platforms	Integration of AI across various government agencies	Seamless service delivery, reduced duplication

Predictive crisis management will also be given significant attention. Building resilient society will depend heavily on AI's capacity to predict calamities, whether they be economic, natural, or health-related. AI may be used by governments to predict economic downturns, estimate the consequences of pandemics, and pinpoint regions most vulnerable to the effects of climate change. AI-based early warning systems for natural catastrophes have already been implemented in nations like South Korea, establishing a standard for others.

Building interoperable digital ecosystems will be crucial. The future of AI in public administration is focused on developing smarter, more equitable, and more resilient governance systems; this calls for not only technological investment but also institutional transformation, ethical safeguards, and inclusive policy frameworks. With the right strategies, AI can become a cornerstone of democratic, effective, and citizen-centered governance in the decades to come. The true potential of AI in public administration lies in its ability to connect siloed departments and data sources into a unified, intelligent governance system. As governments transition to whole-of-government AI platforms, they must deal with interoperability, cybersecurity, and data governance issues holistically.

CONCLUSION

As we navigate the evolving relationship between Artificial Intelligence (AI) and public administration, it becomes evident that we are at the threshold of a profound transformation—one that redefines the fundamental nature of governance. The integration of AI-driven predictive analytics is not merely a technical enhancement of existing systems; it is a reimagining of how public institutions think, act, and serve.

This transition holds the promise of improving transparency, responsiveness, and efficiency across all levels of government.

However, while the potential benefits are immense, realizing them fully requires a nuanced, multi-dimensional approach. The impact of AI must be understood not only in terms of technological capability but also through the lenses of public values, democratic accountability, and social equity. As such, the future of AI in public administration hinges on striking a careful balance between innovation and governance, autonomy and oversight, and efficiency and ethics.

One critical dimension of this transformation is the cultural shift required within public institutions. Public servants, traditionally trained in bureaucratic processes, must now acquire digital competencies and an understanding of data ethics, algorithmic governance, and AI functionalities. This necessitates widespread investments in capacity building, workforce reskilling, and leadership development to ensure that public sector professionals can effectively collaborate with and supervise intelligent systems. Moreover, fostering a culture of innovation within public institutions will be essential to sustain the momentum of AI adoption.

Another essential factor in ensuring the long-term success of AI-driven public administration is citizen trust. Public perceptions of AI systems—particularly concerns related to surveillance, loss of human touch, or algorithmic bias—must be addressed proactively. Establishing transparent AI governance policies, ensuring public participation in decision-making processes, and promoting algorithmic explainability can help build the public's confidence in AI-powered services. Citizen-centric AI should not only deliver services more efficiently but also empower individuals by enhancing accessibility, personalization, and inclusivity.

The role of interdisciplinary collaboration also becomes increasingly significant. The development and deployment of AI in governance require the joint efforts of data scientists, ethicists, legal experts, sociologists, technologists, and policy-makers. Such collaboration fosters well-rounded solutions that take into account both technical efficacy and societal implications. In this context, academia and civil society have a critical role to play in fostering public dialogue, evaluating AI systems, and developing normative frameworks that promote fairness, accountability, and transparency.

Global experiences have shown that there is no one-size-fits-all approach to AI in public administration. What works in a technologically advanced city-state may not be feasible or culturally appropriate in a developing country with limited digital infrastructure. Therefore, policy transfer and adaptation must be guided by contextual realities, institutional readiness, and resource availability. International cooperation—particularly through knowledge exchange platforms, multilateral organizations, and AI ethics consortia—can accelerate equitable and responsible AI adoption across diverse regions.

The integration of AI also opens opportunities for evidence-based policy experimentation. Governments can leverage AI to simulate the potential outcomes of new regulations, social programs, or infrastructure investments before they are implemented. This "sandbox" approach not only minimizes risks but also facilitates more agile and responsive policy-making. As governments confront increasingly complex challenges such as climate change, public health crises, and social inequality, the ability to anticipate, model, and act in real time becomes indispensable.

However, the transformative journey of AI in public administration is far from linear. It must be approached with humility, continuous learning, and adaptability. Governance frameworks must remain flexible enough to accommodate new AI paradigms, emerging ethical concerns, and rapid technological changes. At the same time, it is imperative to safeguard core democratic values—such as equity, inclusion, participation, and justice—against the unintended consequences of automation and digital governance.

In essence, this chapter argues that the responsible application of AI in public administration is not just a technical challenge, but a deeply ethical and strategic one. It calls for a vision of governance where technology serves humanity—not the other way around. AI should be seen not as a silver bullet but as a tool—one that, when guided by sound policy, robust oversight, and collective wisdom, can greatly enhance the public sector's ability to serve society more effectively and equitably.

To conclude, the future of AI in public administration will be shaped by the decisions we make today. As researchers, policymakers, practitioners, and citizens, we all have a stake in ensuring that the AI revolution in governance unfolds in a manner that is inclusive, ethical, and sustainable. With foresight, collaboration, and a steadfast commitment to public good, AI can become a powerful enabler of the next generation of governance—one that is not only smarter but also fairer, more resilient, and truly transformative.

REFERENCES

Angwin, J., Larson, J., Mattu, S., & Kirchner, L. (2016, May 23). Machine Bias: There's software used across the country to predict future criminals. And it's biased against Blacks. ProPublica. Retrieved from https://www.propublica.org/article/machine-bias-risk-assessments-in-criminal-sentencing

Budd, J., Miller, B. S., Manning, E. M., Lampos, V., Zhuang, M., Edelstein, M., & McKendry, R. A. (2020). Digital technologies in the public-health response to COVID-19. *Nature Medicine, 26*(8), 1183–1192. DOI: 10.1038/s41591-020-1011-4 PMID: 32770165

Cath, C. (2018). Governing artificial intelligence: Ethical, legal and technical opportunities and challenges. *Philosophical Transactions. Series A, Mathematical, Physical, and Engineering Sciences, 376*(2133), 20180080. DOI: 10.1098/rsta.2018.0080 PMID: 30322996

Dunleavy, P., Margetts, H., Bastow, S., & Tinkler, J. (2006). *Digital Era Governance: IT Corporations, the State, and E-Government*. Oxford University Press., DOI: 10.1093/acprof:oso/9780199296194.001.0001

Heeks, R. (2001). Understanding e-Governance for Development (i-Government Working Paper Series, No. 11/2001). Institute for Development Policy and Management, University of Manchester. https://doi.org/DOI: 10.2139/ssrn.3540058

Hood, C. (1991). A public management for all seasons? *Public Administration, 69*(1), 3–19. DOI: 10.1111/j.1467-9299.1991.tb00779.x

Joshi, A., Kumar, V., Chauhan, N., Kumar, A., & Singh, R. K. (2024). *The Intersection of AI, ML, and Industry: A Review of Emerging Trends in Real-World Applications,* 2024 4th International Conference on Advancement in Electronics & Communication Engineering (AECE), GHAZIABAD, India, 2024, pp. 769-773, doi: DOI: 10.1109/AECE62803.2024.10911386

Joshi, A., Kumar, V., Chauhan, N., Kumar, A., & Singh, R. K. (2024). The intersection of AI, ML, and industry: A review of emerging trends in real-world applications. In 2024 4th International Conference on Advancement in Electronics & Communication Engineering (AECE) (pp. 769–773). IEEE. https://doi.org/DOI: 10.1109/AECE62803.2024.10911386

Joshi, A., Kumar, V., Thakur, G., Chauhan, N., & Singh, R. K. (2025). A primer for governance. In Kumar, R., Abdul Hamid, A., Ya'akub, N., Nyamasvisva, T., & Tiwari, R. (Eds.), *Leveraging futuristic machine learning and next-generational security for e-governance* (pp. 45–86). IGI Global Scientific Publishing., DOI: 10.4018/979-8-3693-7883-0.ch003

Joshi, A., Thakur, G., Kumar, V., Singh, Y., & Joshi, D. (2025). Harnessing Big Data Visualization in Bioinformatics: From Data to Discovery. In Choudhury, A., Kaushik, K., Kumar, V., & Singh, B. K. (Eds.), *Cyber-Physical Systems Security. Studies in Big Data* (Vol. 154). Springer., DOI: 10.1007/978-981-97-5734-3_12

Kempeneer, S. (2021). A big data state of mind: Epistemological challenges to accountability and transparency in data-driven regulation. *Government Information Quarterly*, *38*(3), 101578. Advance online publication. DOI: 10.1016/j.giq.2021.101578

Lebovits, H. (2018). Automating inequality: How high-tech tools profile, police, and punish the poor [Review of the book Automating Inequality: How high-tech tools profile, police, and punish the poor, by V. Eubanks]. *Public Integrity*, *21*(4), 448–452. DOI: 10.1080/10999922.2018.1511671

Margetts, H., & Dorobantu, C. (2019, April). Rethink government with AI. *Nature*, *568*(7751), 163–165. DOI: 10.1038/d41586-019-01099-5 PMID: 30967667

Singh, B. P., & Joshi, A. (2024). Ethical Considerations in AI Development. In Kumar, R., Joshi, A., Sharan, H., Peng, S., & Dudhagara, C. (Eds.), *The Ethical Frontier of AI and Data Analysis* (pp. 156–179). IGI Global Scientific Publishing., DOI: 10.4018/979-8-3693-2964-1.ch010

Sun, T. Q., & Medaglia, R. (2019). Mapping the challenges of Artificial Intelligence in the public sector: Evidence from public healthcare. *Government Information Quarterly*, *36*(2), 368–383. DOI: 10.1016/j.giq.2018.09.008

Voigt, P., & von dem Bussche, A. (2017). *The EU General Data Protection Regulation (GDPR): A practical guide*. Springer International Publishing., DOI: 10.1007/978-3-319-57959-7

Wirtz, B. W., Weyerer, J. C., & Geyer, C. (2019). Artificial Intelligence and the Public Sector—Applications and Challenges. *International Journal of Public Administration*, *42*(7), 596–615. DOI: 10.1080/01900692.2018.1498103

Zuiderwijk, A., Chen, Y.-C., & Salem, F. (2021). Implications of the use of artificial intelligence in public governance: A systematic literature review and a research agenda. *Government Information Quarterly, 38*(3), 101577. Advance online publication. DOI: 10.1016/j.giq.2021.101577

Chapter 12
AI-Driven Governance:
Predictive Analytics and Blockchain for Smart Public Administration

R. N. Ravikumar
https://orcid.org/0009-0009-3705-1681
Marwadi University, India

S. Aarthi
https://orcid.org/0009-0006-9064-2091
Marwadi University, India

ABSTRACT

This chapter explores how Artificial Intelligence (AI) and blockchain technologies are transforming public administration into a transparent, efficient, and citizen-centric ecosystem. It examines the role of predictive analytics in enabling proactive decision-making and resource optimization, while blockchain ensures data integrity, trust, and decentralization. Through real-world case studies of Estonia and Singapore, the chapter highlights successful implementations of these technologies in digital identity systems, smart urban planning, and public service delivery. It also addresses ethical, legal, and governance challenges, proposing strategic frameworks for responsible adoption. The chapter offers a roadmap for future-ready, technology-driven governance that is inclusive, accountable, and resilient.

INTRODUCTION

The fast pace of development of Artificial Intelligence (AI) and Blockchain technologies is reshaping the domain of the public administration due to an increased

DOI: 10.4018/979-8-3373-3760-9.ch012

level of transparency and efficiency with the implementation of effective and data-oriented governance. With the power of predictive analytics, especially predictive analytics, AI can be used to find patterns in large volumes of information to predict social behaviors, resource requirements and policy effects and allow governments to transform their approach to the more reactive model of decision-making to a proactive approach. In the meantime, blockchain offers a decentralized system and results in data integrity, traceability, and trust as essential requirements in the areas of identity management, the public procurement system, and voting systems as public services. Collectively, the technologies can provide revolutionary power in the aspect of smart governance through entailing improved service provision, corruption reduction, and citizen participation (Mahammad & Kumar, 2022b). This chapter will discuss synergetic use of AI and blockchain in the sphere of public administration and how to implement them into policy framework, operational planning, and ethical challenges. This aims at setting a background knowledge of how these innovations are influencing a path of governance that is smarter, more accountable and more inclusive.

The Rise of Data-Driven Governance

Over the past few years, due to the numerous advances in digital technologies and the rapid increase in the volume of information, government operations have significantly changed, with the transition toward the concept of data-driven governance. Data analytics has brought public administration to the point where it is able to enhance policy formulation, resource allocations, delivery of better services to the people and tracking the success of program efficiency as they occur. Predictive and proactive models fueled by real-time information are replacing the conventional type of decision-making, which was largely reactive and was largely predicated on past information or anecdotal information.

This reality is spurred by the growth of structured and unstructured data which flow in organised forms as well as non-organised forms provided by different sources and sources such as IoT devices, social media platforms, available databases and citizen interactions. All governments across the globe are becoming cognizant of data as a strategic asset and hence investing in data infrastructures like data lakes, data analytics and digital dashboards to enable them to maximize the potential of data (P. Kumar et al., 2023). Moreover, data-driven governance enables higher accountability and transparency due to the possibility of evidence-based reporting and measurable results of performance. The new paradigm does not sound bad as only that; it contributes to enhanced administration effectiveness and increases the trust geared towards citizens by transforming the services more towards citizen demands and expectations. Therefore, data has taken centre stage in the future of smart and responsive governance systems.

The Strategic Value of AI and Blockchain in Governance

Artificial Intelligence (AI) and Blockchain technologies stand at the forefront of innovations driving the modernization of public administration. AI, through machine learning and predictive analytics, enables governments to uncover hidden patterns, forecast social and economic trends, and automate complex decision-making processes. By doing so, public institutions can anticipate challenges such as health crises, traffic congestion, or resource shortages and take pre-emptive actions. AI-powered systems also enhance public engagement by offering personalized services through chatbots, recommendation systems, and adaptive platforms that cater to individual citizen needs.

Blockchain complements AI by introducing a secure, transparent, and immutable ledger system for storing and verifying data. In sectors such as voting, identity verification, and public procurement, blockchain ensures that records are tamper-proof and accessible, thus minimizing fraud and enhancing public trust. Moreover, smart contracts automate rule-based transactions without human intervention, reducing delays and increasing efficiency in government workflows(R. Kumar et al., 2024). Together, AI and blockchain form a powerful duo for digital transformation in governance. While AI drives intelligence and automation, blockchain enforces integrity and trust. Their combined use supports a decentralized, transparent, and responsive government ecosystem capable of meeting the growing demands of a data-centric and citizen-focused society.

Background of the Study

The fast development in digital technologies radically changed the relationship between governments and citizens, resource management and providing the public services. Conventionally created systems of governance, which are characterized by inefficiencies and slow responsiveness, among other shortcomings, are becoming challenged by the waves of a data-driven world. Artificial Intelligence (AI) and blockchain technology have become one of the most potent instruments that can transform the system of the public administration anew.

With AI, the predictive analytics are being made available to governments to allow a glimpse into the future of trends and risks, and decisions are then being made based on the return of the decisions. The practice is quite different to the historically reactive politics. In the meantime, blockchain brings decentralized and tamper-free structures where data integrity, transparency, and social confidence can be guaranteed, especially in such fields as the management of digital identities, public procurement, and voting (A. Kumar et al., 2024). Combined, these technologies immensely have an opportunity to transform to present smart, safe, and government-centric ecological governance. Nonetheless, the adoption of these high-tech systems is also posing some ethical, legal, privacy of data, and acceptability issues. This paper discusses the role of AI and blockchain in transforming the world of government administration, providing the strategy of implementation, ethical implications, and applying in real life, which can demonstrate the practical opportunities and barriers to next-generation governance.

Literature Review

AI and blockchain have been areas of high scholarly and policymaking interest in the past few years and are already integrated into some aspects of the public administration process. (Srivastava et al., 2025)Looking at AI in governance, studies have pointed out that AI could help in decision-making by using predictive analytics to allow governments to be proactive in meeting their societal needs, better resource distribution, better service delivery and so on (Chohan & Hu, 2020). Real-life applications like pattern identification using large data sets and making real-time predictions have been carried out using machine learning models in important fields like public health, traffic control, and social amenity division (A. Kumar et al., 2025). In parallel, block chain literature focuses on its ability to trust experienced on the systems that are public by promoting transparency, immutability and decentralization of the system (Saxena et al., 2025). Other uses of the technology whereby digital identities, smart contracts, and transparent procurements are promoted are capable of exploiting the technology to decrease fraud and wastage in administrative functions.

The scholars also mention the contribution of blockchain to reinforcement of accountability and strengthening of citizen control over their personal data. The interdisciplinary studies have just begun to interact with the merging of AI and blockchain, so there is the possibility of maintaining a highly potent infrastructure in governing that appears to be secure and intellectually fired up. Nonetheless, the current research literature also considers great challenges, such as bias of algorithms, data privacy risks, ethical concerns, and gaps in regulation (Sagar et al., 2025). Policymakers are increasingly agreeing on the necessity of bipolar governance structures to manage the innovation in harmony with the legal, social, and ethical protection of safety and responsibility of the implementation in the segments of the general interest.

Objectives of the Chapter

To explore the role of AI and predictive analytics in transforming public administration from reactive to proactive decision-making.

- To examine how blockchain technology enhances transparency, data integrity, and decentralization in public service delivery.
- To present implementation strategies for integrating AI and blockchain within existing government frameworks, including infrastructure and workforce readiness.
- To analyze ethical, legal, and governance considerations critical to the responsible deployment of AI-blockchain systems in the public sector.
- To showcase real-world case studies (e.g., Estonia and Singapore) that demonstrate the practical benefits and challenges of smart governance.
- To identify benefits and limitations of predictive tools in public sector applications and how to mitigate associated risks.
- To propose strategic policy guidelines and roadmaps for sustainable and inclusive adoption of emerging technologies in governance.
- To foster a future-ready governance model that is citizen-centric, secure, scalable, and aligned with democratic and human rights principles.

FOUNDATIONS OF PREDICTIVE ANALYTICS IN GOVERNANCE

Predictive analytics in governance is the process of conducting predictive analytics in governance to predict future events and trends associated with the public administration. The opportunities that are promised with the help of predictive models to governments are based on the ability to anticipate the challenges, allocate resources more efficiently, or create policies that are responsive to new needs of the society based on historical data as well as real-time. In contrast to conventional analytics that lack foresight, predictive analytics is forward looking, and therefore helps decision-makers adopt proactive, rather than reactive decisions in their governance.

Predictive analytics involves analyzing data and can be used in practically all areas of public administration-the number of hot spots in a crime center, traffic jams, in certain parts of the city, even disease outbreaks or economic meltdown (Javed et al., 2018). Such insights can help in evidence-based policymaking, enhancement of service delivery and risk management. The success of predictive hermeticity is dependent on the quality, mixed data, and the combination of AI algorithm, which can recognize complex, nonlinear trends. With its smart features that include real-time intelligence, automation and responsiveness, predictive analytics becomes an essential pillar of smart governance, in which governments enable great values to community and to their operations to be performed through digital transformation. Figure 1 illustrates the contrast between conventional analytics marked by reactive decision-making and limited foresight and predictive analytics, which supports a forward-looking, proactive governance approach.

Figure 1. From reactive to proactive: The role of predictive analytics

Understanding Predictive Models for Policy Decisions

Predictive models refer to statistical and machine learning frameworks which are applied to predict the future output given some past and current data. These models help the people in public administration to be able to predict patterns in society, risks, and create more informed and data-supported approaches. Regression analysis, decision trees, neural networks, and ensemble predictive models are common forms of predictive models that can be tailored to answer a variety of policy questions, based on a policy question (such as resource allocation versus public health forecasting). As an example, the regression models can be applied to project the unemployment rates according to the economic indicators, whereas such classification models as decision trees may be aimed at predicting who is likely to miss school or default the loans among the citizens. Such knowledge enables officials to plan interventions more effectively, give funds more effectively and make social programs more efficient. In order to operate, predictive models should be constructed using clean data that are relevant and representative (Johnson et al., 2020). Also, they are to be validated constantly and updated to make them accurate and timely. With the combination of a real-time data-streams, such models enable governments to be fast on their feet and transform previous reactive posture to anticipatory policy formulation. With this, predictive analytics is important as it allows efficient and citizen-centric anticipatory government.

Benefits and Limitations of Predictive Tools

Predictive analytics can be used in a very useful way in public administration facilitating effective and quick decision making. They assist in anticipating patterns like crime incidences, health pandemic, or traffic jam thereby enabling them to plan new resources and distribute services better. It can also be used in customized programs, fraud control, natural disaster management and developmental objectives such as climate adaptation and economic development accuracy (Levenda et al., 2020). Their performance however is affected by the quality and accuracy of input data. Discriminatory or obsolete data may result in un-ideal findings and promote inequalities. Moreover, the lack of transparency and stakeholder trust in terms of opacity of certain AI systems is constrained. Forecasting instruments require human checks and ample governance including ethical rules because of the need of fairness and accountability of the decision-making process (Nurmandi & Younus, 2023). The table 1 presents the main opportunities and risks related to the application of the predictive analytics tools in the context of the government. It offers an impartial summary so that the policymakers, technologists, and administrators can learn the potential transformative nature of using AI-based forecasting systems in the governmental operations as well as limitations surrounding it.

Table 1. Benefits and limitations of predictive analytics tools in public administration

Aspect	Benefits	Limitations
Decision-Making	Enables data-driven, proactive policy decisions	May oversimplify complex social problems if not contextually tuned
Efficiency	Optimizes resource allocation and reduces response time	Dependent on data availability and quality
Service Delivery	Improves personalization and targeting of public services	Risk of excluding marginalized groups if models are biased
Fraud Detection	Identifies anomalies and prevents misuse in public welfare, taxation, etc.	Requires continuous monitoring to avoid false positives/negatives
Scalability	Can be deployed across multiple departments and scaled nationally	High initial investment in infrastructure and expertise

continued on following page

Table 1. Continued

Aspect	Benefits	Limitations
Public Trust	Enhances transparency through measurable outcomes	Opaque models can reduce trust if not explainable or accountable
Policy Planning	Supports long-term forecasting for sectors like health, transport, and environment	Ethical and legal implications regarding surveillance and data usage

BLOCKCHAIN FOR TRANSPARENCY AND DECENTRALIZED GOVERNANCE

The use of blockchain technology has become one of the revolutionary factors in the field of public administration, as it implies the use of a decentralized, unchangeable ledger mechanism with a significantly increased level of transparency, trust, and accountability. In contrast to centralized systems, blockchain provides an opportunity to store information in a distributed network, and records thus created are resistant to changes, trackable, and proved with high security as a result of the consensus-building processes (Ahrweiler et al., 2025). This has a tremendous effect especially in those parts of the government that deal with people like land registration, procurement, identity confirmation, and voting systems where reports of fraud and manipulation of data have always been a challenge.

Blockchain supports citizen trust through the ability to conduct unimpeachable audit trails, eliminating chances of corruption. Smart contracts, contracts executed automatically via computer code inscribed on the blockchain, go further to automate even more administrative procedures like payments of welfare checks or licenses authorization so that they are efficient and follow set rules obviating the presence of any third party. Inclusive governance can also be achieved using blockchain to allow inclusive decisions to be made by the creation of secure digital identities that allow real-time voting by the stakeholders (Pereira et al., 2018). Nevertheless, mainstream adoption would still have difficulty with scalability, regulatory certainty and tech preparedness. Nevertheless, the potential to transform the public sphere through blockchain consists in the possibility to achieve not only more efficient but also much more just, transparent, and accountable to the people they are dealing with, systems.

Key Features of Blockchain Relevant to Public Administration

Blockchain technology provides a bundle of solutions which best suits the requirements of the public administration especially in improving transparency, security, and accountability. Among its most important characteristics is immutability, a transaction or record in the blockchain cannot be changed or discarded. It is thus very suitable in keeping tamper free public records, like land titles, tax filings or social benefits. Another fundamental aspect is transparency so that authorized stakeholders can see records in real time, thus working to prevent corruption and to facilitate auditability (Rao & Manvi, 2023). Decentralization does away with central controlling authority, where the power is shared by different nodes. This minimises single points of failure and improves the flexibility of the system. The security is incorporated with the help of cryptographic algorithms, which is why blockchain has a high resistance to cyber-attacks and frauds. Further, traceability allows all activities on the chain to be recorded in time stamped chronological order leading to a comprehensive and verifiable activity record. These features are strong building blocks of the systems of the government that intend to promote trust and participation of citizens. Whether in voting, licensing or procurement, blockchain can provide a paradigm shift a move towards transparent bureaucracy and citizen-verifiable and citizen-centered systems of governance.

Use of Smart Contracts and Identity Systems

One of the technologies that have brought efficiency in decentralized governance is smart contracts and blockchain identities system. Smart contracts constitute a self-enforcing code on a blockchain to enforce agreed outlines and gets rid of manual control. They are able to simplify such processes in public administration as tax returns, cash transfers or subsidy payment, and approvals of permits. As an example, they can process welfare payment automatically after eligibility is certified and this will make them transparent and curtail the incidences of corruption. In the meantime, blockchain-based digital identity systems offer verifiable and secure IDs that are critical to inclusive governance, particularly among the individuals who are not formally identified. These identities integrate records of various departments, eliminate double up and provide real-time service provision. Additionally, they provide ownership of data to the citizens as a way of encouraging privacy and shares with consent. A combination of such technologies results in an open, trustful, and efficient ecosystem of administration, which is based on automation and responsibility.

IMPLEMENTATION STRATEGIES FOR AI-BLOCKCHAIN SYSTEMS

The imposition of the AI and blockchain systems in the sphere of the public administration presupposes the systematic and multi-stage methodology incorporating the complex of merging the technology, policy, and involvement of the stakeholders. The initial action plan is to provide a transparent governance model that would define positions, roles and data responsibilities, privacy regulations, and compliance channels(Mahammad & Kumar, 2022a). Governments are supposed to recognize the most essential issues in the sphere of the public sector in which the AI-based-predictive models and the blockchain technologies can bring tangible improvements e.g., welfare allocation, fraud prevention, or urban planning. Subsequently, it is important that data infrastructure should be updated so as to provide interoperability across departments and the large data demands of AI systems. At the same time, the selection of blockchain platforms should occur according to scalability, the mechanism of consensus, and the possibility of smart contracts. It is also recommended that they initiate pilot programs in specific regions to prove functionality, determine risks, as well as, user feedbacks. It is also important to have capacity building (Mazzi, 2025). To assist with the sustainability of AI integration, civil servants, data officers and legal advisors should be trained on the ethics of AI, the mechanics of blockchain and cybersecurity. Lastly, citizen input and openness should not be lost (Elliott, 2025). Trust is established and proven through the means of deploying open data initiatives, audit processes, as well as public dashboards, making the use of AI-blockchain solutions compliant with democratic principles and the objective of public service.

Designing Interoperable and Scalable Platforms

The effective implementation of AI and blockchain in undergoing public administration hinges on the creation of interoperable and well-extended platforms. Interoperability makes sure that the data can be safely transferred and processed between multiple government departments, legacy systems, and emerging digital services without using the same type of platform to conduct the transfer. This entails the deployment of open standards, API, and module infrastructures that would enable simple integration and upgrading of technologies without interfering with prevailing operations (Gosain et al., 2023). It must also be scalable particularly in the systems operating at the national level that is required to accommodate a high amount of data and interactions. Blockchain platforms should have the capability of doing a large number of transactions, low latency, and consensus algorithm optimisation. Scalable cloud infrastructure or edge computing solutions are crucial in the case of AI systems so that they can manage the real-time analytics and data-intensive tasks (Mahammad & Kumar, 2023). Further, Data governance, cybersecurity measures, and regulatory compliance necessitate design of the platform. Privacy guarantee of the data given the need to allow data sharing to produce predictive opportunities is another problem, and architectural decisions need to be made carefully. There are also the possibilities of exploring mixed solutions by combining both private and publicly operated block-chains, especially by governments that want flexibility and control. Finally, the infrastructure of digital public services is scalable and interoperable platforms that allow never-ending innovation, cooperation between agencies, and citizen-centric governance in the digital era.

Workforce Readiness and Change Management

Making a shift to AI and blockchain-powered governance involves not only preparing the organizational system in a technological context but the workforce that is prepared, agile, and future-ready. Technical/ethical aspects of these technologies should be comprehended by the public employees. This is initiated through extensive capacity-building initiatives on data literacy, AI modeling, blockchain architecture, cybersecurity and digital ethics. Other than technical training, change management is required to deal with institutional inertia and resistance (Agbese et al., 2021). A great number of the organizations operating in the realm of public sphere are grounded in the principles of traditional workflows which is why it is highly important to develop a culture of innovation and adaptability. Leadership is key in this respect as it drives digital transformation throughout, fosters experimentation and aligns personnel to the strategic vision. The governments should set AI governance bodies, block chain policies and digital transformation teams and encourage team work and reskilling to provide inclusive, efficient and human centered AI-driven Governance.

ETHICAL, LEGAL, AND GOVERNANCE FRAMEWORKS

These frameworks are required by the adoption of AI and blockchain in governance because of their quality and their being ethical, legal, and governance. These guarantee the responsible use of data, the rights of citizens and maintain democratic principles of transparency.

Ethically, governments should tackle issues of algorithm bias and explainability of Artificial Intelligence and loss of privacy of data. The government agencies should embrace ethical usages of AI which include fairness, accountability, inclusivity, and transparency. As far as blockchain is concerned, some of the ethical risks are surveillance exposure, identity abuse, and fairness in receiving the benefits of decentralized services (Batool et al., 2024). Laws Since laws such as the GDPR or the Digital Personal Data Protection Act in India currently exist to protect data, they have to be adapted to the novelties of technology. They may require new laws to govern AI choices in governance, the responsibility in automated systems and to establish communal norms of blockchain smart contracts. Transparency regimes regarding cross-nation transfer of data and identification online also becomes essential.

The governance systems must incorporate the oversight structure and citizen advisory structures and audit to instil compliance and citizen trust (Atmaja, 2025). All these structures support participatory governance and allow constant evaluation of technological effect. In sum, these frameworks should be adjusted to changes in technology to make sure that innovations in the field of public administration are ethical, legal and do not contradict good of the society. Table 2 provides some of the major ethical, legal and governance concepts that should guide the practice of Responsible AI and blockchain implementation in governance, this can be referred to by a legislator, a lawyer or a technologist that designs citizen-friendly and citizen-centric digital governance.

Table 2. AI-blockchain governance - key frameworks

Dimension	Key Considerations	Relevance to AI-Blockchain Governance
Ethical	- Algorithmic fairness - Transparency - Non-discrimination - Explainability	Ensures unbiased decisions, protects citizen rights, and promotes trust in automated systems
Legal	- Data privacy laws (e.g., GDPR) - Liability and accountability - Digital consent	Provides a legal framework for data use, smart contracts, and individual protections
Governance	- Oversight bodies - Public auditability - Citizen redress mechanisms	Ensures accountability, public involvement, and continuous review of tech deployments

Algorithmic Fairness and Accountability in AI Systems

Algorithmic fairness and accountability are also important toward achieving the principle of the technology serving all citizens in an equally beneficial way as AI becomes a part of public administration. Predictive policing, welfare allocation, or service entitlements models powered by AI should not contain any biases that are likely to strengthen unfair social, economic, and racial gaps (Singh et al., 2022). They are based on these biases which in terms of historical information or the way an algorithm has been constructed, give unfair results and, in effect, they can disadvantage members of marginalized groups. To be fair, clear model development, diverse dataset, and frequent auditing will be necessary. Such methods as fairness-aware learning and explainable AI (XAI) may be useful in the detection and elimination of biased decisions (Asrifan et al., 2025). Accountability mechanisms, such as impact assessments, independent oversight, and the right to explanation should also be set in effect by governments so that citizens could comprehend the decision-making processes towards them. The objectives of the non-discrimination, equality, and inclusiveness should inform the AI system in the public sector. The establishment of frameworks of redressal and review, wherein the citizens can contest with such automated decisions, is also important. When fairness and accountability are incorporated into AI governance citizens will acquire trust towards the systems, a sense of legitimacy regarding the systems, and will make sure that the advantages of AI are fairly distributed among all members of society.

Data Privacy and Legal Compliance

When using AI and blockchain in the sphere of public administration, one must be careful about data safety and street-legal regulations. Such technologies are also usually based on the usage of great volumes of personal and sensitive information, and the issue of privacy protection is central. The critical parts of data collection, storage, and processing must be assisted by the governments and be done within the Legal framework, which can be the General Data Protection Regulation (GDPR), Digital Personal Data Protection Act (India) or other regional data protection systems (Ahrweiler et al., 2025). The most common harm that AI systems may have (unless effectively regulated) is invasive surveillance, profiling, or citizens data misuse. Laws and regulations need to specify limits of data usage, require minimum use of data, and must secure them with user consent. Although blockchain increases the level of transparency, its implementation has its problems like the irrevocability of the data and the impossibility of having the right to forget rules (Gao & Janssen, 2020). Data Protection Authorities are to be introduced by the governments, legal standards to be set on AI, and Data Protection Impact Assessment (DPIA) to be held on all the services driven by AI. Both AI algorithms and blockchain architectures have to be constructed with regard to privacy-by-design principles. Finally, the balance between innovation and the legal protection enhances confidence among citizens and a commitment of the digital governance to freedom of individuals and the rule of law.

FUTURE-READY PUBLIC ADMINISTRATION WITH EMERGING TECHNOLOGIES

The future of public administration is covered in adopting changing technologies that generate an agile, inclusive and resilient governance. Quantum computing, edge

AI, Internet of Things (IoT) and Decentralized Autonomous Organizations (DAOs) are some of the innovations that will continue transforming the practice of government and citizen interaction as the digital ecosystem continues to adapt. Quantum computing can have the opportunity of solving many optimization issues within the fields of traffic networks, energy allocation, and climate mapping. Edge AI allows the possibility of real-time decision making at the data generation point that can be used in smart infrastructure of the city and emergency response systems. In the meantime, IoT offers dense, real-time data flow of physical landscapes, leading to predictive governance throughout health, waste management, and monitoring of the environment. The use of the Blockchain technology in the form of DAOs will enable the decentralisation of administrative functions so as to feature more participatory and automated models of governance (Ghosh et al., 2016). With a logical mix, these innovations can create more proactive, citizen-oriented and transparent services provided by the government. In order to turn into future-ready, public institutions should make investments into digital infrastructure, promote partnerships between the state and the business world, continuously transform legal and ethical frameworks. It is not that adoption of these technologies is a strategic option, but rather a need towards establishing responsive, effective, and trusted governance in an ever-interdependent globe.

The Role of Quantum and Edge Computing in Smart Governance

The areas where smart governance is headed next are quantum and edge computing and they provide significantly higher functionality than mainstream digital infrastructure. Quantum computers use quantum bits (qubits) to solve complex problems exponentially quickly with respect to classical computers. In government, it can transform such areas as traffic optimization in cities, epidemic modeling, national security modeling and planning of resource distribution. With a high degree of simulation, governments will be able to model myriad policy options, which increases both long-term planning and crisis management (Agu et al., 2024). In contrast, edge computing instead takes computing closer to where the data are found, i.e., sensors, IoT devices, and mobile terminals, to enforce real-time decision-making at the edge of networks. This is primarily essential in smart cities, disaster management, and environmental monitoring where low latency and localized processing is paramount, as well as in the public transport structure (Hasan et al., 2022). Edge computing improves privacy, bandwidth requirements and decreased reliance on centralized severs by decentralizing data processing. Combined with AI edge computing allows having autonomous systems capable of responding in real-time to the needs of the new population. In combination, quantum and edge computing can achieve the twin advantages of extensive computational capability and immediate actionability to enable governments to create responsive, flexible and robust structures of governance relevant to the needs of today and which are upscale to deal with the demands of tomorrow. The figure 2 highlights key domains where predictive analytics supports governance, including real-time decision-making, epidemic modeling, traffic optimization, autonomous systems, resource distribution, and national security demonstrating its broad utility in smart public administration.

Figure 2. Applications of predictive analytics in public governance

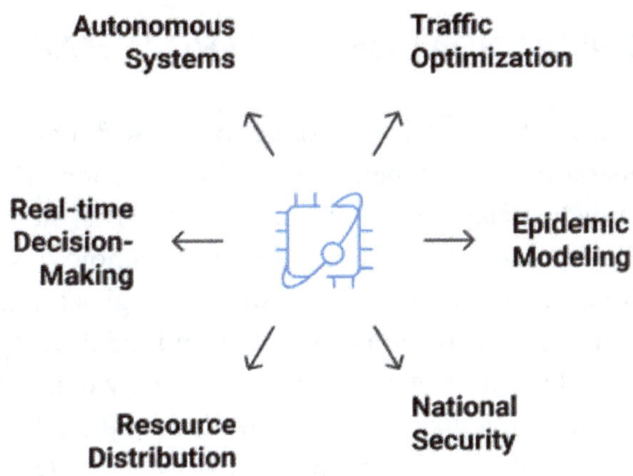

AI-Augmented Decision Support for Policymakers

With the use of AI, policymaking is changing through Decision Support Systems (DSS) that offer real-time, evidence-based guidance to govern complex decision making in government. Such systems apply machine learning, natural language processing, predictive analytics to process unprecedented volumes and diverse data-sets: social media trends, economic indicators, healthcare statistics, and feedback to ensure cross-sector operability. In the context of policymakers, AI-strength DSS provide an instrument to model policy effects, evaluate risk contexts, and maximize resource optimization on numerous variables (Adewusi et al., 2024). This will enable evidence-based governance where decisions are not just determined by gut feeling or past knowledge but are confirmed by unceasing experimentation of existing and predicted statistics (Jobin et al., 2019). Also, the AI will facilitate the regulatory impact assessment, budgeting, and crisis response planning by detecting the trends the human eye can overlook. The tools of visualization based on DSS platforms help to simplify complicated data in favor of transparent communication between the government and people. Nonetheless, these systems have to be constructed with ethical constraints, so there is clarification, bias prevention, and responsibility in auto suggestion. Responsibly implemented, AI-augmented DSS do not cut out the role of human judgment, but enhance it to the status of smarter collaborators to help policymakers make more informed decisions faster and with greater fairness to the common good.

POLICY RECOMMENDATIONS AND ROADMAP

In order to realize the effective introduction of AI/blockchain into the sphere of public administration, governments should implement a visionary policy vision and embrace a launch strategy. It is advisable that the first step be to determine the scope, goal, and governance models of emerging technologies in the public sector which is done through national strategies. Such strategies are expected to focus on interoperability, the standardization of the data and the development of the digital infrastructure in all departments. Second, institute new legal provisions that modernize the data protection legislation, explain the responsibility of algorithms, and identify the blockchain-based documents and smart contracts in the court. These reforms must also be accompanied by the need to trust global norms in order to support international co-operation (Margetts, 2022). Third, make an investment in maintaining capacity by conducting training of civil servants, via digital literacy and ethical awareness. Innovation sandboxes and public-private partnerships may speed up the deployment of pilots and ramp up effective models. Fourth, set up autonomous monitoring and ethical review committees to guarantee responsible use of AI and blockchain technologies, with respect to transparency, inclusion, and privacy. Last, it is recommended that the roadmap is to consist of the short-term pilots, mid-term integration plans, and long-term scaling strategies, and the periodic assessment and citizen feedback loops (Morley et al., 2020). Governments can develop stable and citizen-centric governance systems through consistent policy roadmap using secure and smart technologies.

Strategic Guidelines for AI-Blockchain Adoption

The effective use of AI or blockchain technology in the management of a civil service presupposes the presence of a properly organized implementation plan in which well-defined priorities, scalable architecture, and powerful governance are the premises (Agarwal et al., 2025). Strategic guidelines should start with intensive needs analysis, locating possible areas where the given technologies can bring real value, which can be either fraud detection, predictive welfare delivery, or digital identity verification. Governments are urged to embrace a phased implementation strategy in putting up small scale pilot projects to test possibilities and effectiveness prior to expanded implementation (Socol & Iuga, 2024). The interdepartmental collaboration can also be centralized by creating a central point of coordination inside the government and procurement of technology that should be standardized and regulation must be implemented (Reshi et al., 2023). There should be policies that are technology-neutral and this can allow variances in bringing tools and platforms perceived as most appropriate to the prevailing demands at a given time in the public sector. Ethical AI frameworks, smart contract governance and blockchain interoperability frameworks are needed to avoid segregation. Also vital is the need to develop assessment standards that will be used to measure effectiveness, fairness and efficiency of implemented systems (Wagner et al., 2024). The planning should be both repetitive and dynamic so that the generation of technology and demands should be incorporated swiftly. Through a clear roadmap and set of principles, it will be possible to embrace the power of AI and blockchain in a manner that produces a positive value to the society in a way that does not sacrifice accountability and democratic ethos via institutional compromise.

Building Trust and Public Engagement

The integration of AI and blockchain into the work of governments is also not just a technological problem but a social one whose success depends on the trust of the population and their involvement in the processes. Since the mentioned technologies are used to affect the decision-making and provision of services, due consideration must be given to the fact that citizens need to know how these technologies will operate, which data is being processed, and how their rights are secured. Governments should emphasize transparency when developing trust and AI algorithms and blockchain entries should be scrutinize, explainable, and even auditable (Bai et al., 2022). It involves the use of algorithmic transparency tools, release of impact assessment and the right of explanation of automated decisions to the citizens. People engagement ought to be integrated into the lifecycle of technologies as they are advised to be included in the design of policies to their implementation, and feedback gathering. Engager media through interactive platforms, consultation and literacy campaigns on digital means can promote inclusive contribution, especially across disadvantaged groups that are likely to be left out in the digital transitions (Balcerzak et al., 2022). Creation of citizen advisory boards, open-data programs and grievance redressal systems are other steps which further empower the civic supervision. Governments can foster a culture of digital trust by making intriguing technologies understandable, and citizens engaged as participants (Rathnayake et al., 2022). Finally, the people-centered governance should be of the technology. Feeling informed, empowered and safeguarded, citizens are more likely to lend a hand and make AI-blockchain projects succeed.

CASE STUDY SECTION

Like AI and blockchain technologies, the addition of these technologies into the sphere of public administration is not theoretical anymore, and such countries as Estonia or Singapore have established international standards of proper smart governance as being secure, transparent, and citizen-based. These countries show how with a well-planned approach, digital transformation can change the efficiency and responsiveness and inclusivity of systems of government, revolutionising them. As one of the leading digital governance countries, Estonia has created the X-Road platform the layer of decentralized blockchain-secured data exchange that allows the governments and the private sector to seamlessly and securely interoperate (Beck et al., 2018). The platform supports services, such as digital identity, e-taxation, e-health, e-voting, and lowers the bureaucratic overhead and allows citizens to manage their data. Its success shows the potential how blockchain infrastructure can create trust, improve service delivery and democratic transparency. Comparatively, Singapore has given a lot of emphasis on the use of AI-driven predictive data to manage its cities and to ensure their safety. With the programs of a Smart Nation and predictive policing, Singapore also uses real-time data and AI models to maximize traffic, prevent crime hot areas, and proactively manage public services (Nanayakkara et al., 2021). In the combination, these two case studies can serve as a source of worthy insights into the effective application of AI and blockchain to governance since they present rather different but still complementary models of constructing operating, safe, and structures of public administration.

Case Study 1: Estonia's X-Road and e-Governance System

Estonia is commonly regarded as a world leader when it comes to digitally-based governance, and more than 99% of the governments services in that country are to be found on the internet. At its core is X-Road, the decentralized cross-layer of data exchange supporting a secure messaging platform between state agencies, commercial platforms, and individuals. Governed since 2001, X-Road is the foundation behind Estonia e-Governance by providing interoperability and data integrity and privacy without the need of centralized databases. In 2024, 98% of Estonian citizens had a digital ID that enabled them to have safe access to the services of e-Tax, e-Residency, digital prescriptions, e-Voting, and several others. These solutions save up to 70% of administrative expenses and savings in processing time, and digital signatures save the government an estimated 2% of GDP every year. KSI Blockchain is part of the Estonian infrastructure that provides timestamped, tamper-proof logs of all access to any data or modifications to it (Gottschalg-Duque, 2024). When the data of a citizen is accessed by another citizen or member of the government it is made know to the citizen leading to transparency and control. The introduction of X-Road has also minimized the level of bureaucracy 96% of prescriptions related to medical prescriptions and 95% of tax transactions are handled online. They have also made cross border data exchange possible with other countries, and Finland, in particular, has shown how scalable and collaborative Estonia system can be. The Estonia experience in the context of blockchain and its digital identity systems shows that such an approach may lead to the most efficient, transparent, and citizen-centred public administration (Dwivedi et al., 2021). It has become an example to other countries that want to establish intelligent government systems that do not violate the privacy of citizens yet facilitate smooth service provisions. The Figure 3 visualizes the effectiveness of Estonia's digital governance, highlighting key performance indicators such as 99% online service coverage, 98% digital ID adoption, 70% administrative cost savings, and high digital processing rates for prescriptions (96%) and tax transactions (95%).

Figure 3. Impact of Estonia's X-Road e-Governance System

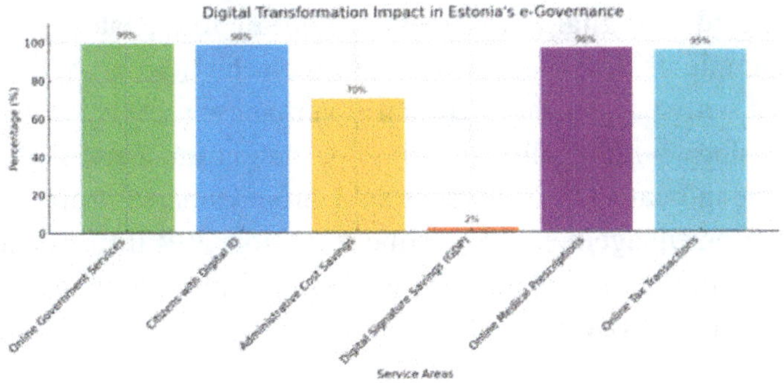

Case Study 2: AI-Powered Predictive Policing and Urban Management in Singapore

Singapore has staked its claim to leading edge city governance through the use of AI and data analytics in the service of public administration as part of the Smart Nation Initiative, which began in 2014. When more than 80% of the whole population dwells in the housing facilities constructed by the government and enjoys the digital services, the AI infrastructure of Singapore has a significant importance in the context of the city planning, safety, and streamlining of the services. A prime example of the flagship technology is the predictive policing system whereby the population density, history of crime, and behavioral models are analyzed through AI which then identifies the high-risk areas. The ministry of home affairs states that predictive patrol routing has achieved more than 15% reduction in some types of crime within the identified districts (Gou & Deng, 2023). Real-time detection of suspicious behaviors is performed with the help of surveillance cameras and AI-based video analytics, which result in a more responsive incident response and more effective allocation of resources. Meanwhile, the AI-enhanced traffic management system in Singapore, employs the usage of sensor networks and machine learning algorithms to regulate the traffic. This has led to 20% efficiency in peak-hour traffic and commutes are minimized by 8-12 minutes on average.

AI can also be used in dealing with wastes and water conservation, with the smart sensors and cigarette predictions models previously increasing the use of resources by 25%. Such solutions have strong backings such as data privacy legislations and responsible AI models such as the Model AI Governance Framework that was published in 2019. Although the issue of surveillance has not yet been eradicated, citizens continue to hold positive attitudes as 84% of people are still happy with the services offered by digital government, according to the latest surveys (Huang, 2023). The example of Singapore shows that with the help of AI it is possible to build intelligent, active, and balanced urban governance systems, which combine the power of technology with legality and civic participation. The Figure 4 illustrates key performance indicators of Singapore's AI-driven smart governance, including 80% public housing engagement, 15% crime reduction, 20% traffic efficiency gains, 10% average commute time savings, 25% resource optimization, and 84% citizen satisfaction with digital government services.

Figure 4. Impact of AI-powered urban governance in Singapore

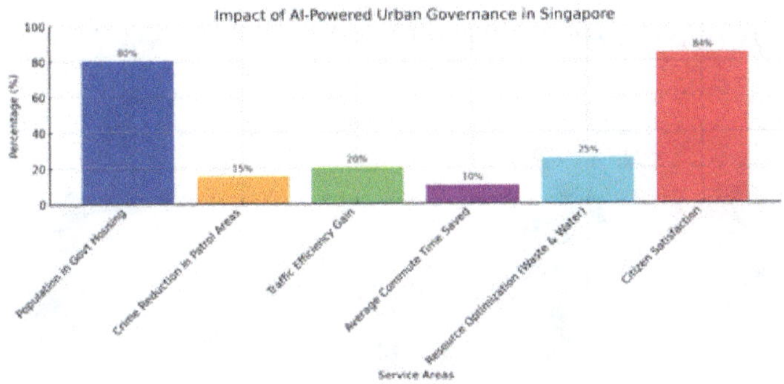

Comparative Analysis: Estonia vs. Singapore in Smart Governance

Estonia and Singapore present two excellent examples of smart governance using the new technologies. In Estonia, blockchain is used in providing 99% of its public services online and at the same time 98% of its population makes use of online IDs. Its network model embraces transparency and the privacy of data. Singapore deploys AI-based predictive analytics through its Smart Nation program to realize a 15% decrease in crime in its focus borders and 20% enhancement in vehicular flow. Whilst Estonia focuses on citizen control and trust through secure and distributed systems, Singapore is focused on dedicated real-time responsiveness and urban efficiencies through integrating AI in a centralized approach, both of which perform exceptionally well in different aspects of digital governments (Khan et al., 2020). The Figure 5 compares key performance metrics of Estonia's blockchain-based governance with Singapore's AI-driven urban management. Estonia leads in online service coverage (99%) and digital ID usage (98%), while Singapore shows strong results in crime reduction (15%), traffic efficiency (20%), and citizen satisfaction (84%), highlighting different strategic strengths in smart governance adoption. The table 3 is a comparison of the two systems of Estonia that the X-Road e-Governance system is and Singapore: AI-enhanced urban governance projects. It brings out the disparities and similarities in the aims, technology orientation, execution, effect, and citizen participation and has important implications on how different models of governance can make use of emerging technologies successfully.

Figure 5. Comparative performance of Estonia and Singapore in smart governance

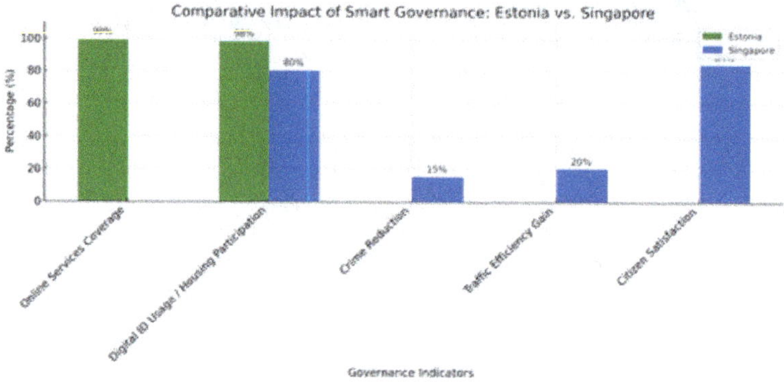

Table 3. Comparison of smart governance models: Estonia vs. Singapore

Aspect	**Estonia: X-Road and e-Governance**	**Singapore: AI-Powered Urban Management**
Primary Focus	Decentralized digital infrastructure and secure data exchange	AI-driven predictive analytics for urban planning and public safety
Key Technology	Blockchain-enabled interoperability (X-Road, KSI Blockchain)	Artificial Intelligence, machine learning, sensor networks
Service Coverage	99% of public services available online	AI applications across traffic, crime prevention, utilities, and surveillance
Citizen Participation	98% digital ID usage; strong control over personal data	84% citizen satisfaction; limited transparency in surveillance systems
Transparency Mechanism	Real-time logs, citizen notification of data access	AI ethics framework; less emphasis on explainability to end users
Efficiency Gains	70% reduction in administrative workload; 2% GDP saved through digital services	20% improvement in traffic efficiency; 15% reduction in crime in targeted areas
Scalability	Cross-border data exchange with Finland and others	National-level AI integration with smart city infrastructure
Ethical Safeguards	Strong privacy-by-design and legal protections	National AI Governance Framework (2019), but surveillance concerns persist

CONCLUSION

Artificial intelligence and blockchain integration in the sphere of public administration should be considered a paradigm shift in the work of the government, its decisions, and interaction with citizens. Relevance of these technologies toward a more transparent, efficient, secure, and citizen-centric governance environment has been discussed in this chapter. With predictive analytics, AI enables public institutions to speculate on social requirements, deploy funds otherwise spent and be prepared to deal with social challenges. Unlike the old models of governance which are based on hindsight data, predictive analytics provides a prospective manner of governance that sharpens responsiveness in policies, provision and delivery of services and agility in operations. And blockchain as a decentralized ledger technology augments AI by integrating trust and accountability in government work.

Be it land registry and digital identity, the procurement and voting blockchain guarantees tamper-proof records, and automation of calculations via smart contracts, as well as citizen data security. It promotes the trust of citizens as it is transparent and can be audited and lessens possibilities of corruption and manipulation. The chapter also underlined the importance of embracing AI and blockchain combination, which promises considerable improvement to the decision-making process and collaborative, data-based policy making in the field of public policy. These technologies cannot do without implementation strategies. The governments need to focus on interoperable platforms, long-term infrastructure as well as capacity building so as to have smooth interrelation between the departments and services. Workforce readiness is also a vital aspect as training civil servants in the field of AI ethics, blockchain security, and change management are necessary to adoption in the institution.

Furthermore, developing ethical, legal, and governance regulations will guarantee that burgeoning technologies are put into practice without restraint. Such challenges as algorithm bias, data privacy, and explainability, as well as regulatory compliance, have to be dealt with in an organized manner to stop undesirable consequences and subserve democratic principles. An example of the successful application of AI and blockchain using different governance models was demonstrated in the comparative case studies of the countries-Estonia and Singapore provided in the chapter. The X-Road system in Estonia shows that blockchain is capable of decentralizing the management of the data and encourage trust, efficiency, and international collaboration. On the other hand, the Smart Nation project in Singapore demonstrates the strength of AI at predictive policing, urban planning, and optimization of the level of public service in real time.

Although the strategies in the two countries (Estonia and Singapore) differ in terms of decentralized trust and citizen control, centralized efficiency and responsiveness, the success of the tailored approaches to digital governance is nonetheless seen in the two countries. Moreover, the chapter closed with the note that one should prepare their future with new technologies like quantum computing, edge AI, and IoT. Such technologies provide governments with powerful innovations in simulation, real-time decision-support and massive automation, unprecedented in the past. The augmented decision support systems that include artificial intelligence are also transforming the relationship between the policymakers and the data to bring more rapid, inclusive, and well-informed policy-making.

Finally, it is the wise use of AI and blockchain that should be entrenched in strategic thinking, ethical vision, and citizen participation. Systems will be alien to public trust where they lack transparency, explanative Ness, inclusiveness, and even compatibility with basic rights. Governments should go beyond being technology users and become custodians of a digital future of the people holding high principles of privacy, justice, and accountability. To sum up, AI and blockchain provide a great chance to reinterpret the area of public administration. The right tools can be used to achieve smarter, more responsive and equitable governance systems built around the needs and right of the people with the right frameworks, infrastructure, and the right kind of societal discourse.

KEY ACHIEVEMENTS AND FUTURE SCOPE OF THE WORK

This chapter has been able to provide an insight into how the potential synergy between AI and Blockchain can be a transforming force in revolutionizing the practice of public administration, focusing on their applicability to the elements concerning predictive governance, transparency, and citizen empowerment. Perhaps the greatest accomplishment is providing evidence of how predictive analytics, fueled by AI, can empower governments to stop making reactive decisions, and start making proactive decisions, thus preferentially allocating all resources, delivering more comprehensive services, and better management of their crises. Also, the incorporation of blockchain makes data secured, accountable, and prevents fraud, especially in applications, like smart contracts, digital identity systems, and safe voting systems. The experience of Estonia and Singapore demonstrates comparative verification based on real-life, showing different, but working examples of AI- and blockchain-based governance. Additionally, the manuscript also describes thorough implementation strategies or measures, including interoperable infrastructures, workforce readiness, and ethical and legal frameworks, which furnish a realistic course of action of transforming the public sector. As a future research direction, the paper speculates the potential move towards the study of next-generation blocks like quantum computing, edge AI, IoT, and Decentralized Autonomous Organizations (DAOs), which shows potential in speeding up computation, real-time decision arbitration and automation of governance. Future scope is also to create the AI augmented DSS to help the policy-makers, the enforceable citizen engagement model as well as the trust mechanisms in the forms of transparency, moral and legal protection. As a whole, the work develops the healthy base of creating a strong, demonstrative, and digitally elevated public management system.

REFERENCES

Adewusi, B. A., Adekunle, B. I., Mustapha, S. D., & Uzoka, A. C. (2024). A conceptual model for responsible AI integration in public-facing digital services and platform governance. *Int. J. Sci. Res. Comput. Sci. Eng. Inf. Technol*, *10*(3), 735–767.

Agarwal, H., Agarwal, S., Husain, F., & Kumar, R. (2025). Next-gen video watermarking with augmented payload: Integrating KAZE and DWT for superior robustness and high transparency. *AppliedMath*, *5*(2), 53.

Agu, E. E., Abhulimen, A. O., Obiki-Osafiele, A. N., Osundare, O. S., Adeniran, I. A., & Efunniyi, C. P. (2024). Discussing ethical considerations and solutions for ensuring fairness in AI-driven financial services. *Int. J. Frontline Res. Multidiscip. Studies*, *3*(2), 1–9.

Ahrweiler, P., & Späth, E. Siqueiros Garcia, J. M., Capellas, B. L., & Wurster, D. (2025). Inclusive technology co-design for participatory AI. In Artificial Intelligence, Simulation and Society (pp. 35–62). Springer Nature Switzerland.

Asrifan, A., Akbar, A., Nur, M., Amu, R. W., & Pajarianto, H. (2025). AI integration in public administration. In *Advances in Public Policy and Administration* (pp. 95–122). IGI Global.

Atmaja, S. A. (2025). Ethical considerations in algorithmic decision-making: Towards fair and transparent AI systems. Riwayat. *Educational Journal of History and Humanities*, *8*(1), 620–627.

Bai, Y., Hu, Q., & Seo, S.-H., & Kang Kyubyung and Lee, J. J. (2022). Public Participation Consortium Blockchain for Smart City Governance. *IEEE Internet of Things Journal*, *9*(3), 2094–2108.

Balcerzak, A. P., & Nica, E., Elżbieta, R., Poliak, M., Klieštik, T., & Sabie, O.-M. (2022). Blockchain technology and smart contracts in decentralized governance systems. *Administrative Sciences*, *12*(3), 96.

Batool, A., Zowghi, D., & Bano, M. (2024). AI governance: A systematic literature review. In *Research Square*.

Beck, R., IT University of Copenhagen, Müller-Bloch, C., King, J. L., IT University of Copenhagen, & University of Michigan. (2018). Governance in the blockchain economy: A framework and research agenda. *Journal of the Association for Information Systems*, *19*, 1020–1034.

Chohan, S. R., & Hu, G. (2020). Success factors influencing citizens' adoption of IoT service orchestration for public value creation in smart government. *IEEE Access : Practical Innovations, Open Solutions*, *8*, 208427–208448.

Dwivedi, V., Norta, A., Wulf, A., Leiding, B., Saxena, S., & Udokwu, C. (2021). A formal specification smart-contract language for legally binding decentralized autonomous organizations. *IEEE Access : Practical Innovations, Open Solutions*, *9*, 76069–76082.

Elliott, M. T. J. (2025). Schools of AI in the public sector: Fairness and accountability concerns. Proceedings of the AAAI/ACM Conference on AI, Ethics, And, 7(2), 11–13.

Gao, Y., & Janssen, M. (2020). Generating value from government data using AI: An exploratory study. In *Lecture Notes in Computer Science* (pp. 319–331). Springer International Publishing.

Ghosh, S., Zheng, Y., Lammers, T., Chen, Y. Y., Fitzmaurice, C., Johnston, S., & Li, J. (2016). Deriving public sector workforce insights: A case study using Australian public sector employment profiles. In *Advanced Data Mining and Applications* (pp. 764–774). Springer International Publishing.

Gosain, M. S., Aggarwal, N., & Kumar, R. (2023). A study of 5G and edge computing integration with IoT- A review. *2023 International Conference on Computational and Sustainable Engineering Solutions(CISES)*, 705–710.

. Gottschalg-Duque, C. (2024, July). Towards the use of blockchain technology in SEI, a Brazilian electronic document and process management tool. Anais Do II Colóquio Em Blockchain e Web Descentralizada(CBlockchain 2024).

Gou, C., & Deng, X. (2023). A blockchain-based security model for cloud accounting data. *International Journal of Ambient Computing and Intelligence*, *14*(1), 1–16.

Hasan, A., Putri, E. R. M., Susanto, H., & Nuraini, N. (2022). Data-driven modeling and forecasting of COVID-19 outbreak for public policy making. *ISA Transactions*, *124*, 135–143. PMID: 33487397

Huang, X. (2023). Review on research of blockchain's impact on bookkeeping, fraud detection and trust of auditing process. Advances in Economics. *Management and Political Sciences*, *22*(1), 60–65.

Javed, B., Khan, Z., & McClatchey, R. (2018). An adaptable system to support provenance management for the public policy-making process in smart cities. *Informatics (MDPI)*, *5*(1), 3.

Jobin, A., Ienca, M., & Vayena, E. (2019). The global landscape of AI ethics guidelines. *Nature Machine Intelligence*, *1*(9), 389–399.

Johnson, P. A., Acedo, A., & Robinson, P. J. (2020). Canadian smart cities: Are we wiring new citizen-local government interactions? *Can. Geogr.*, *64*(3), 402–415.

Khan, Z., Abbasi, A. G., & Pervez, Z. (2020). Blockchain and edge computing–based architecture for participatory smart city applications. *Concurrency and Computation*, *32*(12).

Kumar, A., Bhatia, A., Kumar, S., Kumar, R., & Yadav, V. (2025). Sentimental analysis using natural language processing. *AIP Conference Proceedings*, *3224*, 20054.

Kumar, A., Saini, R., & Kumar, R. (2024). A comparative analysis of machine learning algorithms for breast cancer detection and identification of key predictive features. *TS. Traitement du Signal*, *41*(1).

Kumar, P., Kumar, R., Singh, K. B., & Kumar, M. (2023). Identification of the Problem and Research Methodology. In AI in Education: Ethical Challenges and Opportunities. The Ethical Frontier of AI and Data Analysis (pp. 289–308). IGI Global.

Kumar, R., Hamid, A., Bakar, A., Inayah Binti Yaakub, N., Kumar, P., Kumar, M., & Kumar, R. (2024). *Futuristic E-governance Security with Deep Learning Applications* (Kumar, M., Ed.). IGI Global.

Levenda, A. M., Keough, N., Rock, M., & Miller, B. (2020). Rethinking public participation in the smart city. *Can. Geogr.*, *64*(3), 344–358.

Mahammad, A. B., & Kumar, R. (2022a). Design a Linear Classification model with Support Vector Machine Algorithm on Autoimmune Disease data. 2022 3rd International Conference on Intelligent and Management (ICIEM), 164–169.

Mahammad, A. B., & Kumar, R. (2022b). Progression of Digital Healthcare With Deep Learning and Blockchain Methods for Smart Cities. In Advances in Deep Learning Applications for Smart Cities (pp. 248–266).

Mahammad, A. B., & Kumar, R. (2023). Scalable and security framework to secure and maintain healthcare data using blockchain technology. *2023 International Conference on Computational and Sustainable Engineering Solutions(CISES)*, 417–423.

Margetts, H. (2022). Rethinking AI for good governance. *Daedalus*, *151*(2), 360–371.

Mazzi, F. (2025). AI governance and environmental sustainability. In *Oxford Intersections*. AI in Society. Oxford University PressOxford.

Morley, J., Floridi, L., Kinsey, L., & Elhalal, A. (2020). From what to how: An initial review of publicly available AI ethics tools, methods and research to translate principles into practices. *Science and Engineering Ethics*, *26*(4), 2141–2168. PMID: 31828533

Nanayakkara, S., & Perera, S., Sepani, S., Weerasuriya, G. T., & Bandara, H. M. N. D. (2021). Blockchain and smart contracts: A solution for payment issues in construction supply chains. *Informatics (MDPI)*, *8*(2), 36.

. Nurmandi, A., & Younus, M. (2023). Toward world smart government rank. J. Gov. Polit.

Pereira, G. V., Parycek, P., Falco, E., & Kleinhans, R. (2018). Smart governance in the context of smart cities: A literature review. *Information Polity*, *23*(2), 143–162.

Rao, K. P. N., & Manvi, S. (2023). Survey on electronic health record management using amalgamation of artificial intelligence and blockchain technologies. *Acta Informatica Pragensia*, *12*(1), 179–199.

Rathnayake, I., Wedawatta, G., & Tezel, A. (2022). Smart Contracts in the construction industry: A systematic review. *Buildings (Basel, Switzerland)*, *12*(12), 2082.

Reshi, I., Khan, M., & Shafi, S. Sholla Sahil and Assad, A., & Shafi, H. (2023). AI-powered Smart Contracts: The dawn of web 4. O. In TechRxiv.

Sagar, M. S., & Srivastava, S., Rajeev, K. and Saxena, A. (2025). The evolution of industry 5.0: Harnessing artificial intelligence and communication technology. *AIP Conference Proceedings*, *3224*, 20064.

Saxena, A., Gupta, M., Srivastava, S., & Kumar, R. (2025). Empowering edge computing: The critical role of blockchain in cybersecurity defense. *AIP Conference Proceedings*, *3224*, 20063.

Singh, C. B., Gupta, A., & Kumar, D. R. (2022, April). Diabetes care survey using supervised and unsupervised machine learning. 2022 3rd International Conference on Intelligent and Management (ICIEM).

Socol, A., & Iuga, I. C. (2024). Addressing brain drain and strengthening governance for advancing government readiness in artificial intelligence (AI). *Kybernetes*, *53*(13), 47–71.

Srivastava, S., Ahmed, T., Saxena, A., & Kumar, R. (2025). A novel machine learning hybrid model for heart disease risk assessment. *AIP Conference Proceedings*, *3224*, 20058.

Wagner, J. K., Doerr, M., & Schmit, C. D. (2024). AI governance: A challenge for public health. *JMIR Public Health and Surveillance, 10*, e58358. PMID: 39347615

KEY TERMS AND DEFINITIONS

Algorithmic Fairness: The principle that automated decision-making systems should treat individuals equitably, without bias or discrimination.

Artificial Intelligence (AI): The simulation of human intelligence processes by machines, especially computer systems, including learning, reasoning, and self-correction.

Blockchain: A decentralized digital ledger technology that records transactions across multiple computers so that the record cannot be altered retroactively.

Decentralized Governance: A system where decision-making and service delivery are distributed across multiple nodes or authorities rather than being controlled by a single entity.

Digital Identity: An online or electronic identity that can be used to verify a person's credentials, often secured and authenticated using blockchain or cryptography.

Edge Computing: A computing paradigm that processes data near the source of generation rather than relying on centralized cloud infrastructure.

Interoperability: The ability of different systems, applications, or devices to communicate, exchange, and make use of data effectively and securely.

Predictive Analytics: A branch of data analytics that uses historical data, statistical algorithms, and machine learning techniques to forecast future outcomes or trends.

Quantum Computing: An advanced form of computing that uses quantum-mechanical phenomena like superposition and entanglement to perform operations on data.

Smart Contracts: Self-executing contracts with the terms of the agreement directly written into code and deployed on a blockchain.

Compilation of References

Aazam, M., Zeadally, S., & Harras, K. A. (2018). Fog computing architecture, evaluation, and future research directions. *IEEE Communications Magazine*, *56*(5), 46–52. DOI: 10.1109/MCOM.2018.1700776

Abaas, G., & Robbins, S. (2024, July). Artificial intelligence implementation in human resources: Ethical challenges and performance benefits. https://doi.org/DOI: 10.13140/RG.2.2.20436.21125

Abeywardena, I. S., & Perera, C. (2020). Blockchain-based data integrity architecture for smart agriculture. *Sensors (Basel)*, *20*(18), 5324. Advance online publication. DOI: 10.3390/s20185324 PMID: 32957594

Acharya, S., Khan, H. A. U., Karri, R., & Dvorkin, Y. (2024, February). MaDEV-IoT: Cyberattacks on EV charging can disrupt power grid operation. In *2024 IEEE Power & Energy Society Innovative Smart Grid Technologies Conference (ISGT)* (pp. 1-5). IEEE.

Adejumo, A., & Ogburie, C. (2025). Strengthening finance with cybersecurity: Ensuring safer digital transactions. World Journal of Advanced Research and Reviews, 25.

Adewumi, A. P., & Abasilim, U. D. (2024). Digital Competency and Public Sector Digital Transformation in Nigeria. *ACM International Conference Proceeding Series*, 56–66. DOI: 10.1145/3680127.3680131

Adewusi, B. A., Adekunle, B. I., Mustapha, S. D., & Uzoka, A. C. (2024). A conceptual model for responsible AI integration in public-facing digital services and platform governance. *Int. J. Sci. Res. Comput. Sci. Eng. Inf. Technol*, *10*(3), 735–767.

Adkisson, R. (2008). Nudge: Improving Decisions About Health, Wealth and Happiness, R.H. Thaler, C.R. Sunstein. Yale University Press, New Haven (2008), 293 pp. *The Social Science Journal*, *45*, 700–701. DOI: 10.1016/j.soscij.2008.09.003

Agarwal, H., Agarwal, S., Husain, F., & Kumar, R. (2025). *Next-Gen Video Watermarking with Augmented Payload : Integrating KAZE and DWT for Superior Robustness and High Transparency*. 1–25.

Agarwal, P., & Goel, S. (2024). Exploring the impact of artificial intelligence on work-life balance: A secondary data analysis. *Madhya Bharti - Humanities and Social Sciences, 85(14)*, January–June. Retrieved from https://www.researchgate.net/publication/378268820

Agarwal, H., Agarwal, S., Husain, F., & Kumar, R. (2025). Next-gen video watermarking with augmented payload: Integrating KAZE and DWT for superior robustness and high transparency. *AppliedMath*, *5*(2), 53. DOI: 10.3390/appliedmath5020053

Agu, E. E., Abhulimen, A. O., Obiki-Osafiele, A. N., Osundare, O. S., Adeniran, I. A., & Efunniyi, C. P. (2024). Discussing ethical considerations and solutions for ensuring fairness in AI-driven financial services. *Int. J. Frontline Res. Multidiscip. Studies*, *3*(2), 1–9.

Ahmed, B., Shabbir, H., Naqvi, S. R., & Peng, L. (2024). Smart agriculture: Current state, opportunities, and challenges. *IEEE Access : Practical Innovations, Open Solutions*, *12*, 12345–12359. DOI: 10.1109/ACCESS.2024.3356789

Ahmed, S. (2025). Enhancing Data Security and Transparency: The Role of Blockchain in Decentralized Systems. International Journal of Advanced Engineering. *Management Science*, *11*(1), 593258.

Ahrweiler, P., & Späth, E. Siqueiros Garcia, J. M., Capellas, B. L., & Wurster, D. (2025). Inclusive technology co-design for participatory AI. In Artificial Intelligence, Simulation and Society (pp. 35–62). Springer Nature Switzerland.

Ahsan, M. M., & Siddique, Z. (2022). Industry 4.0 in healthcare: A systematic re- view. *International Journal of Information Management Data Insights*, *2*(1), 100079. DOI: 10.1016/j.jjimei.2022.100079

Ajayi, A. J., Agbede, O. O., Akhigbe, E. E., & Egbuhuzor, N. S. (2024). Enhancing Public Sector Productivity with AI-Powered SaaS in E-Governance Systems Article Info Received : 03-12-2023 Accepted : 04-01-2024 Page No : 1243-1259. *International Journal of Multidisciplinary Research and Growth Evaluation*, 1243–1259.

Alabdulatif, A. (2025). GuardianAI: Privacy-preserving federated anomaly detection with differential privacy. . *Array (New York, N.Y.)*, *26*, 100381.

Alahe, M. A., Wei, L., Chang, Y., Gummi, S. R., Kemeshi, J., Yang, X., & Sher, M. (2024). Cybersecurity in smart agriculture: Threat types, current status, and future trends. *Computers and Electronics in Agriculture, 226*, 109401. Advance online publication. DOI: 10.1016/j.compag.2024.109401

Al-Ansi, A. M., Garad, A., Jaboob, M., & Al-Ansi, A. (2024). Elevating e-government: Unleashing the power of AI and IoT for enhanced public services. *Heliyon, 10*(23). Advance online publication. DOI: 10.1016/j.heliyon.2024.e40591 PMID: 39654738

Alcadipani, R., Cabral, S., Fernandes, A., & Lotta, G. (2020). Street-level bureaucrats under COVID-19: Police officers' responses in constrained settings. *Administrative Theory & Praxis, 0*(0), 1–10. DOI: 10.1080/10841806.2020.1771906

Alcaraz, C., & Zeadally, S. (2018). Critical infrastructure protection: Requirements and challenges for the Internet of Things. *Journal of Network and Computer Applications, 110*, 41–60. DOI: 10.1016/j.jnca.2018.02.008

Alharbi, F., Hussain, F. K., & Hussain, O. K. (2020). Trust-based decision making for smart contracts in IoT. *IEEE Internet of Things Journal, 7*(5), 3991–4004. DOI: 10.1109/JIOT.2020.2970643

Ali Syed, T., Alzahrani, A., Jan, S., Siddiqui, M. S., Nadeem, A., & Alghamdi, T. (2019). A comparative analysis of blockchain architecture and its applications: Problems and recommendations. *IEEE Access : Practical Innovations, Open Solutions, 7*, 176838–176869. DOI: 10.1109/ACCESS.2019.2957660

Aljumah, A., & Ahanger, T. A. (2020). Cyber security threats, challenges and defence mechanisms in cloud computing. *IET Communications, 14*(7), 1185–1191. DOI: 10.1049/iet-com.2020.0083

Almesafri, A., & Habes, M. (2023). Understanding the Use of Artificial Intelligence (AI) for Human Resources in the Dubai Government. *Lecture Notes in Networks and Systems, 620 LNNS*, 417–428. DOI: 10.1007/978-3-031-26953-0_39

Alqahtani, A. H. (2024). An incremental hybrid adaptive network-based IDS in Software Defined Networks to detect stealth attacks. *arXiv preprint.* /arXiv.2404. 01109DOI: 10.48550

Aluga, M. A. (2020). Coronavirus Disease 2019 (COVID-19) in Kenya: Preparedness, response and transmissibility. *Journal of Microbiology, Immunology, and Infection, 2019*(April), 2019–2021. DOI: 10.1016/j.jmii.2020.04.011 PMID: 32331980

Alwakeel, A. M. (2021). An overview of fog computing and edge computing security and privacy issues. *Sensors (Basel), 21*(24), 8226. Advance online publication. DOI: 10.3390/s21248226 PMID: 34960320

Alzoubi, M. M. (2024). Investigating the synergy of Blockchain and AI: enhancing security, efficiency, and transparency. Journal of Cyber Security Technology, 1-29.

Andrikopoulos, S., & Johnson, G. (2020). The Australian response to the COVID-19 pandemic and diabetes – Lessons learned. *Diabetes Research and Clinical Practice, 165*, 108246. DOI: 10.1016/j.diabres.2020.108246 PMID: 32502693

Angwin, J., Larson, J., Mattu, S., & Kirchner, L. (2016, May 23). Machine Bias: There's software used across the country to predict future criminals. And it's biased against Blacks. ProPublica. Retrieved from https://www.propublica.org/article/machine-bias-risk-assessments-in-criminal-sentencing

Antoun, J., Kabir, M. E., Moussa, B., Atallah, R., & Assi, C. (2020). A detailed security assessment of the EV charging ecosystem. *IEEE Network, 34*(3), 200–207. DOI: 10.1109/MNET.001.1900300

Antwi, B. O., Adelakun, B., Fatogun, D. T., & Olaiya, O. P. (2024). Enhancing audit accuracy: The role of AI in detecting financial anomalies and fraud. *Finance & Accounting Research Journal, 6*(6), 1049–1068. DOI: 10.51594/farj.v6i6.1235

Apostolaki, M., Zohar, A., & Vanbever, L. (2017). *Hijacking bitcoin: Routing attacks on cryptocurrencies. In 2017 ieee symposium on security and privacy (sp).*, DOI: 10.1109/SP.2017.29

Arora, A., Vats, P., Tomer, N., Kaur, R., Saini, A. K., Shekhawat, S. S., & Roopak, M. (2024). Data-Driven Decision Support Systems in E-Governance: Leveraging AI for Policymaking. *Lecture Notes in Networks and Systems, 844*, 229–243. DOI: 10.1007/978-981-99-8479-4_17

Ashton, K. (2009). That 'Internet of Things' thing. *RFID Journal, 22*(7), 97–114.

Asrifan, A., Akbar, A., Nur, M., Amu, R. W., & Pajarianto, H. (2025). AI integration in public administration. In *Advances in Public Policy and Administration* (pp. 95–122). IGI Global.

Atkinson, C. (2020). G20 leaders must answer to COVID-19. *Science, 368*(6487), 111. DOI: 10.1126/science.abc1025 PMID: 32273441

Atmaja, S. A. (2025). Ethical considerations in algorithmic decision-making: Towards fair and transparent AI systems. Riwayat. *Educational Journal of History and Humanities, 8*(1), 620–627.

Attard-Frost, B., Brandusescu, A., & Lyons, K. (2024). The governance of artificial intelligence in Canada: Findings and opportunities from a review of 84 AI governance initiatives. *Government Information Quarterly*, *41*(2). Advance online publication. DOI: 10.1016/j.giq.2024.101929

Atzori, L., Iera, A., & Morabito, G. (2010). The Internet of Things: A survey. *Computer Networks*, *54*(15), 2787–2805. DOI: 10.1016/j.comnet.2010.05.010

Aulia, S. R., & Lin, W.-S. (2025). Embracing the digital shift: Leveraging AI to foster employee well-being and engagement in remote workplace settings in the Asia Pacific region. *Asia Pacific Management Review*, *30*(3), 100339. DOI: 10.1016/j.apmrv.2024.12.003

Awashreh, R. (2018). Palestinian NGOs: External governance, stakeholders, and accountability. *Journal of Governance and Public Policy*, *5*(2). Advance online publication. DOI: 10.18196/jgpp.5296

Awashreh, R. (2024). Be aware: Navigating challenges in AI-driven higher education. *International Journal of Interdisciplinary Educational Studies*, *20*(1), 203–218. DOI: 10.18848/2327-011X/CGP/v20i01/203-218

Awashreh, R. (2025). Omani public governance in the age of artificial intelligence. In *Public governance practices in the age of AI* (pp. 137–166). IGI Global., DOI: 10.4018/979-8-3693-9286-7.ch007

Awashreh, R., & Al Ghunaimi, H. (2024). Navigating burnout in the public sector: Strategies for enhancing employee well-being and organizational performance. *Evolutionary Studies in Imaginative Culture*, *8*(3), 212–225. DOI: 10.70082/esiculture.vi.1855

Awashreh, R., Al Ghunaimi, H., & Hassiba, A. (2025). Leveraging blockchain and smart contracts for advancing sustainability in the GCC's circular economy. *Pakistan Journal of Life and Social Sciences*, *23*(1), 4221–4234. DOI: 10.57239/PJLSS-2025-23.1.00334

Awashreh, R., & Al Naqbi, S. (2023). Societal and internal auditing: Establishing good governance framework in Palestinian local governments. *Migration Letters : An International Journal of Migration Studies*, *20*(7), 1–22. DOI: 10.59670/ml.v20i7.4254

Awashreh, R., Al-Naqbi, S., & Gharib, M. (2024). Ethical decision making by Arab universities' advisory and shadow committees: Forms of corruption, implications, and solutions. *Kurdish Studies*, *12*(1), 4197–4209. DOI: 10.58262/ks.v12i1.301

Awashreh, R., & Hamid, A. A. (2025). The role of entrepreneurial leadership in driving employee innovation: The mediating effect of knowledge sharing. *Cogent Business & Management, 12*(1), 2466812. DOI: 10.1080/23311975.2025.2466812

Awashreh, R., & Ramachandran, B. (2024). Can artificial intelligence dominate and control human beings? *International Research Journal of Multidisciplinary Scope, 5*(4), 427–438. DOI: 10.47857/irjms.2024.v05i04.01569

Awashreh, R., & Ramachandran, B. (2025). A study on ethical implementation of AI in collegiate studies using fuzzy implication. *Pakistan Journal of Life and Social Sciences, 23*(1), 3998–4013. DOI: 10.57239/PJLSS-2025-23.1.00317

Aysolmaz, B., Müller, B., & Meacham, D. (2023). The public perceptions of algorithmic decision-making systems: Results from a large-scale survey. *Telematics and Informatics, 79*, 101954. DOI: 10.1016/j.tele.2023.101954

Babšek, M., Ravšelj, D., Umek, L., & Aristovnik, A. (2025). Artificial intelligence adoption in public administration: An overview of top-cited articles and practical applications. *AI, 6*(3), 44. https://doi.org/10.3390/ai6030044

Babu, N. S., Marda, K., & Mishra, A., & Edupub Services. (2024). The impact of artificial intelligence in the workplace and its effect on the digital wellbeing of employees. *Journal for Studies in Management and Planning, 10*(4), 1–32. DOI: 10.5281/zenodo.10936348

Baharmand, H., Saeed, N., Comes, T., & Lauras, M. (2021). Developing a framework for designing humanitarian blockchain projects. *Computers in Industry, 131*, 103487. DOI: 10.1016/j.compind.2021.103487

Bai, Y., Hu, Q., & Seo, S.-H., & Kang Kyubyung and Lee, J. J. (2022). Public Participation Consortium Blockchain for Smart City Governance. *IEEE Internet of Things Journal, 9*(3), 2094–2108.

Bakir, V., Laffer, A., McStay, A., Miranda, D., & Urquhart, L. (2024). On manipulation by emotional AI: UK adults' views and governance implications. *Frontiers in Sociology, 9*. Advance online publication. DOI: 10.3389/fsoc.2024.1339834 PMID: 38912311

Balcerzak, A. P., & Nica, E., Elżbieta, R., Poliak, M., Klieštik, T., & Sabie, O.-M. (2022). Blockchain technology and smart contracts in decentralized governance systems. *Administrative Sciences, 12*(3), 96.

Banik, S., Kothamali, P. R., & Dandyala, S. S. M. (2024). Strengthening cybersecurity in edge computing with machine learning. *Revista de Inteligencia Artificial en Medicina, 15*(1), 332–364.

Bar-Gil, O., Ron, T., & Czerniak, O. (2024). AI for the people? Embedding AI ethics in HR and people analytics projects. *Technology in Society*, *77*, 102527. DOI: 10.1016/j.techsoc.2024.102527

Basnet, M., & Ali, M. H. (2023). Deep reinforcement learning-driven mitigation of adverse effects of cyber-attacks on electric vehicle charging station. *Energies*, *16*(21), 7296. Advance online publication. DOI: 10.3390/en16217296

Batool, A., Zowghi, D., & Bano, M. (2024). AI governance: A systematic literature review. In *Research Square*.

Beck, R., IT University of Copenhagen, Müller-Bloch, C., King, J. L., IT University of Copenhagen, & University of Michigan. (2018). Governance in the blockchain economy: A framework and research agenda. *Journal of the Association for Information Systems*, *19*, 1020–1034.

Begum, A., & Kumar, D. R. (2022). *Design a Linear Classification model with Support Vector Machine Algorithm on Autoimmune Disease data*. DOI: 10.1109/ICIEM54221.2022.9853182

Benabou, A., Touhami, F., & Demraoui, L. (2024). Artificial intelligence and the future of human resource management. In *Proceedings of the 2024 International Conference on Intelligent Systems and Computer Vision (ISCV)*. https://doi.org/ DOI: 10.1109/ISCV60512.2024.10620146

Benfarhat, I., Goh, V. T., Siow, C. L., Sheraz, M., & Chuah, T. C. (2025). Temporal convolutional network approach to secure Open Charge Point Protocol (OCPP) in electric vehicle charging. *IEEE Access*. Advance online publication.

Bennett, C., & Raab, C. (2003). *The Governance of Privacy: policy instruments in global perspective.*

Berlan, D. (2010). Street-level Bureacracy. *Guidance Note*, *5*, 1–5.

Bhanye, J., & Shayamunda, R. (2024). *The Promise of Civic-Tech: Digital Technologies and Transparent, Accountable Governance BT - Digitalisation and Public Policy in Africa : GovTech and CivicTech Innovations* (G. Onyango & G. Karuri-Sebina (ed.); hal. 93–122). Springer Nature Switzerland. DOI: 10.1007/978-3-031-75079-3_5

Bhattar, P. L., & Pindoriya, N. M. (2024). False data injection attack with max-min optimization in smart grid. *Computers & Security*, *140*, 103761. Advance online publication. DOI: 10.1016/j.cose.2024.103761

Bhumichai, D., Smiliotopoulos, C., Benton, R., Kambourakis, G., & Damopoulos, D. (2024). The convergence of artificial intelligence and blockchain: The state of play and the road ahead. *Information (Basel), 15*(5), 268.

Bielawski, R., Gaynier, R., Ma, D., Lauzon, S., & Weimerskirch, A. (2020). *Cybersecurity of firmware updates* (Report No. [). U.S. Department of Transportation, National Highway Traffic Safety Administration.]. *DOT HS, 812*, 807.

Bin Rashid, A., & Kausik, M. A. K. (2024). AI revolutionizing industries worldwide: A comprehensive overview of its diverse applications. *Hybrid Advances, 7*, 100277. DOI: 10.1016/j.hybadv.2024.100277

Binns, R. (2018). A survey of predictive policing and machine learning techniques for law enforcement. *International Journal of Law, Crime and Justice, 56*, 65–78. DOI: 10.1016/j.ijlcj.2018.07.003

Blessing, M. (2024, October 16). The role of AI in real-time financial reporting and continuous auditing. ResearchGate. https://www.researchgate.net/publication/384971921

Boholm, Å. (2019). Lessons of success and failure: Practicing risk communication at government agencies. *Safety Science, 118*(May), 158–167. DOI: 10.1016/j.ssci.2019.05.025

Bol, J., Brown, C. V. C., & LaViers, L. (2023). Employee preferences for artificial intelligence-driven performance evaluation systems in a post-COVID-19 workspace. [Working paper]. Tulane University & Grand Valley State University. https://www.utm.utoronto.ca/pac/media/353/download?inline

Bonduki, M. R. P. C., & Cunha, M. A. (2022). Coordination of the Digital Transformation of Governments in Federalist Context: Hierarchy, Markets and Network-Based Instruments? Effects on Subnational Governments? digital service delivery. *ACM International Conference Proceeding Series*, 528–533. DOI: 10.1145/3560107.3560315

Bonomi, F., Milito, R., Zhu, J., & Addepalli, S. (2012). Fog computing and its role in the Internet of Things. In *Proceedings of the First Edition of the MCC Workshop on Mobile Cloud Computing* (pp. 13–16). ACM. https://doi.org/DOI: 10.1145/2342509.2342513

Bose, S., Sharma, P., & Kumar, R. (2022). Edge computing in smart agriculture. *IoT Edge Systems Journal, 7*(3), 45–56.

Boyd, K. (2025, January 15). Fostering employee wellbeing and improving productivity at Microsoft with Microsoft Viva Insights. Microsoft. https://www.microsoft.com/insidetrack/blog/fostering-employee-wellbeing-and-improving-productivity-at-microsoft-with-microsoft-viva-insights/

Bozdal, M., Samie, M., Aslam, S., & Jennions, I. (2020). Evaluation of CAN Bus security challenges. *Sensors (Basel)*, *20*(8), 2364. Advance online publication. DOI: 10.3390/s20082364 PMID: 32326272

Brodkin, E. Z. (2008). Accountability in Street-Level Organizations. *International Journal of Public Administration*, *31*(3), 317–336. DOI: 10.1080/01900690701590587

Brummer, M., & Ueno, H. (2024). Crisis and choice in digital transformation: COVID-19 and the punctuated politics of government DX in Japan. *Asia Pacific Journal of Public Administration*, *46*(4), 360–391. DOI: 10.1080/23276665.2023.2282472

Budd, J., Miller, B. S., Manning, E. M., Lampos, V., Zhuang, M., Edelstein, M., & McKendry, R. A. (2020). Digital technologies in the public-health response to COVID-19. *Nature Medicine*, *26*(8), 1183–1192. DOI: 10.1038/s41591-020-1011-4 PMID: 32770165

Buterin, V. (2013). Ethereum white paper. *Google Scholar, 1*, 22–23. https://github.com/ ethereum/wiki/wiki/White-Paper

Calado, S., & Veloso, C. M. (2025). Artificial Intelligence in Accounting. In *Empowering Value Co-Creation in the Digital Era* (pp. 75–102). IGI Global., DOI: 10.4018/979-8-3373-1742-7.ch004

Camilleri, M. A. (2024). Artificial intelligence governance: Ethical considerations and implications for social responsibility. *Expert Systems: International Journal of Knowledge Engineering and Neural Networks*, *41*(7). Advance online publication. DOI: 10.1111/exsy.13406

Cao, Y., Xiao, C., Cyr, B., Zhou, Y., Park, W., Rampazzi, S., & Mao, Z. M. (2019, November). Adversarial sensor attack on LiDAR-based perception in autonomous driving. In *Proceedings of the 2019 ACM SIGSAC Conference on Computer and Communications Security* (pp. 2267–2281). ACM. ,

Cardoso, H. R., da Silva, L. G., & Melo, B. L. A. (2022). E-government: Administrative morality and the new public arena of the network society. *Law of Justice Journal*, *36*(1), 45–73. DOI: 10.5335/rjd.v36i1.13461

Carter, L., & Bélanger, F. (2005). The utilization of e-government services: Citizen trust, innovation and acceptance factors. *Information Systems Journal*, *15*(1), 5–25. https://doi.org/https://doi.org/10.1111/j.1365-2575.2005.00183.x

Cath, C. (2018). Governing artificial intelligence: Ethical, legal and technical opportunities and challenges. *Philosophical Transactions. Series A, Mathematical, Physical, and Engineering Sciences, 376*(2133), 20180080. DOI: 10.1098/rsta.2018.0080 PMID: 30322996

Chang, V., Golightly, L., Modesti, P., Xu, O. A., Le Minh, T. D., Hall, K., & Kobusińska, A. (2022). A survey on intrusion detection systems for fog and cloud computing. *Future Internet, 14*(3), 89. Advance online publication. DOI: 10.3390/fi14030089

Cheng, S. C., Chang, Y. C., Fan Chiang, Y. L., Chien, Y. C., Cheng, M., Yang, C. H., Huang, C. H., & Hsu, Y. N. (2020). First case of Coronavirus Disease 2019 (COVID-19) pneumonia in Taiwan. *Journal of the Formosan Medical Association, 119*(3), 747–751. DOI: 10.1016/j.jfma.2020.02.007 PMID: 32113824

Chen, Y. Z., Huang, Z. G., Xu, S., & Lai, Y. C. (2015). Spatiotemporal patterns and predictability of cyberattacks. *PLoS One, 10*(5), e0124472. Advance online publication. DOI: 10.1371/journal.pone.0124472 PMID: 25992837

Chen, Y.-C., & Ahn, M. J. (2023). Artificial intelligence and public values: Value impacts and governance in the public sector. *Sustainability, 15*(6), 4796. https://doi.org/10.3390/su15064796[REMOVED HYPERLINK FIELD]

Chen, Z. (2023). Ethics and discrimination in artificial intelligence-enabled recruitment practices. *Humanities & Social Sciences Communications, 10*, 567. DOI: 10.1057/s41599-023-02079-x

Cheong, H., Lyons, A., Houghton, R., & Majumdar, A. (2023). Secondary qualitative research methodology using online data within the context of social sciences. *International Journal of Qualitative Methods, 22*, 1–19. DOI: 10.1177/16094069231180160

Chhatre, R., & Singh, S. (2024). AI and organizational change: Dynamics and management strategies. *[Preprint]*. https://doi.org/DOI: 10.13140/RG.2.2.16082.98246

Chik, W. B., & Sugumaran, H. (2024). Legal governance of artificial intelligence in healthcare devices and services in Singapore. In *Research Handbook on Health, AI and the Law: Research Handbooks in Health and Medical Law* (hal. 373–391). DOI: 10.4337/9781802205657.00030

Chlingaryan, A., Sukkarieh, S., & Whelan, B. (2018). Machine learning approaches for crop yield prediction and nitrogen status estimation in precision agriculture: A review. *Computers and Electronics in Agriculture, 151*, 61–69. DOI: 10.1016/j.compag.2018.05.012

Chohan, S. R., & Hu, G. (2020). Success factors influencing citizens' adoption of IoT service orchestration for public value creation in smart government. *IEEE Access : Practical Innovations, Open Solutions*, *8*, 208427–208448.

Christidis, K., & Devetsikiotis, M. (2016). Blockchains and smart contracts for the Internet of Things. *IEEE Access : Practical Innovations, Open Solutions*, *4*, 2292–2303. DOI: 10.1109/ACCESS.2016.2566339

Commission, E. (2019). *Ethics Guidelines for Trustworthy AI*. https://ec.europa.eu/digital-strategy/our-policies/european-approach-artificial-intelligence_en

Commission, E. (2021). *Proposal for a Regulation Laying Down Harmonised Rules on Artificial Intelligence (Artificial Intelligence Act)*. https://digital-strategy.ec.europa.eu/en/library/proposal-regulation-laying-down-harmonised-rules-artificial-intelligence

Criado, J. I., & O.de Zarate-Alcarazo, L. (2022). Technological frames, CIOs, and Artificial Intelligence in public administration: A socio-cognitive exploratory study in Spanish local governments. *Government Information Quarterly*, *39*(3). Advance online publication. DOI: 10.1016/j.giq.2022.101688

Dahri, N., Yahaya, N., Al-Rahmi, W., Aldraiweesh, A., Alturki, U., Almotairi, S., Shutaleva, A., & Soomro, R. B. (2024). Extended TAM based acceptance of AI-Powered ChatGPT for supporting metacognitive self-regulated learning in education: A mixed-methods study. *Heliyon*, *10*, e29317. DOI: 10.1016/j.heliyon.2024.e29317 PMID: 38628736

Das, O., Zafar, M. H., Sanfilippo, F., Rudra, S., & Kolhe, M. L. (2024). Advancements in digital twin technology and machine learning for energy systems: A comprehensive review of applications in smart grids, renewable energy, and electric vehicle optimisation. *Energy Conversion and Management: X, Article*, 100715.

Dayanikli, G. Y., Hatch, R. R., Gerdes, R. M., Wang, H., & Zane, R. (2020, May). Electromagnetic sensor and actuator attacks on power converters for electric vehicles. In *2020 IEEE Security and Privacy Workshops (SPW)* (pp. 98-103). IEEE.

Deepu, T., & Ravi, V. (2021). Supply chain digitalization: An integrated mcdm ap- proach for inter-organizational information systems selection in an electronic sup- ply chain. *International Journal of Information Management Data Insights*, *1*(2), 100038. DOI: 10.1016/j.jjimei.2021.100038

Dehrouyeh, F., Yang, L., Ajaei, F. B., & Shami, A. (2024). On TinyML and cybersecurity: Electric vehicle charging infrastructure use case. *IEEE Access*. Advance online publication.

Demestichas, K., Peppes, N., & Alexakis, T. (2020). Survey on security threats in agricultural IoT and smart farming. *Sensors (Basel), 20*(22), 6458. Advance online publication. DOI: 10.3390/s20226458 PMID: 33198160

Demestichas, S., Demesticha, M., Peppes, N., & Alexakis, E. (2021). Cybersecurity strategies for IoT-based agriculture: A comprehensive review. *Sensors (Basel), 21*(15), 5105. Advance online publication. DOI: 10.3390/s21155105 PMID: 34372338

Desikan, S. J., Singh, S. K., & Jayanthiladevi, A. (2025). BACHAAV: Machine learning-augmented human-AI and cryptographic architecture for threat detection in IoT-enabled oil and gas industrial networks. *International Journal of Information Technology : an Official Journal of Bharati Vidyapeeth's Institute of Computer Applications and Management, 17*, 1–12. DOI: 10.1007/s41870-025-01234-5

Development, S., & Goals, S. D. (2022). *Leaving no one behind in the hybrid digital society*. 113–163. DOI: 10.18356/9789210019446c009

Development, L. E. (2021). *Chapter 3*. 87–111.

Development, S., Goals, S. D., & Nations, U. (n.d.). *5. The Future of Digital Government : Trends*. Insights and Conclusions.

Dey, S. (2025). *Leveraging AI and Blockchain for Digital Transformation.*, DOI: 10.4018/979-8-3693-8664-4.ch013

Dey, S., & Khanra, M. (2020). Cybersecurity of plug-in electric vehicles: Cyberattack detection during charging. *IEEE Transactions on Industrial Electronics, 68*(1), 478–487. DOI: 10.1109/TIE.2020.2988129

Dhanaraju, R., Kumar, P., & Roy, S. (2023). Emerging challenges and countermeasures for IoT-driven smart agriculture. *Journal of Network and Computer Applications, 210*, 103620. Advance online publication. DOI: 10.1016/j.jnca.2022.103620

Díaz-Rodríguez, N., Del Ser, J., Coeckelbergh, M., López de Prado, M., Herrera-Viedma, E., & Herrera, F. (2023). Connecting the dots in trustworthy Artificial Intelligence: From AI principles, ethics, and key requirements to responsible AI systems and regulation. *Information Fusion, 99*, 101896. DOI: 10.1016/j.inffus.2023.101896

Djalante, R., Lassa, J., Setiamarga, D., Sudjatma, A., Indrawan, M., Haryanto, B., Mahfud, C., Sinapoy, M. S., Djalante, S., Rafliana, I., Gunawan, L. A., Surtiari, G. A. K., & Warsilah, H. (2020). Review and analysis of current responses to COVID-19 in Indonesia: Period of January to March 2020. *Progress in Disaster Science, 6*, 100091. DOI: 10.1016/j.pdisas.2020.100091 PMID: 34171011

Djatmiko, G. H., Sinaga, O., & Pawirosumarto, S. (2025). Digital Transformation and Social Inclusion in Public Services: A Qualitative Analysis of E-Government Adoption for Marginalized Communities in Sustainable Governance. *Sustainability (Switzerland)*, *17*(7). Advance online publication. DOI: 10.3390/su17072908

Doran, T., Maurer, K. A., & Ryan, A. M. (2017). Impact of Provider Incentives on Quality and Value of Health Care. *Annual Review of Public Health*, *38*, 449–465. DOI: 10.1146/annurev-publhealth-032315-021457 PMID: 27992731

Dunleavy, P., Margetts, H., Bastow, S., & Tinkler, J. (2006). *Digital Era Governance: IT Corporations, the State, and E-Government*. Oxford University Press., DOI: 10.1093/acprof:oso/9780199296194.001.0001

Dwivedi, V., Norta, A., Wulf, A., Leiding, B., Saxena, S., & Udokwu, C. (2021). A formal specification smart-contract language for legally binding decentralized autonomous organizations. *IEEE Access : Practical Innovations, Open Solutions*, *9*, 76069–76082.

Dwivedi, Y. (2009). An analysis of e-Government research published in Transforming Government: People, Process and Policy (TGPPP). *Transforming Government: People. Process and Policy*, *3*, 7–15. DOI: 10.1108/17506160910940704

Edelmann, N., Haug, N., & Mergel, I. (2023). *Digital Transformation in the Public Sector*. DOI: 10.4337/9781802202595.Digital.Transformation.in

ElKashlan, M., Aslan, H., Said Elsayed, M., Jurcut, A. D., & Azer, M. A. (2023). Intrusion detection for electric vehicle charging systems (EVCS). *Algorithms*, *16*(2), 75. DOI: 10.3390/a16020075

Elkhail, A. A., Refat, R. U. D., Habre, R., Hafeez, A., Bacha, A., & Malik, H. (2021). Vehicle security: A survey of security issues and vulnerabilities, malware attacks and defenses. *IEEE Access : Practical Innovations, Open Solutions*, *9*, 162401–162437. DOI: 10.1109/ACCESS.2021.3126672

Elliott, M. T. J. (2025). Schools of AI in the public sector: Fairness and accountability concerns. Proceedings of the AAAI/ACM Conference on AI, Ethics, And, 7(2), 11–13.

El-Rewini, Z., Sadatsharan, K., Sugunaraj, N., Selvaraj, D. F., Plathottam, S. J., & Ranganathan, P. (2020). Cybersecurity attacks in vehicular sensors. *IEEE Sensors Journal*, *20*(22), 13752–13767. DOI: 10.1109/JSEN.2020.3014723

Emerson, K. (2020). A Note From the Editor. *Perspectives on Public Management and Governance*, *3*(3), 183. DOI: 10.1093/ppmgov/gvaa015

Evans, D. (2011). *The Internet of Things: How the next evolution of the Internet is changing everything*. Cisco IBSG.

Ezeji, C. L. (2024). Artificial intelligence for detecting and preventing procurement fraud. *International Journal of Business Ecosystem and Strategy*, *6*(1), 63–73. DOI: 10.36096/ijbes.v6i1.477

Ezzeddine, F., Saad, M., Ayoub, O., Andreoletti, D., Gjoreski, M., Sbeity, I., . . . Giordano, S. (2024, July). Differential privacy for anomaly detection: Analyzing the trade-off between privacy and explainability. In *World Conference on Explainable Artificial Intelligence* (pp. 294-318). Cham, Switzerland: Springer Nature.

Falas, S., Konstantinou, C., & Michael, M. K. (2021). A modular end-to-end framework for secure firmware updates on embedded systems. [JETC]. *ACM Journal on Emerging Technologies in Computing Systems*, *18*(1), 1–19.

Farayola, O. A. (2024). Revolutionizing banking security: Integrating artificial intelligence, blockchain, and business intelligence for enhanced cybersecurity. *Finance & Accounting Research Journal*, *6*(4), 501–514.

Feltham-King, T., & Macleod, C. (2020). Multi-layered risk management in under-resourced antenatal clinics: A scientific-bureaucratic approach versus street-level bureaucracy. *Health Risk & Society*, *22*(1), 31–52. DOI: 10.1080/13698575.2019.1697432

Feng, L., Chiam, Y. K., & Lo, S. K. (2017). Text-mining techniques and tools for systematic literature reviews: A systematic literature review. In *2017 24th asia-pacific software engineering conference (apsec)* (pp. 41–50). IEEE.

Fernqvist, S. (2018). Street-level bureaucracy and categorization processes in social workers' encounters with parents who have financial and cognitive difficulties. *Nordic Social Work Research*, *8588*, 1–12. DOI: 10.1080/2156857x.2018.1547218

Ferrara, E. (2024). Fairness and bias in artificial intelligence: A brief survey of sources, impacts, and mitigation strategies. *Sci*, *6*(1), 3. DOI: 10.3390/sci6010003

Ferreira da Silva, C., & Moro, S. (2021). Blockchain technology as an enabler of consumer trust: A text mining literature analysis. *Telematics and Informatics*, *60*, 101593. DOI: 10.1016/j.tele.2021.101593

Ferreira, A. (2021). Regulating smart contracts: Legal revolution or simply evolution? *Telecommunications Policy*, *45*(2), 102081. DOI: 10.1016/j.telpol.2020.102081

Filippi, P. D., & Hassan, S. (2018). Blockchain technology as a regulatory technology: from code is law to law is code. *CoRR, abs/1801.02507*. https://arxiv.org/abs/1801.02507. Firouzi, F., Farahani, B., & Marinšek, A. (2022). The convergence and interplay of edge, fog, and cloud in the ai-driven internet of things (iot). *Information Systems, 107*, 101840. DOI: 10.1016/j.is.2021.101840

Fitriani, N. A., Loilatu, M. J., & Kurniawan, D. (2023). *Leadership in a Time of Pandemic: Dealing with the COVID-19 Outbreak BT - Proceedings of Seventh International Congress on Information and Communication Technology* (X.-S. Yang, S. Sherratt, N. Dey, & A. Joshi (eds.); pp. 379–388). Springer Nature Singapore.

Floridi, L., Cowls, J., Beltrametti, M., Chatila, R., Chazerand, P., Dignum, V., Luetge, C., Madelin, R., Pagallo, U., Rossi, F., Schäfer, B., Valcke, P., & Vayena, E. (2018). AI4People—An Ethical Framework for a Good AI Society: Opportunities, Risks, Principles, and Recommendations. *Minds and Machines*, *28*(4), 689–707. DOI: 10.1007/s11023-018-9482-5 PMID: 30930541

Food and Agriculture Organization of the United Nations. (2010). *"Climate-smart" agriculture: Policies, practices and financing for food security, adaptation and mitigation.* https://www.fao.org/3/i1881e/i1881e00.htm

Friedman, H. H. (2023). Cognitive biases and their influence on critical thinking and scientific reasoning: A practical guide for students and teachers. SSRN *Electronic Journal*. https://doi.org/DOI: 10.2139/ssrn.2958800

Fusi-Schmidhauser, T., Preston, N. J., Keller, N., & Gamondi, C. (2020). Conservative Management of COVID-19 Patients—Emergency Palliative Care in Action. *Journal of Pain and Symptom Management*. Advance online publication. DOI: 10.1016/j.jpainsymman.2020.03.030 PMID: 32276101

Gallinucci, E., Golfarelli, M., & Rizzi, S. (2015). Advanced topic modeling for social busi- ness intelligence. *Information Systems*, *53*, 87–106. DOI: 10.1016/j.is.2015.04.005

Gamble, G. (2024). AI's role in enhancing wellbeing in the workplace and beyond. Global Wellness Institute. https://globalwellnessinstitute.org/global-wellness-institute-blog/2024/05/07/ais-role-in-enhancing-wellbeing-in-the-workplace-and-beyond/

Ganesan, S., Patel, D. K., & Chokhalingam, R. (2024). Security of electric vehicle charging stations. *International Journal of Electrical and Computer Engineering Research*, *4*(4), 1–7.

Gao, Y., & Janssen, M. (2020). Generating value from government data using AI: An exploratory study. In *Lecture Notes in Computer Science* (pp. 319–331). Springer International Publishing.

García-Horta, J. B., & Guerra-Ramos, M. T. (2009). The use of CAQDAS in educational research: Some advantages, limitations and potential risks. *International Journal of Research & Method in Education*, *32*(2), 151–165. DOI: 10.1080/17437270902946686

García-Madurga, M.-Á., Gil-Lacruz, A.-I., Saz-Gil, I., & Gil-Lacruz, M. (2024). The role of artificial intelligence in improving workplace well-being: A systematic review. *Businesses*, *4*(3), 389–410. DOI: 10.3390/businesses4030024

Garcia-Segura, L. A. (2024). The role of artificial intelligence in preventing corporate crime. *Journal of Economic Criminology*, *5*, 100091. DOI: 10.1016/j.jeconc.2024.100091

Gauld, R. (2006). E-government: What Is It, and Will It Transform Government? *Police Quarterly*, *2*. Advance online publication. DOI: 10.26686/pq.v2i2.4193

Gaur, A. S., Sharan, H. O., & Kumar, R. (2024). AI in education: Ethical challenges and opportunities. In *The ethical frontier of AI and data analysis* (pp. 39–54). IGI Global., DOI: 10.4018/979-8-3693-2964-1.ch002

Gebresenbet, G., Bosona, T., Patterson, D., Persson, H., Fischer, B., Mandaluniz, N., & Nasirahmadi, A. (2023). A concept for application of integrated digital technologies to enhance future smart agricultural systems. *Smart Agricultural Technology*, *5*, 100255. Advance online publication. DOI: 10.1016/j.atech.2023.100255

Gehem, M., Usanov, A., Frinking, E., & Rademaker, M. (2015). *Assessing cyber security: A meta analysis of threats, trends, and responses to cyber attacks*. The Hague Centre for Strategic Studies.

Ghosh, S., Zheng, Y., Lammers, T., Chen, Y. Y., Fitzmaurice, C., Johnston, S., & Li, J. (2016). Deriving public sector workforce insights: A case study using Australian public sector employment profiles. In *Advanced Data Mining and Applications* (pp. 764–774). Springer International Publishing.

Giechaskiel, I., & Rasmussen, K. (2019). Taxonomy and challenges of out-of-band signal injection attacks and defenses. *IEEE Communications Surveys and Tutorials*, *22*(1), 645–670. DOI: 10.1109/COMST.2019.2892419

Gil-García, J. R., & Pardo, T. A. (2005). E-government success factors: Mapping practical tools to theoretical foundations. *Government Information Quarterly*, *22*(2), 187–216. https://doi.org/https://doi.org/10.1016/j.giq.2005.02.001

Gillingham, P. (2019). Can predictive algorithms assist decision-making in social work with children and families? *Child Abuse Review, 28*(2), 114–126. DOI 10.1002/car.2547

Glaeser, E. L., Kominers, S. D., Luca, M., & Naik, N. (2016). Big data and big cities: The promises and limitations of improved measures of urban life. *Economic Inquiry, 54*(1), 1–26. DOI: 10.1111/ecin.12364

Goal, S. D., Index, E. D., Nations, U., States, M., Index, O. S., States, M., Desa, U. N., Egdi, O., & Egdi, C. (2022). *Global Trends in E-Government.* 1–51. DOI: 10.18356/9789210019446c006

Gordon, F. (2019). Virginia Eubanks (2018) Automating Inequality: How High-Tech Tools Profile, Police, and Punish the Poor. New York: Picador, St Martin's Press. *Law. Technology and Humans, 162–164.* Advance online publication. DOI: 10.5204/lthj.v1i0.1386

Gosain, M. S., Aggarwal, N., & Kumar, R. (2023). A study of 5G and edge computing integration with IoT- A review. *2023 International Conference on Computational and Sustainable Engineering Solutions(CISES)*, 705–710.

Gosain, M. S., Aggarwal, N., & Kumar, R. (2023). A Study of 5G and Edge Computing Integration with IoT- A Review. *2023 International Conference on Computational Intelligence and Sustainable Engineering Solutions (CISES)*, 705–710. DOI: 10.1109/CISES58720.2023.10183438

Gou, C., & Deng, X. (2023). A blockchain-based security model for cloud accounting data. *International Journal of Ambient Computing and Intelligence, 14*(1), 1–16.

Grantz, K. H., Claudot, P., Kambala, M., Kouyaté, M., Soumah, A., Boum, Y., Juan-Giner, A., Jemmy, J. P., Cummings, D. A. T., & Grais, R. F. (2019). Factors influencing participation in an Ebola vaccine trial among front-line workers in Guinea. *Vaccine, 37*(48), 7165–7170. DOI: 10.1016/j.vaccine.2019.09.094 PMID: 31623917

Gravenor, N., & Adedoyin, F. F. (2023). Information security threats in the Internet of Things (IoT): A case study of automatic number plate recognition (ANPR) cameras. In *Handbook of Research on Cybersecurity Risk in Contemporary Business Systems* (pp. 291-304). IGI Global.

Grover, P., Kar, A. K., & Janssen, M. (2019a). Diffusion of blockchain technology: Insights from academic literature and social media analytics. *Journal of Enterprise Information Management.*

Grover, P., Kar, A. K., Janssen, M., & Ilavarasan, P. V. (2019b). Perceived usefulness, ease of use and user acceptance of blockchain technology for digital transactions– in- sights from user-generated content on twitter. *Enterprise Information Systems*, *13*(6), 771–800.

Gubbi, J., Buyya, R., Marusic, S., & Palaniswami, M. (2013). Internet of Things (IoT): A vision, architectural elements, and future directions. *Future Generation Computer Systems*, *29*(7), 1645–1660. DOI: 10.1016/j.future.2013.01.010

Gupta, A., & Bansal, R. (2013). E-governance: A step ahead. *International Conference on Advanced Computing and Communication Technologies, ACCT*, 359–362. DOI: 10.1109/ACCT.2013.80

Gupta, M., Abdelsalam, M., Khorsandroo, S., & Mittal, S. (2020). Security and privacy in smart farming: Challenges and opportunities. *IEEE Access : Practical Innovations, Open Solutions*, *8*, 34564–34584. DOI: 10.1109/ACCESS.2020.2974984

Gupta, S., Kumar, R., & Singh, N. (2023). Federated learning for plant disease prediction. *IEEE Access : Practical Innovations, Open Solutions*, *11*, 10522–10535. DOI: 10.1109/ACCESS.2023.3245678

Hachimi, C. E., Belaqziz, S., Khabba, S., Sebbar, B., Dhiba, D., & Chehbouni, A. (2023). Smart weather data management based on artificial intelligence and big data analytics for precision agriculture. *Agriculture*, *13*(1), 95. Advance online publication. DOI: 10.3390/agriculture13010095

Hafel, M., Jamil, J., Umasugi, M., & Anfas, A. (2022). Challenges of E-Government Implementation in The Region Archipelago Characteristics. *JAKPP (Jurnal Analisis Kebijakan & Pelayanan Publik)*, 44–58. DOI: 10.31947/jakpp.v8i1.21282

Hamdare, S., Brown, D. J., Jha, D. N., Aljaidi, M., Cao, Y., Kumar, S., & Kaiwartya, O. (2025). Cyber defense in OCPP for EV charging security risks. . *International Journal of Information Security*, *24*(3), 1–25.

Hamdare, S., Kaiwartya, O., Aljaidi, M., Jugran, M., Cao, Y., Kumar, S., & Lloret, J. (2023). Cybersecurity risk analysis of electric vehicles charging stations. *Sensors (Basel)*, *23*(15), 6716. DOI: 10.3390/s23156716 PMID: 37571500

Hanna, M. G., Pantanowitz, L., Jackson, B., Palmer, O., Visweswaran, S., Pantanowitz, J., Deebajah, M., & Rashidi, H. H. (2025). Ethical and bias considerations in artificial intelligence/machine learning. *Modern Pathology*, *38*(3), 100686. DOI: 10.1016/j.modpat.2024.100686 PMID: 39694331

Hasan, A., Putri, E. R. M., Susanto, H., & Nuraini, N. (2022). Data-driven modeling and forecasting of COVID-19 outbreak for public policy making. *ISA Transactions*, *124*, 135–143. PMID: 33487397

Hashmi, H., Dwivedi, R. K., & Kumar, A. (2023). YOLO-RS: An efficient YOLO-based approach for remote sensing object detection. In *2023 12th International Conference on System Modeling & Advancement in Research Trends (SMART)* (pp. 50–56). IEEE. https://doi.org/DOI: 10.1109/SMART59791.2023.10428504

Hashmi, H., Dwivedi, R. K., & Kumar, A. (2022). An AI & ML based detection & identification in remote imagery: State-of-the-art. *Journal of Automation. Mobile Robotics and Intelligent Systems*, *15*(4), 3–17. DOI: 10.14313/JAMRIS/4-2021/22

Hashmi, H., Dwivedi, R. K., & Kumar, A. (2024). Comparative analysis of CNN-based smart pre-trained models for object detection on DOTA. *Journal of Automation. Mobile Robotics and Intelligent Systems*, *18*(2), 31–45. DOI: 10.14313/JAMRIS/2-2024/11

Heeks, R. (2001). Understanding e-Governance for Development (i-Government Working Paper Series, No. 11/2001). Institute for Development Policy and Management, University of Manchester. https://doi.org/DOI: 10.2139/ssrn.3540058

Heeks, R. (2006). *Implementing and Managing eGovernment: An International Text*. DOI: 10.4135/9781446220191

Herawati, A. R., & Widowati, N. (2023). *The Implementation of Artificial Intelligence in Indonesia's Public Service: Challenges and Government Strategies*. 2471–2480. DOI: 10.46254/au01.20220537

Hill, H. C. (2003). Understanding Implementation: Street-Level Bureaucrats' Resources for Reform. *Journal of Public Administration: Research and Theory*, *13*(3), 265–282. DOI: 10.1093/jopart/mug024

Hirzallah, M. N. Y., & Alshurideh, M. T. R. (2023). The effects of the internal and the external factors affecting artificial intelligence (AI) adoption in e-innovation technology projects in the UAE? Applying both innovation and technology acceptance theories. *International Journal of Data and Network Science*, *7*(3), 1321–1332. DOI: 10.5267/j.ijdns.2023.4.006

Hoetker, G., & Fountain, J. (2002). Building the Virtual State: Information Technology and Institutional Change. *Academy of Management Review*, *27*, 619. DOI: 10.2307/4134407

Holzinger, A., Zatloukal, K., & Müller, H. (2025). Is human oversight to AI systems still possible? *New Biotechnology*, *85*, 59–62. DOI: 10.1016/j.nbt.2024.12.003 PMID: 39675423

Hong, J., Wang, Z., Qu, C., Zhou, Y., Shan, T., Zhang, J., & Hou, Y. (2022). Investigation on overcharge-caused thermal runaway of lithium-ion batteries in real-world electric vehicles. *Applied Energy*, *321*, 119229. Advance online publication. DOI: 10.1016/j.apenergy.2022.119229

Hong, S. (2020). Representative bureaucracy and hierarchy: Interactions among leadership, middle-level, and street-level bureaucracy. *Public Management Review*, *00*(00), 1–22. DOI: 10.1080/14719037.2020.1743346

Hood, C. (1991). A public management for all seasons? *Public Administration*, *69*(1), 3–19. DOI: 10.1111/j.1467-9299.1991.tb00779.x

Huang, X. (2023). Review on research of blockchain's impact on bookkeeping, fraud detection and trust of auditing process. Advances in Economics. *Management and Political Sciences*, *22*(1), 60–65.

Hughes, C., Robert, L. P., Frady, K., & Arroyos, A. (2019). Artificial intelligence, employee engagement, fairness, and job outcomes. In *Managing technology and middle- and low-skilled employees* (pp. 61–68). Emerald Publishing Limited., DOI: 10.1108/978-1-78973-077-720191005

Hujran, O., Alarabiat, A., Al-Adwan, A. S., & Al-Debei, M. (2023). Digitally Transforming Electronic Governments into Smart Governments: SMARTGOV, an Extended Maturity Model. *Information Development*, *39*(4), 811–834. DOI: 10.1177/02666669211054188

Hunt, K., Narayanan, A., & Zhuang, J. (2022). Blockchain in humanitarian operations management: A review of research and practice. *Socio-Economic Planning Sciences*, *80*, 101175. DOI: 10.1016/j.seps.2021.101175

Hu, P., Dhelim, S., Ning, H., & Qiu, T. (2017). Survey on fog computing: Architecture, key technologies, applications and open issues. *Journal of Network and Computer Applications*, *98*, 27–42. DOI: 10.1016/j.jnca.2017.09.002

Hu, Q. (2023). Unilever's practice on AI-based recruitment. *Highlights in Business Economics and Management*, *16*, 256–263. DOI: 10.54097/hbem.v16i.10565

Hussain, A., Yadav, A., & Ravikumar, G. (2024). Anomaly detection using bidirectional long short-term memory networks for cyber-physical electric vehicle charging stations. *IEEE Transactions on Industrial Cyber-Physical Systems*. Advance online publication.

Hussien, H. M., Yasin, S. M., Udzir, S., Zaidan, A. A., & Zaidan, B. B. (2019). A systematic review for enabling of develop a blockchain technology in healthcare application: Tax- onomy, substantially analysis, motivations, challenges, recommendations and future direction. *Journal of Medical Systems, 43*(10), 1–35. https://www.techdemand.io/news/tech-news/blockchain-news/blockchain-in cybersecurity-its-time-to-rethink-and-revolutionize/ https://www.blockchain-council.org/blockchain/blockchain-in-cybersecurity/ https://www.linkedin.com/pulse/how-blockchain-revolutionizing-cybersecurity digialert https://www.infosys.com/insights/cyber-security/cybersecurity-blockchain.html

IBM. (2021). AI-driven performance evaluation: A step towards fairness. Retrieved from https://www.ibm.com

ID. (2020). *Digital Identity and Refugee Services*. https://id2020.org

Index, E. D., & Development, E. (2022). *Regional E-Government Development and the Performance of Country Groupings*. 53–86. DOI: 10.18356/9789210019446c007

Irawan, B., Jafar Loilatu, M., Akbar, P., & Reynaldi, R. (2022). An Exploration Respond of COVID-19 Policy through Social Media in Indonesia. *Policy & Governance Review*, *6*(3), 229. DOI: 10.30589/pgr.v6i3.596

Islam, T., Khatoon, A., Cheema, A. U., & Ashraf, Y. (2023). How does ethical leadership enhance employee work engagement? The roles of trust in leader and harmonious work passion. *Kybernetes*, *53*(6), 2090–2106. DOI: 10.1108/K-09-2022-1343

Jaakkola, H., Henno, J., Mäkelä, J., & Thalheim, B. (2019). Artificial intelligence yesterday, today and tomorrow. *2019 42nd International Convention on Information and Communication Technology, Electronics and Microelectronics, MIPRO 2019 - Proceedings*, 860–867. DOI: 10.23919/MIPRO.2019.8756913

Jack, W., & Suri, T. (2011). *Mobile Money: The Economics of M-PESA*. https://doi.org/DOI: 10.3386/w16721

Jadil, Y., Rana, N. P., & Dwivedi, Y. K. (2022). Understanding the drivers of online trust and intention to buy on a website: An emerging market perspec- tive. *International Journal of Information Management Data Insights*, *2*(1), 100065. DOI: 10.1016/j.jjimei.2022.100065

Jain, D., Dash, M. K., Kumar, A., & Luthra, S. (2021). How is blockchain used in marketing: A review and research agenda. *International Journal of Information Management Data Insights*, *1*(2), 100044. DOI: 10.1016/j.jjimei.2021.100044

Jaiswal, A., & Kumar, R. (2023). Breast cancer diagnosis using Stochastic Self-Organizing Map and Enlarge C4.5. *Multimedia Tools and Applications*, *82*(12), 18059–18076. DOI: 10.1007/s11042-022-14265-1

Jangid, A. (2024). AI and employee well-being: How artificial intelligence can monitor and improve mental health in the workplace. *International Journal of Advanced Research*, *12*(10), 743–764. DOI: 10.21474/IJAR01/19693

Janssen, M., & Van Der Voort, H. (2020). Agile and adaptive governance in crisis response : Lessons from the COVID- 19 pandemic. *International Journal of Information Management*, *102180*(June), •••. DOI: 10.1016/j.ijinfomgt.2020.102180 PMID: 32836637

Janssen, M., Yannis, C., & Zuiderwijk, A. (2012). Benefits, Adoption Barriers and Myths of Open Data and Open Government. *Information Systems Management*, *29*(4), 258–268. DOI: 10.1080/10580530.2012.716740

Javed, B., Khan, Z., & McClatchey, R. (2018). An adaptable system to support provenance management for the public policy-making process in smart cities. *Informatics (MDPI)*, *5*(1), 3.

Jayaraman, R., Chukwu, T. U., & Wang, L. (2020a). Cloud computing in smart agriculture: Current trends and future directions. *IEEE Access : Practical Innovations, Open Solutions*, *8*, 12345–12359. DOI: 10.1109/ACCESS.2020.2967890

Jayaraman, R., Chukwu, T. U., & Wang, L. (2020b). Edge intelligence for smart agriculture: A review. *IEEE Internet of Things Journal*, *7*(8), 7315–7325. DOI: 10.1109/JIOT.2020.2987423

Jayaraman, R., Chukwu, T. U., & Wang, L. (2020c). Energy-efficient IoT for smart agriculture: Challenges and solutions. *IEEE Access : Practical Innovations, Open Solutions*, *8*, 12500–12514. DOI: 10.1109/ACCESS.2020.2971234

Jayaraman, R., Chukwu, T. U., & Wang, L. (2020d). Context-aware IoT middleware for precision agriculture. *IEEE Access : Practical Innovations, Open Solutions*, *8*, 12765–12778. DOI: 10.1109/ACCESS.2020.2974567

Jayaraman, R., Chukwu, T. U., & Wang, L. (2021). Fog computing in precision agriculture: Architecture, applications and future directions. *Computers and Electronics in Agriculture*, *186*, 106195. Advance online publication. DOI: 10.1016/j.compag.2021.106195

Jha, A., Bhattacharjee, R. K., Nandi, M., & Barbhuiya, F. A. (2019). A Framework for Maintaining Citizenship Record on Blockchain. *Proceedings of the 2019 ACM International Symposium on Blockchain and Secure Critical Infrastructure*, 29–38. https://doi.org/DOI: 10.1145/3327960.3332389

Jiang, J., Xie, X., & Fan, L. (2021). Trends of blockchain research in management and business. In *2021 the 7th international conference on frontiers of educational technolo- gies*. In *ICFET 2021* (pp. 228–234). New York, NY, USA: Association for Computing Machinery. DOI: 10.1145/3473141.3473253

Jobin, A., Ienca, M., & Vayena, E. (2019). The global landscape of AI ethics guidelines. *Nature Machine Intelligence*, *1*(9), 389–399.

Johnson, P. A., Acedo, A., & Robinson, P. J. (2020). Canadian smart cities: Are we wiring new citizen-local government interactions? *Can. Geogr.*, *64*(3), 402–415.

Joshi, A., Kumar, V., Chauhan, N., Kumar, A., & Singh, R. K. (2024). *The Intersection of AI, ML, and Industry: A Review of Emerging Trends in Real-World Applications,* 2024 4th International Conference on Advancement in Electronics & Communication Engineering (AECE), GHAZIABAD, India, 2024, pp. 769-773, doi: DOI: 10.1109/AECE62803.2024.10911386

Joshi, A., Kumar, V., Thakur, G., Chauhan, N., & Singh, R. K. (2025). A primer for governance. In Kumar, R., Abdul Hamid, A., Ya'akub, N., Nyamasvisva, T., & Tiwari, R. (Eds.), *Leveraging futuristic machine learning and next-generational security for e-governance* (pp. 45–86). IGI Global Scientific Publishing., DOI: 10.4018/979-8-3693-7883-0.ch003

Joshi, A., Thakur, G., Kumar, V., Singh, Y., & Joshi, D. (2025). Harnessing Big Data Visualization in Bioinformatics: From Data to Discovery. In Choudhury, A., Kaushik, K., Kumar, V., & Singh, B. K. (Eds.), *Cyber-Physical Systems Security. Studies in Big Data* (Vol. 154). Springer., DOI: 10.1007/978-981-97-5734-3_12

Jutla, D. N., Bodorik, P., & Zhang, Y. (2006). Pecan: An architecture for users' privacy- aware electronic commerce contexts on the semantic web. [The Semantic Web and Web Services.]. *Information Systems*, *31*(4), 295–320. DOI: 10.1016/j.is.2005.02.004

Kaefer, F., Roper, J., & Sinha, P. (2015). A software-assisted qualitative content analysis of news articles: Example and reflections. *Forum Qualitative Social Research*, *16*(2). Advance online publication. DOI: 10.17169/fqs-16.2.2123

Kamble, S. S., Gunasekaran, A., & Dhone, N. C. (2020). A blockchain technology implementation for food supply chain transparency. *International Journal of Production Research, 58*(7), 2223–2242. DOI: 10.1080/00207543.2019.1651452

Kamilaris, A., & Prenafeta-Boldú, F. X. (2018). Deep learning in agriculture: A survey. *Computers and Electronics in Agriculture, 147*, 70–90. DOI: 10.1016/j.compag.2018.02.016

Kamil, M., Muhammad, R., Roziqin, A., & Sari, A. E. (2025). Examining Practice Smart City in Local Government: A Smart Governance Perspective. *International Journal of Sustainable Development and Planning, 20*(2), 635–644. DOI: 10.18280/ijsdp.200214

Katsonis, M., & Botros, A. (2015). Digital Government: A Primer and Professional Perspectives. *Australian Journal of Public Administration, 74*(1), 42–52. DOI: 10.1111/1467-8500.12144

Katuu, S. (2025). Blockchain innovations and the contribution of the intergovernmental organizations. *Global Knowledge, Memory and Communication, 74*(1/2), 128–146. DOI: 10.1108/GKMC-07-2022-0179

Kaushal, P. K., Bagga, A., & Sobti, R. (2017). *Evolution of bitcoin and security risk in bitcoin wallets. In 2017 international conference on computer, communications and elec- tronics (comptelix)*. IEEE.

Kavut, S. (2021). Digital Identities in The Context of Blockchain and Artificial Intelligence. *Selçuk İletişim, 14*(2), 529–548. DOI: 10.18094/josc.865641

Kayas, O. G. (2023). Workplace surveillance: A systematic review, integrative framework, and research agenda. *Journal of Business Research, 168*, 114212. DOI: 10.1016/j.jbusres.2023.114212

Kempeneer, S. (2021). A big data state of mind: Epistemological challenges to accountability and transparency in data-driven regulation. *Government Information Quarterly, 38*(3), 101578. Advance online publication. DOI: 10.1016/j.giq.2021.101578

Kennedy, G. (2016). Asia-Pacific news. *Computer Law & Security Review, 32*(2), 375–380. https://doi.org/https://doi.org/10.1016/j.clsr.2016.01.002

Keulemans, S., & Groeneveld, S. (2020). Supervisory leadership at the frontlines: Street-level discretion, supervisor influence, and street-level bureaucrats' attitude towards clients. *Journal of Public Administration: Research and Theory, 30*(2), 307–323. DOI: 10.1093/jopart/muz019

Khan, N., & Daniel, T. (2024). Utilizing AI and Blockchain for Cyber Threat Prediction in Financial Institutions: Tools and Techniques for Cloud Security Posture Management.

Khan, M. A., & Salah, K. (2018). IoT security: Review, blockchain solutions, and open challenges. *Future Generation Computer Systems*, *82*, 395–411. DOI: 10.1016/j.future.2017.11.022

Khan, R., Khan, S. U., Zaheer, R., & Khan, S. (2012). Future Internet: The Internet of Things architecture, possible applications and key challenges. In *Proceedings of the 10th International Conference on Frontiers of Information Technology* (pp. 257–260). IEEE. https://doi.org/DOI: 10.1109/FIT.2012.53

Khan, Z., Abbasi, A. G., & Pervez, Z. (2020). Blockchain and edge computing–based architecture for participatory smart city applications. *Concurrency and Computation*, *32*(12).

Kim, W., Jeong, O.-R., Kim, C., & So, J. (2011). The dark side of the internet: Attacks, costs and responses. *Information Systems, 36*(3), 675–705. . Special Issue on WISE 2009 - Web Information Systems Engineering.DOI: 10.1016/j.is.2010.11.003

Kim, Y., Hakak, S., & Ghorbani, A. (2024). Detecting distributed denial-of-service (DDoS) attacks that generate false authentications on electric vehicle (EV) charging infrastructure. *Computers & Security*, *144*, 103989. Advance online publication. DOI: 10.1016/j.cose.2024.103989

Kinoshita, A., Takasu, A., & Adachi, J. (2015). Real-time traffic incident de- tection using a probabilistic topic model. *Information Systems*, *54*, 169–188. DOI: 10.1016/j.is.2015.07.002

Kleinberg, J., Lakkaraju, H., Leskovec, J., Ludwig, J., & Mullainathan, S. (2018). Human decisions and machine predictions. *The Quarterly Journal of Economics*, *133*(1), 237–293. PMID: 29755141

Kolade, T. M., Aideyan, N. T., Oyekunle, S. M., Ogungbemi, O. S., Dapo-Oyewole, D. L., & Olaniyi, O. O. (2024). Artificial Intelligence and Information Governance: Strengthening Global Security, through Compliance Frameworks, and Data Security. Available at *SSRN* 5044032.

König, P. D. (2022). Fortress Europe 4.0? An analysis of EU data governance through the lens of the resource regime concept. *European Policy Analysis*, *8*(4), 484–504. DOI: 10.1002/epa2.1160

Kovacevic, A., & Gligoric, N. (2024). Enhancing security of automotive OTA firmware updates via decentralized identifiers and distributed ledger technology. *Electronics (Basel), 13*(23), 4640. Advance online publication. DOI: 10.3390/electronics13234640

Krämer, W. (2014). Kahneman, D. (2011): Thinking, Fast and Slow. *Statistische Hefte, 55*. Advance online publication. DOI: 10.1007/s00362-013-0533-y

Kroon, N., & Alves, M. do C., & Martins, I. (2021). The Impacts of Emerging Technologies on Accountants' Role and Skills: Connecting to Open Innovation—A Systematic Literature Review. *Journal of Open Innovation, 7*(3), 163. DOI: 10.3390/joitmc7030163

Kumar, A., Bhatia, A., Kumar, S., Kumar, R., & Yadav, V. (2025, February). Sentimental analysis using natural language processing. In AIP Conference Proceedings (Vol. 3224, No. 1). AIP Publishing.

Kumar, A., Saini, R., & Kumar, R. (2023). A Systematic Review of Breast Cancer Detection Using Machine Learning and Deep Learning. *2023 10th IEEE Uttar Pradesh Section International Conference on Electrical, Electronics and Computer Engineering (UPCON), 10*, 1128–1133. DOI: 10.1109/UPCON59197.2023.10434530

Kumar, P., Kumar, R., & Kumar, M. (2024). Data Storage in Manual Systems that Challenges in Cloud & Fog Computing-Based Systems Which are Affecting the Online Data-Oriented Application Architecture. *2024 4th International Conference on Technological Advancements in Computational Sciences (ICTACS)*, 723–727. DOI: 10.1109/ICTACS62700.2024.10841028

Kumar, P., Kumar, R., & Kumar, M. (2024, November). Data Storage in Manual Systems that Challenges in Cloud & Fog Computing-Based Systems Which are Affecting the Online Data-Oriented Application Architecture. In 2024 4th International Conference on Technological Advancements in Computational Sciences (ICTACS) (pp. 723-727). IEEE.

Kumar, P., Kumar, R., Singh, K. B., & Kumar, M. (2023). Identification of the Problem and Research Methodology. In AI in Education: Ethical Challenges and Opportunities. The Ethical Frontier of AI and Data Analysis (pp. 289–308). IGI Global.

Kumar, R., Kumar, P., & Elngar, A. (2024). *Scrutinizing Domain-Specific Integrated Web Query Interfaces for Enhanced Security and Reliability in Storage Systems.* DOI: 10.1109/DASA63652.2024.10836405

Kumar, A., Bhatia, A., Kumar, S., Kumar, R., & Yadav, V. (2025). Sentimental analysis using natural language processing. *AIP Conference Proceedings*, *3224*(1), 20054. DOI: 10.1063/5.0246883

Kumar, A., Saini, R., & Kumar, R. (2024). A Comparative Analysis of Machine Learning Algorithms for Breast Cancer Detection and Identification of Key Predictive Features. *TS. Traitement du Signal*, *41*(1), 127–140. DOI: 10.18280/ts.410110

Kumar, A., Saini, R., & Kumar, R. (2024). A comparative analysis of machine learning algorithms for breast cancer detection and identification of key predictive features. *TS. Traitement du Signal*, *41*(1).

Kumar, P., Kumar, R., Singh, K. B., & Kumar, M. (2023). Identification of the problem and research methodology. In *Effective AI, blockchain, and e-governance applications for knowledge discovery and management* (pp. 289–308). IGI Global., DOI: 10.4018/978-1-6684-9151-5.ch001

Kumar, P., Singh, R., & Sharma, S. (2020a). A fog-edge-blockchain architecture for secure smart agriculture. *IEEE Access : Practical Innovations, Open Solutions*, *8*, 106164–106173. DOI: 10.1109/ACCESS.2020.2998790

Kumar, P., Singh, R., & Sharma, S. (2020c). Security and privacy challenges in IoT-enabled smart agriculture: A survey. *Computers and Electronics in Agriculture*, *176*, 105596. Advance online publication. DOI: 10.1016/j.compag.2020.105596

Kumar, P., Singh, R., & Sharma, S. (2021a). Data quality challenges in IoT-enabled smart agriculture. *Computers and Electronics in Agriculture*, *179*, 105834. Advance online publication. DOI: 10.1016/j.compag.2020.105834

Kumar, P., Singh, R., & Sharma, S. (2021b). System integration challenges in IoT-enabled smart agriculture. *Computers and Electronics in Agriculture*, *185*, 106167. Advance online publication. DOI: 10.1016/j.compag.2021.106167

Kumar, P., Singh, R., & Sharma, S. (2021c). Communication technologies for smart agriculture: A review. *Computers and Electronics in Agriculture*, *178*, 105781. Advance online publication. DOI: 10.1016/j.compag.2020.105781

Kumar, P., Yadav, R., & Singh, A. (2021). A blockchain-integrated IoT architecture for secure smart farming. *Journal of Network and Computer Applications*, *187*, 103114. Advance online publication. DOI: 10.1016/j.jnca.2021.103114

Kumar, R., Hamid, A. B. A., Ya'akub, N. I. B., Gaur, M. S., & Kumar, S. (Eds.). (2024). *Futuristic e-governance security with deep learning applications*. IGI Global., DOI: 10.4018/978-1-6684-9596-4

Kumar, R., Hamid, A., Bakar, A., Inayah Binti Yaakub, N., Kumar, P., Kumar, M., & Kumar, R. (2024). *Futuristic E-governance Security with Deep Learning Applications* (Kumar, M., Ed.). IGI Global.

Kumar, R., Kumar, P., Hamid, A. B. A., Nyamasvisva, T. E., Kumar, R., Peng, S., Jain, P., & Elngar, A. (Eds.). (2025). *Deep learning innovations for securing critical infrastructures*. IGI Global., DOI: 10.4018/979-8-3373-0563-9

Kumar, Y., Singh, P., & Patil, A. (2021). Blockchain for smart agriculture supply chain management: A survey. *Computers and Electronics in Agriculture*, *184*, 106123. Advance online publication. DOI: 10.1016/j.compag.2021.106123

Lai, L. S. L., & To, W. M. (2015). Content analysis of social media: A grounded theory approach. *Journal of Electronic Commerce Research*, *16*(2), 138–152.

Lammie, M. (2025). Improving financial crime programs with AI: How to help implement effective models. PwC. https://riskproducts.pwc.com/insights/improving-financial-crime-programs-with-ai-how-to-help-implement-effective/

Landri, P. (2018). *Digital Governance of Education*. Bloomsbury Publishing CN - L. https://digital.casalini.it/9781350006416

Lebovits, H. (2018). Automating inequality: How high-tech tools profile, police, and punish the poor [Review of the book Automating Inequality: How high-tech tools profile, police, and punish the poor, by V. Eubanks]. *Public Integrity*, *21*(4), 448–452. DOI: 10.1080/10999922.2018.1511671

Lee, I., & Lee, K. (2015). The Internet of Things (IoT): Applications, investments, and challenges for enterprises. *Business Horizons*, *58*(4), 431–440. DOI: 10.1016/j.bushor.2015.03.008

Lee, N.-Y., Yang, J., Onik, M. M. H., & Kim, C.-S. (2019). Modifiable public blockchains using truncated hashing and sidechains. *IEEE Access : Practical Innovations, Open Solutions*, *7*, 173571–173582. DOI: 10.1109/AC- CESS.2019.2956628

Lee, T. (2024). Artificial intelligence: Governing Singapore's smart digital journey. *Communication Research and Practice*, *10*(3), 307–315. DOI: 10.1080/22041451.2024.2346430

Leiva, V., & Castro, C. (2025). Artificial intelligence and blockchain in clinical trials: Enhancing data governance efficiency, integrity, and transparency. *Bioanalysis*, *17*(3), 161–176. PMID: 39844748

Leoni, L., Gueli, G., Ardolino, M., Panizzon, M., & Gupta, S. (2024). AI-empowered KM processes for decision-making: Empirical evidence from worldwide organisations. *Journal of Knowledge Management*, *28*(11), 320–347. DOI: 10.1108/JKM-03-2024-0262

Levenda, A. M., Keough, N., Rock, M., & Miller, B. (2020). Rethinking public participation in the smart city. *Can. Geogr.*, *64*(3), 344–358.

Liakos, K. G., Busato, P., Moshou, D., Pearson, S., & Bochtis, D. (2018). Machine learning in agriculture: A review. *Sensors (Basel)*, *18*(8), 2674. Advance online publication. DOI: 10.3390/s18082674 PMID: 30110960

Li, J., & Wang, Z. (2023). Drone-based disease detection using AI. *Computers and Electronics in Agriculture*, *205*, 107–115. DOI: 10.1016/j.compag.2022.107115

Lim, M. (2020). The politics and perils of dis/connection in the Global South. *Media Culture & Society*, *42*(4), 618–625. DOI: 10.1177/0163443720914032

Lin, C., Chen, X., & Hu, S. (2021a). Smart contracts in blockchain-based smart agriculture: Opportunities and challenges. *Information Processing in Agriculture*, *8*(4), 605–615. DOI: 10.1016/j.inpa.2021.01.005

Lin, C., Chen, X., & Hu, S. (2021b). Middleware for IoT-enabled smart agriculture: A survey. *Journal of Network and Computer Applications*, *186*, 103097. Advance online publication. DOI: 10.1016/j.jnca.2021.103097

Lin, I. C., & Liao, T. C. (2017). A survey of blockchain security issues and challenges. *International Journal of Network Security*, *19*(5), 653–659. DOI: 10.6633/IJNS.201709_19(5).01

Lin, J., Yu, W., Zhang, N., Yang, X., Zhang, H., & Zhao, W. (2017). A survey on Internet of Things: Architecture, enabling technologies, security and privacy, and applications. *IEEE Internet of Things Journal*, *4*(5), 1125–1142. DOI: 10.1109/JIOT.2017.2683200

Lin, K., Zhang, Y., & Wang, M. (2022). Architectures and trends in IoT-enabled smart farming: A comprehensive review. *IEEE Access : Practical Innovations, Open Solutions*, *10*, 12345–12367. DOI: 10.1109/ACCESS.2022.3145678

Lin, S., Chen, X., & Hu, J. (2024). Deep learning for livestock monitoring. *Computers in Agriculture*, *9*(1), 23–34.

Lipsky, M. (1979). *Street-Level Bureaucracy : Dilemmas of the Individual*. 1-.

Lipsky, M. (2010). Street-Level Bureaucracy: Dilemmas of the Individual in Public Services. Michael Lipsky. In *Social Service Review*. https://doi.org/DOI: 10.1086/643898

Li, Q., Guan, X., Wu, P., Wang, X., Zhou, L., Tong, Y., Ren, R., Leung, K. S. M., Lau, E. H. Y., Wong, J. Y., Xing, X., Xiang, N., Wu, Y., Li, C., Chen, Q., Li, D., Liu, T., Zhao, J., Liu, M., & Feng, Z. (2020). Early Transmission Dynamics in Wuhan, China, of Novel Coronavirus-Infected Pneumonia. *The New England Journal of Medicine*, *382*(13), 1199–1207. DOI: 10.1056/NEJMoa2001316 PMID: 31995857

Li, S., Da Xu, L., & Zhao, S. (2015). The Internet of Things: A survey. *Information Systems Frontiers*, *17*(2), 243–259. DOI: 10.1007/s10796-014-9492-7

Liu, J., Zhang, S., Liu, H., & Zhang, Y. (2021). Distributed collaborative anomaly detection for trusted digital twin vehicular edge networks. In *Wireless Algorithms, Systems, and Applications: 16th International Conference, WASA 2021, Nanjing, China, June 25–27, 2021, Proceedings, Part II* (pp. 378-389). Springer International Publishing.

Li, W., Li, J., & Zhang, F. (2022). Blockchain and AI-enabled resilient smart agriculture architecture. *IEEE Transactions on Industrial Informatics*, *18*(3), 2131–2142. DOI: 10.1109/TII.2021.3091234

Li, X., & Li, X. (2023). 6G URLLC and blockchain for smart farms. *Future Internet*, *15*(2), 31. Advance online publication. DOI: 10.3390/fi15020031

Li, Y., & Liu, Q. (2021). A comprehensive review study of cyber-attacks and cyber se- curity; emerging trends and recent developments. *Energy Reports*, *7*, 8176–8186. DOI: 10.1016/j.egyr.2021.08.126

Longo, J. (2024). The Transformative Potential of Artificial Intelligence for Public Sector Reform. *Canadian Public Administration*, *67*(4), 495–505. DOI: 10.1111/capa.12587

Losavio, M. (2021). Algorithms of Machines and Law: Risks in Pattern Recognition, Machine Learning and Artificial Intelligence for Justice and Fairness. *Public Governance. Administration and Finances Law Review*, *6*(2), 21–34. DOI: 10.53116/pgaflr.2021.2.3

Lumenalta. (2024, October 13). Ethical considerations of AI. Lumenalta Insights. https://lumenalta.com/insights/ethical-considerations-of-ai

Luna-Reyes, L. F., Gil-Garcia, J. R., & Cruz, C. B. (2006). Collaborative digital government in Mexico: Some lessons from federal web-based inter- organizational information integration initiatives. *Association for Information Systems - 12th Americas Conference On Information Systems, AMCIS 2006, 4*, 2357–2366.

Luntovskyy, A., & Guetter, D. (2018). Cryptographic technology blockchain and its appli- cations. In *The international conference on information and telecommunication technolo- gies and radio electronics* (pp. 14–33). Springer.

Ma, Q., Nadamoto, A., & Tanaka, K. (2006). Complementary information re- trieval for cross-media news content. *Information Systems, 31*(7), 659–678. . (1) SPIRE 2004 (2) Multimedia Databases.DOI: 10.1016/j.is.2005.12.004

Machmud, M., Masmuh, A., & Nasirin, C., Salahudin, Baharuddin, T., & Musa, A. E. Z. (2020). Artificial Intelligence In The Public Health Sector: The Use Of Telemedicine In Indonesia During Covid-19 | PalArch's Journal of Archaeology of Egypt / Egyptology. *PalArch's Journal of Archaeology of Egypt, 17*(7), 10106–10118.

Madan, R., & Ashok, M. (2023). AI adoption and diffusion in public administration: A systematic literature review and future research agenda. *Government Information Quarterly, 40*(1), 101774. DOI 10.1016/j.giq.2022.101774

Mahammad, A. B., & Kumar, R. (2022a). Design a Linear Classification model with Support Vector Machine Algorithm on Autoimmune Disease data. 2022 3rd International Conference on Intelligent and Management (ICIEM), 164–169.

Mahammad, A. B., & Kumar, R. (2022b). Progression of Digital Healthcare With Deep Learning and Blockchain Methods for Smart Cities. In Advances in Deep Learning Applications for Smart Cities (pp. 248–266).

Mahammad, A. B., & Kumar, R. (2023). Scalable and security framework to secure and maintain healthcare data using blockchain technology. *2023 International Conference on Computational and Sustainable Engineering Solutions(CISES)*, 417–423.

Mahammad, A. B., & Kumar, R. (2023). Scalable and Security Framework to Secure and Maintain Healthcare Data using Blockchain Technology. *2023 International Conference on Computational Intelligence and Sustainable Engineering Solutions (CISES)*, 417–423. DOI: 10.1109/CISES58720.2023.10183494

Mahammad, A. B., & Kumar, R. (2023, April). Scalable and security framework to secure and maintain healthcare data using blockchain technology. In *2023 International Conference on Computational Intelligence and Sustainable Engineering Solutions (CISES)* (pp. 417-423). IEEE.

Mahmood, K., Nayyar, Z., & Mushtaq, H. (2018). Role of transformational leadership on e-government switching: Multi-channel and digital divide. *2017 12th International Conference for Internet Technology and Secured Transactions, ICITST 2017*, 475–478. DOI: 10.23919/ICITST.2017.8356453

Mahusin, N., Sallehudin, H., & Satar, N. S. M. (2024). Malaysia Public Sector Challenges Of Implementation Of Artificial Intelligence (AI). *IEEE Access : Practical Innovations, Open Solutions*, *12*(August), 121035–121051. DOI: 10.1109/ACCESS.2024.3448311

Makhmudov, F., Kilichev, D., Giyosov, U., & Akhmedov, F. (2025). Online machine learning for intrusion detection in electric vehicle charging systems. . *Mathematics*, *13*(5), 712.

Manfredi Sánchez, J. L. (2019). Big Data and International Politics. *Baltic Yearbook of International Law*, *18*(1), 52–71. DOI: 10.1163/22115897_01801_005

Manso, P., Moura, J., & Serrão, C. (2019). SDN-based intrusion detection system for early detection and mitigation of DDoS attacks. *Information (Basel)*, *10*(3), 106. Advance online publication. DOI: 10.3390/info10030106

Margetts, H. (2022). Rethinking AI for good governance. *Daedalus*, *151*(2), 360–371.

Margetts, H., & Dorobantu, C. (2019, April). Rethink government with AI. *Nature*, *568*(7751), 163–165. DOI: 10.1038/d41586-019-01099-5 PMID: 30967667

Mastercard. (2024, May 22). Mastercard accelerates card fraud detection with generative AI technology. Mastercard. https://www.mastercard.com/news/press/2024/may/mastercard-accelerates-card-fraud-detection-with-generative-ai-technology/

Mazzi, F. (2025). AI governance and environmental sustainability. In *Oxford Intersections*. AI in Society. Oxford University PressOxford.

McKay, F., Williams, B. J., Prestwich, G., Treanor, D., & Hallowell, N. (2022). Public governance of medical artificial intelligence research in the UK: An integrated multi-scale model. *Research Involvement and Engagement*, *8*(1). Advance online publication. DOI: 10.1186/s40900-022-00357-7 PMID: 35598004

McKelvey, F., & MacDona, M. (2019). Artificial intelligence policy innovations at the Canadian federal government. *Canadian Journal of Communication*, *44*(2), 43–50. DOI: 10.22230/cjc.2019v44n2a3509

Mehta, S., & Gupta, P. (2022). Securing IoT-based smart agriculture with blockchain: A survey. *Future Generation Computer Systems*, *125*, 482–495. DOI: 10.1016/j.future.2021.07.017

Mehta, V., Sharma, P., & Verma, R. (2022). An AI and blockchain model for predicting crop yields. *Computers and Electronics in Agriculture, 195*, 106855. Advance online publication. DOI: 10.1016/j.compag.2022.106855

Meijer, A., & Wessels, M. (2019). Predictive policing: Review of benefits and drawbacks. *International Journal of Public Administration, 42*(12), 1031–1039. DOI 10.1080/01900692.2019.1575664

Mensah, G. B. (2023, November). Artificial intelligence and ethics: A comprehensive review of bias mitigation, transparency, and accountability in AI systems. EGRC Africa Regulation Research Consortium. https://doi.org/DOI: 10.13140/RG.2.2.23381.19685/1

Mergel, I., Edelmann, N., & Haug, N. (2019). Defining digital transformation: Results from expert interviews. *Government Information Quarterly, 36*(4), 101385. DOI: 10.1016/j.giq.2019.06.002

Microsoft. (2022). Workplace analytics: Enhancing employee productivity and well-being. Retrieved from https://www.microsoft.com

Mikhaylov, S. J., Esteve, M., & Campion, A. (2018). Artificial intelligence for the public sector: Opportunities and challenges of cross-sector collaboration. *Philosophical Transactions of the Royal Society A, 376*(2128), 20170357. PMID: 30082303

Miorandi, D., Sicari, S., De Pellegrini, F., & Chlamtac, I. (2012). Internet of Things: Vision, applications and research challenges. *Ad Hoc Networks, 10*(7), 1497–1516. DOI: 10.1016/j.adhoc.2012.02.016

Mitikiri, S. B., Srinivas, V. L., & Pal, M. (2025). Anomaly detection of adversarial cyber attacks on electric vehicle charging stations. *e-Prime-Advances in Electrical Engineering, Electronics and Energy, 11*, Article 100911.

Modise, J. M. (2023). The impacts of employee workplace empowerment, effective commitment, and performance: An organizational systematic review. *International Journal of Innovative Science and Research Technology, 8*(7), 3435. https://www.researchgate.net/publication/376260679

Mogielnicki, R. (2021). Free Zones in Dubai: Accelerators for Artificial Intelligence in the Gulf. In *Artificial Intelligence in the Gulf: Challenges and Opportunities* (hal. 141–159). DOI: 10.1007/978-981-16-0771-4_8

Mohammadi, M., & Bagherzadeh Mohasefi, J. (n.d.). A spatio-temporal graph convolutional model for electric vehicle infrastructure response to cyber attacks. *SSRN*. DOI: 10.2139/ssrn.5191964

Mohasses, M. (2019). How AI-Chatbots Can Make Dubai Smarter? *Proceedings - 2019 Amity International Conference on Artificial Intelligence, AICAI 2019*, 439–446. DOI: 10.1109/AICAI.2019.8701413

Mökander, J. (2023). Auditing of AI: Legal, ethical and technical approaches. *Digital Society : Ethics, Socio-Legal and Governance of Digital Technology*, *2*, 49. DOI: 10.1007/s44206-023-00074-y

Mökander, J., Morley, J., Taddeo, M., & Floridi, L. (2021). Ethics-Based Auditing of Automated Decision-Making Systems: Nature, Scope, and Limitations. *Science and Engineering Ethics*, *27*(4). Advance online publication. DOI: 10.1007/s11948-021-00319-4 PMID: 34231029

Moon, M. J. (2002). The Evolution of E-Government among Municipalities: Rhetoric or Reality? *Public Administration Review*, *62*(4), 424–433. https://doi.org/https://doi.org/10.1111/0033-3352.00196

Moravec, P., & Krumnikl, M. (2017). Developing countermeasures against cloning of identity tokens in legacy systems. In *Computer Information Systems and Industrial Management: 16th IFIP TC8 International Conference, CISIM 2017, Bialystok, Poland, June 16-18, 2017, Proceedings* (pp. 672-684). Springer International Publishing.

Morchid, A., Et-taibi, B., Oughannou, Z., El Alami, R., Qjidaa, H., Jamil, M. O., & Abid, M. R. (2024). IoT-based smart irrigation system for resource-efficient agriculture. *Sustainable Computing : Informatics and Systems*, *35*, 100797. Advance online publication. DOI: 10.1016/j.suscom.2024.100797

Morchid, A., Et-taibi, B., Oughannou, Z., El Alami, R., Qjidaa, H., Jamil, M. O., & Abid, M. R. (2025). IoT-enabled smart agriculture for improving water management: A smart irrigation control using embedded systems and server-sent events. *Scientific African*, *27*, e02527. Advance online publication. DOI: 10.1016/j.sciaf.2024.e02527

Morgan, A. K. (2020). Making COVID-19 prevention etiquette of social distancing a reality for the homeless and slum dwellers in Ghana: Lessons for consideration. *Local Environment*, *00*(0), 1–4. DOI: 10.1080/13549839.2020.1789854

Morley, J., Floridi, L., Kinsey, L., & Elhalal, A. (2020). From what to how: An initial review of publicly available AI ethics tools, methods and research to translate principles into practices. *Science and Engineering Ethics*, *26*(4), 2141–2168. PMID: 31828533

Moro, S., Cortez, P., & Rita, P. (2015). Business intelligence in banking: A literature analy- sis from 2002 to 2013 using text mining and latent dirichlet allocation. *Expert Systems with Applications*, *42*(3), 1314–1324.

Morrison, G. S. (2018). *Threats and mitigation of DDoS cyberattacks against the US power grid via EV charging* (Unpublished master's thesis). Wright State University.

Muhammad, A. E., & Yow, K.-C. (2023). Demystifying Canada's Artificial Intelligence and Data Act (AIDA): The good, the bad and the unclear elements. *Canadian Conference on Electrical and Computer Engineering, 2023-Septe*, 510–515. DOI: 10.1109/CCECE58730.2023.10288878

Muhammad, Z., Anwar, Z., Saleem, B., & Shahid, J. (2023). Emerging cybersecurity and privacy threats to electric vehicles and their impact on human and environmental sustainability. *Energies*, *16*(3), 1113. Advance online publication. DOI: 10.3390/en16031113

Mukonavanhu, T. (2025). An international comparison of the role of artificial intelligence in e-governance towards providing better standards of living. *Electronic Government, an International Journal*, *1*(1), 137–157. DOI: 10.1504/eg.2025.10064176

Munster, V. J., Koopmans, M., van Doremalen, N., van Riel, D., & de Wit, E. (2020). A novel coronavirus emerging in China - Key questions for impact assessment. *The New England Journal of Medicine*, *382*(8), 692–694. DOI: 10.1056/NEJMp2000929 PMID: 31978293

Murikah, W., Nthenge, J. K., & Musyoka, F. M. (2024). Bias and ethics of AI systems applied in auditing: A systematic review. *Scientific African*, *25*, e02281. DOI: 10.1016/j.sciaf.2024.e02281

Murphy, M., & Skillen, P. (2015). The Politics of Time on the Frontline: Street Level Bureaucracy, Professional Judgment, and Public Accountability. *International Journal of Public Administration*, *38*(9), 632–641. DOI: 10.1080/01900692.2014.952823

Mustafa, G., Rafiq, W., Jhamat, N., Arshad, Z., & Rana, F. A. (2025). Blockchain-based governance models in e-government: A comprehensive framework for legal, technical, ethical and security considerations. *International Journal of Law and Management*, *67*(1), 37–55.

Mutiarin, D., Yusuf, M., Lega, M., & Habibullah, A. (2024). Agile Bureaucracy in the Digital Age: Assessing the Public Service Delivery in Jambi City. *International Journal of Public Administration in the Digital Age*, *11*(1). Advance online publication. DOI: 10.4018/IJPADA.356405

Nabeel, M. Z. (2024). AI-enhanced project management systems for optimizing resource allocation and risk mitigation: Leveraging big data analysis to predict project outcomes and improve decision-making processes in complex projects. *Asian Journal of Multidisciplinary Research & Review, 5*(5), 53–91. DOI: 10.55662/AJMRR.2024.5502

Nakamoto, S. (2008). *Bitcoin: A peer-to-peer electronic cash system.* https://bitcoin.org/bitcoin.pdf

Nanayakkara, S., & Perera, S., Sepani, S., Weerasuriya, G. T., & Bandara, H. M. N. D. (2021). Blockchain and smart contracts: A solution for payment issues in construction supply chains. *Informatics (MDPI), 8*(2), 36.

Nasr, T., Torabi, S., Bou-Harb, E., Fachkha, C., & Assi, C. (2022). Power jacking your station: In-depth security analysis of electric vehicle charging station management systems. *Computers & Security, 112*, 102511. Advance online publication. DOI: 10.1016/j.cose.2022.102511

Nelson, C., & Woods, R. H. (2013). Content analysis. In *The Routledge Handbook of Research Methods in the Study of Religion* (hal. 109–121). DOI: 10.4324/9780203154281-16

Neumann, O., Guirguis, K., & Steiner, R. (2024). Exploring artificial intelligence adoption in public organizations: A comparative case study. *Public Management Review, 26*(1), 114–141. DOI: 10.1080/14719037.2022.2048685

Nguyen, L. H., Drew, D. A., Joshi, A. D., Guo, C.-G., Ma, W., Mehta, R. S., Sikavi, D. R., Lo, C.-H., Kwon, S., Song, M., Mucci, L. A., Stampfer, M. J., Willett, W. C., Eliassen, A. H., Hart, J. E., Chavarro, J. E., Rich-Edwards, J. W., Davies, R., Capdevila, J., . . . Chan, A. T. (2020). Risk of COVID-19 among frontline healthcare workers and the general community: a prospective cohort study. MedRxiv *: The Preprint Server for Health Sciences, 2667*(20). https://doi.org/DOI: 10.1101/2020.04.29.20084111

Nguyen, T. T., Nguyen, Q. V. H., Nguyen, D. T., Nguyen, D. T., Huynh-The, T., Nahavandi, S., Nguyen, T. T., Pham, Q.-V., & Nguyen, C. M. (2022). Deep learning for deepfakes creation and detection: A survey. *Computer Vision and Image Understanding, 223*, 103525. DOI: 10.1016/j.cviu.2022.103525

Nicolás, M. A., & Sampaio, R. C. (2024). Balancing efficiency and public interest: The impact of AI automation on social benefit provision in Brazil. *Internet Policy Review, 13*(3). Advance online publication. DOI: 10.14763/2024.3.1799

Ning, H., & Liu, H. (2012). Cyber-physical-social based security architecture for future Internet of Things. *Advances in Internet of Things*, *2*(1), 1–7. DOI: 10.4236/ait.2012.21001

Niu, X., Li, J., Sun, J., & Tomsovic, K. (2019, February). Dynamic detection of false data injection attack in smart grid using deep learning. In *2019 IEEE Power & Energy Society Innovative Smart Grid Technologies Conference (ISGT)* (pp. 1-6). IEEE.

Nosina, K. C., & Swarna Latha, T. (2024). Introduction to Cybersecurity with AI, ML, and Blockchain. In *Next-Generation Cybersecurity: AI, ML, and Blockchain* (pp. 1–21). Springer Nature Singapore.

Nost, E. (2024). Governing AI, governing climate change? *Geo : Geography and Environment*, *11*(1), 1–5. DOI: 10.1002/geo2.138

Novelli, C., Taddeo, M., & Floridi, L. (2024). Accountability in artificial intelligence: What it is and how it works. *AI & Society*, *39*, 1871–1882. DOI: 10.1007/s00146-023-01635-y

Nugus, P., Ranmuthugala, G., Lamothe, J., Greenfield, D., Travaglia, J., Kolne, K., Kryluk, J., & Braithwaite, J. (2018). New ways to get policy into practice: A mixed-method participatory study of care coordination and street-level bureaucrats. *Journal of Health Organization and Management*, *32*(6), 809–824. DOI: 10.1108/JHOM-09-2017-0239 PMID: 30299221

Nyashanu, M., Pfende, F., & Ekpenyong, M. (2020). Exploring the challenges faced by frontline workers in health and social care amid the COVID-19 pandemic : Experiences of frontline workers in the English Midlands region, UK ABSTRACT. *Journal of Interprofessional Care*, *00*(00), 1–7. DOI: 10.1080/13561820.2020.1792425 PMID: 32674701

Odonkor, T. N., Adewale, T. T., & Olorunyomi, T. D. (2021). AI-powered financial forensic systems: A conceptual framework for fraud detection and prevention. *Magna Scientia Advanced Research and Reviews*, *2*(2), 119–136. DOI: 10.30574/msarr.2021.2.2.0055

OECD. (2016). Digital Government in Chile. In *OECD Digital Government Studies*. https://www.oecd-ilibrary.org/content/publication/9789264258013-en

OECD. (2022). *Tackling Policy Challenges Through Public Sector Innovation: A Strategic Portfolio Approach*.

Ogunsola, K. O., Balogun, E., & Ogunmokun, A. S. (2025). Enhancing financial integrity through an advanced internal audit risk assessment and governance model. *International Journal of Multidisciplinary Research and Growth Evaluation*, *2*(1), 781–790. DOI: 10.54660/.IJMRGE.2021.2.1.781-790

Okafor, G. (2020). *Digital government blueprint "a singapore government that is.*

Okatta, C. G., Ajayi, F. A., & Olawale, O. (2024). Navigating the future: Integrating AI and machine learning in HR practices for a digital workforce. *Computer Science & IT Research Journal*, *5*(4). Advance online publication. DOI: 10.51594/csitrj.v5i4.1085

Olutimehin, A. T. (2025). The Synergistic Role of Machine Learning, Deep Learning, and Reinforcement Learning in Strengthening Cyber Security Measures for Crypto Currency Platforms. Deep Learning, and Reinforcement Learning in Strengthening Cyber Security Measures for Crypto Currency Platforms (February 11, 2025).

Oman, Z. U., Siddiqua, A., & Noorain, R. (2024). Artificial intelligence and its ability to reduce recruitment bias. *World Journal of Advanced Research and Reviews*, *24*(1), 551–564. DOI: 10.30574/wjarr.2024.24.1.3054

Omogbeme, A., & Odewuyi, O. (2024, December). Mitigating AI bias in financial decision-making: A DEI perspective. *World Journal of Advanced Research and Reviews*, *24*(3). Advance online publication. DOI: 10.30574/wjarr.2024.24.3.3894

Orlikowski, W. J., & Gash, D. C. (1994). Technological Frames: Making Sense of Information Technology in Organizations. [TOIS]. *ACM Transactions on Information Systems*, *12*(2), 174–207. DOI: 10.1145/196734.196745

Osasona, F., Amoo, O. O., Atadoga, A., Abrahams, T. O., Farayola, O., & Ayinla, B. S. (2024). Reviewing the ethical implications of AI in decision-making processes. *International Journal of Management & Entrepreneurship Research*, *6*(2), 322–335. DOI: 10.51594/ijmer.v6i2.773

Ozkan, B. C. (2004). Using NVivo to Analyze Qualitative Classroom Data on Constructivist Learning Environments. *Qualitative Report*, *9*(4), 589–603.

Pagallo, U., Casanovas, P., & Madelin, R. (2019). The middle-out approach: Assessing models of legal governance in data protection, artificial intelligence, and the Web of Data. *The Theory and Practice of Legislation*, *7*(1), 1–25. DOI: 10.1080/20508840.2019.1664543

Pages, N. C. (2025). Mogens Klitgaard in English: The European Context. *Scandinavian Studies*, *74*(4), 521–528. https://www.jstor.org/stable/40920404

Pande, D., & Taeihagh, A. (2024). A governance perspective on user acceptance of autonomous systems in Singapore. *Technology in Society, 77*. Advance online publication. DOI: 10.1016/j.techsoc.2024.102580

Pandey, R., & Chandu, H. N. (2025). Pharmacy informatics and health information technology a systematic review. *Journal of Neonatal Surgery, 14*(1), 554–560. DOI: 10.52783/jns.v14.1577

Papagiannidis, E., Mikalef, P., & Conboy, K. (2025). Responsible artificial intelligence governance: A review and research framework. *The Journal of Strategic Information Systems, 34*(2), 101885. DOI: 10.1016/j.jsis.2024.101885

Patil, S., Kumar, R., & Singh, N. (2023). Blockchain framework for agri-product traceability. *International Journal of Blockchain Research, 6*(2), 78–89.

Paulus, T., Woods, M., Atkins, D. P., & Macklin, R. (2017). The discourse of QDAS: Reporting practices of ATLAS.ti and NVivo users with implications for best practices. *International Journal of Social Research Methodology, 20*(1), 35–47. DOI: 10.1080/13645579.2015.1102454

Pawar, P. P., Kumar, D., Meesala, M. K., Pareek, P. K., & Addula, S. R., & KS, S. (2024, November). Securing Digital Governance: A Deep Learning and Blockchain Framework for Malware Detection in IoT Networks. In *2024 International Conference on Integrated Intelligence and Communication Systems (ICIICS)* (pp. 1-8). IEEE.

Pereira, G. V., Parycek, P., Falco, E., & Kleinhans, R. (2018). Smart governance in the context of smart cities: A literature review. *Information Polity, 23*(2), 143–162.

Perera, C., Zaslavsky, A., Christen, P., & Georgakopoulos, D. (2014). Context aware computing for the Internet of Things: A survey. *IEEE Communications Surveys and Tutorials, 16*(1), 414–454. DOI: 10.1109/SURV.2013.042313.00197

Pi, Y. (2021). Machine learning in governments: Benefits, challenges and future directions. *JeDEM – eJournal of eDemocracy and Open Government, 13*(1), 203–219. DOI 10.29379/jedem.v13i1.625

Pislaru, M., Vlad, C. S., Ivascu, L., & Mircea, I. I. (2024). Citizen-Centric Governance: Enhancing Citizen Engagement through Artificial Intelligence Tools. *Sustainability (Switzerland), 16*(7). Advance online publication. DOI: 10.3390/su16072686

Pokhrel, S. (2024). No TitleΕΛΕΝΗ. *Αγαη, 15*(1), 37–48.

Prajapati, Y., Suthar, O. P., Gosai, K., & Singh, S. K. (2025). Smart city cybersecurity: Leveraging machine learning for advanced ransomware detection and prevention. In *2025 International Conference on Pervasive Computational Technologies (ICPCT)* (pp. 808–813). IEEE. https://doi.org/DOI: 10.1109/ICPCT59999.2025.9876543

Prescott, K., Baxter, E., Lynch, C., Jassal, S., Bashir, A., & Gray, J. (2020). COVID-19: How prepared are front-line healthcare workers in England? *The Journal of Hospital Infection*, *105*(2), 142–145. DOI: 10.1016/j.jhin.2020.04.031 PMID: 32339615

Puspita, A. F., Palil, M. R. B., Puspaningrum, A., & Suman, A. (2024). Taxing Artificial Intelligence: Value Impacts and Governance in the Tax Sector (Study in Indonesia and Malaysia). *Pakistan Journal of Life and Social Sciences*, *22*(1), 4623–4633. DOI: 10.57239/PJLSS-2024-22.1.00343

PwC. (2023). Impact of artificial intelligence on fraud and scams. PwC UK. https://www.pwc.co.uk/forensic-services/assets/impact-of-ai-on-fraud-and-scams.pdf

Qodir, Z., Jubba, H., & Loilatu, M. J. (2022). Muhammadiyah's Response to Covid-19 in Indonesia: Faith-Based Commitment. *Wawasan: Jurnal Ilmiah Agama Dan Sosial Budaya*, *7*(1), 71–86. DOI: 10.15575/jw.v7i1.13756

Qureshi, R., Asad, M., Tunio, S., Qureshi, S., Ahmed, M., & Ghulam, A. (2023). A survey on security issues and attacks of fog computing. *VFAST Transactions on Software Engineering*, *11*(1), 1–11.

Radanliev, P. (2025). Cyber diplomacy: Defining the opportunities for cybersecurity and risks from Artificial Intelligence, IoT, Blockchains, and Quantum Computing. *Journal of Cyber Security Technology*, *9*(1), 28–78.

Rahman, M. M., Chayan, M. M. H., Mehrin, K., Sultana, A., & Hamed, M. M. (2024, December). Explainable deep learning for cyber attack detection in electric vehicle charging stations. In *Proceedings of the 11th International Conference on Networking, Systems, and Security* (pp. 1-7).

Rahman, M. M., Pokharel, B. P., Sayeed, S. A., Bhowmik, S. K., Kshetri, N., & Eashrak, N. (2024). riskAIchain: AI-Driven IT Infrastructure—Blockchain-Backed Approach for Enhanced Risk Management. *Risks*, *12*(12), 206.

Rahman, R., Ahmed, M., & Anwar, F. (2021). 6G-driven AI architecture for secure smart farming systems. *IEEE Access : Practical Innovations, Open Solutions*, *9*, 165723–165735. DOI: 10.1109/ACCESS.2021.3134567

Rahman, S., Kumar, R., & Singh, N. (2024). ML-driven smart soil monitoring. *Sustainable Agriculture Technologies*, *3*(1), 45–56.

Rahwan, I., Cebrian, M., Obradovich, N., Bongard, J., Bonnefon, J.-F., Breazeal, C., Crandall, J., Christakis, N. A., Couzin, I. D., Jackson, M. O., Jennings, N. R., Kamar, E., Kloumann, I. M., Larochelle, H., Lazer, D., McElreath, R., Mislove, A., Parkes, D. C., Pentland, A., & Wellman, M. (2019). Machine behaviour. *Nature, 568*(7753), 477–486. DOI: 10.1038/s41586-019-1138-y PMID: 31019318

Rakhma, N. A., & Roziqin, A. (2025). Human resource mechanisms in the private and public sectors in Indonesia: What are the differences? *Insights Into Digital Business, Human Resource Management, and Competitiveness*, 377–392. https://doi.org/10.4018/979-8-3693-9440-3.ch016

Rao, K. P. N., & Manvi, S. (2023). Survey on electronic health record management using amalgamation of artificial intelligence and blockchain technologies. *Acta Informatica Pragensia, 12*(1), 179–199.

Rathnayake, I., Wedawatta, G., & Tezel, A. (2022). Smart Contracts in the construction industry: A systematic review. *Buildings (Basel, Switzerland), 12*(12), 2082.

Raza, S., & Guibas, L. (2024, July). Artificial intelligence in human resources: Ethical implications and job performance analysis. https://doi.org/DOI: 10.13140/RG.2.2.19631.75680

Reda, H. T., Ray, B., Peidaee, P., Anwar, A., Mahmood, A., Kalam, A., & Islam, N. (2021). Vulnerability and impact analysis of the IEC 61850 GOOSE protocol in the smart grid. *Sensors (Basel), 21*(4), 1554. Advance online publication. DOI: 10.3390/s21041554 PMID: 33672360

Reshi, I., Khan, M., & Shafi, S. Sholla Sahil and Assad, A., & Shafi, H. (2023). AI-powered Smart Contracts: The dawn of web 4. O. In TechRxiv.

Reuters. (2018). Amazon scraps secret AI recruiting tool that showed bias against women. Retrieved from https://www.reuters.com

Reyna, A., Martín, C., Chen, J., Soler, E., & Díaz, M. (2018). On blockchain and its integration with IoT: Challenges and opportunities. *Future Generation Computer Systems*, *88*, 173–190. DOI: 10.1016/j.future.2018.05.046

Rigotti, C., & Fosch Villaronga, E. (2024). Fairness, AI & recruitment. *Computer Law & Security Review*, *53*(1), 105966. DOI: 10.1016/j.clsr.2024.105966

Roberts, H., Cowls, J., Hine, E., Morley, J., Wang, V., Taddeo, M., & Floridi, L. (2023). Governing artificial intelligence in China and the European Union: Comparing aims and promoting ethical outcomes. *The Information Society*, *39*(2), 79–97. DOI: 10.1080/01972243.2022.2124565

Rodgers, W., Murray, J. M., Stefanidis, A., Degbey, W. Y., & Tarba, S. Y. (2023). An artificial intelligence algorithmic approach to ethical decision-making in human resource management processes. *Human Resource Management Review*, *33*(1), 100925. DOI: 10.1016/j.hrmr.2022.100925

Rodrigues, R. (2020). Legal and human rights issues of AI: Gaps, challenges and vulnerabilities. *Journal of Responsible Technology*, *4*, 100005. DOI: 10.1016/j.jrt.2020.100005

Rohn, E., & Erez, G. (2013). A framework for agro-terrorism intentions detection using overt data sources. *Technological Forecasting and Social Change*, *80*(9), 1877–1884. DOI: 10.1016/j.techfore.2013.04.013

Rose, R. (2005). A global diffusion model of e-governance. *Journal of Public Policy*, *25*(1), 5–27. DOI: 10.1017/S0143814X05000279

Roy, A., Chatterjee, S., & Mohanta, B. K. (2022). AI-powered smart irrigation: A review. *Journal of Cleaner Production*, *350*, 131490. Advance online publication. DOI: 10.1016/j.jclepro.2022.131490

Roy, M. (2017). Cathy O'Neil. Weapons of Math Destruction: How Big Data Increases Inequality and Threatens Democracy. New York: Crown Publishers, 2016. 272p. Hardcover, $26 (ISBN 978-0553418811). *College & Research Libraries*, *78*, 403–404. DOI: 10.5860/crl.78.3.403

Roy, S., Kumar, R., & Singh, N. (2022). Drone-IoT in smart crop monitoring. *Drones in Smart Farming*, *5*(1), 34–45.

Roziqin, A., & Fajrina, A. N. (2021). Understanding Public Sector Innovation from A Local Perspective: Contra War (Contraceptive for Women at Risk) Innovation Study in Malang Regency. *Jurnal Borneo Administrator*, *17*(2), 205–222. DOI: 10.24258/jba.v17i2.803

Roziqin, A., Mas'udi, S. Y. F., & Sihidi, I. T. (2021). An analysis of Indonesian government policies against COVID-19. *Public Administration and Policy*, *24*(1), 92–107. DOI: 10.1108/PAP-08-2020-0039

Rožman, M., Oreški, D., & Tominc, P. (2023). Artificial-intelligence-supported reduction of employees' workload to increase the company's performance in today's VUCA environment. *Sustainability*, *15*(6), 5019. DOI: 10.3390/su15065019

Saadat, S., Maingot, S., & Bahizad, S. (2020, November). Electric vehicle charging station security enhancement measures. In *Proceedings of the 5th IEEE Workshop on the Electronic Grid (eGRID)* (pp. 1–8). IEEE. ,

Saatçı, M., Kaya, R., & Ünlü, R. (2024). Resume screening with natural language processing (NLP). *Alphanumeric, 12*(2), 121–140. DOI: 10.17093/alphanumeric.1536577

Sabella, D., Maloor, K., Smith, N., Vanderveen, M., & Kourtis, A. (2024). Edge computing cybersecurity standards: Protecting infrastructure and applications. *IEEE Access*. Advance online publication.

Sabzi, S., & Vajta, L. (2023). Security and energy consumption considerations of electric vehicles integration in smart grids. *U. Porto Journal of Engineering*, *9*(1), 134–149.

Sadanand, V. K., & Sadanand, T. (2025). Artificial intelligence in India: Navigating social justice, environmental ethics, and legal governance. In *Exploring AI Implications on Law, Governance, and Industry* (hal. 87–118). DOI: 10.4018/979-8-3373-3384-7.ch004

Sagar, M. S., Srivastava, S., Kumar, R., & Saxena, A. (2025, February). The evolution of industry 5.0: Harnessing artificial intelligence and communication technology. In AIP Conference Proceedings (Vol. 3224, No. 1). AIP Publishing.

Sagar, M. S., Srivastava, S., Kumar, R., & Saxena, A. (2025). The evolution of industry 5.0: Harnessing artificial intelligence and communication technology. *AIP Conference Proceedings*, *3224*(1), 20064. DOI: 10.1063/5.0246747

Said, D., Elloumi, M., & Khoukhi, L. (2022). Cyber-attack on P2P energy transaction between connected electric vehicles: A false data injection detection-based machine learning model. *IEEE Access : Practical Innovations, Open Solutions*, *10*, 63640–63647. DOI: 10.1109/ACCESS.2022.3182701

Sakuntala, S. S., Sarakanam, S., Dhavan, A., Taggar, R., & Kohli, G. (2024). The complexity of corruption and recent trends in information technology for combating corruption in India. *Public Administration and Policy*, *27*(2), 126–139. DOI: 10.1108/PAP-05-2023-0058

Salahudin, S., Nurmandi, A., & Loilatu, M. J. (2020). How to Design Qualitative Research with NVivo 12 Plus for Local Government Corruption Issues in Indonesia? *Jurnal Studi Pemerintahan, 11*(3), 369–398. DOI: 10.18196/jgp.113124

Salahudin, S., Nurmandi, A., Sulistyaningsih, T., & Lutfi, M. (2020). Analysis of Government Official Twitters during Covid-19 Crisis in Indonesia Analysis of Government Official Twitters during Covid-19 Crisis in Indonesia. *Talent Development & Excellence*, *12*(June), 3899–3915.

Salako, A. O., Fabuyi, J. A., Aideyan, N. T., Selesi-Aina, O., Dapo-Oyewole, D. L., & Olaniyi, O. O. (2024). Advancing information governance in AI-driven cloud ecosystem: Strategies for enhancing data security and meeting regulatory compliance. *Asian Journal of Research in Computer Science*, *17*(12), 66–88.

Salama, R., & Al-Turjman, F. (2024). Blockchain technology, computer network operations, and global value chains together make up "cybersecurity". In *Smart Global Value Chain* (pp. 150–164). CRC Press.

Salesforce. (2021). AI-powered well-being assistants: Redefining employee care. Retrieved from https://www.salesforce.com

Saner, R., Yiu, L., & Nguyen, M. (2020). Monitoring the SDGs: Digital and social technologies to ensure citizen participation, inclusiveness and transparency. *Development Policy Review*, *38*(4), 483–500. https://doi.org/https://doi.org/10.1111/dpr.12433

Saxena, A., Gupta, M., Srivastava, S., & Kumar, R. (2025, February). Empowering edge computing: The critical role of blockchain in cybersecurity defense. In AIP Conference Proceedings (Vol. 3224, No. 1). AIP Publishing.

Saxena, A., Gupta, M., Srivastava, S., & Kumar, R. (2025). Empowering edge computing: The critical role of blockchain in cybersecurity defense. *AIP Conference Proceedings*, *3224*(1), 20063. DOI: 10.1063/5.0245962

Scholl, H. (2003). E-government: A Special Case of ICT-enabled Business Process Change. In *International Journal of E-Govemment Research* (Vol. 1). DOI: 10.1109/HICSS.2003.1174309

Scholl, H. J. (2022). Digital Government Research: A Diverse Domain. In *Public Administration and Information Technology* (Vol. 38, hal. 51–71). DOI: 10.1007/978-3-030-92945-9_3

Scruggs, D., Timilsina, L., Papari, B., Arsalan, A., Muriithi, G., Ozkan, G., & Edrington, C. S. (2024). Neural network-based cyber-threat detection strategy in four motor-drive autonomous electric vehicles. *IEEE Access*. Advance online publication.

Seak, C.-J., Liu, Y.-T., & Ng, C.-J. (2020). Rapid responses in the emergency department of Linkou Chang Gung Memorial Hospital, Taiwan effectively prevents spread of COVID-19 among healthcare workers of emergency department during outbreak: Lessons learnt from SARS. *Biomedical Journal*, (June), 4–7. DOI: 10.1016/j.bj.2020.06.002 PMID: 32792166

Selten, F. J., & Klievink, B. (2024). Organizing public sector AI adoption: Navigating between separation and integration. *Government Information Quarterly*, *41*(1), 101885. DOI 10.1016/j.giq.2023.101885[REMOVED HYPERLINK FIELD]

Selvakumar, P., Pooja Sudharma, B., Mishra, B. R., & Satyanarayana, P. (2025). Digital government and digital governance. In *Public Governance Practices in the Age of AI* (hal. 1–22). DOI: 10.4018/979-8-3693-9286-7.ch001

Senoo, E. E. K., Anggraini, L., Kumi, J. A., Karolina, L. B., Akansah, E., Sulyman, H. A., & Aritsugi, M. (2024). IoT solutions with artificial intelligence technologies for precision agriculture: Definitions, applications, challenges, and opportunities. *Electronics (Basel)*, *13*(10), 1894. Advance online publication. DOI: 10.3390/electronics13101894

Shamout, F. E., & Ali, D. A. (2021). The strategic pursuit of artificial intelligence in the United Arab Emirates. *Communications of the ACM*, *64*(4), 57–58. DOI: 10.1145/3447723

Sharma, V., Vashishth, T. K., Tiwari, D., Sethi, P., & Sharma, S. (2025, April). Enhancing cybersecurity: A machine learning approach for phishing website detection. In AIP Conference Proceedings (Vol. 3278, No. 1). AIP Publishing.

Sharma, S., Kumar, R., & Singh, N. (2020). 5G-enabled IoT and smart farming: Current status and future challenges. *IEEE Access : Practical Innovations, Open Solutions*, *8*, 123456–123475. DOI: 10.1109/ACCESS.2020.2978901

Sharma, S., Kumar, R., & Singh, N. (2023). 6G-enabled precision agriculture architecture. *IEEE Communications Magazine*, *61*(5), 102–108. DOI: 10.1109/MCOM.2023.3245678

Shaw, K., Golding, S., Knight, J., Chadborn, T., Dempster, L., Finistrella, V., & Hopkins, S. (2019). A unique approach to the development of infection prevention and control resources for front-line health care workers. *Infection Prevention in Practice*, *1*(1), 100004. DOI: 10.1016/j.infpip.2019.100004 PMID: 34368670

Sheikh, A. M., Islam, M. R., Habaebi, M. H., Zabidi, S. A., Bin Najeeb, A. R., & Kabbani, A. (2025). A survey on edge computing (EC) security challenges: Classification, threats, and mitigation strategies. *Future Internet*, *17*(4), 175. Advance online publication. DOI: 10.3390/fi17040175

Shovkovyy, O. (2024). Defining Electronic Bureaucracy and Bureaucratism. *Suranaree Journal of Social Science*, *18*(2). Advance online publication. DOI: 10.55766/sjss-2-2024-257400

Shriya, K., Velmurugan, T., & Kumar, G. (2025). Advancements in financial data protection: How artificial intelligence strengthens security measures in blockchain systems. In *Applications of Blockchain and Artificial Intelligence in Finance and Governance* (pp. 136–149). CRC Press.

Sifat, R. I. (2025). Commentary—AI and Public Policy: Navigating the Possibilities and Limitations. *Politics & Policy, 53*(1). Advance online publication. DOI: 10.1111/polp.70019

Sigfrids, A., Nieminen, M., Leikas, J., & Pikkuaho, P. (2022). How Should Public Administrations Foster the Ethical Development and Use of Artificial Intelligence? A Review of Proposals for Developing Governance of AI. *Frontiers in Human Dynamics, 4*. Advance online publication. DOI: 10.3389/fhumd.2022.858108

Singh, B., Kaunert, C., & Ravesangar, K. (2024). Artificial intelligence and employee well-being: Projecting psychological and physical healthcare. In *Human resource strategies in the era of artificial intelligence* (pp. [page range]). https://doi.org/DOI: 10.4018/979-8-3693-6412-3.ch005

Singh, C. B., Gupta, A., & Kumar, D. R. (2022). Diabetes Care Survey Using Supervised and Unsupervised Machine Learning. *2022 3rd International Conference on Intelligent Engineering and Management (ICIEM)*, 207–210. DOI: 10.1109/ICIEM54221.2022.9853085

Singh, C. B., Gupta, A., & Kumar, D. R. (2022, April). Diabetes care survey using supervised and unsupervised machine learning. 2022 3rd International Conference on Intelligent and Management (ICIEM).

Singh, C. B., Gupta, A., & Kumar, R. (2022, April). Diabetes Care Survey Using Supervised and Unsupervised Machine Learning. In 2022 3rd International Conference on Intelligent Engineering and Management (ICIEM) (pp. 207-210). IEEE.

Singh, S. K., Park, L., & Park, J. H. (2022, October). Blockchain-based federated approach for privacy-preserved IoT-enabled smart vehicular networks. In *2022 13th International Conference on Information and Communication Technology Convergence (ICTC)* (pp. 1995-1999). IEEE.

Singh, A. K., & Patro, B. D. K. (2019). Security of low computing power devices: A survey of requirements, challenges & possible solutions. . *Cybernetics and Information Technologies, 19*(1), 133–164.

Singh, A. R., Kumar, R. S., Rathore, R. S., Pandian, A., Alrayes, F. S., Allafi, R., & Ahmad, N. (2025). AI-enhanced smart grid framework for intrusion detection and mitigation in EV charging stations. . *Alexandria Engineering Journal, 115*, 603–621.

Singh, B. P., & Joshi, A. (2024). Ethical Considerations in AI Development. In Kumar, R., Joshi, A., Sharan, H., Peng, S., & Dudhagara, C. (Eds.), *The Ethical Frontier of AI and Data Analysis* (pp. 156–179). IGI Global Scientific Publishing., DOI: 10.4018/979-8-3693-2964-1.ch010

Singh, S. K., Kumar, M., Khanna, A., & Virdee, B. (2024). Blockchain and FL-based secure architecture for enhanced external intrusion detection in smart farming. *IEEE Internet of Things Journal, 11*(10), 17890–17902. DOI: 10.1109/JIOT.2024.3367890

Singh, S. K., Kumar, M., Tanwar, S., & Park, J. H. (2024). GRU-based digital twin framework for data allocation and storage in IoT-enabled smart home networks. *Future Generation Computer Systems, 153*, 391–402. DOI: 10.1016/j.future.2023.11.019

Singh, S. K., Park, J. H., Sharma, P. K., & Pan, Y. (2021). BIIoVT: Blockchain-based secure storage architecture for intelligent Internet of Vehicular Things. *IEEE Consumer Electronics Magazine, 11*(6), 75–82. DOI: 10.1109/MCE.2021.3112599

Singh, S. K., Vaghela, K., Khanna, A., Virdee, B., & Kumar, M. (2025). SuRaksha: AI-powered blockchain framework for HVAC tamper detection and authentication in smart classrooms. *IEEE Internet of Things Journal, 12*(3), 4567–4579. DOI: 10.1109/JIOT.2024.3456789

Singh, S. K., Yang, L. T., & Park, J. H. (2023). FusionFedBlock: Fusion of blockchain and federated learning to preserve privacy in industry 5.0. *Information Fusion, 90*, 233–240. DOI: 10.1016/j.inffus.2022.09.019

Skute, I. (2019). Opening the black box of academic entrepreneurship: Abibliometric anal- ysis. *Scientometrics, 120*(1), 237–265.

Socol, A., & Iuga, I. C. (2024). Addressing brain drain and strengthening governance for advancing government readiness in artificial intelligence (AI). *Kybernetes, 53*(13), 47–71.

Soetan, T., & Samuel, T. (2025). The role of AI chatbots in mental health support: Improving accessibility to counseling and psychological care. Lab: Timothy Soetan's Lab. Retrieved from https://www.researchgate.net/publication/390177016

Sood, A. (2024, January 12). Crafting effective wellness plans for employees using AI. Occupational Health & Safety. https://ohsonline.com/Articles/2024/01/12/Crafting-Effective-Wellness-Plans-for-Employees-using-AI.aspx

Soundenkar, S., Bhosale, K., Jakhete, M. D., Kadam, K., Chowdary, V. G. R., & Durga, H. K. (2024). AI Powered Risk Management: Addressing Cybersecurity Threats in Financial Systems. Library of Progress-Library Science, Information Technology & Computer, 44(3).

Souter, D., & Van der Spuy, A. (2019). *UNESCO's internet universality indicators: A framework for assessing Internet development*. UNESCO Publishing.

Sriharan, A., Sekercioglu, N., & Mitchell, C.. (2024). Leadership for AI transformation in health care organizations: A scoping review. *Journal of Medical Internet Research, 26*(8), e54556. DOI: 10.2196/54556 PMID: 39009038

Srivastava, S., Ahmed, D. T., & Kumar, D. R. (2024). *Urban Growth Estimation of Moradabad City Using Sentinel-2 Images*. DOI: 10.1109/GlobalAISummit62156.2024.10947888

Srivastava, S., Ahmed, T., Saxena, A., & Kumar, R. (2025, February). A novel machine learning hybrid model for heart disease risk assessment. In AIP Conference Proceedings (Vol. 3224, No. 1). AIP Publishing.

Srivastava, S., Ahmed, T., Kumar, R., & Saxena, A. (2025). A transfer learning based model for brain tumor detection using magnetic resonance imaging. *AIP Conference Proceedings, 3224*(1), 20059. DOI: 10.1063/5.0246542

Srivastava, S., Ahmed, T., Saxena, A., & Kumar, R. (2025). A novel machine learning hybrid model for heart disease risk assessment. *AIP Conference Proceedings, 3224*(1), 20058. DOI: 10.1063/5.0246550

Stallone, V., Wetzels, M., & Klaas, M. (2021). Applications of blockchain technology in marketing-a systematic review of marketing technology companies. *Blockchain: Re- search and Applications, 2*(3), 100023. .DOI: 10.1016/j.bcra.2021.100023

Steinbach, A. (2024). Digital sovereignty. *List Forum fur Wirtschafts- und Finanzpolitik, 50*(1–2), 51–74. DOI: 10.1007/s41025-023-00252-3

Stergiou, C., Psannis, K. E., Kim, B.-G., & Gupta, B. (2018). Secure integration of IoT and cloud computing. *Future Generation Computer Systems, 78*, 964–975. DOI: 10.1016/j.future.2017.08.031

Su, H., Lu, Y., Lyulyov, O., & Pimonenko, T. (2023). Good governance within public participation and national audit for reducing corruption. *Sustainability, 15*(9), 7030. DOI: 10.3390/su15097030

Sung, C. S., & Park, J. Y. (2021). Understanding of blockchain-based identity management system adoption in the public sector. *Journal of Enterprise Information Management, 34*(5), 1481–1505. DOI: 10.1108/JEIM-12-2020-0532

Sun, T. Q., & Medaglia, R. (2019). Mapping the challenges of artificial intelligence in the public sector: Evidence from public healthcare. *Government Information Quarterly, 36*(2), 368–383.

Sun, T. Q., & Medaglia, R. (2019). Mapping the challenges of Artificial Intelligence in the public sector: Evidence from public healthcare. *Government Information Quarterly*, *36*(2), 368–383. DOI: 10.1016/j.giq.2018.09.008

Sutrop, M. (2019). Should we trust artificial intelligence? *Trames*, *23*(4), 499–522. DOI: 10.3176/tr.2019.4.07

Swapnil, M., Garima, S., & Shashank, S. (2024). From Automation to Innovation: Harnessing the Synergy of Generative AI and Retrieval-Augmented Generation for Citizen-centric Governance. *2024 ITU Kaleidoscope. Innovation and Digital Transformation for a Sustainable World, ITU K, 2024*. Advance online publication. DOI: 10.23919/ITUK62727.2024.10772932

Szabo, N. (1997). Formalizing and securing relationships on public networks. *First monday*. Tamburri, D. A. (2020). Design principles for the general data protection regulation (gdpr): A formal concept analysis and its evaluation. *Information Systems*, *91*, 101469. DOI: 10.1016/j.is.2019.101469

Takeda, T., Kato, J., Matsumura, T., Murakami, T., & Abeynayaka, A. (2021). Governance of artificial intelligence in water and wastewater management: The case study of japan. *Hydrology*, *8*(3). Advance online publication. DOI: 10.3390/hydrology8030120

Tangi, L., van Noordt, C., & Rodriguez Müller, A. P. (2023). *The challenges of AI implementation in the public sector*. DOI: 10.1145/3598469.3598516

Tang, L. H., Tang, S., Chen, X. L., Zhang, S., Xiong, Y., Chen, R., & Meng, Q. T. (2020). Avoiding health worker infection and containing the coronavirus disease 2019 pandemic: Perspectives from the frontline in Wuhan. *International Journal of Surgery*, *79*, 120–124.

Tanyıldız, H., Şahin, C. B., Dinler, Ö. B., Migdady, H., Saleem, K., Smerat, A., & Abualigah, L. (2025). Detection of cyber attacks in electric vehicle charging systems using a remaining useful life generative adversarial network. *Scientific Reports*, *15*(1), 10092. DOI: 10.1038/s41598-025-17999-1 PMID: 40128270

Tariq, M., & Pervaiz, H. (2022). 6G and blockchain integration for smart agriculture. *IEEE Access : Practical Innovations, Open Solutions*, *10*, 55676–55689. DOI: 10.1109/ACCESS.2022.3174567

Taylor, P. J., Dargahi, T., Dehghantanha, A., Parizi, R. M., & Choo, K.-K. R. (2020). A systematic literature review of blockchain cyber security. *Digital Communications and Networks*, *6*(2), 147–156.

Thakkar, A., Gupta, A., & De Sousa, A. (2024). Artificial intelligence in positive mental health: A narrative review. *Frontiers in Digital Health*, *6*, 1280235. DOI: 10.3389/fdgth.2024.1280235 PMID: 38562663

Thilakarathne, N. N., Bakar, M. S. A., Abas, P. E., & Yassin, H. (2025a). Internet of Things enabled smart agriculture: Current status, latest advancements, challenges and countermeasures. *Heliyon*, *11*(3), e09876. Advance online publication. DOI: 10.1016/j.heliyon.2025.e09876 PMID: 39959477

Thilakarathne, N. N., Bakar, M. S. A., Abas, P. E., & Yassin, H. (2025b). 6G-enabled AI frameworks for smart agriculture. *Heliyon*, *11*(3), e09877. Advance online publication. DOI: 10.1016/j.heliyon.2025.e09877 PMID: 39959477

Thiru, S., Hashmi, H., Hemavathi, S., Vekariya, D., Pandey, A. K., & Abdel-Rehim, W. M. F. (2022). Vehicular cloud data collection for intelligent transportation systems. In *2022 Fourth International Conference on Emerging Research in Electronics, Computer Science and Technology (ICERECT)* (pp. 1–6). IEEE. https://doi.org/DOI: 10.1109/ICERECT56837.2022.10060170

Tian, F. (2017). A supply chain traceability system for food safety based on HACCP, blockchain & Internet of Things. In *2017 International Conference on Service Systems and Service Management* (pp. 1–6). IEEE. https://doi.org/DOI: 10.1109/ICSSSM.2017.7996119

Toosi, A. N., Calheiros, R. N., & Buyya, R. (2014). Interconnected cloud computing environments: Challenges, taxonomy, and survey. *ACM Computing Surveys*, *47*(1), 7. Advance online publication. DOI: 10.1145/2593512

Topol, E. J. (2019). *Deep medicine: How artificial intelligence can make healthcare human again*. Basic Books.

Trajkovski, G. (2024). Bridging the public administration–AI divide: A skills perspective. *Public Administration and Development*, *44*(5), 412–426. DOI: 10.1002/pad.2061

Transparency International. (2022). The corruption risks of artificial intelligence. Transparency International. https://knowledgehub.transparency.org/assets/uploads/kproducts/The-Corruption-Risks-of-Artificial-Intelligence.pdf

Tshuma, G., Kritzinger, E., & Singh, S. (2024). A Framework for Promoting Digital Transformation and the Adoption of Enterprise Architecture in South Africa's Public Sector. *IFIP Advances in Information and Communication Technology*, *709*, 16–30. DOI: 10.1007/978-3-031-66986-6_2

Tummers, L., & Bekkers, V. (2014). Policy Implementation, Street-level Bureaucracy, and the Importance of Discretion. *Public Management Review*, *16*(4), 527–547. DOI: 10.1080/14719037.2013.841978

Tyagi, N. K., & Goyal, M. (2021). Contextualizing Electronic Governance, Smart City Governance and Sustainable Infrastructure in India: A Study and Framework. In *Digital Cities Roadmap: IoT-Based Architecture and Sustainable Buildings* (hal. 163–191). DOI: 10.1002/9781119792079.ch5

Ulnicane, I., Eke, D. O., Knight, W., Ogoh, G., & Stahl, B. C. (2021). Good governance as a response to discontents? Déjà vu, or lessons for AI from other emerging technologies. *Interdisciplinary Science Reviews*, *46*(1–2), 71–93. DOI: 10.1080/03080188.2020.1840220

UNDCO and WHO. (2020). Strategic Preparedness and Response Plan on COVID-19 by WHO. *Printed in Geneva, Switzerland.*, *12*(February), 20.

UNDP. (2023). A Shared Vision for Technology and Governance. *A Shared Vision for Technology and Governance*. DOI: 10.18356/9789213585214

Unilever. (2019). AI-driven hiring: Removing bias in recruitment. Retrieved from https://www.unilever.com

Upadhyay, N. (2020). Demystifying blockchain: A critical analysis of challenges, applica- tions and opportunities. *International Journal of Information Management, 54*, 102120. Vayansky, I., & Kumar, S. A. (2020). A review of topic modeling methods. *Information Systems*, *94*, 101582. DOI: 10.1016/j.is.2020.101582

Upreti, K., Verma, A., Mittal, S., Vats, P., Haque, M., & Ali, S. (2023). A Novel Framework for Harnessing AI for Evidence-Based Policymaking in E-Governance Using Smart Contracts. *Communications in Computer and Information Science, 1921 CCIS*, 231–240. DOI: 10.1007/978-3-031-45124-9_18

Vakkuri, V., Kemell, K.-K., Tolvanen, J., Jantunen, M., Halme, E., & Abrahamsson, P. (2022). How Do Software Companies Deal with Artificial Intelligence Ethics? A Gap Analysis. *ACM International Conference Proceeding Series*, 100–109. DOI: 10.1145/3530019.3530030

Van den Hoven, J. (2020). Responsible AI and the role of transparency and accountability. *AI and Ethics*, *1*(1), 21–39. DOI: 10.1007/s43681-019-00003-9

Vargo, S. L., & Lusch, R. F. (2004). Evolving to a New Dominant Logic for Marketing. *Journal of Marketing*, *68*(1), 1–17. DOI: 10.1509/jmkg.68.1.1.24036

Vashishth, T. K., Sharma, V., Kaushik, V., & Sharma, K. K. (2025). Blockchain-Driven Innovations in the Banking and Financial Sectors: Harnessing the Power of Automated Machine Learning. In Utilizing AI and Machine Learning in Financial Analysis (pp. 555-578). IGI Global Scientific Publishing.

Vashishth, T. K., Sharma, V., Kaushik, V., Singh, A., & Kaushik, S. (2025). Exploring Quantum Challenges and Opportunities of Quantum Machine Learning Adoption in Finance. Machine Learning and Modeling Techniques in Financial Data Science, 437-460.

Vashishth, T. K., Sharma, V., Kumar, B., & Sharma, K. K. (2024). Cloud-Based Data Management for Behavior Analytics in Business and Finance Sectors. In Data-Driven Modelling and Predictive Analytics in Business and Finance (pp. 133-155). Auerbach Publications.

Vashishth, T. K., Sharma, V., Kumar, B., Sharma, K. K., Chaudhary, S., & Panwar, R. (2025). Blockchain for Securing Federated Learning Systems: Enhancing Privacy and Trust. Model Optimization Methods for Efficient and Edge AI: Federated Learning Architectures, Frameworks and Applications, 299-320.

Vashishth, T. K., Sharma, V., Samania, B., Sharma, R., Singh, S., & Jajoria, P. (2025). Ethical and Legal Implications of AI in Cybersecurity. In Machine Intelligence Applications in Cyber-Risk Management (pp. 387-414). IGI Global Scientific Publishing.

Vashishth, T. K., Sharma, V., Sharma, K. K., Kumar, B., Chaudhary, S., & Panwar, R. (2024). Intelligent Resource Allocation and Optimization for Industrial Robotics Using AI and Blockchain. In AI and Blockchain Applications in Industrial Robotics (pp. 82-110). IGI Global.

Vashishth, T. K., Sharma, V., Sharma, K. K., Kumar, B., Chaudhary, S., & Panwar, R. (2024). Security and Privacy Challenges in Blockchain-Based Supply Chain Management: A Comprehensive Analysis. In Achieving Secure and Transparent Supply Chains with Blockchain Technology (pp. 70-91). IGI Global.

Vashishth, T. K., Kumar, B., Alam, M. S., Sharma, V., & Chaudhary, S. (2024). The Impact of Artificial Intelligence on the Future of Computing: A Comparative Study. In *Applications of Block Chain technology and Artificial Intelligence: Lead-ins in Banking, Finance, and Capital Market* (pp. 1–17). Springer International Publishing.

Vashishth, T. K., Sharma, V., Kaushik, V., Bagar, V. K., Sharma, R., & Kumar, R. (2025). Importance of Using AI and ML in the Financial Sector for Risk Prevention and Management. In *Utilizing AI and Machine Learning in Financial Analysis* (pp. 509–530). IGI Global Scientific Publishing.

Verma, S., Sharma, R., Deb, S., & Maitra, D. (2021). Artificial intelligence in marketing: Systematic review and future research direction. *International Journal of Information Management Data Insights, 1*(1), 100002. DOI: 10.1016/j.jjimei.2020.100002

Vike, H. (2018). Street-level bureaucracy and crosscutting cleavages in municipal worlds. *Comparative Social Research, 33*, 245–263. DOI: 10.1108/S0195-631020180000033016

Vogels, E. A. (2021). The future of predictive policing: Ethical considerations and implications. *The Journal of Law and Technology, 36*(3), 142–159. DOI: 10.1080/10465788.2020.1782689

Vohnsen, N. H. (2015). Street-level planning; the shifty nature of "local knowledge and practice.". *Journal of Organizational Ethnography, 4*(2), 147–161. DOI: 10.1108/JOE-09-2014-0032

Voigt, P., & von dem Bussche, A. (2017). *The EU General Data Protection Regulation (GDPR): A practical guide*. Springer International Publishing., DOI: 10.1007/978-3-319-57959-7

von Lucke, J., Fitsilis, F., & Gagnon, S. (2024). Using Artificial Intelligence in Parliament - Initial Results from the Canadian House of Commons. *CEUR Workshop Proceedings, •••*, 3737.

Wagner, J. K., Doerr, M., & Schmit, C. D. (2024). AI governance: A challenge for public health. *JMIR Public Health and Surveillance, 10*, e58358. PMID: 39347615

Walczak, S. (2021). Predicting crime and other uses of neural networks in police decision making. *Frontiers in Psychology, 12*, 587943. https://pmc.ncbi.nlm.nih.gov/ PMID: 34690848

Waller, M. A., & Fawcett, S. E. (2013). Data science, predictive analytics, and big data: A revolution that will transform supply chain design and management. *Journal of Business Logistics, 34*(2), 77–84. DOI: 10.1111/jbl.12010

Wandabwa, H. M., Naeem, M. A., Mirza, F., & Pears, R. (2021). Topical affinity in short text microblogs. *Information Systems, 96*, 101662. DOI: 10.1016/j.is.2020.101662

Wang, C., Cheng, Z., Yue, X.-G., & McAleer, M. (2020). Risk Management of COVID-19 by Universities in China. *Journal of Risk and Financial Management, 13*(2), 36. DOI: 10.3390/jrfm13020036

Wang, J., Zhou, M., & Liu, F. (2020). Reasons for healthcare workers becoming infected with novel coronavirus disease 2019 (COVID-19) in China. *The Journal of Hospital Infection, 105*(1), 100–101. DOI: 10.1016/j.jhin.2020.03.002 PMID: 32147406

Wang, Y.-S., & Liao, Y.-W. (2008). Assessing eGovernment systems success: A validation of the DeLone and McLean model of information systems success. *Government Information Quarterly, 25*(4), 717–733. https://doi.org/https://doi.org/10.1016/j.giq.2007.06.002

WHO, U. (2020l). Social Stigma associated with COVID-19. *World Health Organization, February*, 1–5.

WHO. (2019). 2019 NOVEL CORONAVIRUS (2019-nCoV) STRATEGIC PREPAREDNESS AND RESPONSE PLAN FOR THE SOUTH-EAST ASIA REGION 1. In *World Health Organization South-East Asia*. https://doi.org/.DOI: 1037//0033-2909.I26.1.78

WHO. (2020a). Biomedical Equipment for COVID-19 Case Management Invetory Tool. *World Health Organization, 25*(June), 1–34.

WHO. (2020b). COVID-19 STRATEGY UPDATE. In *World Health Organization* (Issue April). https://doi.org/DOI: 10.1146/annurev.genet.37.050203.103207

WHO. (2020c). Critical preparedness, readiness and response actions for COVID-19. In *World Health Organization Interim Guidance*. Issue March.

WHO. (2020d). Investing in and building longer-term health emergency preparedness during the COVID-19 pandemic. *World Health Organization, 6*(July), 1–30.

WHO. (2020e). Maintaining essential health services: Operational guidance for the COVID-19 context. *World Development, 1*(June), 1–55.

WHO. (2020f). Mental Health and Psychosocial Considerations During COVID-19 Outbreak. *World Health Organization, January*, 1–6.

WHO. (2020g). Operational Planning Guidelines to Support Country Preparedness and Response. *World Health Organization, 22*(May), 1–30.

WHO. (2020h). Overview of public health and social measures in the context of COVID-19. *World Health Organization Interim Guidance, 18*(May), 1–8.

WHO. (2020i). Preparing for large-scale community transmission of COVID-19. *World Health Organization Westren Pacific Region*, (February), 1–8.

WHO. (2020j). Rapid Hospital Readiness Checlist. *World Development*, *25*(June), 1–19.

WHO. (2020k). The COVID-19 Risk Communication Package For Healthcare Facilities. *WHO*, 1–11.

Wimmer, M. A., Grimm, R., Jahn, N., & Hampe, J. F. (2013). *Mobile Participation: Exploring Mobile Tools in E-Participation BT - Electronic Participation* (M. A. Wimmer, E. Tambouris, & A. Macintosh (ed.); hal. 1–13). Springer Berlin Heidelberg.

Wirtz, B. W., Jan, C. W., & Geyer, C. (2019). Artificial Intelligence and the Public Sector—Applications and Challenges. *International Journal of Public Administration*, *42*(7), 596–615. DOI: 10.1080/01900692.2018.1498103

Wirtz, B. W., Langer, P. F., & Fenner, C. (2021). Artificial intelligence in the public sector: A systematic literature review and research agenda. *International Journal of Public Administration*, *44*(13), 1103–1128. DOI: 10.1080/01900692.2021.1947319[REMOVED HYPERLINK FIELD]

Wolfert, S., Ge, L., Verdouw, C., & Bogaardt, M.-J. (2017). Big data in smart farming: A review. *Agricultural Systems*, *153*, 69–80. DOI: 10.1016/j.agsy.2017.01.023

World Economic Forum. (2024, October 14). Why corporate integrity is key to shaping the use of AI. *Emerging Technologies*. Retrieved from https://www.weforum.org/stories/2024/10/corporate-integrity-future-ai-regulation/

Wright, J. (2024). The Development of AI Ethics in Japan: Ethics-washing Society 5.0? *East Asian Science, Technology and Society*, *18*(2), 117–134. DOI: 10.1080/18752160.2023.2275987

Xiao, J., Fang, M., Chen, Q., & He, B. (2020). SARS, MERS and COVID-19 among healthcare workers: A narrative review. *Journal of Infection and Public Health*, *13*(6), 843–848. DOI: 10.1016/j.jiph.2020.05.019 PMID: 32493671

Xu, A., Lin, Y., & Zhao, L. (2023). Digital twin and edge intelligence in precision agriculture: A survey. *Computers and Electronics in Agriculture*, *195*, 106937. Advance online publication. DOI: 10.1016/j.compag.2022.106937

Xu, K., Zhang, Y., Li, Y., & Wu, K. (2023). Decentralized AI with blockchain for smart agriculture. *Journal of Network and Computer Applications*, *202*, 103396. Advance online publication. DOI: 10.1016/j.jnca.2022.103396

Xu, Z., Liu, Z., & Luo, H. (2025). Can artificial intelligence technology help achieve good governance? A public policy evaluation method based on artificial neural network. *SAGE Open*, *15*(1), 1–15. DOI 10.1177/21582440251317833[REMOVED HYPERLINK FIELD]

Yadav, J., Misra, M., & Goundar, S. (2020). An overview of food supply chain virtuali- sation and granular traceability using blockchain technology. *International Journal of Blockchains and Cryptocurrencies*, *1*(2), 154–178. DOI: 10.1504/IJBC.2020.108997

Yadav, J., Misra, M., & Goundar, S. (n.d.) Autonomous agriculture marketing informa- tion system through blockchain: A case study of e-nam adoption in india. In *Blockchain Technologies* (pp. 115–138). Applications and Cryptocurrencies., DOI: 10.1142/9789811205279_0005

Yadav, J., Misra, M., Rana, N. P., & Singh, K. (2021a). *Exploring the synergy between nano*. Technology & People.

Yadav, J., Misra, M., Rana, N. P., Singh, K., & Goundar, S. (2021b). Netizens' Behavior to- wards a blockchain-based esports framework: A tpb and machine learning integrated approach. *International Journal of Sports Marketing & Sponsorship.*

Yaga, D., Mell, P., Roby, N., & Scarfone, K. (2018). Draft blockchain technology overview (nistir-8202). *National Institute of Standard and Technology, 59.*

Yang, K., Wang, R., Jiang, Y., Song, H., Luo, C., Guan, Y., & Shi, Z. (2018). Sensor attack detection using history based pairwise inconsistency. *Future Generation Computer Systems*, *86*, 392–402. DOI: 10.1016/j.future.2018.01.008

Yaqoob, A., & Robbins, S. (2024). Ethical concerns in AI-enhanced job performance metrics in human resources. [Preprint]. https://doi.org/DOI: 10.13140/RG.2.2.36584.28163

Yaqoob, I., Salah, K., Jayaraman, R., & Al-Hammadi, Y. (2021). Blockchain for health- care data management: Opportunities, challenges, and future recommendations. *Neural Computing & Applications*, ●●●, 1–16.

Yu, L., & Li, Y. (2022, April). Artificial intelligence decision-making transparency and employees' trust: The parallel multiple mediating effect of effectiveness and discomfort. *Behavioral Sciences (Basel, Switzerland)*, *12*(5), 127. DOI: 10.3390/bs12050127 PMID: 35621424

Zahidi, F., Kaluvilla, B. B., & Mulla, T. (2024). Embracing the new era: Artificial intelligence and its multifaceted impact on the hospitality industry. *Journal of Open Innovation*, *10*(4), 100390. DOI: 10.1016/j.joitmc.2024.100390

Zainab Kabba, S. D. (2015). NVivo 12: Up and Running. *IT Services, University of Oxford*, 1–68.

Zang, X. (2016). Research on Street-Level Discretion in the West: Past, Present, and the Future. *Chinese Political Science Review, 1*(4), 610–622. DOI: 10.1007/s41111-016-0041-z

Zechmeister, I., Österle, A., Denk, P., & Katschnig, H. (2002). Incentives in financing mental health care in Austria. *The Journal of Mental Health Policy and Economics, 5*(3), 121–129. PMID: 12728199

Zhang, C., & Kovacs, J. M. (2012). The application of small unmanned aerial systems for precision agriculture: A review. *Precision Agriculture, 13*(6), 693–712. DOI: 10.1007/s11119-012-9274-5

Zhang, X., Chen, H., Li, Y., & Wu, K. (2021). Blockchain-based trusted data sharing in 6G-enabled IoT smart agriculture. *IEEE Internet of Things Journal, 8*(12), 9872–9883. DOI: 10.1109/JIOT.2020.3045678

Zhang, Y., Kumar, R., & Singh, N. (2021). Digital twin-based smart farming. *Precision Agriculture Technology, 12*(4), 56–67.

Zhao, W., Alwidian, S., & Mahmoud, Q. H. (2022). Adversarial training methods for deep learning: A systematic review. *Algorithms, 15*(8), Article 283. Kure, H. I., Sarkar, P., Ndanusa, A. B., & Nwajana, A. O. (2025). Detecting and preventing data poisoning attacks on AI models. *arXiv preprint*. /arXiv.2503.09302DOI: 10.3390/a15080283

Zhao, J., & Gómez Fariñas, B. (2023). Artificial intelligence and sustainable decisions. *European Business Organization Law Review, 24*, 1–39. DOI: 10.1007/s40804-022-00262-2

Zhao, X., Chen, L., & Zhang, H. (2023). AI-based smart irrigation optimization in agriculture. *Agricultural Systems, 194*, 103284. Advance online publication. DOI: 10.1016/j.agsy.2022.103284

Zhou, K. Q. (2022). Zero-day vulnerabilities: Unveiling the threat landscape in network security. *Mesopotamian Journal of CyberSecurity, 2022*, 57–64.

Zhou, L., Guo, H., & Deng, G. (2019). A fog computing based approach to DDoS mitigation in IIoT systems. *Computers & Security, 85*, 51–62. DOI: 10.1016/j.cose.2019.03.014

Zuiderwijk, A., Chen, Y.-C., & Salem, F. (2021). Implications of the use of artificial intelligence in public governance: A systematic literature review and a research agenda. *Government Information Quarterly*, *38*(3), 101577. DOI 10.1016/j.giq.2021.101577[REMOVED HYPERLINK FIELD]

About the Contributors

Pradeep Kumar is a Postdoctoral Researcher at Infrastructure University, Malaysia, and currently serves in the Department of College of Computing Sciences & IT at Teerthanker Mahaveer University, Moradabad. With 12 years of experience in the field of computer applications, he has contributed significantly to academia and research. He earned his Ph.D. in Computer Applications from Babasaheb Bhimrao Ambedkar Bihar University, Muzaffarpur, Bihar (India), and completed his M.Tech in Computer Science and Engineering from Uttarakhand Technical University, Dehradun. Dr. Kumar's primary research area is Blockchain Technology, with a focus on enhancing web security processes. His expertise bridges theoretical knowledge and practical applications, contributing to secure and decentralized digital ecosystem advancements.

Abu Bakar A. Hamid chose academia as his profession in 1992, beginning as a lecturer and later rising to a Professor of Marketing and Supply Chain Management. He holds a BBA and an MBA from Northrop University (USA) and a PhD from the University of Derby, UK. He has demonstrated an excellent record of teaching and supervision for more than 25 years in the academic field, at both undergraduate and postgraduate levels. Above all, his achievement in graduating more than 35 PhD candidates proves his ability, capability, and passion in postgraduate supervisions. He has also produced impactful research and publications which directly strengthen his expertise in his area of interest. In particular, he has published more than 300 articles in competitive international journals, proceedings, books, and book chapters. He also managed to secure several competitive national grants and consultancies for various projects. Such commitment is truly a landmark of an academician. His accolades, academic recognition, and leadership demonstrate his level of professorship. His notable contributions are recognized locally and internationally, as proven by the multiple invitations he has received to be an invited speaker, reviewer, editor in journals, external assessor, and internal or external examiner. With such calibre, he has much to contribute to any academic institution in the world.

Parma Nand (Ph.D. -- IIT Roorkee, M.Tech -- IIT Delhi, B.Tech -- IIT Delhi) has more than 30 years of experience with Innovative ideas, Industry linkages & Institution building capabilities. He was a member of the Executive Council of IEEE UP section (R-10), member of the Executive Committee IEEE Computer and Signal Processing Society, member of the Executive India Council Computer Society, LMISTE, LMSCRS, Chairman of the Computer Society of India, Ghaziabad section. He led NAAC & NBA accreditation successfully. Served as a NAAC Assessor in the capacity of Chairperson and as an NBA Evaluator. Got the Best Teacher award from Union Minister, the Best Student's Project Guide Award from Microsoft, and the best faculty award from Cognizant. His areas of interest are AI/ML, Block Chain Technology, Cyber Security & Business/Data Analytics, Algorithms, Wireless and Sensor Networking. He received research/consultancy funding from government and private organizations and organized multiple reputed International Conferences, delivered many keynote talks, and focused on holistic academic growth, & has a proactive approach in life. Published more than 155 + research papers in various International Conference & Journals and 6 Books are indexed in Scopus and Web of Science. More than 125 patents are published & 31 are granted.

Rajeev Kumar is a renowned academician and administrator with over 15 years of expertise in advancing professional education. He currently serves as a Professor in the Department of Computer Science and Engineering at Moradabad Institute of Technology, Moradabad, Uttar Pradesh, India. Prof. Kumar's impressive academic credentials include a Ph.D. and a D.Sc. (Post-Doctoral Degree) in Computer Science, and a Postdoctoral Fellowship from Malaysia. He has further enhanced his expertise with certifications in Data Science and Machine Learning using Python and R Programming from IIM Raipur and advanced certifications from IBM and Google. As a senior member of IEEE, Prof. Kumar plays an active role in the IEEE Young Professional Committee and is also associated with the ACM, Computer Society of India (CSI), and SMIEEE. With core expertise in Artificial Intelligence, Cloud Computing, e-governance, and Networking, Prof. Kumar has significantly contributed to advancing academic programs. His efforts include curriculum design, delivering expert talks, and participating in high-impact leadership training programs. He has played a pivotal role in NAAC SSR preparations and has represented his institution at prestigious international academic forums in London, Mauritius, Malaysia, and Dubai. As a dedicated mentor, Prof. Kumar has guided ten scholars to complete their Ph.D. research, with four more pursuing their doctorates under his supervision and five pursuing post-doctorates from Malaysia. His exceptional guidance has earned him the Best Project Supervisor award three times. His commitment to research and innovation has cultivated a vibrant academic culture, leading to the successful incubation and development of numerous prototypes.

***

Mohammad Al-Khaldy is an Assistant professor of Business Intelligence and Data Analytics at University of Petra, Jordan. He completed his PhD in Atrificial Intelligence and Data Science for the University of Hull -United Kingdom - 20017. Alkhaldy's research interests include data analytics, machine learning, predictive analytics, NLP, and decision support systems. His research has been published extensively in academic journals and conferences. Alkhaldy taught a variety of courses in Artificial intelligence and business intelligence, including Data Mining, Business Analytics, Computer Programming, Intelligent business systems, Data Visualization, and machine learning. Alkhaldy is a member of Jordan Computers Society, and Arab Robotics & AI Association. He also a reviewer for several other academic conferences and journals.

Amjad Aldweesh is a computer associate professor interested in the Blockchain and Smart contracts technology as well as cyber security. Amjad has a Bachelor degree in computer science. He has a MSc degree in advanced computer science and security from the University of Manchester with distinction. Amjad is the second in the UK and the first in the middle east to have a PhD in the Blockchain and Smart contracts technology from Newcastle University.

Raed Atef is an independent researcher and consultant. He has served as a faculty member, researcher, and consultant with various organizations. He is actively involved in consulting, research, and training with government agencies, NGOs, and the private sector. He has collaborated with several universities and published numerous research papers and studies.

Sudhitri Bari is the engineering student from Marwadi University, Rajkot, Gujarat. His research is under the supervision of Dr. Sushil Kumar Singh.

Abhay Bhatia is currently affiliated with Roorkee Institute of Technology, Roorkee, Uttarakhand, serving as an Associate Professor in the Department of Computer Science and Engineering. With over 13 years of academic experience, he has worked with several reputed engineering institutions. He earned his B.Tech in Computer Science and Engineering from AKTU (formerly UPTU), followed by an M.Tech in the same field from Rajasthan, and a Ph.D. specializing in Wireless Sensor Networks. Dr. Bhatia is an active IEEE member and serves as a reviewer for multiple journals. His research credentials include over 30+ indexed publications in Scopus, IEEE, and SCI journals. He has delivered guest lectures at various institutions on emerging research topics. His dedication to research is further reflected in his six patents and ten book chapters. Additionally, he has authored books titled Fundamentals of IoT and Mastering, Data Structures: A Practical Approach and Practical Approach to Machine Learning with TensorFlow. His primary research interests include Artificial Intelligence, Machine Learning, and Wireless Sensor Networks.

Pankhuri Bhatia is working as assistant professor in department of management at Kunwar Satyavira College of Engineering and Management. She is found of mandla art and is having academic experience of 3 years. Currently she is pursuing Phd in Management.

Paritosh Biswas is a master's student in the Computer Engineering Department at Marwadi University, Rajkot, Gujarat, India. His research is under the supervision of Dr. Sushil Kumar Singh.

Sónia Calado is a PhD student in Accounting, holding a Master's degree in Auditing and Finance, with a specialisation in Taxation and Corporate Finance. With over 25 years of professional experience, 25 years in the private sector and 5 in public administration, she also serves as CEO of a private accounting firm. Her research interests include taxation, regulatory compliance, and digital transformation, with a particular focus on the intersection of emerging technologies such as AI and blockchain with public administration. She explores how these technologies can enhance digital identity systems, fiscal responsibility, and corporate governance in SMEs and developing economies, aiming to contribute to more efficient, transparent, and inclusive public sector management.

Puneet Chauhan is currently working in WithSecure Oyj as a Security Program and Operations Manager.

Kajal Choudhary working as an assistant professor in IIMT Univresity, Meerut, U.P, India.

Hina Hashmi Assistant Professor, Department of CSE-AIML Moradabad Institute of Technology, Moradabad, India Dr. Hina Hashmi is a passionate academician and researcher with over a decade of teaching experience and a strong background in Artificial Intelligence, Machine Learning, and Computer Vision. Holding a Ph.D. in Content-Based Video Classification, Dr. Hashmi's research focuses on deep learning, spatiotemporal analysis, and object detection from remote sensing data using advanced models like Faster R-CNN, YOLO, and 3D CNNs. She began her academic journey with a Bachelor's degree in Computer Applications from Sri Ram Group of Colleges, followed by an MCA with distinction from Teerthanker Mahaveer University, where she was also honored as a Gold Medalist. She later completed a BTC (Basic Training Certificate) and qualified for both the UGC NET (2019) and UPTET (2018), demonstrating her dedication to excellence in education. Currently serving as an Assistant Professor at Moradabad Institute of Technology, Moradabad, India, Dr. Hashmi also contributes significantly in leadership roles such as Program Coordinator for B.Sc. (H)-CS, NAAC Criteria-7 Coordinator, NBA Core Team Member, and Cultural Committee Coordinator. She is also the nodal coordinator for the IIRS START Outreach Programme. Her research interests include developing intelligent systems, automating unstructured data analysis, and enhancing AI-driven decision-making models. She has published extensively in SCIE and Scopus-indexed journals, contributed to conferences including IEEE and CEUR, and authored patents on innovative AI applications like the "IVB-E-Mail" and aquatic life-saving systems. Beyond academics, Dr. Hashmi is recognized for her commitment to empowering women through education and technology, and her efforts contribute to the development of smart, sustainable computing solutions with real-world impact.

Muhammad Nurul Huda is a doctoral student in Government Science at Universitas Muhammadiyah Yogyakarta.

Ankush Joshi, a seasoned professional with 13 years of experience, holds an impressive academic background. His pursuit of knowledge continued with postgraduate qualifications, including an MCA and M.Tech, culminating in a Ph.D. Currently serving as an Assistant Professor at COER University, Roorkee, Dr. Joshi specializes in the dynamic fields of Artificial Intelligence, Machine Learning, and Data Science. His extensive expertise and dedication make him a valuable asset in shaping the academic landscape at COER. He is authored and co-authored more than 10 papers in refereed international journals and IEEE conferences, Served as a reviewer and chaired session in IEEE conferences. He published a book " The Ethical Frontier of AI and Data Analysis" with prestiguous IGI global publisher which is SCOPUS indexed.

Habib Khan is research scholar in School Of Computing, Gachon University, South Korea.

Anil Kumar is Working as Associate Professor in Department of Computer Science & Engineering Roorkee Institute of Technology, Roorkee, Uttarakhand, India. He is having more than 19 years of academic experience and worked with various reputed engineering institutions. He has completed his B.Tech in Information Technology from AKTU (formely UPTU), M.Tech in Computer Science and Engineering from Rajasthan and Ph.D. in Natural Language Processing. He had reviewed several journals articles too. He is having distinguish record of research papers with more than 15+ International, Scopus and SCI papers. He is also in his bucket as a researcher with research area of NLP, Machine Learning, and Image Processing.

Hanifa Maylasari is lecturer in the Department of Politics and Government Sciences, Diponegoro University. She completed her Bachelor of Government Sciences education at the Faculty of Social and Political Sciences (FISIP) Diponegoro University, graduating in 2019. She got Master's Degree in the Master of Political Sciences Program at the Faculty of Social and Political Sciences (FISIP) Diponegoro University, graduating in 2022. She has experience working as an digital government practitioner of regional government communication and information services for more than 5 years. She has expertise in digital government and politic on media democracy, also has started to actively write national and international books and journals.

Krishanpal Singh is affiliated with the Department of Computer Science and Engineering at Swami Vivekanand Subharti University in Meerut, Uttar Pradesh. His contributions to the field of computer science, reflecting his engagement in both teaching and research activities. Through his role at the university, Mr. Singh plays a vital part in shaping the academic and professional development of students in the discipline. His profile serves as a testament to his commitment to advancing knowledge and fostering innovation within the realm of computer science and engineering.

Ravikumar R. Natarajan is an experienced academician with over 12+ years of teaching and research expertise across institutions in India, the UAE, and the Maldives. He currently serves as an Assistant Professor at Marwadi University, Rajkot, specializing in Machine Learning, Recommender Systems, and AI-driven applications in healthcare and security. He holds a Ph.D. in Machine Learning and Recommender Systems from Amity University, Jaipur, a Master of Engineering in CSE from VMRF University, Salem, and a Bachelor of Engineering in CSE from Anna University. He also has a MiniMBA from the Swiss eLearning Institute. Dr. Ravikumar has authored more than 8+ multiple SCIE/Scopus-indexed journal articles, 25+ IEEE/Springer conference papers, and co-authored a book on Artificial Intelligence. He has also published 9 patents and contributed 10+ book chapters in emerging domains such as Federated Learning, Blockchain, and Digital Twins for

IGI Global, Wiley and Springer publisher. He actively mentors students through initiatives like the Research Activities Club (RAC) and Student Research Internship Training (SRIT), promoting innovation and research culture.

Nilam Adini Rakma is lecturer in the Department of Public Administration, Diponegoro University. She completed his Bachelor of Public Administration education at the Faculty of Social and Political Sciences (FISIP) Diponegoro University, graduating in 2015. She got Masters degree in the Master of Public Administration Program at the Faculty of Social and Political Sciences (FISIP) Diponegoro University, graduating in 2021. She has experience working as an HR consultant and Supervisor of the Learning & Development section of the Human Resource division for more than 5 years. Seh has expertise in the field of human resource management and has started to actively write national and international books and journals.

Ali Roziqin is a Lecturer in the Department of Government Studies, Universitas Muhammadiyah Malang, Indonesia. He obtained his bachelor's degree from the Department of Public Administration at Universitas Diponegoro, Indonesia. He holds a Master of Public Administration from the Universitas Gadjah Mada, Indonesia. His research interests are in bureaucracy, public policy and administration, and public sector innovation. He has published papers in the reputable international journals like Sustainability (MDPI), Local Environment (Taylor and Francis), Frontiers in Communication, Tourism Critiques, Journal of Science and Technology Policy Management, Journal of the Knowledge Economy, and Public Administration and Policy: An Asia-Pacific Journal as well as in IGI Global.

Aarthi S is a dedicated Assistant Professor in Computer Science with over six years of teaching experience. She is currently pursuing her Ph.D. at Marwadi University, Gujarat, and holds an M.Phil. and MCA from Bharathiar University, Tamil Nadu. Throughout her academic career, Aarthi has specialized in programming languages such as C++, Java, and C, and contributed to research in recommender systems and AI-related data privacy. She has published journal articles, contributed to book chapters, and actively participated in technical workshops. Known for her student mentorship and engagement in academic events, Aarthi remains committed to fostering innovation and excellence in computer science education.

Almash Saifi is a dedicated academic professional currently serving as a Lecturer at Swami Vivekanand Subharti University. With a strong passion for innovation and technology, she specializes in the fields of Artificial Intelligence and Machine Learning. Her commitment to education and research reflects in her dynamic teaching style and her efforts to inspire students to explore the transformative potential of intelligent systems. Ms. Saifi continues to contribute to the academic community through her engagement in cutting-edge advancements in AI and ML.

Vikas Sharma is an active academician and researcher in the field of computer science with 7 years of experience. He earned M. Tech degree specialized in Computer Science. He is involved in academic development and scholarly activities. He is member of International Association of Engineers, The Society of Digital Information and Wireless Communications, Global Professors Welfare Association, International Association of Academic plus Corporate (IAAC), Computer Science Teachers Association and Internet Society. His research interest includes Cloud Computing, Artificial Intelligence, Machine Learning; published more than 55 research articles with 4 books and 75 book chapters in edited books. He is contributing as member of editorial and reviewers' boards in conferences and various computer journals and edited books published by Elsevier, CRC Press, Taylor and Francis, Springer, IGI global, Wiley Publication, IET Publication, De Gruyter, River Publication etc.

Harshita Singh is an engineering student from Marwadi University, Rajkot, Gujarat. Her research is under the supervision of Dr. Sushil Kumar Singh.

Sushil Kumar Singh is an Associate Professor in the Department of Computer Engineering at Marwadi University, Rajkot, India. He received Ph.D. degree from Seoul National University of Science and Technology, Seoul, South Korea. He received M.Tech. Degree in Computer Science and Engineering from Uttarakhand Technical University, Dehradun, India. He also received an M.E. degree in Information Technology from Karnataka State University, Mysore, India. He has also been the lab leader of the UCS Lab at the Department of Computer Science Engineering, Seoul National University of Science and Technology, Seoul, South Korea. He has received Best Lab Leadership Award from UCS Lab for 2019-2021. He has more than 12 years of experience teaching in the field of computer science. He has published Four Books: Computer C Programming, Cyber Security, Big Data Analytics, and Mobile Computing. He has also published many high-quality papers (Q1, Top 10% JCR Rank) in international journals and conferences. He has already delivered international lectures in many countries. His research interests include Blockchain, Artificial Intelligence, Big Data, Internet of Things, Smart City Security, and CPS.

Om Prakash Suthar is the Assistant Professor in the Computer Engineering Department at Marwadi University, Rajkot, Gujarat, India.

Tarun Kumar Vashishth is an active academician and researcher in the field of Computer Science with 22 years of experience. He earned Ph.D. Mathematics degree specialized in Operations Research; served several academic positions such as Dy. Director, HoD, NAAC Coordinator, Academic Coordinator, Member Secretary of Department Research Committee, Assistant Center Superintendent and Head Examiner in University Examinations. He is involved in academic development and scholarly activities. He is member of International Association of Engineers, The Society of Digital Information and Wireless Communications, Global Professors Welfare Association, International Association of Academic plus Corporate (IAAC), Computer Science Teachers Association and Internet Society . His research interest includes Cloud Computing, Artificial Intelligence, Machine Learning and Operations Research; published more than 50 research articles & conference papers with 2 book and 80 book chapters. He is contributing as member of editorial and reviewers boards in conferences and various computer journals and edited books published by Elsevier, CRC Press, Taylor and Francis, Springer, IGI global, Wiley Publication, IET Publication, De Gruyter, River Publication etc.

Cláudia Veloso has a PhD in Social Sciences (Economics and Management). She is Professor of Management (Marketing and Finances) at ESTGA - University of Aveiro. She is a researcher at GOVCOPP. She was a Member of the Board of the Centro Hospitalar do Nordeste (ULSNE) and Technical Adviser of the Ministry of Health of Portugal. She participated in 4 R&D projects, published more than 170 publications in peer-reviewed journals, book chapters and proceedings, and won 7 scientific awards.

Index

A

AI-Driven Predictive Analytics 49, 53, 147, 150, 337, 364
AI-driven Systems 298, 299, 300, 301, 302, 303, 309, 313, 314, 316
AI Ethics 127, 130, 131, 145, 202, 224, 225, 227, 240, 313, 315, 319, 336, 338, 364, 365, 370, 371
AI in governance 222, 328, 338, 346
Algorithmic Bias 154, 211, 302, 312, 313, 316, 328, 330, 333, 334, 338
Artificial Intelligence (AI) 2, 16, 43, 50, 51, 55, 72, 73, 75, 78, 80, 84, 87, 91, 96, 113, 114, 115, 118, 120, 121, 122, 125, 126, 127, 128, 131, 133, 134, 135, 136, 137, 138, 139, 140, 141, 142, 143, 144, 145, 152, 156, 173, 174, 175, 178, 179, 180, 182, 184, 202, 204, 205, 206, 210, 223, 224, 227, 246, 247, 250, 258, 270, 274, 297, 299, 300, 301, 303, 305, 312, 315, 318, 319, 320, 321, 322, 323, 324, 325, 326, 327, 328, 330, 333, 335, 337, 340, 341, 342, 343, 345, 353, 364, 365, 366, 368, 371, 372

B

business intelligence 95, 96, 97, 100, 111, 204, 273

C

Citizen-Centric Services 213
Consensus 54, 61, 63, 67, 72, 74, 171, 179, 180, 181, 182, 183, 185, 186, 192, 194, 225, 249, 250, 252, 261, 262, 264, 270, 350, 352
Corruption Reduction 344
Covid-19 123, 134, 139, 275, 276, 277, 278, 279, 280, 281, 282, 283, 284, 285, 286, 287, 288, 289, 290, 291, 292, 293, 294, 320, 331, 332, 340, 369
Cyber Attacks 1, 7, 16, 44, 45, 47, 272
Cyber Security 4, 25, 32, 41, 47, 198, 204, 205, 256, 257, 258, 268, 269, 272, 274

D

data governance 96, 98, 100, 103, 108, 111, 117, 122, 126, 130, 131, 137, 147, 149, 205, 219, 225, 234, 244, 337, 352
Developed Countries 115, 117, 120, 123, 125, 126, 129, 130, 131, 132
Developing Countries 81, 115, 116, 117, 120, 123, 124, 130, 131, 132, 147, 149, 153, 155, 160, 164
Digital Governance 117, 119, 120, 138, 142, 178, 180, 182, 183, 184, 193, 201, 202, 205, 240, 327, 339, 354, 355, 360, 361, 366
Digital Identity 117, 147, 148, 150, 153, 155, 156, 159, 162, 163, 164, 165, 166, 168, 169, 172, 173, 175, 329, 343, 351, 359, 360, 361, 365, 366, 372
Digital Inclusion 50, 148, 149, 151, 167, 175
Digital public services 353
Digital Transformation 116, 117, 118, 126, 133, 134, 135, 143, 144, 147, 173, 174, 209, 246, 345, 348, 353, 360
Distributed Ledger Technology 44, 180, 251

E

Electric vehicle charging infrastructure 42
Electric Vehicles 1, 2, 3, 4, 8, 10, 11, 15, 29, 32, 41, 42, 43, 44, 45, 46
Ethical Decision-making 298, 300, 303, 305, 308, 311, 316, 324
Ethical frameworks 110, 228, 303, 308, 327, 333, 335, 356

H

health workers 232, 275, 276, 277, 278, 279, 280, 281, 282, 283, 284, 285, 286, 287, 288

Hyperledger Fabric 250

M

Machine Learning 2, 5, 13, 15, 16, 18, 19, 21, 22, 24, 26, 28, 31, 37, 38, 40, 41, 42, 44, 46, 52, 58, 59, 64, 65, 73, 78, 79, 80, 85, 86, 89, 90, 96, 98, 100, 102, 105, 108, 109, 110, 113, 118, 134, 138, 143, 163, 167, 180, 187, 192, 204, 205, 206, 207, 210, 212, 218, 220, 230, 243, 245, 246, 274, 302, 307, 312, 321, 323, 328, 330, 341, 345, 346, 348, 357, 362, 364, 370, 371, 372

O

organizational adaptation 95, 97, 100, 111

P

Policy Formulation 327, 344, 349
predictive analytics 2, 5, 25, 49, 53, 63, 95, 96, 97, 98, 99, 100, 103, 107, 111, 112, 147, 150, 156, 158, 164, 175, 207, 209, 210, 211, 212, 213, 214, 215, 216, 217, 218, 219, 220, 222, 223, 225, 229, 234, 241, 242, 243, 244, 247, 308, 327, 328, 330, 331, 332, 337, 343, 344, 345, 346, 347, 348, 349, 357, 363, 364, 365, 366, 372
Predictive Governance 147, 149, 151, 153, 217, 220, 222, 228, 234, 235, 237, 239, 240, 241, 242, 243, 356, 366
Proactive Governance 209, 210, 211, 241, 348
Public Administration 49, 50, 51, 53, 54, 55, 95, 96, 97, 98, 110, 113, 114, 118, 121, 122, 124, 126, 127, 130, 134, 135, 137, 138, 140, 142, 145, 147, 148, 152, 155, 161, 170, 172, 209, 211, 212, 217, 219, 221, 223, 229, 234, 238, 240, 241, 243, 289, 290, 291, 292, 327, 328, 329, 330, 333, 334, 335, 336, 337, 338, 339, 340, 341, 343, 344, 345, 346, 347, 348, 349, 350, 351, 352, 354, 355, 357, 358, 360, 361, 362, 365, 366, 368
Public Infrastructure 1, 2, 3, 4, 7, 8, 40, 106
Public Service Delivery 140, 164, 209, 213, 234, 241, 242, 331, 343, 347
Public Services 109, 115, 116, 117, 118, 119, 120, 127, 128, 131, 132, 133, 135, 147, 156, 160, 162, 163, 164, 172, 210, 213, 214, 216, 223, 237, 243, 259, 287, 291, 328, 329, 332, 333, 334, 335, 336, 344, 345, 349, 353, 360, 363, 364

S

Self-Sovereign Identity 188, 200
Smart Cities 2, 3, 29, 30, 235, 327, 356, 369, 370, 371
Smart Contracts 27, 28, 50, 54, 74, 79, 85, 86, 89, 144, 158, 163, 175, 177, 179, 181, 182, 183, 184, 185, 186, 190, 192, 193, 195, 196, 200, 202, 250, 259, 271, 301, 319, 345, 346, 350, 351, 352, 354, 358, 365, 366, 368, 371, 372
Smart Governance 137, 153, 183, 344, 347, 348, 356, 360, 362, 363, 364, 371
Street-level bureaucracy 275, 277, 278, 290, 291, 293
Stress Reduction 312, 316

www.ingramcontent.com/pod-product-compliance
Lightning Source LLC
LaVergne TN
LVHW062329300926
849161LV00007B/1628